'The author's insights into the individual paintings are remarkable, but what really gives the book its pep is the author's picking apart of the scanty evidence about Caravaggio's private life, the prostitutes and friends who people his paintings, and the seedy world of late-Renaissance Rome through which he swaggered'
Andrew Holgate, *Sunday Times*, Books of the Year

'Remarkable ... Sheds fresh light on the painter whose hot temper was as renowned as his work ... uncovers details on pivotal events during the artist's turbulent career'
Roya Nikkhah, *Sunday Telegraph*

'Highly readable ... thorough and elegant ... *Caravaggio* has done the artist proud' Ian Thomson, *Spectator*

'Andrew Graham-Dixon's absorbing biography leaves no stone unturned ... he is an entertaining art historian' *Economist*

'Graham-Dixon's excellent new book ... the complexity of Caravaggio's character as well as his art is vividly evoked by Graham-Dixon throughout this book ... Graham-Dixon's biography will surely quickly establish itself as the outstanding introduction to Caravaggio's life and art'
Brian Allen, *Standpoint*

'Andrew Graham-Dixon brings the bad-boy genius of the seventeenth century to life as vividly as if he were one of today's pop stars. His book is scholarly, perceptive and very well written' John Richardson

'An entertaining read ... an engaging and well-written account of Caravaggio's life' Sheila McTighe, *Art Quarterly*

'A beautifully paced narrative ... its tremendous narrative drive ... steers the story fluently and plausibly between the pitfalls of academic dryness and overdone speculation. As a human story it is ultimately tragic'
Charles Nicholl, *Sunday Times*

ABOUT THE AUTHOR

For more than twenty-five years, Andrew Graham-Dixon has published a weekly column on art, first in the *Independent* and more recently, the *Sunday Telegraph*. He has written a number of acclaimed books, including *A History of British Art* and *Renaissance*, and is twice winner of the Hawthornden Prize, Britain's top prize for writing about art. He is one of the leading figures in broadcasting in the UK, having presented seven major television series on art for the BBC.

ANDREW GRAHAM-DIXON

Caravaggio

A Life Sacred and Profane

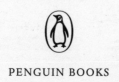

PENGUIN BOOKS

PENGUIN BOOKS

Published by the Penguin Group
Penguin Books Ltd, 80 Strand, London WC2R ORL, England
Penguin Group (USA) Inc., 375 Hudson Street, New York, New York 10014, USA
Penguin Group (Canada), 90 Eglinton Avenue East, Suite 700, Toronto, Ontario, Canada M4P 2Y3
(a division of Pearson Penguin Canada Inc.)
Penguin Ireland, 25 St Stephen's Green, Dublin 2, Ireland (a division of Penguin Books Ltd)
Penguin Group (Australia), 250 Camberwell Road,
Camberwell, Victoria 3124, Australia (a division of Pearson Australia Group Pty Ltd)
Penguin Books India Pvt Ltd, 11 Community Centre,
Panchsheel Park, New Delhi – 110 017, India
Penguin Group (NZ), 67 Apollo Drive, Rosedale, Auckland 0632, New Zealand
(a division of Pearson New Zealand Ltd)
Penguin Books (South Africa) (Pty) Ltd, 24 Sturdee Avenue,
Rosebank, Johannesburg 2196, South Africa

Penguin Books Ltd, Registered Offices: 80 Strand, London WC2R ORL, England

www.penguin.com

First published by Allen Lane 2010
Published in Penguin Books 2011

009

Copyright © Andrew Graham-Dixon, 2010
Maps copyright © Alan Gilliland, 2010

Typeset by Jouve (UK), Milton Keynes
Printed in Great Britain by Clays Ltd, St Ives plc

A CIP catalogue record for this book is available from the British Library

ISBN: 978-0-241-95464-5

www.greenpenguin.co.uk

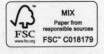

*To the memory of my mother, Sue, who first awoke
my love of reading, writing and looking at art*

Contents

List of Illustrations

All works are by Michelangelo Merisi da Caravaggio (1571–1610), unless otherwise stated.

9. *Perseus and Andromeda* by Giuseppe Cesari (1568–1640), 1602, Kunsthistorisches Museum, Vienna, Austria/The Bridgeman Art Library. Oil on Canvas, 20.4 x 15 in. (51.8 x 38.2 cm).

10. *Boy Peeling a Fruit*, c. 1592–3, The Royal Collection © 2009, Her Majesty Queen Elizabeth II. Oil on canvas, 24 x 19 in. (61 x 48.3 cm).

11. *Boy with a Basket of Fruit*, c. 1593–4. Galleria Borghese, Rome, Italy/ Alinari/The Bridgeman Art Library. Oil on Canvas, 27.6 x 26.4 in. (70 x 67 cm).

12. *Boy Bitten by a Lizard*, c. 1595, National Gallery, London, UK. © The National Gallery, 2010. Oil on canvas, 26 x 19.5 in. (66 x 49.5 cm).

13. *Boy Bitten by a Crayfish* by Sofonisba Anguissola (1532–1625), c. 1554, Museo di Capodimonte, Gabinetto dei Disegni, inv. 1030, Naples, Italy. Photo: Scala, Florence, courtesy of the Ministero Beni e Att. Culturali. Drawing.

14. *Self-Portrait as Bacchus*, c. 1593–4, Galleria Borghese, Rome, Italy/Lauros/The Bridgeman Art Library. Oil on Canvas, 26.4 x 20.9 in. (67 x 53 cm).

15. *Bacchus and Ariadne* by Titian (Tiziano Vecellio) (c. 1488–1576), 1520–23, National Gallery, London, UK. © The National Gallery, 2010. Oil on canvas, 69.5 x 75.2 in. (176.5 x 191 cm).

16. *The Cardsharps*, 1595, Kimbell Art Museum, Fort Worth, Texas, USA/Art Resource, NY/Scala, Florence. Oil on canvas, 37⅛ x 51⅛ in. (94.2 x 30.9 cm).

17. *The Gypsy Fortune-Teller*, 1595, Pinacoteca Capitolina, Palazzo Conservatori, Rome, Italy/The Bridgeman Art Library. Oil on canvas, 59.5 x 45.7 in. (151.2 x 116 cm).

18. *Portrait of Cardinal Francesco Maria del Monte* by Ottavio Leoni (1578–1603), 1616, Museum Purchase, Collection of the John and Mable Ringling Museum of Art, The State Art Museum of Florida, a division of Florida State University, USA. Drawing: black chalk heightened with white on blue paper, 9 x 6½ in. (22.9 x 16.5 cm).

82. *The Burial of St Lucy*, 1608, Basilica di Santa Lucia al Sepolcro, Syracuse, Italy. Photo: Scala, Florence. Oil on canvas, 160.6 x 118.1 in. (408 x 300 cm).

83. *The Denial of St Peter*, 1610, Metropolitan Museum of Art, New York, USA/Art Resource/Scala, Florence. Gift of Herman and Lila Shickman, and Purchase, Lila Acheson Wallace Gift, 1997. Oil on canvas, 37 x 49.4 in. (94 x 125.4 cm).

84. *The Martyrdom of St Ursula*, 1610, Intesa Sanpaolo Collection, the Gallery of Palazzo Zevallos Stigliano, Naples. Oil on canvas, 56.3 x 70.9 in. (143 x 180 cm).

85. *Experiment on a Bird in the Air Pump* by Joseph Wright of Derby (1734–97), 1768, National Gallery, London, UK/ The Bridgeman Art Library. Oil on canvas, 72 x 96 in. (182.9 x 243.9 cm).

86. *The Raft of the Medusa* by Theodore Géricault (1791–1824), 1819, Louvre, Paris, France/The Bridgeman Art Library. Oil on canvas, 193.3 x 281.9 in. (491 x 716 cm).

87. Still from *Mean Streets*, directed by Martin Scorsese (1942–), 1973, Taplin-Perry-Scorsese/The Kobal Collection.

Text illustration, p. 325: Sketch of Caravaggio's sword and dagger made by the police officer who arrested him on the evening of 28 May 1605. As reproduced and cited in Maurizio Marini, *Michelangelo Merisi da Caravaggio 'pictor praestantissimus'* (second edition, Rome, 1979), p. 54.

Text illustration, p. 328: *A Knight of Malta being Defrocked* by Wolfgang Kilian (1581–1662), from C. von Osterhausen, Eigentlicher und gründlicher (Bericht, Augsburg, 1650), no. II. Photo: Zentralinstitut für Kuntsgeschichte. Engraving, 5 x 3 in. (12.7 x 7.5 cm).

Maps

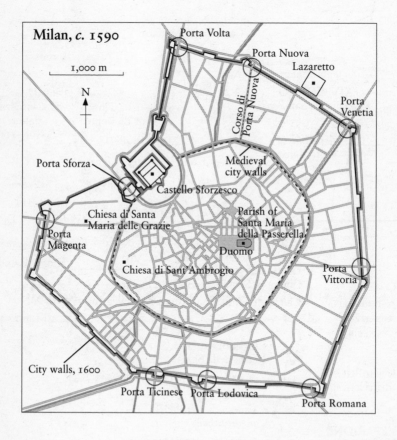

Milan, *c.* **1590**

1,000 m

N

Porta Volta

Porta Nuova

Lazaretto

Corso di Porta Nuova

Porta Venetia

Porta Sforza

Medieval city walls

Castello Sforzesco

Chiesa di Santa Maria delle Grazie

Parish of Santa Maria della Passerella

Porta Magenta

Duomo

Chiesa di Sant'Ambrogio

Porta Vittoria

City walls, 1600

Porta Ticinese   Porta Lodovica

Porta Romana

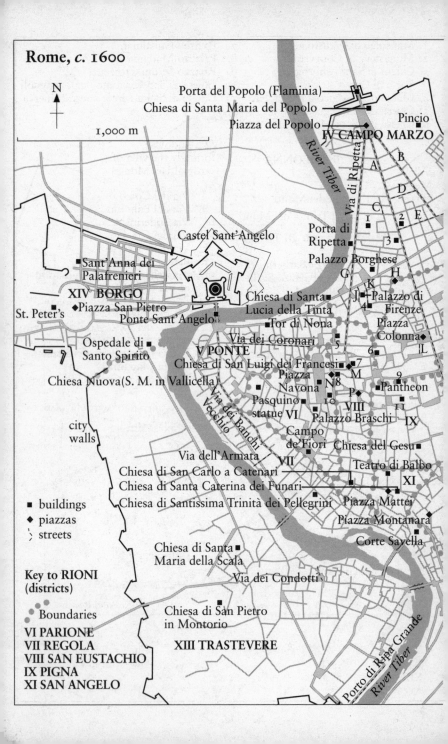

Rome, *c.* 1600

N
1,000 m

Porta del Popolo (Flaminia)
Chiesa di Santa Maria del Popolo
Piazza del Popolo
Pincio
IV CAMPO MARZO

River Tiber

Via di Ripetta

A
B
D
C
I
2
E
3
Porta di Ripetta
Palazzo Borghese
G
K
H
J
4
Palazzo di Firenze
Piazza Colonna

Castel Sant'Angelo

Sant'Anna dei Palafrenieri
XIV BORGO
Piazza San Pietro
St. Peter's
Ponte Sant'Angelo
Chiesa di Santa Lucia della Tinta
Tor di Nona
Via dei Coronari
V PONTE
5
6
L
Ospedale di Santo Spirito
Chiesa di San Luigi dei Francesi
7
Chiesa Nuova(S. M. in Vallicella)
Piazza Navona
M
9
Pantheon
Pasquino statue
Via dei Banchi Vecchio
N 8
P
VIII
11
10
VI
Palazzo Braschi
IX
Via dell'Armata
Campo de'Fiori
Chiesa del Gesu
VII
Chiesa di San Carlo a Catenari
Teatro di Balbo
Chiesa di Santa Caterina dei Funari
XI
Chiesa di Santissima Trinità dei Pellegrini
Piazza Mattei
Piazza Montanara
Corte Savella

city walls

■ buildings
♦ piazzas
⟩ streets

Chiesa di Santa Maria della Scala
Via dei Condotti

Key to RIONI (districts)

Chiesa di San Pietro in Montorio
XIII TRASTEVERE

Porto di Ripa Grande
River Tiber

●● Boundaries
VI PARIONE
VII REGOLA
VIII SAN EUSTACHIO
IX PIGNA
XI SAN ANGELO

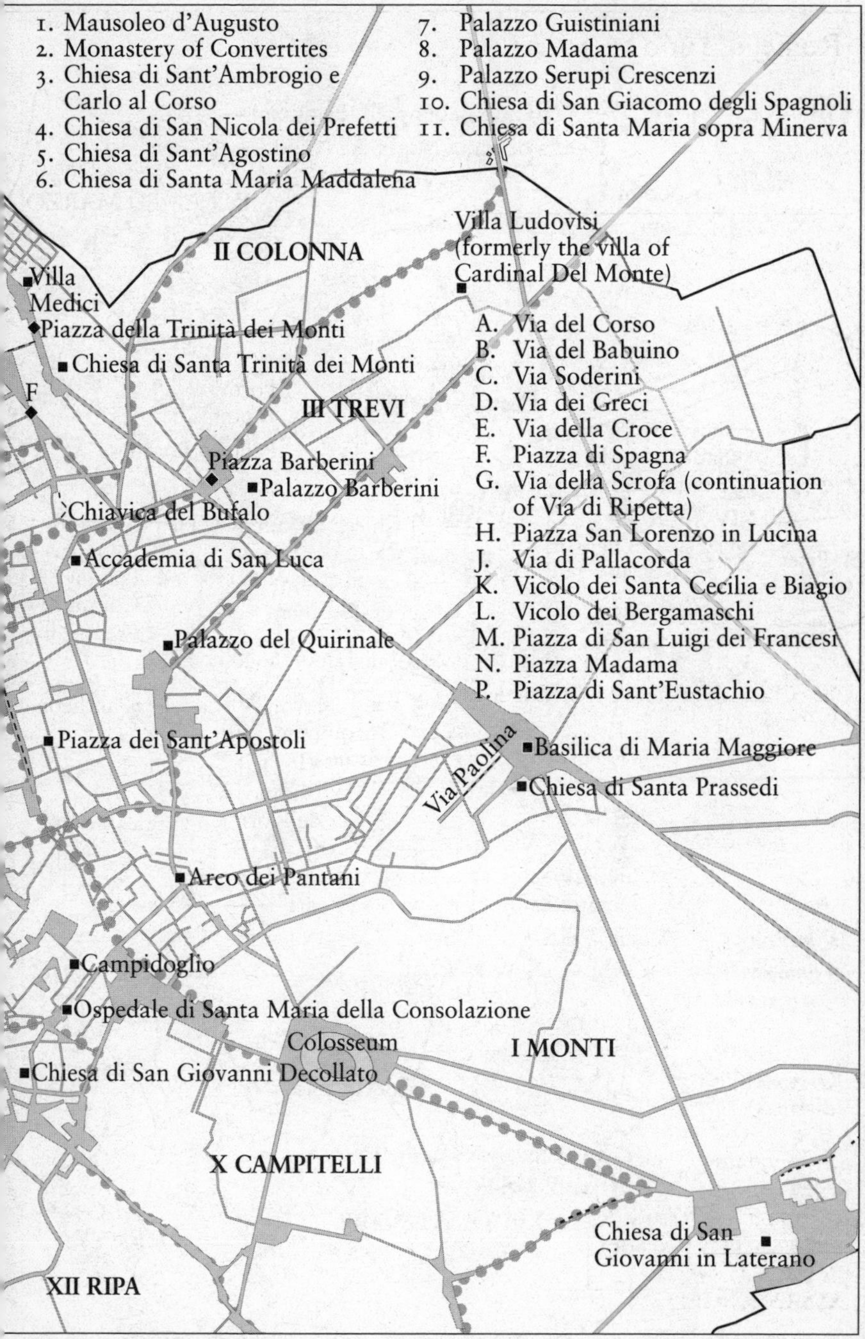

II COLONNA

Villa Medici

Piazza della Trinità dei Monti

Chiesa di Santa Trinità dei Monti

III TREVI

Villa Ludovisi (formerly the villa of Cardinal Del Monte)

F

Piazza Barberini

Palazzo Barberini

Chiavica del Bufalo

Accademia di San Luca

Palazzo del Quirinale

Piazza dei Sant'Apostoli

Via Paolina

Basilica di Maria Maggiore

Chiesa di Santa Prassedi

Arco dei Pantani

Campidoglio

Ospedale di Santa Maria della Consolazione

Colosseum

I MONTI

Chiesa di San Giovanni Decollato

X CAMPITELLI

Chiesa di San Giovanni in Laterano

XII RIPA

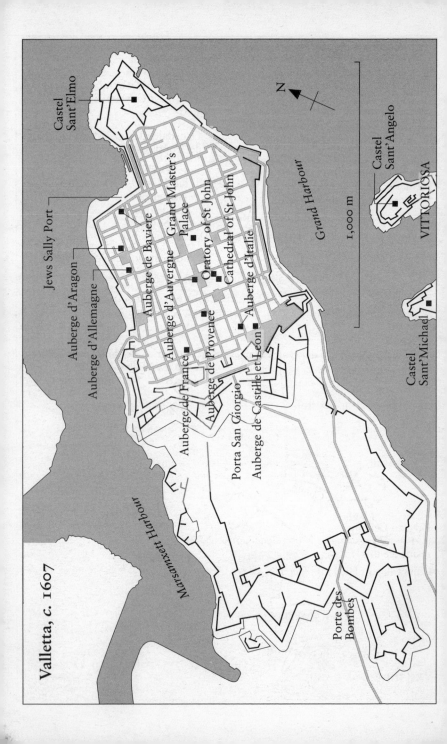

Valletta, c. 1607

Marsamxett Harbour

Castel Sant'Elmo

Jews Sally Port

Auberge d'Aragon

Auberge d'Allemagne

Auberge de Baviere

Auberge d'Auvergne

Grand Master's Palace

Oratory of St John

Cathedral of St John

Auberge d'Italie

Auberge de Provence

Auberge de France

Auberge de Castille et Leon

Porta San Giorgio

Porte des Bombes

Grand Harbour

1,000 m

N

Castel Sant'Angelo

VITTORIOSA

Castel Sant'Michael

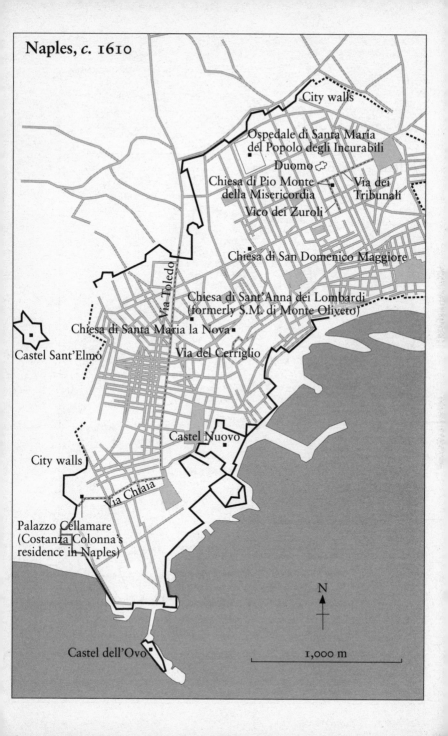

Naples, *c.* 1610

City walls

Ospedale di Santa Maria
del Popolo degli Incurabili

Duomo

Chiesa di Pio Monte
della Misericordia

Via dei
Tribunali

Vico dei Zuroli

Chiesa di San Domenico Maggiore

Chiesa di Sant'Anna dei Lombardi
(formerly S.M. di Monte Oliveto)

Via Toledo

Chiesa di Santa Maria la Nova

Via del Cerriglio

Castel Sant'Elmo

Castel Nuovo

City walls

Via Chiaia

Palazzo Cellamare
(Costanza Colonna's
residence in Naples)

Castel dell'Ovo

N

1,000 m

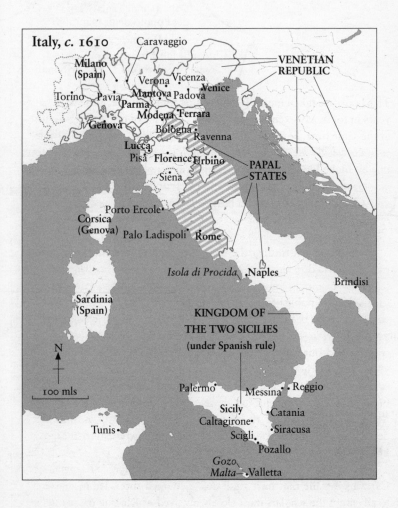

Italy, *c.* 1610

Caravaggio

Milano (Spain)

Verona Vicenza

Torino Pavia **Mantova** Padova **Venice**

Parma

Modena **Ferrara**

Genova

Bologna Ravenna

Lucca

Pisa Florence Urbino

Siena

Porto Ercole

Corsica (Genova)

Palo Ladispoli **Rome**

Isola di Procida **Naples**

VENETIAN REPUBLIC

PAPAL STATES

Brindisi

Sardinia (Spain)

N

100 mls

KINGDOM OF THE TWO SICILIES
(under Spanish rule)

Palermo Messina Reggio

Sicily Catania

Caltagirone

Siracusa

Scigli

Pozallo

Tunis

Gozo

Malta Valletta

Preface and Acknowledgements

This book has taken me a shamingly long time to write, more than ten years in total. My excuse is that I have had a lot of other things to do at the same time. For the first five of those ten years I was responsible for two weekly articles for the *Sunday Telegraph* (latterly reduced to one, to make life workable); in 2007 I had to stop work on *Caravaggio* almost completely to finish a book about Michelangelo's paintings in the Sistine Chapel; and throughout the past decade I have spent at least five months of every year writing and presenting various television series about the history of art for the BBC.

While often frustrating, the many delays and interruptions have, overall, worked to the book's advantage. Had I delivered my manuscript more quickly, I might have caused my miraculously patient and long-suffering publisher, Stuart Proffitt, considerably less stress. But I would not have been able to take advantage of numerous recent archival discoveries – a set of remarkable finds that cumulatively have transformed our knowledge of Caravaggio, particularly of his later years. Because those discoveries have emerged piecemeal, often in out-of-the-way academic journals or private publications, I have found myself in the unusual and fortunate position of writing about one of the greatest artists ever to have lived fully four centuries after his death, yet able to draw on fresh and important documentary material unavailable to previous biographers.

As a result, I believe I have been able to shed light on aspects of Caravaggio's life that have until now remained shrouded in mystery to all except the scholars most closely involved – including the painter's sexuality, the circumstances that led him to commit the murder of 1606 that cast such a long shadow over the rest of his life, and the events surrounding his imprisonment on the island of Malta. In addition I publish here for the first time some hitherto overlooked descriptions of the Osteria del Cerriglio, the establishment in Naples where he was badly assaulted near the end of his life in a vendetta attack. By returning to other previously discovered documents I believe I have also been able to offer a convincing solution to the riddle of how Caravaggio met his death in the summer of 1610.

My principal focus throughout is on the artist's paintings. I dwell on them at length because they are the main reason to be interested in Caravaggio, notwithstanding the tempestuous drama of his life. Attentive readers will notice that I am less generous in my attributions than many other scholars of Caravaggio's work: I prefer to be too rigorous than over-inclusive. It may be assumed that if I do not mention a particular picture, for example the frequently proposed *Narcissus* from the Barberini Collection, it is because I am not satisfied that Caravaggio painted it. The main exception to this is *The Annunciation* in the Musée des Beaux-Arts in Nancy, which is indeed a Caravaggio, but one so badly damaged as not to be worth discussing here.

I have incurred many debts in writing this book, above all to the community of scholars whose researches have yielded so much new information over the past half-century or so, especially in recent years. I am deeply grateful to Sandro Corradini for helping to guide me through the labyrinth of Rome's criminal archive and for sharing the fruits of his twenty years and more of research there. Maurizio Marini took me on a memorable tour of Caravaggio's old haunts in the artist's quarter of the city and made interesting suggestions, which I have developed, about the significance of damage done to the ceiling of a particular room in a house in the present-day Vicolo del Divino Amore. Maurizio Calvesi generously communicated his insights into the painter's 'pauperist' religious orientation, and the role that members of the Colonna family may have played in the various events of his life. In Naples, Vincenzo Pacelli showed me his archival discoveries concerning Caravaggio's last painting, *The Martyrdom of St Ursula*, and shared some speculations about the painter's final days.

My thanks are also due to Peter Robb, who met me in Naples and sent me on what proved to be anything but a wild-goose chase on the island of Malta. On Malta itself I profited from conversations with

Fr John Azzopardi and Keith Sciberras, who have between them shed much light on Caravaggio's ill-fated attempt to join the Order of the Knights of St John. John T. Spike, who received me at his home in Florence, allowed me to see an advance copy of the CD-ROM catalogue and bibliography that accompanied his monograph on Caravaggio: an invaluable guide to the vast literature on the artist. My old friend Mary Hersov, former Head of Exhibitions at the National Gallery in London, has talked and walked Caravaggio with me far beyond the call of duty.

Helen Langdon, whose own biography of Caravaggio appeared in 1998, has also been extremely supportive throughout the writing of this book. In particular, she generously allowed me to profit from the time-consuming work that she put into combing through Riccardo Bassani and Fiora Bellini's sporadically fascinating but deeply flawed book of 1994, *Caravaggio assassino* – the curate's egg of recent Caravaggio studies – sifting the true not only from the false but also from the outright invented. Helen also set me straight at a particular crossroads in my research into the painter's second and final stay in Naples, for which I am very grateful.

I have not spoken to Sir Denis Mahon in the course of writing my book, but, like everyone engaged in serious study of Caravaggio, I have benefited enormously from his pioneering work. The shades of Walter Friedlaender and Roberto Longhi have given me much assistance along the way, as has that of my old tutor at the Courtauld Institute, Michael Kitson, whose wisdom I sought to absorb along with the smoke of many amiably shared packets of cigarettes. I have drawn rather more lateral inspiration from the work of John Michael Montias, whose *Vermeer and His Milieu* of 1989 is a truly remarkable work. The shape of my own book has been certainly influenced by his, as well as by a meeting with Montias at his home in New Haven in the autumn of 2001. Without laying any claim to Montias's eminence as an archival scholar, I have myself tried to spin a 'web of social history', to use his phrase – to convey, through an account of one man's life and milieu, some sense of an entire lost world, in this case the civilization of Italy at the end of the sixteenth century and the beginning of the seventeenth. Charles Nicholl's books about Marlowe and Shakespeare, *The Reckoning* and *The Lodger*, have been among my other touchstones.

Writing about Caravaggio has been an intellectual challenge, but it has also been an adventure, one which has led me into some fairly unusual situations. With John Azzopardi's generous help and the loan of a slightly rickety ladder, I have inspected the stone well, or *guva*, in which Caravaggio was imprisoned on Malta (I can now laugh at the practical joke of his pretending to lock me in and leave me there, although it seemed less funny at the time). I have duelled (after a fashion) with master-swordsman Renzo Musumeci Greco in his Roman fencing school, in an attempt to understand the sort of manoeuvres that might result in the emasculation of a man during a swordfight. I have walked along the quays of the old port at Valletta with the Maltese naval historian Joseph Sciberras, to learn about transport by *felucca* in Caravaggio's time. I have been allowed to inspect the book of the dead in the parish of Porto Ercole by local historian Giuseppe La Fauci. I have spent some happy hours poring over Caravaggio reproductions with the film director Martin Scorsese, who generously gave his time to open my eyes to the artist's importance for modern cinema. To these and all the others who have gone out of their way to help me – the boy who lowered that ladder down the *guva* on Malta, the sacristan who got the keys to the church of Santa Lucia in Syracuse, the librarians and archivists in London, Rome, Naples, Milan and Malta who found so many books and documents – a heartfelt thank you.

Closer to home, I would like to thank my producer Silvia Sacco for devising a schedule for my television and other work that made the seemingly impossible possible. Without her constant encouragement, moral support and ruthless deadline-setting, I really might never have written the book at all. Without the help of my researchers, I would certainly never have been able to finish it. Opher Mansour did a first-rate job of translating Corradini's essential anthology of archival documents, *Materiali per un processo*, from a mixture of legalistic Latin and often difficult sixteenth- and seventeenth-century Italian vernacular slang. Opher also allowed me to read his enlightening doctoral thesis about censorship in Caravaggio's Rome and unearthed several eyewitness accounts of the plague that ravaged Milan in the mid 1570s. In the very final stages of the book, Nicholas Stone Villani took time away from his own thesis to travel to Italy on my behalf, where he found out the seedy truth about the Osteria del Cerriglio. My principal researcher throughout has been Eugénie Aperghis-van Nispen tot Sevenaer, who has been unfailingly helpful, resourceful and thorough in carrying out what must sometimes have seemed a daunting series of tasks. She also did the picture research for the book and secured the reproduction permissions. While running her marathon, Eugénie was ably assisted by Kasja Berg, who on more than one occasion responded to my plaintive demands for particular texts or documents with exemplary calm and efficiency. My mother and father, far more knowledgeable about music than I ever will be, kindly brought their considerable erudition to bear on Caravaggio's early paintings of musicians and lute-players, greatly to my advantage.

I will always remain affectionately grateful to Roger Parsons, with whom I first began to explore the complexities of Caravaggio's world such an absurdly long time ago. Stuart Proffitt has made extremely valuable suggestions concerning style, structure and approach. Donna Poppy, my copy editor, has improved my original manuscript immeasurably with her rigorous and unsleeping eye for sense, proportion, perspective and detail. Finally I would like to thank my wife, Sabine, who must have read this book ten times while I was writing it once, for contributing so many emendations, corrections and indeed fresh ideas – and also my whole family, for helping me to keep my sanity and managing to keep their own while enduring the difficult birth of this long-gestated child.

London, February 2010

PART ONE
Milan, 1571–92

DARKNESS AND LIGHT

Caravaggio's art is made from darkness and light. His pictures present spotlit moments of extreme and often agonized human experience. A man is decapitated in his bedchamber, blood spurting from a deep gash in his neck. A man is assassinated on the high altar of a church. A woman is shot in the stomach with a bow and arrow at point-blank range. Caravaggio's images freeze time but also seem to hover on the brink of their own disappearance. Faces are brightly illuminated. Details emerge from darkness with such uncanny clarity that they might be hallucinations. Yet always the shadows encroach, the pools of blackness that threaten to obliterate all. Looking at his pictures is like looking at the world by flashes of lightning.

Caravaggio's life is like his art, a series of lightning flashes in the darkest of nights. He is a man who can never be known in full because almost all that he did, said and thought is lost in the irrecoverable past. He was one of the most electrifyingly original artists ever to have lived, yet we have only one solitary sentence from him on the subject of painting – the sincerity of which is, in any case, questionable, since it was elicited from him when he was under interrogation for the capital crime of libel.

Much of what is known about him has been discovered in the criminal archives of his time. The majority of his recorded acts – apart from those involved in painting – are crimes and misdemeanours. When Caravaggio emerges from the obscurity of the past he does so, like the characters in his own paintings, as a man *in extremis*.

He lived much of his life as a fugitive, and that is how he is preserved in history – a man on the run, heading for the hills, keeping to the shadows. But he is caught, now and again, by the sweeping beam of a searchlight. Each glimpse is different. He appears in many guises, moods and predicaments. Caravaggio throws stones at the house of his landlady and sings ribald songs outside her window. He has a fight with a waiter about the dressing on a plate of artichokes. He taunts a rival with graphic sexual insults. He attacks a man in the street. He kills a man in a swordfight. He and a gang of other men inflict grievous bodily harm on a Knight of Justice on the island of Malta. He is himself attacked by four armed men in the street outside a low-life tavern in Naples. His life is a series of intriguing and vivid tableaux – scenes that abruptly switch, as in the plays of his English contemporary William Shakespeare, from comedy to tragedy, from low farce to high drama.

Anyone attempting a biography of Caravaggio must play the detective as well as the art historian. The facts are rarely straightforward and the patterns of intention that lie behind them often obscure. The artist's life can easily seem merely chaotic, the rise and fall of an incurable hot-head, a man so governed by passion that his actions unfold without rhyme or reason (this was, for centuries, the prevailing view of him). But there is a logic to it all and, with hindsight, a tragic inevitability. Despite the many black holes and discontinuities in the shadowplay of Caravaggio's life, certain structures of belief and certain habits of behaviour run through all that he did and all that he painted. The evidence has to be decoded using guesswork, intuition, speculation and above all a sense of historical imagination – a willingness to delve as deeply as possible into the codes and values that lie behind the words and deeds of a far distant past.

A lot has been made of Caravaggio's presumed homosexuality, which has in more than one previous account of his life been presented as the single key that explains everything, both the power of his art and the misfortunes of his life. There is no absolute proof of it, only strong circumstantial evidence and much rumour. The balance of probability suggests that Caravaggio did indeed have sexual relations with men. But he certainly had female lovers. Throughout the years that he spent in Rome he kept close company with a number of prostitutes.

The truth is that Caravaggio was as uneasy in his relationships as he was in most other aspects of life. He likely slept with men. He did sleep with women. But he settled with no one. From a very young age, and with good cause, he suffered from a deep sense of abandonment. If any one thing lay behind the erratic behaviour that doomed him to an early death, it was the tragedy that befell him and his family when he was still just a little boy. The idea that he was an early martyr to the drives of an unconventional sexuality is an anachronistic fiction.

To understand the emotions that drove him and the experiences that most deeply shaped him, it is necessary to begin where he was born: in the town of Caravaggio, in Lombardy, from which he would later take his name. He lived both there and in the nearby city of Milan for the first twenty-one years of his life. His youth is the least documented period of his existence – the darkest time, in every sense, of this life of light and darkness. But in its shadows may be found some of the most important clues to the formation of his turbulent personality.

FACTS AND FICTIONS

There are three early biographies of Caravaggio. All were composed after his death, and each is unreliable for different reasons. The first was written during the second decade of the seventeenth century by Giulio Mancini, a physician from Siena who met Caravaggio in Rome, probably in about 1592, and who knew him well between 1595 and 1600. The second was published in 1642 by Giovanni Baglione, a rival painter who had competed and quarrelled with Caravaggio during his years in Rome, in particular between 1601 and 1606, on one occasion suing him for libel in response to some scabrous verses, on another going so far as to accuse him of hiring paid assassins to kill him. The third was written, three decades later, by an antiquarian and art theorist named Giovanni Pietro Bellori, who had never known Caravaggio and who based his own account on those of the two earlier authors.

Mancini is sporadically informative but frustratingly brief. Baglione is more circumstantial and surprisingly objective, given that he was writing the life of a man whom he suspected of having plotted to murder him. As a rule of thumb, Baglione is the most trustworthy early source. His biography has been shown to be extremely accurate in its presentation of the bare facts. Many later discoveries of original documents concerning Caravaggio have simply confirmed the truth of his original account. Baglione is only really unreliable in his smug, moralizing conclusions, which are plainly coloured by *Schadenfreude*. This is particularly evident in the mean-spirited passages that tell the story of Caravaggio's various falls from grace.

Bellori wrote his life of Caravaggio considerably later. It was published in 1672, more than sixty years after the painter's death. Bellori plainly drew much of his material from Baglione. But he did glean some new facts. He also went to much trouble to see the painter's works *in situ*. He was seduced by their power and their drama, and fascinated by the novelty of Caravaggio's technique. Bellori wrote about the painter's art with far greater sensitivity than either Mancini or Baglione. Yet he was also fundamentally appalled by it. Caravaggio's vivid capturing of poverty and violence – his depictions of Christ and the Virgin Mary as barefoot paupers, his bloodily realistic portrayals of Christian martyrdom – went directly against Bellori's own most cherished beliefs. Bellori upheld the academic principle that art should not represent the world as it is, but as it should be, sweetened and idealized. So although he responded instinctively to Caravaggio's captivating realism, he felt bound to condemn him all the more strongly for it. Bellori crystallized what would remain for centuries the standard academic objection to the painter's work:

> Repudiating all other rules, [Caravaggio] considered the highest achievement not to be bound to art. For this innovation he was greatly acclaimed, and many talented artists seemed compelled to follow him ... Such praise caused Caravaggio to appreciate himself alone, and he claimed to be the only faithful imitator of nature. Nevertheless, he lacked *invenzione*, decorum, *disegno* [draughtsmanship], or any knowledge of the science of painting. The moment the model was taken from him, his hand and his mind became empty.

Bellori went on to say that 'Just as certain herbs produce both beneficial medicine and most pernicious poison, in the same way, though he produced some good, Caravaggio has been most harmful and wrought havoc with every ornament and good tradition of painting.'[1]

6

In other words, the painter might have had a gift for mimicking reality, but there was no depth to him. If Bellori were to be believed, he was little more than a machine for producing optically convincing images – a kind of human camera, with his workshop a prototypical photographer's studio, long before the invention of photography itself. In this way was the myth of Caravaggio as an untutored, thoughtless virtuoso, the master of a debased and pernicious brand of naturalism, attached like an anchor to his posthumous reputation.[2] In fact, he was an extremely thoughtful, inventive painter, a close and careful reader of the texts that he was called to dramatize and to embody in the form of images. But how and where he got his education remains unknown, partly because his three biographers have so little to say about his early life.

MODEST ORIGINS, NOBLE CONNECTIONS

Caravaggio was born three years after the publication of the second, revised edition of Giorgio Vasari's pioneering anthology of artists' biographies, *The Lives of the Most Excellent Painters, Sculptors and Architects*. Vasari's book was the model on which later writers such as Baglione and Bellori based their own collections of artists' lives. In it, he confirmed and sought to extend a great rise in the status of artists within the Italian peninsula during the period now known – also largely thanks to Vasari's efforts – as the Renaissance. Previously the profession of art had been ranked low because it involved work with the hands and was therefore classed as a form of manual labour, a craft rather than a liberal art. But implicit throughout Vasari's thousand and more pages is the belief that the greatest artists deserve to be ranked with poets and philosophers as men of true genius, rightful companions of kings and princes.

As well as raising the reputation of his own profession, Vasari established certain formulae for writing the life of an artist. Particularly famous painters and sculptors, such as Giotto or Michelangelo, are established as miraculous prodigies from an early age: the brilliance of Giotto, for example, is said to have been discovered by the older artist Cimabue, who came upon the young man when he was still a callow shepherd and found him drawing perfectly upon a stone. But no such uplifting fables are attached to the youth of Caravaggio by his biographers. Mancini compresses his early life to just two sentences, and Baglione to a paragraph. Bellori has a tale to tell about the young Caravaggio, but it runs counter to the kind of prodigy stories favoured by Vasari because it is designed to stress the artist's principal failing, as Bellori saw it – his supposed *lack* of intellect, which meant that his work could never rise from mere craft.

Bellori's story tells of Caravaggio's origins as the son of an artisan. Since the painter 'was employed in Milan with his father, a mason, it happened that he prepared glue for some painters who were painting frescoes and, led on by the desire to paint, he remained with them, applying himself totally to painting. He continued in this activity four or five years . . .' Bellori may have meant to imply that this imitative, unreflective training predisposed Caravaggio to his great mistake – that of recognizing 'no other master than the model, without selecting from the best forms of nature'.[3] His moral is certainly blunt: once a craftsman, always a craftsman.

The story is not exactly true but like many stories about Caravaggio it contains elements of the truth. He could never have been employed in tasks such as preparing glue or plaster for his father, because his father died when Caravaggio was only five years old. But the record shows that Fermo Merisi was indeed a mason. This might suggest that the artist's origins were, as Bellori implies, rooted in the humble world of the artisan. But the sources hint at a more complicated truth. There is room for ambiguity because Fermo Merisi's job of mason could encompass different ways of working with stone, and possibly even the vocation of architect.

Baglione's brief account broadly agrees with that of Bellori – he simply says that the artist, 'born in Caravaggio in Lombardy, was the son of a mason, quite well off'.[4] But Mancini makes the artist's background sound considerably grander. According to him, 'He was born in Caravaggio of honourable citizens since his father was majordomo and architect to the Marchese di Caravaggio.'[5] Mancini may have got the gist of his account from the artist himself, in particular the idea that Caravaggio was of better than merely common birth. A number of incidents in the painter's later life indicate that he believed that he came from good stock, and deserved respect on account of that. It is important to establish the truth, because Caravaggio's elevated sense of his own status would lie at the root of many of his future troubles.

Most of the known facts about Caravaggio's youth were published by the scholar Mina Cinotti in 1983.[6] One of the more revealing documents to emerge from her research records the wedding of the artists' parents. On 14 January 1571 Fermo Merisi married a woman called Lucia Aratori. Fermo was born in about 1540 and was a widower, with a daughter named Margherita by his first marriage. Lucia was some ten years younger than him and had not been married before. Fermo was recorded as resident in Milan, but the marriage took place in the town of Caravaggio, where both his bride and the rest of his family lived. It would have been an unexceptional wedding had it not been for the presence, among the witnesses, of the Marchese Francesco I Sforza di Caravaggio. The marchese was a member of one of the leading noble families of Italy, the Sforza, who were former lords of Milan. His wife, the young Marchesa di Caravaggio, was from the enormously powerful Colonna family. These were the most important people in the neighbourhood.

The presence of nobility at the nuptials of the Merisi family turns out to have had precious little to do with Caravaggio's father. Fermo Merisi was just an ordinary stonemason, perhaps reasonably well off but with no great social pretensions. He was certainly *not* an architect. In a number of documents relating to him he is referred to as a *mastro*, designating him as a qualified artisan with the right to set up his own workshop and hire apprentices. He ran this modest business in Milan. His probate inventory lists 'some old iron mason's tools', but does not include any books or instruments that would indicate a knowledge of the theoretical aspects of architecture. His retention of an independent workshop makes it unlikely that he was in the direct employ of the Marchese di Caravaggio. Caravaggio's paternal grandfather, Bernardino Merisi, was himself no higher up the social scale. He too had run a small business. He was a wine merchant and vintner based at the family home in Porta Seriola, in the north-east quarter of Caravaggio.

There were in fact close links between Caravaggio's family and the noble Colonna dynasty, but all on the side of the painter's mother.[7] Her father, Giovan Giacomo Aratori, was an *agrimensor*, or 'surveyor', whose job it was to help resolve disputes over land ownership. He was also involved in buying and selling land. His work brought him directly into contact with the Colonna, who owned much property in the region. Whereas Caravaggio's father and paternal grandfather worked with their hands, Giovan Giacomo was a professional rather than an artisan. His work required more literacy than that of a mason, as well as a knowledge of geometry and arithmetic. In 1570, a year before the birth of his grandson, the future painter, he was made a member of the college of land surveyors of the Duchy of Milan.

Giovan Giacomo Aratori also played his part in the religious life of Caravaggio. The most celebrated event in the history of this sleepy little agricultural town had occurred in 1432, when a peasant girl working in the fields was reputed to have had a vision of the Virgin Mary. According to legend a freshwater spring had miraculously gushed from the spot where she experienced her vision, and a shrine had been subsequently erected to the honour of the wonder-working 'Madonna della Fontana'. By the second half of the sixteenth century, the shrine of Santa Maria della Fontana had become the most significant religious institution in Caravaggio. It was administered by a body of *scolari*, to which Giovan Giacomo was elected at various times from the mid 1560s onwards.

In addition, he held important positions in the local *comune*, as councillor, treasurer and emissary to the Spanish authorities (the Duchy of Milan, including the town of Caravaggio, was at that time part of the vast Habsburg empire, controlled by Philip II of Spain from the Escorial, his palace and monastery outside Madrid). Giovan Giacomo's many responsibilities meant that he was a familiar figure among the local nobility. He acted directly as an agent for the Marchese Francesco Sforza I di Caravaggio, served as a legal witness for the Sforza family and collected rents on their behalf. Some documents connect him directly to the marchese, others to the marchese's wife, Costanza Colonna.

There were yet more intimate links between the Colonna family and the Aratori clan. Giovan Giacomo's daughter Margherita, Caravaggio's maternal aunt, was wet-nurse to the Sforza children. She lived in the Colonna household for many years and breastfed Costanza Colonna's sons, including the future adventurer and sometime militant Knight of the Order of St John, Fabrizio Sforza Colonna. In 1584, as a reward for her service, Costanza gave Margherita a small estate in Fara d'Adda, near the town of Caravaggio. As late as 1601 Margherita was still in regular touch with the marchesa, writing letters to her in Rome – at a time when Caravaggio, elsewhere in the city, was receiving some of his most important commissions.

Costanza Colonna would be called on many times by Caravaggio. Always she would respond. She would be a constant support to him in times of crisis, giving him shelter when he was on the run and shielding him when he was under sentence of death. Yet, unlike any of his other noble allies or protectors, she would never try to acquire a painting by his hand. All the evidence suggests that she genuinely cared for him, perhaps even loved him as a child of her own. Her influence and that of her family, with its tentacular network of feudal and familial alliances, reaching right across the Italian peninsula, can be sensed throughout Caravaggio's life – but especially during his later and more troubled years.

Social class, in particular questions of 'nobility' and 'virtue', would be at issue in many of Caravaggio's future disputes and quarrels. These were matters of intense debate in medieval and Renaissance Italy. In northern Europe the aristocracy took its own pre-eminence for granted and assumed that nobility was a quality that could only truly inhere in those fortunate enough to be born into the upper, landed classes. There, a nobleman was easily identified: a man of virtue and pure blood, who had the right to bear arms in the service of his monarch, who was a skilled swordsman and horseman and would never dirty his hands with trade. In Italy the situation was more ambiguous, because Italian society was more fluid and its ruling elites more diverse, made up of imperial knights, communal knights, magnates and other types of feudal lord. It was also an increasingly urbanized society, and that too led to the blurring of social distinctions. From the second half of the fourteenth century onwards, urban patriciates sought to tighten their hold on government. The men who made up those bodies, which included merchants, moneylenders, textile manufacturers and other drivers of early capitalism, were themselves intensely class conscious. They founded their own dynasties, staked their own claims to *nobilità* – so much so that the very term itself became, in Italy, shifting and unstable. As early as the fourteenth century, writers ranging from the poet Dante to medieval jurists had struggled to define the concept. Legal definitions based purely on titles conferred by the monarchy or the church were countered by those who preferred to regard nobility as a moral quality to which, in theory, almost anyone could aspire.[8]

What position did Caravaggio's maternal grandfather occupy within this world of subtly shaded social distinctions? Giovan Giacomo Aratori is referred to in the documents of the time as *signor*, *messer* or *dominus*. While his social status was certainly higher than that of anyone on the Merisi side of Caravaggio's family, neither he nor his descendants possessed any actual titles. He was a member of what might be called the upper, professional bourgeoisie, while the likes of Bernardino and Fermo Merisi belonged to the petty, trade bourgeoisie. Mancini's statement that Caravaggio was born into a family of 'very honourable citizens' – *cittadini* is the word he uses in Italian – was entirely accurate.

But in the small world of Caravaggio, where the artist spent much of his youth, his status may to him have seemed grander than that. As we have seen, his maternal grandfather was a highly respected man, but other factors may have conspired to make him feel that both he and his family were blessed by aristocratic favour. Maybe Costanza Colonna showed particular favours or kindnesses to Caravaggio's mother, Lucia, sister to her own children's wet-nurse. Lucia's early years of motherhood were hard indeed, marked by bereavement and loss. Costanza Colonna too had suffered a difficult time during the early years of her marriage to Francesco I Sforza. She had been married off, as the custom then was among the nobility, at the age of thirteen. The duties of a wife had at first been abhorrent to her, so much so that she had at one point threatened suicide. Did Costanza Colonna feel a particular sympathy for Lucia and her young children during the harsh years of their early upbringing? It is impossible to know for sure, but she certainly took a particular interest in Caravaggio's wellbeing later in his life. Perhaps the date of his birth had something to do with it too, because as far as anyone in Christendom was concerned – but especially a Colonna – he was born at an auspicious time.

THE ANGEL WITH SWORD AND SHIELD

Caravaggio grew up as Michelangelo Merisi. It was an evocative name for a future artist – the same Christian name as that of the most famous Italian sculptor and painter of all, Michelangelo Buonarrotti, who had died just seven years earlier. But Caravaggio's parents did not have that in mind when they named their son. They called him Michelangelo for reasons of faith and superstition. He came into the world on 29 September 1571. His parents named him after the Archangel Michael, whose feast day it was.

This was a charged and momentous time in the history of Christendom. Throughout the 1550s and 1560s the Christian powers of the western Mediterranean were threatened by the forces of Islam – led first by the Ottoman Sultan Suleiman 'The Magnificent', and then by his successor, Selim II. The bitter and bloody conflict between Muslim and Christian reached a climax at exactly the moment of Caravaggio's birth. In 1570-71 Christian Cyprus, a strategically vital island fortress long controlled by the Venetians, fell into Ottoman hands. The garrison stationed at Famagusta, the last Christian stronghold in Cyprus, fought bravely before being forced to surrender. The survivors of the siege were cruelly massacred. Churches and cathedrals were converted into mosques, their stained glass smashed, their paintings and sculptures destroyed, their belltowers turned into minarets. Pope Pius V was appalled not only by the atrocity and its immediate consequences, but also by the possibility that the Ottomans might gain control over the principal trade routes of the Mediterranean. He joined forces with the Venetians, and together the allies sought additional support wherever they could find it. Missions were sent to Spain, to Portugal and to all the independent states of Italy. The princely families of southern Europe rallied together and thousands of soldiers were pressed into service. The result was no mere political alliance, but a self-styled Holy League for the defence of Christendom against the infidel.

Under the command of Don Juan of Austria, illegitimate brother of Philip II of Spain, a vast fleet of galleys – most of them constructed, in record time, within the great dockyard-cum-factory production-line that was Venice's Arsenale – set out to humble the Turkish navy. Eight days after Caravaggio's birth, on 7 October 1571, the two sides met in the Greek Gulf of Corinth, then known in the west as the Gulf of Lepanto. The result was the last great sea battle fought between galley-rowed ships. Both sides suffered heavy casualties. Eight thousand Christians died, and many more Turks. But, while the fleet of the Holy League survived the battle all but intact, the Ottoman fleet was destroyed and its commander-in-chief killed. One of the heroes of the battle was the commander of the papal forces, Marcantonio Colonna, father to Costanza Colonna, father-in-law to Francesco I Sforza, who had been witness at the wedding of Fermo Merisi and Lucia Aratori. After the victory, the pope declared that the Virgin Mary herself had interceded with God on behalf of the Holy League. Henceforward, the day of the victory was to be remembered as the Feast of Our Lady of Victory. Marian cults across Catholic Europe received a huge boost to their popularity. In Venice the day was declared a permanent *festum solemnis,* to be marked every year by a procession led by the doge, and by celebratory masses. All across Italy, churches were built in honour of Santa Maria della Vittoria. Devotion to the Rosary reached a new pitch of intensity.

The Battle of Lepanto was a triumph to salve the wounds of a Christian world that had been sundered by the Reformation some half a century before. The Protestant king of faraway Scotland, James VI, was so carried away by the news that he wrote an epic poem to celebrate the great Catholic victory (though he felt compelled to add a prefatory disclaimer that Don Juan of Austria, hero of his verses, should still be regarded as 'a foreign papist bastard'). Meanwhile, Costanza Colonna's father, Marcantonio, made his triumphal entry into Rome. He rode into the city on a white horse, a modern-day Mark Antony stealing the glory of the caesars of old. But he also had the decorum to temper that show of pride with a spectacular display of humility. Having processed in triumph, he exchanged the armour of victory for rags and set forth on a pilgrimage to give thanks to Our Lady of Loreto.[9]

Michelangelo Merisi had been born on a day full of promise for zealous Christians, whose world was under threat. Archangel Michael had been the guardian angel of the Hebrew nation, and was associated with the protection of the faithful from harm. He had also been adopted, in Christian times, as the principal saint of the Church Militant. In depictions of the Last Judgement, he weighs the souls of the blessed and the damned, separating good from evil. In such paintings he is commonly shown wearing chain-mail and armed with a sword and shield, symbols of the archangel's ancient association with knights and crusades, and holy wars against the infidel.

Michelangelo was a fitting Christian name for any child within the sphere of the Colonna family, defenders of the faith and warriors against heresy – but all the more so in the case of a child born not just on the saint's name day, but on the eve of a great battle between Christian and Muslim in which the head of the Colonna family himself would take a leading role. When victory at the Battle of Lepanto followed within just over a week of his birth, the hopes and prayers attendant on his baptism were answered. Perhaps he was thought of as a child who had brought good luck. Perhaps that was another reason why, despite his difficult personality and frequent lapses into criminal behaviour, Costanza Colonna would always stand by him.

TOWN AND CITY

The artist's early life was divided between the town of Caravaggio and the city of Milan. The contrast between the two could hardly have been greater. Set in the fertile plains of Lombardy, Caravaggio was a quiet place, architecturally undistinguished, which had once been a Roman outpost. The activities of the town revolved around agriculture, which was vital to the booming prosperity of the region. Since the later Middle Ages the entire area had been intensively developed. Irrigation channels, networks of stream and canal that still criss-cross the fields today, had been systematically introduced. Better understanding of crop rotation had transformed the area into a prime producer of cereals. Large plantations of mulberry trees were grown as feed for silkworms, silk being the essential raw material for Milan's booming textile industry. The people of Caravaggio lived and worked by the rhythms of nature. They were known for their phlegmatic character, their solid business sense and their piety, the symbol of which was, from the 1580s onwards, the construction of the great shrine dedicated to Santa Maria della Fontana. Caravaggio was tranquil bordering on dull, a place where it felt as though nothing much had happened for a hundred years and more.

Milan, the great city, two hours' ride away, had a population of 100,000, much the same as that of London or Paris at the time. Milan was noise and bustle, trade and industry, a populous and prosperous city – the place where Fermo Merisi, Caravaggio's father, went to work each day with his mason's tools of iron. It was a city known for the skill of its stone-workers and the ingenuity of its sword-makers. Milanese armour, Milanese swords and Milanese daggers were renowned as the finest in Italy. The men of the city were famous for their swordsmanship, a skill at which Caravaggio would come to excel.

The men of Milan were also known for their singular reluctance to marry. 'In Italy marryage is indeede a yoke, and that not easy, but so grevious, as brethren no where better agreeing, yet contend among themselves to be free from marryage.'[10] Distrust of matrimony was common enough in sixteenth- and seventeenth-century Italy, especially among the upper classes, to have provoked many such comments from visitors. Italian humanists, including Petrarch and Leonbattista Alberti, had railed against marriage as a distraction to the intellect and a potential cause of economic ruin. Nowhere was the misogynistic cult of celibacy stronger than in Lombardy. It did not necessarily entail sexual abstinence, merely a refusal to be yoked to any single woman. The rate of celibacy among the Milanese aristocracy reached unprecedentedly high levels in the second half of the seventeenth century, so much so that it has been calculated that more than fifty per cent of all high-born males in the city never married at all.[11] Caravaggio would never marry either, although it is impossible to establish whether this was another example of the painter imitating aristocratic *mores*, or simply the result of his restless temperament.

The traveller Thomas Coryat visited Milan in 1608, by which time Caravaggio was long gone from the city. But the Englishman's vivid account, published in 1611 under the title *Coryat's Crudities*, describes the metropolis much as it had been when Caravaggio was young. Coryat noted Milan's conspicuous opulence, and the many luxury trades that thrived there: 'No City of Italy is furnished with more manuary arts than this. Their embroderers are very singular workemen, who worke much in gold and silver. Their cutlers that make hilts are more exquisite in the art than any that I ever saw. Of these two trades there is a great multitude in the city: Also silkemen do abound here, which are esteemed so good that they are not inferiour to any of the Christian world.'[12]

He grouped the city's armourers and sword-makers together with its embroiderers and silk-workers, perhaps implying that all were working in different branches of the Milanese fashion industry. The ability to fight was certainly just as important, to a young man out to impress, as the clothes that he wore. Swordsmanship was part of that intangible code of pseudo-chivalric skills and values encompassed by the Italian words *virtù* and *nobilità* – although in Caravaggio's Italy it was never easy to tell whether a young man's aspirations to virtuous nobility were rooted in fact or fantasy.

Coryat was also struck by the number of churches in Milan and impressed by the city's close links with some of the most dynamic figures of early Christianity. He visited the church of St Ambrose, where the relics of Ambrose himself, Bishop of Milan in the fourth century, were preserved. He seems not to have visited Santa Maria delle Grazie, the Dominican friary for which Leonardo da Vinci, more than a hundred years before, had painted his famous *Last Supper* (another English traveller, Fynes Moryson, who visited Milan in 1618, noted that 'in this Monastery ... in the place where the Friers eate, the supper of our lord is painted with wonderfull art'). But Coryat did pay a trip to Milan's cathedral, 'an exceeding glorious and beautifull Church, as fair if not fairer then the Cathedrall Church of Amiens', where he witnessed 'one of the nayles wherewith Christ was crucified, as they affirme'. He then climbed the cathedral tower to get a view of the whole city and the plains beyond, the little town of Caravaggio somewhere in their midst. As he did so, looking out and beyond the city's nine great gates, he encompassed the whole world of the artist's childhood:

> There I observed the huge suburbs, which are as bigge as many a faire towne, and compassed about with ditches of water: there also I beheld a great part of Italy, together with the lofty Apennines; and they shewed me which way Rome, Venice, Naples, Florence, Genoa, Ravenna &c. lay. The territory of Lombardy, which I contemplated round about from this tower, was so pleasant an object to mine eyes, being replenished with such unspeakable variety of all things, both for profite and pleasure, that it seemeth to me to be the very Elysian fieldes, so much decantated and celebrated by the verses of Poets, or the Tempe or Paradise of the world. For it is the fairest plaine, extended about two hundred miles in length that ever I saw, or ever shall if I should travell over the whole habitable world: insomuch that I said to my selfe that this country was fitter to be an habitation for the immortall Gods than for mortall men.

Milan was built on a circular plan. At the centre of the circle stood the massive, intimidating Castello Sforzesco. This daunting structure had originally been built as a palace for the mighty Sforza dynasty. It is an epitome of the Renaissance architecture of tyranny, with its dark and towering walls covered with diamond rustication, like the studs on a knuckleduster. When Milan came under Habsburg control in the 1530s, the patronage of the Sforza came to an end. Caravaggio knew the building as the fortress from which the city's Spanish governors nervously ruled, ever on the lookout for insurrectionists within and heretics without. Hostile, watchful suspicion was a frame of mind deeply ingrained in the Spanish rulers of Milan. They knew how important it was that they maintained their grip on the city. Whoever controlled Milan controlled the overland route from Italy to the rest of Europe. Milan would be on the front line in the event of any attempted invasion from the Protestant north, so it needed its heavy fortifications. In Caravaggio's day, the principal danger was thought to lie in France and, to a lesser degree, Switzerland. For all the animosity between the Milanese and their occupiers – caused to a large extent by taxes and grain levies on the local people to feed the Spanish troops – the religious and political interests of Catholic Spain and

Catholic Italy were as one in the face of such perceived threats from the Protestant north.

Milan had been a strategically important city since the days of the Roman empire, when Julius Caesar and Pompey had at different times made their residence there. Unlike the caesars of the past, Philip II of Spain did not go so far as to live in Milan. But he jealously guarded his power over the city. He had inherited both his crown and his empire from his father, Emperor Charles V. There is no more vivid document of the larger world of *realpolitik*, of the patterns of religious and political division that fractured Europe in Caravaggio's time, than the long 'Instruction' that the ailing Charles V dictated, towards the end of his life, for the benefit of his son. He warned his heir to watch out for the dangers lying in wait throughout the vast range of his territories, from Spain to Naples, from the Netherlands all the way across to Germany and Austria. He gave particular emphasis to the importance of keeping a grip on Milan, a key military outpost at the crossroads of Europe:

Leave German affairs, as I now do, to my brother Ferdinand, but maintain contacts there, for your vigilance must be alert throughout all the possessions of our house. The most constant threat comes from France. Their kings have been and are bound to us by treaties, but remember that they are not true to their undertakings and only keep to their word when they are too poor to go to war ... Keep a good guard on our northern borders with France, and maintain a fleet of galleys in the Mediterranean as a warning both to the Turks and to the French. We need to maintain good relations with Genoa because of its port, so take good care for this.

In the north-east I have strengthened Flanders against France by my annexation of Guelders, Utrecht and Frisia. Still, you must keep money on hand there in case there is need for a sudden mobilisation; the inhabitants are reasonably loyal to us, but do not relax your watchfulness ... I have settled the affairs of Savoy somewhat to the detriment of our ally the Duke, but do not help him to recover the lands occupied by the French even if they are his by right. That could give the French an excuse to press south again against our Milan and if that happens our links with Genoa and Florence and our rule in Naples and Sicily could all be put at risk.

Still Charles V continued, spinning out a web of complex alliances and counter-alliances, seeking to pass on to his son his own, pragmatically paranoid brand of statecraft:

> Further to Italy: do not trust the Pope, who neither honours his word nor has the general interests of Christianity at heart; keep an eye on any strengthening of the Duke of Ferrara's family relationships with the French; Venice is unlikely to form any close attachment to France, Florence is much indebted to our support of the Duke and is safe, but be watchful of Lucca and Siena. Above all, keep Milan and Naples well garrisoned with troops regularly paid to keep them loyal to us. As for the rest, remember that the Swiss covet part of our Franche-Comté; keep on good terms with England but, given the Pope's resentment against that country, very warily; with Scotland, you need have little to do.[13]

Charles V gave Philip II that advice in 1548. By the 1570s relations between Spain and the papacy had somewhat improved, but Europe remained the same fractious place described in the emperor's world-weary anatomy of the continent's political and religious divisions. And Milan, important enough to get two mentions in his long memorandum, remained vital to Spanish interests. Charles V always regarded the city as 'the key to Italy', and his son Philip II never deviated from that view. To lose Milan would not only expose the whole of Spanish rule in southern Italy to danger; it would also separate Spain from its territories in the Low Countries. The caution of Milan's Spanish rulers was exacerbated by their knowledge that the city's defence was in the hands of no more than around 5,000 soldiers. Any hint of trouble – the merest suggestion that the French were fomenting revolt in Genoa, the chance appearance of a group of gypsies from Venice – and a state of emergency was liable to be declared.

On the surface, the city where Caravaggio spent much of his youth was run as it had been during the era of Sforza rule. The Duchy of Milan might have become a vassal of Spain, but its bureaucratic apparatus remained unchanged and the same magistracies held the reins of power. The most significant difference was that the Consiglio Segreto, or 'secret council', that had once advised the Sforza dukes now reported to the Spanish governor. The Senate continued to exercise supreme judicial and administrative authority in the city, but was obliged to do so with a careful eye to Spanish interests.[14] The members of the Senate were jurists drawn from the Milanese patriciate, men with a strong sense of Milanese legal traditions, whereas the governor of the city was one of the highest representatives of the Spanish sovereign, who was naturally disposed to act in accordance with Spain's larger strategic aims. Milanese politics was a balancing act, a fragile equilibrium of occupier and occupied.

Institutional continuity under Spanish rule was mirrored by a continuity of approach to the balance of secular and religious powers. The Sforza had pursued a gradually consistent policy of strengthening civil authority and weakening that of the Church. One of their main aims had been to establish control over ecclesiastical nominations in the Duchy of Milan, so that those whom they considered politically undesirable, or outright hostile, could be excluded from powerful positions such as that of bishop. Under Spanish rule, this strategy was pursued to the point where many other traditional powers of the Church were usurped by the state. Frequently, it was the civil, rather than the religious, authority that tried those accused of heresy, that took responsibility for discipline in the duchy's convents and monasteries, and that assumed the right to punish clerical abuses. This naturally reinforced Spanish power over all areas of life in Milan, but, though its aim was to limit ecclesiastical powers and privileges, it was never intended to weaken the Catholic faith itself.

In his instructions to his viceroys and governors, the fervently devout Philip II constantly stressed that the defence of Catholicism was his absolute priority. He had inherited a medieval Spanish conception of his role as monarch, according to which his first duty was *servicio de Dios*. He was brought up to believe that as king he had been singled out as the instrument of divine will. So, by a self-perpetuatingly circular logic, his policies were held to be those decreed by God and those best calculated to advance the holy mission of Catholicism. Spain's cause *was* the cause of God; and this was true even if Spanish policies clashed directly with those of the supreme ecclesiastical authority, the pope. That was exactly what happened in Milan during the years immediately before and after the birth of Caravaggio. Other circumstances besides conspired to create a mood of incendiary religious fervour, often bordering on hysteria, in the city where the artist spent his formative years.

CARLO BORROMEO

The dominant figure in Milan during Caravaggio's youth was not a Spaniard but an Italian. Carlo Borromeo was a dour and deeply pious man with a fierce sense of mission. He became Archbishop of Milan in 1565. He saw the city as the world itself in microcosm, a place teetering on the brink of damnation, teeming with sinners to be converted and souls to be saved. Like the ascetic Dominican friar Savonarola, who had preached in Florence almost a hundred years before, Borromeo galvanized the Milan of Caravaggio's childhood into regular paroxysms of mass repentance. His appearance, gaunt, hollow-cheeked, charismatically severe, was itself symbolic: a visible sign, like the rags adopted four centuries earlier by St Francis of Assisi, that Borromeo had renounced wealth and privilege to follow directly in the footsteps of Christ and his apostles.

Although he would become one of the most radical reformers of the Catholic faith and way of life, he had first been pressed into the service of the Church by the forces of old-fashioned nepotism. His uncle, Pope Pius IV, appointed him to the position of his own private secretary and elevated him to the rank of cardinal when Borromeo was still barely in his twenties (and despite the fact that he had received no theological training). Yet he soon justified that favouritism. A skilled negotiator, he played a vital part at the end of the Council of Trent. This was the hugely significant nineteenth Ecumenical Council of the Roman Catholic Church – and was, in essence, the Catholic Church's concerted response to the multiple challenges to its authority posed by the Protestant Reformation.

It was at the Council of Trent that the Catholic Church reaffirmed the importance of the sacraments and the role of the priesthood; that it insisted on the importance of good works as well as of faith, in contradiction of Martin Luther's belief in 'justification by faith alone'; that it pronounced its own interpretation of the Bible final, branding any Christian with the temerity to substitute his or her own interpretations a heretic; and that it reaffirmed a multitude of Catholic practices that had been criticized by reformers in the north, such as pilgrimage and the veneration of saints and their relics. These were the basic principles that would underpin the Counter-Reformation, as it became known, the Catholic riposte to Protestant reformers. Yet such was the mood of contention surrounding the questions under debate, in which nothing less than the future of the Catholic Church was at stake, that there were many times when it seemed as though agreement might never be reached. First summoned in 1537, the council was concluded only in 1562–3. Carlo Borromeo was one of the men who saved it, at the last, from breaking down altogether.

He was a hard worker, who rarely slept for more than five hours and often went without food due to the permanent backlog of papal business requiring his attention. But to those who did not know about his punishing regime he may well have seemed like just another corrupt cardinal-nephew, the latest in a long line of such self-serving placemen. The pope appointed him to a dazzling array of positions, including the Protector of Portugal, of Lower Germany and of the seven Catholic cantons of Switzerland; as well as Protector of the Carmelites, Franciscans, Humiliati, Canons Regular of the Holy Cross at Coimbra and of the orders of St John and Christ in Portugal.[15] He was also the absentee abbot of a number of monastic foundations. From these sources and his family estates he derived an annual income of around 50,000 scudi, a princely sum in mid sixteenth-century Italy. He was a keen and energetic huntsman who spent lavishly on his horses and hounds, and equally lavishly on his household, which he turned into a magnificent manifestation of his innate asceticism and sobriety: he kept one hundred and fifty servants and retainers, all dressed from head to toe in a uniform of funereal black velvet.

Borromeo in his youth was a volatile combination of pride and piety, but it would take a personal tragedy to transform him into one of the most fervent and inventively radical priests of the Counter-Reformation. His elder brother, Federico Borromeo, died suddenly in 1562. Carlo, who was administrator of the pope's native diocese, the Archbishopric of Milan, was widely expected to give up his career in the Church, renounce his vows of piety and continue the family line by marrying in order to father a son and heir. Instead, he concluded that all man's earthly hopes and aspirations amounted to no more than a handful of dust. He gave up the trappings of wealth, sacked the majority of his household staff and forbade those remaining in his service to wear garments of silk or to indulge in any other luxuries. He took holy orders and briefly considered retreating from the world altogether, to a monastery. Eventually he decided that it was his role in the divine plan to revive and reform the Roman Catholic Church – and he set about the task with the evangelical zeal of a man convinced that he had God on his side.

It was only after the death of his brother that Carlo Borromeo's influence would really be felt in Milan. In 1565 he was consecrated Archbishop of Milan. He signalled his intentions by making his triumphal entry into the city wearing archbishop's robes, rather than dressed as a cardinal. It was his way of indicating that he came with his own sense of duty and purpose, not as the mere servant of papal Rome. He was determined to make the city and its provinces into the crucible for an extraordinary socio-religious experiment. Under his steely control and watchful gaze, the 900,000 souls of the Duchy of Milan were to be systematically indoctrinated in the ways of his own, deeply ascetic brand of piety. What he attempted was nothing less than a form of forced mass conversion to what he saw as the real and true tenets of Christian faith.

The archbishop had a darkly pessimistic view of human nature. He passionately opposed the doctrine of free will favoured by so many Protestants, and by some within his own church. To him, the idea that man had a God-given ability to choose between good and evil was a pernicious lie. He had a revealing disagreement with another prominent figure in the Counter-Reformation Catholic Church, the Bolognese theologian Gabriele Paleotti. Paleotti argued that 'Since God created human volition free and its own arbiter, it can be forced by no chains, but only sparked with the help of God's grace.' In Borromeo's bleaker view, human nature is 'already tainted by sin' – the Original Sin of Adam and Eve – and 'is by itself so inclined to evil that we easily neglect and forget to do good'. Borromeo's stern conclusion was that 'we need help and stimulants to live well, and always someone to remind us of it.'[16] What that sentence portended, for the people of Milan, was a systematic attempt to change their way of life and transform their habits of thought. Borromeo saw himself as a spiritual successor to St Ambrose. Just as Ambrose had defied the Roman emperor, so Borromeo challenged the Spanish governors of Milan with the aim of asserting his own authority as the city's spiritual leader.

One of his first acts was to reassert the ancient right of the Archbishop of Milan to maintain a private army. Borromeo's so-called *famiglia armata*, or 'armed family', which was a corps of armed men drawn from his own household, became a key weapon in his fight to reform what he regarded as the rotten state of the city. The archbishop claimed wide-ranging powers, so that those suspected of any offence that he judged to touch on public morality – such as heresy, blasphemy or sodomy – were liable to receive the not so tender attentions of his 'family'. He revived the defunct civil and criminal tribunals of the archiepiscopal curia, and reopened ancient prisons for the confinement of those found guilty in Milan's ecclesiastical courts. Borromeo's insistence on the unrestricted use of his *famiglia armata*, and his extension of ecclesiastical authority into areas of life long regulated by the secular courts and justice system, led to numerous clashes with the city's Spanish rulers. At the climax of one particularly acrimonious row over jurisdiction, Borromeo went so far as to excommunicate the Spanish governor, the Marqués de Requesens. When Requesens retaliated, Borromeo himself was nearly exiled from the city.

Borromeo saw to it that the Spanish Inquisition, which operated in Spain's offshore Italian possessions, Sardinia and Sicily, was excluded from Milan. He was able to clip and curtail Spanish power in a number of such ways, largely because he had strong support in Rome. He removed jurisdiction over alleged religious crimes from Milan's Spanish rulers, insisting that he himself should be the final judge in all such cases. But he also slowly won the grudging respect of the pious Philip II – to whom he explained, in a long and persuasive letter, that his aim was not to usurp Spanish power but to strengthen the Roman Catholic Church.[17]

For two decades, throughout the formative period of Caravaggio's life, the archbishop pushed through a multitude of Church reforms intended to control the hearts, souls and minds of the people at large, measures that ranged from the introduction of new confessionals to the segregation of men and women in church. He made no secret of his distaste for self-styled elite clerical associations such as the Theatines or the Barnabites. He actually suppressed one of the orders nominally under his protection, the Humiliati, on the grounds that its membership was restricted to a corrupt, self-serving clique of aristocrats. He was promptly shot in the back at close range by a disgruntled Humiliatus, but survived the attack unharmed – an escape subsequently attributed, by his hagiographers, to divine intervention.

Borromeo was an obsessive regulator and centralizer, and he did his best to turn his clergy into a spiritual equivalent of the *famiglia armata* – a body of Christian soldiers animated by a single purpose and method. All priests with a pastoral duty were obliged to preach every Sunday and feast day. Reports were gathered from every parish in the diocese and underperforming priests were summoned to the archbishop's presence to practise their skills in front of him (they also had to leave a written copy of their sermon behind for his perusal). Not least because Milan was on the frontier with partly Protestant Switzerland, Borromeo was determined to turn his diocese into a shining demonstration of revitalized Roman Catholicism – a beacon to those who had erred, the brilliance of which might persuade them to mend their ways. He built new churches by the score and trained up an army of new priests to spread the word of God to their congregations. He founded diocesan seminaries and many schools. By the time of his death some 40,000 children in the diocese of Milan were being educated at any one time, an unprecedentedly high proportion of the juvenile population.[18] Caravaggio's own family would be directly involved in the Borromean spiritual experiment: his only brother became a priest. No one in Milan and its surroundings was left untouched by the archbishop's plans for spiritual revival.

Borromeo saw sinfulness everywhere and envisaged his priests as an army of spiritual stormtroopers taking the battle to the devil. No detail was too small to escape his eye, especially in the design of churches, which he saw as machines for the purification of an evil world. He wrote entire volumes of instructions about the minutiae of ecclesiastical architecture, the so-called *Instructiones*, in which he pronounced on matters ranging from the precise amount of space church architects should allow for each member of the congregation ('one cubit and eight ounces square' exactly, four square feet in modern terms) to the appropriate scale and decoration of the entrances: 'the middle doorway must be distinguished by its width and ornamented with sculptures of lions ... to represent the Temple of Solomon and the vigilance of bishops.'[19] Borromeo was particularly concerned to ensure that men and women be separated from one another in church. He devised movable screens to be erected between groups of male and female worshippers, to prevent them exchanging glances with one another – often, in Borromeo's view, the first occasion for sin. He also sought to set strict controls on the clothes worn by worshippers, especially female worshippers, whom he berated for coming to church dressed for seduction, as if they were going to Carnival rather than participating in a holy ritual.

The mass of directives issued from the archiepiscopal palace of Milan must have occasionally wearied even the most conscientious of the Milanese clergymen whose task it was to enforce them. Here for example is the archbishop on the intricacies of the holy-water stoup, its placement, its design, its necessary accessories:

> [The holy-water stoup] should not be put outside, but rather inside the church, accessible to those who enter and at their right hand, if possible. One font should be placed on the side where men enter and another ... where the women enter. These [stoups] should not be near the wall but distant from it in proportion to the space that is there. They should be supported ... on a small pillar, or some type of base on which nothing profane appears. There should be a sprinkler on a small metal chain hanging from the rim ... it should not terminate with a sponge rather than bristles. It may terminate with a sponge only if it is enclosed in a silver, tin, or brass-perforated knob that has bristles on the outside.[20]

The bristles about which Borromeo was so particular symbolized the cleansing branches of hyssop that purify the souls of the faithful in the ancient biblical psalm (Psalm 50): 'Sprinkle me with hyssop and I shall be cleansed; wash me and I shall be made whiter than snow.'

Many years later, near the end of his life, when Caravaggio was a fugitive from justice in the Sicilian town of Messina, he was offered some holy water in a little church. The story is told by Francesco

Susinno, a Messinese writer of artists' lives. It suggests that Caravaggio may still have carried with him some sardonic remembrance of the obsessive concern with the purification of souls that had coloured so much of his childhood and youth in Milan: 'One day he went into the church of the Madonna of Pilero with certain gentlemen, and the politest of them stepped forward to offer him some holy water. Caravaggio asked him what it was for, and was told 'to cancel venial sins'. 'Then it is no use,' he said. 'Because mine are all mortal.' That terse remark captures the darkest of the painter's moods – the sullen conviction that nothing, certainly no holy water, could ever wash *his* soul clean or whiten the stain of *his* sins.

'*EGO TE ABSOLVO*'

For Carlo Borromeo, confession was the Church's greatest weapon in the war on sin and evil. His highest priority was to regularize and control the administering of the sacrament of penance – which he believed could be used not only to mould the individual conscience but to redesign society. In Borromean Milan the hearing of confession was restricted to trained teams of diocesan confessors, who were allowed to operate only under direct licence from the archbishop himself. Each confessor was obliged to attend weekly classes to hone his confessional technique and receive the latest instructions from Borromeo. The archbishop told his confessors that they were even more important than the parish priests when it came to the saving of souls; he told them that they 'have the souls in their hands' and 'speak to Jerusalem's heart'.[21]

In 1566 a new Roman Catechism had been composed, under Borromeo's supervision, in which the sacrament of penance had been described as 'the fortress of Christian virtue'. It had preserved the Roman Catholic Church from the attacks of the devil and his heretical minions, and it was to be considered responsible for 'whatever today's Church has preserved in holiness, piety and religiosity'.[22] Borromeo went to great lengths to ensure that 'the fortress of virtue' remained pure of carnality or corruption. He popularized a new article of furniture for the administering of the sacrament, the confessional box, to create a physical separation between confessor and penitent – and thus avert any danger of unclean thoughts polluting their necessarily intimate relationship. It placed the confessor in his own kind of indoors fortress, making him invisible to the penitent and, it was hoped, immune to temptations and blandishments.

The archbishop's suspicious view of human nature extended to his own priests and confessors. In the late 1570s, when a woodworker named Rizzardo Taurini was commissioned to build five confessionals for the new Jesuit church of San Fedele in Milan, he provoked Borromeo's rage by fractionally curtailing one of the partitions at the bottom of the standard double sentry-box design. The Jesuit provost of San Fedele recalled the archbishop's outraged protest – 'the confessor can easily touch the woman's feet with his own.' Borromeo repeated the objection several times, to the evident exasperation of the provost, who found the archbishop's insistence on the moral dangers inherent in a proximity between two people's feet more than faintly absurd. 'He greatly insisted on this,' the provost remembered, 'as if lust enters the body through one's shoes, and he is unaware that in his confessionals the woman's mouth is close to the confessor's ear.'[23] The Jesuit knew a truth that Borromeo did not want to acknowledge: no matter how strong the grilles and walls of any confessional box, nothing could absolutely prevent priests and penitents from harbouring feelings for one another. The partitions intended to separate man from woman might even enhance the illict thrill of such emotions. This exchange between the worldly provost and the archbishop reveals the paranoid fear of sinfulness – and the corresponding desire to close off almost every avenue of human sensuality – that lay at the heart of Borromean piety.

Borromeo believed that confession was nothing less than an instrument, given to him by God, to purify the world. The sacrament of penance already gave the confessor a fearsome weapon for the discipline of each soul – the power to grant or withold absolution. But Borromeo enhanced that power by putting checks in place to ensure that penance was true and not merely a matter of words and assurances. He insisted that confessors make enquiries about their penitents with their parish priests. Those priests in turn were instructed to tell confessors of any conditions that might disqualify a particular penitent from absolution – adultery, for example, or cohabitation out-side wedlock. If absolution were not granted, the penitent would soon find himself or herself before the episcopal magistrates, and under the threat of imprisonment.

Borromeo also ordered his confessors to interrogate their penitents for any knowledge they might have of heretics, or of anyone harbour-ing prohibited books. This cast the net wide, since such was the repres-sive cultural effect of the Counter-Reformation that the list of banned books – the Index – included many of the works now considered part of every Italian's intellectual heritage: Boccaccio's *Decameron*, the poetry of Petrarch and Ariosto, the political theory of Machiavelli, to name just some.[24] Anyone who made too public a display of owning any of those books was likely to find themselves given away to the authorities.

The situation in Milan was not unique, in that harsh measures against heresy were being taken in cities all across Italy, but it was extreme. For example, when the Roman Inquisition recommended that Catholic confessors should encourage their penitents to inform on heretics, Borromeo applied the condition with particular severity. In Milan any confessor too fastidious to enquire about heresy was summarily excommunicated; and if a penitent *did* confess to know-ledge of heretical activities, he or she was immediately sent to higher authorities to give further information about these enemies of the faith – to supply names and addresses, to give details of what they had done or might be planning to do. Only then might the penitent return to their confessor to hear the consoling words, '*Ego te absolvo.*'[25]

Borromeo did not entirely succeed in his efforts to turn Milan into a model Tridentine police state. Even though he had the firm support of the pope and, eventually, Philip II of Spain, some of his attempts to redesign the Milanese way of life met with angry resistance. He tried in vain to ban dancing on feast days and Sundays, and in 1579 he even attempted to kill off the exuberantly joyful pre-Lenten tradition of Carnival. To the disgust of many Milanese citizens, he prohibited all jousts, tournaments, masquerades, plays and dances, and declared the automatic excommunication of all those participating in or attending such spectacles. Borromeo regarded Carnival as the devil's work, a dis-solute rite lodged like a parasite at the beginning of the holy season.

His prohibition was backed up by the threat that his confessors would exploit their information-gathering networks to identity those who had taken part in the celebrations. But this time he had gone too far. Borromeo's attempt to shut down the festive life of the city was met with panic by the civic authorities and rage by the people. Rome and Spain both had to intervene to prevent a popular uprising and Borromeo was forced, reluctantly, to acknowledge that there were limits to his power. In the end, the Milanese were content to fall short of spiritual perfection.

THE POWER OF THE IMAGE

For all his inflexibility, Borromeo was an immensely charismatic and transformative individual. He changed his world, and has been rightly remembered as one of the most dynamic figures in the history of the Roman Catholic Church. In the words of Ludwig von Pastor, author of *The History of the Popes*, 'he stands as a milestone in the history of the Church, at the boundary line between two epochs, the dying Renaissance and the triumphant Catholic reform.'[26] As the first resident Archbishop of Milan for nearly a century, he cast a giant shadow over the city throughout the 1570s and early 1580s.

There is good reason to believe that the acts and ideas of Carlo Borromeo played a profound part in the formation of Caravaggio – an artist whose greatest gift would be an unprecedentedly stark and vivid naturalism, deeply attuned to the ideals of Counter-Reformation piety that permeated the city of his youth. Borromeo embodied more than just a particularly direct and messianic form of piety. His faith was rooted in an intense, spectacularly visual imagination. Borromeo's way of believing in Christ – which involved putting Christ at the centre of his life not in an abstract way, but as actually as possible – depended essentially on a process of mental projection identical to that required in painting pictures.

In early life Borromeo had been strongly influenced by the founder of the Jesuits, St Ignatius Loyola. He had read and followed Loyola's *Spiritual Exercises*, a work that placed great emphasis on the role of visualization in Christian meditation. Loyola specifically advised his readers to visualize Christ's sufferings, insisting that the necessary prelude to any deep and serious meditation on Christ's Life and Passion was a mental process that he termed 'composition, seeing the place'. What that involved was, in effect, a kind of internalized version of the act of painting itself: 'In contemplation or meditation on visual things, as in contemplating Christ our Lord, who is visible, composition will be to see by the eye of the imagination a physical place where that thing is found which I wish to contemplate. By a physical place I mean, for example, a temple or mountain, where Jesus Christ, or Our Lady is found, according to that which I wish to contemplate.'[27]

The Ignatian belief in the power of visualization carried within it the implication that if worshippers can see the image of Christ in their mind's eye, then they can empathize with his sufferings all the more fully – opening themselves to that emotional involvement which leads to the deeper forms of meditative experience. But the idea was not new to Loyola. It goes back to the Middle Ages, and finds especially powerful expression in the writings of the early followers of St Francis of Assisi. A good example is an early Franciscan tract entitled the *Little Book on the Meditation on the Passion of Christ Divided According to Seven Hours of the Day*, which describes the exercise thus: 'It is necessary that when you concentrate on these things in your contemplation, you do so as if you were actually present at the very time when he suffered. And in grieving you should regard yourself as if you had our Lord suffering before your very eyes, and that he was present to receive your prayers.'[28]

A late thirteenth-century guide to prayer entitled *Meditations on the Life of Christ*, probably written by a Franciscan friar from Tuscany, vividly demonstrates how such practices developed. The process involved ever more complicated and detailed visualizations, so that a succession of almost cinematic images would follow, one after another, in the mind:

> reflect on the benignity of the Lord in having to sustain persecution so soon and in such a way . . . He was carried to Egypt by the very young and tender mother, and by the aged saintly Joseph, along wild roads, obscure, rocky and difficult, through woods and uninhabited places – a

very long journey. It is said that couriers would take thirteen or fifteen days; for them it was perhaps two months or longer. They are also said to have gone by way of the desert, which the children of Israel traversed and in which they stayed forty years. How did they carry food with them? And where did they rest and stay the night? Very seldom did they find a house in that desert. Have pity on them, for it was a very difficult, great and long exertion for them as well as for the Child Jesus. Accompany them and help to carry the Child and serve them in every way you can . . . Here there comes a beautiful and pious, compassionate meditation . . . These and other things about the boy Jesus you can contemplate. I have given you the occasion and you can enlarge it and follow it as you please.[29]

The rise of this form of popular devotion was closely linked to the development of painting, from the thirteenth to the fifteenth centuries and beyond. Throughout Western European Christendom, and especially in Italy and the Low Countries, artists competed with each other to create convincing illusions of actual presence, developing new techniques such as mathematically calculated perspective to paint ever more convincing images of the life and sufferings of Christ. Painters made their pictures as realistic as they could in order to assist worshippers in their own acts of mental picture-building. The common goal was to summon up the events described in the New Testament as vividly as possible, so that devout Christians might imagine themselves present as actors at the scene – mourning the dead Christ, for example, or helping to tend him as an infant on the Holy Family's flight to Egypt, as the author of *Meditations on the Life of Christ* had written. Religious painting and religious meditation were, in fact, branches of the same activity.[30]

But by the middle years of the sixteenth century the relationship between art and religious contemplation in Italy had become less straightforward. In the more sophisticated artists' circles, the idea of appealing to the popular devotional imagination with images of painstaking realism was regarded with disdain. Art became seen instead as an idealized, generalized language for the expression of higher thought. Michelangelo, the outstanding painter-sculptor of the High Renaissance, deliberately distanced himself from the pious naturalism of earlier religious painting, which he associated above all with the oil painting traditions of Flanders: 'They paint in Flanders,' he contemptuously remarked in the 1540s, 'only to deceive the external eye, things that gladden you and of which you cannot speak ill. Their painting is of stuffs, bricks and mortar, the grass of the fields, the shadows of trees, and bridges and rivers, which they call landscapes, and little figures here and there. And all this, though it may appear good to some eyes, is in truth done without *reason*, without symmetry or proportion, without care in selecting or rejecting.' It was a form of painting, he concluded, fit only for 'young women, monks or nuns, or certain noble persons who have no ear for true harmony'.[31]

But Michelangelo's subtle, poetically allusive and metaphorical ideal of art seemed, to many in the Roman Catholic Church, to be increasingly out of tune with the times. His use of the idealized nude figure was considered scandalous and his famous cycle of paintings for the Sistine Chapel ceiling was systematically censored in the late 1550s with the addition of a multitude of decorously placed fig leaves. Religious art was a highly controversial subject. Protestant reformers had attacked religious images altogether, on the grounds that they violated the Second Commandment ('Thou shalt not make to thyself any graven image'). The Catholic clerics who assembled at the Council of Trent had their own counter-argument, based on centuries of Church tradition. They resoundingly defended religious paintings and statues as divinely ordained tools for transmitting the messages of the Bible to the illiterate poor. But, at the same time, they acknowledged that many religious artists had forgotten their fundamental role to aid and assist devotion. It seemed clear to most of the leading formulators of Counter-Reformation policy that artists had become so caught up in abstruse ideas, so concerned to demonstrate their own ingenuity and originality, that they had forgotten the humility required of them as servants of the will of God. Not only was the Sistine Chapel ceiling censored, but the Venetian artist Paolo Veronese was publicly castigated for including all kinds of irrelevant details in a painting of *The Last Supper*. The Venetian Inquisition, which called Veronese to account for himself, was outraged by the presence in that picture of parrots, dwarfs, buffoons and, worst of all, Germans (regarded with detestation throughout Italy ever since Charles V's army led by Lutheran *Landsknechts* had sacked Rome in 1527). The painter was forced to find an ingenious solution to the dilemma, which he did by changing both title and subject: Veronese's *Last Supper* became instead a depiction of *Christ in the House of Levi*.

Such developments marked a great shift in attitudes. During the Renaissance religious artists had come to believe that, within fairly loose constraints of Christian orthodoxy, they were free to interpret and depict the stories of the Bible as they liked. As a result of the Counter-Reformation, the Roman Catholic Church set new and stringent limits on the presumed freedom of artists. The principal aim of this policy was to replace the Renaissance cult of freedom and originality with the ideals of artistic duty and responsibility. The second half of the sixteenth century witnessed a widespread call to order – a movement intended to take religious art back to the values of an earlier and supposedly purer time. Carlo Borromeo was at its forefront. As well as containing recommendations of every kind about church architecture and decoration, his *Instructiones* set out his views on art with typical forthrightness. No animals or other distracting details should be included, unless actually mentioned in the biblical text that the artist had been instructed to illustrate. In the seventeenth chapter of his book, devoted to the correct representation of sacred events, Borromeo determined the appropriate fines and punishments for artists who failed to meet the strictest standards of decorum. In Milan, errant artists as well as heretics were liable to come to the attentions of the archbishop's *famiglia armata*. No painter could be in any doubt about what was required of him. Images should be clear and direct. It was the job of art simply to educate spectators and move them to penance.

Borromeo's influence on art in his native Milan is well documented. Simone Peterzano, the feeble late Mannerist painter with whom Caravaggio would sign a contract of apprenticeship, developed a sparer and more austere style in direct response to Borromeo's pronouncements. The archbishop himself owned a collection of paintings that, to judge by its contents, he is likely to have used in his meditations. According to an inventory of 1618, these included an *Adoration of the Magi* by Titian, an *Agony in the Garden* by Antonio Campi and an *Annunciation to the Shepherds* by Jacopo Bassano (all three paintings can be seen, today, in Milan's Pinacoteca Ambrosiana). Such works reflect his taste for the art of Venice and the Veneto, and his marked preference for small-scale devotional pictures. But the most intriguing aspect of Borromeo's taste, for the student of Caravaggio, is his implicit rejection of high art in favour of more traditional, popular visual representations aimed squarely at the promotion of mass piety. Within five years of becoming Archbishop of Milan, he had sold his entire personal collection of art and given the proceeds to charity. This was an act consistent with his personal asceticism, indicating that Borromeo shared the widespread belief – propounded by supporters and opponents of the Reformation alike – that money spent on 'dead' images of Christ, i.e. paintings, could be yet better spent on Christ's 'living' images, namely the real flesh-and-blood poor.

THE SACRED MOUNTAIN

Borromeo was not against religious art *per se*, but he had forceful likes and dislikes. There was a powerfully retrospective cast to his thought. He believed that the best solution to the problems of the modern Catholic Church lay in a return to the past. As a corollary to that, he favoured popular spectacle over the intellectual abstractions of supposedly sophisticated 'High' Renaissance art. Long after he had sold his own paintings, Borromeo continued to sponsor and support particular forms of popular Christian visual spectacle – events and phenomena that were literally 'vulgar', in the sense of being aimed directly at the *vulgus*, the crowd, the general mass of people. Borromeo himself staged numerous theatrical performances of his own extreme ideal of Christian faith. In times of trouble or pestilence for the city, he would march barefoot through the city of Milan with thousands of his supporters, all in sackcloth and ashes. Such processions might themselves be seen as a form of choreographed visual art.

Borromeo's theatricality was another reflection of his belief in the value of constantly remembering and re-enacting the life of Christ – whether actually or in the mind's eye. It was deliberately unsophisticated, direct and immediate, and that was part of its point. Borromeo was intentionally attempting to revive the emotive methods of the itinerant medieval friars such as Francis of Asissi and his followers. The teachings of Francis had unleashed a flood of early Renaissance painting on the walls of churches throughout fourteenth- and fifteenth-century Italy, clear images bringing Christ's message to the poor. But Francis had also helped to found yet more popular and rabble-rousing forms of artistic expression – not only penitential processions of the kind imitated by Borromeo, the pious medieval equivalent of performance art, but also a very particular type of folkish *mise-en-scène* in which painted statues were arranged to conjure up events from the Bible. The first and most widely copied example of this was the crib that Francis created at the monastery of Greccio for the Christmas of 1223: a three-dimensional mock-up of the Nativity, complete with painted carvings of Mary, Joseph and the infant Christ, it was all done, in his words, 'to bring home to the people of Greccio what the birth of Christ at Bethlehem was like'.

Francis's innovation of celebrating the Nativity with the creation of a crib proliferated and mutated. Over the following centuries it produced other, far more elaborate traditions of folk art, including the so-called *sacro monte*, or 'sacred mountain'. It was here that several of the most vital elements of popular piety – including the practice of empathetic visualization of the life of Christ, the ideal of religious meditation and a much enlarged version of the sculptural arrangement devised by St Francis in the crib – all came together in a single carefully orchestrated experience.

The earliest *sacro monte* came into being at the end of the fifteenth century when a Franciscan friar named Bernardino Caimi decided to re-create the sites of Christ's life and passion – ranging from Bethlehem to Nazareth, from Gethsemane to Mount Sion – in the mountains above the town of Varallo, in what is today the Piedmont region. Caimi received papal permission and support for his plan, which involved the construction of numerous chapels linked by mountain paths. Each chapel was to contain polychrome figures acting out the stories of the Bible. Eventually a total of forty-five such chapels were built, allowing pilgrims who climbed up to them to travel even further in spirit – journeying all the way from Original Sin, where they would encounter Adam and Eve tempted by the serpent, to Golgotha, 'the place of the skull', where Christ was crucified. Carlo Borromeo spent the last days of his life on just such a pilgrimage, ascending the mountain at Varallo and praying day and night among its painted figures.

Somewhat decayed, and much restored during the intervening centuries, these sculptures remain *in situ* today. Some of the figures are carved; others are formed from terracotta or stuffed fabric. The effect is inconsistent but full of lively touches of naturalism, somewhere between sculpture and waxwork theatre. The chapel of the Massacre of the Innocents is particularly vivid and gruesome, with its goitred executioner and grieving mothers, its floor strewn with dismembered babies. The *sacro monte* took the kind of interior, spiritual journey advocated for centuries in manuals of prayer and meditation, and turned it into an actual, physical itinerary, with suitably moving or horrifying scenes for the traveller moving up the mountain to witness at each new point of arrival. The sacred mountain gave a palpable form and structure to the instructions contained in devotional handbooks such as the fifteenth-century Venetian text *The Garden of Prayer* – books that, like the Franciscan prayer manuals before them and Ignatius's *Spiritual Exercises* afterwards, counselled the worshipper to summon up a chain of places and images as vividly as possible within the space of the mind:

> The better to impress the story of the Passion on your mind, and to memorize each action of it more easily, it is helpful and necessary to fix the places and people in your mind: a city, for example, which will be the city of Jerusalem – taking for this purpose a city that is well known to you. In this city find the principal places in which all the episodes of the Passion would have taken place – for instance, a palace with the supper-room where Christ had the Last Supper with the Disciples, and the house of Anne, and that of Caiaphas, with the place where Jesus was taken in the night, and the room where he was brought before Caiaphas and mocked and beaten ... And then too you must shape in your mind some people, people well known to you, to represent for you the people involved in the Passion – the person of Jesus himself, the Virgin, Saint Peter, Saint John the Evangelist, Saint Mary Magdalen, Anne, Caiaphas, Pilate, Judas and the others, every one of which you will fashion in your mind.[32]

The sacred mountain was designed to ease the process of devotional visualization. The worshipper must make the physical effort of ascending from one chapel to another, but once inside each space he or she would find that the job of visualization had already been accomplished. The images at Varallo were begun by the artist Gaudenzio Ferrari in the late fifteenth century, but they were ultimately destined to be created, re-created and continually restored in a centuries-long collaborative process involving generations of sculptors, craftsmen and architects. What those images did was, precisely, to re-create scenes from the Bible as if enacted by 'people well known to you'.

The most skilfully carved and painted of the figures have a shocking actuality about them. This is not art that seeks to idealize or generalize life; it is art that aspires to the condition of a simulacrum of life itself. Collectively, the chapels of the *sacro monte* exemplified an ancient, pious fairground form of realism – a type of art that has in general been overlooked or avoided by most art historians precisely because of its naked and self-conscious 'vulgarity'. Yet the art of the *sacro monte* also had strong roots in traditions of high artistic realism going back to the start of the Renaissance. This was a tradition that had produced the sculpturally immediate, emotionally vivid and highly theatrical fourteenth-century paintings of Giotto – which themselves had strong links with certain forms of sacred drama, miracle plays and the like, promoted by the Franciscans and other orders of mendicant friars; as well as the startlingly lifelike fifteenth-century sculptures of Donatello, creations such as the *Mary Magdalen* or the *Habakkuk*, which struck his contemporaries as so eerily imbued with human presence that he was even suspected of necromancy.

This tradition of the work of art as, essentially, a speaking likeness intended to bring the Bible to life was displaced during the later Renaissance – or, at least, it was so transformed by the values and imperatives of the High Renaissance, of Michelangelo and Raphael and the Mannerists who came after them, that its original, uncanny effects were greatly diminished. Yet it continued to thrive away from the perceived centres of art such as Rome or Florence. In Emilia-Romagna and throughout Lombardy, unsettlingly realistic groups of figures were created by a school of sculptors working in the malleable and highly expressive medium of terracotta. Their art is still insufficiently appreciated, but a sculptor such as Guido Mazzoni from Modena, whose breathtakingly emotive works can still be seen in churches across northern Italy – and indeed as far south as Naples – deserves to be ranked alongside any of his better-known contemporaries. The traditions of the highly realized terracotta sculpture, and of the *sacro monte*, played a crucial role in shaping the imagination of pious Italians in the fifteenth, sixteenth and seventeenth centuries.

Both traditions were also deeply influential on Caravaggio. Caravaggio's mature paintings, such as *The Crucifixion of St Peter* and *The Conversion of St Paul*, are blatantly rooted in the traditions of popular pious realism that produced the sculptures of the sacred mountain and the freestanding groups created by Mazzoni and other such masters. So clear and direct is the connection, so manifest the visual resemblance, that it might even be said that his principal strategy as a religious artist was to translate the effects of these two particular branches of theatrical sculpture into the painting of his time. The way in which he paints the wrinkled faces and bodies of his protagonists has its exact parallel in the wizened physiognomies conjured from clay by the masters of terracotta sculpture in Lombardy and Emilia-Romagna – so much so that some of the older faces in his painting might almost have been copied direct from sources in terracotta sculpture.

Caravaggio's fondness for going into gruesome, visceral detail – his depiction, for example, of the gouts of blood that spurt from the decapitated tyrant's head in *Judith and Holofernes* – also vividly testifies to the affinity between his art and the rowdy, bloody, popular spectacle of much *sacro monte* imagery. But even more telling is his constant habit of framing and composing scenes as though confined within a single, small, contained, theatrical space. There is very little landscape in Caravaggio, very little feel of the open air. The scenes he depicts are mostly to be imagined taking place indoors. He habitually collapses the immensity of the world to the confines of a room in which he can control the action and rigorously limit the cast of actors – a space analogous to the densely packed, theatrical spaces devised by the creators of the popular, pious, sculptural *mises-en-scène*.

To say this is to deny neither Caravaggio's virtuosity nor his powers of invention. The way in which he adapted the conventions of popular sculpture to painting, the way in which he made them thoroughly *pictorial* – above all through his use of light and shade – was so original that it gave painters nothing less than a whole new grammar and vocabulary. The very idea of looking *back*, past the etiolated late Mannerism of his day, past the art of the High Renaissance, to vivid and robust traditions of popular religious sculpture – that too was a profoundly original move. It ran directly counter to the prevailing aesthetic orthodoxy of late Renaissance thought, as expressed by Giorgio Vasari in his *Lives of the Artists* – namely, the belief that art should continually evolve and progress, and that it was the duty of every artist to increase that forward momentum, whether he did so incrementally or through some great leap of innovation.

There was admittedly room for a degree of retrospection within Vasari's fundamentally teleological view of history. As he tells the tale of a great rebirth, or *Rinascita*, in Italian art, Vasari allows that the earliest masters, such as Giotto or the Pisano family, had been obliged to look back to the art of classical antiquity to rekindle the painting and sculpture of their own day. In articulating that belief, he was adapting a commonplace of the poet Petrarch's thought – the idea that the classical past was a 'golden age' that could be recovered and eventually surpassed thanks to the efforts of humanist scholarship – and applying it to the discipline of art history. Because Vasari was the very first art historian, his notion of art as essentially progressive has proved peculiarly persistent. But the idea that an Italian artist born in the sixteenth century might have thought it worthwhile to look back past the art of Michelangelo and Raphael, not to the classical world but to the art of the earlier Renaissance, and even to the popular arts of the Middle Ages – that would have shocked and bewildered Vasari. He would have regarded such a preference, for the old and the popular over the new and sophisticated, absurd and perverse. Yet Caravaggio exhibited and proclaimed just such a preference. It might even be said that he was the first self-conscious primitivist in the entire history of post-classical Western art. The force, imagination and ingenuity with which he asserted his position made his art seem all the more iconoclastic and persuasive – compelling the admiration of subsequent painters as diverse as Rembrandt and Rubens, Ribera and Zurbarán.

How was it that Caravaggio came to formulate his aggressively retrograde strategy? The most plausible solution would seem to lie in the painter's roots in Borromean Milan. Caravaggio's reinvention of devotional religious painting along the lines of a direct, theatrical, visceral, popular art would take place not in Milan but in Rome, and it would happen more than a decade after Borromeo's death. But it would represent, none the less, a strikingly faithful translation, into the field of art, of the imperatives of Carlo Borromeo's piety. In matters of piety Borromeo was a dramatist, a populist and – for all his innovations in church architecture and furnishing – a primitivist. The religious art that Caravaggio was destined to create could hardly have been more closely aligned to the beliefs and sensibilities of the charismatic Archbishop of Milan.

There are certainly elements of Caravaggio's religious painting of which Borromeo would not have approved. The full-breasted figure of the Virgin Mary in Caravaggio's *The Madonna of the Palafrenieri* would doubtless have offended his sense of decorum. He would have been disturbed altogether by the painter's intense sensuality, by his feel for the flesh and blood of the human body and by his sensitivity to the suggestions implicit in the least exchange of glances. Yet even here, Borromeo may have exerted a subtle influence on the painter. Caravaggio paints with a strong and unmistakable sense of the perils and the powers of looking. His pictures both embody and evoke an acute and piercing gaze. Caravaggio sees what he sees with such intensity – even if it is only an image in his mind's eye, an image conjured from the imagination – that he makes seeing itself seem a compulsive and potentially fraught act. It is as if he feels at every moment that to see is also to possess and, potentially, to *be* possessed. This is why Caravaggio's paintings have a destructive effect on pictures by other artists hung anywhere near them in art galleries. They exert such a sensually charged, magnetic attraction that they seem almost as though backlit, or somehow illuminated from within, while the pictures around them – even those of great artists, whether Rembrandt or Poussin or Velàzquez – appear by comparison to recede, to retreat from the gaze.

Pablo Picasso was another artist whose pictures project such deep intensity of looking that they have an obliterating effect on other works of art. In his case, the phenomenon seems to have been linked to a powerfully distinctive way of seeing learned from the culture in which he grew up – the male-dominated and intensely Catholic society of late nineteenth-century Andalusia, where they even had a phrase for this kind of looking, the *mirada fuerte* (which literally means 'strong gazing'). It has been succinctly characterized by the historian David Gilmore: 'When the Andalusian fixes a thing with a stare, he grasps it. His eyes are fingers holding and probing . . . the sexual element is present also . . . The light of the eyes is highly erotic . . . In a culture where the sexes are segregated to the point of mutual invisibility, the eye becomes the erogenous zone par excellence . . .'[33] The explanation for Caravaggio's own intensity of looking may also lie in the distinctive milieu of his youth, the milieu of Borromean Milan – a place where, just as in Picasso's Andalusia, rigorous attempts were made to keep men and women apart.

If the dangers inherent in the sense of touch disturbed Borromeo, he was yet more disturbed by the opportunities for corruption furnished by the sense of sight. In the words of the *Methodus Confessionis* – the sixteenth-century confessor's manual that Borromeo himself recommended to his Milanese clergy – sight was described as the most dangerous of all the senses precisely because it was superior to the rest and had the ability to 'incite man to many sins'.[34] In a sermon delivered in the Lombard town of Lecco on 2 July 1583, Borromeo went even further. Reflecting on the murky biblical tale of the rape of Dinah (Genesis 34), he argued that the origins of all such sexual crimes lay within the sense of sight. Dinah was at fault for the rape, he decreed, because she had allowed herself to be seen and had underestimated what can happen when men are given sight of the flesh that they sinfully covet. The eyes, he pronounced, 'are like two gates to the castle of our body. So when they are in the Devil's control, he is also the master of our heart, and can introduce into our soul whatever he wants . . . consequently, since the eyes can introduce great mischief into the soul, they are to be guarded with the utmost diligence. For "death has come up through our windows" [Jeremiah 9:21]: therefore we have to keep them shut.'[35]

It was remarkable advice to give to any congregation. To avoid sin, close your eyes. Take Borromeo's views one step further and the logical thing to do would be to inflict blindness systematically on the whole Christian community to keep it pure of lust and other evil thoughts. He was also of course perfectly capable of taking exactly the opposite line, especially when it came to images of the kind to be encountered on the sacred mountain at Varallo. There, Carlo Borromeo would counsel the faithful to open their eyes as wide as possible – as he did, in the days before his death – and drink in the spectacle of Christ's suffering. For all his contradictions, one thing is certain. At the centre of the paranoid and extremist edifice of Borromeo's religious thought there was a profound, superstitious belief that the sense of sight was the most direct route to the soul.

The evidence of his art suggests that Caravaggio was profoundly shaped by the insistent, manic ocularity of Borromean piety. He would surely have been a very different artist had he not been exposed to the very particular nexus of Milanese attitudes that linked seeing with guilt-ridden sensuality on the one hand, and salvation on the other. His pictures certainly speak of an intense sensitivity to every aspect of visual experience. So too do his notorious arguments and quarrels. Nearly all of the disagreements that would mark and mar Caravaggio's life would turn on a glance taken amiss, a perceived slight or insult implying a potential loss of face. When he looked at people, nothing missed his attention and sometimes his sensitivity may have fooled him into seeing things that really were not there. When people looked back at Caravaggio, they did so at their peril.

PLAGUE

In the summer of 1576, when Caravaggio was almost five years old, the city of Milan was struck by an outbreak of bubonic plague. A census taken at the end of that year in the Milanese parish of Santa Maria della Passerella records the presence there of Fermo Merisi and his wife Lucia. Also listed were Fermo's daughter by his first marriage, Margherita, as well as Giovan Battista Merisi, Caravaggio's brother, four years old at the time. Mysteriously, there is no mention of Caravaggio himself, or of his two-year-old sister, Caterina, or of his still younger sibling, Giovan Pietro.[36]

It is possible that by November or December they had already been evacuated from the city to the relative safety of the countryside, although it is not clear why they alone should have been sent away, leaving the equally vulnerable Giovan Battista at risk. Perhaps the censor missed their presence in the household; perhaps they were not there on the day that he came; perhaps Fermo and Lucia hurriedly managed to conceal at least some of their children when the censor visited, making it easier to evacuate them, unnoticed, at a later date. The movement of people and goods was strictly controlled in time of plague, and almost as soon as the contagion had become apparent, in August, Carlo Borromeo had issued edicts prohibiting anyone from leaving the city. At the end of October, as the disease appeared to abate, this quarantine was briefly lifted – although even then only a select group of wealthier families was allowed to leave. Is it possible that Caravaggio's parents took advantage of their contacts with the Colonna family to secure safe passage for their children, away from Milan, at that time? All that the historical record shows, for sure, is that the whole family had moved to their home in Caravaggio by the autumn of 1577 at the latest.[37] Whatever the subsequent course of events, there is no reason to believe that the artist was not living with his parents in Milan when the outbreak struck in August of 1576. So he is likely to have witnessed much of the horror of the epidemic, especially during its early months, at first hand.

The symptoms of bubonic plague (*yersinia pestis*) are grim and unmistakable. On infection, plague bacteria swiftly multiply in the sufferer's lymphatic system, affecting tonsils, adenoids, spleen and thymus. Within a day or two, the victim suffers fevers, chills and headaches. Vomiting and diarrhoea follow. But the most decisive sign of plague, the true mark of death, is the appearance of the so-called 'buboes' – swellings caused by internal bleeding that appear in the neck, groin and armpits, at the point of the lymph nodes, oozing both blood and pus. Damage then quickly spreads throughout the victim's underlying tissue, until the whole body is covered in dark, purplish blotches. The majority of sufferers die within about four days of contracting the disease.

To the young Caravaggio and his contemporaries, the plague was a visitation, a mysterious curse, like a torture from the bowels of hell inflicted on the living. What could be more appalling than this death by spontaneous internal putrefaction, this sudden consuming of the body from within? Bubonic plague was carried by rats and transmitted to human beings by fleas that jumped from those rats, but no one in Caravaggio's world was aware of that fact. The concept of infection was understood and so was the importance of quarantine, so that houses known to be plague-ridden were locked from the outside, their inhabitants forbidden to leave until the contagion had passed (when all those trapped within were usually found dead). But, although the precise cause of the disease was unknown, human intuition had groped towards an understanding that the illness might in some way be linked to hygiene. Public proclamations issued at regular intervals by Milan's health office in the late 1570s give no fewer than seven accounts of the true cause of the plague, and although they differ widely it is striking how many of them involve rumours about unclean bedding or clothes – which no doubt did, indeed, harbour the fleas that carried the disease. The plague was said to have begun in Venice, originating with Jews trading in used household goods; to have been brought from Mantua by a Jew who had come from that city to Milan selling – again – used household goods; to have been caused by a citizen of Mantua, a man carrying the disease who had spent the night in a Milanese inn and thereby infected the bedding on which he had slept; to have been transmitted by a dirty shirt, worn by a traveller and unwisely confiscated by an innkeeper in part settlement of his bill; and so on.[38]

As well as carrying inklings of the truth about the actual mechanisms of infectious transmission, these stories vividly demonstrate the extent to which plague was liable to stir up a hornets' nest of prejudice. There was a long, ignoble history of such accusations. During the fourteenth century, when all of Europe suffered unprecedented mortality rates from outbreaks of the Black Death, as plague became known, the rumour was put about that Jews were deliberately spreading the disease. The idea of a *pestis manufacta*, a plague-inducing substance secretly manufactured by the enemies of Christianity, took hold of the popular imagination. In the lower Rhineland and parts of

Provence, many Jews suspected of such terrorist acts had been interrogated and tortured, and when confessions had been extorted from them entire Jewish communities had been systematically liquidated.[39] There was no such response to the Milanese plague of the 1570s, but there was a recurrence of rumours about the role of *untori* – unguent-spreaders – in creating the epidemic. According to a Jesuit eyewitness, Paolo Bisciola, 'it is said that there were certain men who went about touching the walls, gates, and streets with artificial unguents, which opinion many affirmed through the discovery one morning that almost all of the gates and *cadenazzi* of the Corsa di Porta Nuova, had been smeared, and the walls in various places had been soiled by unguents.'[40] The presumed culprits, this time, were not the Jews but the Spanish. For a while, the people of Milan convinced themselves that their hated rulers were to blame for the evil that afflicted them. The Spanish governor of Milan felt compelled to pass legislation that forbade anyone from repeating the accusation – which only made the Milanese population even more jittery.

In truth, the Spanish government *was* partly to blame, although not in the way so luridly imagined. The plague had actually been brought from Sicily to Milan by the entourage of Don Juan of Austria, illegitimate brother of Philip II of Spain and hero of Lepanto: the group had arrived in the city in August 1576, with several of its members already close to death. The inner circle of the Milanese Senate knew this, and so did members of the city's Health Tribunal. The plethora of alternative official explanations was a smokescreen created partly to protect the reputation of the Spanish royal family and preserve the *status quo*.[41] The dirty laundry, the flea-infested bedding, really *was* theirs; but this had to kept from the people at large or riots might ensue.

Any risk of the truth coming out was dispelled when Carlo Borromeo involved himself in the situation. From his perspective, the plague was a God-given opportunity to force home his severe spiritual message; and, as far as he was concerned, there was absolutely no ambiguity about its source. It had nothing to do with bedlinen or shirts or phantom *untori* going around wiping poison on gateposts. It certainly had nothing to do with the Spanish or the visit of Don Juan. Its source was human sin. The Milanese had neglected their souls, had confessed too infrequently, had debauched themselves at Carnival and had indulged in luxuries. The plague was being visited upon them by a vengeful God, and even if it seemed terrible it was truly a blessing in disguise – a call to universal repentance that could not be ignored.

Borromeo was so prominent a figure in the events of the plague of 1576–8 that it would eventually be nicknamed after him – remembered forever as *la peste di San Carlo*. It brought out, in equal measure, his extreme piety and his fondness for the exercise of bureaucratic control. In the first two months of the epidemic, when as many as 10,000 people are thought to have died, the city almost fell into a state of anarchy. There was inadequate provision for the disposal of so many corpses and during 'the terrible September' of 1576 – the month of Caravaggio's fifth birthday – carts heaped high with bodies rolled along the cobbled streets of the town at all hours of the day and night. Piles of half-naked cadavers were left in open view. The much feared *monatti*, or 'gravediggers', public health officials whose responsibility it was to collect the dead and purge houses of disease, were said to be running amok. Dark tales abounded of the *monatti* pillaging the houses they were supposed to make safe, and raping the few female survivors they found there.

Faced with a city descending into nightmare, Borromeo requested and duly received a brief from Pope Gregory XIII giving him full authority to redirect all the energies of his clergy to the alleviation of the plague. He mobilized his private army and summoned all the priests and monks of his diocese to a vast congregation. To each was assigned a different task. No more corpses were to be left outside. Every victim was to be given a proper burial, 'with crosses and lights'.[42] Borromeo also organized partial quarantines, especially for women, whom he regarded not only as more likely to occasion sin but as the primary carriers of plague (because, he said, they talked so much and constantly visited each other's houses). On his orders, many of the women of the city were confined within their homes for long periods of time or held in purpose-built isolation cabins. Such measures were not always entirely effective: because women continued to live in terror of the *monatti*, they often failed to disclose the presence of plague or the existence of the dead, with the result that the disease continued to spread, albeit behind closed doors.

Borromeo's most successful strategy against the disease was the reopening of Milan's *lazzaretto*, one of the first great penitentiaries for the plague built in Italy. This was a vast moated structure that had originally been constructed during the late fifteenth century on the orders of Francesco Sforza, following an outbreak of plague in 1483-5. The *lazzaretto* – so named after Lazarus, who had been raised from the dead by Jesus and who was often portrayed in art as a plague victim, spotted with buboes – had been left empty for more than fifty years. But it served Borromeo's purposes well. Into its compound of 288 rooms were squeezed nearly all of Milan's homeless and destitute (a nearby monastery was also conscripted to accommodate any overspill, confining the spread of the disease to great effect). In its regimented spaces, those who remained healthy could be segregated from those who fell ill. The bodies of the deceased were kept in plague pits at the centre of the compound, to be taken away at regular intervals for mass burial. Death was being bureaucratically managed, to Borromeo's satisfaction. Most important of all, the whole itinerant population of the Milanese diocese was now being held in one place.

The man whom Borromeo installed in charge of the *lazzaretto* was a Franciscan friar named Fra Paolo Bellintano, who later published a detailed account of his methods. Under his stewardship, the *lazzaretto* became a kind of centralized fortress for the management of plague. He employed a team of *sbirri* – policemen, or constables, recruited like himself from within the Franciscan order – to maintain discipline within the *lazzaretto* itself, and enforce their own standards on those working with plague victims in the city at large. The *sbirri* were, he wrote, an essential part of his tactical plan:

Many needs arose during the day which could not be remedied without these. I dare to say that without them Milan would have become a den of thieves. How would I have been able to hold back so many *monatti* who cleaned out the houses without fear of justice? Decrees and proclamations could have been made without end, and they would not have feared a thing. But they saw that almost every day I had people whipped, birched, imprisoned, scourged, tied to a column, and that I imposed other punishments besides. And they did not want to become familiar with all this [i.e., suffer the same fate themselves].[43]

As a result, he noted with tight-lipped satisfaction, the behaviour of the *monatti* was soon much improved.

Bellintano's account of the methods applied within the *lazzaretto* graphically demonstrates how the terrors of the plague were used to scourge the collective Milanese soul. The people were being punished for their attachment to the pleasures of Carnival, yet Bellintano himself takes a positively carnivalesque relish in the ways that he and his *sbirri* devised to ensure their penitence. He tells the story of how, one night, the inmates put on a secret dance to raise their spirits. One of his fellow Franciscans, Fra Andrea, got wind of the party and determined to puncture the festive mood. He went to the plague pit in the middle of the *lazzaretto* and retrieved the bloated corpse of an old woman. As he heaved her on to his shoulders, a great belch of air was expelled from her swollen guts. Unperturbed, he told her to keep quiet and get ready for a dance. He went to the room where the inmates were dancing and asked to join their party. When they opened the door, he threw the dead body into their midst, shouting out 'Let her dance too!' There then followed a brief sermon, after which, Bellintano drily observes, 'the dance ended.'[44]

Public counterparts to such dark, private theatricals were the processions organized by Carlo Borromeo. Believing that the only way to salvation was passionate identification with the suffering body of the Lord, he staged a series of re-enactments of Christ's journey to Calvary. In October 1576 he announced three days of fasting and ordered that Milan's most prized relic, a nail said to come from the True Cross on which Christ had been crucified, be taken out of the Cathedral:

> His holiness performed the three processions dressed *di mestitia*, with a large rope around his neck, barefoot and hooded, dragging his clothes on the ground, and with a large Crucifix in his arms. And on the Sabbath he carried the Holy Nail in procession, supplicating God by the merits of His Most Holy Passion to turn away the ire he had conceived against this people, and use them with mercy. He went in the same habit, and manner, as the previous days, but was also accompanied by about a thousand flagellants, who beat themselves continuously, causing great pity in whoever saw them. All the portable relics of the city were also carried in procession that day. But that which most moved

the people to tears, penitence and dolour was [the sight of] the illustrious Cardinal in such sad and mournful dress, that great black cross on which he carried the Holy Nail, the blood that was seen to issue from his feet. When the procession was finished he preached a public sermon almost three hours long, with such spirit and fervour that he was like another St Paul. I believe there were few who did not weep. When the days of prayer were over he carried it all through the city once more, especially in those places where the disease was worst. On this journey he spilt much blood from his feet, and was accompanied by barefoot priests and monks, with ropes around their necks.[45]

The author of this eyewitness description, the Jesuit Paolo Bisciola, describes how huge crowds were exhorted to join in these mass demonstrations of faith. He also notes, without apparent irony, that 'on these occasions, the plague grew very much.' Bisciola's account is also interesting for its visual detail. He says that Borromeo ordered temporary altars, lit with candles, to be set up throughout the streets of the city, 'so that to walk in the streets was like walking in church'. As autumn advanced, and as the nights drew in, the city seemed ablaze with 'the lights of piety and religion'. On a multitude of outdoor altars 'there burned a great quantity of candles and much incense'. Flame and shadow: Milan had become a city of chiaroscuro.

The artist was five when the plague reached its height, and only a year older when it reached into his life and tore his family to pieces. The sequence of events is charted in a series of documents from the archives. On 20 October 1577 the death was recorded, in Caravaggio, of the artist's father, Fermo Merisi, his paternal grandfather, Bernardino Merisi, and his (unnamed) grandmother. The document states that they died within a day of each other. An earlier document, of 17 August 1577, indicates that Caravaggio's uncle Pietro had died earlier in the year. The document in question is a claim to Pietro's estate, which indicates that he died without having made a will, that is, unexpectedly. It also provides the only explicit link to the plague, stating that Pietro lived in Milan but was in Caravaggio because of the epidemic sweeping the city.[46]

The archive contains no description of the events that took place in the Merisi household in late October 1577. It was not a notary's job to paint pictures of human suffering. But the art of Caravaggio's maturity would be saturated in the ineradicable memory of night terrors. It would be an art of paroxysm and abandonment, filled with images of turmoil in dark places. Towards the end of his life, working in Sicily – the place where Milan's great plague had started – he would paint a huge altarpiece of the *The Resurrection of Lazarus*. He himself chose the subject of the picture. It would be a meditation on death and salvation – a work that, though shaded by ambiguity, has a miraculous story to tell. But nothing could change the story of Caravaggio's own early years. No miracle had raised his father, his grandfather, his uncle, from the dead. By the age of six, Caravaggio had lost almost every male member of his family.

THE BAD APPRENTICE

By 18 February 1578 the plague finally abated. A fifth of the population of the diocese of Milan was dead and everyone else was trying to reassemble their lives. On that day Caravaggio's mother, Lucia, signed a document in which she assumed legal guardianship of all four of her children. It shows that the family was now resident in Caravaggio.

Nearly a year later, on 21 January 1579, another document shows that Fermo Merisi, her late husband, had died intestate. It apportions his estate and parts of his parents' estate too. They had also died intestate, on the same night as him, creating a tangle of legal complications. There had evidently been some dispute between Lucia and Fermo's three half-brothers – a quarrel about who was to get what. Arbitration was necessary. The largest property at issue, Bernardino's house and land in Porta Seriola (together with his business premises), went to the half-brothers. In exchange Lucia and her children were relieved of Fermo's debts, which amounted to 1,737 lire.[47] They were also granted four modest landholdings, which the document goes on to list:

1. 7 *pertiche* of land in Canigio Nuovo (which is divided, with three quarters going to Fermo's brothers, the rest to Lucia's children);
2. land and a vineyard in Rovere, 8 *pertiche*;
3. 2½ *pertiche* of land on the road to Calenzano;
4. an orchard outside Porta Prato, 1 *pertica*.

One *pertica*, in Lombardy at that time, was the equivalent of approximately 6,500 square feet. So altogether the Merisi family, Fermo's wife and her four children ended up with roughly 18.5 *pertiche*. That is 120,250 square feet, just under three acres. The land's value amounted to about 3,000 imperial lire, or 500 gold scudi: not a lot of money.

Nothing is known about Caravaggio's early education but he certainly received one. An inventory of his possessions made several years afterwards, when he was a fully fledged painter working in Rome, reveals that he owned several books. The pictures that he would paint, later in life, are without doubt the works of a questing, curious and literate mind. His brother Giovan Battista, who was destined for the Church, would later study at the Jesuit Collegio Romano in Rome. The Jesuits were among the most intellectually demanding of the religious orders, so Caravaggio's brother must have been given at least the rudiments of an education in classical and Italian literature. Numerous grammar schools had been set up across the diocese of Milan at the instigation of Carlo Borromeo, who believed that educated souls were less likely to stray into temptation. Caravaggio's brother probably attended one such school, which makes it more likely that Caravaggio did too.

By 1583 Giovan Battista Merisi had decided that he was destined for the Church. He was following in the footsteps of his father's brother, Ludovico, who was a priest. By 1584, it seems, Caravaggio had decided to become a painter. On 6 April of that year, at the age of thirteen, he signed a contract of apprenticeship with Simone Peterzano. The contract was signed in Milan, where Peterzano had his workshop, and it spelled out the nature of Caravaggio's commitment to his *dominus*, or 'Master', and described what he was to expect in return:

> The said Michelangelo will stay and live with the said Master, Simone, to learn the art of painting for the next four years beginning from today, and that the said Michelangelo will train in that art night and day, according to the custom of the said art, well and faithfully, and that he will commit no deceit or fraud upon the goods of the said Master, Simone.
>
> The said Master, Simone, is required and obliged to support the said Michelangelo in his house and workshop, and instruct him in that art

all that he can, so that at the end of the four years he will be qualified and expert in the said art, and know how to work for himself. The said Michelangelo is required to give and pay to the said Master, Simone, for his recompense, twenty-four gold scudi at the rate of six imperial lire to the scudo, to be paid in advance every six months by the said Michelangelo to the said Master, Simone, of which he now receives ten scudi in advance payment, of which Michelangelo promises to pay the remainder.

These were not exactly standard terms. Caravaggio and his family had to pay Peterzano 24 gold scudi each year of the apprenticeship, six months in advance – a total of 96 scudi. Payment for apprenticeships was not an invariable part of such contracts, in that the apprentice's labour was regarded as recompense to the Master for his tuition. When the Master also provided board and lodging, as in Caravaggio's case, some payment from the apprentice was customary, but Peterzano's fee on this occasion was unusually high. For example, when the painter Gerolamo Lomazzo had been apprenticed in Milan in 1556, he had been required to pay just 8 gold scudi a year. Peterzano's only other known apprentice, Francesco Alicati, was actually *paid* 24 scudi a year for his contributions in the workshop.[48] The implication is that Alicati already had some skills in painting, whereas Caravaggio had none.

Simone Peterzano was an eclectic and mediocre artist who was originally from Bergamo but preferred to stress his links with Venice, where he may have been trained. He claimed to be a disciple of Titian, the most celebrated painter of Renaissance Venice, and sometimes even signed his pictures *titiani alumnus*, 'pupil of Titian'. A number of contemporary sources refer to him as Simone Veneziano.[49] The most extensive surviving example of his art is to be found in the presbytery of the Certosa di Garegnano, north-west of Milan. There, he and his workshop painted a monumental fresco cycle depicting scenes from the life of Christ. Work was begun in 1578 and finished in 1582, so the resulting pictures are a reasonable guide to Peterzano's style as it was when he took Caravaggio on as his apprentice just two years later. It is a flaccid, bloodless late variant of Mannerism, exemplified by *The Adoration of the Shepherds* at Garegnano – an exercise in saccharine piety, complete with a cast of lumpen shepherds whose decorously draped forms, in various postures, were perhaps meant to demonstrate virtuosity but only reveal Peterzano's inadequacies as a painter of the human anatomy. At the centre of the picture a sober and dignified Joseph, the sole convincing figure, is joined by a slack-jawed, pinheaded Mary. Both kneel in adoration of a mannequin baby Jesus, while unconvincing angels circle overhead.

What Peterzano's fresco cycle communicates more vividly than anything else is his determination not to cause offence. His pictures embody the Tridentine timidity that infected so much Italian painting in the years that immediately followed the Counter-Reformation. Before he had begun work on the Garegnano fresco cycle, the artist had been made to sign a contract obliging him to follow the new rules of decorum laid down by the Council of Trent: 'All the human figures, and above all the saints, should be executed with the greatest honesty and gravity, and there should not appear torsos, nor other limbs or parts of the body, and every action, gesture, clothes, attitude and dra-pery of the saints should be most honest, modest and full of divine gravity and majesty.'[50] Peterzano was careful to follow these instruc-tions – all the more careful, no doubt, because Carlo Borromeo him-self was known to visit the charterhouse at Garegnano to practise the spiritual exercises. It might be said that he painted according to the negative principles of Borromean piety, in the sense that his overrid-ing priority was to avoid courting controversy or violating decorum. It would be Caravaggio's genius to express that same piety in boldly positive terms, to create an art of agonized humility and bleeding flesh that would stir up controversy wherever it was seen. In short, there is no trace of a debt to Peterzano's work in the art of Caravaggio's matur-ity. Were it not for the existence of the actual contract of apprentice-ship, there would be no reason whatever to connect the two men.

So what did Caravaggio learn during his apprenticeship? It might be supposed – it is the conventional view – that he received a trad-itional grounding in the techniques of Renaissance painting. In other words, he learned to prepare and grind colours; he learned how to draw; and he learned how to paint in *buon fresco*, the 'true fresco' technique, like Peterzano himself. But Caravaggio never painted a fresco and no single drawing exists by his hand. X-rays of his oil paintings show that he did not even use preparatory drawings on the canvas, as a guide for the brush. In other words, there is almost no resemblance between his daringly improvisatory techniques and those that would have been taught in the studio of an artist such as the safe, dull and cautious Simone Peterzano.

It seems that something must have gone awry during Caravaggio's apprenticeship. He was a painter of extraordinary innate talent, a unique virtuoso when it came to conjuring the illusion of three-dimensional reality within the two dimensions of painting. Yet his earliest known works, while forceful, are relatively gauche and crude. Those pictures were done after 1592 and they were done in Rome. If someone with his gifts really *had* applied himself to the study of art in Milan for four whole years from 1584 to 1588 – working 'day and night', as the contract says – he should have been far better than he actually was by then. The breakneck pace of Caravaggio's subsequent acceleration, from uncertain beginnings to full-blown mastery, begs further questions. Was it perhaps only in the early 1590s that he first took painting seriously? Is it possible that he began his career with the merest smattering of an education, and taught himself most of what he knew about painting on the job? Could it be that he spent much of his presumed apprenticeship playing truant?

The hypothesis has the virtue of helping to explain Caravaggio's extreme technical originality. It is easier, in some ways, for a man to reinvent painting if he has almost nothing in the way of conventionally ingrained techniques to impede him. His contemporaries described him as a difficult young man who liked to settle disagreements with violence and who was prone to disappear for days on end. There is no reason to believe that he was anything but an unruly teenager. Even if he did absorb some of the rudiments of art, he is unlikely to have been a model student. What evidence we have suggests that he was probably a very bad one.

'THEY COMMITTED A MURDER'

The bare bones of the archive – and they are pretty bare, for this part of the painter's story – indicate that these were difficult years for the whole Merisi clan. On 25 August 1584 the richest and most influential member of the family, Giovan Giacomo Aratori, went to his grave. On 7 June 1588 Caravaggio's youngest brother, Giovan Giacomo, died of unknown causes. By this time the painter's apprenticeship, such as it was, had finished. He was back in Caravaggio by 25 September 1589, to sell a parcel of land. He was not quite eighteen, so the sale could take place only with his mother's permission, which she gave. There were more land sales the following year. On 30 May and 20 June 1590 Caravaggio and his brother, the future priest Giovan Battista, parted with all of their remaining property in Canigio Nuovo, 'to clear debts [accumulated] by them or their mother, or by the said Michelangelo by entering into a contract'. The brothers had no option, it seems, but to eat into their rapidly dwindling capital.

There is a hint of trouble too in the fact that legal responsibility for this sale had been suddenly passed from the brothers' mother, Lucia, to their uncle, the priest Ludovico Merisi, who was their next closest relative. Was Lucia ill or incapacitated in some way? It seems so. On 29 October 1590 she made her will, bequeathing her entire property in equal proportions to her three surviving children. Exactly a month after that she died.

There were two more sales and then – on 11 May 1592 – the final division of Lucia's estate between Caravaggio and his two siblings. Giovan Battista got some land and the family's two houses in Porta Folceria. Caterina got some land as well as an undertaking from Giovan Battista that he would pay her dowry of 200 lire. Caravaggio was excused from any obligation to either of them and took nothing except the cash from last land sale. It looks like the behaviour of a man who wanted to cut all ties with his past. Not long after the division of the property, he would leave Caravaggio and Milan, never to return.

By the middle of 1592 he had raised altogether 1,957 imperial lire from the family's capital – the equivalent of 600 gold scudi, or about six times the cost of his apprenticeship. By the end of the same year, he would have run through it all. No one knows what he did with the money, just as no one knows exactly what he was doing with his life during and after his apprenticeship. He was twenty-one years old in 1592. By the same age his namesake, Michelangelo Buonnarotti, had established himself as one of the leading artists in Italy. Yet, as far as anyone has been able to establish, Michelangelo Merisi, soon to be known as Caravaggio, had not even painted a picture.

All this suggests he was not so much a slow developer as a reluctant one. Perhaps he did not even want to be an artist. Perhaps he explored other possibilities, such as becoming a mercenary or soldier of fortune. He was good with a sword, and the alacrity with which he would later jump at the chance to become a Knight of Malta suggests he may always have nurtured romantic fantasies about becoming a knight at arms. Another distinct possibility is that he had got into bad company and was just living it up during these years, with no thought to the future – until the money finally ran out. Children often define themselves in opposition to one another, and the fact that Caravaggio's brother was chosen for the priesthood is in itself suggestive. If Giovan Battista was the good little boy, maybe Caravaggio had taken the role of the rogue. It would not have been surprising. He had grown up with barely a single close male role model. In fact almost all the men closest to him – the men who might have controlled him, helped him, shown him how to live – had died of the plague.

There was no shortage of opportunities for getting into trouble in Milan. Carlo Borromeo was not just flourishing his priestly rhetoric when he called it a city of sin. Milan had a reputation as a violent place, infested with vagabonds, conmen, pimps and whores. Street crime was rife and the murder rate soared during the 1580s and 1590s. The Spanish governor was constantly issuing proclamations about the need to clean up the city and offering rewards for the capture of bandits, muggers and murderers. There are passages in the writings of Caravaggio's biographers which suggest that he got involved – and got out of his depth – in this dangerous Milanese underworld. Bellori baldly states that 'being disturbed and contentious, because of certain quarrels he fled from Milan.'[51] But that is not the last word from him on the matter, because on the front page of his copy of Baglione's biography of Caravaggio (still preserved in the Vatican Library), he wrote a further note, just as bald but more informative: 'he ground colours in Milan and learned to colour and because he had killed one of his companions he fled the country.'[52]

Baglione, who seems to have known nothing about Caravaggio's life in Milan, is silent on the subject. Mancini, in *his* life, was keen to tell the version of the story that Caravaggio himself wanted the world to believe, sweeping any suggestions of ill-doing under the carpet of a single brisk sentence: 'At a young age he studied diligently for four to six years in Milan, though now and then he would do some outrageous thing because of his hot nature and high spirits.'[53]

Mancini too left some scribbled, marginal mutterings that throw more light into this dark corner. There is a manuscript copy of Mancini's life of Caravaggio in the Marciana Library in Venice that contains a number of barely legible lines of disconnected prose: 'They committed a murder. Prostitute tough guy gentleman. Tough guy hurts gentleman prostitute slashes insult into the skin with knife. Policeman killed. They wanted to know what the accomplices ... He was in prison for a year and then he wanted to see his property sold. In prison he didn't confess he came to Rome and said no more about it.'[54]

It is with this gnomic, fragmented record – this mangled account of mysterious skulduggery and impenetrable misdeeds – that Caravaggio's life in Milan comes to a close.

PART TWO
Rome, 1592–5

VIOLENT TIMES

'Whore, bitch, tart! I throw a bowl of shit in your face! Go on, fuck yourself with a horsewhip! I'll stick the handle of my paintbrush up your arse!'

These are the words of an artist scorned, addressed to a courtesan who refused to sleep with him. They are preserved in a deposition in the State Archives of Rome for 1602.[1] The man was before the magistrates for abuse and physical assault. As well as insulting and beating her, he had actually knifed the woman. She had been badly injured, cut deeply to the face. The facial wound was an example of a *sfregio*, a slash with the blade inflicted as a mark of shame – doubly damaging to a courtesan, whose face was her fortune.

There are many such tales in the annals of the lives of the artists who thrived, floundered or failed in Counter-Reformation Rome. Here is another example.

An artist catches his mistress in the company of his own younger brother, an assistant in his workshop. He pursues his brother to St Peter's, where they are busy on a commission, and breaks two of his ribs with a crowbar. He then tries to kill him with his sword, but the brother escapes and seeks sanctuary in a church. Meanwhile, the artist sends his servant to the house of his offending mistress, with instructions to give her a *sfregio*. He finds her in bed and slashes her face with a razor.[2]

Neither of these stories directly concerns Caravaggio. The first is about a now forgotten painter whose misdemeanours took place at the start of the seventeenth century. The second involves the flamboyant sculptor Gianlorenzo Bernini, who caught his brother *in flagrante*

63

with his mistress in 1638. More than thirty years and a gulf of talent separated the two artists but they behaved in an identically hot-headed way. Both men acted in the heat of the moment, spurred on by a slight to their honour – a loss of face punished, with terrible literalness, by cuts and slashes to the actual faces of their victims.

During his own fourteen years in Rome, Caravaggio would become embroiled in more than his fair share of assaults, disputes and bloody vendettas. He was a violent man, but it is important to remember that he lived in a violent world. Throughout seventeenth-century Italy – throughout seventeenth-century Europe – an inflammatory code of honour prevailed. The *fama* of an individual, by which was meant not only his fame or reputation but also his good name, was paramount. Any insult to it had to be paid for, and the price was often blood. Caravaggio went to greater extremes than his contemporaries, in life as in art. He was no angel, even if he had been named after one. He had a hot temper and was forever spoiling for a fight. But he was not the freak or absolute exception that he has often been painted to be – both by his enemies and by those who have claimed to idolize him.

IN ROME

Having cut all ties with his family, the artist travelled to Rome in the autumn of 1592. Bellori says that Caravaggio went there via Venice, 'where he came to enjoy the colours of Giorgione, which he then imitated'.[3] A brush with Venetian art at this formative moment in his life seems likely, although Bellori overplays Caravaggio's indebtedness to Giorgione. Giorgione's work had inspired Titian, the most celebrated painter of Renaissance Venice. But that axis of Venetian painting – rich, brightly coloured, with a strong sense of paint as eloquent, material *stuff*, to be pushed about with the fingers as well as manipulated by the brush – did not hold the young Caravaggio's attention. Aside from his innate sense of pictorial drama, he would have little in common with either of those great masters. Only in the paintings of his very last years would he move towards the impressionistic manner of Titian's later work.

If any Venetian painter touched him to the core it was Jacopo

Tintoretto. Tintoretto's brooding, monumental religious canvases, full of dramatic contrasts of light and dark – lightning strikes of supernatural illumination that shiver like spiritual electricity – are the only late sixteenth-century Italian paintings to prophesy elements of Caravaggio's own mature style. Simone Peterzano, who liked to think of himself as a painter in the Venetian mould, may well have inspired his unruly apprentice to visit the city. If so, he contributed to the final eclipse of whatever dim influence his own art might have had on Caravaggio's imagination.

The trip to Venice remains hypothetical, but highly plausible. According to such a version of events, the young Caravaggio arrives in Rome with his memory full of vast, dark pictures teeming with images of humanity *in extremis*. This helps to make sense of his subsequent development. The preferred, monumental scale of his work as well as the ambition behind it; the extreme sense of light and dark; even the distinctive, low-toned palette that Caravaggio would make his own – where could he have got the first glimmerings of all this, if not from Venice, and Tintoretto?

For the next fourteen years Caravaggio would be at the heart of Roman Catholic Christendom, achieving fame and notoriety in equal measure. The most vivid late sixteenth-century account of the city was written by the French essayist and philosopher Michel de Montaigne, who spent several months there in late 1580 and early 1581. That was ten years before Caravaggio's time. But the city Montaigne described was, by and large, the city that Caravaggio knew.

Montaigne was immediately struck by the ugliness and poverty of the surrounding countryside: 'The approaches to Rome, almost everywhere, look uncultivated and barren, either for want of soil, or, what I consider more likely, because this city has hardly any labourers and men who live by the work of their hands.'[4] The few labourers who *were* to be encountered in the fields tended to be migrant workers, from the mountains of northern Italy: 'When I came here I found on the way many groups of villagers who came from the Grisons and Savoy to earn something in the season by labouring in the vineyards and the gardens; and they told me that every year this was their source of income.'[5]

Rome was a city of migrants. Its shifting population was drawn from every corner of the Christian world – priests seeking preferment, pilgrims seeking salvation, courtesans seeking riches. 'It is the most universal city in the world,' proclaimed Montaigne, 'a place where strangeness and differences of nationality are considered least; for by its nature it is a city pieced together out of foreigners; everyone is as if at home.'[6]

It was also a suspicious city. On arrival, Montaigne's baggage was seized. The books in his travelling library were meticulously inspected by Rome's customs officials. They were looking for forbidden texts, for evidence of heresy, and, although they found little to concern them, Montaigne was struck by the severity of their regulations: 'the rules were so extraordinary here that the book of hours of Our Lady, because it was of Paris, not of Rome, was suspect to them, and also the books of certain German doctors of theology against the heretics, because in combating them they made mention of their errors.'[7] Much to Montaigne's annoyance, the authorities confiscated a book 'on the histories of the Swiss, translated into French, solely because the translator – whose name, however, is not given – is a heretic . . . it is a marvel how well they know the men of our countries.'

More than half a century had passed since the Lutheran troops of Emperor Charles V sacked the city in 1527. But Rome had still not recovered. Thousands had died during the Sack and many others had abandoned their homes. Montaigne was struck by the contrast between the splendour of the papal court – 'remarkable houses and gardens of the cardinals . . . palaces divided into numerous apartments, one leading to another'[8]– and the squalid, neglected condition of so much of the rest of the city.

Relics and reminders of ancient Rome were everywhere, so that 'in many places we were walking on the tops of entire houses . . . in truth, almost everywhere, you walk on the top of old walls which the rain and the coach ruts uncover.'[9] But so mangled were the tangible remains of the classical past that Montaigne felt the totality of its destruction more keenly than anything else: 'those who said that one at least saw the ruins of Rome said too much, for the ruins of so awesome a machine would bring more honour and reverence to its memory: this was nothing but its sepulchre. The world, hostile to its long domination, had first broken and shattered all the parts of this wonderful

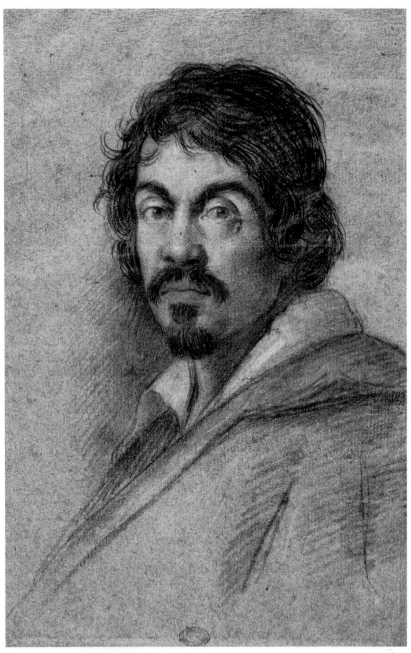

1. *Portrait of Caravaggio* by Ottavio Leoni. A Roman barber named Luca described the painter just as he appears here: 'a stocky young man, with a thin black beard, thick eyebrows and black eyes . . . dressed all in black'.

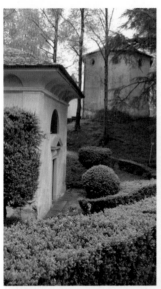

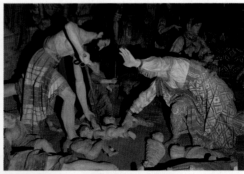

2/3. The *sacro monte* at Varallo, in modern Piedmont. In a series of chapels linked by mountain paths, polychrome figures play out stories from the Bible in vivid and often bloody *mises-en-scène*.

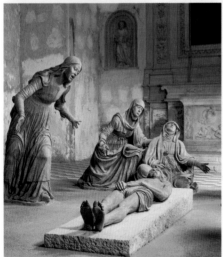

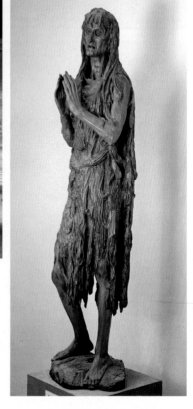

4. *The Lamentation* by Guido Mazzoni. Caravaggio was influenced by this intense form of realism. He knew Mazzoni's work well and painted a picture for the Neapolitan church that housed this very sculpture.

5. *Mary Magdalen* by Donatello. Donatello's disconcertingly lifelike sculptures may also have shaped Caravaggio's imagination.

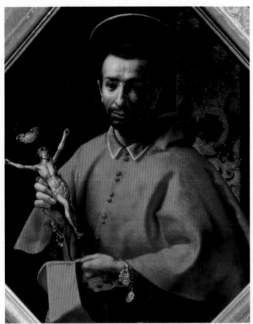

6. *Carlo Borromeo* (detail) by Carlo Dolci. Dour and ascetic, Borromeo was the dominant force in Milan during Caravaggio's formative years. He would remain legendary in the city for centuries.

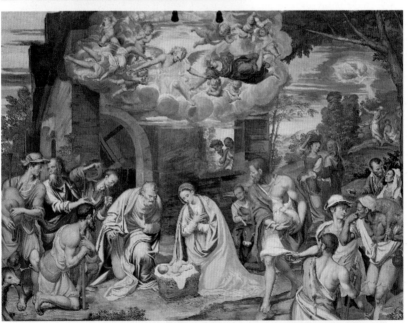

7. *The Adoration of the Shepherds* (detail) by Simone Peterzano. The young Caravaggio signed a contract of apprenticeship with Peterzano, but just what he learned from this feeble disciple of Titian is not clear.

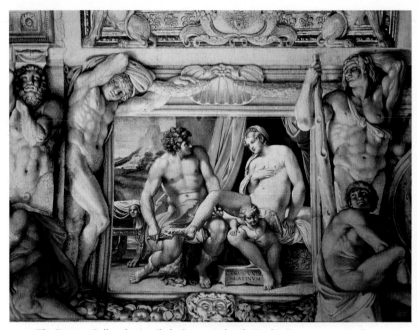

8. The Farnese Gallery by Annibale Carracci (detail). For his Farnese patrons, Carracci daringly revived pagan and erotic mythology in Counter-Reformation Rome.

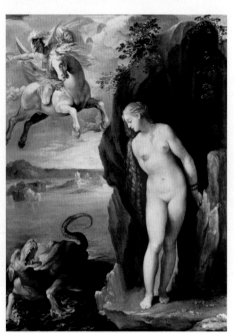

9. *Perseus and Andromeda* by Giuseppe Cesari. The young Caravaggio spent some unhappy months as an assistant to Cesari, who used him to paint fruit and flowers.

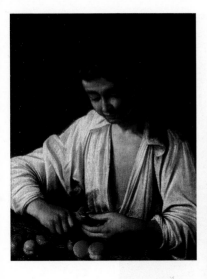

10. *Boy Peeling a Fruit*. This may be one of Caravaggio's earliest surviving pictures. If so, it shows how little progress he had made as a painter by his early twenties.

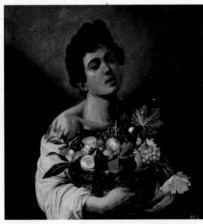

11. *Boy with a Basket of Fruit*: 'a blushing, smooth-skinned adolescent, with dark curly hair and an expression of amorous intensity on his face' who may represent the Groom in the biblical Song of Songs.

12. *Boy Bitten by a Lizard*. In the language of the Italian street the bitten finger represented the wounded phallus.

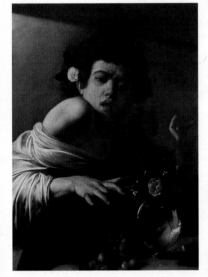

13. *Boy Bitten by a Crayfish* by Sofonisba Anguissola.

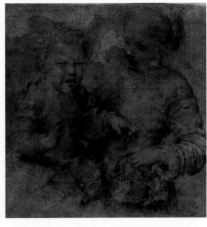

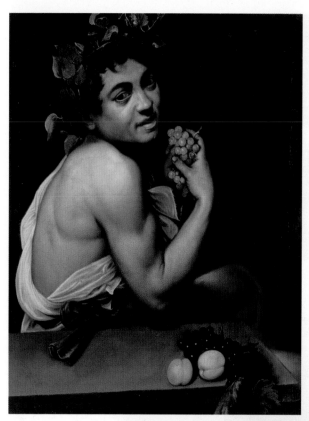

14. *Self-Portrait as Bacchus*. 'The picture has a sorceror's apprentice feel to it, with hints of illicit goings on . . .'

15. *Bacchus and Ariadne* by Titian.

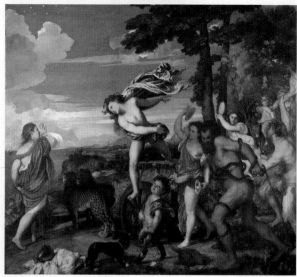

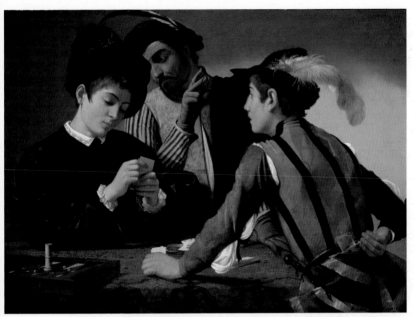

16. *The Cardsharps.* A young aristocrat is cheated by two feral and predatory conmen.

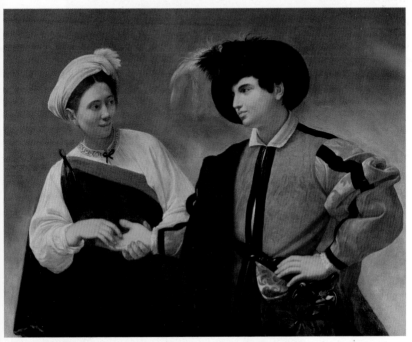

17. *The Gypsy Fortune-Teller.* 'A sweet siren, she enchants with smooth incantations.'

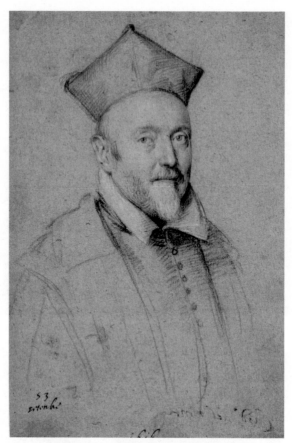

18. *Cardinal Francesco Maria del Monte* by Ottavio Leoni.
Friend to writers, musicians, artists and scientists, del Monte
was Caravaggio's first patron.

19. The Palazzo
Madama in Rome,
where Caravaggio
lived for several
years under del
Monte's protection.

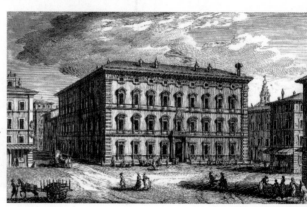

body; and because, even though quite dead, overthrown, and disfigured, it still terrified the world, the world had buried its very ruin.'[10]

Like any other migrant worker from the north, Caravaggio would have entered the city through the Porta del Popolo, into the Piazza del Popolo. In those days the great square was flanked on its northern side by the church and monastery of Santa Maria del Popolo, and on the south by a line of ordinary houses. Attempts had recently been made to aggrandize this main avenue of entry to the city. In 1587 an obelisk had been erected in the middle of the square. A marble fountain had been added too, but still the piazza was anything but grand. A traveller just arrived might get something to eat from one of the fritter vendors at the foot of the obelisk. He might sit with his back to the stump of a classical column – there were several protruding from the ground, like broken teeth – to munch his snack. There was a drinking trough nearby, used by farmers bringing pigs and goats to market, and a watering place where women did their laundry in the open air.

Much of Rome was still down at heel, as it had been when Montaigne visited. But by the time of Caravaggio's arrival the city was in the throes of a great transformation. In the spring of 1585 a devout Franciscan, Felice Peretti, Cardinal of Montalto, had been elected Pope Sixtus V. Energized by the same sense of mission as the formidable Carlo Borromeo – with whom he collaborated on an edition of the writings of St Ambrose – he set out to rebuild Rome both spiritually and physically. The edicts of the Counter-Reformation, handed down at the Council of Trent, were to be scrupulously observed. The fabric of the city itself had to be transformed into the visible symbol of a triumphantly reaffirmed Catholicism.

Under Sixtus V and his immediate successors, the appearance of Rome was dramatically altered. Seven grand new radial avenues were created to link the seven principal Christian basilicas and to ease the passage of pilgrims through the city. Many of the ancient Christian sites of Rome – including the catacombs, the tombs of the early martyrs – were excavated and restored. The dome of St Peter's, begun by Bramante nearly a century earlier, continued by Antonio da Sangallo and finally redesigned by 'the divine' Michelangelo, had at last been completed. Within a year of Caravaggio's arrival a gleaming ball topped by a golden cross had been mounted above its lantern.

As if to justify Montaigne's assertion that ancient Rome still 'terrified the world', its vestiges were yet more thoroughly subjected to Christian zeal. Prominent remains of antiquity were appropriated – moved, transformed, sometimes defaced and demolished – to demonstrate the eternal triumph of a resurgent Catholic Church over paganism and heresy alike. Sixtus V's principal architect, Domenico Fontana, transported a vast obelisk from the Circus of Nero to the square of St Peter's. Inscriptions were added to its base, declaring that a monument erected to the impious cults of the ancient gods had been brought to 'the threshold of the apostles' and consecrated to 'the undefeated cross'.[11] The old Renaissance spirit of admiration for the art and literature of the classical past began to be regarded with a distrust that bordered on outright hostility.

The same, severe repudiation of pagan antiquity had been expressed by one of the most prominent commissions of Sixtus's predecessor, Gregory XIII: Tommaso Laureti's painting *The Triumph of Christianity* – a fresco decoration for the Sala di Costantino in the Vatican Palace, completed in the mid 1580s. In a chilly atrium, a statue of Mercury lies shattered at the foot of an image of Christ on the Cross. The fragments of stone that symbolize the destruction of the ancient gods – hand, torso, decapitated head – have been placed in the foreground, at the start of a brutally insistent single-point perspective scheme. The vanishing point of the picture is like a black hole, where all energy converges. The painter rushes the eye from pagan idol to redeeming Christ and beyond – to a glimmering avenue of architectural mystery that stands, by implication, for the ineffable mystery of the one true faith.

CLEMENT VIII

Caravaggio arrived in Rome some seven or eight months after the election of a new pope. Clement VIII was determined to carry on the work begun by his predecessors, albeit in a somewhat less militant style. He was a shrewd, cautious and deeply pious man, whose pontificate was marked by a relaxation of hostility towards the culture and mythology of antiquity. In the private sphere, at least, it became permissible to commission paintings on profane subjects from the artists of the city. So it was that during the 1590s the Bolognese painter Annibale Carracci covered the ceiling of the Palazzo Farnese – the palace of Cardinal Odoardo Farnese, one of the richest men in all Italy – with a dizzying cornucopia of nudes re-enacting the loves of the gods on earth, in the air and in the water. There had been nothing like this joyful celebration of Eros in Rome since the Renaissance.

Clement VIII had been elected, on 30 January 1592, on the strength of his supposed moderation. In practice, he would tread a fine line between political pragmatism and Counter-Reformation zeal. He could be ruthless in the suppression of heresy and dissent, so the Rome that Caravaggio knew could hardly be described as a haven of creative and intellectual freedom. It was under Clement's pontificate that the speculative mystic Giordano Bruno – who believed in a thousand different worlds spinning through space, but denied the existence of God – was burned at the stake in 1600. Clement was not actively hostile to Philip II of Spain, but he set out to emancipate the papacy from what he perceived as undue Spanish influence. Rival French and Spanish factions lobbied tirelessly for influence in Rome, and at times their disagreements spilled over into street fights and public brawls. Clement steered a skilful middle course. He cultivated closer relations with France, acknowledging the legitimacy of Henri IV's claims to the throne and thus paving the way for the French king to renounce Protestantism and return to the Catholic fold. He then brokered the peace of Vervins of 1598, which effected a rapprochement between Henri IV and Philip II.

The French king's conversion was a tremendous coup for the Catholic Church and would come to be considered the greatest triumph of Clement's reign. (The pope also courted James I of England, whose queen, Anne of Denmark, was already a convert to Catholicism, but to no avail.) At home he did his utmost to restrict the powers of the aristocracy, reining in the feudal barons of the Papal States at every opportunity. In 1597, when the venerable Este dynasty failed due to the lack of a male heir, he promptly claimed title to the family's fiefdom of Ferrara and incorporated it into the papal states. Clement revised the Vulgate, promulgated a new edition of the *Index librorum prohibitorum* and took his duties as Bishop of Rome no less seriously than his role as supreme pontiff. He curbed prostitution, introduced a general ban on the carrying of weapons in public, outlawed duelling, made libel a capital offence and sought to enforce the strict celibacy of his clergy. The papal *sbirri*, the constabulary, were a vital tool in his control of the city. They were the equivalent of the Bishop of Milan's *famiglia armata*, but even more numerous. They were given wide-ranging powers, including the power to stop and search anyone suspected of heresy, of bearing arms or of being out after curfew without good cause. They did much of their work at night and were known for the dark cloaks that they wore to conceal themselves as they tailed their suspects, or paid unannounced visits to the houses of witnesses and potential informers.

Punishment, by contrast, took place in broad daylight. Death by execution was a grim public spectacle, a theatre of retribution designed to instil fear and the spirit of penitence into all who witnessed it. In 1581 Montaigne had observed the last moments of 'a famous robber and bandit captain' by the name of Catena:

> they carry in front of the criminal a big crucifix covered with a black curtain, and on foot go a large number of men dressed and masked in linen, who, they say, are gentlemen and other prominent people of Rome who devote themselves to this service of accompanying criminals led to execution and the bodies of the dead; and there is a brotherhood of them. There are two of these, or monks dressed and masked in the same way, who attend the criminal on the cart and preach to him; and one of them continually holds before his face a picture on which is the portrait of Our Lord, and has him kiss it incessantly. At the gallows, which is a beam between two supports, they still kept this picture against his face until he was launched. He made an ordinary death, without movement or word; he was a dark man of thirty or thereabouts . . .[12]

After the criminal's death, his body was cut into pieces. At this point, Montaigne notes, 'Jesuits or others get up on some high spot and shout to the people, one in this direction, the other in that, and preach to them to make them take in this example.' Such executions were still very much part of life in the Rome that Caravaggio knew.

Religious observance was not a matter of choice. At Easter everyone living in Rome was obliged to take Communion and procure a ticket of evidence from the priest who administered the sacrament. Procuring the ticket – proof of orthodoxy, and necessary to pass muster with the police – was itself part of a system of surveillance and involved a separate visit to the priest, who was obliged to write down the name and address of each communicant. But he also had to write down other details, noting for example who lived where and with whom, and listing their servants. It was, in effect, an annual census. It is because Counter-Reformation Rome was such an intensely controlled society that so much is known about those who lived there.

As in the Milan of Caravaggio's youth, great importance was attached to the question of what people should see, or be allowed to see. In a world where even the death of a criminal could be orchestrated as a grisly spectacle, religious art was inevitably subject to all kinds of supervisions. At the very start of his pontificate (1592–1605, therefore coinciding almost exactly with Caravaggio's years in Rome) Clement proved particularly keen to establish himself as a ruthless enforcer of the doctrines laid down by the Council of Trent. On 8 June 1592, some four months after his election, he issued the papal Bull *Speculatores domus Israel*, declaring a 'Visitation' of all churches of the city of Rome. The clergy would be inspected and so would the fabric and decoration of their churches, including works of art.

It was to be no comprehensive survey. The churches Clement actually visited are listed, in order, in the so-called Secret Vatican Archives (Archivio Segreto Vaticano). He started at the top, with St Peter's itself on 3 July 1592. He then went on to Santa Maria Maggiore, followed by San Giovanni in Laterano. By the time the Visitation had finally petered out, four years later, only twenty-eight churches had been covered. The reason was not dilatoriness but Clement's meticulous attention to detail. He insisted on visiting every church himself, and interrogating any suspect members of his clergy personally. Even though he surrounded himself with an entourage of four cardinals and three bishops – including Audwyn Lewis, the Bishop of Cassano, a Welsh Catholic who had left England in 1579 – the work of inspection was painfully slow. Its eventual abandonment may be taken as further proof of Clement's common sense.[13] Although deeply concerned for the well-being of the Church, Clement was not a man in the same obsessive mould as Carlo Borromeo. He stopped, perhaps knowing that his point had been made. The mere threat of the Visitation had reminded the Roman clergy to pay close attention to the works of art in their churches, and to use their powers of censorship if necessary. Caravaggio's career would be directly affected as a result. Several times during his years in Rome he would experience the humiliation of having a painting intended for the altar of a Roman church rejected on the grounds of indecency or impropriety.

IN THE ARTISTS' QUARTER

Like his immediate predecessors, the new pope was determined both to stabilize the foundations of the Catholic Church and to reassert the Eternal City as the radiant centre of Christendom. The beauty of Rome's churches must compel faith and crush heresy. That is why the city was filled with artists. Painters, sculptors and architects throughout Italy, and further afield, knew that there was more than enough work to go round in Rome. As Florence had been during the fifteenth century, and as Paris would be at the peak of Louis XIV's power, Rome under Clement VIII was the artistic capital of Europe. The artists of the city were so numerous – at a rough estimate, there were 2,000 of them, out of Rome's total population of around 100,000[14] – that they had their own quarter.

This was an area of a little more than two square miles situated, roughly, between the Piazza del Popolo and the Piazza di Spagna. Artists tended to arrive in groups – whether from Naples or Bologna, Lombardy or Emilia-Romagna, Flanders or France – and to board together to save money; it was not unusual for two or three to share a room, using the space both as bedroom and workshop. Rome could be stiflingly hot, which placed a premium on the lower, cooler floors of rental accommodation. But that suited the traditionally hard-up community of painters, who preferred the less expensive upper floors anyway, because there was more light there to paint by. They particularly favoured houses backing on to the Pincio, the hill perched above the Piazza del Popolo.

Different national groups of artists ran in gangs and swapped racial insults with their rivals. There were stereotypes to fit all. Germans were crude, the Flemish were drunks, and the French were violent thugs hiding behind a veneer of fake refinement. The Italians themselves, according to the exiled English earl encountered in Rome by the hero of Thomas Nashe's novel of 1594, *The Unfortunate Traveller*, were addicted to 'the art of epicurising, the art of whoring, the art of poysoning, the art of sodomitry'.[15]

An Englishman like Nashe grouped all Italians together, but for them the matter of national belonging was less clear cut. Italians had some sense of communal identity but an even sharper feeling for the distinctions that set them apart from one another. The Bolognese were known to hate the Tuscans, while most Romans treated Sicilians as if they were little better than peasants. Neapolitans were said to be obsessive about horsemanship. The Milanese, as we have seen, were famously keen swordsmen, and naturally unruly – although 'Lombards' as a group were often stereotyped as sluggish provincials, heavy of mind and body thanks to their rustic diet.

In 1589 the writer Giovanni Botero went so far as to propose a north–south fissure in the Italian temperament: 'Those who live in northern countries but not in the extreme north, are bold but lack cunning; southerners on the other hand are cunning but not bold . . . They are as the lion and the fox; whereas the northerner is slow and consistent in his actions, cheerful and subject to Bacchus, the southerner is impetuous and volatile, melancholy and subject to Venus . . .'[16] The personality of Caravaggio would be hard to locate on this particular map. He does not fit either profile, and in fact he would make his sense of his own singularity the subject of one of his earliest paintings – a self-portrait *as* Bacchus, but a Bacchus who is suffering and full of melancholy.

CITY OF MEN, CITY OF WHORES

The chronology of Caravaggio's early years is impossible to establish with precision, although we can work out that he changed his address frequently – ten times or so between 1592 and 1595. The houses changed but the milieu was always the same: the dark network of alleyways clustered around the Piazza del Popolo; the narrow streets bordering the Palazzo Firenze, home of the Medici's ambassadors to Rome; the Piazza Navona, which had once been the stadium of Domitian and still preserved its ancient double-horseshoe outline; the Campo de' Fiori, the marketplace.

This artists' quarter was a dangerous area of the city. Fights were common and fists were not the only weapons used. In an attempt to deter armed violence, the papal police made a public example of anyone caught wielding a *pugnello*, the short-handled dagger that was so often Exhibit A in the cases brought before Rome's criminal tribunals. At the corner of Via del Corso and Via dei Greci, in full shaming view of the city whose laws he had violated, the arrested suspect would be subjected to the *strappado*, an excruciating form of rope torture. The victim's hands were tied behind his back, with another loop of rope passed beneath his joined arms. He was then hauled into the air and left dangling for half an hour, the full weight of his body gradually pulling his arms further and further back and behind him. The inevitable result was dislocation of both shoulders. Victims eventually recovered but they did not forget the pain in a hurry. A painter subjected to the *strappado* could not work for weeks.

At night Caravaggio, his friends and his enemies shared the streets with the city's prostitutes. Rome's whores and courtesans had long been one of the sights of the city. In the early 1580s Montaigne had noted a craze for open-topped carriages especially adapted for the purpose of erotic ogling: 'One preacher's joke was that we turned our coaches into astrolabes . . . To tell the truth, the greatest profit that is derived from this is to see the ladies at the windows, and notably the courtesans, who show themselves at their Venetian blinds with such treacherous artfulness that I have often marvelled how they tantalise our eyes as they do; and often, having . . . obtained admission, I wondered at how much more beautiful they appeared to be than they really were . . .'[17]

By Caravaggio's time the prostitutes were so numerous that they had been coralled by papal edict into their own enclosure by the Tiber, the Ortaccio di Ripetta – a name which joked that the place was a kind of reverse Eden, since the literal meaning of *ortaccio* was 'evil garden'. But they would escape after dark to ply their trade in the ill-lit streets around the Piazza del Popolo. They were an embarrassment to the authorities because their very presence in such great numbers represented a blatant betrayal of Christian ethics at the very heart of the Catholic world.

Rome was not just an overwhelmingly male city; it was a city full of young and unattached men competing desperately with one another for favours. The city's whores were a much needed outlet for the accumulated sexual energy of this male-dominated, testosterone-fuelled society. But they were also, often, an occasion for violence in themselves. Some girls offered certain services for free to clients whom they liked, which could easily breed resentment. For an artist, the service might be posing naked for a picture (painting the nude model was officially illegal and this was one way of getting around the rules). But if the girls' pimps discovered such an arrangement, there was generally trouble.

The young artists who came to Rome to make a name for themselves lived on top of each other, competed for the same work, drank in the same taverns, frequented the same restaurants and bought their materials – paints, canvases, stretchers – from the same artists' supplier. His name was Antinoro Bertucci and he had a street stall on the Corso. Painters and sculptors of all nationalities would meet there, to buy what they needed for the next day's work and to discuss the latest gossip and news – to find out about workshop vacancies, to learn who was in and who was out with this or that influential prelate or cardinal. A visit to Antinoro's in the evening was also a good way to dodge the curfew regulations, because the paint-seller kept a fire burning at all hours. Going out for heat and light was a legitimate excuse for breaking curfew, so if a gathering should be interrupted by the police everyone would say they had gone to Antinoro for that reason. 'We were at Antinoro's because our fire had gone out' is a phrase that recurs in the witness statements of Rome's artists.

The ultimate ambition of every artist was the same: namely to work for the cardinals closest to the pope, to secure the most important commissions and win lasting fame – along with the money and security that went with it. The rules of the game were by no means straightforward. Everybody knew of mediocre artists who had been promoted above their abilities, and of deserving painters who had been overlooked. In a world where competition and rivalry were intense, resentment flourished easily, so Antinoro's was a rumour factory as well as an artists' supply shop. Stories of sabotage abounded – of the scaffolding that collapsed in the night, of the painter whose rival poisoned his colours with acid so that all his blues turned green in a matter of days. Once an artist got a reputation for bad luck or inefficiency, once it got around that he had 'the evil eye', his commissions would soon dry up.[18]

Though they disagree in some details, taken together Caravaggio's early biographers paint a convincing picture of a young man struggling to find his way in a harsh and unfamiliar world. During these first years in Rome he had contacts to ease his passage into the city: his uncle, Ludovico Merisi, the priest, was living there in 1591–2, Costanza Colonna in late 1592. But he seems to have fended mostly for himself, moving restlessly from one studio to another in search of employment – and quite possibly instruction too.

Baglione reports that 'in the beginning he settled down with a Sicilian painter who had a shop full of crude works of art.'[19] Bellori, in his marginal notes to Baglione's life, gives the Sicilian painter a name of sorts – Lorenzo Siciliano, whose line of work was painting crude bust-length heads for general sale. According to Bellori, in Lorenzo's workshop 'Caravaggio painted heads for a groat apiece and produced three a day.' The 'heads' in question may have been portraits of the famous men of the past, a subject in vogue among collectors of art since the middle years of the fifteenth century. The mercenary soldier and intellectual Federigo da Montefeltro, ruler of Urbino, had turned his private study into a gallery of such pictures, encompassing figures as various as Cicero and St Thomas Aquinas. If Caravaggio did paint his own versions of such subjects, none is known.

It was while staying with Lorenzo Siciliano that Caravaggio met an ambitious but unpredictable young Sicilian artist called Mario Minniti. According to the eighteenth-century biographer Francesco Susinno, who had access to sources now lost or destroyed, the young Minniti had been forced to flee Syracuse, via Malta, to get away from unspecified troubles. Arriving in Rome, he lodged with a hack painter from Sicily, in whose studio he befriended Caravaggio. Susinno implies that they were united in their dissatisfaction with the type of work which 'that coarse artisan' demanded of them, and dreamed together of rising to greater things. They became close friends, Minniti even posing for the impoverished Caravaggio – who could ill afford a model – on several occasions. His moon-shaped, mumpish face can be recognized in a number of early works. Minniti would also prove to be a useful contact much further along the pitted track of Caravaggio's life.

According to Mancini, during this period Caravaggio also lodged with a beneficed priest of St Peter's named Pandolfo Pucci, from the town of Recanati. He may have been introduced through his connections with the Colonna: the priest was household steward to a member of the Peretti family, and the Peretti and the Colonna were close. Mancini says that Pucci gave the artist a room and allowed him to paint there in exchange for domestic chores. The deal was not to the painter's satisfaction, and not only because he was not the sort of man to take pleasure in doing the housework: 'Worse, he was given nothing but salad to eat in the evening, which served as appetizer, entrée and dessert – as the corporal says, as accompaniment and toothpick. After a few months he left with little recompense, calling his benefactor and master "Monsignor Salad".'[20]

Mancini records that during his time with the parsimonious Pucci, Caravaggio 'painted some copies of devotional images', which the priest took home to Recanati with him when he left Rome in 1600. No trace of them has been found. Lost too is 'a portrait of an innkeeper who had given him lodgings' as well as another, unnamed portrait mentioned by the biographer. But the young Caravaggio's painting of a 'boy who is peeling a pear with a knife', also mentioned by Mancini, has perhaps survived.

There are at least ten versions of a similar subject, all showing the same rudimentary composition. The painting in the British Royal Collection, which is thought to have been acquired by Charles II, is conceivably the original picture described by Mancini. It was already recorded in the James II inventory of the collection as a work by 'Michael Angelo', which indicates that it was regarded as an autograph Caravaggio as early as the seventeenth century. An adolescent boy in a white shirt sits at a table on which various fruits, including cherries, peaches and nectarines, are scattered. The boy's shirt is spotlessly white, his hands unblemished, details suggesting that he is of noble birth. He peels not a pear but a green Seville or Bergamot orange, a bitter fruit. Perhaps this symbolizes his determination to choose the path of virtue, to avoid the sweeter temptations that life has to offer, or perhaps it is an emblem of the disappointments and difficulties that lie ahead even for a boy like this, blessed by wealth and fortune – a characteristically sour note for Caravaggio to have struck. But the mood of the painting is anything but ominous, so it might be unwise to burden it with too much hidden meaning. If it is indeed an autograph work, this undistinguished genre picture confirms just how little progress Caravaggio had made as a painter by the early 1590s. The handling is crude, the boy's expression wooden. Only in the extreme contrast of light and shade – the whiteness of the shirt, the depth of the shadows – can some presage of Caravaggio's later work be discerned.

THE BROTHERS CESARI

For the rest of his early time in Rome, Caravaggio appears to have been very much out on his own. Having left Monsignor Salad to his greens, he probably spent some time in the studio of a Sienese painter called Antiveduto Gramatica.[21] Gramatica was an artist of limited gifts about whom little is known save for the fact that his father had a questionable sense of humour. After predicting his son's premature birth, he registered his prescience by giving him his joke of a name – *antiveduto*, meaning 'foreseen'.

Caravaggio may have entered his studio in early 1593. In the same year Gramatica became a member of the guild of painters, the Accademia di San Luca. He was prolific, turning out small-scale devotional pictures, portraits and copies of portraits by the score. Particularly popular were his copies of a series of *Famous Men* then at the Villa Medici. Caravaggio, whose work for Lorenzo Siciliano had probably included similar pictures, may have painted his own copies of the Villa Medici 'heads' while in Gramatica's studio. If so, it is possible that he now came to the attention of his future protector, the Medici cardinal Francesco Maria del Monte, for the first time.

The next studio in which Caravaggio found work was more exalted.

It was that of Giuseppe Cesari, otherwise known as the Cavaliere d'Arpino, one of the most prominent artists in Rome in the 1590s. Giuseppe Cesari was only three years older than Caravaggio but far more successful. He was from a family of artists: his father, Muzio, was a painter. His brother, Bernardino, was his chief assistant and may also have acted as workshop manager. When he was a boy, Giuseppe had shown such precocious gifts as a draughtsman that his mother had taken him to Rome. At the age of just thirteen he had found work as a colour mixer for Niccolò Circignani, who was then directing the decoration of the Vatican Loggie for Pope Gregory XIII. He soon graduated to the painting team and made enough of a name for himself to win several important independent commissions in Rome during the later 1580s. Following the death of his most influential patron, Cardinal Farnese, in 1589, he accepted an invitation to carry out a series of paintings for the Certosa di San Martino in Naples, including a monumental canvas, *The Crucifixion*. He returned to Rome in 1591 and on Clement VIII's accession became the pope's leading painter.

Cesari's art was a limp but occasionally elegant hybrid of High Renaissance and Mannerist styles. As a painter of religious subjects, he answered the Counter-Reformation call for clarity, grace and decorum. But in his smaller, erotically charged mythological pictures, he experimented with complicated poses and frequently arcane symbolism. He painted the rape of Europa and the judgement of Paris, as well as the naked Diana and her companions surprised by the huntsman Actaeon. A composition of Perseus swooping from the skies to rescue an alluring and unusually languid Andromeda from the clutches of a diminutive lapdog of a dragon proved especially popular; several versions survive.

Caravaggio probably began working for the Cesari brothers in the middle of 1593. It was an eventful time for his new employers. In late 1592 Bernardino Cesari had been sentenced to death for associating with known bandits and had run away to Naples. But by May of the following year he was back in Rome, having secured a papal pardon thanks to the intervention of Cardinal Paolo Emilio Sfondrato, one of several powerful patrons of the Cesari workshop. Giuseppe now needed all the help he could get. The studio was busy: the papal treasurer, Bernardo Olgiati, had commissioned the decoration of an entire chapel in the church of Santa Prassede. Figures of the prophets, sibyls and doctors of the Church were required, as well as a *Resurrection* and a monumental *Ascension*. There was also a commission to decorate the vault of the Contarelli Chapel, in the church of San Luigi dei Francesi, with small scenes set into an intricate stuccowork design. Six years later Caravaggio would win the commission to paint two large canvases for the walls of the very same chapel – works that would instantly establish him as the most original religious artist of his time, and forever overshadow the earlier contributions of the Cesari workshop. But in 1593 he was just another apprentice painter from Lombardy with everything to prove.

The sources say that Caravaggio was employed to paint 'flowers and fruit'. Artists from northern Italy had recently begun to work in the relatively new field of still life painting. It was a genre of secular art – albeit frequently with undertones of religious meaning – that had its roots in post-Reformation Flanders and Holland. But its popularity had begun to spread southwards across Europe during the late sixteenth century. The Spanish played a part in disseminating this new taste, buying works of art in their northern territories and taking them to the cities that they controlled in Italy. It is likely that Caravaggio had seen Dutch or Flemish still life paintings during his time in Milan, and perhaps that was why Giuseppe Cesari marked him out for the same line of work. It is likely that he would have contributed the decorative festoons of frescoes by the Cesari workshop, as well as painting canvases for direct sale to private clients. Cesari also bought and sold Dutch and Flemish cabinet pictures, which suggests that he was well aware of the new taste among Roman collectors for the novelties of landscape and still life painting. But the supply of such pictures from the north was inevitably limited. Who better than an artist from Lombardy – a man from fertile Caravaggio, surrounded by the orchards that supplied Milan – to create homegrown depictions of flowers, fruit and vegetables?

There may have been an element of condescension about Cesari's decision to channel Caravaggio's energies towards still life – a trace of dismissive preconception about painters from the north. It was not unknown for Lombard artists to be caricatured as rustic provincials,

country bumpkins of painting, unacquainted with the grand traditions of Renaissance art. Artists were ranked according to a strict
hierarchy determined by subject matter. At the top were those who
specialized in paintings of the human figure shown in heroic or significant action – paintings from the Bible or mythology. Lower down
the scale came portraits, then paintings of animals. Then came another
relatively new genre, the landscape, followed last and least by the
humble still life. Such distinctions mattered a lot, especially to a man
as touchy and as self-conscious about his own status as Caravaggio.

There are strong indications that he resented the lowly nature of the
work that he was given to do in the Cesari studio. Bellori suggests that
he already had the ambition to work in the higher reaches of art, but
had to take whatever employment he was offered simply to survive:

> Since models, without which he did not know how to paint, were too
> expensive, he did not earn enough to pay his expenses. Michele was
> therefore forced by necessity to work for Cavaliere Giuseppe d'Arpino,
> who had him paint flowers and fruit, which he imitated so well that
> from then on they began to attain that greater beauty that we love
> today. He painted a vase of flowers with the transparencies of the water
> and glass and the reflections of a window of the room, rendering
> flowers sprinkled with the freshest dewdrops; and he painted other
> excellent pictures of similar imitations. But he worked reluctantly at
> these things and felt deeper regret at not being able to paint figures.[22]

Shorthand notes in the manuscript of Mancini's biography yield
several tantalizing glimpses of Caravaggio in the Cesari workshop.
They are obscure and hard to interpret, but suggest that the painter's
relationship with his employers was fraught. At first they rescue him,
but then they let him down or betray him in some unspecified way.
There is a reference to Caravaggio in poor and ragged clothing. Then
Bernardino Cesari takes him into the 'Torretta', which was the name
of the building in which the Cesari workshop was housed. He is put
up on a straw mattress on a raised platform, presumably some kind
of minstrels' gallery in one of the rooms. He boards there, in all, for
eight months. But at a certain point something bad happens, although
Mancini's notes do not say what that something was. Giuseppe Cesari
is a witness: 'Giuseppe sees and is petrified and in order to distract

him makes him retreat and flee so he does not appear.' Following this nameless act and its enigmatic aftermath, the Cesari brothers seem to feel that Caravaggio's presence in their workshop has to be concealed. Mention is made of 'C. G.', short for Giuseppe Cesari, painting a picture of St Joseph on which Caravaggio perhaps collaborates; but wherever this takes place, Cesari is very keen that Caravaggio should not be seen. Then Caravaggio gets kicked by a horse so badly that his leg swells alarmingly, but a surgeon is not called because he still must not be seen by anyone. A Sicilian friend who owns or runs a shop – more likely to be Lorenzo Siciliano than Mario Minniti – takes him to the hospital of the Consolazione. The Cesari brothers never go to visit him and he never goes back to them.[23]

Mancini's finished life of Caravaggio is much less circumstantial than his notes, except on the subject of the artist's stay in the hospital of the Consolazione. During his convalescence there, Caravaggio is said to have painted 'many pictures for the prior, who brought them to Seville, his home'. Reversing the chronology suggested by his jottings, Mancini then asserts that it was *after* his illness that the painter 'stayed with Cavaliere Giuseppe'. But whatever the precise sequence of events, a clear enough picture emerges of Caravaggio during this time of evident hardship. He is proud and touchy. He is growing in ambition, but increasingly disgruntled. He has not lost his knack for getting into trouble. He grudgingly performs his duties as a still life painter.

SELF-PORTRAIT AS BACCHUS, BOY WITH A BASKET OF FRUIT

None of the still lives that Caravaggio painted while he was with the Cavaliere d'Arpino seem to have survived. But there are two early pictures with a provenance that places them in the Cesari workshop. Both contain carefully worked still life elements, although neither is a pure still life painting: *Boy with a Basket of Fruit* and the so-called *Sick Bacchus*, or *Self-Portrait as Bacchus*.

They must have been done for Giuseppe Cesari in 1593–4, because both were still in his possession as late as 1607, the year when he unwisely clashed with the covetous papal nephew Scipione Borghese. Borghese was an avid art collector, as well as a great admirer of Caravaggio's work, who had long had his eye on Giuseppe Cesari's considerable backroom stock. He made an insultingly low offer for the pictures, and when Cesari had the temerity to refuse, Borghese used his influence to have the troublesome painter-dealer arrested on trumped-up charges. He then appropriated Cesari's entire collection of 105 paintings. The two pictures by Caravaggio have been in the Borghese collection ever since – and may still be seen in the Galleria Borghese today.

They are unusual works, with more than a hint of awkwardness about them, especially the *Self-Portrait as Bacchus*, which two of Caravaggio's early biographers found sufficiently memorable to single out from the rest of his juvenilia. Mancini refers to 'a beautiful Bacchus who was beardless',[24] while Baglione mentions 'a Bacchus with different bunches of grapes, painted with great care but a bit dry in style'.[25] 'Dry' seems a more appropriate epithet than 'beautiful'.

The ancient god of wine and mystic revelry holds a bunch of white grapes in his right hand. At the same time he brings up his shadowed left hand to clasp and even crush them, as in a wine-press. The bloom on the grapes, which dusts them with a layer of whiteness and dulls the reflected light caught in their opalescent skins, is echoed by the dry and whitish lips of the god himself. His pallour is an enigma, which the dark pools of his eyes – mocking and mysterious – do nothing to dispel. The still life that lies before him has an unsettling pathos. Two ripe, furred peaches lie beside a bunch of purple grapes on a forbiddingly cold and otherwise bare ledge of stone. Vine leaves trail off into darkness.

The title frequently used in modern times, *Sick Bacchus*, is a legacy of the Italian art historian Roberto Longhi. Longhi believed that Caravaggio painted it as an allegorical self-portrait just after his discharge from the hospital of the Consolazione. Whether the work alludes to the artist's illness is open to question, but it is certainly a self-portrait. Baglione groups it with a number of other, long-since vanished 'portraits of himself in the mirror'. The distorted right shoulder of the figure, so close to the picture plane as to seem almost touchable, may reflect the painter's use of a faintly convex mirror. The effect is at once intimate and disconcerting. The promise of a close relationship is held out by the figure's proximity, but denied by the cool evasiveness in his eyes. His right leg, so lost in semi-darkness as to have become little more than a blur, is half raised, which suggests that he could be about to get up. Sensual gratification is the half-promised gift that he brings. But he might disappear at any moment, leaving behind just darkness and the taste of ashes, not of wine.

Why would Caravaggio have painted himself like this? What might he have meant by it? The notion that he intended the work as a record of his own illness is ingenious, but there is a better and simpler explanation for the artist's liverish complexion. The picture is set at night, the time for Bacchic revelry. The light that flares so brightly on the figure's shoulder, giving his face its greenish cast, is simply the light of the moon.

The significance of this hypnotizing self-portrait is best sought in its symbolism, although that is anything but straightforward. In one sense Bacchus is an apt alter ego for an artist, because according to his legend he is subject to fits of divine inspiration. Caravaggio was not the first painter to associate himself with the god of wine. In Borromean Milan, the city of his upbringing, a group of painters, including the well-known artist and theorist Gian Paolo Lomazzo, had formed a mock-academy dedicated to the cult of Bacchus. The young Caravaggio's appropriation of the same Bacchic symbolism may have been his way of announcing his strong sense of his own capabilities, in which case there may have been an element of personal manifesto involved in the play-acting. It is tempting to imagine that he painted this truculent picture to show Giuseppe Cesari that he could be much more than a hack studio assistant.

While Bacchus symbolizes inpiration, he also stands for disorder, anarchy, an unruly surrender to the senses. He is passion, opposed to the reason embodied by Apollo. He is the enemy of civilization, capable of laying waste to an entire society: in Euripides' tragedy *The Bacchae* he destroys Thebes by luring its people into the mountains to join in his revels. The city's outraged king, Pentheus, is torn limb from limb by the god's intoxicated female followers, the Bacchantes. Pentheus' mother, Agave, is at their forefront, bearing her son's head aloft in triumph. In her ecstasy she sees him as a lion, fit to be slaughtered.

The madness and the maenadism associated with the myth had been painted most memorably – and most disconcertingly – by Titian in his celebrated *Bacchus and Ariadne*, now in London's National Gallery. As Bacchus leaps down from his chariot to join the mortal woman with whom he has suddenly fallen in love, his rowdy mob continues with its orgy. The god's followers include the fat Silenus, drunk beyond coherence, and a young satyr with glazed eyes who drags behind him, as if it were a toy, the severed head of a sacrificed calf. It had been Titian's achievement to distil the violence and weirdness of the Bacchic cults to a single image. He had conjured up a Renaissance equivalent to the frenzy described in Catullus' famous 64th poem – which was, almost certainly, one of his principal sources:

> Bacchus was rushing up and down with his dancing band of satyrs ... looking for you, Ariadne. Some of them were waving thyrsi with covered points, some were tossing about the limbs of a mangled steer, some were girding themselves with writhing serpents; some were bearing in solemn procession dark mysteries enclosed in caskets, mysteries which the profane desire in vain to hear. Others were beating tambourines with uplifted hands, or were raising sharp ringings from cymbals of rounded bronze ...

All this is relegated to the background of Caravaggio's self-portrait, which, in its dryness, restraint and small scale, is a world away from Titian's seductively orgiastic mythology. But it is there by implication. The violence that impends, the rending of the flesh, the drunkenness, the cannibalism – these things lurk in the teasing expression on the painter's face. Might he have actually painted the picture behind his master's back? Could it have been an act of truancy from the demeaning drudgery of the pure still life painting to which he had been assigned in the Cesari workshop? It has a sorceror's apprentice feel to it, with its hints of illicit goings on, after dark and away from prying eyes. By the light of the moon, the young painter dares to dress up as a god of misrule.

Boy with a Basket of Fruit is a fresher, brighter painting. But there is maybe more to this work too than at first meets the eye. The viewer is confronted by a blushing, smooth-skinned adolescent, with dark curly hair and an expression of amorous intensity on his face. On the admittedly slender evidence of a later self-portrait by Mario Minniti, it is possible that this was one of the pictures for which Caravaggio persuaded his new Sicilian friend to model. The boy carries a woven basket filled to overflowing with fruit – a cornucopia by comparison with the mere pair of peaches and the solitary bunch of grapes perched before the figure of Caravaggio-as-Bacchus. The basket contains four bunches of grapes, one red, two black and one green, as well as three apples, a peach and a pair of medlars. A pomegranate, split open to reveal its purple seeds, and four figs, two green and two black – the latter so ripe that they too have split to disclose the yellow and purple flesh within – also appear.

The picture has been interpreted in a number of sharply differing ways. It is plainly a kind of demonstration piece, painted to exhibit the young Caravaggio's skill in depicting not only fruits and foliage, but also the human face and form. Some writers have regarded it as a straightforward genre painting, a portrait of a handsome young fruit-seller plying his trade. Others claim to detect echoes of classical literature[26] – in particular, the fables of Pliny the Elder, whose *Natural History* is the principal source of information about the painters of antiquity. Pliny's encyclopedic book contains several stories and parables intended to demonstrate the heights of virtuosity reached by the artists of ancient Greece, as they competed to create an art of perfectly deceptive illusionism:

> The contemporaries and rivals of Zeuxis were Timanthes, Androcydes, Eupompus, Parrhasius. This last, it is recorded, entered into a competition with Zeuxis. Zeuxis produced a picture of grapes so dexterously represented that birds began to fly down to eat from the painted vine. Whereupon Parrhasius designed so lifelike a picture of a curtain that Zeuxis, proud of the verdict of the birds, requested that the curtain should now be drawn back and the picture displayed. When he realised his mistake, with a modesty that did him honour, he yielded up the palm, saying that whereas he had managed to deceive only birds, Parrhasius had deceived an artist.[27]

Pliny adds that, as a riposte to Parrhasius, Zeuxis also painted a picture of a child holding grapes. Once more the birds tried to eat the fruit, but this time Zeuxis felt he had failed. He disconsolately pointed out that if his picture had been perfectly lifelike, the birds would have been too frightened by the painted boy to peck at the painted grapes in his hands.

It was not uncommon for Italian artists of the fifteenth and sixteenth centuries to create their own versions of lost paintings from the classical past. So perhaps Caravaggio's choice of subject was intended to evoke that same picture of a child holding grapes by Zeuxis – and, indeed, to surpass it. No birds would ever dare to pick at the fruit in *this* basket. The blushing boy, whose tunic has slipped off his shoulder, is tremblingly alive. There is a slight awkwardness in the handling of his anatomy – an uncertainty in the juncture of his collarbone and right shoulder, which seems as a result unnaturally enlarged – but he is a compelling presence none the less. While the basket of fruit advertises Caravaggio's ability to capture different tones, textures and colours, the figure of the boy demonstrates a yet rarer gift: the ability to suggest human emotion. Those ardent, intently gazing eyes are filled with longing, even love. This striking intensity of feeling is inconsistent with the notion that the picture is simply a genre painting, a snapshot of daily life. Neither can it be readily explained by reference to the classical past.

How should we think about this remarkable face? Those who subscribe to the romantic myth of Caravaggio as a social and sexual outsider, boldly expressing the love that dares not speak its name, are obliged to twist the fruit-bearer's expression of amorous yearning into the come-hither eyelash-flutterings of a rent boy. Howard Hibbard's biography of Caravaggio, published in 1983, contains a brief but exemplary statement of this line of argument: 'There is a soliciting aspect to this picture, and since some of Caravaggio's other paintings of the 1590s are apparently homosexual in implication, we may read at least unconscious elements of this kind into the *Boy with a Basket*, whose fruits have various potentially symbolic meanings.'

Although Hibbard's interpretation is, I believe, thoroughly misguided, it contains an element of truth. There *is* a link between the figure's mood of sensual abandon and the luscious fruits that he bears, many of which – especially the figs, apples and pomegranate – had ancient sexual connotations. But the explanation for that lies not in the artist's supposedly devil-may-care determination to flaunt his homosexuality. It lies in the words of an ancient Persian love poem, absorbed long ago into the Judaeo-Christian tradition and known as the Song of Songs or the Song of Solomon, the most flagrantly erotic text in all of the Old Testament.[28] It takes the form of a poetic dialogue between two lovers, the Bride and the Groom, who express their feelings for one another in imagery of a rich and fecund natural world.

The Groom compares his beloved to a garden: 'A garden inclosed is my sister, my spouse; a spring shut up, a fountain sealed. Thy plants are an orchard of pomegranates, with pleasant fruits . . .' (4:12–13). For her part, the Bride describes the Groom as 'white and ruddy, the chiefest among ten thousand. His head is as the most fine gold, his locks are bushy, and black as a raven . . . His mouth is most sweet: yea, he is altogether lovely. This is my beloved, and this is my friend, O daughters of Jerusalem' (5:10–16). Finally, the Groom describes the fruition of their desires: 'How fair and how pleasant art thou, O love, for delights! This thy stature is like to a palm tree, and thy breasts to clusters of grapes. I said, I will go up to the palm tree, I will take hold of the boughs thereof; now also thy breasts shall be as clusters of the vine, and the smell of thy nose like apples; and the roof of thy mouth like the best wine for my beloved, that goeth down sweetly, causing the lips of those that are asleep to speak' (7:6–9).

The iconography of Caravaggio's painting is extremely close to that of the Song of Songs. The boy's basket is filled with the fruits described in the poem, while the boy himself has all the attributes of the Groom, with his ruddy cheeks, his hair 'as black as a raven'. So tender and languorous is his gaze that he might readily be imagined actually reciting the verses of the Song of Songs to his beloved. His lips are parted, as if to speak or sing.

The Song of Songs was a controversial religious text among Christians and Jews alike precisely because of its profound eroticism. In the first century AD one of the rabbis to argue most passionately for its inclusion in Jewish scripture, as the 'Holy of Holies', also condemned the secular practice of singing it in banqueting halls, which suggests that sacred interpretation of the text had long been shadowed by suspicion of its sensuality.[29] By the time Caravaggio painted his *Boy with a Basket*, in the late sixteenth century, Christian Church fathers had spent considerably more than a millennium teasing out what they had come to see as the redemptive symbolism of the poem's tale of love. The Groom's passion for the Bride was held to express Jesus Christ's boundless love for his holy mother, Mary. The metaphor of the Bride as an 'inclosed garden' was easily transformed into a symbol of Mary's virginity.

But, to judge by the remarks of St Teresa of Avila, who wrote her own commentary on the Song of Songs in 1573, such forms of allegorical interpretation were not always easily understood by congregations in the world of the Catholic Counter-Reformation. As she noted, bawdy laughter at the sexual connotations of the poem's language might easily interrupt even the most solemn, sacerdotal reflections on the Song of Songs: 'Indeed, I recall hearing a priest ... preach a very admirable sermon, most of which was an explanation of those loving delights with which the bride communed with God. And there was so much laughter, and what he said was so poorly taken, that I was shocked.'[30]

Caravaggio's painting, like that priest's sermon, has also provoked ribald comments and has inevitably been susceptible to erotic interpretation. That ambiguity has perhaps always been part of its meaning. To borrow a phrase applied to Caravaggio's work as a whole by his contemporary Cardinal Ottavio Paravicino, it is a picture that seems poised 'between the sacred and the profane' – in this case, concealing a devout message within an apparently profane, secular subject. To those who would be blind to its spiritual dimensions, the painting was designed to remain a merely enchanting parade of sensual delights – a picture of a boy with a puzzlingly languorous expression on his face, carrying a basket of fruit. But to those who knew how to see through the sensual surface, the boy reveals himself as the Groom in the Song of Songs and therefore as the type of the young Jesus Christ, an image at once of love and vulnerability.

He is bare from the shoulder, not only because he is rapt in symbolic love for his divine mother, but also in anticipation of his crucifixion, the sacrificial gift of love he bears to all humanity. The shadows that flicker on the wall behind him, set against the light that illuminates his face, are shadows of death from which his own image, and with it the promise of eternal life, radiantly emerges. The same Christian message, that eternal life can be salvaged from the jaws of death, lurks in his basket of fruit. Withered, worm-eaten leaves of the vine contrast with ripened bunches of grapes. From death, once more, shall come life. The fading foliage is decay, transience, the passing of all things here on earth. The grapes are wine, the wine of the Eucharist that is the sacrificial blood of Christ. The picture offers not only a gift but a stark contrast of alternatives. What will you have? Death or life? Darkness or light?

BOY BITTEN BY A LIZARD

Caravaggio's *Self-Portrait as Bacchus* and *Boy with a Basket of Fruit* are subtle and ambitious paintings, not the work of a painter likely to be satisfied with long hours and low pay working as another artist's fruit and flower specialist. They corroborate Bellori's assertion that Caravaggio 'worked reluctantly' at whatever hack work was assigned to him and 'felt deeper regret at not being able to paint figures'.

With the *Bacchus*, Caravaggio asks to be taken seriously, to be recognized as a painter not only of inspiration and intelligence but of something more than that. The picture announces Caravaggio's spirit of unruly unpredictability, and shows for the first time the face of a man quite capable of overthrowing the tired artistic conventions of his time. With the *Boy with a Basket*, he demands to be regarded as better than a mere still life painter, and expresses the hope that one day – one day soon – he might be allowed to try his hand at devotional pictures.

Even this early in his career, at a time when so much of his life and personality are obscure, certain things are clear. Caravaggio wants to paint the human figure and he wants to treat what, for his contemporaries, are the deepest and most serious subjects – the great Christian themes of salvation and damnation. His art is both sensually and intellectually seductive. It is carefully calculated to appeal to the more discerning and well-educated type of Roman patron – someone likely to be high up in the hierarchy of the Roman Church, keenly attuned to the subtle devotional symbolism of a picture such as the *Boy with a Basket*, or to respond to a secular, mythological painting like the *Self-Portrait as Bacchus*.

So it is no coincidence that the young Caravaggio should have gravitated towards the company of churchmen. The more he could infiltrate the higher circles of the Roman clergy, the more likely he would be to win meaningful patronage. At first he had stayed with the unsatisfactory Pandolfo Pucci, 'Monsignor Salad'. Around the beginning of 1595, after eight months in the Cesari workshop and a spell in hospital, he lodged once more with a man of the cloth. According to Mancini, the struggling Caravaggio found support from a certain 'Monsignor Fatin Petrigiani, who gave him the comfort of a room in which to live'.[31]

There were no fond farewells to Giuseppe Cesari. Whether Caravaggio left Cesari's employ before or after the murky events that led to his hospitalization, they parted on bad terms. Whatever the personal reasons for the bad blood between them, professional jealousy also probably played a part. There are hints, in Mancini's manuscript notes, that Cesari deliberately attempted to hold his talented young apprentice back for fear of being outshone. The perennially abrasive Caravaggio was a born innovator who had little time for the art of most of his contemporaries (he would later say as much in one of his several appearances before the Roman magistrates), so likely regarded the fey late Mannerism of Cesari's mature style with naked contempt. Cesari's prestige among the most influential Roman collectors and patrons can only have made Caravaggio's own position all the more galling to him. Being studio assistant was bad enough, but being studio assistant to an overrated mediocrity must have been more than his pride could stand.

Accusations of arrogance echo through the early biographies of Caravaggio. 'Michelangelo Merisi was a satirical and proud man,' writes Baglione; 'at times he would speak badly of the painters of the past, and also of the present, no matter how distinguished they were, because he thought that he alone had surpassed all the other artists in his profession.'[32] Bellori explicitly says that pride drove Caravaggio to leave Cesari and strike out on his own. At this point Bellori introduces another character into the narrative, a well-known painter of amusing bizzareries named Prospero Orsi, who suddenly appears as the rebellious Caravaggio's sidekick, egging him on to rebellion and independence: 'When he met Prospero, a painter of grotesques, he took the opportunity to leave Giuseppe in order to compete with him for the glory of painting. Then he began to paint according to his own inclinations; not only ignoring but even despising the superb statuary of antiquity and the famous paintings of Raphael, he considered nature to be the only subject fit for his brush.'

Bellori treats Caravaggio's rejection of Cesari as if it had been the publication of a manifesto. In his eyes, Caravaggio had not just turned away from one man's influence; he had repudiated the entire classical and Renaissance canon and abandoned those principles of selection and idealization on which all truly great and lasting works of art must be founded. He describes it as an act of foolhardy hubris. 'As a result, when he was shown the most famous statues of Phidias and Glykon, in order that he might use them as models, his only answer was to point towards a crowd of people, saying that nature had given him an abundance of masters.'

The idea that anyone would have taken the time to call the young Caravaggio's attention to the sculptures of classical antiquity is probably fanciful. The neatness of his rejoinder strengthens the suspicion that this is parable, rather than fact (Bellori in effect admits as much when he concedes that 'A similar story is told about the painter Eupompus'). Yet the fiction is revealing because it contains, in a nutshell, the academic artist's innate distrust of Caravaggio's startling naturalism. The painter is cast as gifted but fatally proud, a man bent on dragging art down into the gutter – leading it towards the mere unthinking replication of reality. The same attitude, softened by time but equally misguided, lies behind more recent attempts to expose the presumed trickery behind Caravaggio's art – the suggestion that the painter must have used some kind of lens to achieve his effects, or the hypothesis that it was all (literally) done with mirrors. The one grain of truth in Bellori's account may lie in what it has to say about the sheer strength of early audience response, favourable or otherwise, to the seductively lifelike qualities of Caravaggio's paintings.

Having left the Cesari studio, Caravaggio certainly needed to sell his paintings. His stay with Monsignor Petrigiani may not have lasted long. Baglione says that, soon after leaving Cesari, Caravaggio 'tried to live by himself' and that he painted some self-portraits at this time, lacking the funds to hire a model. 'He also painted a boy bitten by a lizard emerging from flowers and fruits; you could almost hear the boy scream, and it was all done meticulously.'[33]

There are two extant versions of this subject, one in the Roberto Longhi Foundation in Florence, the other in the National Gallery, London. Technical analysis, as well as its slightly more crude and direct style, suggests that the Longhi picture was created first, probably in late 1594 or at the start of 1595.[34] The handling of the drapery is more assured in the London picture, which also points to a slightly later date. Yet the very existence of this second, slightly more sophisticated variation indicates that Caravaggio had scored enough of a success with his original version to create a market for replicas.

Once again, Caravaggio paints a single figure in an interior lit by raking light. But this time he animates the figure, having him actively recoil in pain and, as Baglione says, utter an almost audible scream. The painter emphasizes the effects caused by his use of a single light source, pushing the contrast between light and dark to an unprecedented degree.

The subject is a moment of compressed drama. A young man has been unpleasantly surprised during what should have been a quiet moment of unalloyed pleasure. Reaching out towards the selection of fruit laid out on the table before him – two bright red cherries, some figs and some grapes are visible – he finds that he himself is being bitten, by a creature that has been lurking unseen. The animal, a lizard, buries its fangs into the fleshy part of his middle finger. The boy's face, startled and flushed with the sudden consciousness of pain, is strongly illuminated. His bare shoulder and tensed right hand, from which the lizard still dangles, are thrown into sharp relief.

There is a slightly clumsily painted pink rose behind the boy's ear, while the artist has also included a vase on the table in front of him, which is three quarters full of water and contains another rose and some stalks of flowering jasmine. Light slows and thickens to a texture like that of milk in the depths of the water. Reflections play in the convex surface of the vase, and two drops of condensation trickle down its fatly curved side. This is a piece of painting that evokes Giorgio Vasari's description of a work by the young Leonardo da Vinci, the most famous painter to have worked in Caravaggio's home town of Milan – a picture of the Virgin 'in which, besides the marvellous vividness, he had imitated the dewdrops so that the picture seemed more real than life'.

The exquisite still life is a naked demonstration of skill – a reminder that when Caravaggio painted it he was working for the open market and therefore, in a sense, crying out his wares. He included the detail to impress his mastery of certain virtuoso techniques in oil painting on his prospective Roman audience – ways of painting the reflection and refraction of light, of capturing the precise wetness and viscosity of a drop of sweat, a drop of water or a drop of blood, which could make the practice of art seem almost like a form of magic. Despite Vasari's encomium to Leonardo, such skills were primarily associated with artists from Flanders. Jan van Eyck had been the first Renaissance master to master them, followed by Rogier van der Weyden, Hans Memlinc and others. Caravaggio's inclusion of such effects in his own work advertised his roots in Lombardy, in northern Italy, where Flemish art was better known than in the rest of the peninsula. His handling of the vase and its reflections indicate that he was familiar with the work of later Flemish masters such as Jan Bruegel.

But the still life detail *is* only a detail, a grace note in a picture designed primarily as a vehicle for the depiction of a human being gripped by sudden, strong emotion. Contrary to Bellori's assertion that Caravaggio turned away from all artistic tradition to pursue an art rooted solely in study from life, the figure of the boy is extremely sculptural. He was painted from a model, but he also evokes that very tradition of classical statuary which, according to Bellori, Caravaggio despised. The most obvious precedent for the boy who screams in pain was the celebrated classical statue of *Laocoön* and his sons, wrapped in the coils of snakes, which had been excavated in Rome less than a hundred years earlier. Even the lizard may have been inspired by a classical sculpture, namely the so-called *Apollo Sauroctonus*, or *Lizard Apollo*, which is now in the Louvre but was probably in Rome in Caravaggio's time. The reptile climbing up a tree trunk in that sculpture is shown from the same, sharply profiled angle – seen as if from above – as Caravaggio's lizard.

The German art historian, painter and engraver Joachim von Sandrart, who travelled widely in Italy between 1628 and 1635, gave *Boy*

Bitten by a Lizard a prominent place in the short account that he wrote of Caravaggio's early years. To judge by its tone, he must have spoken to artists or collectors who still remembered the picture's thrilling impact from some forty years before: 'In the beginning, he painted many faces and half-length figures in a sharp, dry manner. One of these is that of a child with a basket of flowers and fruit, from which a lizard emerges, biting the hand of the child who begins to cry bitterly, so that it is marvellous to look at and it caused his reputation to increase notably throughout Rome.'

Sandrart mistakenly refers to the picture's vase of flowers as a basket. Perhaps he confused its still life, in his memory, with that in the earlier *Boy with a Basket*. But his report vividly demonstrates the extent to which the exploits of the young Caravaggio were still remembered, still talked about, in Rome even as late as the 1630s. His informants, whoever they were, also gave him to understand its startling combination of emotional intensity and artistic naturalism as a gauntlet thrown down at the feet of Giuseppe d'Arpino and his followers: 'Because Arpino generally painted large works in fresco, which does not in itself have the same strength of colour or the intrinsic truth of oil colours, and because Caravaggio was very excellent in the latter, he offered Giuseppe and many others a challenge which resulted in endless quarrels. This brought them to swords' points . . .' Sandrart also tells the story that Caravaggio painted a picture in the Roman church of San Lorenzo in Damaso, next to an altarpiece by Giuseppe d'Arpino, in which 'he represented a nude giant who sticks out his tongue at Giuseppe's work as if he wished to ridicule it.'[35] The tale of the nude giant with the mischievous tongue is certainly apocryphal, nor is there any other evidence to suggest that Caravaggio and Giuseppe Cesari, the Cavaliere d'Arpino, ever came to blows (if they had, Cesari might never have lived to a ripe old age). But there is perhaps a glimmer of fire behind all the smoke. In Sandrart's telling of the story, Caravaggio becomes far more than a disgruntled studio assistant with the nerve to walk out on his boss. He becomes a rival, someone who turns away from his former master's style and subject matter because he has his own ideas.

The most original aspect of *Boy Bitten by a Lizard* is the fact that it depicts an ordinary person – someone distinguished by no particular signs of rank or status – in the grip of a strong emotion. One of the few known precedents for this lay in late sixteenth-century Bolognese art. Giorgio Vasari tells of a female painter called Sofonisba Anguissola, originally from Cremona, who created a drawing for Tommaso de' Cavalieri – once a close friend of the great Michelangelo – in which she depicted 'a little girl laughing at a boy who is weeping because one of the cray-fish out of a basket full of them, which she has placed in front of him, is biting his finger; and there is nothing more graceful to be seen than that drawing, or more true to nature'.[36]

Vasari's story about another work of art may shed light on the meaning of Caravaggio's. The introduction of a faintly malevolent laughing girl complicates the story of a boy bitten by surprise. Perhaps Anguissola may have intended some playful allusion to the hazards of adult love that lie in store for every child. This, in turn, may begin to suggest the symbolic intentions that lay behind Caravaggio's own choice of the theme. Is the presence of erotic temptation implied in his *Boy Bitten by a Lizard*? There is reason to think so.

There is an air of abandonment about the boy, imparted both by his languid state of undress and by the rose in his hair. Roses are traditional emblems of romantic love, but the other blossoms present in the picture add a less innocent note to its symbolism. Jasmine was a traditional symbol of desire (Caravaggio would include the same flower in his later portrait of a well-known Roman courtesan). The boy's clothing, such as it is, a wispy piece of white drapery, might be no more than a twisted bedsheet. He who reaches for cherries and apples has grasped at sexual temptation. Now he is receiving his just reward. A sexual subtext lurks, as the lizard had done, in that pile of luscious fruit. The animal is zoologically inaccurate – real lizards have no teeth – but charged with metaphorical potency. A toothless reptile has been transformed into the very image of the *vagina dentata*.

It would have required no great ingenuity on the part of Caravaggio's contemporaries to unlock his meaning. In the sign language of the Italian street – symbolism in its most vivid, popular form – the bitten finger represented the wounded phallus. The English diarist John Evelyn witnessed a quarrel between two boatmen in seventeenth-century Genoa, at the end of which one of them 'put his finger in his mouth and almost bit it off by the joynt, shewing it to his antagonist as an assurance to him of some bloodie revenge'.[37] The threat on that occasion, as Evelyn euphemistically hints, was castration. A different fate can be understood to lie in store for Caravaggio's decadent young man: in Rome, city of courtesans, the reward for promiscuity was venereal disease. 'The French disease', they called it in Italy (although the French themselves preferred to think of it as 'the Pox of Naples').

Boy Bitten by a Lizard is a *vanitas* painting, a reflection on the pitfalls that await those who give themselves up to the pleasures of the flesh. It is a work of art that functions in a way exactly analagous to the action which it depicts. An apparently innocuous image, full of sweet fruit and lingering sensual detail, hides the sourest of morals. The message of the picture might seem unnecessarily severe, but it should be remembered that Caravaggio's target audience was the higher Roman clergy. They needed the alibi of moral reflection to enjoy – let alone purchase – a picture such as this.

GYPSIES AND ROGUES AND A CARDINAL SNARED

For all his ingenuity, Caravaggio did not enjoy immediate success with *Boy Bitten by a Lizard*. According to Mancini, the painter was forced to sell the work for next to nothing. In Baglione's yet bleaker telling of the story, Caravaggio failed to find a buyer for any of the pictures that he painted after leaving the Cesari workshop: 'He was unable to to sell these works, and in a short time he found himself without money and poorly dressed.'

Desperate for money, the artist went to the picture-dealers of Rome. According to Baglione, 'some charitable gentlemen expert in the profession came to his aid, and finally Maestro Valentino, a dealer in paintings at San Luigi dei Francesi, managed to sell a few.'[38] This 'Maestro Valentino' was actually Costantino Spata, who did indeed have a shop in the piazza bordering San Luigi dei Francesi, the so-called 'church of the French'. He befriended Caravaggio and Prospero Orsi. He sold their pictures on commission and was seen drinking with them on several occasions.[39]

Costantino Spata played a vital role in Caravaggio's career. It was through him that the painter came to the attention of one of his most important supporters, his principal patron during his early years in Rome. Baglione tells the story in a few words: 'This was the means by which he met Cardinal del Monte, an art lover, who invited him to his home.'[40] Cardinal del Monte would nurture Caravaggio through the next few crucial years of his life. Not only would he house, clothe and protect him, but he would introduce him to a circle of the most powerful and influential collectors in Rome, and negotiate the difficult waters of higher Church patronage on his behalf.

Del Monte, the 'art lover', whose palace was just around the corner from the Piazza di San Luigi, was one of Spata's clients. Did the dealer and the painter think up a deliberate strategy to get the cardinal's attention? Did Spata even advise Caravaggio on *what* to paint, helping to bait the hook that would land the big fish? Certainly, the work that Caravaggio created for his new dealer to try to sell was markedly different from anything he had painted before.

The two pictures with which Caravaggio and Spata successfully tempted del Monte, *The Gypsy Fortune-Teller* and *The Cardsharps*, still exist. The first is to be found in the Capitoline Museum in Rome (a later and even finer version of the same composition, painted for a friend of del Monte, is in the Louvre). The second is in the Kimbell Art Museum in Fort Worth, Texas. Between them, they mark a radical new departure for Caravaggio, and indeed they are among the most innovative pictures created anywhere in Europe in the late sixteenth century.

Each painting shows a scene of trickery and deceit, enacted by half-length figures. 'Genre picture' was the less than satisfactory term eventually settled upon by art historians to describe such works. But the genre picture in this vein did not exist until Caravaggio invented it. Although there had been shadowy precedents for such work, in prints and drawings and in marginal details of paintings about other things, *The Gypsy Fortune-Teller* and *The Cardsharps* introduced a new concept to art: the low-life drama. Hung together in a single room in del Monte's Roman palace, their influence was soon felt far and wide. The taste for such pictures grew rapidly and spread across all of Europe. Caravaggio's tricksters spawned a whole world of painted rogues, created by a multitude of artists including Bartolomeo Manfredi in Italy, Rembrandt in Holland and Georges de La Tour in France.

The differing dimensions of the two canvases suggest that they were not painted as a pair, although both are offspring of the same idea. In *The Gypsy Fortune-Teller*, a sharply dressed young man with a sword at his hip has fallen under the spell of a smiling young Romany traveller. She fixes him with an intense and slightly nervy stare. He returns her hypnotic gaze with a dreamy, half-lost expression of his own. Shadows play on the dun-coloured wall behind the two figures. The precise nature of the action was explained by Mancini: 'I do not think I have seen a more graceful and expressive figure than the Gipsy who foretells good fortune to a young man ... he shows the Gipsy's slyness with a false smile as she takes off the ring of the young man, who shows his naivete and the effects of his amorous response to the beauty of the little Gipsy who foretells his fortune and steals his ring.'[41] Under the pretence of reading the young man's palm, the streetwise confidence trickster is actually robbing him.

The Cardsharps plays a variation on the same theme, a gentleman fooled out of his money. The scene is a gambling den, in which we encounter the second of Caravaggio's fresh-faced, rich young men, playing a game of cards. He is dressed in sumptuous black silk over a lace-trimmed shirt – sleek finery that has drawn the attention of not one but two urban predators. The yellow-and-black stripes of their costumes suggest the image of a pair of wasps buzzing around a honeytrap. Some honey has already been extracted, to judge by the detail of a backgammon board, pushed to the edge of the gaming table. Having failed at one game, the young gentleman is trying to win back his losses at another. His optimism is undimmed, to judge by the halfsmile that plays on his lips. But he cannot possibly win. The young cheat sitting opposite him has a choice of extra cards tucked into his belt behind his back. The other peeks over the young gentleman's shoulder and signals in code to his partner in crime, letting him know exactly what will be required to ensure a winning hand.

The older of the two conmen, with his holed, threadbare glove and black cloak – perfect for melting into the unlit gloom of Rome's streets by night – is the spying accomplice described in numerous books and pamphlets of the time. There was a thriving literature devoted to the tricks of the street and, in particular, the devices of the card cheat. A popular Italian treatise on gambling, entitled *The Book on Games of Chance* (*Liber de ludo aleae*), was written by the mathematician, astronomer and failed card-player Gerolamo Cardano (1501–76). Countless other texts listed the various techniques used by cheats at the gaming table. One of the most widely read, a work first published in England in 1552 under the title *A Manifest Detection of the Most Vile and Detestable Uses of Dice-play, and Other Practices Like the Same*, contains a more or less exact description of the ruse played out in Caravaggio's *Cardsharps*: 'Of this fraternity there be that called helpers, which commonly haunt taverns or ale-houses, and cometh in as men not acquainted with none in the company, but spying them at any game will bid them God-speed and God-be-at-their-game, and will so place himself that he will show his fellow by signs and tokens, without speech commonly, but sometime with far-fetched words, what cards he hath in his hand, and how he may play against him. And those between them both getteth money out of the other's purse.'[42]

There is a narrative and symbolic affinity between the two pictures painted for Cardinal del Monte and the work that immediately preceded them, *Boy Bitten by a Lizard*. All three tell of a man undone by his own vices, of youth suddenly clouded by the prospect of disease, loss or debt – a pattern that the artist had perhaps experienced during his own youth in Milan. But what made *The Gypsy Fortune-Teller* and *The Cardsharps* so startlingly original was their unprecedentedly close focus on the world of the street and the gambling den.

The subject matter of these paintings was highly topical. Counter-Reformation Rome was a city in which all manner of thieves, rogues and scoundrels thronged. Their presence was a symptom of social crisis. Recurrent plague not only destroyed lives, but ravaged economies in the cities and states where it struck. The number of displaced and unemployed people had grown alarmingly during Caravaggio's lifetime. Sixteenth-century Italy had also been racked by an almost constant state of war, resulting in a large, permanently uprooted population of mercenaries. When they had money such men gambled, drank and whored. If the recruiting officer did not call, they were liable to turn to crime. In Rome, ever a magnet for the poor in need of alms, they often masqueraded as pilgrims.

A vivid picture of this confusing world, where scurrility often dressed itself in the clothes of virtuous indigence, is painted by a set of notarial documents dated February 1595 (probably only a year or so before Cardinal del Monte purchased *The Gypsy Fortune-Teller* and *The Cardsharps*), which record the interrogation of a young man in the prison on the Sistine Bridge, in the centre of Rome. 'I am called Pompeo,' the boy declared. 'I was born in Trevi near Spoleto, I am about 16 years old, I have no occupation, I was arrested by your men in the church of S. Giacomo degli Spagnoli, because I was begging for alms during Mass.' When he was asked if he knew anything about other beggars in the city, and whether they formed a single sect, or many, he gave the following answer: 'Sir, among us poor beggars there are different confraternities [*compagnie*, a word normally used to refer to religious confraternities] . . . the first is called the Confraternity of the Grencetti, those who, while they are begging for alms in the churches in a crowd, cut purses . . . The second is called the Confraternity of the Sbasiti, and includes those who pretend to be ill and lie on the ground as if they were dying and keep groaning and demanding alms. The third is called the Baroni, who are healthy and upright, and are sturdy beggars who do not want to work.' By the time he had finished, Pompeo had listed no fewer than nineteen groups of fraudulent beggars. They included the Formigotti, who pretended to be discharged soldiers; the Rabrunati, who faked epilepsy by eating soap and then foaming at the mouth; and the Pistolfi, who posed as priests to extract 'donations' from their victims.[43]

The same set of documents also contains the testimony of another man claiming familiarity with different groups of criminals at work in Rome in the 1590s. His name was Girolamo, and to Pompeo's nineteen categories of villain he added seventeen more, including the Marmotti, who affected to have been struck dumb, and the Spillatori, who – like Caravaggio's *Cardsharps* – sought out the gullible in taverns and inns and cheated them out of their money using marked cards and loaded dice. Girolamo disagreed with Pompeo's (presumably) ironic comparison of such groups of criminal specialists with religious confraternities. 'They are not confraternities [*compagnie*] but crafts [*arti*], like shoemakers, goldsmiths and so on.'

The exact status of these texts is questionable, and the precision with which they reflect actual criminal activity in Caravaggio's Rome is open to debate. Peter Burke, who translated and republished them, notes that 'these documents cannot now be found in the Roman archives, and are best known though a copy made a few years later, which used to be in the former Imperial Library in Berlin', with 'the rather literary title of the "delightful examination" of rogues, "*Il dilettevole essamine de' guidoni, furfanti o calchi*"'.

It is likely that the documents are altered transcripts of reported speech; and almost certain that they have been liberally 'improved' by the late sixteenth-century writer who gave them their present form. Many of the practices that they record, such as the use of soap to feign epilepsy, were (and still are) used by real fraudsters. They are part of an oral history of fraudulence that certainly has a basis in fact. But other elements seem to have been exaggerated. Analysis of the certain testimonies of known criminals that still *are* to be found in the Roman archives presents a less well-organized and significantly less colourful picture of criminal activity – gangs of crooks robbing at random when the opportunity presents itself, fencing stolen goods to the city's Jewish pedlars and immediately eating and drinking away the proceeds.[44]

For all that, the tales told by 'Pompeo' and 'Girolamo' contain their own kind of truth, halfway between fact and fiction. What these stories reveal above all is a particular set of stereotypes about the seamy side of life in Rome, in which a certain sector of the city's elite wished to believe: that criminals were so well organized as to constitute a dark, mirror-version of normal society, complete with 'fraternities' or 'guilds' of particular ill-doers; that they had, in effect, created a kind of inverted world of their own, a *mondo alla rovescia*, or 'world upside down' (a phrase of the time which anticipates the modern term 'underworld'); that any apparently needy beggar might easily turn out to be a crook.

There was something of a craze for the classification of rogues in Caravaggio's Italy. Tommaso Garzoni's *La piazza universale di tutte le professioni del mondo* (*Universal Marketplace of the World*), a compendium published in 1585, had listed seventeen types of false beggar, including five that appear in the accounts of 'Pompeo' and 'Girolamo'. There is strong evidence that such reports tended to multiply at times of genuine social crisis, especially when the existing structures of poor relief were being put under intense pressure by plague or famine. There were several occasions during the 1580s and 1590s – the plague of Caravaggio's childhood, in 1576–7, being a prime example – when the sheer number of beggars and indigent people at large threatened to overwhelm the ability of the Italian states to function. Tough measures against itinerant beggars and 'vagabonds' were periodically introduced throughout the late sixteenth century: in Florence in 1576, in Milan the following year, in Genoa in 1582, in Palermo in 1590 and in Rome throughout the 1590s. The stories that circulated about 'fraudulent beggars', the growing literature devoted to their typology and taxonomy, were partly a reflection of reality and partly a reflection of deep anxiety within the governing classes of society. They multiplied in much the same way as stories about supposed illegal immigration or welfare fraud multiply in right-wing newspapers today, at times when the economy or social services come under strain.

The medieval Christian attitude to the poor had been essentially supportive. Every poor person was to be seen as the living image of the impoverished Christ himself, and helped accordingly. St Francis of Assisi had gone so far as to declare himself married to 'Lady Poverty'. But by the late sixteenth century such attitudes had undergone a sea change. In many states – including the papal states – the poor were viewed with increasing distrust and hostility. In some places they were simply driven out by edict. Elsewhere the great *lazzaretti*, the plague hospitals of the Middle Ages and Renaissance, were converted into poor houses where the indigent were coralled and forced to do menial work.

The ruling and religious elites of the day were bitterly divided by the issue. The more authoritarian wing of the Catholic Church favoured rigorous means of social control and repression. But there were also those more sympathetic to the ancient medieval view – orders such as the Franciscans and Jesuits – who continued to plead for sympathy with the poor. There was, in other words, a form of right-wing / left-wing split in Caravaggio's Rome over the treatment of poverty. One way to view the growing literature devoted to 'roguery' – whether the writings of Garzoni or the 'improved' trial transcripts attributed to 'Pompeo' and 'Girolamo' – is as propaganda for the right.

All this helps to clarify the most important questions that need to be asked about these two pivotal works in the painter's career. Can the *Gypsy Fortune-Teller* and *Cardsharps* be seen as a plea for sympathy for those afflicted by poverty? Or are they simply a translation into painting of the sinister mechanisms of state control – a *visual* means (*pace* Burke) 'of legitimating the repressive measures' taken against those living on the margins of society?

Caravaggio's pictures were certainly not painted for political ends. They were created to amuse and entertain an art-loving cardinal. But it may be significant that del Monte, who dared to hang these startlingly novel pictures of low-life characters on the wall of his palace, was a Medici supporter who publicly shared the Medici's known sympathy for the 'pauperist' views – as they have been termed – of Filippo Neri and the Oratorians. In other words, he was a man who stood to the left in Rome's divide on the issue of the poor.

Caravaggio was undoubtedly familiar with the overwhelmingly negative picture of the rogue or trickster presented in so much of the moralizing literature of his time. His depiction of the *Cardsharps* is so close to the accounts of card cheats in texts such as *A Manifest Detection*, or the seventeenth-century judge Antonio Maria Cospi's book of advice to magistrates, *Il giudice criminalista* (1643), that he may actually have consulted such works when planning his composition. Cospi's section on the marking of cards is a virtual gloss on the action in *The Cardsharps*:

> I have seen those who have marked the edge of the corner of the card with ink, who bend with the right hand a suit towards the narrower part, and bend the other suit at the same angle, but on the longer side ... Many other observations could be made, not all of which could be foreseen or imagined, but this is enough to awaken the mind of the magistrate, should some suspect cards come into his hands, to observe or discover if there is some other mark on them. This is as much as I can say as regards the eye. There are also those who know the cards by touch,

and these make a little hole with a needle that stands out in relief on the underside of the cards. According to the place where they feel this slight relief, they know which card it is that goes to their opponent or that they take from themselves. Others play with thick cards with such thick colours that they have a certain relief. They keep the tip of the middle finger of the right hand well shaven, so that the skin there is very sensitive, and on touching the card with that finger, they sense those colours and know which card is underneath.[45]

This explains why the cheat's accomplice in Caravaggio's picture has two prominent holes in his glove. The glove has not been worn by use. Its stitching has been unpicked, so that the trained and sensitive middle finger and thumb of the sharper can do their work. But, despite such finely observed details, it would be a mistake to assume that Caravaggio's picture is an overtly moralizing work of art. The artist might have drawn on texts such as Cospi's book for magistrates, but he himself reserved judgement.

Despite Caravaggio's vaunted reputation for realism, he emphatically refused to present his image of cardsharping as a slice of reprehensible reality. This is no snapshot from the scene of a crime. It is a piece of lively, intriguing theatre. The gestures of the crooks – especially the pantomimic semaphore of the accomplice's hand signal – plainly come from the world of drama. In an actual gambling den, such overt gesticulation would soon be discovered. But imagine *The Cardsharps* as a scene from a play, performed for an audience happy to suspend disbelief, to enjoy the sense of superiority that comes from knowing that *they* can see everything that the gulled cardplayer is blind to – and the exaggerated body language of the figures makes perfect sense.

The Cardsharps plays on the threat of *il mondo alla rovescia*, a world turned upside down, where wily guttersnipes win and aristocrats lose. But its message is not morally straightforward. The rich young man will no doubt return to his palace at the end of the game. The scruffy *bravi* robbing him blind – who may indeed be out-of-work mercenaries, to judge by the younger cheat's sword – will no doubt drink their gains away and end up back in the gutter. But for this brief moment they are victorious.

Caravaggio's painting is ambiguous, but contains a hint of where his sympathy – or, at least, his empathy – might lie. He paints the young gull with a form of smooth indifference, as a softly generalized figure of aristocratic insouciance. By contrast, the cheats themselves are live, lithe, fascinating. The older man's concentration is absolute, and touched by a sense of desperation. The younger conman, gazing with fixity at his prey, is as tense and alert as a feral cat. Caravaggio paints his desperadoes like a man who feels *with* them, if not necessarily for them. He understands the deep seriousness of their desire to work their trick, to carry out their strategy without a hitch. When he painted the picture his own predicament was not altogether dissimilar to theirs.

The trickster in *The Gypsy Fortune-Teller* belonged to an even more reviled class of 'vagabond' than the cardsharps. For Cospi, gypsies were the lowest of the low because their habits of thievery were innate rather than learned. His entry on them in *Il giudice criminalista* is an undisguised racist diatribe – a nearly hysterical expression of burgeoning hatred for a people initially welcomed to Italy, in the early fifteenth century, as refugees and pilgrims:

> They are thieves by nature, descended from Cus son of Ham, cursed son of Noah . . . They still feel this paternal curse, wandering dispersed around the world without being able to find a homeland or other permanent place . . . They sell their own sons for food . . . They come from the region between Egypt and Ethiopia and wander through the world, erecting their tents outside cities in fields and highways. They make deception, changes and prognostication from the lines of the hand, and earn their living by these amusing frauds . . . Like beasts, they consider marriage to their own sisters legitimate . . . The women steal chickens, and while they pretend to tell one's fortune by the signs of the hand, rob the peasants and steal the women's purses and handkerchiefs.[46]

English attitudes could be just as virulent. In Thomas Dekker's pamphlet of 1608, *Lanthorne and Candle-light*, gypsies are described as: 'a people more scattered than the Jewes and more hated: beggarly in apparell, barbarous in condition, beastly in behaviour and bloudy if they meete advantage. A man that sees them would sweare they all had the yellow Jawndis, or that they were Tawny Moores bastardes . . .'[47]

But when Caravaggio painted his *Gypsy Fortune-Teller* he went against the grain of such crude stereotypes. His gypsy is a thief, for sure, but she is a far cry from the subhuman monster of Cospi and Dekker. She is a beautiful enchantress, an exotic swindler who steals her victim's heart as surely as she pilfers the ring from the hand he drowsily surrenders to her. Like Caravaggio's cardsharps, she has stepped into his painting straight from the theatre – and emphatically not from the pages of judges or journalists seeking to control a perceived social menace.

Three years before Caravaggio painted the picture, Cesare Ripa published an enormously influential guide to the symbolism of the post-Renaissance world, entitled the *Iconologia*. The book is a description, as its title page says, of 'diverse Images of Virtues, Vices, Affections, Human Passions, Arts, Disciplines, Humours, Elements, Celestial Bodies, Provinces of Italy, Rivers and every region of the world'.[48] The gypsy appears twice in Ripa's encyclopedia of imagery, each time as a woman. On the one hand, she is an emblem of poverty, shown 'with a twisted neck' in the act of begging for alms: 'poverty is represented in the guise of a Gipsy,' explains Ripa, 'because a poorer folk than this is not to be found; for they have neither property nor nobility nor taste, nor hope of anything that can give a particle of that happiness that is the aim of political life.' But she is also a symbol of comedy, of light-hearted resilience to the blows of fortune.

Under this aspect, Ripa notes, 'her dress should be of various colours; in her right hand she should carry the horn which is used as a musical instrument; in her left hand she should have a mask, and she should wear socks on her feet. The diversity of colours signifies the varied and diverse actions dealt with by this sort of poetry, which delight the eye of the mind no less than variety of colours the eye of the body through their expression of the accidents of human life, of virtues, vices and worldly conditions, as found in every quality and kind of people, except those of princely blood.'[49] Here Ripa is distantly following the classical theory of theatrical genres propounded by Aristotle in his *Poetics*. Aristotle's distinction between tragedy and comedy, much parroted by the more prescriptive literary theorists of sixteenth-century Italy, held that tragedy should focus on the actions of the elite – kings and princes – while comedy should concern itself with the behaviour of those at the very bottom of the social heap.

Caravaggio's *Gypsy Fortune-Teller* is smiling poverty personified. But she is no mere emblem. With her turban-like headscarf and long cloak she is, in fact, dressed precisely as a real gypsy in late sixteenth-century Italy. Cesare Vecellio's *Habiti Antichi et Moderni*, or *Costumes Past and Present*, published in 1590, contains a description that tallies more or less exactly with Caravaggio's painting. Vecellio notes that gypsy women 'bind a cloak of woollen cloth over the shoulder, passing it under the arm, and it is long enough to reach down to their feet'. The cloak, known in Italian as a *schiavina*, is defined by the writer as 'a long garment of coarse wool, worn by gypsies and hermits'.[50]

The ancestry of Caravaggio's beautiful gypsy can be clearly traced – in accordance with the assumptions behind Ripa's *Iconologia* – to the world of comic theatre. The gypsy was a stock figure in the performances of Italian Commedia dell'Arte, the popular acting companies of the sixteenth century – so much so that the name *zingaresche*, derived from *zingara*, or 'gypsy', was given to a whole range of comic theatrical productions. A series of French prints known as the *Recueil Fossard* documents the performances of an Italian Commedia dell'Arte troupe given in France in the late sixteenth century. One of those prints, depicting the encounter of the brazen whore 'Peronne' with the louche aristocrat 'Julien le Debauche', bears a striking resemblance to Caravaggio's own *Gypsy Fortune-Teller*.

The connections between Caravaggio's painting and the theatre do not stop there. One of the more celebrated late sixteenth-century performances of a *zingarescha* can in fact be traced directly to the milieu of Cardinal del Monte. In 1589, when the cardinal's Medici patron, the Grand Duke of Tuscany, married Christine of Lorraine, a theatrical festival was staged to celebrate their union. A play entitled *La Pellegrina* was performed, together with six extravagant intermedii involving all kinds of elaborate stage machinery and sets representing both a fiery hell and a cloud-capped Mount Olympus. Shortly after this, according to the diary of an eyewitness, the grand duke invited the Comici Gelosi – one of the leading Commedia dell'Arte troupes – to 'act a comedy of their own choice'. The two leading ladies, Isabella Andreini and Vittoria Piissimi,

> nearly came to blows, for Vittoria wanted to act *Zingara* and the other wished to perform her Pazzia, entitled *La Pazzia d'Isabella* [*The Madness*

of Isabella] – given that Vittoria's favourite part is Zingara and Isabel's La Pazzia. However they finally agreed that the first piece to be acted would be *Zingara*, and that *La Pazzia* would be given another time. And so they performed the said *Zingara* with the same *Intermezzi* as were prepared for the great play; and indeed whoever has not heard Vittoria perform *Zingara* has neither seen nor heard something marvellous, and certainly all were very satisfied with the play.[51]

Cardinal del Monte attended this actual performance, and it is quite conceivable that Caravaggio himself had first-hand experience of the Gelosi on stage. The company, which was the most prestigious in Counter-Reformation Italy, had close links with his home city of Milan, where its first recorded performance took place in 1568, just three years before the painter's birth. During its forty-year existence it often played there and in the other principal towns of northern Italy: Florence, Ferrara, Genoa, Mantua and Venice.[52]

It is possible that Caravaggio's painting was actually inspired by the memory or repute of Vittoria Piissimi's celebrated performance as the *Zingara*. In Artemio Giancarli's comedy, written in 1545, the gypsy plays the role of kidnapper, temptress and wily thief. But those who saw Piissimi in the role remembered her, above all, as the temptress: 'a beautiful sorceress of love, she entices the hearts of a thousand lovers with her words; a sweet siren, she enchants with smooth incantations the souls of her devout spectators.'[53] Caravaggio's contemporaries praised his own, painted gypsy in strikingly similar language. In Mancini's eyes, she might have been 'false' and 'sly', but above all she was beguilingly beautiful – the most 'graceful and expressive figure', indeed, that he had ever seen in art. The painter's friend, the poet Gaspare Murtola, went even further. In Murtola's madrigal in praise of Caravaggio's painting, the gypsy is not only an enchantress, she is also the painter's alter ego. Just as she deceives her fresh-faced admirer, so Caravaggio beguiles the world with the freshness and the beauty of his art:

> *Non so qual si piu maga,*
> *O la donna, che fingi,*
> *O tu che la dipingi*

I don't know who is the greater magician,
The woman, who deceives,
Or you, who paint her

The poet rhymes *fingi* with *dipingi*, cheating and painting. So Caravaggio is not merely the painter of rogues, crooks and the enchantresses of the street. He is the painter *as* vagabond. And suddenly all of his subtle counterfeiting has paid off. His illusions have worked their magic, his paintings have been sold – and he has been invited to live in the house of a cardinal. It is the autumn of 1595 and he is twenty-four years old.

PART THREE
Rome, 1595–9

FRANCESCO MARIA BOURBON
DEL MONTE

Caravaggio's patron looks out at posterity from a vivid drawing by the printmaker, painter and master-draughtsman Ottavio Leoni. He has kind but piercing eyes and a fully receded hairline. His thin lips and slightly weak mouth are disguised, not altogether successfully, by a wispy salt-and-pepper beard. Cardinal Francesco Maria Bourbon del Monte was approaching seventy when he sat for the likeness; twenty years had passed since he had taken Caravaggio into his home. But he was still the same inquisitive, thoughtful man whom the painter had known. His epitaph would stress above all that he had always done his best to support 'the good arts'.

Ars longa, vita brevis. The picture was done, in a single sitting of perhaps half an hour, in black chalk with white highlights on fine-grained paper the colour of a hazy blue sky. The cardinal seems to endure the ordeal of keeping still with patience and forbearance: unlike many powerful men, he does not frown and fidget his way through a sitting. There is a mixture of worldliness, compassion and curiosity in his gaze. The finishing touch is a tricorn hat, rendered in dense cross-hatching, perched on the smooth dome of his forehead. It makes him look a little bit like a chess piece come to life.

Francesco Maria del Monte may have been the first father-figure in Caravaggio's life. Giovanni Baglione, terse as ever, described the artist's time with del Monte as a rare idyll in his otherwise troubled existence. 'In these quarters Michelangelo was given room and board, and soon he felt stimulated and confident.'[1] Stimulated and confident: such adjectives were not often applied to Caravaggio by people who actually knew him. This is the only passage in Baglione's biography of Caravaggio where he appears as anything other than mad, bad and dangerous to know. We can sense the painter's genuine relief at having found, at last, a refuge from the storms of his early life.

When Caravaggio met him, del Monte was in his late forties, one of the younger and more energetic cardinals. But, unlike most of those elected to the curia, he was neither particularly rich nor especially aristocratic. He owed his position to a combination of solid family connections, considerable charm and – so jealous contemporaries muttered – outrageous good fortune. Del Monte had been born in Venice, on the Fondaco dei Turchi, in 1549. It is a measure of his family's importance to the city that the great Venetian painter Titian attended his baptism. So too did the notorious poet, pamphleteer and pornographer Pietro Aretino, a man who might be said to have embodied the deepest contradictions of his age. On the one hand, he encouraged Pope Paul IV to fig-leaf the genitalia in Michelangelo's frescoes for the Sistine Chapel; on the other, he wrote such works as *Tales of Nuns, Wives and Courtesans*, the opening scene of which involves numerous nuns, their lubricious mother superior and a copious supply of glass dildos. Also present at the ceremony was the less colourful but widely celebrated architect Jacopo Sansovino.

Despite the pomp that attended his baptism, del Monte would not actually be brought up in Venice. Del Monte's father, Renieri, is known to have been in the service of the dukes of Urbino. Ever since the days of the fifteenth-century soldier-intellectual, Federigo da Montefeltro, the rulers of Urbino had hired out their services as battle-hardened mercenaries to the highest bidder. The Duke of Urbino who employed del Monte's father was particularly active on behalf of the Venetians during the years from 1539 to 1552. Since Renieri went by the title of 'colonel', it seems likely that he was a soldier, who had won the respect of the Venetians by fighting their enemies.[2]

Del Monte was decidedly not a military man, but a student of law and humanities. He and his elder brother, Guidobaldo – later to become a distinguished mathematician and the author of a treatise on perspective – were educated at the courts of the della Rovere family in Pesaro and Urbino. They also studied at Padua, long established as a centre of humanist learning, which was where Prince Francesco Maria della Rovere himself received his education.[3] Del Monte had been named in honour of Prince Francesco Maria. But he later switched allegiances and eventually travelled to Rome, in 1572, in the service of a Sforza cardinal.

Del Monte switched allegiances again in the early 1570s. He won the patronage of Cardinal Ferdinando de' Medici, younger son of Grand Duke Cosimo I, ruler of Florence and Tuscany. Groomed for the Church from an early age, Ferdinando had been made cardinal when he was just fourteen years old. He was a patron of music as well as a discerning art collector, who adorned the gardens of the Villa Medici with ancient Roman sculptures. Del Monte worked for many years as Ferdinando's secretary and assistant. By the mid 1580s he had become his closest confidant. Then, in 1587, both men's lives were transformed by news of a dramatic series of events in the Medici stronghold of Florence. Ferdinando's elder brother, Grand Duke Francesco I, had died of a mysterious illness. The duke's wife had succumbed to the same ailment. In Florence, with its long and murky political history of plot and counter-plot, foul play was inevitably suspected. With Medici power in the balance, Ferdinando felt compelled to renounce his vows and return to Tuscany. He became grand duke, and del Monte his right-hand man. A contemporary witness described the atmosphere at court in the immediate aftermath of Ferdinando's accession. The new grand duke would dine alone, allowing no one save his trusted adviser to share 'his most secret thoughts'. He considered del Monte a kindred spirit, the source added, because he was 'knowledgeable in literature and other learned subjects'.[4]

Ferdinando's resignation from the curia left the ruling family of Florence without a voice in Rome. So in 1588 the new Grand Duke of Florence used his influence with Pope Sixtus V to have del Monte appointed in his place. Del Monte would remain a cardinal for almost forty years, reporting to his Florentine master on the twists and turns of papal politics and promoting the interests of Tuscany whenever he could. His umbilical connection to Florence, and to the court of Ferdinando de' Medici, would have numerous consequences for Caravaggio's career.

The Medici had strong links with the pauperist wing of Counter-Reformation Catholicism. During his years in Rome, Ferdinando had been close to the charismatic churchman Filippo Neri, the dominant religious personality in the city during the second half of the sixteenth century and founder of an order of secular priests known as the Congregation of the Oratory. His style of teaching was informal and direct, inspired by a desire to return to the simplest and most direct forms of Christian belief. He preferred discussion to sermonizing, improvisation to the set text, and had a knockabout, down-to-earth sense of humour. Despite a profound difference in temperaments, Neri was greatly admired by Carlo Borromeo, who on several occasions in the 1560s and 1570s protected him from accusations of heresy. One of Neri's ideals was pilgrimage, which he interpreted as a model for the Christian life itself, as a journey travelled in prayer. As well as the Oratory, he founded the Archconfraternity of the Most Holy Trinity of the Pilgrims and Convalescents – the Santissima Trinità dei Pellegrini – to care for the poor and the sick, and especially the many thousands of destitute pilgrims who travelled to Rome during Jubilee years. The Pellegrini would eventually have their own church, a somewhat severe building constructed between 1587 and 1597 and designed by Martino Longhi the Elder (the father, as it turned out, to one of Caravaggio's most turbulent companions). But much of its energies were devoted simply to health care. For several years Ferdinando de' Medici served honourably as protector of its hospital. Probably as a result of his connections with del Monte and the Medici, Caravaggio would himself develop close links with Neri's Archconfraternity of Pilgrims, and with the Order of the Oratory. Two of his most impressive altarpieces, *The Madonna of Loreto* and *The Entombment of Christ*, would result.

The political alliances of the Medici would also shape the development of Caravaggio's painting. Throughout Cardinal del Monte's long Roman career, but especially during the early years, when he was closest to Caravaggio, the balance of European power was delicately poised between Spain and France. Like other members of the family before him, Ferdinando de' Medici favoured France. He married the Valois princess Christine of Lorraine, the marriage celebrated with great pomp and ceremony in 1589. Just over a decade later the Medici's links with France would become closer still. Ferdinando's niece, Marie de' Medici, would marry Henri IV and become Queen of France. That union could never have taken place without Henri IV's acceptance into the Church of Rome. So throughout the early 1590s del Monte's overriding concern, and the Medici's greatest goal, was to ensure that Henri IV's conversion from Protestantism went ahead as planned. Del Monte's diplomatic style was subtle and self-effacing, but effective. In 1593, when the long-hoped-for event occurred, the Medici cardinal could congratulate himself on having played his part in one of the decisive political events of the age. Clement VIII was deeply grateful for del Monte's help in winning the French king back to the Catholic faith. The cardinal's position within the curia was strengthened as a result.

It was no coincidence that Caravaggio's first major religious commission, secured for him by del Monte – 'his cardinal', as the jealous Baglione put it – would be for San Luigi dei Francesi, the church of the French in Rome. The paintings would be completed in 1600, the year of Henri IV's marriage to Marie de' Medici. The first of them, The Calling of St Matthew, showing the saint roused from spiritual slumber by the coming of Christ, probably alluded to the conversion of the French king. When del Monte looked at the picture, he could reflect on his finest hour as a servant of the Medici, and France.

The cardinal had two official residences in Rome, the Palazzo Firenze, near the old Roman harbour of the Ripetta, and the Palazzo Madama, around the corner from San Luigi dei Francesi. The Palazzo Madama was where he chose to live, and where he gave Caravaggio room and board – presumably on one of the attic floors of the palace, in the servants' quarters. The painter's new surroundings were visible proof of his sudden change of fortunes, a far cry from his mean lodgings with Monsignor Insalata and a world away from the ramshackle platform on which he had been compelled to sleep in the Cesari workshop. The Palazzo Madama was an imposing building in the heart of Rome, its broad façade emblazoned with the famous Medici coat of arms, a shield decorated with six round balls – often, apocryphally, said to symbolize pills, but actually emblematic of bezants, or coins, in allusion to the family's origins as moneylenders. The state rooms of the palace were richly decorated with tapestries and oriental carpets, as well as a small but choice selection of classical sculptures and other hallowed relics of the distant Roman past. These included the most celebrated cameo-glass vessel to have survived from antiquity, the so-called Portland Vase.[5]

Del Monte was forever buying and selling works of art, antiquities, precious stones, sculptures and curiosities. He kept a sharp look-out for anything that might interest his Medici patrons. In 1607 he excitedly reported his acquisition of some fragments of clothing, discovered on the Appian Way, that had once belonged to a Roman consul alive at the time of First Punic War. He was sending them to the grand duke as a gift, he wrote, so that he could study 'the weaving of those times' (as ruler of Florence, a city at the centre of the Italian textile trade, Ferdinando could reasonably be assumed to take an interest in such a find).

The cardinal was an insatiable accumulator of all kinds of things, but above all he accumulated paintings. His collection included allegories and narrative pictures as well as a number of still lives – and, of course, Caravaggio's *Cardsharps* and *Gypsy Fortune-Teller*, those pioneering experiments in the painting of contemporary rogues and tricksters. Inventories show that at his death del Monte owned around 600 paintings, enough to furnish an entire museum. He possessed copies of celebrated pictures by masters of central Italian painting such as Leonardo da Vinci, Michelangelo and Raphael. But he was also drawn to the very different traditions of Venetian painting, owning no fewer than five pictures attributed – possibly with more optimism than accuracy – to Titian. The names of Palma Vecchio and Jacopo Bassano also figure in the lists, alongside that of Giorgione, an artist to whom Caravaggio was often compared in his youth.

The Venetian tradition valued *colore* above *disegno*, emphasizing the primacy of colour rather than design – whereas for the great painters of central Italy, the Tuscan–Roman axis of art for which Giorgio Vasari was such a vocal and persuasive spokesman, drawing was the foundation stone of all excellence. Caravaggio seems to have had almost no interest at all in theories of art. But he shared the Venetian preference for working on canvas, rather than in the medium of fresco. In the ages-old debate about the relative merits of *disegno* and *colore* he might have sided with the Venetians.[6] Not a single independent drawing survives by Caravaggio's hand. Even X-rays of his finished work have failed to yield anything resembling a conventional underdrawing.

The nature of the collections in the Palazzo Madama may have reflected the cardinal's roots in Urbino. Like Federigo da Montefeltro, whose *studiolo* was lined with portraits of famous men, del Monte made a point of collecting images of those whom he admired. By far the greatest part of his collection was made up of portraits, a pantheon of intellectual and spiritual heroes. A late inventory refers to '277 pictures without frames ... of various popes, emperors, cardinals and dukes and other illustrious men and some women'.[7] In addition, the collection contained 67 paintings of saints. These too were portraits of a kind – images of those individuals from sacred history whom the cardinal especially venerated.

The breadth of del Monte's interests was reflected not only in the various rooms of his palace, which contained a well-stocked library and an extensive collection of scientific instruments, but also in the wide circle of his acquaintances. Del Monte collected remarkable men in real life as well as in art. He knew writers, bibliophiles and collectors of rare manuscripts. He knew musicians and composers. He knew alchemists, astronomers and others working on the ill-defined border between medieval belief and modern enquiry.

Inspired by the researches of his own brother, Guidobaldo, del Monte took a lively interest in scientific discovery. He was an early and enthusiastic supporter of Galileo, and played a crucial role in the astronomer's career by helping him to secure the patronage of the Medici. Without the powerful support and protection of Florence's ruling dynasty, some of Galileo's most important work might never have been done. The Palazzo Madama contained a tangible symbol of the scientist's gratitude: the gift of a telescope. Del Monte's views on the controversial hypothesis of a heliocentric universe are unrecorded. But he might have agreed with Cesare Baronio, a prominent member of Filippo Neri's Order of the Oratory, who famously remarked that 'the scriptures teach us how to move to heaven, not how the heavens move.'

Del Monte's interest in science extended to experiment as well as study. He dabbled in alchemy and had a fully equipped laboratory in the Palazzo Madama. Within a year of Caravaggio's arrival in his household, the cardinal acquired a third residence, a country retreat at Porta Pinciana, up in the hills above the western edge of the city, not far from the Villa Borghese. Here del Monte established a pharmaceutical distillery. The distillation of drugs, whether from plants, metals or other substances, was something of a fad in the elite circles of Roman society at the time. In his *Epistolae medicinales*, the Sicilian physician Pietro Castelli (1590–1661) noted that the apothecaries of the day worked not only in their own shops but also in the private households of virtuosi.[8] The efficacy of the resulting cures could be questionable. The German taxonomist and doctor Johannes Faber publicly boasted that the celebrated 'Cardinal Dal [*sic*] Monte' had given him the recipe for a highly effective drug made from the meat of a poisonous snake. But he did not specify whether he had actually put the medicine to the test. Another of del Monte's supposed remedies was rumoured to have killed a man.

Faber's story suggests that the cardinal took an interest in the activities of the Hospital of Santo Spirito, one of Rome's largest and most important institutions for the care of the poor and the sick. Faber was himself a physician of the hospital, which, in his estimate, provided more than 12,000 people with food, shelter and medical care every year. Del Monte was friendly with another doctor working at the Santo Spirito, Giulio Mancini, Caravaggio's future biographer. Mancini, born of humble Sienese parents, had trained in medicine in the city of Padua. He got his job at the hospital in 1595 and probably met the painter in del Monte's house in that same year. That would explain why Mancini knew so much more than the other early biographers about Caravaggio's dark deeds in Milan and his very first years in Rome.

The Hospital of Santo Spirito was closely connected to the papal court. A post there was often the prelude to a successful career in medicine at the highest level, and so it proved in the case of Mancini, who eventually rose to become physician by appointment to the pope.[9] But Mancini's commitment to the relief of the poor seems to have been genuine, rather than just place seeking. When he died he left his considerable fortune to be distributed among the impoverished students of his native Siena. He was known for his unconventional behaviour and beliefs: a French obituarist wrote that Mancini was an amateur astrologer and *un Grand Athé*, 'a great atheist'. Del Monte probably befriended him because of his reputation as an experimental chemist and connoisseur of art. The two men seem to have shared an essentially philanthropic approach to life.

Del Monte was a philanthropist but he was certainly no firebrand of Counter-Reformation piety. In one of his letters he describes an evening spent gambling at the game of hazard at the Farnese Palace, in the company of the cardinal-nephew Pietro Aldobrandini. Having lost heavily – 'I more than he', del Monte noted ruefully – both men finished the evening in the company of a pair of courtesans, listening to music. Overall, the pattern of del Monte's friendships and alliances suggests that he was a worldly, benevolent, diplomatic, curious, open-minded and socially adept man, with a rare sensitivity to genius in other people and a strong sense of Christian charity.

But a considerably more negative picture of him was painted by his contemporary Dirck van Amayden, who composed the principal early biography of del Monte. Amayden's text, which has had a definite influence on the cardinal's posthumous reputation, is so hostile that it amounts to a thinly veiled character assassination. The author's method was a form of devious insinuation. This involved the recounting of various scurrilous tales about the cardinal, followed by half-hearted protestations on the part of the author to the effect that such dreadful things – surely – could not have been true.

The pattern is set by Amayden's discussion of Ferdinando de' Medici's patronage of del Monte. He begins with the phrase 'It is said', eternal refrain of the unreliable reporter. In this case, 'it is said' that del Monte wormed his way into Ferdinando's affection by arranging clandestine trysts between the young Medici buck and the wife of another man, 'the bride of one Cesarino'. The double calumny is followed up instantly by a sly denial of which Shakespeare's Iago would have been proud: 'this nevertheless I would not believe, knowing perfect friendship arises out of virtue, not vice.'[10]

Not only is Amayden's del Monte an accomplice to adultery. He also turns out, at the end of the biography, to be a closet homosexual with a particular fondness for young men. The author's explosion of this bombshell inevitably casts something of a shadow over his earlier, flatly dutiful assertion that del Monte was an intellectually enlightened patron of the arts and sciences who 'was very liberal to painters, chemists and similar'. The scandalized reader is naturally inclined to wonder whether the cardinal might have asked for certain favours, from certain young men, in return for his support. The very last paragraph of Amayden's life of del Monte addresses the question in the author's characteristic style and leaves the matter open:

> He was of unusual sweetness of behaviour, and loved to be familiar with youths, not, however, for a criminal reason, but from natural sociability. This is presumably connected with the fact that he prudently hid it before Urban was elected. When Urban was made pope he threw off all restrictions; in the longed-for reign he indulged his inclination openly, and, though aged and almost blind, more a trunk than a man and therefore incapable of allure, a young man of short stature got a benefice from him.[11]

The image of del Monte in old age as an absurd and enfeebled pederast is hardly flattering. It is also, in all probability, a fiction. Amayden spent his life in the service of Spain, promoting the cause of the mighty Habsburgs with unwavering constancy and taking every opportunity to blacken the names of their enemies. The pro-French faction at the papal court was anathema to him and he had a professionally ingrained hatred of the Medici. So this was a man with every motive to slander the memory of del Monte, whose curial vote had always been cast in favour of the Medici and their French allies. Amayden's story about del Monte belatedly coming out of the closet in 1623, on the accession of Urban VIII, should also be read as a slander aimed at the pope himself. The subtext is that Urban's reign was so licentious that every sin suddenly dared to show its face. This too fits with the hispanophile Amayden's anti-French agenda, since Urban VIII had shown great favour to Cardinal Richelieu, Governor of France under Louis XIV.

Despite its implausibility, Amayden's text has insidiously shaped the legend of Caravaggio. It has fostered a deeply fanciful view of del Monte's household as a louche pleasure palace, subversively lodged at the heart of Catholic Rome. Through the rooms of this imaginary Palazzo Madama passes a parade of freethinkers and sexual outsiders, mostly exquisite young men. The shadowy figure of del Monte, libertine masquerading in a cardinal's robes, looks on with a mischievous twinkle in his eye. Viewed through the lens of this seductive fantasy, many of the pictures that Caravaggio painted during his sojourn with del Monte are correspondingly distorted. They become thrillingly decadent and disappointingly flimsy at one and the same time – mild exhalations of homoerotic yearning, shot through with an abiding spirit of perversity.

The best corrective to Amayden's sweet-tongued libel is an eye-witness description of Cardinal del Monte's household as it actually was in the 1590s, published for the first time in 1991. The recipient of the description was Grand Duke Ferdinando de' Medici. Its author was a musician and gentleman called Emilio de' Cavalieri.[12] It presents a thoroughly believable, down-to-earth picture of the milieu in which Caravaggio, in his mid twenties, found himself:

> Del Monte amazes me in regard to spending that he can live on what he has and do it so honourably. It is true that for his clothing he doesn't spend a *giulio*; he has had only one livery made; his coach is also the first he has had; he makes the best of what he has; he has bought himself a carriage and with this he keeps himself; the mouths he feeds in all don't amount to fifty; he doesn't keep horses or gentlemen but his servants are treated well and given good meals – all that is seen through your highness's favour of a beautiful home, [the fitting out and decoration of] which is now finished; as a cardinal of Rome, he formally receives at table in the morning with his silverware; and he is courted by more Romans than cardinals for his great trafficking, which is all honest, with his metalworkers; and his antechamber is always filled with people; there are no high-ranking clergy. The reason for this is that he is not involved in important transactions and those that come do so only to visit ... I have made this speech so that you will know the truth ...[13]

This account is just as partisan in its way as that of Amayden (Cavalieri was a close friend of the cardinal and would later name him as one of his executors), but it has the disorderly ring of truth about it. Del Monte was anything but well off by the standards of most Roman cardinals. His residences were Medici property, not his own. His recorded income was approximately 12,000 ducats a year, by no means a great deal of money for a man in his position, so Cavalieri's sympathetic description of the household's thrifty but somewhat threadbare imitation of late Renaissance courtly pomp tallies well with the known facts. The reference to del Monte's 'trafficking ... with all his metalworkers' suggests necessary financial dealings conducted on the side. The insistence that 'he is not involved in important transactions' with the pope or his fellow grand clerics may have been meant to reassure the grand duke that del Monte was sticking purely to Medici-approved business.

Cavalieri was from an old Roman family associated both with the arts and with artists. The legendary Michelangelo had been close to his father, Tommaso de' Cavalieri, and had given him a highly finished presentation drawing – possibly *The Rape of Ganymede* of 1532, now in the Royal Collection at Windsor – as a token of his affections. Emilio himself was a composer and impresario, principally employed at the Medici court from the late 1580s as master of ceremonies for the elaborate entertainments known as *intermedii*, dramatizations of myth and legend, set to music.

Del Monte and Emilio de' Cavalieri probably met when the latter was orchestrating the unusually lavish spectacles that marked Grand Duke Ferdinando's marriage to Christine of Lorraine in 1589. By the early 1590s they had become firm friends. Del Monte was in Florence in 1595 to see a production of Cavalieri's *Gioco della Cieca*, an early experiment in musical drama inspired by antiquity.[14] Over the next ten years the composer often visited the cardinal in Rome. Cavalieri's letters back to Florence are a valuable source of information about del Monte's deep immersion in the musical culture of his time, illuminating his tastes and responses to the music that moved him. They also shed some oblique shafts of light on the very first picture that Caravaggio painted for his new benefactor: a compellingly ambiguous depiction of a group of musical performers, about to give a concert.

'IF MUSIC BE THE FOOD OF LOVE'

Painted around the end of 1595, *The Musicians* is one of the artist's most puzzlingly unorthodox creations. Four young men wearing classical drapery have been crowded into an airless interior. The central figure meets the spectator's gaze with a languorous, distracted look, absent-mindedly fingering the strings of the lute that he cradles in the crook of his right arm. Behind him, a dark-haired boy holding a barely visible cornetto – a hybrid instrument of the Renaissance, with a trumpet-like mouthpiece and the fingerholes of a recorder – looks up in a way that suggests the troupe has been disturbed while rehearsing.

A third young man, pressed so close to the foreground that he might almost be on the point of falling out of the picture, studies a sheaf of music. He is presumably the singer, and therefore the star attraction. But he looks as though he is still learning his song and his back is conspicuously turned to the viewer. He wears his costume carelessly, as if he knows that nothing much is going to happen for a little while yet. The folds of white cloth in which he is draped have fallen off his shoulder and become ruched up under the purple silk bow meant to hold them in place, leaving him almost naked from the waist up. The somewhat ragged group is completed by a curly-haired boy, sitting to the lutenist's right, who has a pair of Cupid's wings strapped to his back and a quiver full of arrows hanging at his right shoulder. But firing darts of love is plainly the last thing on his mind. He looks down and helps himself to some grapes, as much out of boredom as hunger.

The picture is not in good condition, having suffered considerable damage during the two hundred years that it spent in obscurity after disappearing into a series of unknown collections in the early eighteenth century. The violin and the page of music in the foreground have been largely reconstructed by modern restorers; the lute has lost its strings. But the work's fundamental originality and oddity remain undimmed, despite considerable areas of paint loss.

The Musicians was clearly one of Caravaggio's better known early pictures, because both Bellori and Baglione mention it specifically. Baglione says that 'For Cardinal del Monte he painted a Concert of Youths from nature, very well.' Bellori describes it in the same terms: 'the Concert of Youths portrayed from life in half figures'. The young man with the cornetto, at the back, resembles Caravaggio himself, while the lutenist may be his friend Mario Minniti. But the composition as a whole radiates an air of contrivance. It resembles a frieze or bas-relief, rendered in paint. The four boys are so similar in aspect and demeanour that they might be clones of each other. The suspicion lingers that they were all based on the same figure, depicted from different angles and then collaged together to form a single composition. Perhaps when Baglione and Bellori talked of Caravaggio portraying from life and painting from nature they were not talking about the artist's processes – the use of models, and so on – but trying to capture the distinctive *mood* of his picture. For all its artifice, it does have a certain clumsy lifelikeness. And that is precisely what made it so different from most earlier paintings of similar subjects.

By the late sixteenth century there was a long-established tradition of so-called 'concert' pictures. The genre had originated in Venice, and in its early form it is exemplified by the so-called *Le Concert Champêtre* of around 1510, now in the Louvre. Once thought to have been painted by Giorgione but now generally attributed to Titian, it is a tender and lyrical fantasy. A young man in fine clothes strums at his lute while conversing with a shepherd. Two naked women are present alongside them, one filling a glass jug with water, the other breaking off from playing on her recorder to listen to the two men's conversation. The action takes place outside, in a golden, idealized landscape based loosely on that of the Veneto itself. The precise meaning of the *Concert Champêtre* (if it has one) is open to debate, but the allegorical thrust of Titian's dreamlike vision is clear enough. It has its roots in the ancient, classical fantasy of pastoral retreat. The city sophisticate retreats to nature and finds there a world as pure as the clearest spring water, and a harmony as sweet as that of the most beautiful music. In Arcadia, he retunes the strings of his very being.

Alongside this idealizing tradition of musical picture, there was another and more prosaic sort of painting that showed singers and musicians in mid performance. Sometimes such works were enlivened by touches of bawdy humour. In Callisto Piazza's *Concert* of circa 1525, a group of performers is crowded into a shallow space, together with a single, male member of their audience. The most prominent of the musicians, a woman playing a lute, wears a low-cut bodice and has a coquettish expression on her face. Her admirer, who has evidently been enjoying the performance in more ways than one, wheels to face the viewer of the painting with a knowing look in his eye. The artist has furnished him with a phallic prop in the form of a sheathed dagger, fastened at his hip, which points towards the girl at an angle carefully calculated to indicate just what he has in mind.

Caravaggio's *Musicians* cannot easily be squeezed into the existing tradition of sixteenth-century musical paintings. It is certainly not a pastoral in the Venetian mode. Nor does it depict an actual performance, showing instead the preparations for one. There was no precedent for this. The presence of the boy with wings has prompted speculation that the picture might have been intended as an allegory of Music and Love. But that offers no real explanation for Caravaggio's most obvious departure from convention. Why should he have chosen to depict this rather ramshackle scene of musicians rehearsing?

Solutions to the enigma may be found in the unusually broad and experimental musical tastes of his patron. Cardinal del Monte was actively involved in music at the papal court throughout the 1590s. Clement VIII put him in charge of a far-reaching reform of liturgical music, and he served as Protector of the Sistine Choir.[15] Music was also an essential part of life at his various residences. In one of his letters back to Florence, Emilio de' Cavalieri gives a richly evocative description of an impromptu concert that took place one day in 1602 at del Monte's country house at Porta Pinciana. The admired soprano Vittoria Archilei was the surprise guest at an afternoon party, together with her husband and accompanist. Also present were cardinals Paravicino and Acquaviva, who had ostensibly come to see a vineyard in the grounds of del Monte's estate. Archilei was prevailed on to sing. She stunned her small audience with the naked emotion of her performance – so much so that even Cavalieri, who had helped to train her famously expressive voice, was surprised. He reported that because she was 'in a wild mood and singing in a vaulted room, I have never heard her in more beautiful voice. She gave so much satisfaction that Acquaviva said to me: "I for shame did not weep." Paravicino said he never thought such refinement was possible. They are both musicians.'[16]

Such expressions of dumbfounded pleasure go beyond the courtly formulas of polite approval. Archilei had clearly given an unusually affecting performance, but that is not the only explanation for the strength of response she received. Its surprise lay essentially in the fact that she sang on her own, in public, to the simplest of instrumental accompaniments. By the early 1600s, medieval polyphony – many voices singing different lines of music simultaneously – had been the overwhelmingly dominant mode of music for centuries. Monody, in which a single melodic line is carried by a solitary singer, was still relatively uncommon in concert performance. The solo voice accompanied by the solo instrument was unfamiliar, arresting. As the rapturous response to Archilei's singing shows, its potential was only just being developed.

The polyphonic and monodic modes are at opposite ends of music's emotional spectrum. Polyphony subsumes the individual voice within a choral harmony, reflecting the desire to conjure up an essentially otherworldly sound, such as the singing of the angelic host. Words are hard to distinguish in the layers of polyphonic singing. Syntax dissolves and sense is sacrificed for an effect of transcendence. By contrast, monody puts precise meaning and specific human emotions at the heart of music. The single melodic line, the solo voice, is easily understood. To follow its meanderings is to follow the contours of feeling expressed by words and music together (the theme of Vittoria Archilei's song would, almost certainly, have been unrequited love). It might be said that while polyphony aspires to heaven, monody expresses man.

'The solo voice contains all the purity of music, and style and melody are studied and appreciated more carefully when one's ears are not distracted by more than one voice.'[17] Baldassare Castiglione's *Book of the Courtier* of 1528 shows that the fashion for the solo voice had roots in an earlier period of the Renaissance. Further proof of this lies in the fact that the Flemish composer Adrian Willaert, choirmaster at St Mark's Basilica in Venice in the 1530s, had rearranged a number of polyphonic madrigals so that they could be sung for the solo voice. What seems to have been most strikingly new in the more experimental singing of Caravaggio's time, seventy years later, was its strong emphasis on vocal expression. This was characterized by the development of the *stile rappresentativo*, a style of monodic singing that followed the natural accents and rhythms of spoken language. It was an innovation that transformed the performance of choral music, and the style in which Vittoria Archilei would have sung.

Emilio de' Cavalieri was himself a composer at the forefront of this shift in musical sensibilities. He understood exactly what was going on in del Monte's house that afternoon in 1602. What he describes, very precisely, is the shock experienced by the listeners as they encounter raw feeling through the medium of music. On this particular occasion, the already unfamiliar experience is amplified by the wildness of the singer's own mood and the cavernous acoustic of a high-ceilinged room. The audience of cardinals Acquaviva and Paravicino is genuinely astonished, and Cavalieri's parting shot – 'they are both musicians' – is meant to underscore the sheer novelty of the performance. These men are experienced listeners and practitioners; they know music very well; but they have never heard music quite like *this*.

The origins of the musical transformation epitomized by Archileo's performance were (and still are) debated. A group of Florentine musicians active in the 1570s and 1580s had built a whole philosophy around the doctrine of a return to monody. For them, this was an extension of the Renaissance ideal of reviving the modes of classical antiquity. Their spokesman had been the humanist author Vincenzo Galilei – father of the scientist and astronomer – who was partly inspired by the mistaken belief that the drama of ancient Greece had been sung rather than spoken. Galilei argued in favour of the perceived simplicity and emotional directness of ancient monody, conjuring the romantic vision of a world in which singers might reclaim the fabled powers attributed to Orpheus. He urged that song and drama should be reunited once more, to tell the stories of ancient legend and move the hearts of men. The ideas expressed in Galilei's *Dialogue on Ancient and Modern Music*, of 1581, would have profound implications for music in Italy and beyond. New and ever more nakedly emotional songs for the solo voice would be written and performed. The *stile rappresentativo* would triumph and the abstract patterns and harmonies of medieval polyphony fall out of fashion. In the music of court entertainment, individual performers separated from the chorus to sing passionate songs of love and death. Such songs would become known as arias, as the old genre of *intermedii* metamorphosed into a new, startlingly dramatic art form that became known, simply, as 'opera'.

Many different musicians and composers claimed a hand in these changes. Cardinal del Monte's friend Emilio de' Cavalieri was prominent among them. Cavalieri was thoroughly disgusted when his rival, the singer and composer Giulio Caccini, took credit for inventing the *stile rappresentativo*. 'Everyone knows I am the inventor of this style,' Cavalieri angrily countered in a letter of 1600.[18] Posterity has sided with Caccini in that particular argument, partly because of his especially close association with the circle of Vincenzo Galilei. But Cavalieri's other big claim, to have written the very first opera, has been more widely accepted. The work in question, a musical drama in three acts entitled *La Rappresentazione di Anima e di Corpo*, was composed in 1600 – at the height of his friendship with Caravaggio's cardinal, and just two years before his sudden death from an unknown illness.

Cardinal del Monte was, then, rather more than a mere amateur of music: through his various musical activities and associations he had assisted at the birth of momentous changes in both composition and performance. By supporting a pioneer like Cavalieri, by hosting events like Vittoria Archilei's remarkable concert, by reordering the priorities of liturgical music at the papal court and by subtly altering the style of the Sistine Chapel Choir itself to favour the expressive qualities of the human voice brought out by the *stile rappresantativo* – by doing so much, del Monte had placed himself at the forefront of musical experimentation at the turn of the seventeenth century.

Del Monte was also friendly with the nobleman and banker Vincenzo Giustiniani, whose palace was directly opposite the Palazzo Madama. Giustiniani was a fellow musical enthusiast, who in 1628 would write *A Discourse on Music* describing the so-called musical *camerino* – a purpose-built private chamber, 'nobly decorated with paintings made for the sole purpose' of setting the right mood and tone for intimate musical performances. One of del Monte's first acts on moving to the Palazzo Madama had been (in his own words) to 'reserve a room for Harpsichords, Guitars, a Chitarrone and other instruments'.[19] By the late 1620s such rooms were a familiar sight in the palaces of the Roman aristocracy. But in the early 1590s, when del Monte had created his own *camerino* at the Palazzo Madama, he had been setting a new trend. To judge by the inventory made after his death, it must have been a headily atmospheric space – a cross between a private concert chamber and a miniature museum on the theme of music. Del Monte's *camerino* contained no fewer than thirty-seven musical instruments, not including the 'chest where the viols are'.[20] On its walls hung four pictures, all of which were listed, simply, as *una musica*, 'a scene of music'. One of these was Caravaggio's *Musicians*.

So why did the painter depart from all the known conventions of the so-called 'concert picture' and depict his musicians as an ensemble of the blatantly unready? Further clues lie in Emilio de' Cavalieri's letters, which show (among much else) that Cardinal del Monte was extremely interested in the technical aspects of singing and performing. One of the most promising singers in his household was a Spanish castrato named Pedro Montoya, to whom Cavalieri gave six singing lessons, some of which del Monte himself must have attended: 'The Cardinal del Monte was amazed because he [Montoya] can already sing to the same standard as Onofrio [probably Onofrio Gualfreducci, a gifted castrato attached to the household of Cardinal Montalto] and if he does not cause trouble, within a month he will surpass Onofrio.'[21]

Caravaggio's painting moodily evokes the milieu of del Monte's household – a laboratory of musical experiment and innovation, where performers rehearsed under the tutelage of the cardinal and his friends, and where the expressive, classically inspired *stile rappresantativo* was taken to new extremes. The space into which Caravaggio's four boys have been crammed evokes the cluttered intimacy of the *camerino* itself. Dressed in their makeshift *all'antica* costumes, they are preparing to take part in a piece of musical theatre of just the kind favoured and supported by del Monte. A single voice will be accompanied by only two instruments, in emulation of that imagined golden age when the songs of Orpheus were heard. The theme of the piece is the intoxicating effect of music on those who are in love. The song studied by the boy with his back to the viewer is no longer decipherable, but it probably expressed some variant of the sentiments voiced by Shakespeare's Count Orsino in *Twelfth Night*: 'If music be the food of love, play on.'

By painting a rehearsal rather than a performance, Caravaggio went behind the scenes of the traditional concert picture. He showed the long hours of preparation and the artifice that made possible the final, polished performance. In doing so, he paid subtle tribute to the active role del Monte himself played in the musical culture of his time.

Once hung in the room that the cardinal had consecrated to music, the picture conjures up a scene in which his own, animating presence is forever awaited. It is the picture of a process that depends on the energies of the patron himself. Only when the cardinal arrives can the final preparations be completed, and the concert begin.

THE LUTE PLAYER AND THE BASKET OF FRUIT

The second of Caravaggio's musical paintings, *The Lute Player*, was commissioned by del Monte's friend Vincenzo Giustiniani and probably painted around 1596. An effeminate young man plucks at the strings of a lute while gazing out at the viewer with an expression of such soulfulness that his eyes seem to be brimming with tears. Two musical part-books and a violin lie on the table before him beside some scattered fruit and a glass carafe full of flowers. The scene is lit by a bright, diagonal shaft of light that casts strong shadows.

The wistful singer has sometimes been taken for a girl. Bellori, for example, described the figure as 'a woman in a blouse playing a lute with the sheet music in front of her'.[22] But the 1638 inventory of Giustiniani's collection unambiguously listed the work as 'a half-length figure of a youth who plays the lute, with diverse flowers and fruits and music books ... from the hand of Michelangelo da Caravaggio'.[23] There would seem little reason to doubt its accuracy. The singer's face is androgynous but the shirt, open almost to the waist, reveals no sign of a cleavage.

It is possible that Caravaggio's *Lute Player* is an idealized portrait of del Monte's promising but potentially troublesome castrato, Pedro Montoya. Montoya joined the Sistine Chapel Choir in 1592 and left in 1600, so he was almost certainly in del Monte's household when the picture was painted. The soft, hairless skin and slightly swollen face of Caravaggio's lutenist are consistent with the hormonal side-effects of castration. There may be a glancing allusion to the pitch of the boy's voice in the part-books that lie on the table before him. The five-staved sheets of an open part-book reveal a number of madrigals. Beneath lies another part-book, prominently marked 'Bassus'. It is closed, perhaps the painter's way of indicating that this particular singer never would be capable of hitting the low notes.

Castrati were much in favour in Rome in the years around 1600. Their rise coincided with that of the professional female singer, and both reflected the new taste for piercingly emotional music arranged for the single voice. In his *Discourse on Music*, Vincenzo Giustiniani noted that 'the famous Vittoria Archilei' had established 'the true method of singing of women', adding that it applied equally well to sopranos singing in falsetto and the castrati of the Sistine Chapel choir.[24] The castrato voice was valued for its sweetness and sensuality, as well as for its clarity of enunciation.[25]

Castrati were encouraged to learn musical instruments so that they might accompany themselves. Such tuition is likely to have been part of the regime in del Monte's household. The cardinal himself played the Spanish guitar, and it is possible that Caravaggio learned the same instrument while living there. A deposition lodged against him by his landlady in 1605 includes the complaint that he came to her house late at night with a group of friends, playing the selfsame instrument and singing lewd songs, and a later inventory of his possessions lists one.

The singer in the *Lute Player* is anything but raucous. He opens his mouth 'not more than is necessary to converse with friends', as a contemporary singing manual advised those performing chamber music of this kind.[26] The picture is in such good condition that the sheet music open on the table is still legible: four madrigals by the Flemish composer Jacques Arcadelt (*c.* 1505-68): '*Chi potra dir*', '*Se la dura durezza*', '*Voi sapete*' and '*Vostra fui*'.[27] Their texts are a compendium of the conventions of the courtly love tradition, shot through with plaintive simile and metaphor – beauty that blinds like the sun, ardent fires of passion, cold unyielding marble of a proud woman's heart. '*Chi potra dir*' is representative:

> Who can express what sweetness I taste
> In gazing on that proud light of my lady
> That shames the celestial sphere?
> Not I, who am unable to find within myself
> The proper words,
> So that, looking on her beautiful face and mien,

So as not to see less well
I would deign to lose together both life and light.[28]

The amorous mood of the song is conveyed by the singer's passionate, voluptuous expression. The beam of light that rakes the room, illuminating the boy's face with its flash of radiance, may be Caravaggio's own metaphor for 'that proud light of my lady'. The melancholy poetry of a song has been translated into the texture of painting.

The prominent still life may have been intended to enhance the bittersweet mood. Faded flowers traditionally symbolized the transience of life and love. Baglione singled them out for particular praise, focusing on 'the carafe of flowers filled with water, in which we see clearly the reflection of a window and other objects in the room, while on the petals of the flowers there are dewdrops imitated most exquisitely'. The flowers have indeed been depicted with meticulous care, each one sharply individuated. But they pose a puzzle because neither they, nor the fruit, can possibly have been painted by Caravaggio himself. The handling is very different in this part of the painting, much harder in the outlines, with a pernicketiness in the finish that is quite alien to his style. The vase of flowers strikes an especially discordant note. The enamelled blooms are piled high in a merely decorative profusion. They have none of the weight, none of the mute and insistent singularity, of things seen and painted by Caravaggio. It is conceivable that the fruit and flowers were added by the Netherlandish painter Jan Bruegel (1568–1625), who was in Rome in the mid 1590s. The second son of Pieter Bruegel the Elder, Jan Bruegel was a favourite of Carlo Borromeo's cousin Cardinal Federico Borromeo, a friend of del Monte who lived close to the Palazzo Madama from 1597 to 1601. With Borromeo's encouragement, Bruegel would later become a specialist painter of flowers in vases. Given that he was certainly in Caravaggio's circle and in Rome at the right time, he is a plausible candidate for authorship of *The Lute Player*'s mysterious bouquet.

Jan Bruegel's patron, Federico Borromeo, was one of the first collectors of still life painting. It was for him that Caravaggio painted his only pure example of the genre, the *Basket of Fruit*, now in the Ambrosiana Library in Milan. Created some time in the later 1590s, it is among the very first autonomous still life pictures, a muffled explosion of morbidity and metaphysical aspiration, and another testament to Caravaggio's extreme originality.

The *Basket of Fruit* was elaborated from the earlier *Boy with a Basket of Fruit*. What it shows, essentially, is the basket without the boy. The weight of the painter's attention on his apparently straightforward theme is palpable. The basket on this occasion contains a considerably reduced ration of produce. There are figs, an apple, a quince, a peach, a pear and four bunches of bloom-clouded grapes. These are the fruits of late summer, ripe to succulence, but also on the turn. There is a dark wormhole in the red-streaked cheek of the apple. Two of the grapes at the apex of the uppermost bunch have shrivelled to raisins. There are black spots as well as bright pearls of dew on some of the foliage. A parched vine leaf has turned thinner than paper, while the peach leaves have curled and dried to dark, perforated twists. The basket of woven straw has been placed on the most minimally suggested of ledges. It overhangs the edge a little, a fact that the painter indicates with the smallest crescent of black shadow. The transience of nature is linked to precariousness. Entropy and the fear of falling are connected in Caravaggio's mind.

The background of the painting is a golden void, reminiscent of a cream-coloured wall in the sun. An early inventory of Federico Borromeo's collection shows that it was kept unframed. This may have been deliberate: it may have been hung high on a wall the same colour as the ground, to emphasize its *trompe-l'œil* effect and make it yet more of a tantalus.[29] In any case, the blank background had been a characteristic peculiarity of Caravaggio's work from the very start of his career. It is the hallmark of an artist utterly uninterested in extraneous detail. For Caravaggio, making images is a way of focusing the mind. To paint something is to isolate it for the purposes of contemplation.

The total isolation of forms in the *Basket of Fruit* might have lent the image a quality of objectivity, akin to that of the contemporary specimen studies in the albums compiled for Cassiano dal Pozzo collectively known as 'The Paper Museum'. But in Caravaggio's hands it has the opposite effect. The objects of his concern have been removed from the world of the merely mundane. The possibility of transfiguration seems to linger in the stillness that surrounds them. The picture implicitly contrasts death with hope. From withered grapes comes wine, just as from the dead body of Christ flowed the blood of salvation. The fruits and leaves are haloed by the golden light, which seems to emanate from several sources. The light gives modelling to some and reduces others to sharp and ragged silhouettes. There is a measure and a rhythm to the arrangement of objects and shapes, which creates the sense that there must be more going on than meets the eye. Leaves droop and curl with an exquisite sense of placement, fastidiously arranged in such a way as to hang clear in the golden air.

Caravaggio exhausted the genre of still life – for himself, at least – in the act of painting his only example of it. Roberto Longhi, searching for words to express the uniqueness of the painting, called it 'a humble biological drama'. It is precisely the picture's dramatic quality that makes it so unusual, and so powerful. The *vanitas* connotations of bruised fruit and the eucharistic implications of grapes come together in the painted basket. But the accumulation of symbols is not enough for Caravaggio, who prefers to express his meaning dynamically. His idea of still life painting is not an assemblage of objects but a theatre of forms. The huddled windfall fruit have a corporeal solidity. The grapes overspill. The foliage is uncannily anthropomorphized. The most daring detail is the single tendril of vine that reaches into the picture from an unexplained point of origin outside its right-hand edge. The blackened silhouettes of leaves hanging from that single, knubbled stalk might almost be hands stretching. They are figures of death or desperation reaching towards the light and life. The work is, in the end, only a still life painting, but it is filled with the same energies, the same sense of agony and paroxysm, as Caravaggio's greatest religious pictures.

The origins of the *Basket of Fruit* remain obscure. It might have been commissioned directly by Federico Borromeo when he lived in Rome, between April 1597 and May 1601. Or it might have been a gift from Cardinal del Monte. In a letter to Borromeo of 1596, del Monte thanks him for certain presents received and expresses his intention to reciprocate with a gift of 'paintings and clocks'. He says he is sorry for the delay, caused by the fact that 'I am dealing with persons with whom I have to arm myself with patience' – which sounds like a reference to the temperamental Caravaggio.

Opinion is also divided on the question of what Borromeo thought of the painting. He singled it out in an intriguing passage in his *Musaeum*, part of a tract entitled '*De Pictura Sacra*', 'Of Sacred Painting', written in 1618: 'Of not little value is a basket containing flowers in lively tints. It was made by Michelangelo da Caravaggio who acquired a great name in Rome. I would have liked to place another similar basket nearby, but no other having attained the incomparable beauty and excellence of this, it remained alone.'[30] Borromeo's reference to flowers instead of fruit has called into question the sincerity of his admiration for the painting. If he had truly loved it, surely he would never have made such an elementary mistake. But it was not uncommon for a churchman to refer to the mystic grapes of Christian belief as *flores vineae*, the 'flowers of the vine' – a phrase inspired by the Song of Songs. Rather than indicating Borromeo's indifference to the picture, the passage may actually reveal his awareness of its deeper connotations.[31]

PAINTINGS FOR PRAYER AND DEVOTION

Federico Borromeo's ownership of the *Basket of Fruit* suggests that with del Monte's support Caravaggio's circle of patrons and collectors soon widened. As well as painting secular subjects, such as *The Musicians* and *The Lute Player* for del Monte himself, the artist created a number of private devotional works – images of the saints, and the Holy Family, intended as aids to prayer and meditation. These too were subtle and original works that did much to enhance his steadily growing reputation for independence of thought and style.

Two of these religious pictures, *The Penitent Magdalen* and *The Rest on the Flight to Egypt*, have been together in the Pamphili Collection in Rome ever since they were first recorded there in an inventory of 1652. Their earlier history is not known for certain but it is likely that their first owner was Donna Olimpia Aldobrandini, whose heir married Prince Camillo Pamphili in 1647, taking all the family pictures with her. Olimpia Aldobrandini was the niece of Cardinal Pietro Aldobrandini, with whom Cardinal del Monte played hazard and frequented the company of courtesans, so she would have been well placed to buy works from Caravaggio in the later 1590s;[32] these two pictures appear to have been part of the unsold stock that the painter brought with him when he moved to the Palazzo Madama. Mancini, the most reliable source of information about the early years, says that both were painted at around the same time as *The Gypsy Fortune-Teller*, when Caravaggio was living in the house of Monsignor Fatin Petrigiani.[33] That would place them in 1595–6, a date consistent with their lightness of palette and slightly soft style.

Bellori thought *The Penitent Magdalen* was a shockingly unorthodox work of art and described it as one of the most extreme examples of Caravaggio's obsession with reproducing raw and unmediated reality:

> Since Caravaggio aspired only to the glory of colour, so that complexion, skin, blood and natural surfaces might appear real, he directed his eye and work solely to that end, leaving aside all the other aspects of art. Therefore, in order to find figure types and to compose them, when he came upon someone in town who pleased him he made no attempt to improve on the creations of Nature. He painted a girl drying her hair, seated on a little chair with her hands in her lap. He portrayed her in a room, adding a small ointment jar, jewels and gems on the floor, pretending that she is the Magdalen. She holds her head a little to one side, and her cheek, neck and breast are rendered in pure, simple, and true colours, enhanced by the simplicity of the whole figure, with her arms covered by a blouse and her yellow gown drawn up to her knees over a white underskirt of flowered damask. We have described this figure in detail in order to show his naturalistic style and the way in which he imitates truthful colouring by using only a few hues.

Neither for the first nor the last time in his life of Caravaggio, Bellori's criticism was mitigated by grudging admiration. Compelled by his own academic dogma to dismiss the work, he none the less responded instinctively to its vivid style and unusual composition.

Mary Magdalen was one of the most popular saints of the Counter-Reformation Catholic Church, which placed a heavy emphasis on the moral responsibilities of each and every believer. She was held up as a shining example of penance and conversion, a beacon for all those languishing in darkness and sin. According to the most prominent part of her legend, she was a prostitute who repented, and 'the woman whom Jesus loved'. The biblical Mary Magdalen was the woman from whose mouth 'seven devils' were exorcised in the gospel of St Luke. But tradition also identified her with Mary, the sister of Martha and Lazarus of Bethany, and with the unnamed repentant sinner blessed by Christ for washing his feet with her tears, drying them with her hair and anointing them with oil (Luke 7:37–50). In the Eastern Church these figures were regarded as separate individuals, but in the West all three were merged into Mary Magdalen. Her fable was further embroidered during the Middle Ages, when she was said to have travelled from the holy land to the South of France, where she 'went into the desert and dwelt there thirty years without knowing of any man or woman'.

In the mid fifteenth century the Florentine sculptor Donatello had carved a harrowingly ascetic sculpture of Mary Magdalen in the wilderness, portraying her as a gap-toothed hermit with withered flesh, wasting away in a hair shirt. But by Caravaggio's time, Donatello's raw immediacy of imagining had fallen out of fashion. The image of Mary Magdalen, epitome of the repentant prostitute, had become fossilized by convention into two basic types: either she appeared as a beautiful nude in a landscape, decorously draped by tresses of her own luxuriant hair, praying before a crucifix and skull; or she appeared as a demure aristocrat reading a book indoors.

Caravaggio rejected both of those stereotypes to create his own, highly distinctive image of Mary Magdalen. The hands of the figure are boneless and the anatomy of her chest and neck unconvincing, but the painter's conception of the subject is impressively original and characteristically dramatic. Caravaggio placed the girl who modelled for the painting on a chair so low that her knees must have been only inches off the ground. As a result, she is seen from above, almost as in a compressed version of a bird's-eye view, so that at first sight it is not quite clear whether she is sitting or lying outflung on the ground. It may have been this extremely unusual perspective, so alien to the pictorial conventions of the time, that led Bellori to think of the work as a perverse exercise in purely optical painting. But it has a poetic point to it. By seating Mary Magdalen so low, Caravaggio emphasizes her humility – the etymology of which, derived from the Latin *humus*, or 'ground', itself expresses the idea of abasement.

Caravaggio's Magdalen is no emblem, but a person in turmoil. She sits in darkness, but above her an abstract wedge of light intrudes, as if to dramatize the light of Christ entering her soul. The painter depicts her in the immediate aftermath of her conversion – the moment just after Christ says, 'Thy faith has saved thee; go in peace.' A single tear trickles down the side of her nose. She has torn off her gold and her jewels and scattered them on the ground. The glass jar beside her, three quarters full, contains the same unguent with which she anointed Christ's feet. It is echoed by the shape of a vase in the damask of her dress, a visual pun that may have its own significance. She is herself like a vessel that has been filled with the spirit of the Lord. Her closed eyes suggest the idea that she is looking within, perhaps even experiencing the transports of mystic vision. She looks as though she is cradling an imaginary child. Perhaps she is thinking about her namesake, the Virgin Mary, and reflecting on the mystery of the mother whose divine child is foredoomed to die.

When Caravaggio reimagined the Magdalen in this way, when he thought about the heart of her story and asked himself how to bring that story to life, he was doing just what Carlo Borromeo had urged the preachers of post-Tridentine Milan to do. The true precedent for his painting lay in images formed from words, rather than paint or stone. There is nothing like his *Penitent Magdalen* in the visual art of late sixteenth-century Italy, but turn to the sermons of the time and close parallels can be found. The following, for example, is a description of Mary Magdalen in the passionate transports of her conversion given in a sermon by Francesco Panigarola, a preacher closely associated with Borromeo: 'now she retraces her steps, her legs stagger, now she starts to take off all her vain ornaments, now to utter cruel invectives against indecent womankind, now to disparage the beauty of the eyes, now to groan, exclaiming, "Oh roof, why don't you fall down and crush me?" Casting down her necklaces and jewels, shaking her tresses, violently wringing her hands, she trembled . . .'[34] Caravaggio's picture is like a still image pulled from the flow of such thoughts. It would always be his practice as a religious painter to rethink sacred story as living drama. Perhaps, when he did so, he often began by remembering the images conjured up in the sermons of his childhood.

The Rest on the Flight to Egypt, always closely associated with *The Penitent Magdalen*, must have been painted at around the same time. Caravaggio employed the same young model, a redhead, in both cases. In the second picture she has metamorphosed from distraught courtesan to exhausted Madonna. She sits cross-legged on the ground, cradling the infant Christ in her lap. The baby sleeps peacefully but the mother's rest is more fitful; Mary's head lolls, her cheek resting on the crown of the infant Christ's head. Her brow is furrowed. There is some hesitancy in Caravaggio's painting here. He has trouble articulating the junctures of chin and neck, neck and shoulder, and her limp hands are only a little more convincing than those of the *Penitent Magdalen*. But there is great tenderness, none the less, in the artist's idea of mother and child. The heavy-headed Mary is a refugee huddled with her baby, snatching a moment of rest while she can. Bellori, that keen if reluctant admirer of Caravaggio's humanity, noted the poignancy of 'the Madonna who, with her head inclined, sleeps with her baby at her breast'.

On the other side of the painting sits a wizened, greybeard St Joseph. Wrapped in folds of heavy brown cloth, he has the weather-worn face of a working man. He rubs one of his bare feet with the other in a way that suggests he is feeling the cold. His head is placed almost disconcertingly close to that of the ass, which stands patiently behind him. The objects beside him, a bundle wrapped in green striped cloth and a flagon of wine sealed with a twist of paper, speak of the family's hurried displacement. Caravaggio's Holy Family is very much in hiding. They nestle close together, within a bower sheltered by undergrowth. Like illegal immigrants seeking to avoid detection, they have made themselves small and unobtrusive.

The painter's biblical source was the Book of Matthew, 2:12–15, which recounts the events immediately preceding Herod's massacre of the innocents: 'the angel of the Lord appeareth to Joseph in a dream, saying, Arise, and take the young child and his mother, and flee into Egypt, and be thou there until I bring thee word: for Herod will seek the young child to destroy him.' Between Mary cradling the Christ child and the figure of Joseph, Caravaggio has included the angel of the Lord – a smooth-skinned adolescent boy, scantily draped, seen from behind, face in half-profile. The only upright form in the painting, the figure resembles a pillar of divine light against the dark clouds that hover over the landscape in the background. The angel plays a violin while Joseph obligingly holds up a musical part-book.

The music being played has been identified. It is the four-voiced *Quam pulchra es et quam decora*, composed by Noel Bauldewyn (*c*. 1480–1520) to a medieval text drawn in patchwork fashion from the verses of the Song of Songs.[35] The angelic music solemnizes the spiritual union of Caravaggio's sleepy mother and child, so they are to be understood as the true husband and wife in the scene. Joseph earnestly contemplates the angel, as if straining to understand the mystical significance of the heavenly vision. But, like the slow and faithful ass with which he has been paired, he does not fully grasp the elusive meaning of the notes that fill the air.

His incomprehension might well have been echoed by many of Caravaggio's contemporaries. Because the painter rendered the notes in the musical part-book without the actual words from the Song of Songs, a vital part of the iconography of his painting was encrypted from the outset. *The Rest on the Flight to Egypt* has an air of secrecy about it. In many respects it is a touchingly direct dramatization of a biblical story. But it is also occluded, a painting of different levels and layers designed to speak fully only to those who have been initiated into its mysteries.

The standing angel is one of the young Caravaggio's most haunting inventions. There was nothing in the Bible or any of the Christian apocrypha to suggest the playing of heavenly music during the Holy Family's flight to Egypt. A music-making guardian angel did appear in medieval miracle plays telling the story. The painter may have seen dramas of this kind, which were traditionally staged at Christmas, and perhaps he intended to evoke popular sacred theatre. But Caravaggio's precise visual source for the angel was far removed from the world of medieval piety. He lifted the figure directly from *The Judgement of Hercules*, a mythological picture of 1596 painted for one of the ceilings of the Palazzo Farnese by Annibale Carracci. That painting, now in the Museo di Capodimonte, Naples, shows the mythical character Hercules choosing between two female figures personifying

Vice and Virtue. It was the scantily clad figure of Vice that Caravaggio daringly chose to transform into his own half-naked angel. Caravaggio's career would be marked by bitter rivalry with a number of other painters, including Annibale Carracci. So it seems likely that he was deliberately courting comparisons between his own work and Carracci's *Judgement of Hercules*, which was painted only a few months earlier.

Appropriation is Caravaggio's pretext for a virtuoso display of his own powers. The thief turns out to be a magician. Annibale's figure is a heavy, sculpturally draped figment of the late Renaissance, a being abstracted from reality into the realm of art. Caravaggio's angelic boy is a type of ideal beauty, but he has been brought down to earth. His feet touch the dark soil, his slender legs shift to transfer his weight to his left side, his curly hair is tousled by the wind. Even his wings, evidently modelled on those of a pigeon, announce Caravaggio's distinctive attachment to actuality. An unnecessary curl of surplus string coils from one of the pegs of the angel's violin, a final grace note of captivating realism. All this serves to emphasize the gulf between Carracci's disembodied spirit of sensuality and Caravaggio's fully realized angel. But the most daring trope of inversion is the transformation of the figure's essential meaning. An embodiment of temptation has been recast as an angel. Vice has been sanctified. The profane is invested with sacred meaning, just as it is in the Songs of Songs. Like the half-concealed text at its heart, *The Rest on the Flight to Egypt* is charged with erotic feeling. The alluring and mysterious angel, sensuality and divinity intertwined, splits the picture like a bolt of lightning.

Shortly after painting *The Penitent Magdalen* and *The Rest on the Flight to Egypt*, Caravaggio created perhaps the most daring of all his early devotional pictures. *St Francis of Assisi in Ecstasy* is now in the Wadsworth Atheneum, Connecticut. The painting is a nocturne, set in a landscape of gloomy indistinctness lit by the first distant gleams of dawn. The painter directs a focusing beam of divine light on to the form of the ecstatic saint, as he swoons into the arms of his guardian angel.

Scholars disagree about who commissioned the picture from Caravaggio. The two candidates are Ottavio Costa, a rich banker, and del Monte himself. There is a case to be made for either, and even for both.

A picture of St Francis by Caravaggio is recorded in Costa's will of 1605, while 'A *St Francis in Ecstasy* by Michel Agnolo [*sic*] da Caravaggio with an adorned gold frame of four palmi' was sold by del Monte's heir in 1627.[36] It is not known if these were one and the same picture, or two versions of the same composition. Cardinal del Monte's Christian name was Francesco, and as we have seen he had a particular fondness for images of the saints. So, though the complications of its early history may never be fully unpicked, the picture now in Connecticut may well have hung at one time in the Palazzo Madama – perhaps not far from Caravaggio's earlier painting of a musical rehearsal. There is a striking resemblance between the boy with Cupid's wings in *The Musicians* and the angel cradling the ecstatic saint in the later picture. The same model probably posed for both figures.

St Francis of Assisi in Ecstasy is a crucial painting in Caravaggio's early development. It announces the stark tenebrism that would become the hallmark of the painter's revolutionary style – that 'boldly dark and black colouring,' in Bellori's words, 'which he used abundantly to give relief to the forms'.[37] It also displays for the first time Caravaggio's lifelong fascination for the strongest and most intense strains of Counter-Reformation Catholic spirituality. It expresses the idea of a transfiguring love of Christ, a love so deep that it becomes a form of mystic self-annihilation.

In Italy during the later years of the sixteenth century, the thirteenth-century Francis was regarded as the saint to emulate above all others. The Counter-Reformation Church looked back to the Middle Ages as a time of powerfully simple piety, uncomplicated by divisive theological speculation. Francis had practised an emotive, theatrical form of preaching, which spoke to the feelings rather than the intellect. He encouraged his followers to venerate nature as God's blessed creation, and held that the only way to follow Christ's message was to live it out in daily life. In prayer, he sought to visualize the events of the New Testament. In public, he would act them out, turning his own body into the living image of Jesus Christ. In sackcloth and ashes, haltered like a beast, he would re-enact the humiliations of the journey on the road to Calvary. The central event of Francis's life was itself a miracle of empathetic identification. One day the saint focused his prayers so strongly on the image of Christ that the wounds of

Crucifixion were miraculously branded on his own body. The idea of the stigmata was in turn burned into the Christian folk memory, becoming the ultimate symbol of the power of prayer and visualization to lead the believer towards God. This is the theme of Caravaggio's picture, and it became a guiding principle of his art. All his religious paintings would be re-enactments or reimaginings, closely akin to the vivid theatricality of Franciscan devotion.

The miracle of the stigmata is most fully described in St Bonaventure's mid thirteenth-century *Life of St Francis*. Bonaventure relates that the saint went up to Mount La Verna, an isolated mountain at the centre of the Apennines, with one of his followers, Brother Leo, to pray and fast. While he was absorbed in devotion to Christ, a seraph with six flaming wings appeared to him in the sky. As the seraph came nearer, Francis saw the figure of a man crucified between its wings:

> He marvelled exceedingly at the appearance of a vision so unfathomable, knowing that the infirmity of the Passion doth in no wise accord with the immortality of a Seraphic spirit. At length he understood therefrom, the Lord revealing it unto him, that this vision had been thus presented unto his gaze by the divine providence, that the friend of Christ might have foreknowledge that he was to be wholly transformed into the likeness of Christ crucified, not by martyrdom of body, but by enkindling of heart. Accordingly, as the vision disappeared, it left in his heart a wondrous glow, but on his flesh also it imprinted a no less wondrous likeness of its tokens. For forthwith there began to appear in his hands and feet the marks of the nails, even as he had just beheld them in that Figure of the Crucified ... The right side, moreover, was – as if it had been pierced by a lance.[38]

St Bonaventure makes a minute distinction here. The Lord makes it known to Francis that he will be transformed into 'the likeness of Christ crucified' not by the mortification of his flesh but by the inner burning of love in his heart – 'not by martyrdom of body, but by enkindling of heart'. It is love, not pain, that transfigures the human being in search of God. Once Francis understands this, the seraph disappears. A wound appears in Francis's heart at that very moment; immediately afterwards the marks of the stigmata appear on the saint's hands and feet.

Caravaggio's composition indicates not only that he had read St Bonaventure's *Life of St Francis*, but that he intended to dramatize the crucial moment in the story – the moment when, as the seraph disappears, the wound appears in the saint's heart. As Caravaggio's saint swoons backwards, he reaches involuntarily with his right hand towards a rent in his habit where a wound in his side has already started bleeding. There are no signs of stigmata in his hands or his feet, and there is no seraph in the sky. There was no precedent, in depictions of St Francis, for including the wound in his side and omitting the others. There was no precedent, either, for the compassionate kneeling angel who cradles the saint in his arms. Caravaggio was also the first artist to depict the saint lying down at the moment of his stigmatization.

In every sense – style, iconography, drama – the painting broke new ground. It certainly gives the lie to the slander that Caravaggio was an untutored Lombard realist, bent solely on dazzling with the mimetic brilliance of his art. *St Francis of Assisi in Ecstasy* is a picture full of subtle, poetic reflections on the deeper meaning of Francis's transfiguring moment of communion with Christ. Barely visible in the gloom behind the angel and the saint, a little group of shepherds is gathered round a campfire, one of them pointing excitedly to the heavens. Here, Caravaggio consciously echoes the traditional imagery of Christ's Nativity – which had itself often been painted as a nocturne – as if to imply that at the moment of his swooning ecstasy Francis really has been reborn in the image of Christ himself. Implicit in this brief moment of death-in-life is, therefore, a second birth for Francis, marking out his destiny to live only in and for Christ – to live as *alter Christus*, or 'another Christ', as his legend had it.

The group of saint and angel echoes another tradition of Christian art, recalling images of the dead Christ cradled in the arms of his mother, the Virgin Mary. Caravaggio's angel is taller than the figure of St Francis, which has sometimes been put down to the painter's youthful clumsiness, but this too is actually a poetic device, enhancing the pathos of the saint's helpless body: in many images of the Virgin mourning Christ's death, including Michelangelo's celebrated marble *Pietà* in St Peter's, the mother's supporting body is much larger than that of her lifeless son. This echo of Christ's death and lamentation may also have been meant to express the idea that it was through the act of meditating on Christ's passion that Francis brought the miracle of his own transfiguration upon himself. By thinking about the dead Christ, he achieved the state of electrifying empathy that summoned forth the blessed vision of the seraph.

Francis was a figure from the relatively recent past. His legend was treasured by Catholics, not least because it seemed such a tangible demonstration of the continuing presence of a miracle-working God in the real and actual world. Protestants disapproved of the veneration of saints and their relics, arguing that too much worship had been displaced from its proper focus on God alone. The destruction of shrines and the suppression of pilgrimage in countries of the Protestant north was, in part, an attempt to stem this perceived haemorrhaging of holiness from the divine centre to the apocryphal margin. But in Catholic Italy, it was feared that such theological purism might rob the world altogether of its Christian magic. To abandon the images and relics of the saints, together with the rituals associated with their veneration, might create the sense of a terminally disenchanted present, cut adrift from the sacred past.

Many of the religious initiatives of the Counter-Reformation addressed this nexus of fear, desire and belief. One of the challenges that the Catholic Church set itself in Caravaggio's time was that of demonstrating that the old and the modern Christian worlds were not distinct and separate eras but formed, instead, a single unbroken continuum. The very fabric of Rome, where so many of the dramas of Christian history had been played out, was itself interrogated for evidence of this. The discovery of the catacombs, burial places of the earliest generations of Roman Christians, led to a boom in the field of what might be called sacred archaeology. The seventeenth-century Bishop of Vaison, Joseph Maria Suarez, examined the mosaics of ancient Rome from a Christian perspective. Antonio Bosio's study of the city's buried architectural bones, *Roma Sotterranea*, was posthumously published in 1632. Another scholar, Antonio Gallonio, spent years studying the instruments and reconstructing the methods of early Christian martyrdom, publishing the results in 1591 as *The Tortures and Torments of the Christian Martyrs*. Gallonio gave the different chapters of his book gorily circumstantial titles – 'Of the Wheel, the Pulley and the Press as Instruments of Torture', or 'Of Instruments Wherewith the Heathen Were Used to Tear the Flesh of Christ's Faithful Servants, to wit Iron Claws, Hooks and Currycombs' – and his text proved immensely popular. The more lavishly illustrated editions bear vivid witness to the author's underlying ambition, that of making the holy deaths of venerable memory seem as gruesomely fresh as yesterday's executions.

The past was not to be thought of as the past. The age of miracles and martyrdoms was not another time, dead and buried, the passing of which was to be mourned; it was part of the present. To go on pilgrimage, as Catholics were encouraged to do, was to reaffirm precisely that belief, because to travel to a holy site was to move through time as well as through space – journeying back through the centuries, in mind and spirit, to relive the events of sacred history as if they were taking place in the here and now. Ascanio Donguidi, Augustinian Canon Regular of San Giovanni in Laterano, one of the principal pilgrimage churches of Rome, published a guidebook for prospective pilgrims in 1600. On approaching St Peter's, he advised,

> You will greatly enjoy thinking about your visit to all the Saints whose relics are kept in that Church. Imagine yourself having found the saints present and alive . . . O with how much great devotion and fervour and joy of heart you would go into Saint Peter's, if you truly believed to find him . . . sitting in his Pontifical Throne, or how you would hurry, even run, if you imagined being able to find present [and alive] in said Church where they are buried, all the Holy Martyrs, Popes, Confessors and Holy Virgins. And [it is not only a figment of your imagination] because it is true that you are going to visit them, and it is very true that they are living a life of glory. And they will listen to your petitions, prayers and supplications and will present them to God.[39]

Not only were the old saints to be venerated, to be conversed with as if they were still alive. It was to be known that their miracles were being actively repeated in the contemporary world, in the lives of new saints elect. Ecstasies of empathetic love akin to those of Francis loomed large in the lives of sixteenth-century penitents, priests and charismatic nuns. St Teresa of Avila's memoirs, published in 1588, famously told of an angel coming to her when she was deep in prayer and piercing her breast with an arrow of divine love: 'It is not bodily pain, but spiritual, though the body has a share in it – indeed, a great share, so sweet are the colloquies of love which pass between the soul and God that if anyone thinks I am lying I beseech God, in his goodness, to give him the same experience.'[40]

Caravaggio's painting was intended to prompt reflections on more than the stigmatization of Francis alone. *St Francis of Assisi in Ecstasy* embodied an ideal of transfiguring Christian love, exemplified not only by St Francis, and by St Teresa, but also – still closer to Roman hearts – by St Filippo Neri, founder of the Oratory. Like Teresa, Neri had been fascinated both by the legends of a saint such as Francis of Assisi, and by the power and authority of the primitive Church. In early life he prayed continually in the catacombs of Rome's most ancient saints of all; and it was in the Catacomb of San Sebastiano that he experienced his own ecstasy and his own divine wound of love:

> In 1544, just before the feast of Pentecost, Philip, while still a layman, was praying to the Holy Ghost in the Catacomb of San Sebastiano, when he seemed to see a globe of fire which entered his mouth and sank down into his heart. At the same time he felt a fire of love which seemed to be a positive physical heat, so that he had to throw himself on the ground and bare his breast to cool it. When he rose he was seized with a violent trembling, accompanied by an extraordinary sense of joy, and putting his hand to his heart, felt there a swelling as big as a man's fist . . . At the same time there began that palpitation of the heart which lasted throughout his life, and made itself felt particularly when he was praying, hearing confession, saying Mass, or giving communion, or when he was speaking on some subject which stirred his emotions. So violent was this palpitation that it was described by those who knew him best as being like the blows of a hammer, while the trembling it caused was such as to shake his chair, his bed, or sometimes the whole room. Yet, when he pressed his penitents to his heart they felt an extraordinary consolation . . .[41]

Such modern stories of saintly ecstasy were well known to those who commissioned and paid for Caravaggio's early devotional pictures. Neri had confided the tale of his blissful ordeal by divine fire to none other than Cardinal Federico Borromeo, owner of Caravaggio's

Basket of Fruit. Near the end of his life, Cardinal del Monte delivered a *laudatio* of St Teresa, on the occasion of her canonization.

Caravaggio's strong and unusual emphasis on the love that burned within Francis's heart expressly evoked the parallels between his legend and those of the modern saints. The sacred past is projected into the present. The holy light that shone on Francis might still shine on anyone with eyes to see. *St Francis of Assisi in Ecstasy* is more than an illustration of an episode in the life of a saint. The picture offers a consoling dream of transfiguration, a condition of oneness with Christ to which anyone might aspire. That is the significance of its most striking detail, the creased and eyes-closed face of the ecstatic saint. Caravaggio painted St Francis as a real, flesh-and-blood human being, a man with sharply defined features, someone who might be easily recognized, even on the dark streets of Rome by night. Not only that – he gave the saint his own face.[42] It is an extraordinary statement of self-identification, but one that would be more than justified by Caravaggio's subsequent religious works. No other painter of his time would do more to revive and proclaim the solemn, ascetic sense of humility at the heart of the Franciscan ideal.

BETWEEN SACRED AND PROFANE

The sacred and the profane are inextricably intertwined in Caravaggio's early work. Pictures of apparently mundane subjects are depth-charged with spiritual yearning, while flashes of intoxicating eroticism dart from pictures of the saints or the Holy Family. The painter dreams of angelic beauty, but can only embody it as one beautiful boy after another. The sensual and sexual appeal of such youthful, smooth-skinned figures as the coquettish, music-playing angel in *The Rest on the Flight*, or the angelic ministrant to St Francis, has been taken as evidence of the painter's homosexuality. The truth is not straightforward. Caravaggio was capable of being aroused by the physical presence of other men. He could not have painted such figures in the way that he did if that were not so. But he was equally attracted to women, as certain other paintings from the late 1590s, such as the transfixing *St Catherine of Alexandria*, plainly demonstrate. Insofar as the art reveals the man, Caravaggio's painting suggests an ambiguous sexual personality. On the evidence of his paintings he was neither heterosexual nor homosexual, terms that are in any case anachronistic when applied to his world. He was omnisexual.

The devouring way in which Caravaggio looked at the world made it all but impossible for him to paint idealized forms. There is a quality of seemingly involuntary vividness in many of the details of his paintings – a quality that, increasingly, he learned to control and to manipulate. This both intrigued and fascinated his contemporaries, and brought a dangerous unpredictability to his pictures. Something base and ordinary might suddenly seem touched by a miracle; a holy mystery could shade into figments snatched from an erotic daydream. Caravaggio's early work is beguiling, in part, because it is so ambiguous and metamorphic. It expresses the truancies of the painter's imagination and allows space for the unregulated responses of the viewer's wandering eye. It speaks of piety but makes concessions to the impious mind, guiltily mingling the pleasures of the world with a genuine sense of devotion.

Caravaggio's more sophisticated patrons were attuned to such subtle ambiguities. The best evidence for this is an intriguing correspondence between a cleric from Vicenza named Paolo Gualdo and Cardinal Ottavio Paravicino. Paravicino, who had been present at Vittoria Archileo's concert, was a friend of del Monte and one of three Roman cardinals certainly linked with Filippo Neri's Oratory. Gualdo was a scholarly cleric with strong connections to the humanist culture of the Veneto in general and Vicenza in particular. He was a friend of the poet Tasso and wrote a biography of the architect Palladio. He was also a lover of painting, who had tried and failed to obtain a picture by Caravaggio.

In one of his letters to Paravicino, Gualdo harks back to that disappointment. Referring to himself in the third person, and writing in a spirit of knowingly ironical self-deprecation, he casts himself in the role of a simple impecunious man of the cloth, motivated by philanthropy as well as the love of art, whose overtures to Caravaggio have been unfairly rebuffed: 'the good priest has a certain discernment when it comes to painting, but not very many jewels to fund his fancy, so this seemed a good occasion to help a *galant'huomo* of the art of painting, and in the process obtain some graceful little picture.'[43]

The allusion to Caravaggio as a *galant'huomo* suggests not only his pre-eminence as a painter but also a degree of social pretension. The term, which was used interchangeably with *valent'huomo*, signified a virtuoso or a man of especial expertise in his chosen field. But it also carried associations of worth and, by extension, honour. Gualdo's letter was written in 1603, but, given that he refers to a small picture, and elsewhere mentions the name of Cardinal del Monte, it seems reasonable to believe that he had the painter's work of the mid to late 1590s in mind.

A yet more interesting letter about Caravaggio was written by Paravicino to Gualdo in August 1603. It is a teasing text, composed in courtly riddles and insinuations, which takes the form of an imaginary encounter between the phantom of Caravaggio and a caricatured version of Paravicino's friend, Gualdo himself, the cleric from Vicenza:

> Michelangelo da Caravaggio, excellent Painter, says that he came as a shade or spirit to Vicenza, and met a *galant'huomo* who loves paintings and who asked him wondrous many questions. He describes, but does not paint with his brush, a priest with the air of a solemnly reformed cleric, a man who, if he did not speak, would appear to be a Theatine. [The Theatines were a Counter-Reformation order of clerics noted for their asceticism and moral severity.] But when he does open his mouth he touches on every topic, and does so in a spirit of gallantry. It seems to me that he has a tincture of all the sciences, says Caravaggio, but since I lack the necessary expertise myself I cannot touch the marrow of his actual knowledge. He describes himself as extremely keen to have something painted, one minute speaking of various churches, the next of having some beautiful work painted for his lordship the Bishop of Padua. But Caravaggio would have made for him some painting that would have been in that middle area, between the sacred, and the profane – a kind of picture that he would not have wanted to see from a distance . . .

The aim of the letter is to tease Gualdo and to puncture, with the lightest of touches, his holier-than-thou pretensions – which had themselves been expressed in a spirit of ironic self-parody. Caravaggio and his art are merely the tools employed to that ludic end. But, for all its cryptic circumlocutions, Paravicino's letter reveals much about the risky pleasures enjoyed by keen-eyed connoisseurs of Caravaggio's painting.

The whole passage turns on the play between appearance and reality. The figure of Gualdo seems at first to be a severe and utterly correct Counter-Reformation cleric, but he then discourses with gallantry on every subject under the sun, showing that he has a more restless mind than first appearances had suggested. He is not necessarily irreligious, although he thinks about more than religion alone. But even this second Gualdo, *galant'huomo* himself of art and all the sciences, may not be everything that he seems, since the fictional Caravaggio of the letter confesses that he himself lacks the wherewithal to judge the true extent of his knowledge.

A similar contrast between seeming and being is drawn in the second part of Paravicino's tale, about the imaginary commissioning of a picture. Gualdo says that he is thinking of a painting to be given to a church, or to his superior, the Bishop of Padua. But Caravaggio sees through the smokescreen of Gualdo's request and understands what would *really* please him. He decides not to paint an altarpiece, a monumental and unimpeachably pious type of painting. That is because a public work of art, designed to be seen and read from a distance, would not suit a man of Gualdo's personality. Instead, Caravaggio will paint for him something very different – a work that might appear devout but will also appeal to a taste for profane pleasures. It will be a picture for private contemplation, 'not one that he would have wanted to see from a distance', because it would yield its secrets and pleasures only when viewed at close quarters. Such a picture, it is archly implied, would be the exact complement to Gualdo, because it would be just as slippery as the man himself. For the priest who is not entirely priestly, for the man who is not all he seems, Paravicino has found the perfect gift: a work by Caravaggio.

BACCHUS AND HEAD OF THE MEDUSA

None of the artist's pictures are more teasingly poised between the sacred and the profane than the *Bacchus* that he painted sometime in 1597 or 1598 for his patron Cardinal del Monte. This later Bacchus is very different from the *Self-Portrait as Bacchus* – the malingering reveller, impersonated by the artist himself, painted during his apprentice days of discontent. The model, this time, seems to have been Caravaggio's Sicilian friend Mario Minniti. He is a swarthy, ruddy-cheeked, well-fed god of wine, crowned with a wreath of grapes and vine leaves. An air of Dionysian mystery still clings to him, but he is very much the Greek god in his Roman incarnation. Wearing a toga, he lounges on a *triclinium*, as the ancient Romans did when feasting.

There is a decanter on the table in front of him, two thirds full of a wine so darkly crimson that it looks almost black. There are bubbles at its surface and its level is askew, a minute touch of realism that makes the moment captured in the painting seem ever more fleeting. The wine is still swinging in the heavy bowl of the decanter. The boy-god has just set it down, after pouring a glassful of the liquid into the fine-stemmed Venetian goblet that he holds, delicately, in his left hand. He offers the wine to the viewer of the painting. His expression is gently quizzical, his half-raised eyebrow both invitation and challenge: unriddle me if you can.

The *Bacchus* is a sophisticated, courtly work of art, calculated to catch the eye and then hold it. It is an enigma embodied as a rich store of captivating details. Viewed from a certain perspective, the picture seems ripe with sensuality, bordering on outright lubricity. The barely draped boy might be no more than an elaborately wrapped sexual gift. Does he himself not hint at that possibility, with the suggestive play of his right hand in the knot of black ribbon that binds his clothes?

That would be the profane approach to the picture. But there is space for a devout approach too. There is another way of undoing that knot. Bacchus is the god of wine and of autumnal fruitfulness, and in keeping with that Caravaggio has given him another of his overflowing baskets of fruit. The black grapes have never seemed so lustrous, the figs so ripe. But the foliage once more is withered, the apple worm-eaten, the quince and the plum bruised. The pomegranate has split and collapsed, disgorging its fleshy seeds. Once more, a sense of eucharistic implication hovers in the still air. Summer has become autumn and the sere leaves at the basket's edge are the presage of death to come. But there is hope here too: the transcendent promise of eternal life is contained in the glass of wine held so carefully by the boy-god – and with such precise metaphorical intent – directly above the basket of decaying fruit.

According to the Neoplatonic thought of the Renaissance, classical myth was alive with shadowy anticipations of Christian truth. The legend of Dionysus, who died to be reborn, was regarded as a pagan prophecy of the coming of Christ. So it was that the figure of Dionysus/Bacchus became associated with the Saviour himself. Caravaggio's Bacchus has sad, solemn eyes. Those aware of his Christian aspect might also have noted how the toga that drapes him so loosely also resembles a winding sheet. The wine that he offers is the wine of his blood, an allusion lightly pointed by the heart-shaped shadow, angled towards the figure's heart, cast by the decanter. The apparent promise of physical delight has been transfigured, changed to a metaphysical gift.

The picture plays on the deceptive nature of appearances, yet also flaunts the very deceptions that brought it into being. As he had done in *The Musicians*, Caravaggio allows the viewer to peer behind the scene of his own artifice. The model's face and hands are sunburned, to indicate that he is someone who has to go out into the world and earn a living under the harsh noonday sun. There are crescents of black dirt under the fingernails of his left hand. His Roman bed of repose has been created by the expedient of draping white sheets over a somewhat grubby cushion decorated with blue ticking, part of which shows through. This is not *really* Bacchus, but a young man playing his part.[44]

The *Bacchus* soon found its way into the collections of the Medici in Florence. It is likely that del Monte specifically commissioned it as a gift for the grand duke. But the present does not seem to have gone down well. The god with dirty fingernails and sunburned skin may have struck the Medici as a joke in poor taste, or perhaps they were scandalized by the picture's close focus on the sensual body of a half-naked boy. Either way, the picture disappeared from view as soon as it entered the Medici collections. When it finally resurfaced, some four hundred years later, in a basement storeroom of the Uffizi Galleries, not only had it never been catalogued, it had never even been framed.

In 1598 del Monte gave another painting by Caravaggio to his Medici protector. Baglione writes that the artist created 'a head of a terrifying Medusa with vipers for hair placed on a shield, which the Cardinal sent as a gift to Ferdinando, Grand Duke of Tuscany'.[45] Unlike the Bacchus, the *Medusa* was enthusiastically received and prominently displayed in the Medici collections. It is one of Caravaggio's most startling inventions. Painted on to a circular piece of canvas stretched over a convex shield of poplar wood, the picture conjures up the legendary monster at the instant when she breathes her last. In Greek myth, the serpent-haired Medusa turned all who gazed upon her to stone, until the hero Perseus, looking only at her reflection in his brightly polished shield, cut off her head. In Caravaggio's painting, thick jets of blood spurt from the horrible creature's neck, which has been neatly severed just below the jaw. Her eyes stare and her mouth opens in a soundless scream. The snakes of her hair coil convulsively, each writhing in its own separate corkscrew agony of death.

The dying monster with arrestingly masculine features is yet another of the artist's self-portraits.[46] '*Item*: a convex mirror', reads one of the entries in an inventory of Caravaggio's possessions. The distortions of the painter's face as it appears in the *Medusa* indicate that he used a convex mirror to paint it. As in a convex reflection, the cheeks and forehead have been slightly broadened and elongated. Caravaggio deepens the game further by making his own convex reflection, painted on to a convex shield, look as though it is actually *concave*. The shadow cast by the Medusa's head creates the illusion of a curved circular surface scalloped away from the viewer, like a shallow bowl.

Caravaggio treated the commission as a pretext for the display of his own special skills and techniques – so much so that the picture might almost be regarded as his own emblem, or *impresa*. Just as the face is the painter's own, studied from life, the snakes too were painted from actual, wriggling specimens. It is a mark of Caravaggio's pragmatism that the snakes are not vipers, but watersnakes of a type commonly found in the Tiber. He must have asked a fisherman to net some for him.

Just as Perseus had slain the snake-haired Gorgon, Caravaggio set out to vanquish every other artist to have attempted the subject. The

Medusa is a work of such flourish and bravado that it has the look of a painting submitted for a prize. Giorgio Vasari had argued that without the intense spirit of competition between Florentine artists there could have been no Italian Renaissance. His *Lives of the Artists* is full of accounts of such rivalry, and tales of actual contests that had taken place between artists in earlier times – for example, the story of Ghiberti and Brunelleschi competing for the commission to create a set of bronze doors for the Baptistry in Florence, or that of Michelangelo and Leonardo da Vinci working, side by side, on two enormous battle paintings for the council chamber of the city's town hall. By commissioning the *Medusa*, Cardinal del Monte was consciously arranging another such competition. He was pitting Caravaggio against the celebrated Leonardo himself: not only was Leonardo's *Medusa* one of his most famously idiosyncratic creations, it also happened to be in Florence, in the collection of the Medici. The work is lost now, surviving only in the form of a vivid account in Vasari's life of Leonardo. The story begins with Leonardo's father asking him to paint something on a shield of fig wood:

And afterwards, having given it a coat of gesso, and having prepared it in his own way, he began to think about what he could paint upon it, that might be able to terrify all who should come upon it, producing the same effect as once did the head of the Medusa. For this purpose, then, Leonardo carried to a room of his own into which no one entered save himself alone, lizards great and small, crickets, serpents, butterflies, grasshoppers, bats, and other strange kinds of suchlike animals, out of the number of which, variously put together, he formed a great ugly creature, most horrible and terrifying, which emitted a poisonous breath and turned the air to flame; and he made it come out of a dark and jagged rock, belching forth venom from its open throat, fire from its eyes, and smoke from its nostrils, in so strange a fashion that it appeared altogether a monstrous and horrible thing; and so long did he labour over making it, that the stench of the dead animals in that room was past bearing, but Leonardo did not notice it, so great was the love that he bore towards art.[47]

Caravaggio also studied live animals in the process of creating his own monster, but otherwise his *Medusa* could hardly have been more different to that described by Vasari. Leonardo's painting sounds complicated and full of circumstantial detail, conjuring up rocks and crags, a theatrical entrance on the part of the monster, and even the air itself thick with fire and smoke, just the sort of picture that mirrored his restless mind. By contrast, the brilliance of Caravaggio's *Medusa* reflects the painter's remorseless pursuit of a realist conceit. Leonardo had painted a picture of the Medusa that seemed wittily appropriate as the decoration of a shield. Caravaggio did something bolder and conceptually far more pure. He created a painting that sought to transcend painting and become the very thing that it depicts. His *Medusa* is not a painting *of* a shield, or at least it pretends not to be. It pretends to *be* the shield itself, held in Perseus's hand at the very instant when he has killed the Medusa. It is a painting meant to be admired at close quarters, passed round from hand to hand. To look at the picture thus would be to *become* the conquering hero himself – to gaze, through his eyes, at the reflection of the Medusa, as she in turn watches herself die, in her own reflection, in the shield's mirror.

The best way to grasp the true nature of Caravaggio's illusion – to complete the circle of gazes demanded by the painter's conceit – would indeed be actually to hold it. Did Ferdinando de' Medici do just that, and smile at the ingenuity of Caravaggio's idea? Certainly, the sense that this was not a picture like other pictures, a picture simply to be hung on a wall, persisted among later generations of the Medici. An inventory of the family's armoury from 1631 reveals that it was displayed as part of a suit of armour arranged to look like a standing knight at arms. It was brandished by the figure, in fact, just like a real shield.

Caravaggio's *Medusa* was designed to transform its owner into Perseus himself. To give such a picture to a Medici was to pay him a comfortingly familiar compliment. The Perseus myth had been assimilated into the mythology of Medici power in the middle years of the sixteenth century, when the family had assumed absolute control over what had once been the Florentine republic. Benvenuto Cellini's chillingly persuasive, larger-than-life bronze of *Perseus*, brandishing a scimitar and holding up the Medusa's head, was a public symbol of Medici might – a vivid demonstration of exactly what would happen to anyone with the temerity to resist Medici rule. Caravaggio's

Medusa, reviving those old associations with the lightest of touches, is a clever piece of praise as well as a virtuoso work of art.

But its biggest compliment of all is paid implicitly to the painter himself. He it is who personifies the Medusa, the monster who might be defeated but whose magical powers, none the less, loom larger than anything else in her legend. With eyes wide open and mouth agape, the painter takes on her role and in doing so claims for himself her dark powers of enchantment. Whomsoever the Medusa looks at, she freezes, preserving them forever in a single, charged instant of being. From the flux of life she takes a moment and makes it last for all time. That is what Caravaggio does too. Her magic is his magic, a petrifying art.

IN THE LABORATORY
OF THE ALCHEMIST

Sometime around 1599 del Monte invited Caravaggio to his villa near the Porta Pinciana and commissioned him to decorate the ceiling of the Tesoretto, a narrow, rectangular room next to the distillery where the cardinal conducted his alchemical experiments. A hidden, private space, it is reminiscent of the *studiolo* of Francesco de' Medici in the Palazzo Vecchio in Florence, a chamber like a jewellery box, which had been richly decorated in the Mannerist style by Giorgio Vasari and his assistants in the late 1560s. Francesco de' Medici himself appears in one of those paintings, in the character of an alchemist. Although Caravaggio did not actually paint Cardinal del Monte surrounded by his phials and retorts, he did create a kind of portrait of the alchemically inclined mind. *Jupiter, Neptune and Pluto* is a wall painting but it was executed in the unusual and fugitive medium of oil on plaster, which strengthens the suspicion that Caravaggio had never learned to paint in fresco, despite his supposed apprenticeship to Peterzano. The picture, which is still *in situ* and in surprisingly good condition, was first described by Bellori:

> In Rome in the Ludovisi Gardens near the Porta Pinciana, they attribute to Caravaggio the *Jupiter, Neptune and Pluto* in the casino of Cardinal del

Monte, who was interested in chemical medicines and adorned the small room of his laboratory, associating those gods with the elements and with the globe of the world placed in their midst. It has been said that Caravaggio, reproached for not understanding either planes or perspective, placed the figures in such a position that they appear to be seen from sharply below, so as to vie with the most difficult foreshortenings . . .[48]

For the first and last time Caravaggio flirted with out-and-out Mannerism.[49] The picture's primary function might almost be, as Bellori insinuates, to demonstrate difficulties triumphantly overcome. The plunging perspective is of a type known as *di sotto in sù*, literally meaning 'of above, from below', executed here with light-hearted bravado. Jupiter, mounted on an eagle, reaches a hand into the translucent celestial sphere at the centre of the ceiling's painted sky. The frowning figure of Neptune, mounted on a rearing seahorse, is yet another of Caravaggio's self-portraits.[50] The most dramatically foreshortened figure is that of Pluto, whose carefully painted penis is uncircumcised and surrounded by a dark bush of pubic hair. The Mannerist painter Giulio Romano had painted a similarly vivid *di sotto in sù* depiction of male genitalia – the undercarriage of a flying charioteer – in his mid sixteenth-century decorations of the Palazzo del Te in Mantua. Caravaggio's bawdy fantasy of airborne larking about belongs squarely in the same tradition.

There is an allegorical alibi for the emphatic phallus. The overarching theme of the painting is the procreative role of the three elements. From their seminal confluence, everything in the known universe depends. The picture reflects a particular twist in sixteenth-century alchemical theory. During the middle years of the century, the card-playing astronomer Gerolamo Cardano had proposed a revision of the ancient Aristotelian belief in the four elements of Fire, Air, Water and Earth. Cardano argued that fire should not properly be regarded as an element, thereby reducing their number to three. Caravaggio followed this refinement, presumably advised by del Monte.

Michelangelo had made dramatic use of *di sotto in sù* perspective for his depictions of *God Separating Light and Darkness, God Creating the Sun and Moon* and *God Calling Forth Life from the Waters* on the ceiling of the Sistine Chapel. The subject of Caravaggio's painting for del Monte is, in essence, a profane version of the same story, told at the start of the Book of Genesis. Caravaggio's use of the same device may have been his way of mischievously pointing up the parallel between the most famous cycle of religious frescoes in all of Rome and his own, rather more playful ceiling decoration.

Caravaggio was always highly responsive to circumstance and milieu. Throughout his life, his art would be deeply coloured by the different social, political and religious environments that he encountered. Entering the circle of Cardinal del Monte, living in his palace, absorbing his ideas, listening to his musicians, looking at his art collections – those experiences are all clearly reflected in Caravaggio's paintings of the late 1590s. His work becomes more sophisticated, and more intellectually rarefied. Certain details, such as the exquisite wine glass held up by Bacchus, with its delicately blown stem and the whirlpool patterning of its shallow bowl, express his palpable delight in a previously unknown world of beauty and luxury.

The work of this period is also marked by a spirit of experiment. The artist is trying out new ideas and striving to impress, so much so that he occasionally paints against the grain of his own dark and intense personality. The mythical Mannerist comedy of *Jupiter, Neptune and Pluto* would not be repeated. But the fact that Caravaggio was prepared to undertake a commission so alien to his own sensibility demonstrates his determination to succeed.

Away from his painting room, and away from the company of Cardinal del Monte, Caravaggio was still the same turbulent young man who had committed nameless misdeeds in Milan. Those who knew him at this time thought of him as a person split asunder, a man who contrived to live two opposing lives. Karel van Mander, a Dutch painter in Rome, described him as a piece of living chiaroscuro:

There is . . . a certain Michelangelo of Caravaggio who is doing remarkable things in Rome . . . he . . . has risen from poverty through his industry and by tackling and accepting everything with farsightedness and courage, as some people do who refuse to be held down through timidity or through lack of courage but who advance themselves candidly and fearlessly and who boldly pursue gain – a procedure which, if it is taken in honesty, in a proper manner, and with discretion, deserves no censure. For Fortuna will offer herself by no means frequently of her own accord; at times we must try her, prod her, and urge her ...

But again there is beside the grain the chaff, to wit that he does not pursue his studies steadfastly so that after a fortnight's work he will swagger about for a month or two with his sword at his side and with a servant following him, from one ball-court to the next, ever ready to engage in a fight or argument, with the result that it is impossible to get along with him. All of which is wholly incompatible with our Art. For certainly Mars and Minerva have never been the best of friends. Yet as regards his painting, it is such that it is very pleasing in an exceedingly handsome manner, an example for our young artists to follow ...[51]

Caravaggio lived his life as if there were only Carnival and Lent, with nothing in between. His pictures are the legacy of his lenten days. To encounter his carnivalesque alter ego it is necessary to consult the records preserved in the labyrinthine vaults of Rome's Archivio di Stato: a paper city within the city of stone, made up of witness statements and accusations. Through smokescreens of rumour, denial and furtive insinuation, this other figure comes clearly into view, accompanied by his friends, his lovers and his enemies.

PAINTERS, SWORDSMEN AND WHORES

On 11 and 12 July 1597 three men were summoned to appear before the Tribunal of the Governor of Rome and interrogated in connection with a case of assault. It was literally a cloak-and-dagger affair. A young man called Pietropaolo, apprentice to a barber-surgeon, had been hurt in a fight on the Via della Scrofa. Following the incident, he had been detained in prison because he refused to reveal the identity of his attacker. Violent crime was on the increase in Rome and steps were being taken to limit the unlicensed bearing of arms. Pietropaolo's silence irked the authorities. They were also interested in the discovery of a black cloak near the scene of the crime. Someone had handed it into the barber's shop where the apprentice worked. Who was that person? Might he be able to shed light on the matter?

The investigators would soon discover that the man who found the

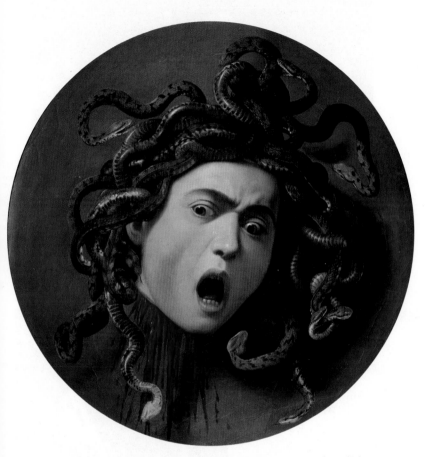

20. *Medusa*. 'Whomsoever she looks at, she freezes. From the flux of life she takes a moment and makes it last for all time. That is what Caravaggio does too. Her magic is his magic, a petrifying art.'

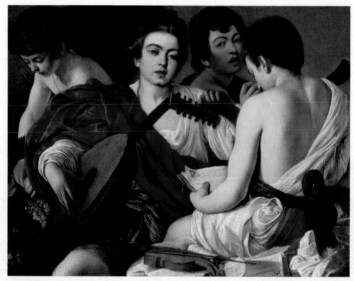

21. *The Musicians*. By painting a rehearsal instead of an actual performance, Caravaggio went behind the scenes of the traditional concert picture.

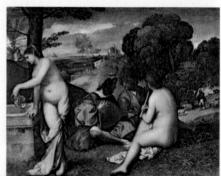

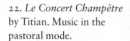
22. *Le Concert Champêtre* by Titian. Music in the pastoral mode.

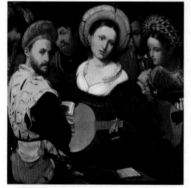

23. *Concert* by Callisto Piazza. Music as erotic stimulus.

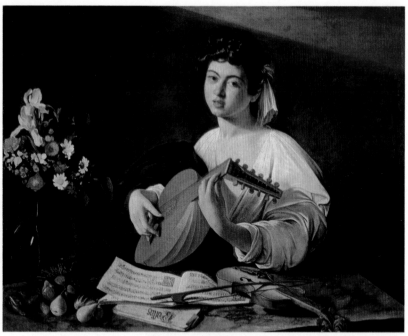

24. *The Lute Player*. This may be Pedro Montoya, a castrato favoured by del Monte. His swollen cheeks are consistent with the hormonal effects of castration.

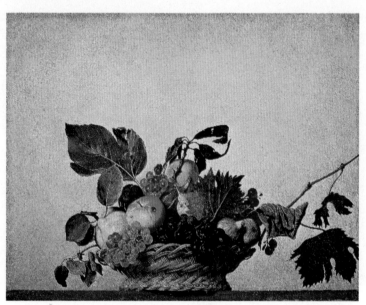

25. *Basket of Fruit*. Caravaggio's only surviving pure still life painting.

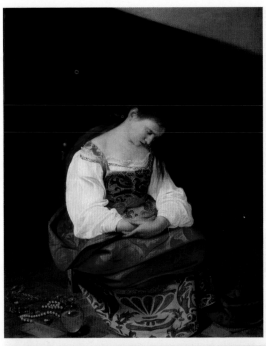

26. *The Penitent Magdalen.* In a paroxysm of repentance, she has torn off her gold and her jewels and scattered them on the ground. By seating the Magdalen so low, Caravaggio emphasized her humility.

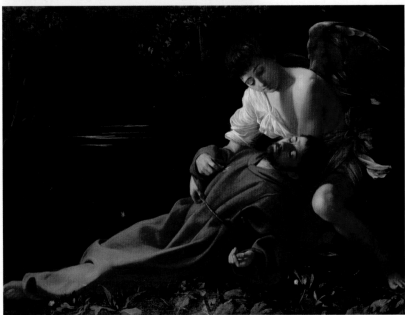

27. *St Francis of Assisi in Ecstasy.* 'The picture offers a consoling dream of transfiguration, a condition of oneness with Christ.' It seems to be a self-portrait.

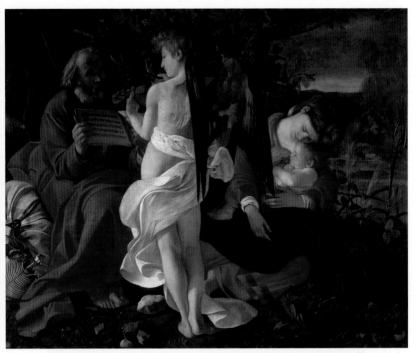

28. *The Rest on the Flight to Egypt.* A scantily draped adolescent angel stands between Mary and Joseph. Caravaggio borrowed the figure from a composition by Annibale Carracci (below).

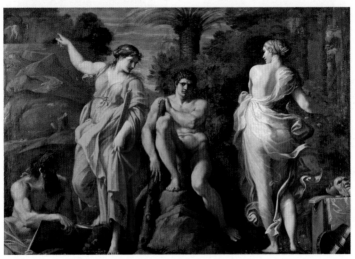

29. *The Judgement of Hercules* by Annibale Carracci.

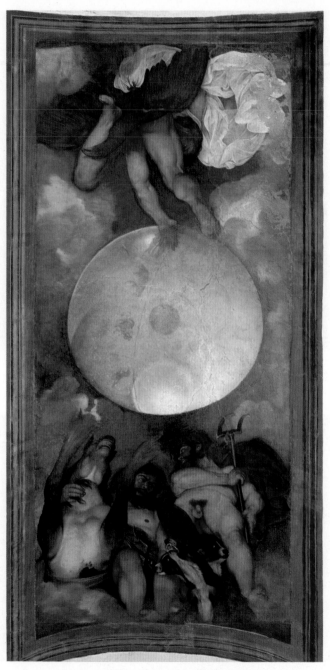

30. *Jupiter, Neptune and Pluto*. Decorations for the ceiling of del Monte's alchemical laboratory, in his house near the Porta Pinciana.

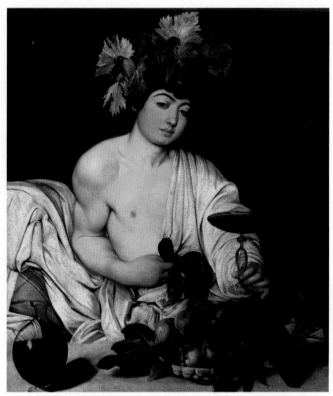

31. *Bacchus*. The model for Caravaggio's second depiction of the god of wine was probably his Sicilian friend and fellow painter, Mario Minniti.

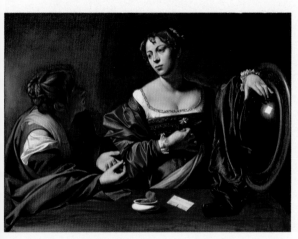

32. *Martha and Mary Magdalen*. Fillide Melandroni, not so penitent courtesan, modelled for the Magdalen. Her friend Anna Bianchini possibly sat for the figure of Mary's sister Martha.

33. *St Catherine.* Fillide also posed for this depiction of the Christian martyr Catherine. 'She leans towards the wheel and its vicious spikes of grey steel as if leaning towards a lover.'

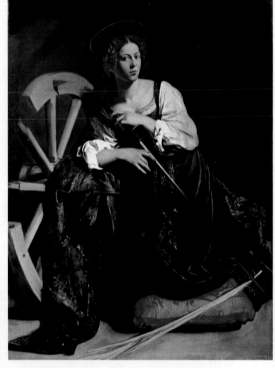

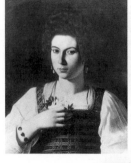

34. *Portrait of Fillide Melandroni.* She kept this portrait with her until her death. It later passed into the German national collections and was destroyed by fire during the Second World War.

35. *Judith and Holofernes.* Fillide once more, frowning with concentration as she plays the part of the Old Testament biblical heroine beheading a tyrant.

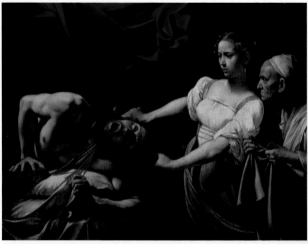

cloak was Michelangelo da Caravaggio, artist in the service of Cardinal del Monte. Because he had friends in high places, they decided not to call him until their preliminary enquiries were complete. Instead, they called two of the friends with whom he had been seen on the evening of the fracas, namely Prospero Orsi, the painter of grotesques, and the picture-dealer Costantino Spata. In the event, Caravaggio himself never would be asked to testify in connection with the case. But the words of those who were summoned give us vivid glimpses of the life that he led, at night, in the streets of Rome.[52]

It is with the testimony of Pietropaolo's employer, a barber-surgeon called Luca, that the case records begin. 'I am a barber, and I practise the profession of barber here by the church of Sant'Agostino,' Luca told the court. What did he know about the article of clothing that had been handed into his shop? Luca answered that a *ferraiuolo* – a black cloak, fastened with iron hooks – had been given to his apprentice, Pietropaolo, on the night in question. Luca himself was busy having dinner with his father and some others, but later Pietropaolo showed him the cloak and told him that a certain painter had brought it. 'He told me his name, but I can't remember it.' When pressed to say if he knew the painter in question, Luca said that certainly he did: 'One time he came into my shop to be spruced up, and another time he came to have a wound dressed . . . he had been in an argument with one of the grooms of the Giustiniani or Pinello families.'

When the case investigator expressed scepticism that Luca could not remember the man's name, he protested that it was the truth: 'Really, sir, I do not recall it.' Then, as if ashamed of his own memory lapse, he gave a startlingly precise physical description of the painter whose injuries he had treated, and whose beard he had trimmed. All is carefully transcribed in the spidery handwriting of a court notary. Suddenly here is Caravaggio, caught in the flashbulb glare of a barber's memory: 'This painter is a stocky young man, about twenty or twenty-five years old, with a thin black beard, thick eyebrows and black eyes, who goes dressed all in black, in a rather disorderly fashion, wearing black hose that is a little bit threadbare, and who has a thick head of hair, long over his forehead.'

Returning to the matter of the lost-and-found cloak, Luca remembered Pietropaolo telling him that another man had been present when it was handed in – 'a certain Costantino, who buys and sells paintings and whose shop is attached to the Madonella next to San Luigi dei Francesi'. All this happened shortly after Pietropaolo had been assaulted, and the fact that he was looking after the shop suggests that he cannot have been very badly injured. Luca made no mention of his apprentice's wounds. Instead, he stressed that the cloak had never belonged to his apprentice in the first place. He probably hoped the whole investigation would come to nothing, so that normal business could be resumed.

Costantino Spata was the next witness called by the court. 'I am a seller of old paintings and I have a shop at San Luigi,' he declared. He had been there for four years, since 1593, always on the same premises. He lived over the shop with his wife, Caterina Gori, and their four children, two adolescent girls and two little boys. The boys went to school, to the '*Letteratura*'. Costantino had no assistant and he did not employ members of his family in the business, so when he went out the shop was closed.

Having established these particulars, the investigator asked him to recall the events of the previous Tuesday evening, the night of the fracas. Costantino said that, having been in his shop all day, he closed up at sunset, when the *Ave Maria* sounded. Just as he did so, two painters whom he knew walked by.

> One of them was Monsignor Michelangelo from Caravaggio who is the painter of Cardinal del Monte, and lives in the house of the said cardinal, and the other was a painter called Prospero, who comes from I know not where but lives near Monsignor Barberini over a boarding house . . . he is of small stature, with a little black beard, and is around twenty-five to twenty-eight years old. They asked me if I had eaten and I said yes but they said they hadn't eaten and wanted to go to dinner at the Tavern of the Wolf ['*all'hostaria della Lupa*'], where we all went together, and I stopped there with them while they ate.

After dinner the three companions left the tavern. Moments later, the trouble erupted. 'We all heard someone coming towards us from the Piazza San Luigi, yelling out and saying "ahi, ahi".' Caravaggio and Prospero headed off in the direction of Sant'Agostino, while Costantino hurried homewards. As he was walking, a running man passed him. For the rest of his testimony, Costantino stonewalled the investigators. He never really saw the man who was in such a hurry. He could not judge his height or make out how he was dressed. He could not even tell if he had a cloak, or if he was wearing a hat on his head. He did not see if either of the painters had picked up a cloak. He did not have his glasses with him, and without his glasses he could not see very well. Besides, it was dark.

Prospero Orsi, the last witness to be called, corroborated Costantino's story. He also went into more detail about Caravaggio's decidedly marginal involvement in the evening's events. Half an hour before the sounding of the *Ave Maria*, Prospero recalled, Caravaggio had come round to his place. They had gone out to eat. After dinner, they were walking along the Via della Scrofa when they heard shouts coming from the Piazza San Luigi – 'screams and laments, someone saying "ohime, ohime" and other words'. But because they were still some way off, because it was getting dark and there was very little street lighting, Prospero could not really see what was going on. Moments later a man sprinted past him. What did he look like, this man? 'Sir, I cannot say who that man was. I didn't see his face, I didn't see his clothes, because he passed like a shadow.'

After the man ran past them, Prospero and Caravaggio carried on walking in the direction of the Pantheon. They came across a black cloak lying on the ground. Prospero didn't touch the cloak, so he could not say of what material it was made. Caravaggio picked it up and said he would give it to a neighbour. With those words, he turned around and went back to the corner of Sant'Agostino and gave the cloak to a young man at the barber's shop there. 'I don't know the young man's name because I don't go to that barber's shop,' Prospero added. The two artists wandered back towards San Luigi dei Francesi, where they bumped into Costantino again. He was closing his shop for the night. Prospero parted with Caravaggio at the Palazzo Madama and went home. The investigator enquired whether any of the parties involved had been bearing arms. 'Costantino and I were not carrying weapons of any kind,' Prospero said. But Caravaggio was wearing a sword. 'He is the only one to carry a sword, because he is in the service of Cardinal del Monte. Before he used to carry it by day. Now he only carries it sometimes when he goes out at night.'

Caravaggio's remark that he would give the cloak to 'a neighbour', and his immediate decision to hand it in at Luca's shop, indicate that he (unlike his conveniently short-sighted and confused friends) had immediately recognized the running man. Caravaggio knew that it was Pietropaolo, because he himself went to the barber-surgeon's shop on the corner of Sant'Agostino.[53] He assumed the cloak was his and took it straight to the apprentice's place of work – only to find that Pietropaolo had run so fast that he was there to receive it himself.

The enquiry was dropped and the case was closed, unsolved. It was a trivial matter. But the testimonies of those involved, fragmented and confused, reveal much about Caravaggio and the milieu in which he moved. He might have gone up in the world, but he had not forgotten his old friends. He still kept company with Prospero Orsi, who had pushed him to leave the Cesari workshop, and with Costantino Spata, the hard-pressed picture-seller with many mouths to feed. Taking advantage of his newfound status as member of a cardinal's household, Caravaggio was now carrying a sword openly in the streets of the city. He was not afraid to use it. He had been to the barber-surgeon's at least once, to have his wounds dressed, following a fight with a groom attached to another noble Roman household. History does not relate whether the groom's injuries were worse than his.

The barber-surgeon's account of Caravaggio's physical appearance closely matches descriptions of the painter in other early sources. Bellori, echoing Vasari's idea that artists resemble their own work, wrote that 'Caravaggio's style corresponded to his physiognomy and appearance; he had a dark complexion and dark eyes, and his eyebrows and hair were black; this colouring was naturally reflected in his paintings . . . driven by his own nature, he retreated to the dark style that is connected to his disturbed and contentious temperament.'[54] Bellori's Caravaggio is the epitome of the melancholy artist, born under the sign of Saturn: dark looks, dark temperament, dark art. But the evidence of the criminal archive suggests a more literal explanation for Caravaggio's sartorial style. People who went dressed in dark colours did so to avoid detection, especially at night. To describe a man as someone who wore black when the *Ave Maria* sounded was to mark him out as a trouble-maker. Like the dark cloak that may or may not have belonged to Pietropaolo, Caravaggio's black clothes were a form of urban camouflage, designed to enable him to disappear into the poorly lit streets of the city at night. He pursued the same strategy on the streets as he did in the studio. In life as in art he hid what he wanted to hide in the shadows.

Bellori also confirmed Luca's description of the 'disorderly' and 'threadbare' state of Caravaggio's clothing. But he added an interesting twist to it. 'We cannot fail to mention his behaviour and his choice of clothes, since he wore only the finest materials and princely velvets; but once he put on a suit of clothes he changed only when it had fallen to rags.' Caravaggio was one of those who liked to play the gentleman, to put on airs and graces and set himself above the people at large – even though his actual status remained highly ambiguous.

So the dark, threadbare Caravaggio was wearing a sword by night in 1597. He was evidently still doing so in spring of the following year: on 4 May 1598 he was arrested for bearing arms in a public place at eleven o'clock at night. A certain lieutenant Bartolomeo, attached to the Bargello of Rome, reported that 'I encountered Michelangelo da Caravaggio between the Piazza Navona and the Piazza Madama, carrying a sword, without a licence, and also a pair of compasses, so I took him and put him in prison at the Tor di Nona.' The following day, after a night in jail, Caravaggio was in court. Asked to account for his actions, he replied with righteous indignation. 'I was arrested last night . . . because I was carrying a sword. I carry the sword by right because I am Painter to Cardinal del Monte. I am in his service and live in his house. I am entered on his household payroll.'[55] Unusually, the notary transcribing the day's evidence capitalized the word 'painter', perhaps in an attempt to capture the self-important stress that Caravaggio had placed on the word. Because he had such powerful contacts, the magistrate had no choice but to release him. The case was dismissed.

Joachim von Sandrart, a German etcher and art historian, wrote a brief account of Caravaggio's life that contains a short but telling paragraph about the painter's years in Rome. According to Sandrart, Caravaggio liked to go about 'in the company of his young friends, mostly brash, swaggering fellows – painters and swordsmen – who lived by the motto *nec spec, nec metu*, "without hope, without fear".'[56] A number of those friends can be identified from contemporary sources. Prospero Orsi and Costantino Spata seem to have been among his more peaceable companions. Caravaggio's Sicilian friend, the painter and occasional model Mario Minniti, must also be included. He was no stranger to violence but he lacked Caravaggio's positive relish for it. According to his biographer, Francesco Susinno, Minniti was close to Caravaggio during his early years in Rome but eventually abandoned him; 'he settled down and got married, because he found the turbulent adventures of his friend too much to stomach.'[57]

Orazio Gentileschi was among the more volatile 'painters and swordsmen' with whom Caravaggio kept company. Orazio was a gifted artist in his own right, but a difficult man with a short temper, whose reputation was under a cloud. In 1615 Grand Duke Cosimo II of Tuscany – son and heir to Cardinal del Monte's patron, Ferdinando de' Medici – considered bringing Orazio to Florence as an artist and asked his agent in Rome, Piero Guicciardini, to file a report on the painter's character. The resulting reference was less than favourable: 'he is a person of such strange manners and way of life and such temper that one can neither get on nor deal with him.'[58]

Some ascribed the fiery temperament of painters to the toxic qualities of the materials that they used. Lead white and vermilion were particularly poisonous. The mere touch or smell of either might cause a variety of symptoms including depression, anxiety and increased aggressiveness. Those suffering from 'Painter's Colic', as it was called, also tended to drink heavily. While wine alleviated some symptoms, it exacerbated others, and was itself the catalyst for innumerable brawls and scraps in the artist's quarter. Most of the people around Caravaggio were involved in some kind of violent incident at one time or another. Orazio Gentileschi's own daughter, Artemisia, herself a painter, was raped by another artist. His name was Agostino Tassi. The enraged Orazio subsequently accused Tassi of 'repeatedly deflowering' his daughter. Artemisia's matter-of-fact testimony, given at Tassi's trial on 9 May 1611, gives a very clear view of the real violence that stalked the lives of so many of Caravaggio's contemporaries.

Artemisia told the court that she was with her sister, Tuzia, when the attack took place:

After midday dinner the weather was wet and I was painting a portrait of one of Tuzia's children for my own pleasure, when Agostino came by. He was able to get inside because there were masons in the house and they had left the door open. When he found me painting he said, 'Not so much painting, not so much painting,' and he took the palette and brushes out of my hand and threw them around, saying to Tuzia, 'Get out of here.' When I said to Tuzia to stay and not leave me with him as I had motioned to her before, she said, 'I don't want to stay and argue, I want to be off.' Before she left Agostino put his head on my breast and after she had gone he took me by the hand and said, 'Let us walk about a bit because I hate to be sitting down.' As we walked up and down the room some two or three times I told him that I felt unwell and that I thought I had the fever, and he answered, 'I have more fever than you,' and after walking up and down two or three times, each time going past my bedroom door, when we came to the door of the bedroom he pushed me inside and locked it.

Once it was locked, he pushed me on to the edge of the bed with one hand on my breast, and he put one of his knees between my thighs so that I could not close them, and he lifted my clothes, doing so with much difficulty. He placed one of his hands with a handkerchief over my throat and my mouth so that I could not scream ... and with his member pointed at my vagina he began to push it into me, having first put both his knees between my legs. I felt a terrible burning and it hurt me very much, but because of the gag on my mouth I could not cry out, though I tried as best as I was able to scream and call Tuzia. And I scratched his face and pulled his hair and before he could put it inside me again I grabbed his member so tightly that I even removed a piece of flesh. But none of this deterred him and he continued what he was intent upon, staying on top of me for a long time and keeping his member inside my vagina. And after he had finished his business he got off me.

Seeing myself free I went to the table drawer and took out a knife and moved towards Agostino saying, 'I want to kill you with this knife because you have dishonoured me.' And he opened his tunic saying, 'Here I am,' and I threw the knife at him; he shielded himself otherwise I would have hurt him and might easily have killed him. The outcome was that I wounded him slightly on the chest and he bled little because I

had scarcely pierced him with the point of the knife. Then the said Agostino fastened his tunic and I was weeping and lamenting the wrong he
had done me and to pacify me he said, 'Give me your hand and I promise
to marry you as soon as I am out of the mess I am in.' He also said to me,
'I warn you that when I take you as a wife I want no foolishness,' and I
answered him: 'I think you can see whether there is foolishness.'

One of the most persistent trouble-makers in Caravaggio's own
immediate circle was the architect Onorio Longhi. He was just two
years older than the painter and they had much in common. Onorio
was from Viggiù, near Varese in Lombardy, close to where Caravaggio
himself had been brought up. Longhi's family had links with the Colonna dynasty. Onorio's father, Martino, also an architect, had been
called to Rome to work for the Colonna family. After Martino's death
in 1591, Onorio took on the family architectural practice, overseeing
the completion of the church of Santa Maria in Vallicella in Rome,
among other significant commissions. In between, he found plenty of
time to get into trouble with the law. He was constantly in court,
charged with disturbing the peace and a variety of other offences.
G. P. Caffarelli, whose four-volume *The Families of Rome* was written
between 1603 and 1615, described Onorio as 'a little lawless leader for
the youth' (*'e un poco scapo scelerato per la gioventu'*).[59] He certainly
seems to have been the ringleader of the group or gang that included
Caravaggio. The architect and the painter were often seen together.
Longhi was brash and talkative and generally took the lead, while
Caravaggio tended to be more taciturn and veiled.

'I am a gentleman ... and I don't care about anything, I just go to
eat and drink.' That was how Onorio defiantly introduced himself in
a witness statement given in court on 4 May 1595.[60] Like Caravaggio,
he was all the more dangerous because he had connections with a
powerful household. As a *servitore* of the Colonna family, he too
could defy the general ban on carrying weapons issued by Pope Clement VIII. 'I don't carry a sword by day or by night,' Longhi declared in
a witness statement of 1595. 'Instead my servant, who accompanies
me, carries it.'[61] Two years earlier, in 1593, a prostitute named Margarita Fanella had testified that Onorio was armed at least part of the
time – 'sometimes yes and sometimes no I have seen him carry it [his

sword] in the street when he goes around with other gentlemen.' Also according to Margarita, 'he has a little blonde beard, that he grows quite thick ... he goes dressed in rich dark velvet.'[62] It comes as no surprise to learn that he too was one of those who dressed in black after the sounding of the *Ave Maria*.

One cause for his many court appearances was a festering dispute with his brother Stefano, which broke out into actual violence on more than one occasion. Onorio had been away when their father had died, and he believed that Stefano had failed to pay over his full share of the inheritance. In 1599 Onorio succeeded in having Stefano imprisoned for four or five months for non-payment of the debt. In the autumn of 1600 Stefano issued a counter-suit, in which he claimed that on 7 July 1598 Onorio had come to his lodgings with three armed companions, possibly including Caravaggio, and had tried to break down the door, shouting, 'You cuckolded thief, I want you to die by these hands!'[63]

That was by no means the only accusation levelled against Onorio. The investigators who looked into Stefano's counter-suit of 1600 also examined evidence linking him to a number of other unsavoury incidents. They were particularly interested in a long-standing grievance between Onorio and a certain widow called Felice Sillano. Under questioning, Onorio told them that he knew her and that she was a respectable woman. But he denied that he had once tried to beat her door down while shouting, 'You whore, you slut, you coward!'[64] That interrogation itself went back to an older, unresolved case. Another set of transcripts, from 1599, reveal that Felicita Silano (*sic*) had already sued Onorio – together with 'Claudio, the stone-cutter' – for threatening behaviour:

It is now two nights ago that the said Onorio came to my doors saying: 'Open, you baggage and slag.' Having left, he came back and wanted to kick down the door, threatening me with further insults. He said that if I spoke he would beat me over the head with his sword. This same Claudio came and did the same thing five or six months ago, inciting others, and particularly Onorio, to cause trouble at my door. I am not a woman to put up with such treatment, and therefore I am now bringing the matter before the court.[65]

The record of the outcome does not survive; probably, the case petered out.

One of Longhi's biographers said of him that 'he was naturally bizarre and had a head that smoked.'[66] The quarrel with his brother and the dispute with Felice Sillano were a fraction of his misdemeanours, which ranged from the extremely serious to the utterly trivial. He would be present when Caravaggio committed murder. But he was just as likely to be found getting into fights with passers-by who made the mistake of bumping into him in the street, or shouting insults at tradesmen for showing him insufficient respect. Case transcripts for 1595 record a scuffle in a cake-maker's shop, after he had gone in to buy 'a certain type of soft white meringue'.[67]

The violent words and deeds of Caravaggio and his contemporaries may now seem random and chaotic. In fact, the behaviour recorded in Rome's criminal archive conformed to a particular set of codes. To attack a woman's house, to threaten to break down her doors, was also to insult her honour, because, according to the mores of the time, people's dwellings represented the occupants themselves. A common way to cast aspersions on someone's name was to commit the crime of *deturpatio*: daubing paint – or sometimes excrement – on to the doors or windows of their home. In such cases the front of the house metaphorically represented the face. But the locked home also represented the human body, secure in virtue, hence Artemisia's emphasis, in her account of being raped, on the carelessness of the masons who had been working on her house. By insisting that it was they, not she, who had left the door open, she was emphasizing that Agostino's violation of her home and her body was none of her doing.

Even an act as apparently gratuitous as Longhi's attack on a maker of meringues had its own significance. It was Longhi's way of asserting that he was a *valent'huomo*, a cut above the common herd. Deportment books of the time encouraged gentlemen and aristocrats to cultivate a deliberate air of insolence towards the lower orders. In 1616 Giovanni Bonifacio published a manual on deportment entitled *L'arte de' cenni*, in which he argued that gesture and facial expression themselves amounted to a language as complex as that of human speech. Bonifacio devoted fifty-eight sections to the eyes alone, itemizing different types of wink and squint, differentiating between the promise of a raised eyebrow and the threat of a frown. He also went into some detail about the significance of the out-thrust elbow. To walk with arms akimbo gave the impression of strength, he noted, it being the demeanour of someone prepared to thrust through the mass of ordinary people, to 'push their way through crowds'.[68] Anthony Van Dyck captured this modishly insouciant arrogance in his portraits of swaggering English aristocrats at the court of Charles I. Van Dyck's portraits were painted in London in the 1630s and 1640s, but they evoke an aggressive air of sharp-edged hauteur that had been fashionable among 'gentlemen' throughout Europe for decades – the same style of threatening superiority that was being aped by men such as Onorio Longhi, and indeed Caravaggio himself, in Rome at the turn of the seventeenth century. They too were men who walked around with their elbows – and often their swords – out-thrust.

It would however be a mistake to regard Longhi as a simple thug. He was a man of learning, a poet as well as an architect, who used his literary skill to curry favour with the great and the good. When Ferdinando de' Medici's first son was born, Onorio marked the occasion with a witty poem full of satirical jibes against the Spanish. He associated with writers and musicians, as well as the likes of Caravaggio. Men working in the liberal professions, who could dream of rising through the social hierarchy, were attracted to the mock-chivalric ethos of his circle. Some of his companions were genuinely high-born, the sons of Rome's leading families. Others were simply out-of-work soldiers. Most lived around the Campidoglio, between the Piazza dei Sant'Apostoli and the Piazza Montanara.

But Longhi was also undoubtedly dangerous. Perhaps the most telling detail in descriptions of him in the archive is the fact that he often went around the streets of Rome on horseback, as if he were a knight and his servant were his page. Onorio and Caravaggio and those who ran with them – or against them – did not just copy the clothes and the manners of the aristocracy. They behaved like modern, debased versions of the 'veray parfit gentil knights' of the old romance tradition. Instead of wandering through the forests of Arthurian legend, doing battle with monsters and saving damsels in distress, they frequented the streets and taverns of Rome, picking fights with pimps and vying for the favours of whores.

This topsy-turvy translation of courtly manners and codes of honour, from high-flown literature to the most ordinary milieux of modern life, was by no means restricted to Italy. It became a *leitmotif* of seventeenth-century prose, poetry and drama across Europe. The misapplication of chivalric codes of honour to the circumstances of modern life is the great theme – the essential running joke – around which the whole of Cervantes's picaresque novel *Don Quixote* revolves. The Don might be aged, Sancho Panza fat and ridiculous, and they might inhabit a gentler and more absurd world than the Rome of Pope Clement VIII; but their escapades are none the less close parodies of the scrapes and adventures in which Caravaggio, Onorio Longhi and their companions were habitually embroiled. A man with a barber-surgeon's basin on his head is mistaken for a rival knight, and beaten by Don Quixote until he bleeds. The action takes place on a dusty road in provincial Spain – but events very much like it took place every day in Caravaggio's Rome.

Tommaso Garzoni's *Piazza universale* of 1585 includes a vivid characterization of Rome's ragged army of self-appointed knights errant, marauding through the city:

> Every day, every hour, every moment, they talk of nothing but killing, cutting off legs, breaking arms, smashing somebody's spine ... For study, they have nothing other than the thought of killing this or that person; for purpose, nothing more than to avenge the wrongs that they have taken to heart; for favour, nothing more than serving their friends by butchering enemies ...[69]

The author goes on to describe a day in the lives of such 'dregs-of-knaves ... scum-of-scoundrels'. Armed with an improbably extensive arsenal of weaponry, they sally forth into the city to do their worst. Despite, perhaps, some element of caricature, Garzoni paints a convincing picture of Caravaggio's life, as it must have been, during his Carnival months, when he would 'swagger about ... with his sword at his side ... ever ready to engage in a fight or argument'.

The day begins in the piazza and ends, more often than not, in the whorehouse:

> In the morning they get out of bed and straightaway pull on their hose, put jacket and breastplate on their back, hats on their heads, gauntlets

or hunting gloves on their hands, sword and dagger at their side, arquebus in a bag and its iron balls in their breeches. And thus, armed like St George, they swagger out of the house, make a circuit of the piazza and, with four companions, make themselves master of the field . . .

Then they go in a group to walk about the district, bullying everyone they meet, demanding the right of way, and with their plumes, whether black or white, they flutter fearlessly about, so that they will be taken for the boldest swordsmen on earth. Then they stop on a street corner and here, drawn up in a circle, they make fun of whoever passes, and mockingly salute whomever they like with their hats, deride the farmers, poke fun at the masters, and stop their servants by force . . . They also make it their custom to go out in the piazza and, as ruffians, stop to look at the peasant-girls and the countrywomen, whom they harass . . . Then they go to where the whores and procuresses are found: there they play a bit with Laura, strut about with Betta, and mess around with Rosa. With Cieca they have an argument, pinching a pair of clogs and taking away her shoes, or giving her some slaps on the head, pinching her buttocks, biting her breasts, and making her howl like a wretched bitch. On the way home they meet some other *bravi*, by whom they are punished as they deserve . . .

There is no written evidence to place Caravaggio in the company of any particular Laura or Betta, any Rosa or Cieca, but he was certainly friendly with a number of prostitutes, some of whom modelled for him. His favourite was a dark-eyed girl destined to become one of Rome's most famous courtesans. Caravaggio painted her portrait, perhaps in exchange for favours received, which she would bequeath to her richest lover and patron, a Florentine nobleman named Giulio Strozzi. It later passed into the collection of Cardinal del Monte's friend Vincenzo Giustiniani, in whose collection it was catalogued as 'a courtesan called Fillide', and eventually the work entered the collections of the Kaiser-Friedrich Museum in Berlin. It was destroyed during the Second World War, but black-and-white photographs survive. They show a smouldering beauty, in understated finery, with a look of wary self-possession about her. She could be a sister to Edouard Manet's hard-faced nineteenth-century whore *Olympia*. She clutches a posy of jasmine blossoms, symbol of erotic love, to her breast.

'Fillide' was Fillide Melandroni. The literary land of Arcadia was peopled with pure and innocent shepherdesses named Fillide (or Phyllida, as the name is often anglicized), but this was her real name. Someone, once, had dreamed of a bright future for her – her father perhaps, whose own name, Enea, conjured up the epic deeds of Aeneas recounted by the Roman poet Virgil.

Fillide was born in Siena, but in early adolescence she was uprooted to Rome. Her father had died when she was still young, so money was scarce. Her aunt Pietra was already waiting on tables in a taverna in the city; perhaps it was she who encouraged the family to move there in search of better prospects. Fillide made the journey with her mother, Cinzia, and her brother, Silvio. They arrived on a rainy day in February 1593, less than a year after the young Caravaggio had first come to the city. They shared their coach with the Bianchini family. Sibilla Bianchini had a son called Matteo and two daughters, Alessandra and Anna. Anna was the same age as Fillide.

The two families lodged together in the same house on Via dell'Armata. Close by was the church of Santa Caterina, patron saint of their home town, Siena. Not long after arriving in Rome, the two mothers, Cinzia and Sibilla, put their daughters to work as prostitutes. In April 1594 the two girls were arrested together for being out after curfew, on suspicion of soliciting. The investigating magistrates called them 'Donna Anna' and 'Donna Fillide', which made them sound more grown-up than they really were. They were fourteen and thirteen years old, respectively.[70]

Caravaggio painted his portrait of Fillide around 1598, by which time she was seventeen or eighteen, and when she and Anna Bianchini were still going around together. According to a witness statement made in that same year, Anna was 'smaller rather than bigger' and had 'long red hair'.[71] There is an outside possibility that she was the girl who modelled for *The Penitent Magdalen* and the sleeping Virgin Mary in *The Rest on the Flight to Egypt*.

Fillide first appears in a devotional painting of about 1598, *Martha and Mary Magdalen*, now in the collection of the Detroit Institute of Arts. The picture is badly damaged and of questionable quality: the brightly illuminated Magdalen is puffy and distorted and clumsily portrayed, giving her a pop-eyed appearance, but it is certainly by Caravaggio.

The painter shows the moment when the Magdalen, urged on by her sister Martha, forswears her life of harlotry. The shadowy Martha, viewed in half-profile, is another figure who may possibly have been modelled by Fillide's friend, Anna Bianchini. Like preachers of the time, Martha counts on her fingers the reasons to repent. But her sister has already decided to devote herself to God. Fillide as Mary Magdalen once again holds a flower to the bodice of her scarlet silk dress. This time it is not perfumed jasmine but orange blossom, symbol of purity. A gap-toothed ivory comb and a precariously propped-up convex mirror – probably the same convex mirror in which Caravaggio studied his own distorted features to paint the screaming *Medusa* – here symbolize worldly vanities renounced. The mirror also evokes the prophecy of St Paul: 'Now we see through a glass darkly, but then we shall see face to face' (1 Corinthians 13:12). Her mind has turned away from the things of this world, and towards the next.

The ring on the wedding finger of her left hand symbolizes her decision to embrace chastity and become a bride of Christ. The finger sticks out at an angle, as though dislocated or nerve-damaged. Another figure by Caravaggio for which Fillide modelled, that of the slightly later *St Catherine*, suffers from the same slight deformity of the same finger: Fillide must have had a damaged hand.

The painter could easily have disguised or corrected the flaw, but he chose to preserve it on both canvases. Why? The most likely explanation is that he intended it as an advertisement of his militant naturalism. To animate the old stories of Christianity, to make them seem as though taking place in the present day, he had developed his own unique method: he would systematically restage the sacred dramas, using real, flesh-and blood people, and paint the results. The crooked finger was there to call attention to the most distinctive aspect of his practices: his reliance on the study of actual models carefully posed in the stage setting of the studio.

Martha and Mary Magdalen was probably painted for Olimpia Aldobrandini.[72] The picture's subject may have reflected Olimpia's own charitable activities. Gregory Martin, an English Catholic priest who was in Rome in the 1580s, observed that a group of noblewomen had formed an association for the reform of whores. Regardless of their own safety, they would go into the Ortaccio di Ripetta, the 'evil garden', and plead with prostitutes to mend their evil ways: 'honest and wise matronnes of Rome ... match them selves with the famous or rather infamous and notorious sinful wemen of the citie, such as sometime Marie Magdalen was, and so by their wordes and behaviour and promises and liberality towards them, they winne them to honest life, and by Gods merciful hand working with exceeding charity they plucke them out of the deepe pitte of dayly fornication, as it were raysing dead stinking carcasses out of their graves.'[73] Perhaps Olimpia Aldobrandini was one of these modern-day Marthas. The reformed prostitutes were known as *convertite*, or convertites. 'These be therefore so called,' noted Martin, 'bycause they are converted from their naughty life, and of common whores and harlots made good Christian wemen ...'

'I'LL GET YOU NEXT TIME'

The young Fillide Melandroni could pose as the Magdalen, but actually it seems that repentance was the last thing on her mind. During the years when Caravaggio knew and painted her, she was often in trouble with the authorities, and not solely for prostitution. On 4 December 1600 a Roman court investigated an accusation of assault made against her and another courtesan, Tella Brunora. The litigant was a third prostitute, Prudenza Zacchia, who lived directly 'behind the monastery for the Convertites of the city'. All three of the women involved worked for the same pimp, a man called Ranuccio Tomassoni from Terni. Caffarelli, in *The Families of Rome*, described Ranuccio as 'a good young man, and good in his conduct', but others disagreed. Caravaggio, for one, would become his deadly enemy.

Ranuccio belonged to a family of soldiers and mercenaries with long-established links to the Farnese dynasty. One of Ranuccio's brothers, Giovan Francesco, had served with honour under the general of the pontifical army, Giovan Francesco Aldobrandini. Another brother, Alessandro, had fought in Flanders. Ranuccio himself never saw military service, although he often carried a sword in the evenings. His excuse was that he was in the service of Cardinal Cinzio Passeri Aldobrandini.[74] But his real job was running an unruly gang of prostitutes. If any of his girls' clients turned nasty, it was as well to be armed. As well as taking a cut of their earnings, he took payment in kind from those he favoured. This sometimes caused trouble, as an investigation of December 1600 revealed.[75]

Prudenza Zacchia was called first by the court. She had recently been charged with throwing a brick at an agent of the Governor of Rome, but this time she was the injured party. She claimed that Fillide and Tella had been conducting a vendetta against her:

> Your Honour should know that yesterday evening, at about the first hour of the night, the two accused came to look for me, and not finding me, they gave my mother several kicks, and went out. Nothing else happened yesterday evening. This morning I was in the house of Ranuccio, who lives at the Rotonda [i.e. next to the Pantheon]. The said Fillide, the accused, came to this said house and attacked me with a knife, which she had in her hand, and was restrained by Ranuccio. She came at me in every way, and gave me many blows, and tore off a lot of my hair. Then she left . . .
>
> Later I was in a downstairs room in my own house, when both of the accused arrived and entered the house by force. In coming in they gave my mother, who was at the door, a shove. The said Fillide came at me with a knife to disfigure me, and she hauled me up by the mouth to give me a scar. I defended myself with my hand, which she cut on the wrist and wounded me, as your Honour can see . . . and as soon as they saw that I was bleeding, they went with God. Later they went out again to have a go at me, and if they hadn't been restrained by certain gentlemen . . . they would have gone at me again. Then the said Fillide came up to the window, and started to taunt me, saying that she wanted to scar me all over. I am making a complaint about this . . .

Other testimony fleshed out the story. Geronimo Mattei told the court that he had been warming himself by the fire downstairs in Ranuccio's house earlier that morning. 'Ranuccio was in bed together with a woman called Prudenza Zacchia . . . and a woman called Fillide came into the house and ran upstairs to the said Ranuccio and Prudenza, and as soon as she saw the said Prudenza she began saying, "Ah, you slag, you baggage, there you are!" and at the same time she ran to the table and took a knife and went to the said Prudenza, saying, "Whore, I'm going to scar you everywhere."'

Geronimo intervened and took the knife from Fillide, but he could not prevent her from attacking Prudenza again. This time, 'she tore lots of hair from her head.' Later on, he told the court, 'I was passing by the said Prudenza's house, just behind the monastery of the Convertites, when Prudenza called out to me and showed me a wound in her hand, saying that Fillide and Tella had attacked her in her house, and that Fillide had taken a knife to scar her, and had wounded her in the hand . . .' It is not hard to imagine how Fillide might have acquired the bent and damaged finger of her own left hand.

There was one more witness, a man called Cesare Pontoni. He was a close friend of Ranuccio and Giovan Francesco Tomassoni, and often testified in cases where they were involved. He had witnessed only the last incident in this serial fracas. Cesare told the court that he was walking down the street when he saw Fillide shouting at Prudenza. Fillide was at the window of Tella's house, which was opposite where Prudenza lived. Prudenza was standing in her own doorway. 'You dirty whore!' Fillide screamed. 'I hurt your hand, when I wanted to stab you in the mouth, but I'll get you next time!' Moments later Fillide advanced on Prudenza with a stone in her hand, yelling, 'You dirty whore! I want to cut you! I want to cut you!'

The interpretation of the case is clear enough. Prudenza and Fillide were vying for Ranuccio Tomassoni's affections. Amongst the elaborate rituals of insult and injury, the crucial terms in the court documents are *sfregio* and the related verb *sfregiare*. Literally, a *sfregio* was a facial scar, but in the honour code of the time it also carried the figurative meaning of a serious affront to a person's reputation. When Fillide said, repeatedly, that she wanted to cut Prudenza in the face, she was expressing a desire to dishonour and shame her. She uttered her threats publicly because she wanted her intentions to be known in the public arena of the street – the theatre in which reputation was made and harmed. Prudenza repeated those threats in court for the same reason. To accuse someone of the intention to inflict a *sfregio* was to alert the law to a potentially serious offence.

In the event, the many threats of wounds to Prudenza's face seem not to have actually been carried out, perhaps because Fillide's main aim was to frighten her rival. If she had actually cut her in the mouth, or sliced off her nose – a not unheard-of tactic in the more extreme revenge assaults – Prudenza would have become damaged goods. That would not have pleased Ranuccio. The impression that emerges from the testimony is that, for all her apparent wildness, Fillide knew what she was doing and remained in control throughout. Probably because nobody was seriously hurt, the case seems to have come to nothing.

Caravaggio's name does not appear in the trial transcripts involving Fillide, Tella, Prudenza and Ranuccio, so these documents shed little direct light on the painter's future quarrels with the pimp. But they shed a good deal on the murky world in which both men moved. Ranuccio's contacts and alliances may also be significant. His family's patrons, the Farnese, were supporters of Spain against France, so the Tomassoni clan was closely connected with Rome's pro-Spanish faction. This was true of Ranuccio's friends too. Politics could have been one cause of bad blood between him and Caravaggio. But the artist's relationship with Fillide may have been another: a mere painter was hardly a desirable client for Ranuccio's most beautiful courtesan.

PAINTING FILLIDE

Fillide had been miscast as the virtuous heroine of *Martha and Mary Magdalen*, which is perhaps why that picture seems less than completely convincing. On two other occasions Caravaggio painted her more as the historical record suggests she truly was – tough, passionate, with a capacity for violence. Even though she only appears in devotional pictures, her presence in them tips the balance of his art from sacred to profane.

In 1598 or 1599 Caravaggio painted a startlingly sado-erotic *Judith and Holofernes*, with Fillide in the leading role. Like that of David and Goliath, the biblical story of Judith was a parable of underdog virtue triumphing over tyrannical might: the Jewish heroine of the tale seduces the ruthless Assyrian general and then slays him, with his own sword, in his tent. It was a subject that had been treated by many celebrated artists. Michelangelo had depicted Judith and her maidservant elegantly bearing aloft the tyrant's severed head, as his corpse writhed in darkness, in one of the four paintings at the corners of the

Sistine Chapel ceiling. The great Florentine Renaissance sculptor Donatello had created a famous bronze *Judith* in which the heroine hacks implacably at the neck of her victim. But even Donatello's stark and visceral image pales by comparison with Caravaggio's clinically violent conception of the subject.

Once again, the painter brought a scene from the biblical past into the world of his own time, but never before had he done so with such brutal, shocking immediacy. Sanctified execution in an Assyrian tent has become murder in a Roman whorehouse. The bearded Holofernes, lying naked on the crumpled sheets of a prostitute's bed, is a client who has made a terrible mistake. He wakes up to realize that he is about to die. Fillide pulls on his hair with her left hand, not only to expose his neck but to stretch the flesh taut so that it will part more easily under the blade. In her right hand, she holds the oriental scimitar – Caravaggio's one concession to historical accuracy – with which she has just managed to sever her victim's jugular. She frowns with grim concentration, as he screams his last, and as the blood begins to spray from the mortal wound in bright red jets. A theatrical swag of dark red drapery hovers directly above the act of murder.

Caravaggio has imagined the whole scene as a fantastically extreme version of the kind of violent incidents in which he and his companions were often embroiled. 'I want to cut you! I want to cut you!' Fillide would yell at her rival Prudenza. Here, the threat is fully carried out. The heroine's grizzled maidservant, readying herself to bag up the bloody trophy of a severed head, reinforces the impression that the action is indeed taking place in a darkened brothel somewhere in Rome. She is the stock figure of the procuress, the whore's wizened partner in corruption.[76] Caravaggio adds a sexual frisson to the thrill of bloody violence: beneath the diaphanous fabric of her tight-fitting bodice, Fillide's nipples are visibly erect. It is the sort of detail that Cardinal Paravicino may have had in mind when he made his remark about pictures that he 'would not have wanted to see from a distance'.

Judith and Holofernes divided Caravaggio's contemporaries. Annibale Carracci's succinct condemnation of the work encapsulated the reservations of all those who found Caravaggio's realism rude and indecorous. 'When pressed to speak his opinion on a *Judith* by

Caravaggio, he replied "I don't know what to say except that it is too natural."⁷⁷ Artemisia Gentileschi, by contrast, was fascinated by it. During the second decade of the seventeenth century, she made a name for herself by painting numerous versions of the same subject in a darkly tenebristic style directly modelled on Caravaggio's own. She gave an idiosyncratic twist to the theme by using it to take public revenge on the man who had raped her, painting herself as the sword-wielding heroine and Agostino Tassi as her victim.

In 1599 Fillide Melandroni appears once more in Caravaggio's art, as *St Catherine of Alexandria*. The masterpiece of his early career, it is another picture that simmers with violent sexuality. Less shocking than the *Judith and Holofernes*, but equally striking, it encapsulates the intense and powerfully inverted eroticism with which the Counter-Reformation Church infused the idea of martyrdom. The haloed saint is isolated in a bare, featureless, dark room illuminated by a single light source coming from the left. She kneels on a red damasked cushion and wears splendid robes of purple, to indicate her royal birth. The mood is intimate, suspenseful. She holds the viewer's gaze.

The saint is alone with the attributes decreed by her legend. A martyr's palm lies crosswise on the floor at her feet. Beside her is the spiked wheel on which the Roman emperor Maxentius had intended to break her body, painted from an ordinary Roman cartwheel of coarse-grained oak. (A section of it is broken, because God sent a thunderbolt to shatter it before it could be used on the saint.) The actual instrument of her death was a sword. Caravaggio, with the expertise of a swordsman, has furnished Fillide with a weapon appropriate to her sex – a light, thin, perfectly deadly rapier. He did not have such a sword himself, so he borrowed one. The hilt is so intricate that it must have been painted from a real example.

The picture's subject is a yearning for death so strong that it resembles sexual desire. The saint leans towards the wheel and its vicious spikes of grey steel as if leaning towards a lover. A fold of extraneous drapery has wrapped itself around the longest and darkest of the wheel's spikes. She caresses the pommel of the sword and runs a finger lovingly along its blood-groove. Death by the sword is her consummation. To be penetrated by its steel is to be married, forever, to Christ. Her face is flushed, her eyes excited.

The composition is austere, the forms monumental, the paint handled with a subtle brilliance. The soft-focus depiction of the muted drapery around the wheel-spike anticipates the work of Velàzquez, and in fact Caravaggio would rarely repeat such levels of virtuosity. But it is not hard to see why some of the artist's contemporaries might have been troubled by such a picture. Was it really a picture of St Catherine, rapt in the joyful embrace of death? Or was it just a picture of a sexy modern girl, with some studio props, alone in a room? In truth, it was both. Caravaggio's technique opened his art to ambiguity because it exposed the painter himself directly to reality. His responses inevitably coloured every image that he created, whatever its mythical construction might be. Caravaggio could turn Fillide into Mary Magdalen, into Judith, into St Catherine, but the transformation could never be absolute. After all, it was Fillide that he saw in the room, Fillide with her damaged hand, breathing softly and looking back at him, with her wide appraising eyes, as she tried to hold the pose.

By the end of the 1590s Caravaggio had invented a new style and a new approach to painting, and in the three pictures for which Fillide posed he arrived at something like a fixed, settled method. In some early works he had used a light ground, like other painters from Lombardy. But in these later paintings he used a dark ground and worked from dark to light, a technique that he may have seen for the first time in the art of Tintoretto. It suited him in a number of ways. A dark ground enabled him to focus only on the essentials of a scene, as he imagined it. Dark paint creates an illusion of deep shadow around the principal forms and therefore also does away with the need to paint background detail: Bellori, in his biography of the painter, noted that Caravaggio 'left the ground visible in the half-tones', meaning that in places he could model form simply by leaving the canvas in the unpainted state in which it had been prepared. (The technique is visible, for example, in the frame of the mirror in *Martha and Mary Magdalen*.) Caravaggio was fond of short-cuts and liked to work quickly, which suggests another reason behind his extreme tenebrism: quite apart from their expressive effect, pools of darkness, like visible ground, simply mean that there is less to paint.

Caravaggio's habitual impatience is manifest too in his frequent practice of working wet-in-wet rather than waiting for each layer of oil paint to dry. He was unique among the painters of his time in making no preparatory drawings for his pictures, preferring to block out his compositions directly on the primed canvas. Having posed his models, he often marked the exact positions of heads and other contours by making light incisions in the base layer of paint, presumably so that he could reset the models' positions after every break in the work. No other artist of his time used such incisions. Caravaggio's exceptional working procedure argues strongly for the hypothesis that he learned little from his master, Peterzano, and was largely self-taught.[78]

Caravaggio did not draw because his method of composition was essentially theatrical – proto-cinematic, it might be said, because lighting was also involved. He composed by staging scenes, or fragments of scenes, that he knitted together, collage-like, on his canvas, using shadow to mask the joins. The scenes involved objects, models, props. Fillide knelt on a real purple cushion, leaned against a real wheel and held a real sword while Caravaggio painted her. Sometimes, not surprisingly, the absence of preparatory drawing led him to make a mistake in posing his models: halfway through *Judith and Holofernes*, he realized that a head half severed would look more detached from the neck and trunk of the body than the head of his very alive model. X-rays show that he painted over the first head of Holofernes, reposed the man and painted him again to achieve the necessary degree of grisly separation.

Caravaggio's method also involved setting lights, or at least controlling illumination in some way. Joachim von Sandrart gave a short description of his technique, saying that 'as he wished to effect a more perfect roundness and natural relief, he regularly made use of gloomy vaults or other dark rooms which had one small source of light from above; so that the darkness, by means of strong shadows, might leave power to the light falling upon the model, and thus produce an effect of high relief.'[79] There is evidence of it in *Martha and Mary Magdalen*. The brilliant square of light reflected in the surface of the convex mirror is Caravaggio's 'source of light from above' made visible on the canvas. Bellori noted that Caravaggio began to work in this way at around the time that he painted the *St Catherine* and other pictures close to it in date, in 1598–9. His pictures from these final years of the sixteenth century 'have a darker colour', he observed, 'as Michele [*sic*] had already begun to darken the darks'.

Bellori went on to give his own account of how Caravaggio achieved his famously extreme contrasts of light and dark:

> the colouring he was introducing was not as sweet and delicate as before, but became boldly dark and black, which he used abundantly to give relief to the forms. He went so far in this style that he never showed any of his figures in open daylight, but instead found a way to place them in the darkness of a closed room, placing a lamp high so that the light would fall straight down, revealing the principal part of the body and leaving the rest in shadow so as to produce a powerful contrast of light and dark. The painters then in Rome were greatly taken by this novelty, and the young ones particularly gathered around him, praised him as the unique imitator of nature, and looked on his work as miracles.[80]

A BROTHERLESS MAN

Many of Caravaggio's pictures of the later 1590s look like demonstration pieces. Each new work shows a new difficulty overcome. But with the *St Catherine* of 1599 Caravaggio had reached a higher level of mastery and assurance. He painted the picture for del Monte, who had a special devotion to the martyr, probably because she was the patron saint of scholars. Perhaps this was the work that persuaded the cardinal that his protegé was ready for bigger commissions.

It was at this otherwise propitious time, for reasons unknown, that Caravaggio finally severed all links with his family. In 1594 his sister Caterina had married a 'maestro Bartolommeo Vinizzoni' – 'maestro' indicating that he was an artisan of some kind. Caravaggio had not attended the wedding. He had also been avoiding his brother, Giovan Battista, the priest, who was in Rome studying moral theology with the Jesuits from the autumn of 1596 to the winter of 1599. Before Giovan Battista went back to Lombardy, to be ordained as a subdeacon in the province of Bergamo, he decided to call on Caravaggio. Giulio Mancini tells the strange story of what happened when the two brothers met:

> Caravaggio had an only brother, a priest, a man of letters and of high morals who, when he heard of his brother's fame, wanted to see him and, filled with brotherly love, arrived in Rome. He knew that his brother was staying with Cardinal del Monte, and being aware of his brother's eccentricities, he thought it best to speak first to the Cardinal, and to explain everything to him, which he did. He was well received by the Cardinal, who told him to return in three days. He did so. In the meantime, the Cardinal called Michelangelo and asked him if he had any relatives; he answered that he did not. Unwilling to believe that the priest would tell him a lie about a matter that could not be checked, and that would do him no good, he asked among Caravaggio's compatriots whether he had any brothers, and who they were, and so discovered it was Caravaggio who had lied. After three days the priest returned and was received by the Cardinal, who sent for Michelangelo. At the sight of his brother he declared that he did not know him and that he was not his brother. So, in the presence of the Cardinal, the poor priest said tenderly: 'Brother, I have come from far away to see you, and thus I have fulfilled my desire; as you know, in my situation, thank God, I do not need you for myself or for my children, but rather for your own children if God will do you good as I will pray to His Divine Majesty during my services, as will be done by your sister in her chaste and virginal prayers.' But Michelangelo was not moved by his brother's ardent and stimulating words of love, and so the good priest left without even a goodbye.[81]

Mancini neither comments on the story nor explains it in any way. But the structure of his telling, which is like a fable, may contain clues about what he believed was going on. Three times Caravaggio is asked to recognize his brother, the priest, and three times he refuses him. Like St Peter denying Christ three times 'before the cock crows twice' (Mark 14:66–8), Caravaggio denies his brother, himself Christ's servant on earth. The implication is that religion, somehow, lay at the heart of the matter. Was Caravaggio ashamed to look his pious brother in the eye? Mancini may have thought so.

Ottavio Leoni drew a portrait of Caravaggio at around this time. He has the dark, dishevelled hair and bushy eyebrows described by Luca, the barber-surgeon. But it is his expression that seems most striking. His mouth is set and sullen. There is determination and truculence in his eyes, but there is sadness there too – a look of profound loneliness, and abandonment.

PART FOUR
Rome, 1599–1606

THE ST MATTHEW CHAPEL

For the priests at San Luigi dei Francesi, the Contarelli Chapel had been nothing but trouble. For years the chapel – the fifth one along on the left, in the national church of the French – had been little better than a building site. Not only did it make the church look bad, the priests complained, it was giving Rome's French community a bad name.

The saga had begun in 1565, when a French cardinal named Mathieu Cointrel (or Matteo Contarelli, as his name was Italianized) had paid a considerable sum to acquire the chapel, where he intended to be buried. Contarelli had already given generously during the construction of San Luigi dei Francesi, footing the bill for its fine marble façade, designed by Giacomo della Porta. But despite his best efforts his own chapel was still all but bare of decoration when he died in 1585.

The cardinal himself had contracted Girolamo Muziano, a competent but unexceptional painter, to paint frescoes on its two lateral walls and decorate its vault. Muziano had prevaricated for years, only to renege on the commission with almost nothing painted. In 1587 the executor of Contarelli's will, Virgilio Crescenzi, had commissioned a marble altarpiece from a Flemish sculptor, Jacques Cobaert. Crescenzi had also persuaded Giuseppe Cesari to fresco the walls and ceiling. Cesari had completed the frescoes on the vault by 1593, when Caravaggio was part of his studio, but he never got round to the rest because he was deluged by other assignments, including several from the pope himself. Meanwhile the sculptor, Cobaert, was said to be working away, although there was nothing to show for it. Thrilled by the importance of the commission, but paralysed by self-doubt, he toiled for years on what he hoped would be his *magnum opus*. His contract was renewed in 1596, yet as the end of the sixteenth century approached there was still no sign that he would ever actually deliver the work. Those close to him remarked that Cobaert was becoming ever more paranoid and secretive.

In 1597 the patience of the long-suffering priests had finally snapped. With the Jubilee year of 1600 fast approaching, they had sent a petition to the pope:

> Most Blessed Father, the French community of the Church of San Luigi in Rome ... humbly represents that the chapel ... founded in this church by the late Cardinal ... and provided by him with one hundred gold scudi per annum for two chaplains, has been closed for more than twenty-five years and is at present still closed. And if Your Holiness does not bring His authority to bear in the matter, there is a danger that the chapel will never be completed, because Signor Abbate Giacomo Crescenzi, the executor of the will of the above-named Cardinal since the retirement of his father Virgilio Crescenzi ... has not finished it and excuses himself on the grounds of difficulties with the sculptor, the painter and other things. Thus the soul of the deceased has been cheated of its masses and the church of San Luigi similarly cheated of the endowment which was destined for the chapel. All of this is a discredit to the divine service and a shame for the community, and it leads people to believe that the neglect is the fault of the community when they see the chapel continually boarded-up and closed while various other churches in Rome are constructed from their foundations up ... the heirs and sons of the Crescenzi, accumulating [revenues] year after year and day after day, have bought many and various offices in the Cancelleria, real estate and other things without doing anything which relates to the will of the testator and without even having anniversary services said for the soul of the deceased ...[1]

As a result of this tirade, Clement VIII ordered the Crescenzi to surrender Contarelli's legacy and entrusted responsibility for the chapel to the governing body of the Fabbrica di San Pietro – the works office of St Peter's. Giuseppe Cesari was approached again and asked to finish what he had begun, but he pleaded overwork. Del Monte, whose palace was directly opposite the church, followed these developments carefully. Del Monte was friendly with the Crescenzi family. He busied himself behind the scenes, pulled the right strings and somehow won the commission for Caravaggio, an artist as yet untried in the public arena of large-scale religious painting. 'With the support of his Cardinal he got the commission for the Contarelli chapel in San Luigi dei Francesi,' Baglione noted, with a touch of bitterness. On 23 July 1599 Caravaggio signed a contract with the two rectors of the church in which he undertook to complete the side panels for the chapel by the end of the year for a fee of 400 scudi.

It was a daunting challenge for a young and relatively inexperienced artist. So far Caravaggio had never painted a picture with more than four figures in it. None of his previous canvases had been more than four or five feet across. Suddenly, he would have to produce two monumental paintings, each more than ten feet in width and almost the same in height. He had, it is true, painted a number of devotional pictures, but he was known principally as a painter of genre scenes with a talent for still life. Now he was being invited to create complex religious narrative paintings. It was a chance to compete with the greatest artists of the past. But if it went wrong, Caravaggio's failure would also be very public.

The subjects of the two lateral pictures for the Contarelli Chapel had been prescribed by Cardinal Cointrel himself. He had wanted his burial chapel to be dedicated to St Matthew, his name saint, and so the two pictures on either side of the altar were to tell stories from the apostle's life. The painting on the left was to show Matthew, the tax collector, being summoned by Christ. That on the right was to show the saint's glorious martyrdom at the hands of a pagan assassin. Cointrel had also had very particular ideas about how these scenes might be depicted, which are reflected in the unusually circumstantial wording of an attachment to one of the contracts for the painting of the chapel:

For the St Matthew Chapel ... At the right side of the altar, that is, on the side of the gospel, there is to be a painting 17 palmi high and 14 palmi long in which is painted the same St Matthew in a store or large room used for tax collection with various items pertaining to such an office, with a counter such as tax collectors use, with books, and monies that have been received, or as shall seem best. From this counter St Matthew, dressed as a practitioner of his trade would be, should rise in order to follow Our Lord who passes along the street with his disciples and calls him to the apostolate; and the attitude of St Matthew should show the painter's skill, as should also the rest. On the left side, that is, of the epistle, there should be another painting of the same height and length as above in which is painted a long wide space in the form of a temple, with an altar raised up on the top of three, four, or five steps: where St Matthew dressed in vestments to celebrate the mass is killed by the hands of soldiers and it might be more artistic to show the moment of being killed, where he is wounded and already fallen, or falling but not yet dead, while in the temple there are many men, women, young and old people, and children, mostly in different attitudes of prayer, and dressed according to their station and nobility, and benches, carpets, and other furnishings, most of them terrified by the event, others appalled, and still others filled with compassion.[2]

The level of detail in these instructions shows how carefully painters had to tread in Rome at the end of the sixteenth century. In the event Caravaggio took artistic licence, but he remained faithful to the spirit of the patron's recommendations. None of the documentary sources specifies the medium in which the works were to be carried out, although such was the pre-eminence of fresco in the traditions of Rome's Christian art that its use was probably assumed. But frescoes must be painted *in situ*, the pigment applied directly to a fast-drying layer of wet plaster. The technique would have required Caravaggio to depart from his studio practice – the painting of live models posed in carefully controlled light conditions. Reluctant to abandon the procedures that had already won him admirers, Caravaggio purchased two large canvases and set to work in his usual way.

True to his method of transposing the biblical past to the present day, Caravaggio imagined *The Calling of St Matthew* taking place in a dingy room somewhere in modern Rome. Christ and St Peter have just entered the dim and plainly furnished office of Matthew, the tax-gatherer. Here they encounter five men, grouped around a table set close to a bare wall relieved only by a single window. The window's shutter is open, but little light penetrates through its four dull panes, which are made not of glass but of oilskin held in place by crossed strings. There are coins on the table as well as a moneybag, an open account book and an inkwell from which the stem of a quill pro-trudes. A transaction is taking place.

At the far end of the table, a young man sitting in a savonarola chair is absorbed in calculation. He is the taxpayer, who has settled his dues and is now receiving a small amount of change. His shoulders are hunched as he counts the meagre handful of coins before him and prepares to draw the money in. Directly behind him, a bespectacled old man wearing a fur-trimmed coat peers down at the table, as if to check that all the sums have been done correctly. Next to them sits Matthew himself, accompanied by his page, a round-faced boy who leans with friendly familiarity on his master's shoulder. Caravaggio's Sicilian friend, the painter Mario Minniti, posed for this figure. Oppos-ite sits another young man in fine page's livery, his striped black and white sleeves flashing and shimmering in the half-dark of the room. He is presumably the taxpayer's minder. Tradition has it that this fig-ure was also modelled by a painter, Lionello Spada. But the identifica-tion may be apocryphal, a flight of fancy inspired perhaps by the sword – *spada*, in Italian – that he wears at his side.

The biblical account of Matthew's election to the apostolate is terse in the extreme: 'And as Jesus passed forth from thence, he saw a man, named Matthew, sitting at the receipt of custom: and he saith unto him, Follow me. And he arose, and followed him' (Matthew 9:9). Caravaggio has painted the moment at the heart of this truncated nar-rative, when Christ has just spoken his simple two-word command. Matthew, at once astonished and compelled, points to his own chest as he gazes up into the eyes of the Saviour. There is incredulity in his expression and a question frozen on his lips: 'Who, me?' He con-tinues, absent-mindedly, to count out one last coin of the taxpayer's change, but he knows in which direction his destiny is taking him. He braces his legs, preparing to stand up and step into his new existence. The command is irresistible, its outcome inevitable. Christ fixes the tax-collector with a hypnotizingly intense stare. Even as he reaches out towards Matthew, he has already begun to leave the room. His bare feet, half hidden in deep shadow, are turned away from the com-pany of men back towards the outside world. In a moment he will have left, taking his new apostle with him. All has been done that needed to be done.

Matthew and his companions, grouped around the coin-strewn table, might almost be gaming in the tavern of the *Cardsharps*, painted for Cardinal del Monte five years earlier. The disconsolate man paying his taxes and raking back a pile of change looks like a gambler who has just won an annoyingly small pot. Indeed that was exactly what the seventeenth-century writer Joachim von Sandrart took him for, years after the picture was painted. 'Christ is represented in a dark room,' he wrote, 'which he has entered with two of His followers and finds the tax collector Matthew in the company of a gang of rogues with whom he is playing cards and dice, and sitting about drinking. Matthew, as if afraid, conceals the cards in one hand and places the other on his breast; in his face he reveals that alarm and shame which is the result of his feeling that he is unworthy to be called to the Apostolate by Christ. One of the other men takes his money from the table by sweeping it with one hand into the other, and attempts to sneak away; all of which seems true to life and nature itself.'[3]

Sandrart plainly failed to give the painting his full attention, but none the less his misinterpretation evokes a mood that Caravaggio intended to create. The tax-gatherer's office, with its basement gloom and its cast of mercenary characters, is a convincingly seedy den of iniquity. Christ brings light into this darkness, just as he brings illumination and divine purpose to Matthew's dreary, money-grubbing existence. The picture's main light source is high and to the right, to suggest daylight flooding in from above, perhaps through an open door and down a flight of stairs. It flashes on to the face of Matthew, along a diagonal parallel with the line traced by Christ's golden halo and his outstretched, spotlit, beckoning hand. It is the light of ordinary mundane reality, yet it is also the light of God.

The Calling of St Matthew is built on contrasts, and not only the contrast of light and shade. Whereas Matthew and his companions are dressed in foppish modern finery, Christ and the solemn, reproving figure of St Peter go barefoot and wear simple, timeless robes. They belong to a different time and place, and a different moral and spiritual universe. They might be an apparition or a dream, projected from the distant sacred past into a profane Roman present.

With *The Calling of St Matthew* Caravaggio was staking his claim to a place in the great Italian tradition of monumental religious painting.

He had the confidence to weave an overt reference to that tradition into the very fabric of his picture. The hand that Christ holds out to Matthew is a direct paraphrase of one of the most celebrated images of Michelangelo's Sistine Chapel ceiling, a detail appropriated from *The Creation of Adam* in which the animating finger of God reaches towards the languid hand of the first man. Yet it is the hand of Adam, not God, that Caravaggio has chosen to give to his own solemnly beckoning figure of Christ. This apparent homage to Michelangelo is actually a statement of Caravaggio's independence of thought, and the detail adds a subtly appropriate layer of meaning to the picture. Caravaggio's Christ becomes a second Adam, made in God's image but purged of sin, calling Matthew to his redemption: 'For as in Adam all die, even so in Christ shall all be made alive' (1 Corinthians 15:22).

The hand of Christ is not the only such allusion in the painting. The grouping of figures around the table has been calculated to resemble a profane version of the Last Supper. The young man counting his change, oblivious to the call of Christ, clutches a bag of money in his shadowed left hand. He is like Judas with his fifty pieces of silver. It is from the company of worldly Judases, to that of Christ the Saviour, that Matthew has been called.

The painting is poetical and metaphorical, although the piety of which it speaks is harsh, direct and forbidding. It also has a haunting quality, the character of a personal renunciation: in *The Calling of St Matthew*, Caravaggio revisited the world of his own early genre paintings, but only to consign that world to darkness. The picture was the artist's first public demonstration of his formidable naturalism, but it is less like a depiction of real life than a dream of escaping reality altogether, of being called away from a life of vice, suddenly and inexplicably, and summoned into the presence of God. Did Caravaggio himself dream of being chosen like this – of being rescued from his own unruly, imperfect nature?

The painter fought long and hard with the second of his pictures for the Contarelli Chapel, *The Martyrdom of St Matthew*. His struggle became common knowledge among the gossiping artists of Rome. Bellori, writing seventy years afterwards, knew enough to declare that Caravaggio 'did it over twice',[4] a claim confirmed when the picture was examined during conservation in 1966. X-ray photographs reveal the painter's aborted first composition, in which the bearded martyr stood before the altar, hands outstretched to protect himself from the assault of three armed men. As one of the assassins prepared to attack, another strode in from the side, sword at the ready. A third stepped in with his back to the viewer, as if entering the scene from directly in front of the picture. Shocked spectators looked on. In this initial attempt, the figures were considerably smaller than in the completed version. The architecture, square columns and pilasters with heavy cornicing, was correspondingly more prominent. The painter was perhaps struggling to depict the scene as it had been described in Contarelli's instructions: 'a long wide space in the form of a temple ... where St Matthew dressed in vestments to celebrate the mass is killed by the hands of soldiers'.

Unhappy with his first effort, Caravaggio painted it out and rethought his approach. Now he was determined to give his composition a focal point, to make an image that would be at once more monumental and more dynamic. He made two fundamental changes to the composition that had displeased him: he greatly increased the scale of the individual figures, and he reduced the number of executioners from three to one. The story of murder and martyrdom was in this way compressed to a single brutal act. In the finished work a snarling youth wields a sword over the prone figure of Matthew, who lies at the base of a simple stone altar. The saint, whose chasuble is splashed with blood, has already been wounded. The assassin grasps him by the wrist, subduing Matthew at the same time as turning his body towards him, the better to administer the *coup de grâce*. In the first version of the painting the killers had been represented as athletic youths stripped to the waist. In the final version the single assassin is nude save for a loincloth. A high, raking light falls on the scene, catching his pale skin and accentuating his musculature. It also catches Matthew's white vestments and his helpless upturned face.

Caravaggio's final composition resembles a centrifuge, with peripheral forms and figures seeming to fly off in all directions, driven away by the violence at the centre. On the right-hand side a statuesque altar-boy screams, open-mouthed. To the left several onlookers recoil, including two men in shadow. One raises his hands in a gesture of instinctive shock and revulsion, while the other simply stares, transfixed. Behind them two *bravi*, one armed with a sword and wearing a plumed hat, look back as they prepare to flee the scene. Two more distant figures, isolated against the darkness, have already taken flight. One is shown in half-profile while the other is shown in full-face, picked out by a sudden shaft of light. He turns back to stare at the killing, his eyes full of sadness, regret, guilt. His features are unmistakably those of Caravaggio himself.

The painter's treatment of the foreground was long regarded as a puzzle. To the right-hand side, two nearly nude figures huddle together on a fold of striped blanket. Opposite them, another reclining nude supports his weight on both hands while dangling his right leg into a dark area of void space. The near-nudity of Matthew's assassin might be explained by the fact that he is pagan, but why should these other figures be half naked in church at the celebration of Mass? It has been argued that they are no more than an expedient compositional device, and that their function is essentially to swell the small crowd of witnesses.[5] A more plausible explanation, advanced by Giovanni Urbani in his report on the cleaning of both Contarelli Chapel pictures in 1966, is that the nudes should be regarded as recent converts to Christianity who are about to be baptized.[6] The evidence suggests that his hypothesis is correct.

The principal source for the story of Matthew's martyrdom was the popular compendium of saints' lives known as *The Golden Legend*. There it is told that Matthew travelled to Ethiopia, where he converted many people to Christianity. His followers built him a church, where he baptized the king and queen and their daughter, Ephigenia, who entered a religious order. Matthew's martyrdom was the work of the king's successor, Hirtacus, who came to the throne determined to marry Ephigenia. When Matthew counselled her to remain a bride of Christ, Hirtacus ordered that the troublesome priest be killed. The story emphasizes that Matthew's martyrdom was the direct consequence of his missionary zeal: in earlier Italian pictorial narratives of the saint's life, the image of his killing was often immediately preceded by a depiction of him baptizing new converts.[7]

Conversion and baptism were themes highly appropriate to the national church of the French, whose own king had himself been so recently converted to Catholicism. The setting of Caravaggio's painting is a baptismal chapel, with steps leading down from the altar to a lustral pool, around the edges of which the naked converts have gathered. The significance of the painting's architecture was long unrecognized, for the simple reason that hardly any such baptismal chapels have survived. But they were once a common sight in Italian churches, especially in the north. In Rome, where baptism by aspersion was the general practice, stepped pools were not necessary. But in Milan, where they practised the Ambrosian rite of baptism by full bodily immersion, such chapels contained a deep pool at the base of the altar. The liturgically precise Archbishop of Milan, Carlo Borromeo, writing in his *Instructiones fabricae et supellectilis ecclesiasticae*, described an arrangement that closely corresponds to the setting of *The Martyrdom of St Matthew*: 'a baptistery should be in the centre of the chapel. It should be eleven cubits wide and deep enough so that the descent to it from the floor of the chapel consists of at least three steps. By the descent and moderate depth it should resemble a sepulchre.'[8] It seems that Caravaggio painted the kind of baptismal chapel that he remembered from his childhood in Milan.

Borromeo's instruction that the baptistry should resemble a sepulchre reflects the Christian belief that baptism and death are closely connected: to be baptized is to enter a new life in Christ, and to die is also to embark on the journey to a new existence – eternal life among the blessed. Baptism and death by martyrdom were even more intimately linked in Christian theology, in part because of the belief that the wound in Christ's side had flowed with water as well as blood during the Crucifixion. The early Church father, Tertullian, commented that this was 'to make us, in like manner, called by water, chosen by blood. These two baptisms He sent out from the wound of his pierced side in order that they who believed in his blood might be bathed with the water; they who had been bathed in the water might likewise drink the blood.'[9]

These ideas are woven together in *The Martyrdom of St Matthew*. The artist has imagined Matthew, missionary to the heathen, being murdered in the very act of conducting Mass during the sacrament of baptism. As he dies his blood flows into the baptismal pool. In this detail, murder is sanctified to a holy rite. The saint's death is a baptism of blood, a rebirth into immortality. Above, invisible both to the assassin and to the saint's shocked congregation, an angel perched on a heavy outcrop of cloud descends to thrust the palm of martyrdom into Matthew's open right hand.

Caravaggio's hard-won solution to the challenge of the picture combined theological subtlety with dramatic immediacy and narrative plausibility. The murderer, all but naked like the circle of converts awaiting baptism, has sprung up from their midst. He turns out to have been a pagan in disguise, lurking among the ranks of the faithful.

The principal visual inspiration for *The Martyrdom of St Matthew* is often said to have been Titian's famous *St Peter Martyr*, which had been painted for an altar in the Venetian church of SS Giovanni e Paolo.[10] That work must have been in Caravaggio's mind as he devised his own image of martyrdom, since his fallen saint and executioner are undeniably close to the same figures in Titian's composition. Yet the effect of his crowded tableau of figures is closer still to the three-dimensional sculptural *mises-en-scène* of popular religious art in his native Lombardy. *The Martyrdom of St Matthew* resembles nothing so much as the chapel sculptures of the sacred mountain at Varallo, near Milan – in particular, perhaps, the many figures assembled in a frozen re-enactment of *The Massacre of the Innocents*. Caravaggio's picture is like a partial, spotlit memory of that crowd scene.

Caravaggio's self-portrait as one of the fleeing onlookers in the *Martyrdom* is partly a kind of signature, in line with well-established Renaissance convention. A hundred years earlier Luca Signorelli had included himself as a solemn witness at the end of the world, in his fresco cycle of scenes from the Book of Revelation in Orvieto Cathedral. Caravaggio too is a witness. Including himself in the scene may have been his way of proclaiming that he really did see it all unfold, just like this, in his mind's eye. But there is perhaps more to it: he is not only an observer, but also a participant, a furtive accessory to the dreadful act. Like the converts in the foreground of the painting, he has stripped naked to be baptized; unlike them, he has gathered his blanket around him and taken to his heels. The self-portrait, in this instance, reads like a *mea culpa*. If Caravaggio had actually been there, he suggests, he would have had no more courage than anyone else. He would have fled like the others, leaving the martyr to his fate. According to the logic of his own narrative, he remains unbaptized and therefore outside the circle of the blessed. He is a man running away, out of the church and into the street.

A BACK-STABBING, AND OTHER MISADVENTURES

On 4 July 1600 the painter received a final payment of 50 scudi for *The Calling* and *The Martyrdom of St Matthew*. The two pictures were complete by that date, but may not have been set into the walls of the chapel until the autumn. Only in December did the carpenter employed to do the work submit his bill:

> for lining the two pictures which are on either side of the chapel of Cardinal Contarelli, which are both 14½ palms broad and 15 palms long; for fixing the laths in the wall so that the boards may be nailed, for putting three [laths] for each picture ... and for dividing the fir-wood boards, by 50, all my own material – it amounts to 20 scudi 20 baiocchi. For making the frames of the said pictures of my own white-poplar timber – it amounts to 20 scudi and 20 baiocchi.[11]

The pictures for the Contarelli Chapel were compellingly original public works of art. At a stroke they brought Caravaggio's new style of painting to a much broader public. His matchless sense of drama and his use of extreme contrasts of light and dark would prove intoxicatingly influential. The painting of such seventeenth-century masters as Rembrandt in Holland, Georges de La Tour in France, Ribera in Spain, even the work of much later Romantic artists such as Géricault and Delacroix, all are inconceivable without the pictorial revolution first unleashed by Caravaggio in his two pictures of scenes from the life of St Matthew. It is no exaggeration to say that they decisively changed the tradition of European art. But in their own time, they were controversial.

Caravaggio's rival, imitator and future biographer Giovanni Baglione went to see the pictures as soon as they were installed. His account of the visit conveys the impact of Caravaggio's work on those who first saw it. But it also hints at the jealousies aroused by the sudden rise to fame of a previously little-known painter from Lombardy. Baglione went to see the pictures with Federico Zuccaro, the president of Rome's art academy, the Accademia di San Luca. Sixty years old, Zuccaro was an *éminence grise* who aspired to the mantle of Michelangelo while painting late Mannerist monstrosities.[12] He claimed to be unimpressed by Caravaggio's work, as Baglione reported with evident pleasure:

> This commission with the paintings done after life . . . made Caravaggio famous, and the paintings were excessively praised by evil people. When Federico Zuccaro came to see this picture, while I was there, he exclaimed: 'What is all the fuss about?' and after having studied the entire work carefully, added: 'I do not see anything here other than the idea of Giorgione in the picture of the saint when Christ calls him to the Apostolate'; and, sneering, astonished by such commotion, he turned his back and left.[13]

At first sight Zuccaro's response seems as puzzling as it is petty. Caravaggio's monumental, tenebristic *Calling of St Matthew* has little in common with the works of Giorgione, painter of *The Tempest*, *The Sleeping Venus* and the *Three Ages of Man*. But Zuccaro's phrase, 'the idea of Giorgione', suggests that he meant to invoke the Venetian master first and foremost as a stereotype – the embodiment of a particular approach to painting. It is by no means certain that the crusty academician was familiar with Giorgione's actual works. But he certainly knew Giorgio Vasari's life of Giorgione, which had emphasized the painter's absolute dependence on the evidence of his own eyes. According to Vasari, Giorgione 'would never represent anything in his works without copying it from life'.[14] Vasari was a partisan of the Tuscan–Roman approach to art, with its strong emphasis on idealized forms, usually realized in the medium of fresco; his portrayal of Giorgione as a slavish naturalist was part of a systematic damning of the great Venetian oil painters with faint praise. So in declaring that Caravaggio was merely another Giorgione, Zuccaro was tarring him with the same brush: the comment was shorthand for saying that Caravaggio had no faculty of invention or imagination, that he was a painter who brought everything down to the level of mundane actual life, even the sacred mysteries. The curmudgeonly and conservative Zuccaro may well have been genuinely disturbed by the painter's decision to depict Matthew in his tax office as if he were a character in a low-life genre scene. If so, he would not be the last to take offence at Caravaggio's perceived sins against decorum.

In certain circles of the Roman art world Caravaggio would always be seen as an unwelcome outsider. Not only did Zuccaro criticize him for being an empty-headed naturalist, but he also implied that Caravaggio was polluting the pure and noble traditions of Roman painting with a seditious foreign idea – 'the idea of Giorgione' – brought in from Venice. Caravaggio's dark and monumental oil paintings would certainly have looked extremely Venetian in the chapel of a Roman church in 1600, because only in Venice, where dampness and humidity discouraged fresco painting, was it common to see such large works of religious art carried out in oil on canvas. Caravaggio's painting must have seemed truly foreign, alien.[15]

Caravaggio may not have been unduly concerned by Zuccaro's dislike for his work, but it was hardly a good omen. The Accademia di San Luca was an influential organization that could play an important role in a painter's career. He seems to have tried to be a part of it. A few years earlier he had been one of 105 artists to participate in the religious devotion known as the Forty Hours, annual celebrations in honour of St Luke. At that time he was not yet a member of the academy, although there is evidence to suggest that he may have joined some time after 1600.[16] He was, however, never admitted to its inner circle.

The Contarelli paintings divided opinion, but they instantly established Caravaggio as one of the leading painters of the city. However, there is no sign that success mellowed him. His life on the streets of the city was more turbulent than ever. At some point during the winter of 1600 – the precise date is unknown – he clashed with one of Rome's many unemployed mercenaries. Both men drew their swords. The painter outfought the soldier, who retired hurt. Caravaggio's friend, the notoriously hot-headed Onorio Longhi, was also involved. The injured man prosecuted and the legal document that records the affair also notes that it was settled out of court. Caravaggio must have compensated the man for his injuries:

In favour of Michelangelo Caravaggio, summoned and prosecuted for a sword wound which he had inflicted on the hand of Flavio Canonico, a former sergeant of the guards at Castel Sant'Angelo, with the complicity of Onorio Longhi, without danger to life, but with a permanent scar ... the most Illustrious and Reverent Lord, the Governor [of Rome], in view of the accord and reconciliation obtained from the aforesaid Flavio who was the injured party, ordered that the lawsuit ... and all other documents existing against the aforesaid [Caravaggio] for the above mentioned cause shall be cancelled and annulled and that the same [Caravaggio] shall not be molested any further on the ground of the aforesaid incident ...[17]

Flavio Canonico was not Caravaggio's only victim that winter. On 19 November 1600 the painter was charged with a nocturnal assault on a young art student named Girolamo Spampa from Montepulciano in Tuscany. This is what Spampa told the court:

You should know that last Friday night, three hours after nightfall, while returning from the Academy [the Accademia di San Luca], where I had been studying, when I got to the Via della Scrofa – Messer Orazio Bianchi was with me – and I was knocking at the candlemaker's door to get some candles, the defendant came up with a stick and began to beat me. He gave me a good many blows. I defended myself as best I could, shouting: 'Ah, traitor, is that a way to act!' Some butchers arrived with lights, and then Michelangelo drew his sword and made a thrust at me, which I parried with my cloak, in which he made a gash, as you can see, and then fled. Then I recognized him, whereas previously I had not been able to recognize him.[18]

Spampa's description of the attack was confirmed by his companion, Orazio Bianchi, who gave his own town of origin as Lyon in France; he was the moderately accomplished religious painter Horace Le Blanc. Le Blanc's finest hour would come in 1622, long after his return from Italy, when he was commissioned to design sets for the triumphal entry of Louis XIII and Anne of Austria into Lyon. His decorously idealized paintings, and the pattern of his later career, when he served for years as master of Lyon's guild of painters, identify him as a pillar of the academic establishment. Although he was only about twenty years old in 1600, he was already a member of the Accademia di San Luca.

Caravaggio's attack on the industrious young Spampa and his aes-
thetically conservative friend was not a spur-of-the-moment fracas: it
was a premeditated assault that reeked of vendetta. Caravaggio had
clearly lain in wait for the young student, tailing him through the dark
Roman streets as he made his way home from the Accademia di San
Luca. Revenge attacks of this sort were often carefully calculated. The
convention was that the punishment should fit the crime. Is it possible
that Spampa, keen to nail his colours to the mast of the academy, had
been parroting Federico Zuccaro's criticisms of the Contarelli Chapel
pictures? Had Caravaggio been tipped off by one of his own friends and
allies? If so, his response had a certain brutal logic to it. Spampa had
been guilty of back-stabbing. So Caravaggio attacked him from behind.

The case went no further, perhaps because of lack of evidence, perhaps
because Cardinal del Monte intervened on Caravaggio's behalf. But there
were other incidents besides, including one sighting of the painter that
suggests he himself had been on the receiving end of a beating.

In late October 1600 trouble had broken out again between Caravaggio's friend Onorio Longhi and Onorio's brother Stefano. The
pair were still arguing over their contested inheritance. Stefano had
charged Onorio with assault and threatening behaviour. In the course
of a three-day investigation of his grievances and accusations, the
court looked into a number of incidents in which Onorio had been
involved. Caravaggio's presence is mentioned. The evidence is confused and fragmentary, but presents a vivid picture of the painter's life
on the streets of Rome in the first year of the new century.[19]

During the investigation, Onorio Longhi was asked to cast his
mind back to an altercation involving himself, Stefano and others that
had taken place earlier that year. Under cross-examination, he conjured up the vibrancy of Rome in the high summer in holiday mood,
packed with men watching sport and spoiling for a fight:

Yes, sir, if I remember correctly, in July I was at the French tennis court
at Santa Lucia della Tinta to see a match between two fencers, one of
whom is called Cencio Abruzzese and the other is a Bolognese, whose
name I don't know. After I had seen the two fencers fight, I went on to
Piazza Navona, where some people were playing ball. I went up to
watch them play. I met Vicenzo da Ascoli, a fencer, Livio Freta, who

had been the judge of the said combat, Fulvio Scocimarro da Riete and Geronimo Roncalli, a merchant; there was one other with them, who they say is from Terni, but I don't know his name or anything else. They asked me what I thought about the fight between the two fencers, and who struck the most blows. I told them in my opinion Cencio had struck the most; then the man from Terni suggested that I hadn't seen well, or that I didn't understand much. I told him that he had gambled away ten scudi on the first hit, and in response the said Stefano made a mistake and threw a punch at me, then he put his hand to his sword. For my honour and defence I put my hand to my sword too. We threw so many punches that I don't know who was hit, because we were separated by many, and I was alone. But according to what I heard from the Duke of Acquasparta, who brokered a peace between us, he told me that he was hurt a little in the hand.

The magistrate then told Onorio that he was not asking about that fight, but another one that had taken place on the Via della Scrofa near the harbour of the Ripetta, the whore's part of town.[20] It was a brawl that had started because someone had called out 'Testicles for a penny' (a double-edged provocation, since the Italian word for testicles, *coglione*, could also signify a moron or imbecile). Longhi remembered that fracas too and described it:

Sir, I was walking down the street with some friends of mine. We were talking among ourselves and I said to them that bollocks were one a penny. Someone happened to be passing, accompanied by a certain painter whom I didn't know at all. He took it as meant for himself and told me not to speak to him like that, saying that he ate bollocks like me fried. We went at each other with our fists, and were separated. Then I went off on my own business, because after the fist-fight, those two took up stones to throw, but I didn't throw back because we had been separated.

Longhi insisted that nothing else happened and that no one else came to blows, but the magistrate continued with his cross-examination:

Who else was present at the scene?
    With him, that is, the one who came to blows with me, was one Marco Tullio, a painter, and with me was Michelangelo Merisi, the painter, who separated us.

Was Caravaggio armed at the time?

At the time Messer Michelangelo was convalescing, so he had his sword carried by a boy. This boy had the sword and was with him when the fight occurred, but Messer Michelangelo never took it out of the scabbard.

Did anyone else take up the scabbard and throw it, and if so, at whom?

When Messer Michelangelo was separating us, my adversary drew the scabbard to himself. I don't know what he did with it then and whether he threw it at me or not.

Did Michelangelo have the sword in its scabbard? Why was the scabbard thrown?

I don't know about that, because Messer Michelangelo was so ill he could barely stand, and when he saw the sword without its sheath he went off about his own business.

Suddenly the magistrate changed tack, perhaps revealing his main reason for enquiring into this otherwise apparently trivial affair. Longhi was asked to give the name of the man from Terni, the one with whom he had fought. He replied that he was not sure, but that he had heard that the man was called Luca Ciancarotta. At this point, the cross-examiner abruptly brought up the name of Ranuccio Tomassoni, also from Terni.

Had Longhi ever had an argument with the said Ranuccio? If so, when had he quarrelled with him, and over what?

No, sir, I've never had any words with Ranuccio Tomassoni from Terni. Even if he is a little related to the said Stefano, he is my friend and we've never had any disagreements in the past.

Had he ever tried to attack Ranuccio, alone or in company?

No, sir, no such thing, because, as I said, Ranuccio is my friend. We ate together only a few days ago. And I've never had any arguments or attacked him.

A swordfight on a tennis court; the painter barely able to walk, 'convalescing' probably not from illness but from injuries sustained in some fight or other; an argument involving testicles; a rivalry with a group of men from Terni. These events would soon enough be replayed – low farce turning to tragedy – in the lives of Caravaggio and Ranuccio Tomassoni. Stirrings of the trouble that lay ahead between the two men can be sensed behind the evasive testimony of Onorio Longhi.

Longhi did know Ranuccio Tomassoni well enough to be on first-name terms, as he had claimed. Just two weeks after the investigations of late October 1600, he was up before the magistrates again. The case at hand was his alleged assault of Felice Sillano, which by then had rumbled on for more than two years. Part of the investigation turned on whether a particular witness could possibly have recognized Longhi at night. When challenged, the witness turned to him and said 'I know you by your voice, because I've heard you talking with Messer Ranuccio at the Rotonda [the Pantheon], and seen you playing tennis in the Vicole de' Pantani.'[21] Longhi may once have been on good terms with the philandering, tennis-playing pimp. But their friendship had soured by the summer of 1600, perhaps because of Caravaggio's relationship with Fillide Melandroni, or perhaps because Ranuccio had taken the side of Stefano Longhi in the brothers' long-running battle over their inheritance.

In the archives of the tribunal of the Governor of Rome is another illuminating document, in effect an early seventeenth-century restraining order. On 17 November 1600 a sculptor called Hippolito Butio, of Milan, gave his pledge that Longhi would neither attack, nor cause to be attacked, a whole host of people.[22] The list included the long-aggrieved Felice Sillano as well as Stefano Longhi and Flavio Canonici (sic), whose hand Caravaggio had marked with 'a permanent scar', and Ranuccio Tomassoni.

There is a strong sense, in all this, of battle lines being drawn. A dangerous pattern of alliances was forming, a web of personal and patriotic rivalries. Caravaggio and Onorio Longhi stand on one side of the street, while Tomassoni and his henchmen from Terni gather on the other.

TWO PAINTINGS FOR TIBERIO CERASI

Meanwhile, in the autumn of 1600 Caravaggio had been offered another important commission. Two more lateral pictures were required, this time on the subjects of *The Conversion of St Paul* and

The Crucifixion of St Peter, for a chapel that had been acquired by Monsignor Tiberio Cerasi in the Church of Santa Maria del Popolo. It was another exceptional opportunity for the artist to excel on a public stage. The Augustinian foundation of Santa Maria del Popolo, at the northern edge of Rome, marked the start of one of the principal routes of pilgrimage through the city. Caravaggio was well aware that over the years millions of pilgrims would see his depictions of Peter and Paul, the beloved Princes of the Apostles. With the help of Cardinal del Monte, he was becoming famous.

Caravaggio's new patron, Monsignor Tiberio Cerasi, was a rich man. Born in 1544, he had made his fortune practising law at the papal court. Since 1596 he had been Treasurer-General to the Apostolic Chamber, responsible for authorizing papal expenditure. During the same period Cardinal Vincenzo Giustiniani was the Depositary-General, whose job it was to receive and distribute the funds. The two men were often brought together by their work. It may have been Giustiniani, close friend of Cardinal del Monte and owner of *The Lute Player*, who first suggested that Cerasi employ Caravaggio to paint two pictures for his burial chapel in Santa Maria del Popolo.

Caravaggio may also have been favoured by the religious order that owned the church, the Augustinian Friars of the Congregation of Lombardy. They were from his corner of Italy, and would have had every chance to admire his new pictures in San Luigi dei Francesi, which was only a short walk from their door. St Augustine himself had regarded human beings as essentially helpless recipients of divine mercy, measured out according to the inscrutable logic of a predestined universe, so an Augustinian community may have been impressed by the painter's *The Calling of St Matthew*, which shows a sudden, inexplicable shining of divine grace into the life of a sinner.

Cardinal Giustiniani's involvement in the commission is confirmed by the contract for the new work. He is described in the role of banker, making the first payment to Caravaggio on Cerasi's behalf. The document is dated 24 September 1600:

Michael Angelo [*sic*] Merisi da Caravaggio ... outstanding painter of the city, contracts with Tiberio Cerasi to paint two pictures on cypress wood, each with a length of ten Roman palmi and a width of eight,

representing the Conversion of St Paul and the Martyrdom of St Peter,
for delivery within eight months, with all figures, persons, and ornaments which seem fit to the painter, to the satisfaction of his Lordship.
The painter shall also be obliged to submit specimens and designs of
the figures and other objects with which according to his invention and
genius he intends to beautify the said mystery and martyrdom. This
promise the said painter has made for an honorarium and price of 400
scudi in cash ... [having received] 50 scudi in the form of a money
order directed to the Most Illustrious Vincenzo Giustiniani ... For all
this the parties have pledged themselves ... They have renounced to the
right of appeal, in perfect consent and have taken their oaths respectively: the Prelate according to the custom of his rank, by touching his
breast; Messer Michel Angelo [sic], by touching the Bible ... [23]

Tiberio Cerasi had only acquired the burial chapel in Santa Maria
del Popolo in July, barely more than two months earlier, and clearly
wanted to avoid the kinds of delay that had plagued the decoration of
the Contarelli Chapel. He may also have suspected that he did not
have long to live. Two years earlier he had signed his last testament, in
which he declared the Hospital of Santa Maria Consolazione to be
the *erede universale* and residuary legatee of his will.[24] His father,
Stefano Cerasi, had worked there as a physician, and Tiberio had
always kept close ties with the institution.[25] In his will, Cerasi wrote
that his love for the hospital was greater than his poor bequest could
convey. He was a man with his mind on the next world, determined
to be in credit when the final reckoning came. He would die while
work was still in progress on the paintings for his chapel, but the
results would surely have pleased him. Caravaggio's dark and solemn
style was well suited to his penitential mood.

Saints Peter and Paul were deeply revered in Rome. Their heads
were reputedly preserved in St John Lateran, their bodies buried
before the high altar of St Peter's. It was believed that they had both
been martyred in the city on the same day, baptizing the Roman
Church with their blood. Because they were regarded as 'the founders
of the Apostolic See',[26] the stories of their lives were often presented
together, but it was unusual to see depictions of the particular episodes prescribed by Cerasi placed side by side. The conversion of Paul

was not usually paired with Peter's martyrdom, but with Peter receiving the keys from Christ.

There was one notable precedent for the chosen arrangement. In the 1540s, in the Pauline Chapel, next to the Sistine Chapel, Michelangelo had painted his last pair of monumental frescoes, a *Conversion of St Paul* and a *Martyrdom of St Peter* for Pope Paul III. They are forbiddingly gloomy pictures, part of Michelangelo's long retreat from ideal beauty. By commissioning Caravaggio to repeat the same juxtaposition of themes in his own burial chapel, Cerasi was implicitly setting him in competition with the ghost of the most celebrated Renaissance artist of all.

To this challenge, the patron added another. In addition to Caravaggio's lateral panels of Paul and Peter, he commissioned a painted altarpiece for his chapel. The artist chosen was the Bolognese painter Annibale Carracci, who had recently completed the breathtaking cycle of mythological paintings for the ceiling of the Palazzo Farnese. The subject for his new work was to be *The Assumption of the Virgin*. Carracci and Caravaggio were the two most talented painters in Rome. Cerasi had secured the services of both, beginning what he must have hoped would be a thrilling battle for pre-eminence.

Carracci was the senior of the two, some fifteen years older than Caravaggio. Before starting work, he looked at his rival's new pictures in the nearby church of the French and probably assumed that Caravaggio would repeat the pattern of his *Calling* and *Martyrdom of St Matthew*: making the past seem present, painting from carefully posed models, using intense contrasts of light and shade. During the course of his considerably longer career, Carracci himself had flirted with similar methods and devices. But now his sense of competition pushed him to the opposite extreme.

Painting *The Assumption of the Virgin*, Carracci reverted to the pure, sweet style of the High Renaissance. He brightened and softened his colours and ruthlessly eliminated any hint of real life. Swathed in drapery the colour of a summer's sky, arms outspread, an expression of beatific serenity on her perfectly round face, Carracci's Virgin Mary rises from the tomb like an ecstatic doll. Her feet rest on a cushion of winged cherubim's heads, while a decorous cast of bearded apostles has been arranged, below her, in various standard poses of politely expressed wonderment. The painting is airless and spaceless, all its figures pushed up to the picture plane as if to a sheet of glass. There is no suggestion of the sacred erupting into the world of the everyday. It is a dream of pure transcendence.

Carracci's picture is a point-by-point refutation of all Caravaggio's innovations in the Contarelli Chapel. Harking back to the serenity of Raphael's middle style, it is an insistently retrograde work of art – a doctrinaire assertion of the importance of *disegno*, in the sense both of drawing and of idealized composition. But it also anticipates the swooning, aerially propelled visions of the incipient Baroque – the style that in Italy at least would for a time triumph over Caravaggio's harsh brand of pious naturalism. *The Assumption of the Virgin* is a reminder of the powerful tides of taste against which Caravaggio was swimming.

Annibale Carracci delivered his work on time, to the approval of Tiberio Cerasi, and it was duly installed on the altar of the chapel in Santa Maria del Popolo. Caravaggio struggled with his own commission. Working on panels of cypress wood, as the contract had stipulated, was very different from his usual practice of working on canvas. Oil paint does not penetrate panel in the same way that it works its way into the weft of a canvas. The resulting surface is more reflective, with more emphatically succulent colours and shadows that do not recede as fully into darkness. According to Baglione, Caravaggio persevered with the two panel pictures, but they 'were painted in a different style' and 'did not please the patron'. Cerasi rejected them and the artist had no choice but to start again, this time in his preferred medium of oil on canvas. His abortive first efforts were sold on, Baglione added, to Cardinal Sannesio.

Only one of these unsatisfactory compositions survives. The attribution to Caravaggio has sometimes been questioned, but is now generally accepted. The dimensions of the panel are very close to those of the two oil paintings that the painter eventually completed for the Cerasi Chapel. Allowing for the painter's use of an unfamiliar support, the style is convincing. The model for the angel reappears in at least one of Caravaggio's later works.

It is not hard to see why Tiberio Cerasi rejected this first *Conversion of St Paul*. The composition is a clutter and a jumble. As the bearded Paul squirms on the ground, shielding his eyes from the dazzling celestial vision, his horse rears up and foams at the mouth. The saint's aged retainer, clutching a shield decorated with a crescent moon and wearing an absurdly elaborate plumed helmet, resembles a baffled spear-carrier in a comic opera. Hearing a noise like a thunderclap, but seeing nothing, he brandishes his weapon at thin air. The young, bearded Christ descends from the heavens, reaching down to the stricken Paul with a gesture of grave compassion. He and the angel accompanying him lean awkwardly across a snapped branch of a laurel, like a pair of parachutists stuck in a tree. This cumbersome arrangement probably reflects some actual studio contrivance. A ladder and a length of rope may have been used to help the models assume their poses for this part of the *mise-en-scène*.

Once again, the artist's memories of the popular religious art of Lombardy are much in evidence. The picture bears a strong resemblance to some of the more overcrowded scenes enacted by the busy mannequin figures in the chapels of the *sacro monte* tradition. The painting is more upright than the Contarelli Chapel canvases, yet Caravaggio has tried to squeeze almost as much dramatic action into the narrower compass allowed for by the cramped dimensions of the Cerasi Chapel. As a result, the forms and figures seem bizarrely compressed, with heaven and earth forced into a weird and unconvincing proximity.

During his early struggles with the Cerasi Chapel commission, Caravaggio was handicapped by an apparent inability to get away from the famous prototype of Michelangelo's restless and turbulent *Conversion of St Paul* in the Pauline Chapel. The rearing horse and reeling saint, the figure of Christ descending from the heavens, arm outstretched – he borrowed and adapted all these elements from Michelangelo's far larger and more densely populated painting, as if he were setting out to create a condensed version of the earlier work. It was only when Cerasi rejected the painting out of hand that Caravaggio reconsidered and found a diametrically different solution. For his second *Conversion of St Paul*, he went back to basics. He returned to oil on canvas and went back to the biblical source of the story, to find a new way of getting to its heart and bringing it to life.

The tale of Paul's conversion is told in the Acts of the Apostles. The

Roman citizen Saul of Tarsus, the future St Paul, was travelling to Damascus with letters of authority to persecute the Christians. A harsh and ruthless man, 'breathing out threatenings and slaughter against the disciples of the Lord', he was abruptly stopped in his tracks by a miracle:

> And as he journeyed; he came near Damascus: and suddenly there shined round about him a light from heaven: And he fell to the earth, and heard a voice saying unto him, Saul, Saul, why persecutest thou me? And he said, Who art thou, Lord? And the Lord said, I am Jesus whom thou persecutest . . . And he trembling and astonished said, Lord, what wilt thou have me to do? And the Lord said unto him, Arise, and go into the city, and it shall be told thee what thou must do. And the men which journeyed with him stood speechless, hearing a voice, but seeing no man. And Saul arose from the earth; and when his eyes were opened, he saw no man: but they led him by the hand, and brought him into Damascus. And he was three days without sight, and neither did eat nor drink' (Acts 9:1–9).

Caravaggio's own revelation, on rereading these words, may have been as sudden. The story is essentially a parable played out between the twin poles of his own art – a tale of light and darkness. Lost in the shadows of evil and ignorance, a vicious man is suddenly bathed by the light of God and his soul is washed clean. In the moment of his ecstatic vision the divine light enters him, invades and permeates his whole being. Filled with this inner illumination, the light of truth and faith, he becomes blind to the mundane world about him. There are striking parallels with the story of Matthew called by Christ as Caravaggio had imagined it in the Contarelli Chapel. But this time the metaphor of illumination, which the painter had brought to the bare text of Matthew's gospel, is there in the biblical account itself: 'there shined about him a light from heaven'. In that phrase, he found his key to understanding the nature of Paul's conversion. Turning his back on the tumult and drama conventionally associated with Paul's conversion, Caravaggio created a picture of unprecedented calm. Gone are the creakingly theatrical figures of Christ and the angel, replaced by a spectral radiance that is the light of God. There is no noise, no clamour, no comedy of misapprehension here – just simple ignorance contrasted with miraculous divine illumination, an irresistible tide of light that floods the saint and changes him forever.

Paul's retainer stands quietly to one side, lost in his thoughts and half lost in the shadows. A hard-faced balding man with a furrowed brow, he tends with calm solicitude to the horse from which his master has fallen. Below, almost beneath the animal's hooves, the figure of Paul lies on his back with his eyes closed like a man dreaming of his lover. His arms are open wide, embracing the light that envelops him, filling him with truth and wisdom and humanity. He is considerably younger than the wizened, bearded Paul of the rejected version. This Paul is very much the tough Roman soldier described in the Acts of the Apostles – a hard-bodied athlete with a granite jaw who has suddenly been melted by the love of God. His sword lies by his side, resting in folds of red drapery as if to symbolize the rivers of Christian blood that he had meant to shed when he set out for Damascus.

In the moment of Paul's ecstasy, the world is brought to a standstill. A physical journey has turned into a spiritual odyssey. Caravaggio's decision to purge the story of visible narrative was brave and unorthodox, but expressive. Bellori, missing the point with perfect eloquence, described the picture as 'the Conversion of St Paul, in which the history is completely without action'. On the contrary: the action has been completely internalized, so that we see or sense it unfolding within Paul's soul. He is being moulded by the light that models his figure with its soft and gentle rays. In the chiaroscuro that plays along the length of his outstretched left arm, in the shafts woven through the tips of his fingers, in the gleams reflected in the dull sheen of his fingernails, light itself becomes palpable – something he feels, accepts, draws into the depths of his body.

This is a painting to be understood intuitively, instinctively. It is not an intellectual picture, nor one that shows any interest in beauty as conventionally understood. It is designed to speak not to the rich or theologically learned but to the poor – to roughshod peasants and sunburned labourers, ordinary people who had made the long pilgrimage south to Rome and found themselves, at last, inside the city walls. The composition is dominated by the solid, heavy form of the patiently standing horse, lifting a heavy hoof so as not to tread on the prone body of its master. The animal is no thoroughbred, but a stocky piebald beast of burden. Caravaggio paints the weight and density of its powerful flank. He paints the animal's patience and loyalty. He even conjures up a feeling of the heat that emanates from its slow, heavy body – in rural parts, in the little town where he had been brought up, poor people kept their livestock in their homes in the winter months to keep themselves warm. This is an essential part of the picture's plainspeaking intimacy. It is like a hearth, inviting cold bodies to gather round and warm themselves in the act of devotion.

The horse evoked other folk memories too. Like the benign ox and ass in traditional depictions and plays of the Nativity, the animal standing quietly in the dark recalls the manger in which Christ was born. Seen through half-closed eyes, the animal's groom might almost be St Joseph. The association adds another level of meaning to the scene. In the moment of his conversion Paul is helpless yet blessed, bathed by the light of God, just as Christ was in his infancy.

Behind all this is the old idea of the *Imitatio Christi*, which was central to the ethics of the old pauperist orders such as the Franciscans. To understand Christ's message is to become like him, to follow in his footsteps – to undergo a profound, internal metamorphosis. At the instant of his inner rebirth as a Christian, Paul mystically experiences the whole life of Christ, its beginning and its end. He becomes, in his own mind, both Christ the blessed child and Christ the doomed adult, sacrificed to save mankind. In the movements of his body are reflected the motions of his soul. He reaches his arms out like a baby. As he does so, his gesture mimes the Crucifixion.

The theological justification for pairing St Paul's conversion with St Peter's martyrdom was the belief that each event represented a mystical death. At his conversion, Paul dies to the world to be reborn in Christ; at his martyrdom, Peter literally dies, to meet his rewards in heaven. Such symmetry is implicit in the relationship between Caravaggio's two paintings. The prone body of Paul, cruciform in a gesture of spiritual empathy, is echoed by the actually crucified body of Peter.

According to legend, Peter insisted that he be crucified upside down because he felt unworthy to die the same death as Christ. In *The Crucifixion of St Peter*, Caravaggio shows him already nailed to the cross, defiantly half rearing up as his executioners toil to raise him into place. He exhales against the pain, stomach muscles tensing, and looks away out of the picture. His eyes are fixed on the actual chapel's altar, as if to stress that death by martyrdom is another form of participation in the rite of the Mass. Even as his own blood is shed, he trusts that he will be saved by the flesh and blood of Christ. The rock in the foreground is the symbol of his hard, enduring faith, cornerstone of the Church itself: 'thou art Peter, and upon this rock I shall build my church; and the gates of hell shall not prevail against it' (Matthew 16:18–19).

The action takes place in some dim corner of a nocturnal world lit only by the flash of God's grace. The light falls on Peter and the straining figures of his three executioners, but the martyr alone is alive to its message of salvation. The others grunt and sweat under the burden of his weight, grimly immersing themselves in the practical business of hoisting up a human body nailed to a cross. They look as though they are trying not to think about what they are actually doing – or pretending to themselves that it might be some more innocent and straightforward task, such as erecting a fence-post, or heaving the joist of a house into place.

The executioners are insensitive to the point of insentience, blind to the mystical significance of the death they so callously arrange. Their figures are pushed up so close to the front edge of the picture that they seem almost to spill out into the real world. Like *The Conversion of St Paul*, *The Crucifixion of St Peter* is a painting aimed squarely at poor and ordinary people. It is a challenge as well as a call to conscience: viewers are brought into its space and invited to take the place of Peter's executioners, at least in the mind's eye – to make good their failings, to show compassion and mercy, to open up to the light of God.

The Renaissance scholar and connoisseur Bernard Berenson, who published a short and rather tetchy book about Caravaggio in 1951, was offended by the aggressive directness of the picture:

> But for the noble Titianesque head of the victim, the rest is a study in the raising of a heavy weight without the aid of machinery. Of the chief performers, the one who acts as crane and the other as booster, we see the back of one and the buttocks of the other. We do not see their faces. No need. They are mere mechanisms. Hard to conceive a more

dehumanized treatment of the subject. No doubt the arrangement of the four figures as crossed diagonals taking up the entire canvas was a happy thought ...[27]

The executioners were certainly intended to shock. The presence of these coarsely posed, unmistakably low-brow figures underscored Caravaggio's total rejection of High Renaissance and Mannerist elegance. This is all the more apparent in the Cerasi Chapel, where Annibale Carracci's large and centrally placed altarpiece perfectly embodies the traditions to which Caravaggio's work is so brutally opposed. Carracci had sought to pre-empt his rival by creating a work designed to reassert the values of idealized beauty, splendid colour and lofty transcendence. In doing so, he may have hoped to sow seeds of self-doubt in Caravaggio's mind. But the younger painter was only spurred on to a more blatant statement of his own, very different priorities. In place of Carracci's emotionless splendour of effect he offered up his own spare, low-toned, militantly 'poor' art. Carracci had used rich colours, colours that literally embodied wealth and magnificence, like the celestial blue of the Madonna's cloak, painted in the costly medium of ultramarine. In stark contrast, Caravaggio kept rigorously to a palette of humble, ordinary, cheap colours: the earth colours, ochre and umber, carbon black, lead white, verdigris. The use of costly ultramarine was actually specified by Cerasi, who doubtless wanted posterity to know that no expense had been spared. But Caravaggio used the colour in such a way as to reject its rich associations. The dying Peter's robe, lying in a heap in the bottom corner of the *Martyrdom*, has been painted in murkily shadowed ultramarine. As Bellori noted, Caravaggio avoided more brilliant vermilions and blues, and even when he did use them generally 'toned them down'.[28]

The lives of Christ and his followers were neither rich nor splendid. Their deaths were brutal. Caravaggio insists on these home truths in every detail of the Cerasi Chapel paintings, whether it be the glint of the crouching executioner's spade or the black dirt so deeply ingrained in the upturned heel and ball of his left foot. Like Carlo Borromeo preaching in rags, the art of Caravaggio expressed an aggressively harsh piety. With *The Conversion of St Paul* and *The Crucifixion of St Peter*, he took his uncompromisingly severe style of painting to an ascetic extreme. As a parting gesture to his rival, as if to stress the depth of his disdain for Carracci's brand of vapid magnificence, Caravaggio contrived a cunning insult: the rump of St Paul's proletarian carthorse is pointedly turned towards Carracci's *Assumption of the Virgin*.

IN THE HOUSE OF THE MATTEI

Caravaggio finished his two lateral paintings for the Cerasi Chapel towards the end of 1601. Earlier in the year he had left the household of Cardinal del Monte to accept the hospitality of another powerful figure in the Roman Curia, Cardinal Girolamo Mattei.

The Mattei were powerful. They lived in a honeycomb complex of houses and palaces built over the ruins of the ancient Roman Teatro di Balbo, in the heavily populated district of Sant'Angelo, between the Tiber and the Campidoglio. The adjoining residences of the various branches of the family formed an entire block, known as the Isola dei Mattei. At its centre, looking out across the Piazza Mattei, was the massive Palazzo Mattei, home to Cardinal Girolamo.

Caravaggio moved there some time before 14 June 1601, when he gave his address on agreeing a contract for an altarpiece of *The Death of the Virgin*, for the church of Santa Maria della Scala in the district of Trastevere in Rome: he is described as 'Michelangelo Merisi from Caravaggio, painter of the city, living in the palace of the illustrious and reverend lord cardinal Mattei'. The terms of the contract allowed him twelve months to paint the new altarpiece. He would complete the work eventually, but not until long after that deadline had passed.

Caravaggio probably remained in the household of the Mattei family until at least the beginning of 1603. His precise movements are hard to track following his departure from the household of Cardinal del Monte, who was himself friendly with the Mattei and may have been instrumental in the artist's move. Caravaggio's change of address should not be seen as marking a break between him and del Monte. The painter continued to rely on his old protector for support. On the evening of 11 October 1601 Caravaggio was stopped for carrying arms without a licence in the district of the Campo Marzio. The policeman who made the arrest reported that the painter 'insisted that he was on the household roll of the Cardinal del Monte, and because he did not have a licence and I did not know if it was true, I took him to prison at the Tor di Nona.'[29] Nothing came of it and the painter was soon released, probably with del Monte's help. For his part the Medici cardinal seems to have remained on good terms with his protégé, continuing to make allowances for his erratic behaviour.

Cardinal Girolamo Mattei was one of three brothers. Although he was not the eldest, his elevated position in the Roman curia meant that it was he who lived in the principal family palace. He was a member of the strictest order of Franciscan friars, the Observants. Cardinal Mattei was noted for his dislike of conspicuous display and may have influenced Caravaggio's turn towards a harsh and simplified language of Christian painting in 1601. The pictures for the Cerasi Chapel, so stark and ascetic, were finished when Caravaggio was living in the Palazzo Mattei.

Girolamo's two brothers, Ciriaco and Asdrubale, shared a house close to the Palazzo Mattei. Ciriaco was a year older than the cardinal, while Asdrubale was ten years younger. Both men had added to their considerable inherited wealth by marrying advantageously. They were known as enthusiastic collectors of ancient Roman sculpture and as connoisseurs of contemporary art. The family account books show that it was they, rather than their brother the cardinal, who commissioned paintings from Caravaggio. For Asdrubale he created a painting of St Sebastian that has long since been lost. For Ciriaco he painted no fewer than three gallery paintings on sacred themes, all of which survive.

The archives of the Mattei family show that Caravaggio was paid by Ciriaco at the start of January 1602 for 'A painting of Our Lord Breaking Bread'. This is The Supper at Emmaus, now in the National Gallery in London. The painting tells the biblical story of the risen Christ, days after the crucifixion, sharing a meal with two of his astonished followers. According to the gospel of Luke, at first they did not recognize him: 'And then it came to pass, as he sat at meat with them, he took bread, and blessed it, and brake, and gave to them. And their eyes were opened, and they knew him; and he vanished out of their sight' (Luke 24:30–31). Caravaggio paints the moment just before the vanishing. Dressed in robes of red and white, colours that symbolize his triumphant resurrection, Jesus reveals his identity with a gesture of gentle benediction. In the act of blessing the square and solid loaves of bread, he both confirms that he has indeed risen from the dead and affirms his own bodily presence in the Eucharist. The claws of a scrawny boiled chicken, pathetic image of mortality, are contrasted with the life-giving hands of Christ. A simple meal has become a sacrament.

The Bible says that the village of Emmaus 'was from Jerusalem about threescore furlongs', but Caravaggio imagined a place much closer to home. His *Supper at Emmaus* is served up in a rough Roman tavern, the kind of place where the painter would meet his friends and start arguments with his enemies. As the Saviour announces himself, a hardbitten innkeeper looks on with an expression of uncomprehending suspicion, as if he might be wondering whether this pale, plump-faced young man and his ragged companions will be able to pay their bill.

Meanwhile the two disciples are frozen in the throes of astonished, dawning recognition. One has his back to us. As he prepares to lever himself upright, his hands are braced on the arms of the same savonarola chair that Caravaggio had used in *The Calling of St Matthew*. At the point of his bony elbow, there is a small rent in his rough green tunic, through which his white undershirt shows. The other disciple, who wears a pilgrim's shell on his mantle, spreads his arms as wide as he can, measuring the extent of his amazement like an angler demonstrating the size of a fish that got away. His gesture also mirrors the Crucifixion, as if to shape the question springing to his mind. How is it possible that a man whom he so recently saw nailed to the cross, a bleeding corpse, should live and breathe and speak once more?

The hands of Christ and the wondering apostle seem to reach out of the painting, through the membrane that separates illusion from reality. The effect is worked through skilful foreshortenings of perspective. The apostle's outspread arms plot the whole depth of the picture. His right hand, half lost in the darkness, seems blurred by movement. His other hand, so close to the picture plane as to seem almost touchable, is sharply in focus. From the tip of Christ's thumb, back along the dappled sleeve of his red shirt to his shoulder, his arm is a piece of art that measures distance, in graded lights and darks, with such illusory precision that it is almost impossible to look at the painting and believe it truly flat.

Yet Caravaggio's intense realism is also, on this occasion, shot through with a strong sense of the uncanny. It is as if the painter has asked himself a series of direct, straightforward questions about the story that he was given to depict. What happens to the world when a miracle takes place? How might it be possible to tell, should the risen Christ suddenly come among us? What do things actually look like at such moments? *The Supper at Emmaus* contains Caravaggio's answers to those questions.

The idea that divine visitations are inevitably accompanied by thunderclaps and clouds of angels is dismissed as naive and childish. Caravaggio, himself so keen-eyed and attentive to every last nuance of visual experience, imagines the process to be subtler than that. God is light, so he announces his presence among men in the elusive forms of a shadowplay. The innkeeper cannot see it, but by standing where he does he casts a shadow on the wall that gives Christ a dark but unmistakable halo. Below, a basket of fruit is balanced precariously on the leading edge of the table. It is the same basket that Caravaggio had painted for Federico Borromeo, and its contents are nearly the same too – a worm-eaten apple, a pomegranate and fig, withered grapes and trailing vine leaves, embodying decay but also symbolizing the hope of Christian redemption. The fruit and the teetering basket cast a second meaningful shadow, this one shaped like the tail of a fish, the ancient mnemonic sign for Christ used by his earliest followers. Caravaggio's painting suggests that those who would prefer to be saved, rather than damned, might do well to pay attention to such details. Even those in the presence of a miracle might easily miss it.

Bellori unwisely chose to single out *The Supper at Emmaus* as an example of the painter's thoughtless literalism and lack of decorum: 'in addition to the vulgar conception of the two Apostles and of the Lord who is shown young and without a beard, the innkeeper wears a cap, and on the table is a dish of grapes, figs and pomegranates out of season. Just as certain herbs produce both beneficial medicine and most pernicious poison, in the same way, though he produced some good, Caravaggio has been most harmful and wrought havoc with every ornament and good tradition of painting . . .' The biographer concluded this little homily with the reflection that many other painters had been bewitched by the 'error and darkness' of Caravaggio's painting, 'until Annibale Carracci came to enlighten their minds and restore beauty to the imagination of nature'.[30]

Bellori's misreading of *The Supper at Emmaus* does at least have the virtue of highlighting some of the picture's most effective devices. The writer found his eye drawn to Caravaggio's wicker basket of fruit, so beautifully painted, only to complain that the fruits within were 'unseasonal'. He clearly felt they should have been the fruits of Easter, the time of Christ's crucifixion. Guilty of the very literalism for which he blamed Caravaggio, Bellori was oblivious to the symbolic meanings concealed within the basket of fruit, and completely blind to the significant shape of its shadow.

He was also perturbed by the disrespectful figure of the innkeeper, who wears his cap in the presence of Christ. But this is no mere oversight, or vulgar lapse, on the part of the painter; it is a detail essential to his telling of the story. The innkeeper fails to doff his cap because he does not realize whom he serves. He remains in darkness, even though a miracle is taking place before his eyes. In Caravaggio's interpretation, the story of the meal at Emmaus becomes a parable about those who see and those who do not.

Bellori disliked the evident poverty of the two disciples and can almost be heard tut-tutting over that prominent torn sleeve. More telling is his other complaint, about Caravaggio's depiction of Christ as 'young and without a beard'. The painter's decision to depart from the traditional image of a solemn, bearded Christ – such as he had recently painted in *The Calling of St Matthew* – was certainly unusual. But once again, it is essential to his understanding of the story as a tale of hard-won recognition.

The principal source for the story of the Supper at Emmaus is the gospel of Luke, Chapter 24, but there is also a fleeting reference to it in Chapter 16 of the gospel of Mark: 'After that he appeared in another form unto two of them, as they walked, and went into the country.' Caravaggio seized on the three words, 'in another form'. They are the only explanation given in the Bible for the apostles' failure to recognize Christ. Risen from the dead, he took on a different physical appearance. It seems that Caravaggio's inspiration for the picture's main idea – the idea of an unobvious miracle, a miracle that men must struggle to see – had its origins in a careful reading of the Bible.[31]

Back in the 1540s Michelangelo had placed a similarly controversial, young and beardless Christ at the centre of his *Last Judgement*, on the altar wall of the Sistine Chapel. The image was meant to evoke the early traditions of Christian Rome, where Christ had often been depicted in the guise of the sun god, Apollo. There are strong echoes of Michelangelo's Apollonian Christ, judging all mankind at the end of the world, in Caravaggio's own figure of Christ in *The Supper at Emmaus*. In the fresco of *The Last Judgement*, Christ's left arm is turned against the seething mass of the damned, while with his right he beckons the blessed up into heaven. Caravaggio appropriated those same gestures, adapting them with surprisingly little modification for his own figure's act of blessing the bread. It is another formal echo charged with spiritual meaning. Christ's appearance to his two disciples at Emmaus prefigures his final appearance to the whole human race on the day of judgement.

Two more payments were made to Caravaggio by Ciriaco Mattei in 1602, one in July, the other in December. These were for a painting which has been plausibly identified with the *St John the Baptist* now in the Capitoline Museum in Rome. Once again, Caravaggio treated his appointed subject in an unusual and idiosyncratic way. The saint, who is shown during his legendary retreat into the desert, appears without several of his usual attributes. He carries neither a cross nor a banderole. The lamb of God who usually accompanies him has metamorphosed into a sheep with horns. He embraces the animal, which nuzzles his cheek. It was conventional to depict St John as a haggard ascetic in animal furs, but Caravaggio presents him as a cheerfully smiling, ruddy-cheeked adolescent. Most unusual of all, he is stark naked. The boy reclines on a scrap of fur, but his discarded clothes lie around him in a heap.

The picture is so unconventional that even its very subject has been called into question. As early as 1620 the author of a guidebook to the Mattei collection gave the work a mythological title, referring to it as a *Pastor Friso*, which identified the naked young man as a pagan shepherd.[32] A number of subsequent scholars have taken that attribution seriously. Others have argued that Caravaggio intended to depict the biblical Isaac, son of Abraham, stripped for sacrifice and rejoicing after his sudden stay of execution.[33] None of these hypotheses has much merit. Ciriaco Mattei presented the picture to his son, Giovanni Battista Mattei, whose name saint it certainly depicts and for whom it was almost certainly intended from the outset. An inventory of his possessions drawn up in 1616 refers to 'A painting of San Gio: Battista with his Lamb by the hand of Caravaggio',[34] and it is safe to assume that the picture's owner knew its true subject. When Giovanni Battista made his will, seven years later, he gave instructions that the painting 'of St John the Baptist by Caravaggio'[35] be left to none other than Cardinal Francesco del Monte. This implies that the Mattei family felt an abiding sense of obligation to del Monte for releasing Caravaggio into their service.

Although its subject is easily established, the work is still intriguingly unusual. Why did Caravaggio paint John the Baptist in this strange, splay-legged pose? Why is the figure smiling so enigmatically? Why, above all, is he nude? Part of the answer to those questions lies in the art of the immediate past.

During the early years of the seventeenth century, when Caravaggio was forging his style and making his reputation, he gave a great deal of thought to the works of Michelangelo. He had been born just seven years after the death of 'the divine Michelangelo', as Vasari had called him. Like every ambitious painter of his generation, he would have regarded Michelangelo's works as a summit of excellence. And as if to force such comparisons upon him, Michelangelo also happened to be his own namesake. Caravaggio had already been invited to compete with the older artist by the choice of subjects for the Cerasi Chapel. In that case, he had asserted his independence from his predecessor by reconceiving his two canonically Michelangelesque themes in a radically un-Michelangelesque manner. But in other works of the period, he complicated the game of rivalry and homage. *The Supper at Emmaus*, with its Michelangelesque Christ, is just one of several instances. The Capitoline *St John the Baptist* is another.

The picture is a variation on the theme of Michelangelo's *ignudi*, the idealized male nudes which frame the nine great narrative paintings telling stories from the Book of Genesis on the Sistine Chapel ceiling. Michelangelo's male nudes are the only non-Christian elements in the whole of his scheme. They had been included as a compliment to Pope Julius II, who commissioned him to paint the ceiling: they bear festoons of oak leaves and acorns, emblems of the pope's family name, della Rovere. Collectively, they symbolize the idea of a golden age described in the writings of antiquity, the conceit behind them being that the reign of Julius amounted to another such blessed period in the lives of men. But by the second half of the sixteenth century the *ignudi* had become controversial. Their nudity was deemed unbecoming, their pagan symbolism judged suspect, and a painter called Daniele da Volterra was hired to fig-leaf their genitalia.

The pose of Caravaggio's smiling *St John the Baptist* has been directly borrowed from one of the four *ignudi* who frame *The Sacrifice of Noah* on the Sistine Chapel ceiling. The seventeenth-century writer who believed the painting to be an image of a pagan shepherd was probably responding, unconsciously, to its neo-pagan source in the art of Michelangelo, and in this sense the Capitoline *St John* is another of Caravaggio's pictures on the borderline between 'the sacred and profane', in Cardinal Paravicino's phrase. But the true subtlety of the work lies in its double inversion of the famous but controversial prototype that inspired it.

Whereas Michelangelo's nudes collectively represent a languorously beautiful ideal, an imaginary museum of male beauty raised up to the vault of heaven, Caravaggio has clearly painted a picture of a real, flesh-and-blood boy. The fact that the model has been posed just like an *ignudo* emphasizes the gulf between Michelangelo's idealizing aesthetic and Caravaggio's countervailing realism. The flesh of Michelangelo's nudes is chiselled, marmoreally perfect. Caravaggio's adolescent saint is slight and skinny. His ribcage shows through the light-dappled flesh of his side and there is dirt under his toenails. He is an *ignudo* brought down to earth, but not in a spirit of homage. The echo is there to assert Caravaggio's difference, to make it unavoidable.

Caravaggio has also reversed the sense of Michelangelo's nudes in the act of appropriating their form. Those who have seen the Capitoline *St John* as a daringly sexy depiction of a Christian saint, laughing provocatively as he turns to face the viewer, miss the point of the picture entirely. The truth is that Caravaggio has taken Michelangelo's notoriously pagan imagery, a classically phrased compliment paid to a pope, and fully reclaimed it for Christianity. His *ignudo* is no sleepy, sensual emblem of a vanished golden age, but an ecstatic prophet bathed in the light of divine revelation. The naked, rejoicing boy embraces the animal by his side because it has been sent to him by God to show him what will come to pass. He sees in it the destiny of Christ the saviour, with whose fate his own is intertwined, and whom he will one day baptize.

The painter's decision to give the animal horns is unusual, but underscores the significance of the scene. It recalls the image of a sacrificial ram, and may also have been inspired by a detail of the Sistine Chapel ceiling: only a few feet from the *ignudo* whose pose is closest to that of Caravaggio's *St John*, Michelangelo had painted a ram being prepared for slaughter in *The Sacrifice of Moses*. Those who have misinterpreted Caravaggio's picture as an image of Isaac delivered from sacrifice are in one way simply overreacting to a genuine element of the painter's intended meaning. He meant to emphasize the idea of sacrifice by giving the sheep horns, but the sacrifice he had in mind was not that of Isaac but of Christ himself.

In the upper-right-hand corner, barely visible in the shadows, a small detail clarifies the picture's iconography: the foliage of a vine, symbolizing grapes and the wine of the Eucharist. The sacrificial sheep and the vineleaves are the outward signs of the saint's inner contemplation. In his mind's eye, he is looking into the future, seeing Christ's blessed death and the salvation of mankind. That is the reason for the smile on his face. It is the beatific smile of a mystic, a seer.

The last of the three pictures commissioned from Caravaggio by Ciriaco Mattei was *The Betrayal of Christ*. It was paid for on 2 January 1603, and probably painted just a few weeks or months before. The picture has had an eventful history. It remained in the Palazzo Mattei in Rome for nearly two centuries, after which it disappeared into the obscurity of a Scottish private collection. In 1990 it was rediscovered in the possession of the Irish Jesuit Fathers of the house of St Ignatius in Dublin, who placed it on indefinite loan to the National Gallery of Ireland.

The story of Christ's betrayal by Judas is told in all four gospels. Caravaggio followed certain stage directions, but ignored others.

According to Matthew, at the time appointed for Christ's arrest, 'Judas, one of the twelve, came, and with him a great multitude with swords and staves, from the chief priests and elders of the people.' (Matthew 26:47). John adds a detail crucial to Caravaggio's nocturnal conception of the scene, equipping Judas and his men 'with lanterns and torches' (John 18:3). Mark gives the most economical account of the treacherous kiss given to Christ by Judas: 'And he that betrayed him had given them a token, saying, Whomsoever I shall kiss, that same is he; take him, and lead him away safely. And as soon as he was come, he goeth straightway to him, and saith, Master, master; and kissed him. And they laid their hands on him, and took him' (Mark 14:44–6). Only in Luke could Caravaggio have found the idea that Christ showed his foreknowledge of Judas's treachery by flinching at the kiss: 'Judas drew near unto Jesus to kiss him. But Jesus said unto him, Judas, betrayest thou the Son of Man with a kiss?' (Luke 23:48).

Despite his academic prejudices, Bellori often responded instinctively to the sheer humanity and psychological depth of Caravaggio's painted dramas. His is by some distance the most eloquent early account of the picture: 'Judas is shown after the kiss with his hand on the Lord's shoulder; a soldier in full armour extends his arms and his ironclad hand towards the chest of the Lord, who stands still, patiently and humbly, his hands crossed before him, as John runs away behind with outstretched arms. Caravaggio rendered the rusty armour of the soldier accurately with head and face covered by a helmet, his profile partially visible. Behind him a lantern is raised and we see the heads of two other armed men.'[36]

Earlier artists had often envisaged the betrayal as a chaotic crowd scene, confusing the eye with a multitude of soldiers and panicking disciples. Caravaggio's new technique of emphatic chiaroscuro was the perfect editing device for avoiding such unnecessary complications. He used it here as a ruthless means of exclusion, spotlighting the figures at the very centre of the drama and casting everything else into deepest shadow. In his interpretation, the whole story becomes an elemental conflict between good and evil, innocence and malignity. The pale, delicate, emotionally sensitive face of Christ is set hard against the brutish, sunburned face of Judas. There is great sorrow, mingled with resignation, in Christ's half-closed eyes. In the moment of betrayal, Judas seems to lament the fatal move he has only just made. He stares into space like a man possessed, as if he is already haunted by the guilt that will soon drive him to suicide.

To this drama of juxtaposed faces, the painter has added a subplot of hands. Judas reaches out to grasp Christ with his left hand, the sinister side. Christ instinctively shrinks from the clutching embrace. Below, isolated and emphasized by a bright pool of light, Christ's own hands are clasped in a gesture of great pathos. His fingers are entwined, palms pushed away, in a movement that speaks at once of regret and acceptance of his fate. It is a detail that suggests the influence of Cardinal Mattei: the Franciscans placed the concept of *Abnegatio*, the complete denial of self and dedication to others, at the centre of their teaching. According to the Franciscan ethic of the *Imitatio Christi*, 'the imitation of Christ', his calm acceptance of cruelty and torture was a constant source of wonder and inspiration. Caravaggio's *Betrayal of Christ* is one of the most powerfully moving images of that Christian ideal.[37] It is a work that allies Caravaggio, once again, with the deepest strains of severity in Counter-Reformation spirituality.

But there is more to the eloquently compressed composition of the picture than the figures of Christ and Judas alone. To the left, just behind Christ, a terrified disciple runs away into the night. Two soldiers approach from the other side to make the arrest. They are grim and impersonal, as lacking in compassion as the stolid executioners in *The Crucifixion of St Peter*. They stand for the implacable forces unleashed by the act of betrayal. Just enough of the face of the soldier on the right is visible, beneath his helmet, to reveal that Caravaggio used the same model who had sat for the open-armed disciple in *The Supper at Emmaus*. This would have been all the more evident when both pictures hung in Ciriaco Mattei's palace. The effect must have been slightly disconcerting, like watching the same actor playing utterly contrasting roles simultaneously. Did Caravaggio do it on purpose, to demonstrate the versatility of his method? The other soldier is so obscured by the burnished steel of his helmet that almost nothing can be seen of his features. He is faceless as well as pitiless.

The encounter of Judas and Christ is charged with feeling, an exchange through which guilt and saddened acquiescence flow. Those emotions are amplified by the fleeing disciple, whose red cloak billows excitedly above the heads of Christ and Judas, linking his form so closely to theirs that he seems less like a person in his own right than like their psychic emanation – a scream forced out into the night sky by their inner turmoil. But the soldiers feel nothing and they show no capacity for feeling. They are all murderous efficiency, armoured against compassion. Christ, Judas and the disciple are beings of yielding flesh; the soldiers seem made of the very steel that they wear. Bellori was particularly struck by the horrid contrast between dark metal and soft human tissue: 'a soldier in full armour extends his arms and his ironclad hand towards the chest of the Lord.'

Caravaggio took the idea for this vivid distinction from a woodcut of Christ's arrest in the garden of Gethsemane by the German Renaissance artist Albrecht Dürer. In Dürer's image the soldier's chain-mailed arm, which calls to mind the scales of an armadillo, reaches across the kissing Judas to the vulnerable figure of Christ with exactly the same gesture. In his own picture, Caravaggio sharpened that ugly juxtaposition and made it even more shocking. The soldier's black armour, jointed at shoulder and elbow, looks like the carapace of some gigantic insect. His black hand points into Christ's neck like the sting of a scorpion about to pierce its prey.

Caravaggio was in the habit of pillaging prints and engravings for compositional ideas during the early years of the seventeenth century. He probably kept a stock of such images, ready catalysts for his imagination. Dürer's woodcut was not his only source for *The Betrayal*. There is another borrowing in the composition, this time from an engraving actually commissioned by the man for whom the picture was destined, Ciriaco Mattei himself. In 1601 Mattei had asked the engraver Francesco Villamena to commemorate a particularly brutal Roman street battle between members of the city's pro-French and pro-Spanish factions. From this bruising scene of affray, Caravaggio took one detail: that of the crescent-shaped, billowing cloak that connects the fleeing disciple to the figures of Christ and Judas. Once again, the painter makes the detail an organic part of his own, very different composition. The actual borrowing is less interesting than the fact that Caravaggio should have been thinking about a scene of modern-day violence in Rome when he devised the composition of his *Betrayal*. It seems that he envisaged the scene, from the start, as just the kind of fracas with which he was personally familiar – a nocturnal scuffle, with figures crying out in the dark Roman night as the *sbirri* pounce on their man.

At the back right of the scene, set slightly apart from its principal action yet straining to witness it, the painter included his own self-portrait. He holds up a lantern with his right hand, a gesture which some have seen as a proud flaunting of his new and very particular method – a demonstration of exactly that technical revolution in studio lighting which Bellori attributed to Caravaggio when he spoke of him 'placing a lamp high so that the light would fall straight down, revealing the principal part of the body and leaving the rest in shadow so as to produce a powerful contrast of light and dark'. The trouble with this is that the light that Caravaggio holds up is actually rather feeble. It fails to illuminate anything much except for the painter's own face and intent expression. The light that falls across Christ's saddened face and clenched hands, the light that gleams in the metal armour of the soldiers, comes from somewhere else. It is fluid and cannot be easily located.

Caravaggio knew very well that studio lighting, the trick for which he was fast becoming famous, can only ever be a device. What counts is what is done with it. The dim paper lantern in Caravaggio's hand may indeed be the emblem of his method. But its ineffectiveness is significant. The painter brings light to the scene, but in a symbolic rather than a literal sense. The real light-source is his imagination.

DIRTY FEET

Caravaggio was increasingly well known in Rome – the volatile, aggressive painter with the lightning-strike style, who made stories from the Bible look as though they were taking place right here, right now. He was also becoming famous as the painter of feet: the overlapped feet of Joseph, feeling the chill during the flight to Egypt; Christ's bare feet, on the stone flags of Matthew's counting house; the nail-pierced feet of St Peter and the dirt-ingrained feet of his coldly indifferent executioner.

Feet were controversial. Here is a passage from a book about the Christian saints and martyrs, written by the theologian Niccolò Lorini del Monte in the second decade of the seventeenth century:

In sum, feet may be taken by the holy Church as symbolising the poor and humble. In addition to the authority of the Holy Fathers, there are also fundamental reasons [for this], because the poor may be called the feet of the Church, and to caress the feet is to caress the poor of Christ. Because if the feet are the last and most lowly part of the human body, the poor and humble are the last part, and those who hold the last place in the Church. The poor carry the heaviest burdens of the world. They are exposed to all the blows, bumps and knocks . . . And if the feet are a member [of the body], then nude and uncovered they lack rosiness, and it is not a shameful thing to discover them: the poor servants of Christ were not guilty and had nothing of which to be ashamed . . . But yet, as they are vile the poor may be humiliated; nevertheless, God has honoured them so much that he has willed the greatest Heroes of the world serve them, and caress them, and fatten them up with servitude and earthly sustenance.[38]

Lorini's paean to feet was part of a discussion of the life of a popular thirteenth-century saint, Elizabeth of Hungary. The daughter of a king, she was famous for receiving the poor into the apartments of her palace, where she fed them, dressed their wounds and washed their feet as Christ himself had washed the feet of his disciples. Francis of Assisi, whose followers called him *alter Christus,* 'another Christ', had also abased himself at the feet of the poor and needy. In Caravaggio's time wealthy members of certain religious confraternities emulated such venerable examples – clothing, feeding and washing the feet of poor pilgrims coming to Rome. To do so was quite literally to embrace humility, to lower the proud self to the ground in emulation of Christ. The Latin root of *humilitas* is the word *humus,* meaning 'ground'. The word 'humble' is part of the same linguistic family. To honour the foot is to honour the lowest part of the human body, and implicitly to humble the self in the sight of God.

When Caravaggio painted the saints and martyrs with bare feet, he was firmly allying himself with the pauperist wing of the Catholic Church. Not only was he explicitly welcoming the poor into his pictures, making them feel part of the same impoverished family as that of Christ and his followers, he was also implicitly calling on the rich to follow the example of those such as St Francis, the merchant's son, and Elizabeth of Hungary, the princess, who had given away all their worldly possessions to minister to the poor. The message would not always be well received.

The painter was kept busy by other commissions as well as by the demands of the Mattei family during the first three years of the century. Early in 1602, several months before painting *The Betrayal of Christ*, he had learned that he was required once more at the church of San Luigi dei Francesi. Although more than a year had passed since Caravaggio had finished the lateral canvases for the Contarelli Chapel, the completion of the whole decorative scheme had been delayed by the prevarications of Jacob Cobaert. At the end of January 1602 the tardy Flemish sculptor finally delivered his marble altarpiece of Matthew and the angel, still partially incomplete. It was instantly rejected by the increasingly irritable and fractious coalition of Mathieu Cointrel's executors.[39] Just eight days later Caravaggio was asked to replace the sculpted altarpiece with a painting of the same subject. Matthew was to be shown writing his gospel. The contract specified that he must be depicted taking dictation from an angel; those were the only figures required. It was a clear brief, but its execution would prove to be far from straightforward and Caravaggio would end up having to paint two versions of the picture. The root of the problem would be his depiction of the saint's feet.

Caravaggio's first *Matthew and the Angel* for the Contarelli Chapel eventually passed to the Kaiser-Friedrich Museum in Berlin. Like the lost portrait of Fillide, it was destroyed by fire during the Second World War, but a record of its appearance is preserved in black-and-white photographs. Possibly because he knew that his picture was replacing a marble altarpiece, the painter created a powerfully sculptural composition. Matthew and his attendant angel, a tender winged boy who guides the saint's writing hand, form a single monumental group. The evangelist sits with his body twisted effortfully around the great book in his lap. His shoulders are hunched, his neck arched forward so that he can peer at the text. The gleaming white pages of the book and the dark jerkin that he wears obscure and interrupt much of his anatomy. His body is reduced to its component elements: balding, bearded head on a bull neck; gnarled hands and forearm; bare legs and heavy feet; toes thrust almost into the viewer's face. This

Matthew is an aggressively inelegant, proletarian figure, conceived along the lines of St Peter in the Cerasi Chapel and very different from the pale-skinned tax-gatherer or the heroic fallen priest depicted in Caravaggio's earlier pictures for the chapel. The suggestion is that he is both writing and reading for the first time, like a peasant made suddenly and miraculously literate.

The gospel of Matthew was at the centre of a controversy between Catholics and Protestants. In the fourth century, St Jerome had asserted that Matthew wrote in Hebrew. But at the start of the sixteenth century the humanist author Erasmus had questioned whether the received version had really been translated from a Hebrew original. This raised the possibility that the biblical book of Matthew was based on a later, corrupt version of the text – posing a grave threat to the authority of the Church itself. In 1537 a Protestant Hebraist named Sebastian Munster published his own translation of a Jewish manuscript that he claimed was the true text of Matthew's gospel, and which differed from the received version in numerous places. Caravaggio was certainly aware of this: the words in the book on Matthew's lap are written in Hebrew, and he has been careful to ensure that they exactly mirror the sense of the received version approved by the Catholic Church.[40]

Because Matthew has just started writing his gospel, the painter shows its opening lines: 'The book of the generations of Jesus Christ, the son of David, the son of Abraham.' Matthew, aided by the angel, is about to finish the next phrase, 'Abraham begat', which marks the start of the gospel's tracing of the lineage of Christ. As the bloodline leading to the salvation of mankind is announced, Matthew stares in wonder.

According to St Jerome, Matthew was the first of the apostles to write his gospel. By the time Caravaggio painted his picture, this had become part of Catholic tradition. He alludes to it by implication through his emphatic use of chiaroscuro. As the wizened, sunburned figure of Matthew receives the very first divinely inspired Christian text, he is bathed in light. Through him, the whole world will be illuminated. As so often during this phase of his career, Caravaggio defines his own art by contrast with that of Michelangelo. Once more, he has the Sistine Chapel in mind, specifically the vast, sculptural figures of the prophets who sit enthroned at the level of the pendentive arches.

Michelangelo's monumental figures, like Caravaggio's Matthew, are shown in the spasms of divine revelation, reading or writing the prophecies vouchsafed to them by God. Also like Caravaggio's Matthew, they are barefoot, and often accompanied by inspiring angelic figures.

But Caravaggio evokes the comparison with Michelangelo's prophets only to offer his own, opposed conception of divine inspiration. His *St Matthew* perfectly reverses all of the properties of the Michelangelesque figure of the prophet. Michelangelo's prophets are nobly idealized figures, decorously draped, but Caravaggio's Matthew is an ordinary, imperfect human being in working clothes that leave his arms and legs bare. Michelangelo depicts troubled intellectuals, straining to grasp God's veiled meanings, but Caravaggio's sainted peasant is a simple man stunned by the directness of his revelation. Whereas Michelangelo's prophets sit on carved thrones of marble, Caravaggio's apostle sits on a simple wooden chair, the same savonarola chair already used for the *Calling of Matthew* and the *Supper at Emmaus*.

Perhaps the most touching aspect of the painting is the intimacy of the relationship between the stooped saint and the tender young angel, whose wings enfold the whole scene in a hushed embrace. The angel is God's messenger but also the embodiment of Christian love – a love so generous it encompasses even those as ragged and gnarled as the cross-legged, doltish St Matthew. The contrast between the two figures is the contrast between extreme youth and encroaching old age. Frailty is being overcome, an old man is being made young by the teachings of a child, which are the teachings of Christ himself, and the writing of the first word of the first gospel marks the very instant when the Old Testament is being replaced by the New.

Despite or more likely because of its brusque singularity Caravaggio's picture 'pleased nobody', according to Baglione. The *St Matthew* was rejected as soon as it was delivered. Bellori gave the fullest account of events: 'Here something happened that greatly upset Caravaggio with respect to his reputation. After he had finished the central picture of St Matthew and installed it on the altar, the priests took it down, saying that the figure with its legs crossed and its feet rudely exposed to the public had neither decorum nor the appearance of a saint.'[41] That was, of course, precisely Caravaggio's point: Christ and his followers looked a lot more like beggars than cardinals. But the decision of Mathieu Cointrel's executors – who included François Cointrel, his nephew and heir – was final. Saving Caravaggio's blushes, Vincenzo Giustiniani took the painting of *St Matthew* for his own collection. According to Bellori, Giustiniani also prevailed on the congregation of San Luigi dei Francesi to allow the painter to try again.

The resulting picture, his second version of *St Matthew and the Angel*, was accepted without demur. It remains on the altar of the chapel. The character of the painting, and indeed the very fact that it was commissioned at all, suggests that those in charge of the commission had few doubts about the painter's ability. As far as they were concerned, it was merely his taste, and the tenor of his piety, that was suspect: if he was given the right instruction, these could easily be amended.

The second *St Matthew* suggests that Bellori's account of the reasons for the rejection of the first was correct. Matthew the shockingly illiterate peasant has suddenly been turned into Matthew the dignified, grey-haired sage. This scholar-saint kneels at his desk, quill pen at the ready. He is draped in red robes and has been equipped with an expression of dignified attentiveness. Rather than guiding his uncertain hand, the angel now counts off the verses as he dictates them. The pages of the book are no longer visible, but since the angel has got to the index finger of his left hand – number two, in the gestural rhetoric of the time, since Italians counted the number one with their thumbs – it seems that he has once more got to the start of the second verse, and Abraham's begetting of Christ's lineage. The angel's airborne arrival from behind Matthew closely echoes the composition of Tintoretto's *Virgin Appearing to St Jerome*, which Caravaggio may have seen in Venice. There is no suggestion of intimacy here. A message is not vouchsafed tenderly as an act of love, but handed down from on high as an emanation of divine authority.

Caravaggio's second *St Matthew and the Angel* is a much diluted, dutifully toned-down version of his original idea. Matthew's poverty and humility are not rudely proclaimed, but politely whispered. The most tellingly emphatic of the painter's several adjustments relate to the apostle's feet. They are shown in profile rather than thrust towards the viewer, still bare but unlikely to offend anybody.

For the first but not the last time, Caravaggio's work had been censored. His sin when painting the first *St Matthew* had been to make holy poverty and humility unpalatably real. On this occasion his embarrassment was spared by Vincenzo Giustiniani, but Giustiniani's purchase of the first *St Matthew* itself created a paradox. A work of art expressly designed to articulate ideals of popular piety, to appeal to the broadest possible audience, had been deemed unsuitable for mass consumption. Instead, the picture had found a home in the collection of a noted connoisseur. The implication was that there was something dangerous, even seditious, about Caravaggio's emphatically humble vision of the origins of Christianity. In a prominent church, such an intoxicatingly powerful painting might serve as a rallying cry. It might have an influence. Its visual language might help shape the visual language of the Counter-Reformation Catholic Church. But confined to the collection of a rich man, it became something much less potent: an interesting work of art, an experiment in a new style, but altogether too strange and adventurous for anyone but a sophisticate and his friends to appreciate.

LONG LIVE V

Vincenzo Giustiniani was a torchbearer for Caravaggio's intensely ascetic religious art. He had probably helped the painter to win the commission to paint the lateral canvases in the Cerasi Chapel, and if Bellori is to believed it was he who persuaded the executors of Mathieu Cointrel to allow Caravaggio a second attempt at the *St Matthew* altarpiece for the Contarelli Chapel. Now, probably around the start of 1603, Giustiniani commissioned one of Caravaggio's most uncompromisingly pauperist depictions of Christ and his disciples, *Doubting Thomas*,[42] and when it was finished he displayed it prominently in the huge Palazzo Giustiniani, opposite San Luigi dei Francesi, on Via Crescenzi. Its presence there, in addition to that of the first *St Matthew*, meant that the Giustiniani collection was fast becoming an advertisement for Caravaggio's new approach to devotional art. Vincenzo Giustiniani must have hoped that with his support the artist would eventually win papal favour, obtain great public commissions and become one of those painters who transform the depiction of Christian belief. Without him, many of Caravaggio's most remarkable pictures might never have been created.

Doubting Thomas is a raw picture about the palpable proving of faith. Joachim von Sandrart, impressed by the graphic realism of the work, described it as a picture of 'Christ, in whose holy wounds, Thomas, in the presence of the other apostles, is putting his finger. By means of good painting and modelling he was able to show on the faces of all those present such an expression of astonishment and naturalness of skin and flesh that in comparison all other pictures seemed to be coloured paper.'[43] Sandrart was responding not only to the flesh wound in Christ's side but also to the wrinkled and wizened skin of Thomas and his companions. Thin and papery with age, perhaps it was this that elicited his thoughts about other pictures looking like coloured paper. Caravaggio, once the painter of withered autumn fruits, was becoming increasingly the painter of withered human beings, battered by age and poverty.

Like *The Supper at Emmaus*, *Doubting Thomas* was inspired by a legend of the risen Christ. The painter's source was a passage from the gospel of John:

when the doors were shut where the disciples were assembled for fear of the Jews, came Jesus and stood in the midst, and saith unto them, Peace be with you. And when he had so said, he shewed unto them his hands and his side. Then were the disciples glad, when they saw the Lord ... But Thomas, one of the twelve, called Didymus, was not with them when Jesus came. The other disciples therefore said unto him, We have seen the Lord. But he said unto them, Except I shall see in his hands the print of the nails, and thrust my hand into his side, I will not believe. And after eight days again his disciples were within, and Thomas with them: then came Jesus, the doors being shut, and stood in the midst, and said, Peace be unto you. Then saith he to Thomas, Reach hither thy finger, and behold my hands; and reach hither thy hand, and thrust it into my side: and be not faithless, but believing. And Thomas answered and said unto him, My Lord and my God. Jesus saith unto him, Thomas, because thou hast seen me, thou hast believed: blessed are they that have not seen, and yet have believed' (John 20:20–29).

Caravaggio chose a half-length frieze-like composition and a close-up view, further excluding all extraneous detail with his usual blanket of shadow. The story is distilled to its essence. Four faces, arranged in the configuration of a diamond, bear mute witness to the miracle of the Resurrection. Christ gently accepts the indignity of being surgically investigated by his sceptical follower. Holding aside the folds of his burial sheet, he guides Thomas's hand towards him and draws the disciple's forefinger into his open wound. Two fellow-disciples crowd round, eyes fixed on the clinical probing of divine flesh. Christ too looks down, as though assisting at his own autopsy. The place where finger meets wound is a different kind of vanishing point, achieved without the calculations of perspective. All converges at the place where the miracle is proved to be true, and the meta-physical and the empirical meet.

Thomas and his fellow apostles are men in the same mould as the first *St Matthew and the Angel*, earnest, ordinary, with heavily lined brows and sunburned faces. Thomas's sleeve needs restitching at the shoulder. An otherwordly radiance floods the scene, illumination the herald of revelation. Cured of his doubt, Thomas himself looks not at the wound in Christ's side but instead to the light.

There is also, once more, the suggestion of a reminiscence of Michelangelo's paintings for the Sistine Chapel. Thomas's reaching gesture is another of Caravaggio's inverted variations on the fingertip-touching act of generation at the centre of Michelangelo's *Creation of Adam*. In the act of touching Christ, Thomas is born again in unques-tioning faith.

Giustiniani commissioned one other, very different picture from Car-avaggio. It is the single, stunning exception to the prevailingly solemn body of work produced by the artist during these middle years of his career. *Omnia vincit amor*, or *Love Conquers All*, was painted in the summer of 1602. The most nakedly libidinous of the painter's secular mythological works, it is a mischievously joyful celebration of Eros – a laughing proclamation of the power of sexual love.

A smooth-skinned, naked young Cupid, far removed from the wiz-ened saints of Caravaggio's devotional pictures, confronts the viewer with a puckish smile. The figure half sits and half stands, one leg raised and bent at an angle of almost ninety degrees to his body. Awkwardly perched on a table draped with a white sheet, he occupies an interior cluttered with the stuff of intellectual, artistic, military and political endeavour: men may fight and dream, create and aspire, but in the end love will always triumph over all. The picture's symbolism is concisely explained in a 1638 inventory of the Giustiniani collection, where it is listed as 'A painting of a smiling Cupid, in the act of disparaging the world'.[44] The question of whether it may have had other and deeper meanings, both for Caravaggio and for his patron, Vincenzo Giustiniani, has been hotly contested.

The pubescent boy who modelled for the picture also modelled for the *St John the Baptist*, painted by Caravaggio for Ciriaco Mattei at around the same time. Like that other picture, *Omnia vincit amor* is a variation on Michelangelo's *ignudi* in the Sistine Chapel, although the effect on this occasion could hardly be more different. The *St John* is a sanctified version of a Michelangelo nude, spiritually transformed by Christian revelation. This dazzling Cupid in an airless room is devoid of conscience or piety. He embodies a triumphant, amoral, vibrant sexuality.

The figure's pose carries echoes not only of the *ignudi*, but also of famous sculptures, one by Michelangelo, the marble figure of *Victory*,[45] and one by Donatello, the celebrated bronze *David*, the first freestanding image of the male nude since antiquity, a work charged with homoerotic overtones. Caravaggio's sexy adolescent is the extrovert alter ego of Donatello's veiled, ambiguous, naked young man. The most sensually explicit detail of Donatello's bronze is a feather, a plume from the felled Goliath's helmet, that tickles David's inner thigh. The same motif is repeated in Caravaggio's painting, but here the boy's leg is brushed by the tip of one of his own Cupid's wings.

Joachim von Sandrart, a guest of Vincenzo Giustiniani between 1629 and 1635, reported that the marchese prized the *Omnia vincit amor* above all the other works in his collection. He gave an admiring, if not altogether accurate, description of the picture itself, and an arresting account of the manner in which it was originally displayed:

Caravaggio painted for the Marchese Giustiniani a life-size Cupid as a boy of about 12 years old, seated on a globe, and raising his bow in his right hand. On his left are various instruments, a book for studies, a laurel wreath. The Cupid has the brown wings of an eagle. Everything is accurately and clearly designed with bright colours and a three-dimensionality that approximates reality. This painting was among 120 others in a gallery of the most celebrated artists. But, I recall, it was covered with a curtain of dark green silk, and was shown last, after all the others, to avoid eclipsing the other works.[46]

The objects strewn at Cupid's feet and by his side form a dispersed but uniquely haunting still life: a hallucination of things. They allude to the arts, sciences and letters. A compass and triangle, representing architecture as well as geometry, are prominent in the left foreground. A violin and a lute, rendered in extreme foreshortening, are propped on a musical part-book. A manuscript, emblem of literary ambition, lies open and abandoned on the floor. A laurel wreath has been dropped on to an empty cuirass and other scattered pieces of armour, of the same dark steel as that worn by the sinister soldier in *The Betrayal of Christ*. These signs of military glory undone are complemented by the crown and sceptre obscurely nestling in the dishevelled sheets near Cupid's raised calf. Poking out from behind his right thigh is the rim of a celestial globe, blue with gold stars. Astronomy too has been laid low by Cupid, who holds up two arrows – not his bow, as Sandrart had asserted – to symbolize his triumph over all the works and schemes of industrious but easily tempted humanity.

The objects in the painting may have been selected to reflect Vincenzo Giustiniani's own interests and family history. He was an author and a well-known musical amateur with a keen interest in astrology. The Giustiniani also had an illustrious military and political history. According to one ingenious (but incorrect) interpretation, the picture is not even intended to show love's triumph over all worldly endeavours. Instead it is a celebration of Vincenzo Giustiniani's many accomplishments, a Neoplatonic allegory of the passion propelling him and his family to so many different forms of excellence.[47] But if art and culture really were being celebrated, why would their remnants litter the floor like bric-a-brac?

Sandrart's remark about the patron keeping the picture until the end of a tour through his house – saving the best until last – is suggestive.

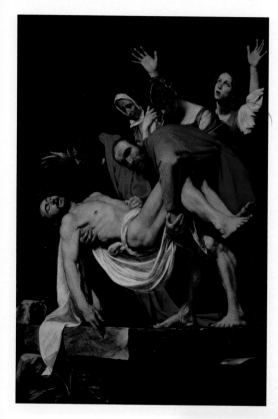

36. *The Entombment.* This stark, strong composition was much admired by the people of Rome, whom Giovanni Baglione described as 'chattering like geese' at its unveiling.

37. *Pietà* by Michelangelo. Caravaggio adapted the limp right arm of Michelangelo's dead Christ for his own version of the same figure in *The Entombment* (above).

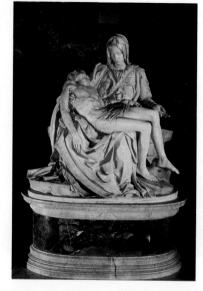

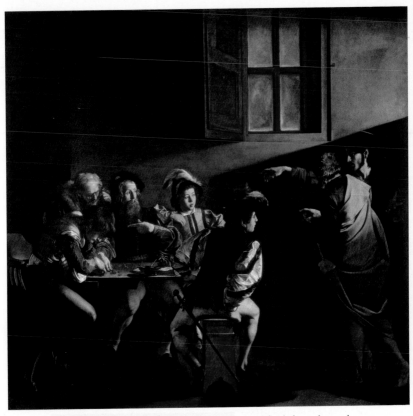

38. *The Calling of St Matthew.* 'And as Jesus passed forth from thence, he saw a man, named Matthew, sitting at the receipt of custom: and he saith unto him, Follow me. And he arose, and followed him' (Matthew 9).

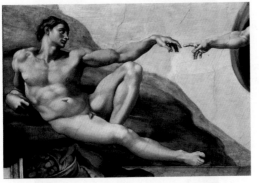

39. *The Creation of Adam* by Michelangelo (detail). Caravaggio modelled the hand of his beckoning Christ (above) on the hand of Michelangelo's Adam.

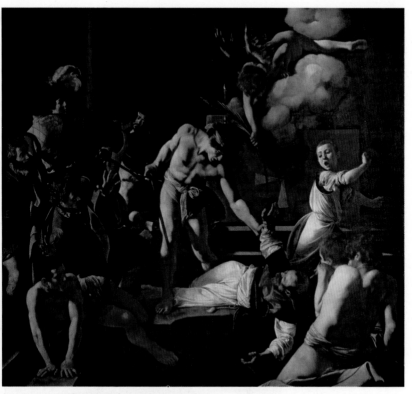

40. *The Martyrdom of St Matthew*. Caravaggio included his self-portrait among those fleeing from the scene of the crime. He looks back as if to regret his failure to help the stricken Matthew.

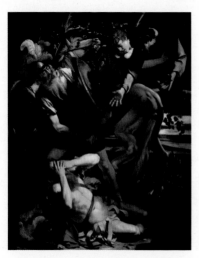

41. *The Conversion of St Paul* (first version). One of Caravaggio's few failures, it was immediately rejected by the patron, Tiberio Cerasi. The reeling servant looks like a spear-carrier in a bad comic opera.

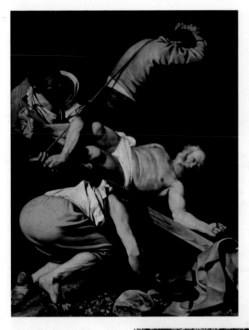

42. *The Crucifixion of St Peter*. Peter insisted that he be crucified upside down, because he felt unworthy of the same death as Christ. His unfeeling executioners impassively hoist him aloft.

43. The Cerasi Chapel (front view). (*above the altar*) Annibale Carracci's *Assumption of the Virgin*. (*left*) *The Crucifixion of St Peter*. (*right*) *The Conversion of St Paul*, with horse's rump aimed at Carracci's Virgin Mary.

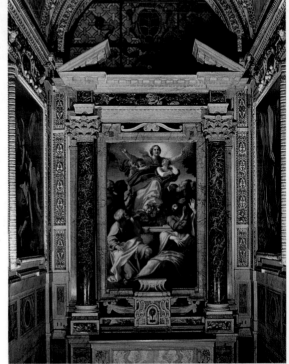

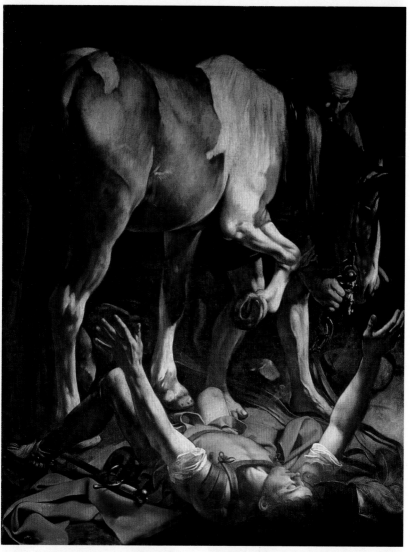

44. *The Conversion of St Paul* (second version). Rejecting the tumult and drama of his first, unsuccessful treatment of the subject (Plate 41), Caravaggio internalized the action so that we sense it unfolding within Paul's soul.

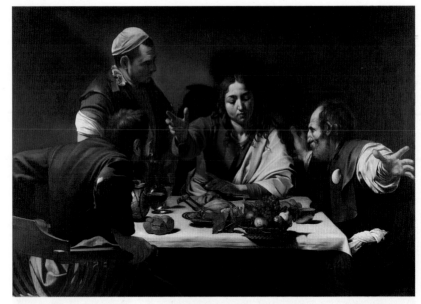

45. *The Supper at Emmaus*. As the risen Christ reveals himself to the two disciples, they react with gestures of awe and astonishment.

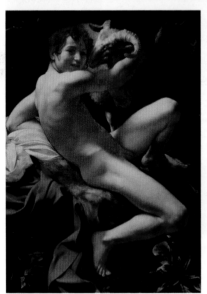

46. *St John the Baptist*. Caravaggio's workshop assistant, Cecco, modelled for this depiction of the saint in the wilderness as a smiling and ecstatic young boy.

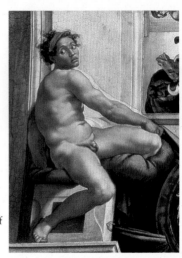

47. *Ignudo* by Michelangelo. The male nudes on the Sistine Chapel ceiling evoke the golden age of classical myth. Caravaggio appropriated motifs from Michelangelo's work throughout his life.

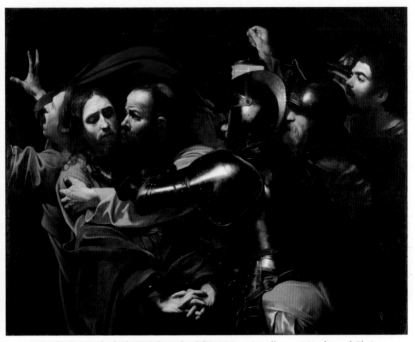

48. *The Betrayal of Christ.* 'The pale, delicate, emotionally sensitive face of Christ is set hard against the brutish, sunburned face of Judas.'

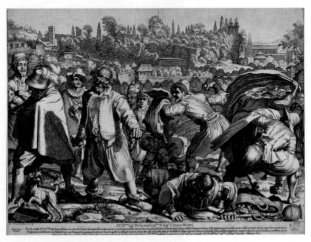

49. *Street Scene* by Francesco Villamena. A notorious battle between Rome's pro-French and pro-Spanish factions. Caravaggio took the billowing cloak for his own nocturnal street scene, *The Betrayal of Christ*.

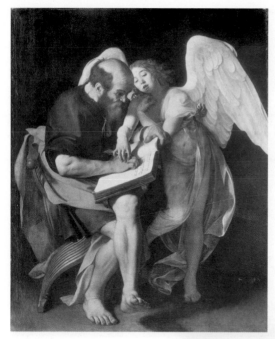

50. *St Matthew and the Angel* (first version). Caravaggio's first, rejected version of the altarpiece. Objections were raised to its lack of decorum. During the Second World War, it met the same fate as the lost *Portrait of Fillide Melandroni* (Plate 34).

51. *St Matthew and the Angel* (second version). More refined but less forceful, the saint has metamorphosed from illiterate bumpkin to dignified sage. The picture still hangs over the altar in the Contarelli Chapel today.

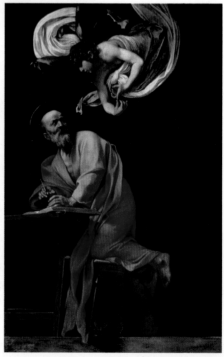

Having shown his guests his splendid palace, his collections of classical statuary, his musical *camerino*, his pictures by the great masters of Italian art, Giustiniani would show them *this* – an allegory of all hubris, creative and intellectual, brought low at the feet of love. An elegant gesture of knowing self-deprecation was surely intended. As rich and influential as he was, as accomplished in the arts, letters and sciences, even he still had to concede – with a graceful smile, of course – that there was a limit to his powers. Before love, all must give way.[48]

But *Omnia vincit amor* was more than just an excuse for that graceful flourish of rhetoric. The picture is arrestingly littered with letter *v*'s. The majuscule in the musical part-book is a *v*. The set square is arranged in the form of a *v*. The compasses form an upside down *v*. The violin and lute fall across each other to form a *v*. The crown and sceptre shape a *v*. So does the curiously awkward arrangement of the Cupid's splayed legs. His wings echo the shape too. They are eagle's wings, which also formed part of the Giustiniani family crest. All these *v*'s are also implicated in an orgiastic series of sexual consummations. The set square pushes at the furled circle formed by the part-book's leaves. The compass straddles the set square. The bow of the violin has slid over the neck of the instrument. The sceptre phallically pierces the circle of the crown. Even the white sheet on which the boy rests has contrived to fold itself, at the point just below Cupid's phallus, into the shape of the female sex.

The phrase *omnia vincit amor* is taken from Virgil's *Eclogues*, where it is followed by the line *et nos cedamus amori*: 'Love conquers all; let us lovers all yield to it.' In Caravaggio's painting, the objects of art and culture have not merely been conquered by love, they have given themselves up to passion. The picture buzzes and pulsates with libidinous energy. It is a mythology shot through with a raucously erotic and life-affirming sense of comedy, a fantasy of learning and knowledge suddenly caught up in the throes of sexual self-abandonment.

But why would Caravaggio have painted such a picture for a Roman nobleman? And why would a man such as Vincenzo Giustiniani have wanted one? There was in fact a long tradition of such erotically charged mythologies in Italian painting. They were usually created on the occasion of family weddings. The earliest examples were painted on the panels of the wedding chests traditionally given by groom to bride in fifteenth-century Tuscany.[49] By the end of the fifteenth century the mythological love painting had emancipated itself from the decoration of wedding chests to become an independent art form. Botticelli's *Birth of Venus* is the most famous example. The goddess of love rises from the sea and steps on to dry land. As she does, a cloak is readied by Venus's handmaiden to wrap her perfect body. A particular bunched fold of that cloak, close to Venus's face, has been painted by Botticelli to resemble the female sex and within it a tiny leaf is folded, an emblem of fertility. There are shades, here, of Caravaggio's vulva-like twist of sheet in *Omnia vincit amor* – and an anticipation of its meaning. *The Birth of Venus* was painted as a gift to a Medici bride. Its message was unambiguous. Like the virgin Venus leaving the sea and arriving on earth, the bride was about to leave her former chastity behind and embark on married life. As she did so, the painting was offered to her as a prayer for the future fertility of the union.

This tradition was still alive in Caravaggio's time, although by then it had mutated into yet more spectacular forms – none more so than the mythological-erotic ceiling painted by Annibale Carracci for the ceiling of the Farnese Palace between 1597 and 1601. A deliberately pagan parody of Michelangelo's Sistine Chapel ceiling, Carracci's Farnese decorations constitute a vast panorama of the loves of the gods, a comical riot of the sexual indiscretions of Jupiter, Juno and a veritable horde of other, amorously inflamed deities. The overarching theme of the ceiling is *Omnia vincit amor*. The work was painted, just like the wedding chests of Tuscan tradition, just like Botticelli's *Birth of Venus*, to celebrate a wedding.[50]

It is highly likely that Caravaggio's own *Omnia vincit amor* was commissioned on the occasion of a wedding in the Giustiniani family. Whether it commemorates a particular event or not, its essential meaning is clear. Vincenzo was a family name among the Giustiniani, so all those orgiastically active *v*'s in the picture may be taken to stand both for the man who commissioned the work and for his many heirs and descendants. Long live the Giustiniani, the picture priapically exclaims: long may they prosper, and long may they procreate.

THE BLACK WINGS OF ENVY

Giovanni Baglione and his friends were not happy to see the painter from Lombardy doing so well. Forty years later, when he came to write his short biography of Caravaggio, Baglione still seethed with a sense of injustice when he thought of his rival winning a string of commissions from Vincenzo Giustiniani and Ciriaco Mattei. As far as Baglione was concerned, Caravaggio's patrons had been fooled by nothing more than clever publicity: 'The Marchese had been put into this frame of mind by Prosperino delle Grottesche, Caravaggio's henchman [Prospero Orsi, the painter of grotesques] ... Moreover, Signor Ciriaco Mattei succumbed to the propaganda ... Thus Caravaggio pocketed from this gentleman many hundreds of scudi.'[51]

Karel van Mander's *Schilderboek* of 1604 includes some pithy remarks on the rivalries that divided Rome's competing factions of artists during the early years of the seventeenth century. According to van Mander, Clement VIII and his papal court commissioned so many new works that they stirred up a frenzy of competition among painters and sculptors: 'a new ardour is kindled; lean Envy secretly begins to flap her black wings and everyone strives to do his best to gain the coveted prize.'[52]

The dark wings of Caravaggio's Cupid certainly fanned the flames of Giovanni Baglione's envy. Infuriated by the acclaim with which Caravaggio's *Omnia vincit amor* had been received – the curtain of green silk later described by Sandrart proof of its status as the *coup de théâtre* of Vincenzo Giustiniani's whole collection – Baglione responded with an act of provocation. On 29 August 1602 he brought a new work to the artists' exhibition held annually in the courtyard of San Giovanni Decollato. Caravaggio was not taking part in the show, but his friend and follower Orazio Gentileschi did have a picture on display. Baglione's painting was an attack on both of them, as Gentileschi would later explain under cross-examination: 'there certainly is some rivalry among us. When I hung a picture of *St Michael the Archangel* in San Giovanni dei Fiorentini [a slip of the tongue; the exhibition took place in San Giovanni Decollato], Baglione showed up and hung one of his opposite, a *Divine Love* that he had done to vie with an *Earthly Love* by Michelangelo da Caravaggio.'

The full title of Baglione's painting, now in the Gemäldegalerie in Berlin, is *Divine Love Overcoming Earthly Love, the World, the Flesh and the Devil*. It is no masterpiece but it is a clever and vicious painting, carefully calculated to try to wound Caravaggio and cloud his reputation. Inverting both the moral and the message of *Omnia vincit amor*, Baglione shows love conquered by virtue. A saint in armour subdues a cowed and cowering Cupid, while the devil skulks in darkness to one side. Although armed with a thunderbolt rather than shield and sword, the figure of *Divine Love* evokes traditional images of Archangel Michael trampling Satan underfoot – a detail that can only have been intended to sharpen Baglione's satire. Caravaggio's own holy namesake is shown exorcizing the erotic and demonic spirits of Caravaggio's art. The resemblance to St Michael may also have been meant as a sideswipe at Gentileschi and his own 'picture of *St Michael the Archangel*'. But Caravaggio was the primary target. Baglione's parody is completed by the emphatically Caravaggesque lighting that flashes across the vengeful angel and the prone, flaccid form of Cupid below.

Not content with satirizing Caravaggio and his art, Baglione even dared to offer his own picture to Vincenzo Giustiniani's brother, Cardinal Benedetto Giustiniani. Yet more galling, it was accepted, and Baglione given the traditional painter's reward of a gold chain. Gentileschi, who would tell this part of the story too in court, was distinctly unamused by the whole affair. He tried to get his own back by telling Baglione that his avenging angel should have been naked and childlike, perhaps deliberately misunderstanding the figure's pointed and satirical resemblance to the Archangel Michael: '[Baglione] had dedicated *Divine Love* to Cardinal Giustiniani and although said picture was not liked as much as the one by Michelangelo – all the same, that Cardinal gave him a neck chain. That painting had many flaws. I told him he had done a grown-up man in armour who should have been nude and putto, so he did another that was completely nude.'

That last remark is only half true. Baglione did paint another *Divine Love*, the version now in the Palazzo Barberini in Rome, but he completely ignored Gentileschi's advice. The second and equally grown-up angel is certainly no naked putto. He still wears armour, albeit modified this time to a breastplate and some wisps of drapery.

The most important change has been made elsewhere, at the bottom of the picture. The devil, previously shown lurking in obscurity, now wheels round with an expression of startled guilt on his face. Despite his staring eyes, his fangs and his pointed ears, he is unmistakably a portrait in caricature of Caravaggio, caught *in flagrante* with a flushed and furtive Cupid. Baglione's second *Divine Love* went beyond satire. It was a visual accusation of sodomy.

Baglione repeated that charge verbally, and in public. He and his friends talked openly about Caravaggio keeping company with a *bardassa* – vulgar Italian slang derived from a Turkish word for a young man who took the female part in sexual encounters with other men. Rome's artists gossiped, so people may have begun to look at Caravaggio's *Omnia vincit amor* in a different light. The identity of the boy who had modelled for Cupid was known. He was Cecco di Caravaggio, who prepared the artist's paint and his canvases.[53] If Baglione was to be believed, not only was he Caravaggio's assistant and model, he was also his catamite.

Half a century later, the story was still current. In about 1650 an English artist called Richard Symonds was shown round the Giustini-ani collection in Rome. He made notes on the pictures, writing down any anecdotes that struck him. He obviously spent a while in front of *Omnia vincit amor*. The *custode* told him that it was one of the most precious pictures in the collection, that it had cost 300 scudi, and that both the Cardinal of Savoy and a member of the Crescenzi family had offered 2,000 ducats for it. But the punchline of the spiel, no doubt regularly trotted out to tourists visiting the palace, was the scandalous relationship between artist and model. Here is a full transcription of the entry in Symonds's travel journal:

> Cupido di Caravaggio / Card di Savoya profe. / 2 milia duboli p[er] / il
> Cupido di Caravaggio / Costo 3 cento scudi. / Checco del Caravaggio
> tis / calld among the painters / twas his boy – / haire darke, 2 wings /
> raie, compasses lute / violin & armes & laurel / Monsr Crechy vuolle
> dare / 2 milia dubole / Twas the body & face / of his owne boy or ser-
> vant / that laid with him.[54]

From the readiness with which the story was believed and then accepted into local legend, it seems that nobody had been particularly surprised to hear about Caravaggio's alleged homosexual proclivities. He was known to be an impetuous man who followed his passions. He kept company with whores and courtesans, such as Fillide Melandroni, and on the evidence of his paintings he was equally alive to the physical charms of men. Caravaggio and Francesco Boneri, alias Cecco, were close: Cecco stayed with him even after he was obliged to leave Rome in 1606. There is a good chance that the rumours were true and that Caravaggio did indeed have a sexual as well as a working relationship with 'his owne boy or servant'.

Whatever the reality, Baglione's accusations were damaging and dangerous. Sodomy was a capital crime in Clement VIII's Rome, and though the authorities were unlikely to investigate the well-connected Caravaggio's sexual behaviour, as long as he was reasonably discreet, the potential harm to his name and prospects was immense. Once an artist had been smeared as a pederast, his work was smeared too. People were liable to stop taking it seriously, seeing it only through the lens of its creator's presumed sexual aberration. This had happened half a century before, notoriously, to an artist named Giovanni Antonio Bazzi. Bazzi had offended the famous chronicler of artists' lives, Giorgio Vasari, who had taken his revenge in print: 'since he always had about him boys and beardless youths, whom he loved more than was decent, he acquired the by-name of Sodoma.'[55] This was all a pure fabrication on Vasari's part, first started perhaps by Bazzi's rival, the Sienese painter Domenico Beccafumi. But the mud stuck, and to this day the artist is known as Il Sodoma, 'the Sodomite'.

Caravaggio was deeply sensitive about his reputation. He never knowingly allowed the least slight to go unpunished. His nocturnal assault on Girolamo Spampa, the art student from Montepulciano, was proof of that. Spampa had probably been recycling Federico Zuccaro's criticisms of Caravaggio's Contarelli Chapel paintings, which he had most likely heard from Baglione in the first place. Either way, Baglione must have been aware of the beating that Caravaggio had given Spampa, which had taken place just eighteen months before. He knew that his satires and smears would not be forgotten. Sooner or later, Caravaggio would retaliate.

The autumn and winter of 1602 passed without incident, as Caravaggio bided his time. Only in spring of the following year did he give vent to his simmering anger. He was stung into retaliation by the unveiling of Baglione's largest work yet, *The Resurrection*, an altarpiece for the principal Jesuit church in Rome, the Gesù. That work is now lost, but, to judge by Baglione's preparatory study in the Louvre, it was a clumsy and grandiose essay in the same proto-Baroque idiom as Carracci's *Assumption of the Virgin*. In the sketch Christ stands heavily on a stage-flat cloud as angelic choirs hymn his heavenward ascent. Below on earth, one of the soldiers guarding the tomb gets drowsily to his feet, while others snooze or look on in laboured poses of amazement.

Baglione could carry off the mock sublimity of a parody like the *Divine Love*. But when he strove for effects of awe-inspiring transcendence, he was undone both by his lack of skill and by the essentially prosaic nature of his imagination. His shortcomings can only have been magnified by the scale of the altarpiece for the Gesù: eight metres high and nearly five across.[56] The picture was in its allotted place by Passiontide 1603, but kept under wraps until Easter Sunday itself, the day of the Resurrection. It seems never to have been much loved. Caravaggio and his friends set the tone for its reception by poking fun at it from the moment it was unveiled. There would be no protests when it was quietly removed from the church towards the end of the seventeenth century, following alterations to the transept altars.

Caravaggio observed (and probably helped to orchestrate) the picture's unfavourable reception with rancorous pleasure. He was already annoyed that Baglione had been given such a prestigious assignment – and all the more irritated because he suspected that Baglione had won the job through the ruse of offering his satire, the *Divine Love*, to Benedetto Giustiniani. Cardinal Giustiniani was a Jesuit and had probably intervened with the general of the order, Claudio Acquaviva, to obtain the commission for Baglione. So when his rival produced his monumental flop, Caravaggio decided that it was the moment to take his revenge. What better time to kick a man than when he is down?

Shortly after Easter Sunday 1603 a couple of newly composed satirical poems caused something of a sensation in the artists' quarter of Rome. Copies were passed round. Impromptu recitals were held. The verses were aimed at 'Gioan Bagaglia' or 'Gian Coglione', 'John

Baggage' or 'Johnny Testicle'. They were not the most ingenious nick-names for Giovanni Baglione, but they were effective. One of the poems also included a swipe at 'Mao', the alias of Tommaso Salini, who was a minor still life painter and Baglione's closest associate.

The first poem is crude and makeshift, a mock-sonnet with all the subtlety of a punch in the face:

> Gioan Bagaglia tu no[n] sai un ah
> le tue pitture sono pituresse
> volo vedere con esse
> ch[e] non guadagnarai
> mai una patacca
> Ch[e] di cotanto panno
> da farti un paro di bragesse
> ch[e] ad ognun mostrarai
> quel ch[e] fa la cacca
> portela adunque
> i tuoi disegni e cartoni
> ch[e] tu ai fatto a Andrea pizzicarolo
> o veramente forbete ne il culo
> o alla moglie di Mao turegli la potta
> ch[e] libelli con quel suo cazzon da mulo più non la fotte
> perdonami dipintore se io non ti adulo
> ch[e] della collana ch[e] tu porti indegno sei
> et della pittura vituperio.[57]

John Baggage you don't even know
That your pictures are mere woman's-work
I want to see
That you won't even earn a counterfeit penny from them
Because with as much canvas
As it would take to make yourself a pair of breeches
You can show everyone
What shit truly is
Therefore take
Your drawings and cartoons
That you have made, to Andrea the grocer's shop

[so he can wrap fruit and veg in them]
Or wipe your arse with them
Or stuff them up the cunt of Mao's wife
Because he isn't fucking her anymore with his donkey cock
Pray pardon me, painter, if I do not worship you
Because you don't merit that chain you wear round your neck
And your painting deserves only vituperation.

Benedetto Giustiniani's award of a gold chain to Baglione evidently still rankled. Rubens, Van Dyck and Rembrandt would all paint themselves wearing chains of gold, symbols of accomplishment and courtly patronage. It was a mark of intellectual distinction, a sign of honour, but it had been conferred on Baglione for painting a picture that explicitly *dishonoured* Caravaggio.

The second poem was rather more carefully constructed, in regular hendecasyllabic lines. Its attacks on Baglione were slightly less sexually graphic, at least until the last line:

> Gian Coglione senza dubio dir si puole
> quel ch[e] biasimar si mette altrui
> ch[e] può cento anni esser mastro di lui.
> Nella pittura intendo la mia prole
> poi ch[e] pittor si vol chiamar colui
> Ch[e] no[n] può star p[er] macinar con lui.
> I color no[n] ha mastro nel numero
> si sfaciatamente nominar si vole
> si sa pur il proverbio ch[e] si dice
> ch[e] chi lodar si vole si maledice
> Io no[n] son uso lavarmi la bocca
> ne meno di inalzar quel ch[e] no[n] merta
> come fa l'idol suo ch[e] è cosa certa.
> Se io metterme volessi a ragionar
> delle [s . . . re] fatte da questui
> no[n] bastarian interi un mese o dui.
> Vieni un po' qua tu ch'[e] vo' biasimare
> l'altrui pitture et sai pur ch[e] le tue
> si stano in casa tua a' chiodi ancora
> vergogna[n]doti tu mostrarle fuora.

Infatti i' vo' l'impresa aba[n]donare
ch[e] sento ch[e] mi abonda tal materia
massime s'intrassi n[e] la catena
d'oro ch[e] al collo indegnamente porta
ch[e] credo certo [meglio] se io non erro
a piè gle ne staria una di ferro.
Di tutto quel che ha detto con passione
per certo gli è p[er] ché credo beuto
avesse certo come è suo doùto
altrime[n]te ei saria un becco fotuto.

Call him Johnny Bollock,
this man who sets about criticizing another man
who could be his master for a hundred years.
I mean in my beloved art of painting,
because he would like to call himself a painter
although he's not even fit to grind colours for that other man.
Using colours isn't as easy as one two three,
even if he shamelessly wants to pretend it's like that.
Everyone knows the truth of the proverb:
Men like to attack those whom they should really be praising.
I'm not one for washing my mouth out,
nor for exalting someone who doesn't merit it,
as he praises his false idol.
If I wanted to start describing
the pathetic things this man has done
a whole month wouldn't be enough, nor even two.
Come here for a moment, you who like to criticize
the paintings of another,
even though you know that your own
are still in your house
because you're ashamed to show them to anyone.
In fact I'm going to stop this humiliation in a minute
because I've just got too much material to work with
especially if I start on that necklace
of gold which you so undeservedly wear round your neck
because I believe, if I'm not mistaken, that you should

really have an iron one attached to your ankle.
As for all that [Johnny Bollock] has said with such passion,
well, it can only be because he's drunk, in my opinion,
as he ought to be,
otherwise he'd just be a fucked-over cuckold.

There was a long and carnivalesque tradition of colourful insult in Rome, embodied by the battered ancient statue known as *Pasquino*, which stood at the corner of Palazzo Braschi to the western side of Piazza Navona. It had long been the custom to attach squibs, satires, scurrilous pieces of graffiti and other outbursts of defamatory rage to the wall next to the statue, under the cover of darkness. There was a collective noun for these libels: *pasquinate*, or 'pasquinades'. Caravaggio, a familiar sight in the Piazza Navona, sword strapped to his side, may well have attached the verses attacking Baglione to the so-called 'speaking statue'. In any case it must have been fairly obvious to anyone who knew about the trouble between the two men that Caravaggio was behind this poetry of scabrous ridicule.

The timing of his attack was unwise. During the early years of the seventeenth century there was a fierce crackdown on libel in Rome, in direct response to the widespread unrest that had followed a notorious trial and public execution. In the summer of 1599 a beautiful young noblewoman called Beatrice Cenci had been sentenced to death for murdering her tyrannical and incestuous father.[58] Her mother, Lucrezia, and her two brothers, Giacomo and Olimpio, had also been convicted as accomplices to the crime. Appeals for clemency were turned down by the pope, and on 11 September of the same year the execution had taken place on a temporary scaffold erected on the Ponte Sant'Angelo. Lucrezia and Beatrice were publicly beheaded, while Giacomo had his flesh torn piece by piece from his body with red-hot pincers. Olimpio was spared because he was still a minor. But he was forced to watch the suffering of the others and roused with cold water on the many occasions when he fainted. A vast crowd was present, including perhaps Caravaggio: artists were encouraged to witness executions so that they might imagine the pains of the Christian martyrs all the more sharply. The sympathies of the people were firmly with the Cenci. It was widely believed that the execution was no more than a judicial murder, designed to enrich Clement VIII and other members of the Aldobrandini family. The pope did not care for justice, it was said. He was just looking for an excuse to sequester the Cenci's estates. There was rioting and seven died in the crush.

The notoriously tough Governor of Rome, Ferrante Taverna, had personally supervised the extraction of Beatrice Cenci's confession. In the immediate aftermath of her trial and execution, he clamped down brutally on the circulation of seditious rumours. At the end of 1599 he issued a decree, *Contro detrattori della fama, & honor' d'altri in lettre d'avisi, versi, prose, o altrimenti,* 'to curb the audacity of those . . . who use their pernicious tongues, in writing newsletters to various parts, filling their papers with lies and calumnies'. Tough penalties would be imposed on anyone who 'defamed, and detracted from honour and reputation . . . under the guise of cleverly written poems, and witty epigrams, or libellous prose, & pasquinades'.[59] A man found guilty of the most serious form of libel could expect a sentence of from seven years to life rowing in the papal galleys. Many of those convicted requested beheading instead.

Within a matter of months of Caravaggio's poems starting to circulate, Baglione and Tommaso Salini – Mao, as he was known – decided to take the case to court on a charge of criminal libel. They prepared their evidence with care. Salini cultivated the acquaintance of a painter who was close to Caravaggio, Filippo Trisegni. In a show of friendship, he lent Trisegni various studio props, including a helmet, and promised to teach him how to paint cast shadows. Eventually Salini managed to wheedle a copy of the first poem out of Trisegni. He then persuaded him to write the second one out for him in longhand. Armed with Exhibit A and Exhibit B in the case for the prosecution, Baglione and Salini struck back at their enemies. On 28 August, Baglione lodged a complaint with the Governor of Rome about some *libelli famosi,* or 'famous libels'. The accused were Onorio Longhi, Caravaggio, Orazio Gentileschi and the hapless Filippo Trisegni. Baglione produced his manuscripts of the offending poems, incriminatingly written out in the hand of Caravaggio's known friend Trisegni, as he addressed his deposition to Judge Alfonso Tomassino, judicial representative of Governor Taverna:

You should know that I am a painter by profession and have been practising this profession here in Rome for a good many years. Now it happens that I have gone and painted a picture of the resurrection of Our
Lord for the Father General of the Company of Jesus, which is in a
chapel of the church of Gesù. When they found out about the said picture, which was this past Easter, the said accused were envious because
they intended, I mean, the said Michelangelo intended to do it himself.
So this Michelangelo out of envy, as I said, and the said Onorio Longhi
and Orazio, his friends and followers, have gone round speaking ill of
me and reproaching my work. And, in particular, they have done some
verses that dishonour and insult me. They gave these round and circulated them among many different people, these being the ones I'm showing you, which I had from the painter Messer Tommaso Salini. He told
me he got them from Filippo Trisegni, also a painter, and that a part of
the said verses were written by Filippo in his presence, being those that
begin 'John Baggage' and end 'your painting deserves only vituperation'
and that the others are those on this quarter page that begin 'Johnny
Bollock' and end 'otherwise he'd just be a fucked-over cuckold'. So I
take action against the above-named and any others that have assisted,
or in whatever way were aware of and found guilty of this fact, asking
that action be taken against them as justice requires, since the above-
named accused have always persecuted, emulated, and envied me seeing
that my works are held in higher esteem than theirs.[60]

Immediately afterwards Mao Salini made his own deposition, flesh-
ing out Baglione's account of events with more detail. Salini particularly relished telling the story of how he had trapped Filippo Trisegni
into helping him obtain copies of the incriminating poems:

I was taking a stroll around with the said Filippo asking him what
painters were saying about the picture that the said Giovanni had
done for the church of Gesù. He told me that Michelangelo of Caravaggio, Onorio Longhi, and Orazio Gentileschi, all three painters, had
put together some verses against the said Giovanni, and against me
since I am his friend, concerning the said painting. And so, a few days
later, the said Filippo with fine words gave me a paper with several
verses written against the said Giovanni, which were on a quarter-
page. Then he told me that the said Orazio had written them together

with Ottavio Padovano [a nickname for Ottavio Leoni], likewise a painter, and that Ludovico Bresciano, also a painter, was going around distributing them to numerous painters. In particular, he had given them to one Mario, in like manner a painter, who lives in Via del Corso.

Then – I don't know how many days later – the said Filippo came to my house one day towards evening to see a painting. After showing it to him, I begged him to tell me a little about the sonnet that he had given me a while back. That was before he gave me the said verses that I mentioned above. Then he told me that he had already given it to me once, and when I said that I had misplaced it he finally wrote the sonnet out for me there in my house on half a page, which if I don't remember badly begins 'John Baggage', telling me that the said Michelangelo and Onorio had written it, and that he had received it from a catamite [*bardassa*] of Onorio and Michelangelo called Giovanni Battista who lives behind the Banchi.

What's more, he told me that the said Michelangelo, knowing that this Filippo had been handed the said sonnets, had warned him to be careful that these sonnets didn't fall into the hands of the said Giovanni or in my hands because trouble would be caused, and that certain young men had done them at his home for their pleasure, telling me also that a certain Bartolomeo, servant of the said Michelangelo, was going around distributing these sonnets to whoever wanted one, and that he had also written others.

What Salini so carefully described was exactly what the new libel law had been brought in to eradicate: a systematic attempt to blacken a man's reputation. The cast of villains was impressive. First there was the naive accomplice, Trisegni, with his 'fine words', taking a malicious pleasure in the whole affair while unwittingly playing the part of a patsy. Then there was the network by which the slanders were distributed. It included the Lombard artist called Ludovico from Brescia and his friend Mario – possibly Caravaggio's old friend from Sicily, Mario Minniti – who took the poems from one artist's studio to the next. An alleged catamite and a servant of doubtful morals were also involved. Finally, at the centre of the conspiracy, were Caravaggio and his shady friends. They wrote the poems at Caravaggio's home, which at this time was the Palazzo Mattei, and they did so out of pure malice, 'for their pleasure'. After Salini's testimony, the judge had little choice but to prosecute.

Less than two weeks later, the black-cloaked *sbirri* swooped. On 11 September 1603 they took Filippo Trisegni while he was having lunch at home in the Via della Croce. Caravaggio was seized in the Piazza Navona the same day. Less than twenty-four hours later, they arrested Orazio Gentileschi at his quarters in Via Paolina. They also searched Gentileschi's rooms and removed certain letters and sonnets, to be used as evidence. The only defendant to escape arrest was Onorio Longhi. He had left town, presumably after a tip-off.

The accused were kept apart, in order to prevent them getting their respective stories straight before the trial. Gentileschi was held at the crumbling Corte Savella. Caravaggio and Trisegni were kept in solitary confinement at the Tor di Nona. Their dark, single cells were on the first floor. Nearby was another prison known as the *galeotta*, so called because it housed convicts who had already been condemned to row in the papal galleys. It was a vivid reminder of the fate awaiting Caravaggio and his associates if Giovanni Baglione had his way.

Filippo Trisegni was the first of the accused to give evidence. He began by pretending that he barely knew Mao Salini: 'I know a painter called Tommaso but I don't know his surname. He lives near me on Via della Croce. I usually call him Mao and I believe he's from Rome.' But there was an immediate surprise in store for him. Salini had provided the court with a note written to him by Trisegni, requesting the loan of an iron helmet. The judge produced the note, which surely implied that Trisegni and his neighbour were closer than he had just said. He had written the note, had he not? Wrongfooted, Trisegni backtracked hurriedly. He could not deny that the note was in his handwriting. On reflection, he added, 'the said Tommaso is a very good friend of mine, who lent me chalks and anything else I needed.'

It was not an auspicious beginning. But Trisegni managed to recover his composure when questions were asked – as he must have known they would be – about certain scurrilous verses. His responses were teasing and ambiguous, clearly intended to deflect attention away from himself, as well as from Caravaggio and the other suspects. He implied that a mysterious man called Gregorio Rotolanti had commissioned the verses from a yet more mysterious and unnamed man, a student of physics or logic – Trisegni was not sure which. Here is the main body of his testimony:

I heard some insulting poems about the said Tommaso told by Gregorio Rotolanti, and since Tommaso is my friend I pretended to like them and begged the said Gregorio to give me a copy. And so I went to his home and he let me copy some verses but I don't remember exactly what they said. The wife of the said Tommaso was mentioned in it and he was called Mao and it said 'Your pictures are woman's work' or something similar and I think they were on a quarter-page. After I copied them I went to see the said Tommaso and told him that he ought to be aware that while he was going around speaking badly of other people's paintings people were speaking badly of him too. Then I told him I wanted to show him something that had been written against him and so I showed him that poem. I gave it to him and [Mao] pressed me to tell him who had given it to me and who had written it, but I never wanted to tell him because I didn't want to cause trouble.

Yet he pressed me and named a lot of people and especially Michelangelo of Caravaggio, Bartolomeo, who was Michelangelo's servant, and Orazio Gentileschi, a man from Parma called Ludovico Parmigianino, another called Francesco Scarpellino, and he asked me if the person could be one of them. I said to him 'It could be any one of them – it might be one of them but I don't want to tell you his name.' I had been waiting for him to teach me how to do figures in cast shadows and then I would have told him. But he never taught me, and so I didn't tell him.

But he did beg me to tell him if I heard anything else about him. And so I spoke to the said Rotolanti, who said that he had another poem against the said Tommaso. Then on the following day we met on Via della Croce and went into the apothecary, where he let me copy some more verses that I think began with, 'Johnny Bollock'. It was in a nice style and well written. But I don't know much about verse and out of several verses I made one. Rotolanti didn't want to give me the original because he said he wanted to learn it by heart. I asked him who had written them and he answered that a young man had written it, a student of logic or maybe physics, a *valent'huomo*, who was really good at it and would write a sonnet or two for a woman for me if I so desired. He told me he was a graduate and wrote exquisite verse. So I returned to see Tommaso about fifteen or twenty days after the first visit and showed him this other poem and left it with him. It was on a quarter-page filled with small handwriting from one side to the other. He told me that he had lost the first one and asked me if I would be kind enough to give him a copy. Since I had learned almost all of it by heart I made him a copy there at his home the way I remembered it.

Trisegni's testimony directly contradicted Salini's deposition to the court. The man whom he claimed had given him the verses, Gregorio Rotolanti, now became a key witness. But he was never called to testify. Perhaps he had gone into hiding, like Onorio Longhi. Or maybe Trisegni had simply invented Rotolanti and his story about the student of physics or logic with a talent for versification.

Gentileschi was next to be questioned by the court. The main purpose was to identify the handwriting of the various documents that the *sbirri* had confiscated at his home. These included a letter to which some playful verses were attached, as well as four sonnets written on a single piece of paper. After having admitted that 'I know how to write but not very correctly', Gentileschi denied that any of the verses produced in evidence were written in his hand. He said that the eight lines of verse attached to the letter were written by a friend of his called Lodovico. As for the four sonnets, 'I say that about six to eight days ago one Giovanni Maggi, an engraver and painter that lives in Vicolo dei Bergamaschi, gave them to me. He dabbles in these things but I don't really know if it's his handwriting. But it could be his handwriting.'

On the next day, 13 September, the magistrate arranged a confrontation between 'Mao' – Tommaso Salini – and Filippo Trisegni. This was common practice when two witnesses had given opposing testimonies. Neither man changed his story. Salini repeated his assertion that Trisegni had listed the names of those who had written the two poems. He stressed once again that Trisegni had told him that he been given some of the verses by the *bardassa*, the catamite 'who lives behind the Banchi'. But Trisegni denied everything and maintained that Salini was lying.

Later the same day Caravaggio was called to give evidence. The notary, Decio Cambio, made his usual careful report of the proceedings, but the painter gave him less work than any of the other witnesses. He was haughty and taciturn. He gave his answers grudgingly and kept them short. At one point he asked, with evident irritation, how much more he would have to listen to, as if to suggest that the enquiry was just an elaborate waste of his time. He declared, improbably, that he had never heard of any scurrilous poems written about Giovanni Baglione and Mao Salini. He claimed that he had not even spoken to Orazio Gentileschi for three years. But he made no pretence of his utter contempt for Baglione's work. That was the one subject on which, dangerously, he became almost effusive. But perhaps the most noteworthy part of his testimony is his grumpy, one-line definition of a good painter.

Here is the full court record of his interrogation:

> *Before His Excellency the Illustrious Alfonso Tomassino assistant examining magistrate and myself . . . Michelangelo Merisi of Caravaggio interrogated under oath by the magistrate.*
>
> *Asked how, under what circumstances, and for what reason he was incarcerated.*
>
> *Answered*:
>
> I was arrested the other day in Piazza Navona but I don't know what the reason and circumstances are.
>
> *Asked what profession he exercises.*
>
> My profession is painting.
>
> *Asked if he knew and knows some painters in Rome and which ones.*
>
> *Answered*:
>
> I think I know almost all the painters in Rome starting with the *valent'huomini*. I know Gioseffe, Caracci, Zucchero [*sic*, for Zuccaro], Pomarancio, Gentileschi, Prospero, Giovanni Andrea, Giovanni Baglione, Gismondo and Giorgio Todesco, Tempesta, and others.
>
> *Asked if all the painters named above are his friends and are all (as they are commonly called) valent'huomini.*
>
> *Answered*:

Almost all the painters I have listed above are my friends, but not all of them are *valent'huomini*.

Asked to identify what he means by the word 'valent'huomo'.

Answered:

By the term *'valent'huomo'* I mean he who knows how to do well, that is, he who knows how to do his art well. So in painting a *valent'huomo* is one who knows how to paint well and imitate natural objects well.

Asked to identify which of them are his friends and which are his enemies.

Answered:

Of those I listed above neither Gioseffe, nor Giovanni Baglione, nor Gentileschi, nor Giorgio Todesco are my friends because they don't speak to me. The others all speak and converse with me.

Asked to specify which of the above-named he considers and holds to be valent'huomini (as they are commonly called) and those which he does not consider as such.

Answered:

Of the painters I listed above as good painters, Gioseffe, Zucchero, Pomarancio and Annibale Carracci; as for the others I don't consider them *valent'huomini*.

Asked if he knows if the above-named painters are judged respectively to be good or bad by other painters, just as he judges and reputes them to be.

Answered:

Valent'huomini are those who are well versed in painting and will judge as good and bad painters those that I judge myself to be good and bad. But those that are bad and ignorant painters will judge as good painters the ignorant just as they are.

Asked if he knows of any person or painter who praises, considers and holds to be a good and virtuous painter one of those painters named above that he esteems is not a good painter.

Answered:

I don't know of any painter that praises and considers a good painter any of those painters that I don't esteem to be good painters.

Then:

I have gone and forgotten to tell you that Antonio Tempesta – he too is a *valent'huomo*.

Asked in particular if any other painter has praised and praises the said painter Giovanni Baglione and who he might be.

Answered:

I don't know of any painter who thinks that Giovanni Baglione is a good painter.

Asked if he has seen any of the works of the said Giovanni Baglione and which ones.

Answered:

I've seen almost all the works of Giovanni Baglione, that is, the big chapel at the Madonna dell'Orto, a painting in San Giovanni Laterano, and recently *The Resurrection of Christ* at the Gesù.

Asked how he judges the above-named painting The Resurrection, and if he knows if it was praised or reproached by other painters.

Answered:

I don't like that painting there at the Gesù because it's a bungle. I think it's the worst he's done and I haven't heard any painter praise the said painting. Of all the painters I've spoken to no one liked it.

Then:

Except that it is praised by someone who's always with him, who's called his guardian angel, who was there praising it when it was unveiled. They call him 'Mao'.

Asked to identify with whom or with which painters he saw that painting The Resurrection.

Answered:

Prospero and Giovanni Andrea. And I saw it on other occasions when I went to the Gesù, but I don't remember if any other painters were with me.

Then:

What am I going to have to hear next about this matter?

Asked if he knows if the said Mao is a painter and if he has done any paintings and if he has seen any of them.

Answered:

Maybe he dabbles in art and still daubs, but I've never seen any work of this Mao.

Asked if he has met and knows Onorio Longhi and Ottavio Padovano.

Answered:

I know Onorio Longhi, who's very much a friend of mine, and I also know Ottavio Padovano.

Then:

But I've never spoken to Ottavio Padovano.

Asked if he has ever had a conversation with the said Onorio Longhi and Orazio Gentileschi concerning the said painting The Resurrection.

Answered:

I've never spoken to Onorio Longhi about the said painting of the Resurrection by Baglione, and it's been more than three years since I've spoken to Gentileschi.

Asked if he knows the painter Lodovico Bresciano and Mario, also a painter.

Answered:

I know a Lodovico Bresciano and a Mario, both painters. This Mario once stayed with me and it's been three years since he left and I haven't spoken to him since. As for Lodovico I've never spoken to him.

Asked if he knows someone called Bartolomeo, who was once a servant of his, and his whereabouts.

Answered:

I know Bartolomeo. He was once my servant who went two months ago to the Castello del Soderino.

Asked if he knows someone called Giovanni Battista, a young man who lives behind the Banchi.

Answered:

I don't know any young man called Giovanni Battista or any young man who lives behind the Banchi.

Asked if he knows how to write verse in the vulgar tongue.

Answered:

Your Excellency, no. I don't dabble in verse either in the vulgar tongue, or in Latin.

Asked if he has ever heard of a poem or composition written in the vulgar tongue in which the said Giovanni Baglione was mentioned.

Answered:

I have never heard it in verse or in prose, in the vulgar tongue, or in Latin.

Asked if he has ever heard of a poem or composition written in the vulgar tongue in which the said Giovanni Baglione was mentioned.

Answered:

I have never heard in verse or in prose, in the vulgar tongue or in Latin, or in any other form, anything where mention of the said Giovanni Baglione was made.

And to his Excellency who said that according to the Bar he was aware that mention had been made of this Giovanni Baglione, and also of the said Mao, in some verses in the vulgar tongue.

Answered:

Never have I received information that mention has been made of Giovanni Baglione or of the said Mao in verse in the vulgar tongue.

Caravaggio's definition of a good painter as 'one who knows how to paint well and imitate natural objects well' is almost comically prosaic. Perhaps he meant it as a deliberately provocative, no-nonsense assertion of his own notoriously direct naturalistic approach. But it is equally likely that he was just playing dumb. Caravaggio knew very well that there was more to painting than the mere reproduction of appearances. But it was not in his interests to appear before the court as an intellectual. After all, intellectuals were the kind of people who might write poetry in their spare time.

Caravaggio's eventual list of *valent'huomini* was influenced by calculation. Most of those chosen were conservative and academically minded painters. None were his friends, least of all Annibale Carracci, with whom he had crossed paintbrushes in the Cerasi Chapel. He included Federico Zuccaro, who had insulted Caravaggio's Contarelli Chapel canvases in the presence of Giovanni Baglione. Zuccaro was president of the Academy, so no wonder Caravaggio wanted the court to think he thought well of him. This was not merely false magnanimity: it was a shrewd attempted alignment with respectability.

Shortly after Caravaggio gave his evidence, Baglione decided to concentrate his attack on Gentileschi. He came back to the court that afternoon with another exhibit for the prosecution. It was an angry letter to Baglione from Gentileschi, written earlier that summer. Baglione had been on a pilgrimage to the shrine at Loreto and Gentileschi had asked him to bring him back some silver figurines of the Madonna. Baglione had given him two figures, but they were in lead, which

Gentileschi had taken as a slight. Having explained the background to the court, Baglione then produced the letter:

To Giovanni the painter,

I am not returning your Madonna figurines as you deserve but will keep them for the devotion they represent. However, I consider you a man with just about enough courage to buy them in lead. Your other actions have shown everyone all the riches you are made of and I don't give a hoot about you.

I'd like you to do me a favour by hanging some offal on that chain you wear around your neck as an ornament to match your worth. I told you that if you sent me one in silver I would pay you for it. I would never under any circumstances send one in lead to a courteous gentleman, like the ones you see worn on hats.

And with this I take leave of you and return your friendship and who is saying this to you cannot be a blackguard.

This was conclusive proof of Gentileschi's enmity. The robust style of the letter also showed that he had misled the court when he said he could barely string a sentence together on paper. Most incriminating of all, however, was the reference to Baglione's chain. 'In the sonnets written against me he mentions a neck chain saying I ought to wear an iron chain instead,' Baglione told the court. 'In this note he also speaks about the neck chain saying I should hang some offal in place of the chain. I steadfastly insist that it must have been him . . .'

The next day, as a final throw of the dice, the examining magistrate recalled Orazio Gentileschi. If he could be made to crack under cross-examination, the case would suddenly be thrown wide open.

At first the magistrate lulled Gentileschi into a false sense of security, asking him a series of questions about other artists, which Gentileschi parried with ease. It was at this point in the trial that he blithely volunteered the story about Baglione bringing his picture of *Divine Love* to the annual artists' exhibition, to compete with his own *St Michael the Archangel*. He presumably wanted to demonstrate that he had nothing to fear from a discussion of the rivalry between them. He was happy to admit to the occasional disagreement with

Baglione, but he also took care to distance himself from Caravaggio, complaining that both men had a habit of looking down on him:

> I haven't spoken to the said Giovanni Baglione since the St Michael affair and especially because he expects me to raise my hat to him on the street and I expect him to raise his hat to me. Even Caravaggio, who's a friend of mine, expects me to salute him, and although both of them are my friends, there's nothing more between us. It must be six or eight months since I've spoken to Caravaggio, although he did send round to my house for a Capuchin's robe and a pair of wings I lent him. It must be about ten days since he sent them back.

Gradually the magistrate turned the conversation towards the incriminating note, although for the time being he kept the document itself up his sleeve. Did Gentileschi ever remember Baglione leaving Rome? Had Baglione ever given anything to him? The accused stumbled slowly but surely into the trap. Gentileschi told the court that Baglione had gone to Loreto and that he had brought him back some lead figurines 'like the ones that are worn on hats'. He had hoped for silver ones, but he had thanked Baglione graciously none the less. What about a note? Had he written a note? Gentileschi pretended to struggle to remember. Baglione had written to him first, as he recalled, saying that he had heard that Gentileschi was complaining about the figurines. He had felt obliged to reply. 'I answered him in a note that I held devotion dear, that I was surprised that he would write these things to me, that I had thanked him in the presence of several people ... and that he shouldn't think I was interested in all that silver nonsense.'

After a little more sparring the magistrate suddenly produced the note itself, to Gentileschi's evident consternation. At first he tried to deny that he had written the note, then realized that the handwriting was so evidently his that he had better own up to it. But when confronted with the line about hanging offal on Baglione's chain, he panicked and half-heartedly denied authorship of the letter once again. Drowning in his own inconsistency, all he could find to cling to was an implausible insinuation that the letter was a forgery. His testimony rapidly descended into incoherence. 'It seems to me,' he stammered, 'yet it doesn't, that I wrote about offal and chains, but the handwriting looks like mine. I recognize this letter by my handwriting. It's true

I wrote about someone who had done something bad and that he face up to it but I don't think I've written about chains and offal.'

At this point the notary reported, '*He got confused*.' Again and again the magistrate pressed him for the truth about the letter, but Gentileschi just went round and round in ever-decreasing circles: 'it doesn't seem to be in my hand, but I know I haven't written this note in this manner: it is like my handwriting but I don't know of having written these things ... the handwriting looks like mine, but I don't think I've written this letter in this way, but it is my handwriting ...' It was not quite a confession, but he must have signed such a testimony with a heavy heart.

But just as the case seemed to have swung decisively against them, the defendants were reprieved. Someone must have told the Governor of Rome to call off his hounds, because on 25 September 1603 Caravaggio was suddenly released from prison. He was bailed under guarantee from the French ambassador, which strongly suggests that Cardinal del Monte, friend to the Medici and to France, had engineered his release. The condition of bail was that he 'was not to leave his habitual residence without written permission ... at the risk of being condemned to the punishment of galley slave'.[61] He was also obliged to make himself available for a further hearing in a month's time. In another document of the same date, Ainolfo Bardi, Count of Vernio, undertook to ensure that Caravaggio would offend 'neither the life nor the honour' of either 'Giovanni Baglione, painter' or 'Tommaso, alias Mau [*sic*]'.[62]

In the event, there were no further hearings and the case was dropped. But that was not quite the end of the affair. By November 1603 Caravaggio's friend Onorio Longhi was back in Rome. He wanted revenge for the ordeal of the lawsuit and tried to pick a fight with Baglione and Salini. This time, Longhi was the one who ended up in court, arrested for threatening behaviour by a *sbirro* who signed himself 'Tullio, assistant to the head of police'. The events leading up to the arrest were described by Salini in his deposition to the court:[63]

> I was in the church of Minerva together with my friend Messer Giovanni Baglione. We wished to hear Mass and while we were waiting I saw Onorio Longhi who was standing in front of us staring at me saying

something very softly with his mouth that couldn't be heard. Then he beckoned me with his head and I went over and asked him what he was calling me for. He started to say, 'I'd like to make you swing from a wooden scaffold, you fucking grass.' To which I answered that he was insulting me so in church but that outside he wouldn't have dared say such a thing. Then, raising his voice, Onorio told me to come outside and said I was a fucker and a grass if I didn't and that I should come out and he'd be waiting for me.

He immediately went out of the rear door of the Minerva and picked up a stone saying, 'Come out, you scum you grass.' Then I told him he was lying through his teeth and that he should put down the brick or we'd be uneven. And then the said Messer Giovanni Baglione came out and held me back and Onorio began to say, 'There are two of you', and a companion of the said Onorio, a procurator from Truffia who lives in Montecitorio, turned towards Messer Giovanni and seeing him with a dagger said, 'Put the dagger down.' Onorio, likewise, said 'Get the dagger off him', . . . and the said procurator approached him [and punched the said Messer Giovanni in the chest[64]] . . . and all at once Onorio threw the brick at Messer Giovanni, which hit his hat but didn't hurt him. Then he turned towards me, but having a stone in my hand I told him to stop or I'd knock him down. All the same he came towards me saying, 'You fucking grass', and so I called him a liar and entered the church and he went off with the said procurator.

Shortly after this, Salini added, Longhi challenged him to a sword-fight again, 'near the door of the friars' cloister'. When he refused to rise to the bait, Longhi went to wait at Salini's home on the corner of Via della Croce. When Baglione and Salini got there, he shouted at them to arm themselves, but still they refused to fight with him. Salini went to see his tailor and Baglione went into 'the baker's shop that sells bread, wine and charcoal'. (Were it not for this aside in Salini's testimony, it might never have been known that bakers in the artists' quarter of seventeenth-century Rome sold charcoal from their bread-ovens to painters.)

The tale of provocation ends there, with Salini trying on shirts and Baglione buying artist's materials and the enraged Longhi left yelling in the street. The story as Salini had told it was confirmed by another eyewitness, Lazzaro Visca, a barber. True to his profession, he added one small tonsorial detail to the picture: the infuriated Longhi had a red beard.

A DAGGER, A PAIR OF EARRINGS, A WORN-OUT BELT

Onorio Longhi left the custody of the *sbirri* with a caution as the enmity between rival factions of artists rumbled on. Caravaggio had not been involved in the latest fracas, if only because he was away from Rome at the time. He had left the city shortly after the collapse of the libel trial, to research a new picture he had been asked to paint.

In early September 1603 the heirs of Ermete Cavalletti had acquired a chapel in the church of Sant'Agostino. Caravaggio was in prison at the time, but immediately after his release Ermete's widow, Orinzia Cavalletti, commissioned him to paint an altarpiece depicting the Madonna of Loreto. Cavalletti's late husband had been particularly devoted to the cult of Loreto, a small town in the Marches, east of Rome, which was home to the fabled Holy House of the Virgin Mary, and during the last year of his life he had organized a pilgrimage to the Holy House, then one of the principal pilgrimage sites in the Roman Catholic world. Caravaggio decided to familiarize himself with the shrine and its legend before starting work on the altarpiece, so he too followed the pilgrims' trail. Orazio Gentileschi may or may not have asked him to pick up a few silver figurines when he got there.

While he was on the road, Caravaggio accepted another commission, this time to paint an altarpiece for the Capuchin church of Santa Maria di Costantinopoli in the town of Tolentino. The picture is lost and was nearly forgotten altogether, but in the late nineteenth century a scholar working in the town's municipal archives stumbled on a letter about it. Dated 2 January 1604, it was sent to the priors of the town by a nobleman from Tolentino, Lancilotto Mauruzi, who was living in Rome at the time. He congratulated them on securing Caravaggio's services and wanted them to know that he was 'a most excellent painter, of great worth, in fact the best in Rome today'.[65] He pleaded with them to treat the artist well, because if he created one of his 'extraordinary' paintings for Tolentino it would forever bring honour to the town. The fate of the work is unknown, but it must have disappeared some time after 1772, when the author of a local guidebook rapturously described it as 'a singular and precious production of Knight Michelangelo Amerigi da Caravaggio, in which, in his strong and dark manner, he depicted St Isidora Agricola piercing a tree with a spike and miraculously bringing forth a fountain: the figure is so natural, seeming to be alive, such is the delicacy of the flesh tones ... there are also other figures, transfixed by the sight of the miracle: in fact one could say it it is a miracle of art, so true to life does it seem.'[66]

Caravaggio went on to Loreto, for how long we do not know, but he was back in Rome by the beginning of 1604. In the aftermath of the libel trial, his life became increasingly unsettled. Having lodged for several years with powerful patrons, first del Monte and then the Mattei family, he was now living in rented accommodation. Not long after his release from prison he had moved into a small two-storey house in the Vicolo dei Santa Cecilia e Biagio (now the Vicolo del Divino Amore), a narrow curved street flanked on one side by the walls of the Palazzo Firenze. The palace was part of the machinery of Medici power in Rome, serving among other things as the post office for Tuscany, and del Monte was often required to be there in the course of his duties. It seems that despite his changed circumstances the painter was still keen to stay close to his protector.

Unlike many Roman streets, the Vicolo was, and still is, unshaded by any large church or monastery. In high summer the sun beats down on to the roofs and through the windows of the houses there, creating dramatically Caravaggesque effects of light and shade. The painter's new home had a cellar and a small courtyard garden with its own well. His landlady, Prudentia Bruni, charged him the modest sum of 40 scudi a year in rent. His reasons for moving are not known. Perhaps he wanted privacy. He was living alone with his one assistant, according to a communion census carried out for the parish of San Nicola dei Prefetti. The document in question, part of a *Status animarum*, or report on 'the state of souls', records that 'Michelangelo, painter' had taken communion as required, together with 'Francesco, his servant'[67] – Cecco, the model for *Omnia vincit amor*, the source of all those rumours about Caravaggio's homosexuality that would still be current half a century later. There must have been talk, but Caravaggio was paying no attention to it.

An inventory of Caravaggio's household contents was drawn up when his tenancy ended abruptly in August 1605, an event that will be described below. The inventorist noted the objects in the order in which he encountered them, so the list of things also describes a sequence of rooms. Like many of the documents concerning Caravaggio, the inventory is fascinating but tantalizing. Reading it is like leafing through a dossier of arbitrarily cropped and framed snapshots of the things a man once owned – the furniture he sat on, the weapons with which he fought, the books he read, the tools he used. But all the photographs are just a little out of focus. Crucial details are missing and there is no one to fill in the gaps:

This is the inventory of all the personal property of the painter Michelangelo from Caravaggio ... First, a kitchen-dresser made of white poplar-wood, with three compartments and an alder frame, containing eleven pieces of glassware, namely glasses, carafes and flasks covered in straw, a plate, two salt-cellars, three spoons, a carving board and a bowl, and on the above-mentioned dresser two brass candlesticks, another plate, two small knives and three terracotta vases. *Item* a water jug. Two stools. *Item* a red table with two drawers. *Item* a couple of bedside tables. A picture. *Item* a small chest covered with black leather, containing a pair of ragged breeches and a jacket. A guitar, a violin. A dagger, a pair of earrings, a worn-out belt and a doorleaf. *Item* a rather big table. *Item* two old chairs and a small broom. *Item* two swords, and two hand daggers. *Item* a pair of green breeches. *Item* a mattress. *Item* a shield. *Item* a blanket. *Item* a foldaway bed for servants. *Item* a bed with two posts. *Item* a chamber-pot. *Item* a stool. *Item* an old chest. *Item* a majolica basin. *Item* another chest containing twelve books. *Item* two large pictures to paint. *Item* a chest containing certain rags. *Item* three stools. *Item* a large mirror. *Item* a convex mirror. *Item* three smaller pictures. *Item* a small three-legged table. *Item* three large stretchers. *Item* a large picture on wood. *Item* an ebony chest containing a knife. *Item* two bedside tables. *Item* a tall wooden tripod. *Item* a small cart with some papers with colours. *Item* a halberd. *Item* two more stretchers.[68]

'Once he put on a suit of clothes he changed only when it had fallen to rags.' Bellori's remark, repeated in one or two other early sources, finds confirmation in the ragged breeches and jacket and the worn-out belt. There is little in the way of cooking equipment, which suggests that neither the painter nor his apprentice spent a great deal of time in the kitchen. It is not surprising to learn that Caravaggio kept books, and a pity that the notary did not list their titles (though if they *had* been identified, a multitude of over-ingenious iconographic hypotheses would have been unleashed on the painter's work). At any rate, their presence gives the lie to the old academic caricature of Caravaggio as an unlettered copyist of appearances.[69] But we cannot tell anything conclusive from what is here about his relationship with his servant: all the references to beds and bedding occur in one place, so it can be inferred that the two men either shared sleeping quarters, or slept in adjoining rooms. But Cecco certainly had his own separate bed, or mattress.

The convex mirror is likely to be the one in which Caravaggio had studied his own, distorted self-portrait while painting the *Medusa*. It is probably the same object that can still be seen, propped up on the table, in the *Martha and Mary Magdalen* in Detroit. The mention of a 'large mirror' is more mysterious: mirrors were extremely expensive in the early seventeenth century, and, given Caravaggio's often-remarked disregard for his own appearance, it is unlikely he would have owned one for reasons of vanity. It was most likely another tool of his studio, which he used to bounce or reflect light, much like a modern cinematographer. The 'large painting on wood' could have been one of the two botched first attempts at the Cerasi Chapel commission.

One thing is clear from the inventory: Caravaggio was living modestly. For all Baglione's allegations of 'the many hundreds of scudi' that he had 'pocketed' from Ciriaco Mattei, there was not much sign of suddenly acquired wealth in the meagre possessions assembled in the little house on the Vicolo dei Santa Cecilia e Biagio. Caravaggio was a very well known painter by early 1604, but his future was by no means assured. When Clement VIII commissioned a series of altarpieces for St Peter's in these, the last years of his pontificate, Caravaggio was not among the artists approached.

Part of the problem was almost certainly his personality. By now he would have been notorious as a proud and difficult man. Baglione and his clique would have been only too happy to reinforce that impression. But there were other, more powerful forces working against Caravaggio. The Catholic Church was moving decisively away from the severe Counter-Reformation piety embodied so powerfully by his work. The religious attitudes that he had grown up with in Milan were falling increasingly out of favour among those in positions of power. Carlo Borromeo's belief that the princes of the Church should clothe themselves in humility and model their lives on those of Christ's own poor disciples was falling terminally out of fashion. Poverty and the poor were there to be controlled, regulated, put in their place. In parallel, the idea that Christian art should exalt poverty was regarded as increasingly eccentric and distasteful by senior churchmen, from the pope downwards. It was the function of art to hymn the majesty of God in his heaven – and therefore to bathe the papal court and the upper hierarchies of the Church in the reflected glory of that higher, celestial court. Like the art of Caravaggio, the art favoured by a newly triumphalist Church was aimed at the poor as well as the rich. But its approach was very different. It did not welcome the poor and the meek or make them feel that they, ultimately, were the inheritors of the earth. It was there to awe, daunt and stupefy them, to impress them with visions of a force so powerful it could not be resisted – and must, therefore, be obeyed.

For all his sensitivity and genius, there could ultimately be no place in this new Baroque sensibility for an artist such as Caravaggio. If anything, his art was becoming even more pared down, more severe, with the passage of time. This pattern of development, begun with the Cerasi Chapel paintings, had continued throughout 1603. In his evidence given at the libel trial, Orazio Gentileschi had remembered Caravaggio returning 'a Capuchin's robe and a pair of wings'. Cecco had worn the wings when he sat for *Omnia vincit amor*. The Capuchin robe, sacred uniform of the Franciscan order, had been worn by the rather older model whom Caravaggio cast in another picture of the same period, *St Francis in Meditation*, now in the Galleria Nazionale d'Arte Antica, Palazzo Barberini, Rome. Nothing is known about why, or for whom, this ascetically morbid picture was painted. The saint kneels alone in darkness beside the simple wooden crucifix that assists his meditations. His torn, patched cloak is the symbol of his piety and of his utter disdain for the things of this world. He holds a skull in his hands, staring deep into the sockets where eyes once were. He is shown lost in contemplation of his own mortality, and of the eternal life that awaits him thanks to Christ's crucifixion at Golgotha, 'the place of the skull'. But the idea of the picture is stronger than its execution. The folds of the drapery have been cursorily painted and the penitential pose seems artificial. Caravaggio had always composed with a strong sense of theatre, but here his work tips over into theatricality.

According to Gentileschi, Caravaggio had returned the borrowed habit at around the beginning of September 1603, so probably the *St Francis* was completed shortly before then. *The Sacrifice of Isaac* is another picture from this time. Less penitentially gloomy, it clothes an Old Testament legend in the same robes of holy poverty. The lined and bald Abraham is cousin to Caravaggio's earlier pauper saints and strongly resembles the uppermost disciple in his *Doubting Thomas*. A simple man of simple faith, he steels himself to do God's bidding, holding his screaming son down as if the boy – modelled by Cecco in yet another guise – were just one more lamb brought to slaughter.

The Sacrifice of Isaac had been the subject of a famous competition in fifteenth-century Florence between Lorenzo Ghiberti and Filippo Brunelleschi, for the commission of a cast-bronze pair of doors for the city Baptistry. Each artist had produced a single bas-relief in bronze, which between them became the two most famous Renaissance treatments of the subject. The eventual winner, Ghiberti, had devised a composition of great elegance and delicacy, setting the scene in a gracefully abbreviated landscape and lending a balletic quality even to the murderous gesture of the Old Testament prophet. Brunelleschi had produced a much brusquer and more violent interpretation of the story, focusing on the action itself, where Abraham plunges the dagger dramatically towards his son even as the angel stays his hand. Brunelleschi lost the competition, but unsurprisingly it was with his vivid, violent, essentially late medieval view of the story that Caravaggio identified. Caravaggio's greatest Dutch admirer, Rembrandt, would give a yet more brutal emphasis to the drama, by showing Abraham's smothering hand clamped over the face of his helpless son.

The Sacrifice of Isaac is also notable for Caravaggio's very last view of landscape: an idyllic glimpse of the Roman *campagna* complete with winding path, avenue of cypresses, a country villa and a distant monastery silhouetted against a fragment of summer sky. From 1604 onwards, his painted world shrinks in on itself, and even events set outside look as though they are taking place in a darkened theatre. Middle tones almost disappear. Increasingly, there is only darkness and light.

A PLATE OF ARTICHOKES
AND OTHER STORIES

Caravaggio would receive just three commissions for large-scale public religious paintings between 1603 and 1606. As the spareness and solemnity of his work became increasingly out of step with the times, he was forced to watch from the sidelines as lesser painters overtook him in the unstable hierarchy of Roman patronage. In reaction, he became ever more aggressive. An eighteenth-century writer of artists' lives, Filippo Baldinucci, recounts the story of Caravaggio's jealous attack on a Florentine painter called Domenico Passignano. Passignano's sin had been to secure the coveted commission to paint an altarpiece for St Peter's. One day his assistant was alone with the unfinished picture, which was still curtained off from public scrutiny, when Caravaggio went to take a look. Showing 'no respect for place or person', he drew his sword, cut a slit in the fabric and poked his head through the hole. His assessment of the work in progress was predictably caustic: 'As bad as I thought, from a painter like him'.[70] The message was presumably passed on to Passignano by his startled apprentice. The legend was soon absorbed into the collective memory of the Italian artist.

Caravaggio was picking fights with other people too. On 24 April 1604 he got into an argument with a waiter at one of his local restaurants, the Osteria del Moro, or 'Tavern of the Blackamoor'. In the course of an altercation concerning artichokes, he smashed a plate against the man's face. Stopping only to have his wound dressed at the barber-surgeon's, the waiter took his grievance straight to court. He gave his name as Pietro de Fossaccia and declared that he was originally from Lago Maggiore. This is his testimony against Caravaggio:

> At about seventeen hours [half past twelve] the above-named defendant with two other men was eating in the Tavern of the Blackamoor, near the Church of the Magdalen, where I am employed as a waiter. I had brought him eight cooked artichokes, to wit, four cooked in butter and four in oil, and the said defendant asked me which were done in butter and which in oil. I replied: 'Smell them, and you will easily know which are cooked in butter and which in oil.' Thereupon, he flew into a rage and without further words seized an earthen plate and flung it in my face. It hit me here in the left cheek, wounding me slightly. Then he got up and snatched the sword of one of his companions, which was lying on the table, perhaps with intent to strike me. But I got away from him, and came here to the office to file a complaint.

A copyist called Pietro Antonio de Madii, from Piacenza, had also eaten at the Tavern of the Blackamoor that lunchtime. He was called as an eyewitness. He partially corroborated the waiter's story. But, in recalling the exact words that had been exchanged, he shed new light on the incident. The verbal precision of his evidence may have reflected the habits of his work, as a transcriber of others' words:

> I was dining at the Tavern of the Blackamoor. On the other side of the room there was Michelangelo da Caravaggio, the painter. I heard him ask whether the artichokes were done in oil or butter, they being all in one plate. The waiter said: 'I don't know', and picked one up and and put it to his nose. Michelangelo took it badly and sprang to his feet in a rage, saying: 'It seems to me, you fucked-over cuckold, that you think you're speaking to some kind of vulgar provincial [*barone*].' And he seized the plate and threw it at the waiter's face. I did not see Michelangelo grasp the sword to threaten the waiter.[71]

Caravaggio was being touchy about status again. The fight may have been sparked by a question about butter and olive oil, but the argument was really about something else. The painter was accusing the waiter of a quasi-racist insult. The Romans were proud of their olive oil – Montaigne had remarked on its quality when he visited the city – and scorned northern Italians for lacking the discrimination to appreciate its fine but faintly bitter taste. Lombards were easily caricatured as cowherds from far-off plains and mountains, who thought a meal was not a real meal unless it was dripping with butter and cheese. The painter accused the waiter of taking him for a *barone*, which has been imperfectly translated above as 'vulgar provincial'. Its literal meaning is 'baron', but used ironically, in the language of demotic insult, it means the opposite – a low parody of an aristocrat, somebody from the sticks who thinks he has taste but actually has none.

Caravaggio responded to the implied slight by hurling a plate at the man's mouth. It was an impetuous act, but as usual the painter had put thought into his violence. The punishment mirrored the perceived crime: 'You think I have no taste? Taste this.' The insult that accompanied the assault, *becco fottuto*, or 'fucked-over cuckold', was the same phrase that had been used at the end of the poem addressed to 'Johnny Bollock'. Caravaggio must have used it fairly frequently.

Despite only three major commissions in these troubled years, Caravaggio certainly had work to do. His altarpiece for *The Death of the Virgin* was years overdue and he still had the picture of the Madonna of Loreto to paint. But he seems to have found it increasingly difficult to concentrate for prolonged periods. In the past he had been a conscientious respecter of deadlines, but now he had a growing reputation for unreliability. It was with the Caravaggio of these years in mind that Karel van Mander wrote his comment about the painter spending a month in the streets for every two weeks in the studio, swaggering about with his sword at his side, 'with a servant following him, from one ball-court to the next, ever ready to engage in a fight or argument'.[72]

It was probably in the summer of 1604, between fights, that Caravaggio painted the hauntingly intense *St John the Baptist* now in the Nelson-Atkins Museum in Kansas City. The picture was almost certainly painted for the Genoese banker Ottavio Costa. There is an early copy in the church of the Oratory of the Confraternity at Conscente, in Liguria, which was a fief of the Costa dynasty. The family had paid for the building of the church, so it may be that Caravaggio's painting was originally destined for its high altar, and subsequently replaced by the copy for reasons unknown. Perhaps Ottavio Costa was so impressed by the work when he saw it that he decided to keep it for his art collection in Rome.

The picture is very different to the *St John the Baptist* painted for Ciriaco Mattei a couple of years before. As in the earlier painting, the saint occupies an unusually lush desert wilderness. Dock leaves grow in profusion at his feet. But he is no longer an ecstatic, laughing boy. He has become a melancholy adolescent, glowering in his solitude. Clothed in animal furs and swathed in folds of blood-red drapery, he clutches a simple reed cross for solace as he broods on the errors and miseries of mankind. The chiaroscuro is eerily extreme: there is a pale cast to the light, which is possibly intended to evoke moonbeams, but the contrasts are so strong and the shadows so deep that the boy looks as though lit by a flash of lightning. This dark but glowing painting is one of Caravaggio's most spectacular creations. It is also a reticent and introverted work – a vision of a saint who looks away, to one side, rather than meeting the beholder's eye. This second *St John* is moodily withdrawn, lost in his own world-despising thoughts. The picture might almost be a portrait of Caravaggio's own dark state of mind, his gloomy hostility and growing sense of isolation during this period of his life.

Only one other painting by Caravaggio can be securely dated to 1604. It is *The Entombment*, a large and ambitious altarpiece for the Oratorian church in Rome, Santa Maria in Vallicella, a few hundred yards west of the Piazza Navona, close to where the Tiber snakes around the Vatican. He finished it some time shortly before 1 September, when the picture is described as 'new' in a document recording that it had been paid for by a man called Girolamo Vittrice. Girolamo commissioned the work for the burial chapel of his uncle, Pietro, who had died in 1600. Like many of the painter's most important patrons, the Vittrice family was closely connected with Filippo Neri's Oratory and therefore directly allied with the emphatically populist, pauperist wing of the Roman Church. Pietro Vittrice had been particularly close to Filippo Neri himself and had strongly supported the core values of the Oratory, with its stress on the importance of charitable works, its antipathy to elaborate ritual and its ambition to revive the simple and direct faith associated with the early Church.

Caravaggio's monumental and dramatic altarpiece for Vittrice's burial chapel was immediately recognized as one of his most accomplished paintings. Baglione baldly stated that 'this is said to be his best work', a judgement that was echoed rather more circumstantially by Bellori:

> One of the best works by Caravaggio is the *Deposition of Christ* [*sic*] in the Chiesa Nuova of the Oratorians which has received well-deserved praise. The figures in the painting are placed on a stone in the opening of the sepulchre. In the centre Nicodemus supports the Sacred Body under the knees, embracing it, and as the hips are lowered, the legs jut out. On the other side St John places one arm under the shoulder of the Redeemer whose face is upturned and his breast deathly pale; one arm hangs down with the sheet and all the nude parts are drawn forcefully and faithfully from nature. Behind Nicodemus are seen the mourning Marys, one with her arms upraised, another with her veil raised to her eyes, and the third looking at the Lord.[73]

Caravaggio had Michelangelo in mind again when he created *The Entombment*. Pietro Vittrice's burial chapel was dedicated to the Pietà, the solitary lamentation of Mary over the dead Christ. Caravaggio deliberately harked back to one of the most hallowed images of that earlier event in the story, namely Michelangelo's marble *Pietà* in St Peter's. The limp right arm of Caravaggio's dead Christ, with its prominent veins, is a direct paraphrase in paint of the same element in Michelangelo's composition. The flesh of the arm gently bulges over the supporting hand of St John, just as it does over the hand of the Virgin Mary in the marble *Pietà*. But in Caravaggio's painting, John's hand inadvertently opens the wound in Christ's side. For the pathos and poetry of Michelangelo's sculpture, in which Mary mourns the man she once cradled as a child, Caravaggio substitutes his own intense morbidity. Caravaggio's dead Christ is punishingly unidealized. He truly is the Word made flesh: a dead man, a real corpse weighing heavily on those who struggle to lay him to rest. John strains not to drop the sacred burden. Nicodemus stoops awkwardly as he clasps the body around the knees in a bear-hug, locking his right fist like a clamp around his left forearm.

Once more, the painter emphasizes the bare feet of Christ and his disciples. Nicodemus's feet, so firmly planted on the tomb slab by the heavy load of the corpse, are veined and creased at the ankle. Christ's feet dangle limply in space. Such details could be controversial else-where, but the Oratorians' sense of decorum was evidently undisturbed by Caravaggio's insistence on holy poverty. Christ's drapery has been given strong emphasis, shining with particular force in the darkness of Calvary. His winding sheet dangles below the tomb slab, touching the leaves of a plant – a juxtaposition perhaps meant to symbolize the hope of new life brought even to the darkness of the grave. Pietro Vittrice had especially venerated the Holy Shroud of Turin, fabled as the winding sheet in which Christ had been interred.

The Entombment is a powerfully sculptural painting. It alludes to Michelangelo's *Pietà* but ultimately looks back again to the poly-chrome *mises-en-scène* of the *sacri monti* and the vivid terracotta sculptures of northern Italian tradition. The figures are tightly grouped, each responding to the tragedy of death in a different way. Caravaggio's Madonna, who has been given a wimple so that she resembles a nun, gazes solemnly at the dead body of her son. The other two female figures are more overtly expressive. Mary Magdalen, eyes uptilted in a trance of sorrow, raises her hands to the heavens. The third Mary bows her head and weeps. Both these figures were modelled by Fillide Melandroni. She had dropped out of Caravaggio's art for a while, but was clearly still part of his life. Her continued presence in Rome at around this time is confirmed by a communion census report of Easter 1603, in which she is recorded as living with her brother and aunt from Siena in the parish of Santa Maria del Popolo. By now she was twenty-two years old.

There is a hint of theatricality about the pair of figures modelled by Fillide, which jars with Caravaggio's prevailing rhetoric of brutal real-ism. Perhaps he was trying to sweeten the bitter pill of his art, at least to a degree. There would be hints of compromise in one or two other Roman pictures of the period, a sign perhaps that his confidence had been knocked by rejection. In fact the whole composition of *The Entombment* has a slightly staged and artificial feel to it, although this may reflect a specific aspect of the image's meaning. There was a trad-ition of painting Christ's entombment not as a dramatic event but as a moment of votive stasis – a presentation of his sacrifical body both to the congregation of the church and, symbolically, to all mankind. Caravaggio's Nicodemus looks directly out of the picture as he and John seem, indeed, to hold Christ's body up to view, and Bellori's description of the painting repeatedly refers to the image of Christ as 'the Sacred Body'. This element of the composition may well have been created to complement the actual liturgy of the Mass, as the painting originally hung directly above the altar in the chapel: at the moment when the priest elevated the host, the actual flesh of Christ, he was obliged by the design of Caravaggio's composition to align it with the painted body of Christ.

STONES THROWN AND A DOOR DEFACED

On 4 June 1604 Caravaggio was sentenced for his attack on the waiter, along with several people convicted of unrelated offences. The other men and women in the dock included a furrier, a launderer and a recent convert to Christianity from Judaism. Their various crimes and punishments are detailed in the judicial Latin of the document, but whereas the entry under Caravaggio's name gives the nature of his offence – wounding a man under the left eye with an earthenware plate – it fails to specify the penalty. Perhaps he was again let off with a warning, thanks to his powerful friends.

On 19 October he was back in prison at the Tor di Nona. This time he and some friends were accused of throwing stones at some police officers. The alleged incident had taken place two days earlier, at 9.30 in the evening, on the Via dei Greci. His fellow defendants were Ottaviano Gabrielli, a bookseller; Alessandro Tonti of Civitanova, a perfume-maker; and Pietro Paolo Martinelli, a courier to the pope. Their testimonies are contradictory, but they give at least a piecemeal picture of the incident.

Caravaggio had eaten with Martinelli and Gabrielli that evening at the Osteria della Torretta, the 'Tavern of the Little Tower'. After dinner they had decided to walk to the Piazza del Popolo. They were halfway there when they were arrested for throwing stones. 'We were arrested because a stone had been thrown and they wanted me to tell who had thrown it, whereas I didn't know,' Caravaggio testified. 'I told the constables, "Go and look for the man who threw the stone, and no more abusive words."'[74] In his version of events, he had been walking along with his old friend Onorio Longhi, as well as the bookseller Gabrielli and someone else whose name he did not know. They had stopped to chat in the street to a girl called Menicuccia – a nickname for the courtesan Menica Calvi – when he heard stones flying through the air. He was under the impression that the stones had been thrown at his friends. He insisted that he was just an innocent bystander.

The pope's courier, Martinelli, distanced himself from the whole affair. He claimed to have walked on ahead with another friend. Ottaviano Gabrielli denied having been present at dinner with the others. He asserted that he was on his way to meet the girlfriend of a friend of his when he got caught up in the evening's events. Gabrielli admitted having been in prison once before, on suspicion of selling prohibited books. On the evening in question, he said, he had witnessed Caravaggio's arrest but had not been involved in the events leading up to it. As the *sbirri* had taken Caravaggio away, the painter had appealed to Gabrielli for help. The bookseller recalled his precise words: 'Go to the house of the Illustrious Cardinal del Monte and speak to Monsignor the Cardinal del Monte, or to his majordomo ... and go to the house of Signora Olimpia Aldobrandini.'[75] Gabrielli had taken the message but had been arrested himself later.

For his part, the perfume-maker said that he had had nothing to do with any of it. He had never been in prison before, he said. It was unfair. He had only been going for a walk on the Via del Babuino. During his one night in jail, he had clearly been struck by Caravaggio's confidence in his powerful patrons. The perfumier remembered the painter saying, 'Whatever happens, I'll be out tomorrow.'

It is clear from Caravaggio's testimony that this had been only one of several run-ins with the police in the autumn of 1604. He was accused of using offensive language to the *sbirro* who had arrested him, Corporal Malanno. Caravaggio answered that the said Malanno had a grudge against him. The policeman was hostile and insulting whenever he bumped into him, the painter complained, but he stoutly denied having called the arresting officer a 'cocksucker' on the night in question.

A month later Caravaggio was stopped again, late at night, walking along a narrow conduit called the Chiavica del Bufalo. The arresting officer filed his report on 18 November 1604:

> Five hours after nightfall at the Conduit of the Bufalo, Michelangelo da Caravaggio, who was carrying a sword and dagger, was halted by my men. When asked if he had a licence, he answered, 'Yes,' and presented it, and so he was dismissed, and I told him he could leave, and said, 'Goodnight, sir.' He replied loudly, 'You can stick it up your arse,' and so I arrested him, since I did not wish to bear such a thing. I ordered my men to take him, and when he was bound he said, 'You and everyone with you can shove it up your arses.' And so I put him in the jail of the Tor di Nona.[76]

As always the evidence is fragmentary, but what we have of it at the end of 1604 strongly suggests a life going awry. Caravaggio is living in rented accomodation with only his apprentice Cecco for company. He has several commissions but works at them in sporadic bursts. He flares up at the merest hint of an insult. He goes looking for trouble late at night and even manages to pick a fight with the police when they are on the point of letting him go.

Winter came and went with little sign of Caravaggio doing much in the way of work: no pictures from his hand are known from these months. His former rival, Annibale Carracci, had fallen into a deep melancholy after the completion of the Farnese Gallery, so deep that it prevented him from working altogether. In the terminology of the time, Caravaggio was choleric rather than melancholic, but he too seems to have been afflicted by some form of painter's block. By early 1605 his debts had begun to mount up. His rent was in arrears. His landlady, Prudentia Bruni, kept sending him reminders that he studiously ignored.

Meanwhile the city was in a state of political flux. Clement VIII took to his bed in February 1605 and died on 3 March after a short illness. The supporters of the French faction in Rome rejoiced when Alessandro de' Medici was elected as Pope Leo XI, but he was frail and old and soon after his election he too died, on 27 April. Rome was a turbulent city at the best of times, but it was doubly unstable whenever the papal throne was empty. During this interregnum normal government was effectively suspended. According to long tradition, a blanket amnesty was given to the inmates of the city's jails. The felons celebrated their newfound freedom with predictable exuberance. The regular civic authorities tried to maintain their grip on the population, but their jurisdiction was frequently contested at such times by the *caporioni*, the heads of the city districts.[77]

Three days after the death of the short-lived Medici pope Leo XI, simmering rivalry between the French and Spanish factions broke out into open street warfare. Soon there was a full-blown riot, with fighting spilling over from the Piazza della Trinità into the Via dei Condotti. The *bargello* of Rome, the city's principal law enforcement officer, tried to restore order with his troops. But he was met, with equal force, by Giovan Francesco Tomassoni, *caporione* of the Campo Marzio district, his brothers Ranuccio and Alessandro, and their own ragtag militia. The ensuing argument revolved around jurisdiction over prisoners. The *bargello* wanted to take a number of men into custody, whereas the Tomassoni demanded that the men be handed over to them, for reasons that are not clear: they were either allies, whom the pro-Spanish Tomassoni intended to set free, or they were enemies, sought for the darker purposes of retribution.

The three Tomassoni brothers ended up in court over the incident. The outcome is unknown, but the testimony given by two eyewitnesses paints a vivid picture of the upheavals in Rome. The first to be called was Lieutenant Antonio Crepella, an officer under the command of the *bargello* who had been assigned to patrol duties on the day in question:

> Sir, I was with the *bargello* of Rome, who was leading the entire constabulary, and we were walking slowly around Rome. When we were in Piazza Trinità we saw a large crowd of people towards Via de' Condotti, who were quarrelling and had their swords out. So we hurried there and the people, when they saw us, ran off in all directions. Chasing after them, we caught seven or eight. We then led them off as prisoners towards Tor di Nona by order of the *bargello* ... and when we were in the Piazza of Cardinal Borghese [Piazza S. Eustachio, in front of the

Palazzo Borghese] the *caporione* of Campo Marzio, Captain Francesco Tommasoni da Terni, appeared in front of us, along with his brother Ranuccio, and another brother whose name I don't know, but who is older than them, with a great crowd of people who were all from the militia, which Francesco captains.

He and his brothers were all three armed with swords, daggers and prohibited pistols. Some of the militiamen were armed with arquebuses, some with halberds, and some with other weapons. Their captain Francesco said to me, 'Hey! What prisoners are these?' I told him they were prisoners who had been fighting in Piazza della Trinità, where there had been people hurt, and someone may have been killed. He replied that I should stop, and that he wanted the prisoners himself, and that I should hand them over to him, because they were taken in his *rione*, and that he wanted to know what was going on, because it was up to him to account for these things. I replied: 'Captain Francesco. Don't get in my way. Let me go, and talk with Captain Girolamo, who is on his way. Don't make [trouble]. These prisoners fought with us, and we can't hand them over to you. Let us take them to prison, then go and talk to the Governor, and get satisfaction.

The said Captain Francesco answered me: 'I want you to leave them with us,' and put his hand to the pistol he was carrying, and his brothers also took their pistols, saying, 'Leave them here! Leave them here, or we'll cut you all into pieces, you fucking pricks!' and their militiamen shouted, 'To arms! To arms! Beat the drum!' One of them pointed his halberd at my chest, saying: 'Get away from here! What are you doing here? Get out of here!' Finally, having surrounded us, the said Francesco, his brothers and the militiamen took the prisoners away from the *sbirri* and led them away themselves. Then they let us go, and I came straight here to the office to give my account.

The next, unnamed witness, another officer under the command of the *bargello*, was asked to identify the participants. He could only indicate Francesco and his brothers. His account differs little from that of the lieutenant, until he comes to the aftermath of the event:

And while we were waiting [at the 'office' where they had gone to report the incident] the *caporione* Captain Francesco Tomassoni came and said, 'Go to the Heavens. The prisoners are mine.' And we said,

'Take them,' but also that he would have to give us an account of it. Then he said, 'Do us a favour, take us to the militia [Tomassoni's own headquarters].' And so we escorted him to his house in Piazza S. Lorenzo in Lucina. When we were inside we told him to make a list of the prisoners with their names and surnames, and someone who was dressed in long clothes began to write it. While they were being written down, I told him to make out the receipt saying that we had consigned them to him, and he replied: 'I don't want to make out a receipt, etc.' Ranuccio, the *caporione*'s brother, came towards me and said: 'I'll talk with my brother Gian Francesco, who's here in a house where the prisoners are, etc.' Then the *caporione* and his people forced us to halt, saying, 'Stop there! Stop there!' and putting their hands to their swords and pointing them at us *sbirri* and prisoners. I know two of them, one of whom was Captain Ranuccio, and another one, an old man who is his relative.[78]

Giovanni Baglione was also a *caporione* during the period of the two Vacant Sees. His area of jurisdiction was the district of Castello. Perhaps his civic duties brought him into contact with the Tomassoni clan. Baglione would later describe Ranuccio Tomassoni as an honourable young man, which suggests that they may have been friends. Honourable or not, Ranuccio and his family were certainly well connected in Rome. When his brother Alessandro died later in the year of an unspecified illness, he was accorded the signal honour of burial in the Pantheon.[79]

On 29 May 1605 Camillo Borghese was elected as Pope Paul V. The new Borghese pope, considerably less severe than his predecessor, allowed the revival of the traditional nepotism of the papal court, ensuring that his nephew Scipione was elected to the cardinalate. The papal nephew loved food and art in equal measure and would soon become an acquisitive collector of Caravaggio's pictures. But private and public domains were very different. The official religious style of the Borghese papacy would be far removed from Caravaggio's simplicity and austerity. For major commissions, the graceful manner of an artist such as Guido Reni was preferred. The ground was being prepared for the soaring majesty of the full-blown Baroque style.

On the eve of Paul V's coronation, Caravaggio was back in jail. He had been stopped yet again for bearing arms. When he failed to produce a licence for his weapons, he was taken to prison – not the Tor di Nona this time but the governor's jail. The name of the arresting officer was Captain Pino. His testimony was brief:

> Last night about seven hours after nightfall [3 a.m], as I was on patrol with my constables at Sant'Ambrogio on the Corso, there came a man by the name of Michelangelo, wearing a sword and dagger. Stopped and asked whether he had a licence to carry the said weapons, he said he had not. I had him arrested and brought to jail, and I now make my report, as is my duty, that he may be punished according to justice.

In the margin of his report, Captain Pino drew a little sketch of the offending sword and dagger. The questioning of Caravaggio followed. The court notary took down his responses and made a note of the outcome:

> I was seized on the street of the Corso in front of the Church of Sant'Ambrogio. It may have been eight hours after nightfall [4 a.m.] for it was light, and I was seized because I had a sword and dagger.
>
> I have no written licence to carry a sword and dagger. However, the Governor of Rome had given oral orders to the captain and his corporal to let me carry them. I have no other licence.
>
> *He recognized the weapons taken from him by the constables.*
>
> *He was allowed to go at large, with three days' time to prepare his report.*[80]

Just what Caravaggio had been doing in the middle of the night is anyone's guess. He is unlikely to have been up to much good. Six weeks later, on 19 July 1605, he was back in the Tor di Nona, having been cautioned for the crime of *deturpatio portae*, or defacing doors. A woman called Laura della Vecchia and her daughter Isabella lodged the complaint.

Deturpatio was a specific legal term that can be translated as 'house-scorning'.[81] It was invariably a response to a perceived slight or injury. House-scorners generally operated in the dead of night, when they were less likely to be disturbed by the police. They often made a lot of noise, shouting insults or singing lewd songs as a prelude to the vengeful assault itself. Then they would throw stones, damaging shutters and blinds. Sometimes they would also hurl animal bladders filled with blood or ink to leave other visible marks of shame. Excrement was often smeared on to doors and door handles. Doodles were drawn, scurrilous graffiti in the shape of erect phalluses or cuckold's horns.

The charges levelled at Caravaggio by Laura della Vecchia and her daughter do not specify which of these methods the painter had employed. The wording of the complaint against him suggests that the worst damage was done to the door of the house. That may in itself suggest the nature of the painter's grievance. House-scorning was an almost exclusively male activity, and the most common perpetrators were men whose amorous attentions had been rejected by women. Had Isabella della Vecchia led Caravaggio on in some way, only to change her mind? Had Laura della Vecchia shut the door of her house – and therefore, metaphorically, the door of her daughter's chastity – against the infuriated painter? Or perhaps Isabella was just one of the many whores with whom the abrasive Caravaggio mingled, and quarrelled. There is reason to believe that sex, in some form, lay at the root of the argument. As the spring turned to summer in the troubled year of 1605, even the painter's relationships with women were going badly.

A CACKLING OF GEESE

Caravaggio did manage to start work on at least one picture in the heat of the Roman summer of 1605: *The Madonna of Loreto*, commissioned for the Cavalletti Chapel in the Roman church of Sant'Agostino some eighteen months earlier. Caravaggio's painting was clearly shaped by his experience of visiting Loreto and its Holy House, which was said to have flown miraculously from Nazareth to Italy in the Middle Ages, eventually touching down in Loreto one night in December 1294. Protestants, predictably, dismissed the cult of Loreto as a sham. Even the credulity of many devout Catholics was strained by a legend according to which the childhood home of Jesus Christ himself had been aerially projected, by the force of miracle, from Nazareth to an obscure wood in the eastern Marches of Italy.

The popularity of the shrine was sustained by its dramatic popular appeal, and by the persuasive rhetoric of its promoters. Louis Richeome's influential tract *Le Pelerin de Lorette* was originally published in French in 1604, the year before Caravaggio painted his picture. Soon translated into Latin, Italian and a number of European vernacular languages, Richeome's text was a bestseller that brought thousands more pilgrims to the doors of the Holy House.

Richeome placed great emphasis on the miracle of the Incarnation and eloquently made the case for regarding Loreto as the holiest of all holy shrines. The following passage is taken from *The Pilgrime of Loreto*, the English translation of his book:

> when we shall have reckoned up by name, the most renowned places of all the world, as well out of profane Writers, as out of the sacred Scriptures, the Chamber of *Loreto* exceedeth them all in this condition, in having been the closet, where the marriage of the Sonne of God with our humane Nature was celebrated in the B. Virgin's womb, the most high and mysterious worke, that the holy Trinity maker of all things, did ever accomplish; for therein God was made man; the Creator, a creature; the supreme cause, an effect; the Word, flesh; the spirit did take a body; the first is become last, and Alpha, Omega . . .[82]

By Caravaggio's time there were two basic conventions for depicting the shrine of Loreto. The Madonna and child might be shown sitting on the roof of the Holy House, as they had been said to do during its magic carpet-like flight from Nazareth to Italy. Or the Madonna might simply be shown standing, holding the Christ child, in a pose derived from an ancient cult statue said to have been carved by St Luke himself that was housed on the altar of the shrine.

Departing from the limited conventions of existing Lauretan imagery, Caravaggio depicted two poor modern pilgrims kneeling at the entrance to the famous shrine. They are husband and wife, or perhaps mother and son. They have come in all humility, as every pilgrim was advised to do, to pray to the Queen of Heaven. Their feet are bare and dirty, their clothing begrimed, patched and poor. They have been rewarded for their honest piety and their weeks on the pilgrimage trail with a vision. The Virgin has chosen to appear to them, in the very doorway of the Holy House of Loreto itself. The infant

Christ appears with his blessed mother, clasped in her arms, a finger of his right hand raised in the gesture of benediction. Haloed by a filigree circle of gold, Mary cranes her neck towards the pilgrims, as if to make sure that she catches every last word of their prayers.

In Caravaggio's time, it was the custom for pilgrims to enter Loreto barefoot, wearing simple clothes. Their immediate destination was the simple dwelling of the Holy House itself, which, like the modest barn of Francis of Assisi's first church, had been shoehorned into a splendid marble architectural casing, itself contained within the vast nave of a later cathedral. Once arrived, the pilgrims were to circle the holy dwelling three times, on their bare knees. Having made this slow crawl towards the hope of salvation, they were finally allowed to enter the shrine.[83]

All this is the implied prelude to Caravaggio's gentle fantasy of a painting. The work is a *tour de force* of naked religious populism: spare to the point of banality, blatant in its appeal to the masses. The gratification that it offers is instant, the idea that it embodies too good to be true. It is the realization, in art, of every pilgrim's dream. At the end of the barefoot, knee-scraping journey, a vision. The door to the Holy House has become the door to Heaven itself. The two weary pilgrims are greeted by the Virgin and Child and implicitly welcomed towards another, better place. They will have no further need of their walking sticks, now they have come this far.

Such is the sheer directness of its appeal to popular piety, *The Madonna of Loreto* has often been regarded as something of an embarrassment – a saccharine, sentimental picture, the only work in Caravaggio's entire *œuvre* with something of the chocolate-box about it. But in its time it was unusual and daring. No artist had ever given such prominence, in a major religious altarpiece, to two such nakedly proletarian figures as the pair of kneeling pilgrims.

There was an old tradition of including portraits of men and women who had paid for certain altarpieces within the work themselves. Such donor portraits, as they have become known, often place the kneeling figures of such pious benefactors to either side of the Virgin and Child. They are included within the scene, yet they are also apart from it, witnesses rather than participants. In *The Madonna of Loreto*, Caravaggio turned this convention on its head, first by making the kneeling figures central to the sacred story (the story's catalyst, even, since it is their faith that has called forth the vision of the merciful Madonna and child), and secondly by depicting them not as wealthy donors but as poor pilgrims who have circled the shrine at Loreto three times on their bare knees. The man's filthy naked feet, turned towards the viewer, emphasize this shockingly complete inversion of an old pictorial tradition.

What might the true donors of the picture, the Cavalletti, have made of all this? Might they not have been disconcerted by Caravaggio's substitution of their images by those of the two poor pilgrims? It would only have required a relatively minor adjustment to the picture for the normal proprieties to be observed. He could easily have painted the standing Madonna and Child with the kneeling figures of Ermete and Orinzia Cavalletti to either side, in the manner of traditional donor portraits. Yet he did not, and no such alteration was asked of him.

Ermete Cavalletti was of course dead by the time Caravaggio finished *The Madonna of Loreto*. But he would most likely have approved of the painter's innovations. Ermete's dedication to the Santissima Trinità dei Pellegrini is proven: as a member of that lay confraternity, he, a rich man, had abased himself in imitation of Christ and washed the feet of poor pilgrims. Caravaggio's painting no less dramatically asserted the pauperist values of that institution. In fact the painter might be said to have repeated that act of self-abnegation, on Cavalletti's behalf, by putting poor pilgrims in place of his rich patrons. The replacement may even imply a kind of wishful metamorphosis, with the kneeling pilgrims as metaphorical portraits of Ermete and Orinzia Cavalletti themselves – transformed, through their humility of heart, into honorary members of the blessed poor.

Whether that too was part of Caravaggio's meaning, there is every indication that the family approved wholeheartedly of his picture. Not only was it accepted without demur and without alterations, but Orinzia Cavalletti arranged for her own burial beneath the floor of the same chapel.

Once again, Caravaggio had painted a monumental altarpiece aimed squarely at the poor and the hungry. The location of the church for which he painted the picture was also part of its message and part of its significance.[84] With the completion of *The Madonna of Loreto*,

Caravaggio now had major works on display in two of the most frequently visited churches on the principal pilgrimage axis through northern Rome. Every year wave after wave of pilgrims would enter the city from the north at the Porta del Popolo. Immediately on their left was the church of Santa Maria del Popolo, for which Caravaggio had painted *The Conversion of St Paul* and *The Crucifixion of St Peter*. The main pilgrimage route from there towards St Peter's then led directly along the Via di Ripetta and its continuation, the Via della Scrofa, to the corner of the Via dei Coronari. Turning right on to that street, in the direction of the Tiber and the Ponte Sant'Angelo, the pilgrim would find himself in one of the most congested thoroughfares in all Rome. The church of Sant'Agostino lay at the start of the Via dei Coronari, so named after its multitude of Rosary-makers' shops, thronged by pious tourists buying Rosaries and other devotional souvenirs of their visit to the Eternal City. Caravaggio knew that he was guaranteed a vast audience of the pious and the humble by virtue of Sant'Agostino's prominent place on the city's Christian itinerary. To the pilgrims who entered the church and walked into the Cavalletti Chapel, he offered a perfected mirror image of their own travels, one in which they could see themselves reaching the wished-for end of every pilgrim's journey.

It was this direct appeal by Caravaggio to the poor, and the central role he gave them in his theatre of Christianity, that most shocked his critics. Writing from the perspective of the later seventeenth century, when the pauperist ideals of the early Counter-Reformation lay in ruins, Bellori cast Caravaggio in the role of a seditious revolutionary. With pictures such as *The Madonna of Loreto* he had opened a Pandora's Box of vulgarity: 'Now began the imitation of common and vulgar things, seeking out filth and deformity, as some popular artists do assiduously ... The costumes they paint consist of stockings, breeches, and big caps, and in their figures they pay attention only to wrinkles, defects of the skin and exterior, depicting knotted fingers and limbs disfigured by disease.'[85]

Bellori's disgust for Caravaggio's 'popular' art, his lazar-house realism, was echoed by Giovanni Baglione. Unlike Bellori, Baglione was a contemporary of Caravaggio, and had gone to see the picture soon after it was installed. His predictable dislike of the work was only intensified by the huge crowds that it drew: 'In the first chapel on the left in the church of Sant'Agostino, he painted the Madonna of Loreto from life with two pilgrims; one of them has muddy feet and the other wears a soiled and torn cap; and because of this pettiness in the details of a grand painting the public made a great fuss over it.'[86]

The word Baglione used for public was *popolani*, which specifically denoted the lower classes: peasants, *hoi polloi*. To convey the kind of fuss they made over the picture, he used *schiamazzo*, which means a din of chattering, but can also be used to describe the cackling of geese.

Bellori and Baglione represented the values of the academy, of idealized classical style. But they spoke not only for a particular notion of decorum in art: they spoke also for power and for wealth, and for forms of religious art that spoke down to, rather than for, the mass of Christian believers. Caravaggio had not painted *The Madonna of Loreto* for them. He had painted it for the *popolani*, and whether they cackled like geese or not, the *popolani* took it to their hearts. Not for nothing is the picture commonly known by its 'popular' title – which is, simply, *The Madonna of the Pilgrims*.

LENA WHO STAYS ON HER FEET
IN THE PIAZZA NAVONA

Precisely when Caravaggio finished and delivered the altarpiece to Sant'Agostino is unknown. It may not have been until the autumn of 1605, or even later: he was probably still working on the picture at the end of July, but could have done no work on it at all in August, because for the whole of that month he was again in trouble with the law.

On 29 July 1605 a junior notary called Mariano Pasqualone accused Caravaggio of assault and grievous bodily harm. The young man arrived, still bleeding, in the legal offices of a certain Paolo Spada, where a clerk of the criminal court took his statement under oath:

I am here in the office because I have been assaulted by Michelangelo da Caravaggio, the painter, as I am going to relate. As Messer Galeazzo and I – it may have been about one hour after nightfall [8.30 p.m.] – were strolling in Piazza Navona in front of the palace of the Spanish ambassador, I suddenly felt a blow on the back of my head. I fell to the ground at once and realized that I had been wounded in the head by what I believe to have been the stroke of a sword. As you can see, I have a wound on the side of my head. Thereupon, the aggressor fled.

I didn't see who wounded me, but I never had disputes with anybody but the said Michelangelo. A few nights ago he and I had words on the Corso on account of a woman called Lena who is to be found standing at the Piazza Navona, past the palace, or rather the main door of the palace, of Messer Sertorio Teofilo. She is Michelangelo's woman. Please, excuse me quickly, that I may dress my wounds.[87]

After Pasqualone's departure from the office, his companion, Galeazzo Roccasecca, who gave his profession as a writer of apostolic letters, added his own witness statement:

I saw a man with an unsheathed weapon in his hand. It looked like a sword or a small pistol. He turned round at once and made three jumps and then turned towards the palace of the Illustrious Cardinal del Monte, which was nearby down the little street where we were. He wore a black cloak on one shoulder only. I said to Messer Mariano, 'What is it? What is it?' and he replied to me, 'I have been assassinated and I am wounded.' I saw that he had a wound in the head and he said, 'I am assassinated ... it could not have been anyone other than Michelangelo da Caravaggio.' And that is the truth.[88]

Some seventy years later Giambattista Passeri wrote a long and circumstantial account of what might have been behind the trouble between Caravaggio and Pasqualone. Passeri was a painter, poet and author of artists' lives, who had clearly been told some version of the story while he was doing his research in the artists' studios of Baroque Rome. Having applied a liberal coat of literary polish to the original anecdote, he included it, as an entertaining diversion, in the first edition of his life of the painter Guercino:[89]

In the first chapel to the left of the entrance in S. Agostino, Caravaggio painted the Holy Virgin with the Child in her arms and two pilgrims adoring her. At that time he lived in the House of the Eight Corners, in one of the little streets behind the Mausoleum of Augustus. Nearby lived a lady with her young daughter, who was not at all unattractive; they were poor but honest people. Michelangelo wished to have the young girl as a model for the Mother of God which he was to paint in this work, and he succeeded in this by offering them a sum of money which was large enough, considering their poverty, to enable him to carry out his wish.

This girl was being courted by a young man who was a notary by profession and who had asked the mother for her daughter's hand in marriage. However, he had always received a negative answer because this simple and naive woman was unwilling to give her daughter to a notary since, as she said, all notaries are surely bound for damnation. The young man was indignant at this refusal, but he nevertheless did not lose track of his beloved. Thus he found out that she frequently went to the house of Caravaggio and remained there for long periods of time posing for him.

Full of jealousy and totally enraged, he contrived to meet the mother one day and said to her, 'My good woman, you're so scrupulous and such a good guardian, and here your lovely daughter, whom you refused to let me marry, goes to this miserable painter so that he can do anything he likes with her. Really, you have made a wise choice and one which is worthy of your class, refusing to let her marry a man like me so that you can make her the concubine of this scoundrel. Now you can just keep her and I hope it will do you a lot of good.' Then turning his back, he left her confused and completely upset.

It seemed to this lady that she had inadvertently done the wrong thing by taking her daughter to Michelangelo, even though she had done so in perfectly good faith, and it also seemed that this notary had good reason, at least from his point of view, for treating her so badly. She went immediately to Caravaggio in tears and complained about what had happened on his account. He smiled bitterly at this accusation and asked her who it was that had so unjustly mistreated her. From her description he easily recognized him as a person whom he frequently met in the street. He consoled the lady with gentle words and sent her home.

He was upset by this incident and, being by nature irritable and violent, the next morning he put a hatchet under his coat and went out to look for this young man. This being Wednesday, market day, he carried the affair right into Piazza Navona, just when a fair was being held there. It took place in front of the church of S. Giacomo degli Spagnoli, near the Triton Fountain. He went up to the notary and gave him such a terrific blow on the head with the hatchet that he fell to the ground unconscious and covered with his own blood. And Michelangelo said, 'Now learn to behave yourself if you don't know how.' After this misdeed he took refuge at San Luigi dei Francesi and remained there for a long time. Fortunately for Caravaggio, the notary did not die from the blow, even though he was unconscious and for a long time remained ill. It was some years before they settled their feud and the indemnity.[90]

In several striking respects, Passeri's account is impressively close to the witness statements given in the immediate aftermath of the attack. Passeri gets Pasqualone's profession right, correctly specifies the place where the attack occurred, describes it as a surprise assault on an unarmed man. So even though his 'poor but honest' female characters sound like the heroines of a fairy story, Passeri's assertion that the young lady at the centre of the dispute was Caravaggio's model is worth taking seriously.

Passeri's description of the two women as virtuous creatures from the world of fable also marks the one serious fault-line between his account and the original witness statements. Although brief, Pasqualone's description of the mysterious Lena suggests that she was actually a prostitute. Two very precise phrases in his testimony may shed light not only on this specific incident, but also on the whole vexed question of Caravaggio's nocturnal existence – the other life that he pursued, so vigorously, in the shadows of the city.

Pasqualone's exact words in Italian when first describing the girl were '*una donna chiamata Lena che sta in piedi a Piazza Navona*' – literally, 'a woman called Lena who stays on her feet in the Piazza Navona'. This way of describing a woman who can always be found standing in a certain place carries an insinuation; the phrase is still current Italian slang for a streetwalker, a whore. There was in fact a known prostitute called Lena Antognetti working in the area at around this time, who was arrested in Piazza Catinara, the present-day Piazza Cairoli, opposite the church of San Carlo ai Catinari, on the night of 1 November 1604.[91] She was apparently on her way home but was stopped for being out after curfew.

The young notary's second remark about Lena is even more intriguing. He baldly says '*e donna di Michelangelo*', which literally means 'she is Caravaggio's woman', but implies a particular form of possession. Pasqualone pointedly does *not* describe Lena as '*la donna di Michelangelo*' but as '*donna di Michelangelo*': not '*the* woman of Caravaggio' but simply 'woman of Caravaggio', a phrase that objectifies her and carries the suggestion that she is one of several such women. Pasqualone might simply have been saying that Lena was one of several prostitutes frequented by Caravaggio,[92] but it is also possible that he meant to imply that she was one of several prostitutes *controlled* by Caravaggio – and that the painter, therefore, was a part-time pimp.

Pasqualone's remarks offer an explanation for much of Caravaggio's seemingly random nocturnal escapades and unpredictable behaviour. His life becomes no less violent, but more logical. Caravaggio certainly used whores as models. He painted Fillide Melandroni and, quite possibly, Fillide's friend Anna Bianchini. He painted Lena the streetwalker, and according to Giulio Mancini, who knew Caravaggio well, at least one other prostitute modelled for him in Rome. Perhaps he and his friends just happened to know a lot of whores and courtesans – after all, such women tended to move in the same circles and live in the same places as painters, sculptors and architects. But it is conceivable that there was more to it than that. Caravaggio needed women to model for him, so rather than be at the mercy of pimps for a reliable supply of girls, why not secure his own small team of whores? He would get free use of female models, which was by no means otherwise easy to arrange. He would not be beholden to anybody, which always made him uneasy. He would earn a bit of extra money on the side, and there would have been some free sex. For their part, the prostitutes would get their own livelihood, and a formidable protector.

Caravaggio used his contacts in high places to ensure that he could carry a sword and a dagger with impunity wherever he went. If he could not always actually produce a licence, he could usually count on Cardinal del Monte, or his majordomo, to get him out of trouble.

Maybe one of the reasons Caravaggio went about armed the whole time was that when he was out on the street, he was also out on duty, looking out for 'his' women.

Many of the known incidents involving him lend at least circumstantial support to the hypothesis. What kind of argument over a whore could have led to a sudden, brutal assault of the kind perpetrated by Caravaggio on Pasqualone? The romantic answer is that both men were in love with the girl. But if that were so, a duel would have been the solution. It would have been a matter of honour, whereas Caravaggio treated his victim with a calculated show of contempt.[93] If, on the other hand, Lena was one of Caravaggio's prostitutes, the shameful attack from behind becomes easier to explain. Pasqualone was perhaps a client who had not paid, or had mistreated the girl in some way, so Caravaggio took his revenge publicly, sending out a clear message to anyone who might be watching.

Seen in this light, many of the smaller or more puzzling details to emerge from the painter's criminal record suddenly come into sharper focus. He is often seen out and about, carrying a sword, in the small hours of the morning. He attacks the house of two women, who have annoyed him in some way that seems to relate to sex. On the evening of the stone-throwing, he stops in the street to chat with Menicuccia, a whore whom he clearly knows well. All of this is consistent with the behaviour of a pimp.

The enmity between Caravaggio and Ranuccio Tomassoni, soon to reach its climax, may have been in some way territorial: certainly Tomassoni was a pimp himself. Caravaggio painted one of Tomassoni's girls, Fillide Melandroni, and, having got her to model for him, perhaps he also tried to persuade her to work for him.

THE CASE OF THE DAMAGED CEILING

At the end of July 1605, concurrently accused of the assault on Pasqualone and the *deturpatio* of Laura and Isabella della Vecchia, Caravaggio skipped bail and fled to the coastal city of Genoa. He probably took letters of introduction with him from some of his patrons and protectors in Rome. Ottavio Costa and Vincenzo Giustiniani, both enthusiastic collectors of Caravaggio's work, had strong links with the city, as above all did the Colonna family, his protectors since boyhood. The Marchesa Costanza Colonna was living in Rome, at the Palazzo Colonna, between 1600 and 1605. The Colonna family had intermarried with one of the great Genoese families, the Doria. As soon as Caravaggio got to Genoa, he sought out one of the marchesa's relations, Prince Marcantonio Doria, who, although it came to nothing, offered him a prestigious commission.

Caravaggio spent the best part of a month away. On three separate occasions between 3 and 19 August, a Roman court notary reported his failure to attend hearings in the case brought by Laura della Vecchia. Repeated summonses were addressed to him and he was eventually fined for contempt.[94] Meanwhile, his movements were being carefully tracked by Fabio Masetti, an agent in Rome working for Cesare d'Este, Duke of Modena.

Masetti was keeping a close watch on Caravaggio in the summer of 1605 because he was trying to get a picture out of him. Earlier in the year Cesare d'Este had conceived the idea of staging another pictorial competition between Caravaggio and Annibale Carracci. This rematch of the Cerasi Chapel contest of 1601 was to have been staged for a 'Chapel of the Madonna' in the newly renovated ducal castle in Modena. The idea was that each artist should paint a scene from the life of the Virgin. Carracci was to paint the altarpiece, Caravaggio a single canvas for one of the side walls. But there were problems from the outset. Carracci was crippled by depression, and Caravaggio had good reason to dislike the terms of the commission: his picture was to be considerably smaller than his rival's, and in March 1605 another of the duke's agents in Rome, Attilio Ruggieri, reported that Caravaggio was trying to wriggle out of the assignment altogether, truculently remarking that the duke would be better off hiring a miniaturist to paint such small figures.[95] Caravaggio's fee was to be just 50 or 60 scudi, compared to the 200 offered to Carracci.

In the end he had stuck with it, and by the summer responsibility for handling the commission had passed from Attilio Ruggieri to Masetti, whose letters from Rome to Modena are a paper trail of mounting frustration. On 17 August, Masetti told the duke that it was impossible to force a painting out of the depressive Carracci, saying that there was nothing for it but to accommodate the painter's strange 'humour'. Meanwhile, he added, 'Caravaggio is in contempt of court, and is to be found in Genoa.'[96] On 20 August, Masetti reported that Carracci continued to be utterly intractable, but that efforts were being made to secure Caravaggio's return to Rome: 'a settlement is now being negotiated for Caravaggio; as soon as it's concluded, I'll be on his back.'[97] Perhaps del Monte was still busy on Caravaggio's behalf – Galeazzo Roccasecca had hinted as much in his testimony for Pasqualone at the end of July.

Masetti's next letter, of 24 August, shows that the Este agent was now trying to put pressure on Caravaggio through del Monte:

> When I heard that Caravaggio had appeared in Rome in hope of a settlement, I petitioned Cardinal del Monte to command him to despatch Your Highness's painting, which he promised me would be ready quickly, though one can't rely on [Caravaggio]. It is said that he is funny in the head ['e uno cervello stravantissimo'; literally, 'he is a very extravagant brain'] and also that Prince Doria sought to have him paint a loggia for him [in Genoa] and wanted to give him 6,000 scudi for it, but that he didn't want to accept, though he had almost promised. It occurred to me to sound out whether, under these circumstances of his non-attendance [in Rome], he would be happy to move there [to Modena], where he could have given every satisfaction to Your Highness. But seeing that he is so unstable I have done no more.[98]

Caravaggio's refusal of a prince's ransom for the small task of decorating a loggia struck Masetti as typically capricious. But the painter had never learned to work in fresco, so he could not have accepted the commission even if he had wanted to. Besides, he had business to attend to in Rome. Apart from anything else, he needed to arrange some more modelling sessions with Lena and finish off the overdue *Madonna of Loreto*.

Caravaggio was indeed back in Rome a week or so before the end of the month. On 26 August he signed a judicial peace with Mariano Pasqualone. Damages had probably been paid, although the legal conventions governing such documents made it sound like a gentleman's agreement: 'the above-named parties, exhorted and persuaded by mutual friends, determined to make peace as befits good Christians . . .'[99]

In exchange for a pardon from the Governor of Rome, Caravaggio put his name to the declaration:

> I, Michelangelo Merisi, having been insulted by Messer Mariano, clerk of the Vicar's Court, as he would not wear a sword in the daytime, resolved to strike him wherever I should meet him. One night, having come upon him accompanied by another man and having perfectly recognized his face, I struck him. I am very sorry for what I did, and if I had not done it yet, I would not do it. I beg him for his forgiveness and peace, and I regard the said Messer Mariano with a sword in his hand as a man fit to stand his ground against me or anybody else. I, Michelangelo Merisi, do affirm all the above.[100]

Pasqualone's lawyers must have insisted on some of the more humiliating phrases in this fulsome apology. Did Caravaggio sign it through gritted teeth? Or did he simply regard it, phlegmatically, as a means to an end? Assault with a lethal weapon was a serious crime. He had been let off lightly. Intriguingly, the judicial peace was actually signed at the Palazzo Quirinale, in the antechamber of the papal nephew, Scipione Borghese. It is possible that the new Borghese cardinal had helped to arrange Caravaggio's truce with Pasqualone. It was at around this time that Caravaggio's darkly penitential depiction of *St Jerome Writing* entered Scipione Borghese's collection. Perhaps the work was a gift, in recognition of a favour received. It is a strikingly sombre painting. The wizened and emaciated figure of Jerome sits in semi-darkness, writing in a great book. His deeply shadowed face and the bald dome of his head are modelled so severely, in chiaroscuro, as to resemble the skull that lies on the desk before him as a *memento mori*. It is a morbid visual rhyme.

Getting on with his life turned out to be more difficult than Caravaggio might have hoped. While he was away in Genoa, his infuriated landlady had taken advantage of his absence to seize his possessions in lieu of rent, and change the locks on the house in Vicolo dei Santa Cecilia e Biagio. This occasioned the inventory of its contents, which was made on 26 August (see p. 271). 'Two large pictures to paint' were included on the list. Perhaps one of them was the half-painted canvas of *The Madonna of Loreto*, still in his studio but now frustratingly inaccessible. The other, most probably, was the incomplete and long-overdue *Death of the Virgin*, which had been commissioned by the jurist Laerzio Cherubini, to serve as the altarpiece for a chapel that he had acquired in the church of Santa Maria della Scala in Rome, all the way back in 1601.

Caravaggio decided to vent his rage on the landlady who had locked him out with another *deturpatio*. Just four days after he had signed his peace with Mariano Pasqualone, he was being prosecuted yet again, for throwing stones at her windows. The attack took place in the small hours of 1 September and later that day Prudentia Bruni was airing her grievances in court:

> Last night at about the fifth hour [1 a.m.], the said Michelangelo came and threw so many stones at the shutters of my windows that he broke them all down one side, as Your Lordship sees.
>
> [The notary adds: *then she showed the wooden shutter broken in one part, and also some stones that were in the said window, which was noted down as evidence.*]
>
> And a little after this he came back with some others, playing a guitar; they stopped on the corner of the alley, and he talked with his companions, but I couldn't hear the exact words they were saying.
>
> The said Michelangelo did this because he rents a house of mine, which is beside my [own] house. Some days ago he wounded a notary of the Vicariate and left. I was owed rent for six [the notary adds: *correction, four*] months, and he had broken a ceiling of mine in the said house, so I had obtained a mandate ... to take the things that were left in the house, giving a security in the form of the deposit, which I did. Because of this he broke my shutters in order to spite me. There were three others in company with him. So I am making this complaint, and demand that they be punished in conformity with justice ...[101]

Four days later the magistrate examined two of the landlady's neighbours, a woman called Francesca Bartoli and a lady called Lucretia, who was the widow of a certain Ferdinando, from Perugia. Each separately denied that she had seen or heard a thing on the night in question. But as Caravaggio's recent neighbours, they of course knew what he was like.

Prudentia Bruni had referred to a damaged ceiling in the rented house. Might it have been caused by the painter's unorthodox working methods? Caravaggio's proto-cinematographic fondness for powerfully directed downlighting must have involved some ingenious studio set-ups. As we have seen, Bellori wrote that he placed 'a lamp high so that the light would fall straight down'. Sandrart echoed Bellori's remark, saying that Caravaggio liked to work in a dark space with a single source of light from above. In practice this might have involved a powerful flame, perhaps a torch made of pitch, the light from which might have been directed by the use of one of the mirrors in the studio. That would certainly have been enough to char the studio ceiling. Or Caravaggio may simply have taken advantage of the powerful, raking sunlight beating down on the roofs of the houses in his street. Perhaps he had got the effect he wanted just by blacking out his windows and smashing a hole in the ceiling to let the sunlight in.

The painter's latest prosecution did nothing to lighten the mood of Cesare d'Este's agent. On 7 September he sent yet another gloomy missive to his master in Modena. Neither of the two required pictures had even been started. There was no hope of getting anything from Annibale Carracci, who was completely incapable of working because of his depression. As for Caravaggio: 'last Saturday, his contempt of court for wounds given to a notary was settled, but now there's some other affair he's involved in.'[102]

Five weeks later, on 12 October, in a desperate bid to stir Caravaggio into action, Masetti gave him an advance of 12 scudi. By that time the painter had managed to find a new place to live, and had probably retrieved his possessions from Prudentia Bruni (though we do not know how the case between them was settled). He had moved into the house of Andrea Ruffetti, a lawyer with an interest in art and literature, in the Piazza Colonna, almost next door to the palace of Caravaggio's very first protector, the Marchesa di Colonna.

The new lodging brought about no more ordered a life. Towards the second half of October, Caravaggio was injured in a fight with a person or persons unknown. The affair was serious enough to warrant investigation. But when the law came calling on him, the bedridden painter was decidedly incommunicative. The investigating officer's report is dated 24 October 1605:

I, the notary of warrants, etc., visited the painter Michelangelo Caravaggio who was lying in bed in the house of Sr Andrea Ruffetti in Piazza

Colonna, wounded in the throat and left ear. Because of the bandages placed on it, this wound could barely be seen, but it is noted here. He was sworn to tell the truth and interrogated by me as to where, by whom and for what reason he was wounded. He replied: 'I wounded myself with my own sword when I fell down these stairs, I don't know where it was and there was no one there.' Although I exhorted him several times to tell the truth, he replied, 'I can say no more.' And I got no other response from him.[103]

Throughout the winter, the Este agent continued to chase Caravaggio for the duke's painting. On 5 November 1605 he reported that 'Caravaggio says the picture is almost ready and that he needs money; I replied that once the appointed thing has been done there will be no want of the money.'[104] But by 16 November, Masetti had capitulated to Caravaggio's demands. On that day he noted paying the artist another 20 scudi 'because the painting will definitely be finished by this coming weekend'.[105]

But it was not ready by the coming weekend. Nor the next. Nor the one after. After a long silence Fabio Masetti wrote one more exasperated letter on 18 January 1606: 'I have given Caravaggio 32 scudi for this thing. He goes red when he sees me.' Cesare d'Este never would get his painting.[106]

'SO MUCH TROUBLE'

Caravaggio is unlikely to have felt any regret over the unfinished and most probably unstarted picture for the ducal palace of Modena, or any embarrassment at taking money for it. By the beginning of 1606 he had already begun work on a far more prestigious commission. He had finally been asked to paint an altarpiece for St Peter's, the central church of Catholic Christendom.

The wheels of papal influence had turned in the painter's favour. Scipione Borghese, pleased with his new picture *St Jerome Writing*, had praised Caravaggio to the pope. According to Bellori, the papal nephew personally 'introduced Caravaggio to Pope Paul V, whom he portrayed seated, and by whom he was well rewarded'.[107] That portrait is lost, although a hamfisted copy of it still survives in the collections of the Palazzo Borghese. With papal favour came papal preferment. Paul V had plans for St Peter's. Caravaggio now became part of them.

In September 1605 the new pope had ordered the final demolition of the ancient nave of Old St Peter's, which still survived beneath the great dome of the new cathedral begun by Bramante and completed by Michelangelo. Seven altars lost in the destruction of the old basilica were moved to the new transept. One of these was owned by the Confraternity of the Palafrenieri, or 'papal grooms', whose patron saint was Anne. By the end of October the members of the confraternity had resolved to commission an altarpiece for their 'altar of St Anne in St Peter's'.[108] Within a month they had been steered towards Caravaggio.

On 1 December 1605 Antonio Tirelli, deacon, gave the painter a down payment of 25 scudi. Caravaggio would receive only another 50 scudi in total, a low fee for such an important work, but the painter was in no position to bargain. He was recently evicted, deeply in debt, scarred by a swordfight and in trouble, yet again, with the law. The commission must have seemed like a God-given chance for him to paint his way out of trouble. The altarpiece was finished and delivered in less than four months.

The Madonna of the Palafrenieri, sometimes known as *The Madonna of the Serpent*, is an unsettling picture. Monumental in scale, almost ten feet tall and more than six across, it shows three figures in a tall room, absorbed in a confrontation with pure evil. The Virgin and the infant Christ together crush the head of a serpent beneath their feet. As the foul creature writhes in its death agonies, St Anne, frail and bent by age, looks on in solemn contemplation. By God's grace, the devil is defeated.

Raven-haired Lena, '*donna di Caravaggio*', was required once again to play the part of the Virgin. Wearing a coral-coloured dress with a deep décolletage, she leans to support her son as he steps forward, his foot upon hers, hers upon the snake. He is a curly-haired, red-headed boy of about four years old. Were it not for the presence of the animal, they might just be mother and son playing a game of walk-on-my-feet as grandmother watches.

The mood of the picture is still and strange. There is no sense of drama, because instead of telling a story Caravaggio was obliged to embody an allegory. The result is like an image from an emblem book staged as a *tableau vivant* by flesh-and-blood human beings. The voluptuously full-breasted Virgin holds her smooth-skinned son under his arms. St Anne, half lost in the shadows, has corded sinews around her neck and collarbone, while the skin of her lined face looks as dry as autumn leaves.

The theme prescribed for the picture was calculated to make a specific theological point. Its origin lay in a much debated passage in the biblical Book of Genesis, in which God curses the serpent that has tempted Eve to eat from the Tree of Knowledge: 'I will put enmity between thee and the woman, and between thy seed and her seed; it shall bruise thy head, and thou shalt bruise his heel' (Genesis 3:15). There was a long tradition of regarding this as a prophetic reference to the Virgin Mary, the so-called 'Second Eve'. By giving birth to Jesus Christ, she would redeem mankind from Original Sin and undo the evil done by the treacherous snake in the garden of Eden – bruising the head of the serpent, as had been predicted in Genesis. But Protestants, suspicious of the cult of the Virgin Mary and concerned that it detracted from the proper worship of Jesus Christ, disputed this interpretation. Martin Luther declared that Christ, and Christ alone, could redeem mankind. The Catholic Church had reaffirmed its position, in a papal Bull of 1569 that proclaimed 'the Virgin crushed the head of the serpent with the aid of him to whom she had given birth.'

Caravaggio's picture was intended to translate word into image, to embody this article of Catholic faith as a vivid picture that all could understand. He was careful, at every point, to emphasize the underlying significance of his allegory. The serpent writhes in uneven, broken coils, while Christ forms a perfect circle with the thumb and forefinger of his outstretched left hand, a circle mirrored by the floating haloes of his mother and grandmother. The serpent is death. Christ is eternal life, perfection incarnate. The humble figure of Anne is there not only because her presence was decreed by the spiritual allegiance of the Confraternity of Palafrenieri, but to reinforce the idea of the Immaculate Conception, the belief that her daughter, Mary, was preserved from Original Sin. In Caravaggio's painting, Anne is shrouded in darkness, while her daughter is bathed in light. That is because

Anne's virtue, great as it had been, was only a dim prefiguration of Mary's radiance.

The Virgin and Christ child seem tense and alert, as they concertedly crush the serpent. Caravaggio himself seems to have approached his task of painting in a mood of wary circumspection, deliberately curbing the aggressive side of his originality and softening the rougher edges of his style: there were no horses' rumps here, no grimy feet thrust in the face of the viewer, no red rags to conventional piety or decorum, or so he hoped. He did his utmost to produce an unimpeachably correct endorsement of the Marian orthodoxy laid down by the Counter-Reformation Church – which can only have made what happened next all the more painful. The story of the picture's reception is told in three prosaic documents in the archives of the Palafrenieri.

On 8 April, Caravaggio delivered the painting and gave a certificate to the deacon of the confraternity. It is the only known example of a statement by the artist written in his own handwriting: 'I, Michelangelo da Caravaggio, am content and satisfied with the picture that I have painted for the Company of St Anne, in faith I have written and underwritten this 8th day of April 1606.'[109] On 14 April the picture was put on display in the confraternity's chapel. The record shows that 1 scudo was paid on that day to a carpenter named Pierfrancesco, for installing the painting on the altar of St Anne in St Peter's. On 16 April, two days later, the picture was removed. Orders were given that it should be taken away and stored in Sant'Anna dei Palafrenieri, the church of the papal grooms. The confraternity records 'payment to two porters to carry the painting of St Anne from St Peter's to their church'. On a spring morning, Caravaggio's monumental altarpiece was loaded into a mule-driver's cart and drawn slowly along the cobbled streets of the city.

To a painter so sensitive about his honour, the humiliation of this sudden reverse must have been deeply wounding. Why was the painting rejected? At around the time when Caravaggio delivered his picture, a dispute had arisen over the Palafrenieri's rights to the altar in St Peter's, but even after its resolution in early May the Palafrenieri made it clear that they still did not want the painting. By the middle of June 1606 they had sold it to Scipione Borghese for 100 scudi. The arrangement suited both parties: the Palafrenieri disposed of the picture that displeased them, clearing a small but tidy profit on their original outlay, and Borghese acquired a new work by the painter he most admired at a knockdown price.

It is possible that the Palafrenieri had simply taken exception to Caravaggio's portrayal of their beloved patron, St Anne, as a withered old lady thrown into deep shadow. The theology behind it allowed her to represent all the ancient generations before the coming of Christ, who had lived in darkness – but the Palafrenieri still might not have liked the overall effect. Their main objections, however, probably centred on the portrayal of the other two figures. The most plausible account of the picture's rejection is given by Bellori, who baldly states that it was taken out of St Peter's 'because of the offensive portrayal of the Virgin with the nude Christ child'.[110]

The infant Christ's nudity may have been thought improper but a wisp of drapery could easily have been added. It was surely Caravaggio's embodiment of the Virgin as Lena in a low-cut dress that really caused the difficulty. Appealing once more to the mass of ordinary Catholics – and especially women, among whom the cult of Mary was strongest – Caravaggio had painted her as the kind of mother with whom real mothers might identify. He had stressed her tenderness, leaning down over the child with gentle solicitude, but in the process he had revealed quite a lot of her cleavage. It is not difficult to see why such a voluptuous Virgin Mary might have caused misgivings. Cardinal Gabriele Paleotti, whose *Discourse on Sacred and Profane Images* was a widely consulted book of rules for the Counter-Reformation artist and patron, wrote that a picture of the Madonna with even the slightest hint of lasciviousness made him 'sick to my stomach'.[111]

There is no reason to doubt Caravaggio's pious intentions. He probably called attention to the Madonna's full breasts to stress her maternal aspect and posed her as he did to impart the touching awkwardness of actual life. But, if so, he miscalulated. The woman in red, leaning forward with her skirts hitched up, was just too real to be allowed into St Peter's. In the eyes of the Counter-Reformation Church, Mary was pure and perfect, the Queen of Heaven. Caravaggio's Mary was just not like that. As Roberto Longhi memorably remarked, she might almost be 'a peasant woman killing a viper in a barn'.[112]

The hellfire Dominican preacher Savonarola had once declared that artists should depict the Virgin as a pauper, not a queen, but that had been in Florence a hundred years before Caravaggio's time, when collective repentance was in the air along with smoke from Savonarola's bonfires of the vanities. In Rome under Pope Paul V such views were not widely held. The Borghese papacy was characterized by a return to pomp and magnificence, a decisive rejection of the austerity that had marked the age of Carlo Borromeo and, to a lesser degree, that of Clement VIII. Caravaggio, whose approach to religious painting had been shaped so powerfully by Borromean ideals of piety, found himself in a difficult position. In one sense his work was favoured by those in power. But in another and more important sense it was deemed entirely unacceptable.

Scipione Borghese, who ended up buying *The Madonna of the Palafrenieri*, clearly liked Caravaggio's powerfully dramatic style. But he did so as a connoisseur. As a cardinal, he looked at it differently. Caravaggio may have had friends among the elite clerics of the Borghese papacy, but they were not prepared to put the weight of the Church behind his visions of holy poverty. The rejection of his altarpiece for St Peter's, and its acquisition for the Borghese collection, fundamentally altered its nature as a work of art. It was secularized, and in the process was also neutered.

The same thing had happened to him once before, in 1602, when Vincenzo Giustiniani had stepped in to buy the first *St Matthew*. But on that occasion the picture had been for a burial chapel in the church of the French and Caravaggio had been invited to paint another version. This time the picture was for St Peter's and he was given no second chance. It was a watershed in his career. Thereafter he became an increasingly isolated figure – an artist whose work would be tolerated, even admired, in private, or at the provincial margins of the Catholic world, but not at its centre.

Despite this enormous setback Caravaggio refused to change his approach. Shortly after delivering *The Madonna of the Palafrenieri*, he finally completed his long overdue altarpiece of *The Death of the Virgin*.[113] This huge and deeply moving picture is stark evidence of the painter's reluctance to compromise, and of his moral resilience.

Never before in the history of Christian painting had Mary, mother of God, been made to seem as poor and frail and vulnerable as this. Wearing a simple red dress, unlaced at the bodice to make her more comfortable in her last moments, she lies stretched out on the make-shift bier of a plank of wood. She looks shockingly dead. The apostles have gathered around her lifeless form, to pay their last respects. They are grave and serious men in the winter of their lives, each expressing pain and sorrow in his own different way. Those nearest the body are the most convulsed by grief. One man cries and rubs at his tears. Another covers his eyes and holds himself by the throat as if to choke off his own sorrow. Two others stare intently at her prone body, as if rapt in contemplation of the miracle that once grew within this mortal flesh.

Caravaggio suggests that the Virgin's own last thoughts had been of that miracle, and that even now she might be dreaming of it. Her right hand rests gently on her own slightly swollen stomach, remembering the sacred baby that once grew in the blessed womb. Standing slightly to one side, St John the Evangelist, his head propped on one hand, is the picture of melancholy reflection. Mary Magdalen sits shuddering with grief on a chair pulled right up to Mary's bed. She must have been the last person to hold the dead woman's hand. As some crowd round the body, others must wait. At the back of the room, more men can be seen, talking quietly among themselves or simply thinking their own grave thoughts. Perhaps they have just come in. Once more, Caravaggio evokes the messiness of actual life. People have always mourned their dead like this, and always will.

The Death of the Virgin is the most bleakly mundane of Caravaggio's sacred dramas, the deathbed scene of a poor and ordinary woman. It drew another of Longhi's pithy metaphors: 'a scene from a night refuge', he called it. The Virgin's dwelling is certainly poor and humble, with its rough plastered wall and simple ceiling of coffered wood. Her feet, bare like those of the apostles, poke out straight and stiff from the folds of her dress. There is perhaps a hint that *rigor mortis* has begun to set in. The copper basin on the floor of the room adds a final note of pathos. The body of the Virgin, too, is an empty vessel, and there is little hint of transcendence.

There is a stratagem behind the painting's apparent mood of hope-less bereavement: it invites the viewer into the darkness and doubt of death. It even dares to suggest – the deepest fear of all, in an age of faith – that perhaps this meagre life is all that there is. But peer into the gloom and all is not as it seems. Just as he had done in *The Supper at Emmaus*, with its mystical shadowplay, Caravaggio weaves a sense of the miraculous into hard and ordinary reality. The signs of salvation have to be looked for, even if at first sight they appear to be lacking. The Virgin's face is much younger than those of the apostles, which indicates that she has been spared by God the ravages of age. The thinnest of haloes, shining in the dark air, encircles her head. Above her a great swag of drapery hangs from the ceiling of the room. Literally, it is the canopy of the Virgin's bed, but spiritually it is a sign from above. Its colour relates to her body, while its form tells the story of her soul. It is being drawn upwards, whirled to heaven by unseen energies.

The church of Santa Maria della Scala, for which the painting was intended, belonged to the order of the so-called Discalced Carmelites, the shoeless Carmelites. This may have encouraged Caravaggio to believe that his uncompromisingly severe depiction of the Virgin and apostles as shoeless paupers might find favour there. But he was once again disappointed. No sooner was his painting delivered than he learned that it too had been rejected.

Giulio Mancini watched the whole situation unfold and even took the trouble to talk to the Fathers of the Carmelite order about why they had rejected the picture. In his biography of Caravaggio, he baldly states that 'the fathers of that church had it removed because Caravaggio portrayed a courtesan as the Virgin.' Had they simply got wind of the fact that the painter had modelled his Madonna on a prostitute, and found it scandalous? Caravaggio would certainly not have publicized his method, since the practice had been explicitly condemned in Cardinal Paleotti's *Discourse on Sacred and Profane Images*.[114] Maybe one of the Carmelite fathers simply recognized the girl in the painting as a local streetwalker, or perhaps one of the painter's enemies helpfully pointed it out to them. She is not Lena, who had modelled for *The Madonna of Loreto* and *The Madonna of the Pala-frenieri*. Mancini seems to have known her identity, although he does not give her a name. In marginal notes to the manuscript of his life of Caravaggio, he elaborates tantalizingly on the bare bones of the story: 'the fathers rejected it because he had painted, in the person of the

Madonna, the portrait of a courtesan whom he loved – and had done so very exactly, without religious devotion.'[115] It is impossible to establish the true nature of Caravaggio's relationship with the girl – lover, pimp or simply employer.

But the model's identity cannot have been the sole reason for the rejection of the painting. One painted face can easily be substituted for another, a detail that could have been altered in less than a day's work. It seems it was Caravaggio's fundamental approach to the subject – essentially, his blunt portrayal of the Virgin as an actual dead woman – that the fathers could not bear. In the autumn of 1606 Mancini talked to the Carmelite fathers and subsequently wrote a letter to his brother in Siena in which he alluded to the picture being 'compromised by its lasciviousness and lack of decorum'. Later in the same document he reiterated that it was 'well made but without decorum or invention or cleanliness'.[116] To say a picture had been created 'without invention' was shorthand for saying that it had been painted from reality rather than the imagination. The other two objections, about cleanliness and decorum, were versions of the same criticism. This was the heart of the fathers' objections. The Madonna had been made to look dirty and indecorous. She had been made to look real.

The best evidence for this is the picture that eventually ended up on the altar of the church. Having sacked Caravaggio, the church fathers passed the commission on to an artist called Carlo Saraceni. Taking his cue from images of the Virgin as the Queen of Heaven, such as Annibale Carracci's *Assumption of the Virgin* in the Cerasi Chapel, he depicted an ecstatic Mary being translated to heaven at the moment of her death. But even that was not a sufficiently happy ending for the Madonna. The Carmelites of Santa Maria della Scala wanted a choir of angels to waft her to heaven, so Saraceni had to cook up a second version of his own sweet confection, adding a topping of cherubs. His picture, finally completed in 1610, can still be seen in the church today. Caravaggio's painting is in the Louvre.

Coming so soon after the rejection of his altarpiece for St Peter's, this second disappointment must have cut Caravaggio to the quick. Looking back on it years later, Mancini wondered if the refusal of *The Death of the Virgin* might not have been the tilting point of the painter's whole life. 'Perhaps consequently Caravaggio suffered so much trouble,' he wrote. It is just an aside, but it should not be taken lightly. Mancini was there at the time. He had seen what happened next. In the immediate aftermath of the two rejections, Caravaggio committed the darkest of his many crimes, the crime that would blight the rest of his life. He killed a man.

DEATH ON A TENNIS COURT

For several years Caravaggio and Ranuccio Tomassoni had been heading obscurely towards their final confrontation on the streets of Rome. Exactly what happened, and why, has been the subject of much speculation, but one thing is certain. On 28 May 1606 Caravaggio killed his enemy in a swordfight.

The earliest account of the murder is contained in a document in the Roman archives, which dates to the day of the killing itself. It was a Sunday, and the anonymous author saw Caravaggio's crime as part of a sinister pattern, as rowdy festivities across the city threatened to spiral dangerously out of control:

> The celebrations began for the [anniversary of the] coronation of the Pope . . . towards evening at Ripa Grande there were celebrations and fighting with boats. In the midst of the festivity and the contest, someone gave somebody else a knock, and was stabbed to death. In Campo Marzio the same evening the painter Michelangelo Caravaggio wounded and killed Ranuccio da Terni with a sword-thrust through the thigh; he had barely confessed before he died, and was buried in the Rotonda [the Pantheon] the next morning. After that his brother, Captain Giovan Francesco, unsheathing his sword, killed another soldier (formerly a captain) of the Castel Sant'Angelo. The above-mentioned Giovan Francesco, Michelangelo and one other were also wounded in the same quarrel.[117]

Until quite recently the only known accounts of the murder were those given by Caravaggio's three principal biographers. They were written long after the event itself, and give only the sketchiest sense of what might really have happened, but each contains vestiges of a complicated truth.

Mancini insinuates, as we have seen, that at the time of the killing Caravaggio was even touchier than usual because he had been upset by the rejection of *The Death of the Virgin*. He also implies that the painter was provoked, and he places the perenially hot-headed Onorio Longhi at the scene of the crime: 'Finally, as a result of certain events he almost lost his life, and in defending himself Caravaggio killed his foe with the help of his friend Onorio Longhi and was forced to leave Rome.'[118]

Baglione moralized the murder, describing it as the predictable outcome of Caravaggio's innate criminality. He also explained its cause. An argument over a tennis match had got out of hand:

> Michelangelo was quite a quarrelsome individual, and sometimes he looked for a chance to break his neck or jeopardise the life of another. Often he was found in the company of men who, like himself, were also belligerent. And finally he confronted Ranuccio Tomassoni, a very polite young man, over some disagreement over a tennis match. They argued and ended up fighting. Ranuccio fell to the ground after Michelangelo had wounded him in the thigh and then killed him. Everyone who was involved in this affair fled Rome . . .[119]

Bellori echoed Baglione's account, adding a colourful account of the fight itself: 'during a tennis match with a young friend of his, they began hitting each other with their rackets. At the end he drew his sword, killed the young man, and was also wounded himself.'[120]

The idea that the fight was in some way connected to a game is seemingly confirmed by two *avvisi*, small booklets that were the rudimentary forerunners of the modern newspaper. They were sold on the streets of the city, especially around the statue of *Pasquino*, to the cry of '*Nove e Avvisi!*', or 'News and Notices!'[121]

One of these *avvisi*, written on 3 June 1606, six days after the murder, establishes the scene of the crime. It also confirms the involvement of the two other men who had been mentioned in the very first report of 28 May. According to the *avviso* of 3 June, Ranuccio Tomassoni's brother, the former soldier and *caporione* Giovan Francesco Tomassoni, had indeed joined the fight, drawing his sword on another soldier. But this *avviso* contradicts the earlier document's statement that the other man had been killed, saying instead that he had been seriously wounded and was now in prison awaiting trial. It also provides his name, and specifies that he was a companion of Caravaggio:

> because of a game near the palace of the Grand Duke [i.e. the Palazzo Firenze] an argument arose between the son of the late Colonel Lucantoni da Terni, and Michelangelo da Caravaggio, the famous painter; Tomassoni was killed by a blow given to him while, retreating, he fell on the ground. Then his brother, Captain Giovan Francesco, and Petronio the Bolognese, Caravaggio's companion, entered the fray; Giovan Francesco seriously wounded Captain Petronio, and wounded Caravaggio in the head. Caravaggio saved himself by running away, and Petronio was put in prison, where he remains.[122]

This would appear to confirm Baglione's account of an argument over a tennis match. The *avviso* mentions a game near the Grand Duke of Tuscany's palace. There were indeed tennis courts directly opposite the Palazzo Firenze: although they have long since disappeared, the street where they once stood is still the Via di Pallacorda, i.e. 'Tennis Street'.[123]

The other *avviso* that mentions the murder was written on 31 May 1606. It does not name Caravaggio's wounded companion, simply describing him as a Bolognese captain serving in the papal fortress of the Castel Sant'Angelo. It confirms that he had been wounded rather than killed, and had now been put in prison. This report also blames the fight on a game, on which money had been wagered. But it also makes the fight itself sound more like an outbreak of gang warfare than a chance fracas. A total of eight people are now said to have been involved, two bands of four:

> On the aforesaid Sunday night a serious quarrel took place in the Campo Marzio, with four men on either side. The leader of one side was Ranuccio of Terni, who died immediately after a long fight; and of the other Michelangelo da Caravaggio, a painter of some renown in our day, who reportedly received a wound, but his whereabouts [are] not known. Severely wounded, however, and taken to prison, was one of his companions whom they call the Captain, from Bologna, and who was a soldier of Castel Sant'Angelo. The incident is alleged to have

been caused by a dispute over a game involving 10 scudi which the dead man had won from the painter.[124]

A number of other documents found in the Roman archives confirm many elements of the accounts given in the two *avvisi*. On 29 May 1606, the notary responsible for the registry of births and deaths in the parish of San Lorenzo in Lucina recorded that Ranuccio Tomassoni had been murdered in the Via della Scrofa.[125] Since the fatal blow had actually been struck on a tennis court in the nearby Via di Pallacorda, this reference must be to Tomassoni's place of death – presumably at the shop of a barber-surgeon, who was unable to stem the flow of blood from the stricken man's wounds. The mortal thigh wound mentioned by several sources is consistent with this. Caravaggio must have caught Tomassoni high in the leg, near the groin, severing or at least seriously rupturing the femoral artery. It is very difficult to stop the bleeding from such injuries, which make the tying of an effective tourniquet all but impossible. Tomassoni would have died quickly, as the sources indicate, but it is unlikely that he would have had time to confess, as the author of the first report of 28 May optimistically suggested.

While Ranuccio Tomassoni's companions were taking him and his brother Giovan Francesco to the barber-surgeon's in the Via della Scrofa, Caravaggio's friends were tending to Captain Petronio Toppa from Bologna. They took him to another barber-surgeon, a man called Pompeo Navagna,[126] who treated him for a cut in his left arm so deep that seven pieces of bone had to be removed before it could be dressed. He had eight stab wounds in his left thigh, one in his left shin, and another in his left heel. Taken altogether, Navagna concluded, these were life-threatening injuries, and despite them Toppa had subsequently been taken to the prison of Tor di Nona for questioning.

Meanwhile, Fabio Masetti was still keeping his eye on Caravaggio and reporting the latest developments back to Cesare d'Este in Modena. In a letter of 31 May he confirmed that Caravaggio had been wounded, and that he had fled Rome. According to Masetti's spies, the painter was on his way to Tuscany, a logical destination, given his links with Cardinal del Monte and the Medici. Masetti even found cause for a certain grim optimism in this sudden turn of events:

'The painter Caravaggio has left Rome badly wounded, having killed a man who provoked him on Sunday evening. I am told that he is heading in the direction of Florence, and perhaps will also come to Modena, where he will give satisfaction by making as many paintings as are wanted.'[127]

On the same day, another letter was written by another representative of the Este in Rome, Pellegrino Bertacchi. He too had heard that a game of tennis had been the cause of all the trouble: 'the fight was over the question of a penalty, while we were playing at racquets, near the [palace] of the Ambassador of the Grand Duke [i.e the Palazzo Firenze].' He had also heard that the painter 'lay down his head, mortally wounded' and that 'two others were dead.'[128] Clearly all kinds of wild rumours were flying about.

But a month later some of the smoke had cleared and the *sbirri* had begun to get to the bottom of the whole murky business. As the *avviso* of 31 May had stated, eight men had been involved. By the end of June the authorities had established the names of everyone on Ranuccio Tomassoni's side. He had been accompanied by his two brothers-in-law, Ignazio and Federigo Giugoli, as well as by his brother Giovan Francesco. Between 28 June and 8 July, summonses were issued to all three, instructing them to appear before the court and remain resident at their customary addresses. Caravaggio's partners in crime were Petronio Toppa, another Bolognese soldier by the name of Corporal Paulo Aldato and – just as Mancini would later report – his old friend Onorio Longhi. There was no need to call Toppa, who was in jail already, still recovering from his injuries. No one seemed to know anything much about Paulo Aldato, save for the fact that he had only one eye. So just two further summonses were sent, to Caravaggio and Longhi.

Caravaggio, by then long gone, would never appear in court to answer the charges against him. But, as Baglione would later write, everyone else involved in the affair had run away from Rome too – everyone else except for the unfortunate Petronio Toppa. Onorio Longhi had fled to Milan. Giovan Francesco Tomassoni was nowhere to be found. Nor were the Giugoli brothers, whose father, Flaminio, paid caution money to the court on their behalf on 27 July.

The continued absence of so many of the participants casts considerable doubt on the story that the fight between Caravaggio and

Ranuccio Tomassoni had been sparked by an argument over a tennis match. If that had been so, why would at least three apparently inno-cent bystanders, namely Longhi and the two Giugoli brothers, have defied court orders and gone into hiding? It made no sense.

The known facts of the case point to a very different explanation of the fight. The pattern of the evening's events could hardly be clearer. Four men on one side, four on the other: two combatants, two seconds, four witnesses. An encounter on a tennis court, a flat field that was often also used as a fencing arena – as on the day back in 1600, when Onorio Longhi watched a fencing match take place on the French tennis court at Santa Lucia della Tinta. The fight between Caravaggio and Ranuccio Tomassoni was no chance row. It was a prearranged duel. The stories about a tennis match, a bet, a disputed call – they were all fabrications, tall tales put about by the partici-pants themselves to hide what had really happened. It was an expe-dient pretence: duelling was illegal in papal Rome, and punishable by death.

By the end of June, when the first summonses were issued, Judge Angelo Turchi and his fellow investigators had rumbled the cover-up of a tennis match. By the second week of July, even some of the par-ticipants had given up pretending that it had been anything other than a duel. On 11 July 1606, a notary recorded Mario and Giovan Francesco Tomassoni's acknowledgment of the writ served against Giovan Francesco. Writing in judicial Latin, he recorded their joint undertaking to do nothing in breach of the peace, in effect a vow not to take the law into their own hands – there were perhaps concerns that a vendetta might develop. He also recorded their plea for the conclusion of the investigation into Giovan Francesco, in 'distant parts'. But the most crucial elements of this document are a couple of scraps of vocabulary. Not once, but twice, Mario and Giovan Franc-esco referred to the dispute between Caravaggio and their late brother as 'a duel'.[129]

By the start of August, Petronio Toppa was well enough to undergo questioning.[130] On 6 August 1606 Toppa called two witnesses in his defence. The first was Captain Francesco Pioveno, of Vicenza, who testified that he had known the Bolognese soldier for about twelve years. He gave a ringing endorsement of his former comrade in arms:

'Captain Petronio, who's been in the wars and has been a soldier with me in these two garrisons, in Lucca and Rome ... I've known him as a soldier, and I've always considered him an honourable soldier.'

The second witness was Francesco fu Menici of Lucca. He gave his profession as a gentleman's valet, although before that he had been a soldier. He had known Petronio Toppa for about eight years. They had fought together in the Hungarian campaigns of the 1590s. Unlike the first witness, Francesco Pioveno, Menici had been in the vicinity of the tennis court on the evening of Ranuccio Tomassoni's death. He said he had not seen the fight itself, but he gave an account of the prelude to it.

On the night in question, Menici said, he had seen his friend Petronio sitting

in front of the Florentine ambassador's, in front of the tennis court. He was with another Bolognese, who had only one eye, but I don't know his name. I think they call him Paulo, but I don't know his name and I don't want to say what I don't know [for sure] ... I don't remember exactly when the argument was, but it was a Sunday, and it could be about a month and a half or two months ago. I wasn't present at the fight and I didn't see who was in it or what happened. I passed through there because I was coming alone from the French ambassador's house, and in passing I saw Captain Petronio and said to him, 'At your service' [this was possibly a deliberate irony, given Menici's profession as a valet] and he returned the greeting and said, 'Where are you going?' I replied, 'I'm going home,' and he replied that he wanted me to wait, because he was waiting to perform a service, and that afterwards he would come too, but he didn't tell me what service he wanted to do, and I replied that I couldn't wait and was in a hurry.

So I left and went towards Campo Marzio, and the man who was with him left him and came with me up to Piazza Campo Marzio past the Manescalco, and said that he wanted to go and see a whore of his nearby. Then I went home. I don't know if that man without an eye, who came with me up to Campo Marzio, returned from there to Captain Petronio. When I passed the captain I saw that there were others around him, besides the one I said, and they were armed with swords ...

Toppa's own testimony and his eventual fate are unknown. But the evidence given by the second witness called in his defence confirms that the contest between Caravaggio and Tomassoni was indeed a duel.

Thanks to the nature of Rome's judicial processes there exist, in addition, four statements by those who saw and acted in the duel itself. Apart from Petronio Toppa, all the men involved had run away from Rome immediately after the swordfight. Having been subsequently summoned, to no avail, all were presumed guilty and sentenced to mandatory exile. Over the following months and years, each sought to bargain the terms of a return. As they did so, they were obliged to account for their actions on the night in question. The resulting evidence is patchily informative, but it does at least clarify the circumstances in which the second swordfight, between Giovan Francesco Tomassoni and Petronio Toppa – the duel within the duel – had started.

Ranuccio Tomassoni's brothers-in-law, Ignazio and Giovan Federico Giugoli, revealed little as they submitted to the due process of law. In their petition for an end to their exile, they admitted that they had been present at the fight in which their kinsman had been killed, but said no more than that. The reason they gave for wanting to return to Rome was that their father, Flaminio Giugoli, who had paid the caution money for them, had died while they were away. They needed to sort out his affairs, or the family would fall into ruin.[131]

Onorio Longhi, from his native Milan, protested his total innocence in the killing. He had witnessed the fight but asserted that he had been there simply to keep the peace (hardly likely, given his record of inflammatory remarks, provocative behaviour and incitement to assault). He too said little of any substance about the duel itself and he finished, like the Giugoli brothers, by invoking his family:

Onorio Longhi in all humility declares to Your Holiness that in 1606 he was banished from Rome, as can be seen in the trial records of the Tribunal of the Governor of that city . . . because he was present at the murder committed by Michelangelo da Caravaggio on the person of Ranuccio Tomassoni, in which deed the speaker was not at fault. On the contrary, he accompanied Caravaggio as his well-wisher, so that no disorder should occur and to exhort him to make peace, as God and his conscience are witnesses. Thus, he has remained conscious of his own innocence and has obtained peace, and at this time is retained in Milan in the service of His Imperial Majesty and desires to return to his fatherland and to his wife and five children in order to serve the Holy Church and Your Holiness.[132]

Giovan Francesco Tomassoni's plea for his own exile to be revoked was more informative. He acknowledged having intervened in the fight between his brother and Caravaggio, and accounted for his own actions in some detail:

When the speaker saw his brother injured, bleeding and thrown to the ground, [any] obligations to keep the peace or pledges not to offend were entirely dissolved. He and the said Michelangelo standing beside each other, he wounded him [Caravaggio] in the head with a sword and would perhaps have killed him in the presence of others, save that the aforementioned Captain Petronio, and others, were present. The said Captain Petronio defended Caravaggio with a naked blade, and he [Giovan Francesco] wounded him several times.[133]

From this patchwork of biographies, letters, *avvisi* and witness statements, a clear picture of the fight can now be established.

Because it is a matter of honour between Caravaggio and his long-standing enemy, they must be allowed to settle it alone. According to custom, the duellists' seconds must promise not to intervene, while Onorio Longhi, the one-eyed Bolognese soldier Paulo Aldato and the Giugoli brothers must undertake to attend simply as witnesses. Once these formalities about 'keeping the peace' have been agreed, the duel can be arranged.

On the evening chosen for the settling of scores, the air is thick with foreboding. Toppa, the painter's appointed second, is ready and waiting in front of the tennis court. As the evening wears on, he is joined by one man and then another. Having briefly wandered off, the one-eyed soldier from Bologna returns to complete the group. Everyone concerned is trying hard to look casual, but they emanate a powerful sense of menace none the less. All are armed with swords, not a tennis ball or racket in sight. Somewhere nearby, Ranuccio Tomassoni is meeting his brother and his two brothers-in-law. As nightfall approaches, the vendetta is about to be settled.

The duel does not last long. Real swordfights are short and sharp, nothing like modern fencing matches. Tomassoni and Caravaggio are wearing no helmets or body armour, because that would have made their story about an argument over a tennis match completely implausible. They use the full width of the court, fighting in a channel formed by the two lines of their witnesses and seconds. At the climax of the duel, Caravaggio seizes the initiative and the tiring Ranuccio Tomassoni stumbles in his retreat. Caravaggio lunges at the groin of his fallen opponent, piercing his femoral artery. Blood spurts in jets from the wound. Caravaggio withdraws his sword and prepares to strike again, but at this moment Giovan Francesco Tomassoni steps out of line to help his 'injured, bleeding' brother. As luck would have it, the rhythms of the fight have placed him right next to Caravaggio at this critical moment. He draws his sword in a flash and strikes the painter in the head, preventing him from inflicting further damage on the stricken Ranuccio. Seeing this violation of 'the peace or pledges not to offend', Petronio Toppa draws his sword and saves Caravaggio's life, at grave danger to his own. As he and Giovan Francesco engage, Onorio Longhi and the one-eyed Bolognese intervene to prevent further injury on both sides.

Meanwhile, Federico and Ignazio Giugoli do what they can to help their brother-in-law. Caravaggio, stunned by his injury, can fight no more. At this point the carnage stops and everyone disperses into the twilit streets. As Ranuccio's friends carry his ominously still body towards the barber-surgeon's on the Via della Scrofa, they unconsciously re-enact Caravaggio's great altarpiece of *The Entombment* in the nearby Chiesa Nuova – solemn depiction of men struggling under the weight of a heavy corpse, stilled mirror-image of the scene in the street outside.

BANDO CAPITALE

None of the witnesses said anything to the investigating magistrate about the causes of the duel. Who had challenged whom, and why?

There are possible answers to those questions too in the extensive

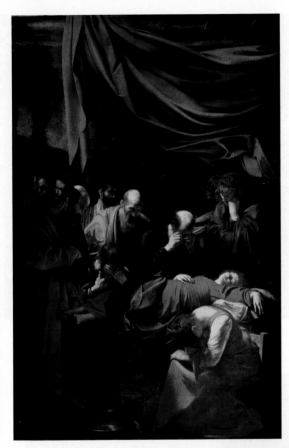

52. *The Death of the Virgin*, in which a prostitute modelled for the Virgin. The picture was rejected by the fathers of Santa Maria della Scala, the last straw that may have triggered Caravaggio to commit murder.

53. *The Death of the Virgin* by Carlo Saraceni, the picture that replaced Caravaggio's rejected altarpiece (above).

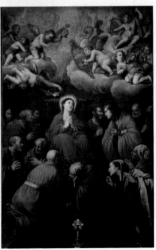

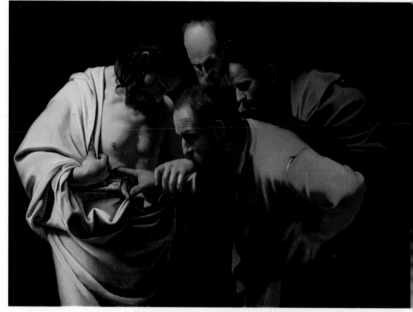

54. *Doubting Thomas*. 'Then saith he to Thomas, Reach hither thy finger, and behold my hands; and reach hither thy hand, and thrust it into my side: and be not faithless, but believing' (John 20).

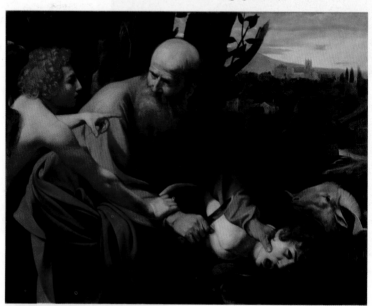

55. *The Sacrifice of Isaac*. Abraham holds his squealing son down as if the boy were a lamb brought to slaughter. These are the last glimpses of landscape in Caravaggio's work.

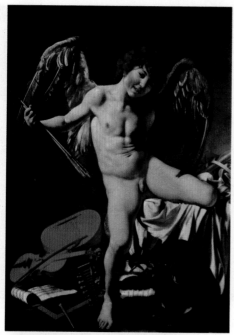

56. *Omnia vincit amor*. 'Love conquers all.' Cupid was modelled by Cecco. An English visitor to Rome was told that ''Twas the body & face / of [Caravaggio's] owne boy or servant / that laid with him.'

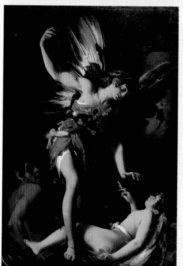

57. *Divine Love* by Giovanni Baglione. The avenging angel triumphs over the devil, who has been caught *in flagrante* with his young catamite. The sodomitic Satan on the left is a libellous caricature of Caravaggio.

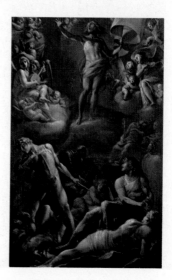

58. Study for *The Resurrection* by Giovanni Baglione. This study preserves the composition of Baglione's lost altarpiece for the Gesù, which Caravaggio mocked openly: 'It's a bungle . . . the worst he has done.'

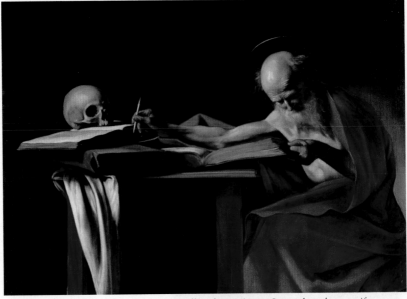

59. *St Jerome Writing*. A penitentially solemn picture. It may have been a gift to Scipione Borghese, papal nephew, for helping Caravaggio obtain a pardon for violent assault in the summer of 1605.

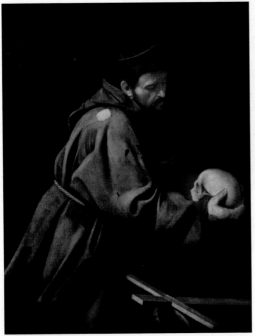

60. *St Francis in Meditation*. The saint is lost in contemplation of his own mortality, and of Christ's crucifixion at Golgotha, 'the place of the skull'.

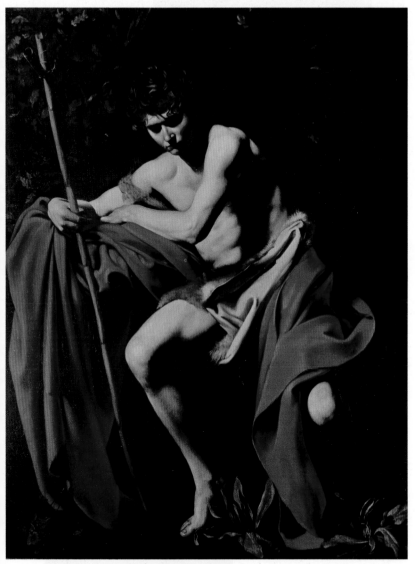

61. *St John the Baptist.* A world away from the earlier St John modelled by Cecco. This glowering adolescent 'might almost be a portrait of Caravaggio's own dark state of mind' during his later years in Rome.

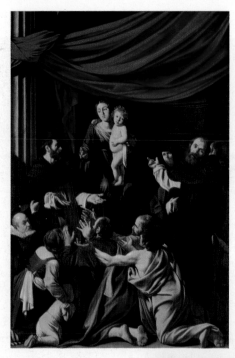

62. *The Madonna of the Rosary*. This altarpiece was greatly admired by Peter Paul Rubens, one of a group of connoisseurs who bought the picture for a prominent church in Antwerp in 1651.

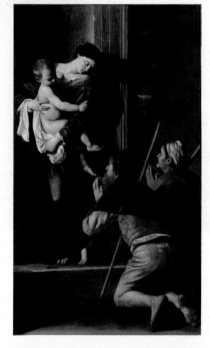

63. *The Madonna of Loreto*. Two humble pilgrims to Loreto, with patched clothes and dirt-ingrained feet, are granted a miraculous vision of the Madonna and child.

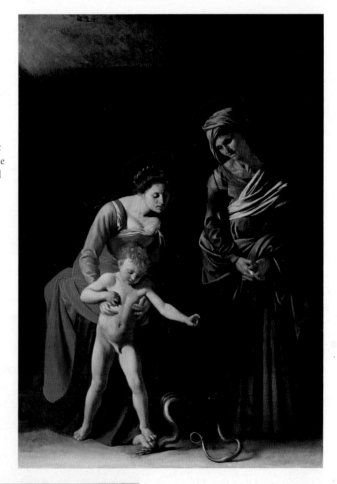

64. *The Madonna of the Palafrenieri.* The Virgin Mary and the infant Christ crush the serpent Satan as St Anne looks on. The picture was turned out of St Peter's, probably because of the Madonna's full cleavage.

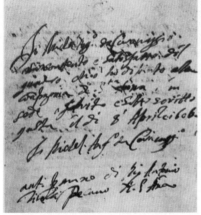

65. The contract for the ill-fated *Madonna of the Palafrenieri.* His blood signature aside (Plate 80), this is the sole surviving example of Caravaggio's handwriting.

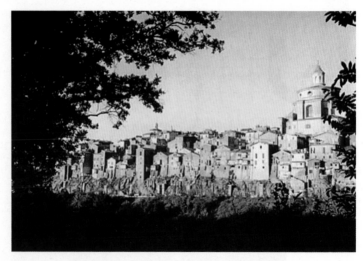

66. View of Zagarolo in the Alban Hills outside Rome. Palazzo Colonna in Zagarolo was Caravaggio's first hide-out after the murder of Ranuccio Tomassoni.

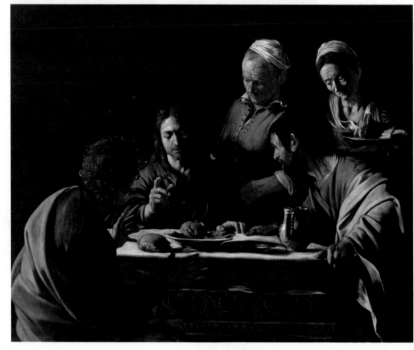

67. *The Supper at Emmaus*. A strikingly different interpretation of a subject Caravaggio had treated so subtly five years earlier (Plate 45). After the murder his style became increasingly bleak, dark and morbid.

but partial dossier of archival evidence about the killing. Fabio Masetti, in his letter to Cesare d'Este of 31 May, had said that Caravaggio had 'killed a man who provoked him', which implies that it was Tomassoni who had challenged the painter. Mancini, the only other source with anything to say on the matter, spoke of Caravaggio 'defending himself', which also suggests that Tomassoni was the initiator of the fight.

The most telling clue to the nature of Tomassoni's grievance may lie in the identity of his chosen witnesses. He chose his brother, a soldier, as his second, and the other men there were his two brothers-in-law. It may be that Tomassoni challenged Caravaggio over a question of family honour – a question, specifically, involving the honour of Ranuccio Tomassoni's wife. Her name was Lavinia. The painter had already stolen or tried to steal one of the pimp's whores, Fillide Melandroni. Had he compounded that insult by starting something with Lavinia Tomassoni too? If so, that would have made Ranuccio a cuckold – a *becco fotuto*, to use one of the painter's favourite phrases. Since nothing has been found in the archives to connect Caravaggio directly with Lavinia Tomassoni, a verbal provocation is more likely to have been the cause of the trouble. Perhaps Caravaggio had heard that Lavinia Tomassoni was being unfaithful to her husband, and had taunted him by repeating that rumour to his face. We may never know exactly what lay behind the duel but some kind of insult concerning Lavinia is the most likely explanation. This would explain why Tomassoni wanted Lavinia's brothers watching when he exacted his revenge – or so he hoped – on the troublesome painter who had dared to cast aspersions on his wife.

Whatever the precise truth, another chain of archival evidence suggests that Lavinia Tomassoni was hardly a model wife and mother. Less than a fortnight after Tomassoni's death, arrangements were set in train for a close friend of the family, the lawyer Cesare Pontoni, to look after the couple's only daughter. Her name was Felicita Plautilla Tomassoni, and she was still only a baby. Tomassoni's widow, Lavinia, made the excuse that she was too young to bring up a child on her own. She said that she wanted to remarry (which she did, as another document in the archive reveals, within less than a year). Lavinia's mother-in-law, Tomassoni's mother, claimed that she was too old to look after the little girl.[134] On 10 October 1606 the legal guardianship of Felicita was ratified and she became Pontoni's ward.[135] Only one other document has been found concerning her, the will of a relation who died on 17 August 1615. This reveals that the girl had by then dropped her first name, Felicita, which means 'happiness' in Italian, and had entered a nunnery. The document refers to her as Sr Plautilla of the convent of S. Silvestro in Urbe.[136]

One other detail suggests that the cause of the fight may have been some kind of sexual insult. Ranuccio Tomassoni bled to death from the femoral artery. Caravaggio had struck him a low blow, aiming perhaps at the groin and missing by just a fraction. Was the artist using his sword as if it were a paintbrush, attempting to mark out the most graphic of sexual insults on the body of his enemy? Wounds were meaningful, as Fillide Melandroni had graphically indicated when threatening to cut the face of her own love-rival, Prudenza Zacchia. A cut to the face was a *sfregio*, but it was by no means the only form of symbolic, premeditated injury that vengeful Italians inflicted upon their enemies.

The practice was sufficiently common to be mirrored in the provisions of the law, where widely differing penalties were specified for different forms of revenge wound. The fourteenth-century statutes of Florence set a fine of 50 lire for the loss of members including the foot, hand, tongue and eye – but for both eyes the penalty was much steeper. The mid sixteenth-century statutes of Caravaggio's native Lombardy valued teeth at 50 lire apiece, and set a fine of 500 lire for the amputation of a hand. The loss of a single testicle was assessed at the same rate as four teeth or a tongue, namely 200 lire. The penalty for castration was understandably more than double that, at 500 lire.[137] It is entirely possible that Caravaggio was not actually trying to kill Ranuccio Tomassoni, but attempting to make mincemeat of his testicles with a duelling sword.

Like many other aspects of the Roman judicial system, sentencing was irregular and inconsistent. All those involved in the duel were sentenced to exile, but the precise sentences are not known and can only be guessed at by the different dates on which the various convicted men petitioned for their return. On this evidence, it seems that those on Caravaggio's side were dealt with more harshly than the supporters of Tomassoni: Giovan Francesco Tomassoni's plea to return, duly granted, was filed on 9 December 1606, and that of the Giugoli brothers less than two years later, but Onorio Longhi felt able to seek his own return only in the spring of 1611.

The most serious penalty was reserved for Caravaggio. As well as being sentenced to indefinite exile from Rome, he was condemned as a murderer and made subject to a *bando capitale*, a 'capital sentence'. This meant that anyone in the papal states had the right to kill him with impunity; indeed there was a bounty for anyone who did so. The phrase meant exactly what was indicated by the etymology of its second word, derived from the Latin *caput*. To claim the reward, it would not be necessary to produce the painter's body. His severed head would suffice.

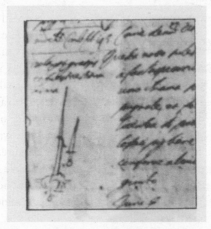

Caravaggio's sword and dagger, drawn by a policeman (see p. 287).

PART FIVE

The Alban Hills, Naples, Malta, Sicily, Naples, Porto Ercole, 1606–10

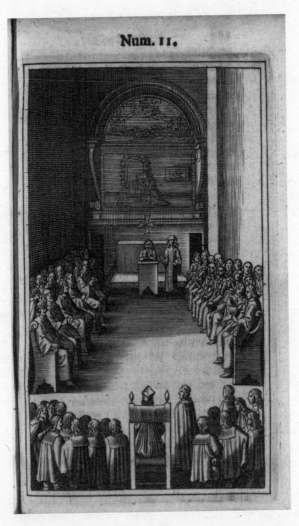

A Knight of Malta being Defrocked by Wolfgang Kilian (detail). The ceremony of *privatio habitus* took place directly beneath Caravaggio's altarpiece, which can just be made out here at the far end of the oratory.

ON THE RUN

Caravaggio had been seriously injured in the swordfight, but he needed to get out of Rome quickly. After having his wounds dressed, he returned briefly to his lodgings in the house of the lawyer Andrea Ruffetti to gather a few necessary possessions – clothes, painting materials, whatever money he could lay his hands on. But it was not safe to stay at Ruffetti's overnight because the *sbirri* knew to look for him there. So, accompanied by Cecco, Caravaggio went to the neighbouring Palazzo Colonna and threw himself on the mercy of his family's first protectress, Marchesa Costanza.

Bleeding, bedraggled, wild-eyed with adrenalin, he confessed to the murder and asked for her help. Despite the seriousness of his crime, she gave it. For all his sins, perhaps in her eyes he was still the lucky child – the boy whose birth on the feast day of the Archangel Michael had once seemed like such a good omen, and whose very name was like a prayer invoking her father's famous victory at the Battle of Lepanto. Caravaggio and Cecco were given a bed for the night. Early next morning the injured painter and his boy left the palace in the marchesa's coach and four, bound for the safe haven of a remote Colonna fiefdom in the Alban Hills. As the carriage clattered through the streets of the city, its blinds were firmly drawn.

No actual account of Caravaggio's flight from the city survives, so all of the above is speculation. But something much like it must have happened. The fact of the matter is that within a day or two of the murder the painter had indeed been spirited out of Rome, deep into Colonna territory.

He probably went first to Zagarolo, and moved between there and Palestrina, both small towns owned and controlled by the Colonna, some twenty miles from Rome and suitably off the beaten track. The Colonna Palace at Zagarolo still looms today over thickly wooded hills, a forbidding fortress in a wild and remote landscape. It is exactly the sort of place where a man in fear of his life might choose to take refuge. Mancini stated categorically that this was, indeed, Caravaggio's first stopping place on his flight from Rome: 'He first reached Zagarolo, where he was secretly housed by the prince.' Bellori echoed Mancini, adding the detail that the painter was being pursued: 'Fleeing from Rome, without money and being followed, he found refuge in Zagarolo under the protection of Duke Marzio Colonna.'[1]

We do not have much information about his first few months of exile. All three early biographies refer to a picture of Mary Magdalen that the artist supposedly painted while he was in the Alban Hills, but it has never come to light.[2] Mancini and Bellori also mention a *Supper at Emmaus* from the same period, which does survive. A solemn and introverted work, it now hangs in the Pinacoteca di Brera in Milan. This second *Supper at Emmaus* is strikingly different from the painting on the same subject in London, created just five years earlier. It seems to announce a change within Caravaggio himself, and certainly marks the transformation of his style. With this troubled picture begins the last phase of the painter's life and work.

The older Caravaggio would often revisit themes and motifs that he had painted before. But only on this occasion did he rework the entire composition of a picture from earlier in his career. The second painting is almost identical in size to the first, the figures are the same scale, and virtually repeated – with the addition, in the Brera version, of the innkeeper's wizened wife, waiting to serve a rack of lamb. The tablecloth and the Turkish rug over which it has been laid are almost the same. But in this later painting it is as if someone has turned off the lights, so deep are the shadows.

Christ is no longer the beardless youth of five years before, the Apollonian judge calmly looking forward to the end of time. He is the conventional type of Jesus, with light beard and shoulder-length hair, but pushed to the point of exhaustion. He is a pained and troubled figure, a Man of Sorrows who has suffered much and struggles even to raise his hand, poised just inches above the table, in the revelatory gesture of blessing.

The first *Supper at Emmaus*, a spotlit drama of sudden recognition, has blurred to an image from a dream. The theatre of Caravaggio's early Roman painting has contracted to a space that seems more like the inside of the artist's mind, a space of memory or mental projection. That some of the figures in the picture almost certainly *were* painted from memory, rather than from life, enhances the effect. The innkeeper resembles the innkeeper in the earlier version of the picture, but seen at one remove or through half-closed eyes. The figure of his wife, so beaten down by existence, was surely based on Caravaggio's recollections of the old woman who had recently modelled for St Anne in the *Madonna of the Palafrenieri*.

The lamb on the dish that she holds is a scrap of meat so shrivelled and inconspicuous that it barely performs the iconographic task required of it – the scantest of allusions to Christ's sacrifice and the death of all flesh. Even the still life on the table has been reduced to a bare, eucharistic minimum, just some broken loaves and a chipped majolica jug. Darkness surrounds the huddled figures seated at this simple meal, but there are no shades of transcendence here: no halo is cast on the wall behind Christ, no pattern of the divine is suggested in the shadows that fall on the drab white tablecloth. The invigorating light of a miraculous dawn has weakened to the feeble gleams of the end of the day.

The paint has been applied thinly and the colours muted to earths and ochres. The faces of all the figures are less sharply differentiated than they are in any of Caravaggio's earlier pictures. Many of the technical departures of the artist's later work are related to his circumstances: he stops painting from models, in all but a few cases, because he has no time to find them or money to pay them, and he paints quickly because he has to move on.

The disciple sitting with his back to the viewer is seen only as a silhouette, a few stray curls of his tousled hair picked out against the folds of Christ's blue-green robe. His hands express surprise but also uncertainty, as if he cannot quite believe the miracle to which he is a witness; his right hand is a shadowy form set against shadows, light glimmering in the interstices between the fingers. This recalls similar passages in the darkest paintings of Tintoretto, and indeed an eloquent Venetian indistinctness enters Caravaggio's painting at this time.

The wiry, sunburned disciple seated to Christ's left is fiercely intent.

He grips the table hard with both hands, grasping for a sense of reality. Can it really be true? Can he really be performing this one last miracle? Can he really have come back from the dead? The tendons in his neck stand out as he stares with desperate intensity at the half-lit face of Christ. But there is a stoop in his shoulders, a defeated weariness about him, suggesting that in his heart of hearts he still cannot quite bring himself to believe in the miracle, that it would be too much to hope for. Christ himself seems about to disappear into the surrounding blackness of the inn – as indeed he does, in the gospel of Luke, at the very moment when the disciples realize who he is. This dark and occluded picture has the quality of a confession. How much harder Caravaggio now finds it to see the possibility of salvation.

One other painting survives from the early months of Caravaggio's exile, a depiction of *David with the Head of Goliath*, which has traditionally been misdated to the end of his life.[3] Its subject is David's well-known act of giant-slaying, recounted in the Old Testament (1 Samuel 17:48–51): a familiar story, but treated by Caravaggio in a strikingly unfamiliar way. The sombre young hero is intriguingly unexultant in his moment of triumph. He holds his grisly prize at arm's-length, staring down almost absently at the trails of blood still pouring from the severed neck of his vanquished foe. Mild disgust is mingled, in David's complicated and contemplative expression, with gentle sadness. Cecco modelled for this figure, as he had for the exuberant *Omnia vincit amor*. But what a change has come over him. He looks older, more drawn. His brow is furrowed and there are bags under his eyes. Exile and flight had taken their toll on him too.

The disembodied head of Goliath seems still to be screaming, in an extension of his death agony. Light glints on his irregular row of front teeth and is reflected in the wetness of his lower lip. The extreme tenebrism of Caravaggio's technique isolates these few charged details, distilling the drama to a compelling vignette while casting everything extraneous into darkness. Having reduced the story to an apparent bare minimum of incident, the painter deepens the meaning of his picture by deftly weaving in other layers of association. David's earlier act of hurling his shot at the giant's head is subtly implied by the way his white shirt has been looped through his belt to shape a kind of sling. His vulnerably naked torso and softly compassionate, almost

Christ-like expression hint at the larger perspective of theological meaning in which the slaying of Goliath was to be understood.

David evokes the youthful Christ, because the story of David slaying Goliath was often seen as an Old Testament prefiguration of Christ subduing Satan. The inscription on the blade of the sword held by David spells out the letters 'H.OC.S'. This is the acronym of a phrase from St Augustine's commentary on Psalm 33, in which he remarks that 'As David overcame Goliath, this is Christ who kills the Devil.' The Latin phrase used by Augustine is *humilitas occidit superbiam*: 'humility kills pride'.

The most insistent of the picture's meanings is carried by its most blatant detail. The death's head of Goliath is a self-portrait, a depiction of Caravaggio himself *in extremis*. There is a terrible, ambiguous intensity behind his fixed stare. He seems, horribly, half dead and half alive, his right eye glazed over and closing while his left eye is still bright with outrage and pain. He is like one of the damned souls glimpsed by Dante in the *Inferno*, an outcast moaning forever in torment.

The last piece in the puzzle of this haunting picture is furnished by the identity of its intended owner. Caravaggio painted the *David and Goliath* for Scipione Borghese, papal nephew and the chief administrator of papal justice – the man who, more than any other, had the power of life and death over Caravaggio himself. The *David and Goliath* was Caravaggio's darkly ingenious plea to the one man who could save him: his way of saying that Borghese was welcome to have his head in a painting, if only he would let him keep it in real life.

Thanks to the help of his protectors, Caravaggio was able to despatch his pictures to Rome. The second *Supper at Emmaus* was sold to the banker Ottavio Costa;[4] the *David and Goliath*, a precious gift to Scipione Borghese, may have arrived in Rome in the same Colonna carriage. It was likely to have been well appreciated: the papal nephew already owned Caravaggio's severe *St Jerome Writing*, which the painter had probably also given to him as a gift, in exchange for helping to resolve the affair of his assault on the lawyer Pasqualone; and within less than a year he would sequester the entire art collection of the unfortunate Giuseppe Cesari, largely in order to get his hands on two early pictures by Caravaggio, the *Boy with a Basket of Fruit* and the moonlit *Self-Portrait as Bacchus*.

News of the *David and Goliath*'s arrival at the Palazzo Borghese was kept quiet. Scipione Borghese did not actually hang the picture for several years, perhaps because he did not want the artist's death's-head petition to him to be too widely known.[5] But as the summer of 1606 turned to autumn, it seems that he was indeed working behind the scenes on Caravaggio's behalf. News of the painter's presence in the Alban Hills had spread to Rome, where it was rumoured that there were plans for Caravaggio to make a swift return. On 23 September the Este agent Fabio Masetti wrote to his masters in Mantua that 'Caravaggio, having committed the murder previously reported, is staying at Pagliano with the plan of coming back soon. I will get repayment from him of the 32 scudi . . .'[6]

But though Caravaggio had support in Rome, he also had enemies. Bellori's brief comment about his 'being followed' on his flight from the city is a reminder that certain people were determined to see him brought to justice. The Tomassoni clan may have sent men after him. Within Rome itself their voices must have been raised against an early pardon for Caravaggio. Whatever deal was being brokered on his behalf, by the end of September it had fallen through and the painter had resigned himself to a lengthy period of exile.

Caravaggio probably used the proceeds of the sale of the second *Supper to Emmaus* to pay his way to Naples. Certainly by early October he was living and working there, where he felt safe enough to show his face in public. But the fear of reprisals stayed with him. He was careful to remain under the protection of the Colonna family, who maintained a powerful presence in the city. With their help, he would attempt to repair his damaged and disordered life.

IN THE CITY OF BEGGARS

Naples at the start of the seventeenth century was the largest city in southern Europe. Its population was 300,000, three times that of Rome, and would soon grow to half a million. Founded by the Greeks in ancient times, and built around the crescent of a natural bay, Naples had always been a port town. Its lifeblood was maritime commerce. Although Muslim corsairs and Barbary pirates continued to make predatory forays from their bases along the African coast, the seas had become safer for Neapolitan traders since the victory of the Christians over the Turks at Lepanto. Ships from Naples travelled to Flanders, Holland, England and Germany, as well as to Sicily, Spain and northern Africa.

The sharp-eyed English traveller George Sandys visited Naples in 1611, just after Caravaggio's time there. He was impressed by the sheer range of foods, fabrics and other materials on sale in the city's many markets:

> The concourse of sundry nations to this haven, doth adde an over-abundance to their native plenty. *Apulia* sends them almonds, oyle, honey, cattell, and cheese. *Calabria* … silke, figges, sugar, excellent wines, minerals, and matter for the building of ships. *Sicilia* releeveth them with corne, if at any time their own soile prove ungrateful … *Africa* furnisheth them with skinnes; *Spaine* with cloth and gold; *Elba* with steele and iron; and we with our countries commodities: so that nothing is wanting.[7]

The city's traders dealt not only in goods but also in people: there were 10,000 slaves within the Neapolitan population.

According to the phlegmatic and worldly Giulio Cesare Capaccio, long-time secretary of the city's administration, Naples was living proof that industry rather than piety was the key to a city's prosperity. 'It is not fate or the stars that determine the greatness of cities,' he proclaimed, 'but commerce and the concourse of people as in Antwerp, Lisbon, Seville, Paris, and Naples.'[8] In his drily patriotic book about the city, the *Guida de' forestieri*, Capaccio anticipated the later Romantic adage 'See Naples and die', asserting that 'there is nobody who does not desire to see it, and who does not desire to die here. Naples is the whole world.'[9] That world included distinct Neapolitan communities of Pisans, Catalans, Ragusans, Germans, Flemings and French. The French and the Ragusans had their own consulates in the city. So too did the English, who ran the city's textile trade.[10]

Like the painter's home province of Milan, Naples was under Spanish rule. The city was the capital of the so-called Kingdom of the Two Sicilies, another part of the immense Spanish empire, which had passed from Philip II to his son, Philip III, in 1598. Travellers approaching from the sea were impressed by the scale and density of the town.

Tier after tier of buildings rose up from the half-moon of the bay's shoreline, stretching into the hills and towards distant Mount Vesuvius, smoking ominously on the horizon. The seaward limits of Naples, like all its boundaries, were marked by high walls of stone. Massive fortifications dominated both skyline and waterfront, embodying Spanish naval and military might. Naples had three castles: the Castel Sant'Elmo, built in the shape of a six-pointed star on the top of the hill above the centre of the city; the Castel Nuovo, which stood beside the shore and was home to the Spanish viceroy; and the Castel dell'Ovo at the south-east corner of the city, so named after the egg-shaped rock on which it was perched.

Naples was a bastion of Habsburg rule over the southern Mediterranean. An army of Spanish soldiers was stationed in its garrisons, a navy of Spanish galleons moored in its harbour. The policy of the city's rulers was driven by two overriding aims: to safeguard the territories of the Spanish empire and subjugate the Neapolitan aristocracy to the will of the Spanish monarch. Under a succession of sternly autocratic viceroys, those aims had been ruthlessly pursued. The old structures of Neapolitan society had been systematically eroded, as the aristocracy, who had been a thorn in the side of Neapolitan rulers for centuries, were stripped of their powers and forced to renounce their ancient rule as despots on their rural estates. Most had been persuaded to leave their fiefdoms in the countryside and move to Naples itself, where they were compensated for the loss of real power with the sybaritic rewards of life at the court of the Spanish viceroy. The Italian historian Benedetto Croce encapsulated their decline in a single, acerbic sentence of his *History of the Kingdom of Naples*: 'Idleness, luxury, rivalry in conspicuous display, the construction of huge palaces, the attendance of large numbers of servants, the abandonment of family and the frequenting of courtesans (a custom copied, apparently, from the Spaniards) led the baronial families, in the course of a few generations, to ruin.'[11]

As the power of the barons dwindled, a new class of professionals and entrepreneurs flourished: lawyers, tax advisers, importers and exporters of grain, moneylenders, traders in luxury goods. Many came from Genoa, others from Tuscany, traditional breeding ground of merchants and financiers. Regardless of background, those involved in trade and finance were routinely referred to as 'Jews' by the habitually anti-

Semitic Neapolitans. The actual Jewish population had been decimated by a systematic campaign of expulsions begun a hundred years before.

The rich dressed in the Spanish manner and travelled through the streets in carriages or covered litters. George Sandys remarked that there were as many litter-bearers touting for work on the streets of Naples as there were boatmen on the busy wharves of London. But the city's most striking feature was its ubiquitous crowd of beggars and paupers. In every street and in every alley thronged a seething, jostling mass of the poor. 'Nowhere in the world,' wrote Capaccio, 'is there anything so obtrusive and undisciplined, the result of the mixture and confusion of so many races . . . miserable, beggarly and mercenary folk of a kind such as to undermine the wisest constitution of the best of republics, the dregs of humanity, who have been at the bottom of all the tumult and uprisings in the city and cannot be restrained otherwise than by the gallows.'[12] He likened the Neapolitan crowd to a constant swarm of insects. Wherever he went, he heard 'a murmuring . . . as if it were the buzzing of bees'.[13]

Despite the city's prosperity, there was work for only a fraction of its ever-growing population. Every day, every week, every year, an unstoppable flood of rural migrants poured into its already close-packed mesh of streets. They came to escape the harshness and uncertainty of life on the land, where petty banditry was rife and where the failure of one crop could doom an entire family to starvation. Their plight had been further exacerbated by new and punitive royal taxes, exacted by the Spanish from the rural peasantry, who abandoned their smallholdings in droves.

As its population climbed inexorably, Naples became caught in a vicious circle that made mass unemployment and grim poverty inevitable facts of life there. The authorities lived in continual fear of social unrest, with good reason. There had been brief, bloody rebellions in 1508 and 1547. To avert the threat of revolution, the viceregal government guaranteed food and provisions even in times of scarcity or famine. Grain was stockpiled in vast quantities to ensure that corn and bread would always be available, at state-controlled prices, to all the inhabitants of the city. Such measures had the inevitable effect of attracting yet more immigrants, thus exacerbating the very crisis the government had intended to alleviate.

In a vain attempt to check the city's growth, the authorities introduced restrictive building ordinances, which prohibited the construction of new dwellings outside the city walls; the intention was to stem the tide of immigrants by the simple expedient of depriving them of anywhere to live. But workers from the countryside continued to flow into Naples, so the new regulations simply meant that living conditions became ever more cramped. It has been estimated that some 21,000 people were squeezed into every square mile of the city.[14]

Even the physical appearance of the population was transformed by this wrenching demographic shift. Pressure on the food supply meant that for the majority pasta replaced vegetables and fruit as the staple diet. Despite the best efforts of the government, many people lived in a state of permanent semi-starvation. Neapolitans became shorter in height and notably more prone to the illnesses and deformities caused by malnutrition: goitres in the throat, rotten teeth, rickets and scurvy. The ragged and homeless were themselves seen as a kind of disease afflicting the body politic. The poorest citizens were known as the *lazzari*. The term literally means 'lepers', but in Spanish-controlled Naples it was used to encompass an entire social underclass, a subproletariat of the destitute. At night they huddled under market stalls, in courtyards, beneath porticoes, anywhere shelter could be found. By day they sought refuge in churches or took to the streets to beg. They were everywhere, complained Capaccio, clogging the very arteries of his city. 'Nothing is more difficult than getting about in Naples, wherever I go and at whatever time.'[15]

The chronic shortage of housing was made yet more acute by the city's many churches and monasteries, by the grand scale of its civic buildings and by the determination of the authorities to maintain large areas of park and orchard in the urban centre. Because space was so precious, it was rigorously exploited. Houses in Naples commonly rose to six storeys, twice as tall as those in any other Italian city. The streets were narrow and they were still arranged in the same tight grid-plan formation that had been laid down by the Greek founders of the settlement more than two thousand years earlier. The centre of the city was dark. Overshadowed by unbroken lines of tall buildings, its congested lanes and alleys were rarely penetrated by direct sunlight. Despite the sunshine of southern Italy, most daily life took place in deep shadow, in a form of civic space not unlike the bottom of a well.

THE SEVEN ACTS OF MERCY

Little is known about Caravaggio's first visit to Naples. The archives of the city have not even yielded his address. He may have stayed on the Via Toledo, in the palace of Luigi Carafa Colonna, Costanza Colonna's nephew. But it is more likely that he and Cecco were given rooms in Costanza's own residence at Chiaia, a grand fortified block of a building on the edge of town, close to the sea. He is securely documented as having stayed there during his second visit to Naples, three years later.

According to Bellori, Caravaggio was deluged with work from the moment he arrived in the city, 'since his style and reputation were already known'.[16] Within days of his arrival he had been commissioned by Niccolò Radolovich, a rich grain merchant from Ragusa, to paint a large altarpiece of 'the Madonna and child, surrounded by choirs of angels, with St Dominic and Francis embracing below, with St Nicholas on the right and St Vitus on the left'.[17] On 6 October he received 200 ducats in advance payment and later the same day opened an account at the Banca di Sant'Eligio, where he deposited the money. Radolovich wanted his picture as soon as possible: the contract specified that the altarpiece was to be delivered by December.

The Radolovich altarpiece has been lost, if it ever existed. None of the artist's early biographers mention the picture, so perhaps it was never painted. Might Caravaggio have had second thoughts about taking on the type of stiff, static and rather old-fashioned composition prescribed by the contract? The Virgin Mary wafted to heaven in clouds of cherubim: hardly a subject to bring out the best in him. Less than three weeks after agreeing the deal with Radolovich, Caravaggio cashed a money order for 150 ducats drawn on his new bank account. Perhaps he took the money out to give his client a refund.

At around the same time, late October or early November, he took on a more prestigious commission: to paint a monumental picture for the high altar of a new church in the heart of Naples. The church was the Chiesa del Pio Monte della Misericordia, close to the cathedral, on the corner of the Via dei Tribunali and the narrow Vico dei Zuroli. The subject of the altarpiece was to be the Seven Acts of Mercy, the good works encouraged by the Christian spirit of charity, such as feeding the hungry and giving shelter to pilgrims. It was a topical theme in Naples, where the plight of the poor was so brutally visible.

The pauperist strain of Counter-Reformation piety, to which Caravaggio had given such uncompromising expression in his Roman altarpieces, was especially strong in southern Italy. The Pio Monte della Misericordia was a lay confraternity devoted to the care of the sick and the needy, an institution at the front line of attempts to alleviate the urban crisis gripping seventeenth-century Naples. It had been founded in 1601 by seven idealistic young noblemen who were dissatisfied with the narrowness and superficiality of life at the court of the Spanish viceroy. Moved by the plight of the *lazzari*, they would meet every Friday at the Hospital of the Incurables, 'to serve and succour those poor invalids with food and sweetmeats'.[18] As their confraternity grew and flourished, they broadened its activities to encompass all seven of the traditional Christian acts of mercy. They also built a church. It had been consecrated in the middle of September 1606, a mere fortnight before Caravaggio's serendipitous arrival in Naples.

The original statute of the Pio Monte had been written in 1603. The document placed great emphasis on the practice of 'corporal mercy', by which was meant hands-on charity, as opposed to the spiritual offering of prayer. It also expressed the confraternity's fiercely independent spirit, insisting on its freedom from ecclesiastical control: 'finally we wish that our Monte be not subject to the ordinary [i.e. the Archbishop of Naples], but that the workings of the Monte be autonomous and free from the jurisdiction of this ordinary.'[19] The papal authorities made the concession, although they insisted on keeping it secret for fear of setting an undesirable precedent.

Caravaggio's new patrons were powerful and persuasive men, with deep pockets. They offered him 400 ducats, twice the fee that had been proposed for the Radolovich altarpiece. They were evidently determined to get their man. Caravaggio had come to Naples in their time of need, at the exact moment when they were looking for a painter to give permanent visual expression to their sense of charitable mission.

The prime mover of the commission was probably Giovanni Battista Manso, the Marchese di Villa, one of the seven founding members of the Pio Monte.[20] Manso was interested in the arts, especially poetry. He was a patron of Giambattista Marino, a poet famous for his restless and unruly nature, who had himself struck up a friendship of sorts with Caravaggio in Rome, and had possibly cast an eye over the scurrilous verses addressed to 'John Baggage'.[21]

Manso was sharp and open-minded, with a keen and speculative intelligence. He was a friend of Galileo and regularly visited Tommaso Campanella, freethinking cleric and author of *The City of the Sun*, during his 27-year imprisonment by the Inquisition. Manso was also friendly with Costanza Colonna's nephew, Luigi Carafa Colonna. Together, in 1611, they would found the Accademia degli Oziosi, one of the leading literary academies of Naples. Manso liked to entertain poets and other writers at his villa in coastal Puteoli, a place he fondly described in his biography of the poet Torquato Tasso: 'on a most beautiful sea-shore . . . a beautiful house somewhat elevated above all the others and encompassed all around by very beautiful gardens'.[22] Many years later Manso would play host to the English poet John Milton on his visit to Naples. Milton described him in a Latin epigraph as 'a very noble and authoritative man'.[23]

Tolerant of outsiders and misfits, interested in intellectual innovators, close to the Colonna family – all this indicates that Manso is likely to have been well disposed to Caravaggio. He was first and foremost an author, a connoisseur of literature rather than painting, but this too points to his involvement in the commission, which seems to have reflected a very literary conception of the subject of the acts of mercy. All seven acts were to be depicted on a single canvas, together with the figure of the Madonna della Misericordia, the 'Virgin of Pity', descending from heaven to give her blessing. Caravaggio would rise to the challenge of this busily elaborate iconography with one of the most compellingly humane pictures of the seventeenth century.

The painter was deeply responsive to the different worlds through which his stormy life would take him. He had an unerringly keen sense of milieu, a sharp eye for all that sets one place apart from another, whether architecture or mood, the quality of light or the quality of human behaviour. That responsiveness was one of the foundations of his art. It was the means by which he made holy legend seem real and true to those who looked at his pictures, embodied in a painted world that looked and felt like *their* world. When in Rome, he had brought the Bible and its stories to Rome. When he moved to Naples, he shifted his visions of the sacred past there too.

The Seven Acts of Mercy is set at the bottom of the crowded well of a Neapolitan street corner. It is night-time, but the street is full of people. In the foreground a beggar half kneels and half crouches, light flaring off his pale naked back. His skin is stretched tightly across his shoulderblades, over the curve of his vertebrae and the cage of his ribs. A young man in silk and velvet clothing, wearing a feather in his cap, looks down at the half-naked pauper with an expression of troubled compassion. They are just two in the midst of a throng. Beside them, an innkeeper gives the nod to a sad-faced pilgrim and a sunburned man looks skyward with pained relief as he slakes his thirst with a trickle of water.

To their right, someone really has seen Naples and died. The corpse is being carried away. Only the dirt-ingrained soles of the cadaver's feet are visible. The face of the dead person's pallbearer is lost in deep shadow. Behind, a swarthy and bearded sexton in plain white vestments is reciting the funeral office. There is a flickering, mobile quality to the light, especially where it falls on the folds of the priest's cassock, which has an almost phosphorescent glitter. Its source is the pair of candles that the priest holds aloft, a torch against the blackness of night. A more mysterious light also falls from above, its source hidden.

Smoke rises from the coarse tallow and the priest chants in a deep, melancholy voice. Next to the departing corpse, a dull-eyed woman bares her breast and gives succour to an old man through the grille of his prison cell. Above, a contemplative Virgin Mary cradles her son and looks down on the scene. The Madonna and child are wrapped in the embrace of two intertwined angels.

'For I was an hungred, and ye gave me meat: I was thirsty, and ye gave me drink: I was a stranger, and ye took me in: Naked, and ye clothed me: I was sick, and ye visited me: I was in prison, and ye came unto me.' The different groups in Caravaggio's painting represent the different forms of charity listed in the gospel according to Matthew (25:36–7). To the six biblical acts of mercy the medieval Church had added one more: the burial of the dead. It was traditional to represent each of the acts separately. But, having been asked to combine them all in one picture, Caravaggio turned an apparent handicap to his own advantage. For a dark and desperately overcrowded town, he created a dark and desperately overcrowded altarpiece.

With the exception of the burial of the dead, which is implicitly set in the present, each of the acts of mercy is enacted by a figure from history or legend. The sunburned man with a desperate need for water is Samson, whose thirst was miraculously quenched from the jawbone of an ass (Judges 15:18–19). The bearded traveller sheltered by the stolid innkeeper is Christ the pilgrim. The young *bravo* with a plumed hat, who evokes bittersweet memories of the finely dressed ne'er-do-wells in Caravaggio's first Roman pictures, is a representation of St Martin of Tours. He has drawn his sword to cut his cloak in half, as the medieval saint had done, to clothe a pauper, in the most frequently recounted episode of his life. The unclothed wretch at the saint's feet has already been given his piece of cloth, which the pauper grasps in his left hand as if to begin covering his nakedness. The blade of St Martin's sword glints in the darkness to the left of the beggar's face. Half lost in the shadows, virtually under the innkeeper's feet, another curly-headed figure squats with his hands clasped in supplication. The solemn and melancholy saint may be about to give away the second half of his cloak to this second beggar. He gives his charity to two people and is presumably meant to embody two different acts of mercy, not only clothing the naked but visiting the sick. Of all the charitable figures, he has been placed closest to the picture plane, and therefore closest to the congregation in the church of the Pio Monte. Literally, he represents St Martin, but he is also an alter ego for the seven young Neapolitan noblemen who had founded the Pio Monte. Like them, he is an aristocrat helping those who have been struck down by sickness and poverty.

The two figures at the right, the half-undressed woman and the greying old man behind the bars of his cell, are drawn from the legends of ancient Rome. They also embody twin acts of charity, namely feeding the hungry and visiting prisoners in jail. The imprisoned Cimon was starving to death when his daughter, Pero, came to him and nourished him with milk from her breast. The subject was known as the *Caritas Romana*, 'Roman Charity', and seen as a classical prefiguration of the Christian spirit of mercy. Since Caravaggio had visited the Palazzo Doria, in Genoa, on his brief flight to the city in the summer of 1605, he must have known Pierino del Vaga's fey Mannerist version of the same subject, in which an elegantly dressed young woman in a windswept cloak smuggles her left breast through the grille of a prison cell with a gesture of improbable grace. Caravaggio's interpretation is harsher, darker, gratingly realistic. Looking around her furtively, as if wary of detection, the dark-haired young woman performs her act of mercy with a troubled and anxious air. The old man who suckles at her breast has been reduced by his plight to a second infancy. Her dress is folded up under his chin like a bib. Two viscous drops of milk are caught in the strands of his beard.

The Seven Acts of Mercy is a picture that collapses time and space, drawing the whole world and all the world's history into its dark centre. Classical antiquity, the Old Testament, the New Testament, the Middle Ages and the present day – every epoch is symbolically represented in the different episodes that crowd the canvas. 'Naples is the whole world,' Capaccio wrote, and in Caravaggio's painting a corner of the city has been transformed into precisely that. This one dark street, this scene of desperation and pain and death, is the painter's microcosm for the brutality of existence itself. Briefly, it has been blessed and transfigured, made other than cruel experience normally proves. Here, the thirsty drink, the homeless are given shelter, and a sword is used not to kill a man but to put clothing on his back.

The embracing angels, themselves a celestial vision of fraternal love, descend earthwards in a rush, bearing the Madonna and Child with them. The leading angel's hand reaches down and into the world of fallen humanity – the highest reaching towards the lowest, the hand of the angel extended towards its visual rhyme, the left hand of the wretch at the very bottom of the painting, itself pressed down on the hard and unyielding ground. But a gulf of darkness and confusion separates the angel from the wretch. In that darkness there is space for the shadow of a doubt.

The tumbling angels and Madonna of Mercy are unusually heavy and corporeal, so emphatically realized that the wings of one angel cast the clearest of shadows on the prison wall. Yet the sense of hectic, jostling movement that ripples through the entire composition has the effect of making everything in it seem unsettlingly provisional. At any moment the celestial vision might disappear, the lights that flare gutter and go out, and the world plunge back into impenetrable night.

THE MECHANICS OF EVIL

Caravaggio painted the monumental altarpiece at breakneck speed, in little more than seven weeks. He received the balance of his fee on 9 January 1607, by which time the painting was probably installed on the high altar of the church of the Pio Monte. The confraternity soon came to see it as one of their greatest treasures. At a group of meetings held in the summer of 1613 the congregation decided that the painting could never be sold at any price. By then, several offers of 2,000 scudi or more – five times the original fee for the work – had already been turned down. One of the would-be purchasers was the Spanish poet Juan de Tassis y Peralta, Conde de Villamediana, but he was forced to content himself with a copy painted from Caravaggio's original.[24] In the 1650s, when the complex of the confraternity's buildings was remodelled, a new centrally planned Baroque church was created with the specific aim of giving Caravaggio's altarpiece yet more prominence, space and light – a rare instance of an entire building being constructed around a single picture.

The *Seven Acts* guaranteed further commissions and more work for Caravaggio. Sometime in the early months of 1607 he agreed to paint another altarpiece, on the subject of Christ's flagellation, for a chapel within the courtyard of a Dominican monastery in Naples.[25] The picture was finished by 11 May 1607, when a final payment of 250 ducats was made.[26] It has remained in Naples ever since, although it is no longer in the chapel for which it was commissioned, but in the Museo di Capodimonte.

With *The Flagellation of Christ*, Caravaggio resumed his old rivalry with Michelangelo. The most celebrated earlier version of the subject had been for the Roman church of San Pietro in Montorio, painted by Sebastiano del Piombo but to Michelangelo's designs. Sebastiano's High Renaissance Christ is sorrowful but withdrawn. He is an idealized victim enduring the blows of a group of animated, mildly grotesque tormentors, in the setting of a grand apsidal chapel supported by marble columns with finely carved Corinthian capitals.

Caravaggio took the same basic composition but made it his own by giving yet more emphasis to the cruelty and suffering implicit in the subject. He moved the viewer much closer to the grim act of torture, enlarging the figures and narrowing the complex architecture of the earlier painting to the truncated shaft of a single pillar in a darkened space. To that shadowy pillar, a reduced cast of torturers strive to bind the spotlit figure of Christ. Naked save for a loincloth and a crown of thorns, he is a strikingly statuesque figure. Just like the Christ of Michelangelo and Sebastiano, he might almost be a sculpture come to life. But he is more beaten down, more nakedly vulnerable. His exhaustion is conveyed by the line of his neck, the way he has wearily allowed the weight of his head to sag on to his shoulder. Too tired to hold himself upright, he has stumbled forward from the base of the pillar.

Responding to their victim's state of collapse with angry determination, two of his tormentors are kicking and yanking him back into place. The torturer at the right, whose face is half hidden by shadow, is tightening the cords with which Christ's arms are bound. The man on the left is pulling his hair to straighten his body for the first blows. He snarls bestially, brandishing a makeshift whip in his other hand.

A third torturer kneels at Christ's feet, binding a sheaf of twigs into a flay. He goes about his work with care, only looking up to see how soon the work of flagellation need begin. Just as he had done in *The Crucifixion of St Peter* for the Cerasi Chapel, Caravaggio focused on the grim mechanics of evil. The kneeling man's shadowed profile is shown in silhouette against Christ's left thigh and bright white loincloth. Placing such emphasis on the proximity of one man's body to another is Caravaggio's way of heightening the horror of the scene. Torture is a misbegotten form of physical intimacy.

His new audience was impressed but also startled by Caravaggio's intense and troubling realism. The shock of their initial reaction can still be sensed in an account of *The Flagellation*, written more than a hundred years later, by the Neapolitan art historian Bernardo de Dominici: 'This work when it was shown to the public attracted much attention, in particular the figure of Christ which was taken from a common and not a noble model as is necessary for the representation of God made Man: everyone, from the amateurs to the professors, was shocked by his new manner: the use of deep and terrible shadows, the truth of the nakedness, the cold light without reflections.'[27]

Apart from his irrelevant complaint about the supposedly ignoble Christ – actually one of the painter's most gracefully sculptural figures – de Dominici's remarks epitomize the Neapolitan response to Caravaggio's art. Pictures such as the *Seven Acts* and *The Flagellation* were greeted with stunned admiration, bordering on bewilderment. They created a sensation and transformed Neapolitan painting virtually overnight. Caravaggio's extreme chiaroscuro and his brutal sense of reality were the catalyst for the birth of a new school of tenebristic painting in Naples. And through this city at the crossroads between Italian and Spanish art, Caravaggio's starkly powerful new style was transmitted to Spain itself. There it would have an even deeper transformative effect on native traditions. The work of the greatest Spanish religious painters of the seventeenth century, Ribera and Zurbarán, is unimaginable without the influence of Caravaggio. The gruesome particularity of Baroque Spain's polychrome statuary, so bloodily realistic in its conjurings of saints martyred and Christ crucified, is also deeply Caravaggesque in spirit.[28] The painter's years of exile and displacement are reflected, obliquely, in the westward spread of his influence.

Two further altarpieces survive from this period. *The Crucifixion of St Andrew*, which now hangs in the Cleveland Museum of Art, may have been even more directly responsible than the *Seven Acts* or *The Flagellation* for the dissemination of Caravaggio's influence in Spain. Bellori records that the picture was acquired by the Spanish viceroy in Naples, Don Juan Alonso de Pimentel y Herrera, Conde de Benavente, and taken by him to Valladolid on his return home to Spain in 1610. Its presence is confirmed by an entry in an inventory of the contents of the palace of the counts of Benavente drawn up in 1653, where it is described as 'a large painting of a nude St Andrew when he is being put on the cross with three executioners and a woman, with an ebony frame' and attributed, in a marginal annotation, to 'micael angel caraballo[sic]'.[29]

The Crucifixion of St Andrew was almost certainly commissioned directly from Caravaggio by the Conde de Benavente himself. The viceroy had a special devotion to the saint, having played a significant role in the early seventeenth-century renovation of the crypt of St Andrew in the cathedral of Amalfi. In 1610, the year of his departure from Naples, he is reported to have made a special pilgrimage to Amalfi, 'moved by devotion to visit the tomb of St Andrew'.[30] It seems highly probable that he commissioned Caravaggio's painting as an aid to his own prayers, and that it was destined from the start for the private chapel of his palace in Spain.

The picture is a harsh and daringly abbreviated depiction of a withered old man dying the cruel death of a martyr. Its true subject is not actually 'St Andrew when he is being put on the cross', as the writer of that Spanish inventory understandably assumed, but the miracle that occurred when his would-be executioners attempted to take him off it. According to *The Golden Legend*, the saint met his death in Patras, in Greece, after incurring the wrath of the Roman proconsul Aegeas. To prolong his agony, Aegeas ordered that Andrew be tied rather than nailed to the cross. For two days he hung there in the scorching sun, continuing to preach his forbidden Christian message to a crowd of twenty thousand. On the third day, the people grew restless and threatened Aegeas with death unless he put an end to the sufferings of 'an old man full of gentleness and piety'. But the saint prayed to God to be allowed to die on the cross, just as Christ had done. When Roman soldiers tried to unbind him, 'they could not touch him, for instantly their arms fell back powerless . . . a dazzling light came down from Heaven and enveloped him . . . and when the light vanished, he breathed forth his soul.'[31]

This is the moment that Caravaggio chose to depict. As the flash of divine light fades, the old man stops breathing and his eyes begin to roll up into his head. This is the parody of a deathbed scene, with the dying man forced to expire, against nature, in an upright position. His livid yellow skin is stretched tight across his ribcage. Wizened and pathetically shrunken, he exhales his last breath. The painter captures that moment when a man does indeed give up the ghost, when he suddenly becomes strange and unfamiliar, no longer like *himself*, as the life slackens out of him and death takes over his mouth, his eyes, his limbs, twisting them into unfamiliar forms.

Might the painter have observed his model, this very man, at the moment of his death? Might he have used his contacts in the Pio Monte della Misericordia to gain access to the Hospital of the Incurables – not to 'serve and succour' the terminally ill, but to paint one of their number? It is an image that reeks of mortality. The dead man's face and neck are sunburned, the rest of his emaciated body pale. He looks just like an actual human being at the end of an actual hard life, a malnourished *lazzaro* who has swapped the hardships of the land for the brutality of the city.

The odour of the geriatric ward hovers too about the figure of the old woman in the bottom-left-hand corner of the painting.[32] Sun-scorched like the saint himself, with a face heavily lined and wrinkled and a goitre in the neck, she frowns with fellow feeling. Her strong and sad eyes are full of pity. Gazing up towards the dying martyr, she plays the part of a chorus of one, standing in for the twenty thousand who had listened as Andrew preached.

The party of Roman soldiers sent to untether the saint from his cross has also been reduced to a solitary figure, a man teetering on a ladder. He struggles to free his arms from the invisible force that has paralysed them. As he does so, he arches away from the saint. The two bodies perform a kind of dance, its symmetry shaping a contrast between life and death. One is curved in tension, balanced against the possibility of a fall. The other is curved involuntarily, by the sideways sag of its own dead weight. Below, the lightly bearded figure of Aegeas looks up wonderingly at the miracle. His armour gleams darkly, evoking memories of the malign armoured soldier in Caravaggio's *Betrayal of Christ*. Two other figures loiter, their faces obscured by darkness. Landscape and sky have been reduced to a cursory smear.

CARAVAGGIO AND RUBENS

The other picture by Caravaggio to surface during his first visit to Naples was a large altarpiece of *The Madonna of the Rosary*. It was first mentioned by Frans Pourbus the Younger, a painter at the court of Mantua who was in Naples in the autumn of 1607. He had seen it for sale along with another painting by Caravaggio, a *Judith and*

Holofernes that has since disappeared. On 15 September he wrote to his master, Vincenzo I Gonzaga, the Duke of Mantua, to inform him that 'I have seen here two most beautiful paintings from the hand of Michelangelo da Caravaggio. One is a *Rosary* and was made as an altarpiece; it is 18 palmi high and they are asking no less than 400 ducats for it. The other is a painting of medium size with half figures and is a *Judith and Holofernes*; they will not let it go for less than 300 ducats. I did not want to make an offer because I did not know the intentions of Your Highness; however, they have promised not to let the painting go until they have been informed of the wishes of Your Highness.'[33]

In the same letter Pourbus implied that the picture had been painted by Caravaggio in Naples, but its tight, dry, highly finished style is utterly at odds with the brusquely abbreviated technique that characterizes the known works of the first Neapolitan period, such as the *Seven Acts* or *The Crucifixion of St Andrew*. Poised and somewhat theatrical, with its crowd of anxious paupers clustered in supplication at the feet of the Virgin and Child, *The Madonna of the Rosary* must have been painted considerably earlier in Caravaggio's career. Figures and forms are clearly delineated, the play of light and shade in the drapery far more sharply defined than such passages in any of the painter's later works. The red drapery bunched above the head of Mary is more precisely described even than the similar swag of red cloth in Caravaggio's last Roman altarpiece, *The Death of the Virgin*.

Caravaggio was an artist compelled to be true to himself, incapable of stretching to the ventriloquistic impersonation of his own earlier manners. As he grew older, his style moved inexorably towards simplification, abbreviation, occlusion. *The Madonna of the Rosary* is closest in spirit and appearance to *The Madonna of Loreto* and *The Entombment*. It breathes the same air of unclouded popular piety as those pictures of 1604.

Given the prominence of St Dominic in the legend of the Rosary, this large and imposing work was perhaps commissioned as the altarpiece of a Dominican church somewhere in or near Rome. Its appearance in Naples can best be explained by another of the rejections that occurred so frequently during the painter's years in Rome. The naked and conspicuously dirty feet of the kneeling paupers in the foreground were probably to blame. Caravaggio may have taken the large and valuable canvas with him when he fled from Rome after the killing of Ranuccio Tomassoni.

Worship of the Rosary had begun in Italy in the early years of the twelfth century. According to tradition, the Virgin appeared in a vision to St Dominic one night in 1208, holding a string of beads in her hand. She showed him how to use the beads in prayer and instructed him to preach the technique to Christians everywhere. Each bead represented a different mystery in the life of the Virgin or of Christ. As the worshipper moved the beads along the string, one by one, he or she was to visualize one particular mystery at a time, to bring it forth in the mind's eye and focus devotion upon it, while reciting the *Ave Maria* and the *Pater Noster*. Protestants disapproved of the Rosary, but during the second half of the sixteenth century the cult went from strength to strength. At a time when the Church was actively seeking to strengthen its hold on the mass of ordinary believers, the distribution of Rosary beads was recognized as a cheap and effective way of encouraging prayer and piety at every level of society.

Caravaggio stressed the inclusive nature of the cult by giving great prominence to the huddled crowd of the poor, reaching out in unison for the strings of beads held out by Dominic in both hands. In most depictions of the subject, the saint is shown himself receiving the Rosary from the Madonna. But here she acts the part of a heavenly overseer, supervising its distribution to the people. Supporting a plump Christ child on her knee, she points down towards the bottom-left-hand corner of the picture, in the direction of a mother who, like herself, is accompanied by her young son. The Virgin seems gently concerned that they should not be forgotten in the clamouring press of people.

On the other side from St Dominic stands St Peter Martyr, distinguished by the head-wound of his martyrdom. He was a Dominican friar, who had been killed by a stone thrown by a heretic. Accompanied by another darkly cowled and inscrutable member of the order, he gestures towards the Madonna and child and looks out at the viewer with a yearning, soulful expression on his face.

One other figure also looks at us. With the bearing and demeanour of an aristocrat, dressed in black and wearing a fine lace ruff, he kneels at Dominic's elbow and stares meaningfully out from the picture. He is presumably its donor, the man for whose chapel it had been commissioned in the first place. Who is he? There is perhaps a clue in the painting's composition. He has been aligned with a massive fluted column. The column was a symbol of the Colonna dynasty, strongly associated with the Madonna of the Rosary ever since the Battle of Lepanto, at which Costanza's father Marcantonio had played a pivotal role. In Rome in the early 1570s, Filippo Neri had attributed victory there to the prayers of the faithful to the Madonna of the Rosary. Various names have been proposed for the donor, including that of Don Marzio Colonna, who had sheltered Caravaggio after his flight to the Alban Hills. But since the commission of the painting remains entirely undocumented, his precise identity remains a mystery.

For whatever reason, the picture had disappointed the man in the lace ruff. Whoever he was, he had turned it down, and so it appeared on the open market in Naples in the autumn of 1607. By that time it was in the hands of two minor painter-dealers, Abraham Vinck and Louis Finson, whose stock also contained the now lost *Judith and Holofernes*. It is not clear whether they had purchased these works or whether they were selling them on commission on the painter's behalf. It was Finson and Vinck who told Frans Pourbus that *The Madonna of the Rosary* would cost the Duke of Mantua 400 ducats, which happens to be exactly in line with the fee Caravaggio had received for the *Seven Acts*. But the deal must have fallen through, because in the end the dealers themselves kept hold of the painting. Finson subsequently took it to Aix-en-Provence and then Antwerp, where he died in 1617.[34] *The Madonna of the Rosary* would eventually become part of the royal collection of the Viennese Habsburgs, and is nowadays to be seen in Vienna's Kunsthistorisches Museum. It is a key picture in the transmission of Caravaggio's style to northern Europe. But one particular chapter in its history introduces the crucial role that would be played in that process by another great artist.

In 1620 or shortly afterwards the picture was bought from the heirs of Finson and Vinck and donated to the principal Dominican church in Antwerp by a group of painters and connoisseurs. It would remain there for more than a hundred and fifty years.[35] The archives of the Dominican Fathers of Antwerp record that the most celebrated Flemish painter of the seventeenth century, Peter Paul Rubens, was a driving force behind the bequest: 'The large painting ... now in the chapel above the altar, is a work of Michelangelo da Caravaggio and was given by various art lovers, including among others, Rubens, Bruegel, Van Bael, Cooymans. Seeing that they could acquire this extraordinary great work of art for a good price, they bought it out of affection for the chapel and to have in Antwerp a rare art work ...'[36]

Rubens was a middle-aged man in the early 1620s, but he had been deeply impressed by Caravaggio's work from the start of his career. Like many other artists from northern Europe, he had travelled to Rome in his youth, forty years before, to study the art of classical antiquity and the Renaissance. While he was there he had been struck, as if by the force of revelation, by Caravaggio's Roman altarpieces. The violence and drama of the works of Rubens's early maturity, such as *The Massacre of the Innocents*, would be deeply touched by Caravaggio's influence. Through Rubens, that influence would be transmitted to Flanders and Holland, where an entire school known simply as 'the Caravaggisti' would come into being. The development of Rembrandt's subtle, shadowy realism would be part of the same story, which can ultimately be traced all the way back to the time of Caravaggio's first visit to Naples, and Rubens's early encounter with his pictures in Rome. In 1607, within just a few months of Pourbus's negotiations on behalf of the Gonzaga to buy *The Madonna of the Rosary* – the very picture that Rubens, over a decade later, would help donate to the Dominicans in Antwerp – Rubens himself was acting for the Duke of Mantua in regard to another painting by Caravaggio that was for sale on the open market in Rome.

The picture in question was *The Death of the Virgin*, another rejected altarpiece from Caravaggio's Roman years. Laerzio Cherubini, who had commissioned the work only to reject it in the summer of 1606, wanted to recoup his outlay. He had put it on the market in January 1607 and it had been snapped up by Caravaggio's future biographer, Giulio Mancini. The fragmentary evidence of Mancini's correspondence suggests that he paid 200 scudi for it, and that he intended to sell it to an unnamed purchaser in his home town of Siena. His letters to his brother, who was helping him with the negotiations for the sale there, show that he was concerned that Caravaggio's indecorous depiction of the Virgin might cause a stir. 'Someone knowledgeable will reprove us, but as it is for the service of God and the embellishment of the city, I will pay no attention to complaints.'[37]

But by the middle of February, Mancini was considering other options. The Duke of Mantua, one of Rubens's most valued patrons, had shown interest in buying the picture. His agent in Rome, Giovanni Magno, had opened negotiations with Mancini and was taking advice about the painting from, among others, Rubens. It seems likely that it may have been Rubens's idea to acquire the picture for Mantua in the first place.

On 17 February, Magno wrote a cautiously encouraging letter to the duke's secretary, Annibale Chieppio, about the potential acquisition. While he himself found *The Death of the Virgin* rather difficult and unpalatable, it had been greatly praised by the experts and connoisseurs: 'Last Sunday I saw the painting by Caravaggio, proposed by Signor Peter Paul Rubens who, when he saw it again, was still more satisfied by it . . . It pleased me to a degree corresponding to the concordant judgement of the professionals. However, because people of little experience desire some pleasure to the eyes, I was more impressed by the testimony of the others than by my own feeling which is not sufficient to understand well certain occult artificialities which place this picture in such high esteem. The painter, however, is one of the most famous for the collectors of modern things in Rome, and the picture is held to be one of the best paintings he has ever made. Thus, presumption is in favour of this painting in many respects, and really one can observe in it certain very exquisite parts . . .'[38]

In Magno's next letter, of just a week later, he told the duke's secretary that the price for the painting had been agreed by Rubens at 280 scudi. Mancini would make a profit of 80 scudi on the deal. He was content with that, and at this point the prospective purchaser in Siena disappears from the story. By the end of March, Magno was writing to confirm that he had taken possession of the picture on behalf of the Duke of Mantua.

Within a week, the painters of Rome had heard about the purchase and were clamouring to be allowed a sight of Caravaggio's painting before it left the city. It had been removed so quickly from its intended altar in Santa Maria della Scala in the summer of 1606, just before the murder of Ranuccio Tomassoni, that almost no one had had a chance to view the work. On 7 April 1607 Magno reported to his masters in Mantua that

> I found it necessary, in order to gratify the painters' guild, to let the purchased picture be seen all week long. Many of the most famous painters have been flocking there with a good deal of curiosity because this picture was the talk of the town, but scarcely anybody had been allowed to see it. It has certainly been a great satisfaction to me to let it be enjoyed by the public because it has been commended for the exceptional art with which it was done. It will be forwarded next week.

In the event, despatch of the painting was delayed because Rubens wanted to be sure that it survived the journey. On 14 April, Magno wrote to say that 'The purchased picture is at Sr Peter Paul Rubens's disposal, ready to be forwarded. But he, in order to preserve it from injuries, is having I know not what sort of case constructed, which will necessarily delay the shipment until after the holidays.' By May, *The Death of the Virgin* had reached Mantua.

FLIGHT FROM NAPLES

Clearly Caravaggio was held in deep regard by his fellow painters in Rome, despite being under capital sentence for murder. But he still had his enemies there. All had not been forgotten and forgiven. There were those who claimed that Caravaggio was still up to no good, still making trouble in the city even though he was in exile from it. Within days of his arrival in Naples, he had been accused, *in absentia*, of another attempted murder back in Rome. It was said that an assassin named Carlo Piomontese, working to Caravaggio's orders, had tried to kill a man who was on his way into church to hear Mass. Carlo Piemontese was a painter, a man also known as *il Bodello*, a nickname for sodomites. The victim of his alleged assault was none other than Caravaggio's old adversary Giovanni Baglione.

Baglione's accusations are to be found in a series of depositions

recorded by a notary in a Roman court of law at the beginning of
November 1606:

> Last Sunday at the 14th or 15th hour I was walking to mass at Trinità
> de' Monti. I was alone, and wearing a sword and a cape. I was walking
> down the stairs toward the Medici gardens when, as I set foot on the
> last step the said Carlo, who was hiding behind a pilaster on the stairs,
> attacked me with an unsheathed sword and struck me a blow that hit
> me on the shoulder, and tore my cloak and coat, as Your Lordship can
> see when I show you here ... [*Then I, the notary, saw a black cloak
> with a cut on the left shoulder, and a coat with a similar cut*] Then he
> aimed a blow at my head, which struck me on the arm with the flat of
> the sword. Seeing myself attacked in this way I put my hand to my
> sword also. In grasping it he wounded me in the said right hand, as you
> can see ... [*Then I, the notary, saw a little scar on the index of the right
> hand*] Then we exchanged some blows and my sword broke, because I
> think that he was wearing a breastplate, or something else of iron. Then
> some people came up, and we separated.[39]

Until this attack, things had gone well for Baglione in the autumn
of 1606. In September he had been knighted as a Cavaliere di Cristo.
In October he had received the further honour of being voted *principe*,
or 'head', of the Accademia di San Luca. Baglione believed that his
success in the elections for that post had provoked the attempt on
his life. Three weeks before the attack, he said in his evidence, Carlo
Piemontese had come to the academy and attempted to disrupt the
vote: 'As he was not one of the Congregation, was under twenty years
of age, and had no reason at all for being admitted, I told him that he
should go outside until the *principe* had been chosen. He answered
me that he was a painter like the others, and as he was there already
he wanted to stay, but he did it in such a way that he was not balloted,
and did not vote in the creation of said *principe*, and nothing else
occurred.'

That earlier incident had passed off without violence, but Baglione
believed his election had continued to gnaw at Carlo Piemontese. The
would-be assassin was friendly with two other painters, Carlo Saraceni and Orazio Borgianni, who were themselves close to Caravaggio.
Baglione believed that the three of them had formed a cabal, to block

his campaign and ensure that a member of Caravaggio's faction be elected instead. When their plans were foiled, they resorted to violence. He knew this, he said, because on the day of the vote for *principe*, his groom had seen Saraceni and Borgianni standing outside the Accademia with Carlo Piemontese, stirring him up into a frenzy. He had also been told – although he did not say by whom – that the mastermind of the whole plot was Caravaggio himself:

> My servant told me that, while he was outside holding my horse, there came out the aforementioned Carlo, Orazio and Carlo Veneziano, and that they incited the said Carlo by saying 'that prick' and other insulting words [about me]. They did this because they wish me ill, now and in the past, and are adherents of Caravaggio, who is my enemy. I heard that he gave them something, and someone else another thing, and told them to kill me, and to bring the news to Caravaggio, who would give them a fine reward.

The final judgement of the case is unknown. Two of the accused, Saraceni and Borgianni, made unusually large donations to the Accademia di San Luca on St Luke's feast day in the following year, which suggests that the affair may have been settled out of court.[40] Baglione's accusation was potentially very damaging for the absent Caravaggio: at the moment of his arrival in Naples, just as he was taking what he hoped would be the first steps on the way to a pardon, his name was once more associated with violence and murderous intent.

But behind the scenes it seems efforts were being made on Caravaggio's behalf by the Colonna and his other allies. In May 1607, some six months after the assault on Baglione and just as Rubens was packing up *The Death of the Virgin* for transport to Mantua, it was again rumoured that he would soon be returning to Rome. The Este agent, Fabio Masetti, still fretting about the 32 scudi he had advanced to him sixteen months earlier, had remained alert for new developments. Reporting back to Modena from Rome on 26 May, he sounded a distinctly hopeful note: 'It has not been possible to recover the money because of a homicide committed by the said painter, on account of which he has been banished. However, as the said homicide was accidental and the painter was badly wounded too, a reprieve is being negotiated and a pardon is hoped for. So, when he is back, I shall not fail to recover the said 32 scudi.'[41]

'The said homicide was accidental' and 'the painter was badly wounded too' – Masetti was no doubt repeating the same arguments, perhaps even the very same phrases, that were being used in Caravaggio's defence. By the start of June, Masetti was sufficiently optimistic to let the painter himself know that he would be waiting for him when he got back to Rome. 'I have written a letter to Caravaggio the painter for the restitution of the 32 scudi,' he informed his superiors in Modena, 'although it was not the first one, and the other time he failed to send a reply.'[42]

Yet again the hapless Masetti was to be disappointed. Caravaggio, painting *The Crucifixion of St Andrew*, once more failed to reply. By the end of June, unpredictable as ever, he had left Naples by boat and was travelling ever further away from the city of Rome. His destination was the island of Malta, southernmost bastion of the Christian faith against Turks and Corsairs, and home to the military Order of the Knights of St John.

Just why Caravaggio took the extraordinary decision to go to Malta is one of the many puzzles of his later years. Piecemeal clues in the historical archive suggest that he went in the hope of finding freedom and forgiveness. He appears to have believed that by allying himself with Malta's formidable militia of warrior knights he might win permanent redemption for his crimes. But in the tough world of the Christian soldier he would be undone, once again, by his own volatility.

THE FRIARS OF WAR

To become a Knight Hospitaller of the Sovereign and Military Order of St John of Jerusalem, Rhodes and Malta, Custodian of the Poor of Jesus Christ and Servant of the Sick, was to join one of the most venerable and powerful organizations in the Christian world. The order's roots lay deep in the medieval past, when the religious zeal of the pilgrim and the aristocratic ethos of chivalry became closely interwoven. In the year 1070 a group of noblemen from Amalfi, in Italy, founded a hospital in the city of Jerusalem to care for fellow Christians weakened by the long pilgrimage to the Holy Land. After the First Crusade, and following the capture of the Holy City, they were formally constituted as a nursing and military order. 'The Friars of War', as they became known, were dedicated both to the service of the sick and to the defence of the Christian faith against the threat of Islam.

Within less than a century, the Knights of St John had established a vast network of hospitals and fortifications along the pilgrim routes leading from Europe to Jerusalem. Over the next two hundred years, they developed into a formidable army of aristocratic Christian warriors, building and defending a long chain of castles to safeguard the land frontiers of the Holy Land, from Asia Minor to Egypt. The Knights of St John were the crack troops of Christendom, but they also bore the brunt of wave after wave of attacks from the armies of Islam. By the end of the thirteenth century they had been made to relinquish almost all of their hard-won possessions. When the Christians were finally forced out of the Holy Land altogether, the knights were the last to leave, finally defeated at the Siege of Acre in 1291.

The history of the order over the next three centuries would be no less bloody and no less embattled. The knights found a new home on the Greek island of Rhodes, a strategically vital maritime base at the crossroads of Europe, Asia and Africa. Having captured the island, they fortified it and set about creating a fleet of fighting ships. From that time on, they were no longer an army of Christian footsoldiers but a naval force. From their base on Rhodes they mounted raids on Turkish shipping and vulnerable coastal settlements, taking slaves and capturing hostages for ransom.

In the Islamic world they were regarded as brutal and pitiless marauders. In their monastic uniform of black robes, proudly emblazoned at the chest with a white eight-pointed cross, the Knights of St John represented a militantly aggressive form of Christianity. Their activities inevitably attracted reprisals. In 1480 a Turkish fleet laid siege to Rhodes, only to be repelled with crippling losses. Forty years later, in 1522, Sultan Suleiman the Magnificent once more sent a flotilla of ships to conquer Rhodes. After six months of attack and counter-attack, the knights were finally defeated and expelled from the island.

In 1530 the Holy Roman Emperor Charles V gave them another new home, on Malta, part of his Two Kingdoms of Sicily. His motives were part religious, part strategic. Charles V wanted to protect the southern flank of Europe and ultimately Rome itself against the might of Islam. His reasoning was that if anyone could hold Malta, the Knights of St John could. He ceded it to them in exchange for an annual tribute of a single falcon.

Thirty-five years later, in 1565, the Turks once more laid siege to an island garrisoned by their most hated adversaries. The Siege of Malta lasted for months and would forever be remembered, both for the ferocity of the fighting and for the atrocities committed on both sides. The official historian of the Order of St John, Giacomo Bosio, included a harrowing account of it in his three-volume *Dell'Istoria della sacra religione*, the last part of which was published in 1602, five years before Caravaggio arrived on Malta. At the height of the siege, Bosio recounted, having captured Fort St Elmo, the Turks proceeded to massacre their Christian captives. The day allotted for the killing was 24 June, the feast day of St John and therefore one of the two most holy days of the year for members of the order (the other being 29 August, the day that marked the saint's decapitation at the whim of Salome). Making grim play of the significance of the date, the Turks turned the killing itself into an obscene parody of a Christian religious festival: 'All the cadavers which by their clothing could be recognized as knights or men of importance were gathered up; and it was ordered that they be stripped nude, decapitated, and that their hands be severed. Then, out of disresepect for the Holy Cross and to make sport of the knights' military overgarments, on each corpse four huge incisions were made with scimitars, making the sign of the Cross on both the fronts and the backs.'[43]

On a later occasion, in a similar spirit of vengeful parody, the Turks crucified a number of headless knights' corpses and floated them into the harbour at Birgu. Bosio wrote that 'after having had them lashed to various pieces of wood with their arms spread apart so as to form, similarly, the sign of the Cross, and bound in such a manner as to make one body tow the other in a long chain, they were then tossed into the sea. The water, it was thought, would carry them and this truly horrible spectacle over to our brethren at Birgu, and it in fact did so.'[44] The intention was to strike terror into the last remnants of Malta's Christian garrison. But the Grand Master of the Order of St John, a doughty Frenchman named Jean de la Valette, responded to the Turks' flotilla of death with a fusillade of his own. He ordered his Turkish captives to be decapitated and had their heads fired from cannons at the Turkish soldiers occupying Fort St Elmo. In the end the knights held firm, despite their crippling losses, and the Turks were forced to withdraw. By the end of the siege just 50 Knights of St John survived. More than 7,000 defenders had lost their lives, but the last great effort of the Ottoman Turks to seize control of the western Mediterranean had been successfully repulsed.

Over the decades that followed there was a surge of new recruits to the Order of St John, lured to Malta by the dream of emulating the exploits of the heroes of 1565. Just six years after the siege, that other famous Christian victory, at the Battle of Lepanto, had fanned the flames of such enthusiasm yet further. Hundreds of young noblemen from the leading families of Europe travelled to Malta to seek knighthood, honour and glory. They wanted to fight, and if necessary die a martyr's death, at the front line of conflict with the forces of Islam.

According to Bellori, Caravaggio too nurtured the dream of becoming a Knight of St John. He was 'eager to receive the Cross of Malta', in the words of the biographer.[45] But why? His art had electrified Naples. According to sources in Rome, steady progress was being made in the negotiation of his pardon. It would seem like an odd moment to travel yet further south, to a barren and rocky island at the farthest frontier of Christendom. It is possible that the fantasy of becoming a knight had long been with him – after all, he was a keen and talented swordsman, who had been brought up in the immediate aftermath of the Battle of Lepanto. Or perhaps he still felt vulnerable to attack or apprehension by a bounty hunter, aware of the price on his head. By papal dispensation the Knights of St John were above the law, subject to their own unique legal code. In Malta, Caravaggio would be safe. Furthermore, if he could win a knighthood he would, *de facto*, have gained pardon for his crimes.

But there was probably more to it than that. Caravaggio had always been extremely touchy about status. At his trial for libel, he had contemptuously dismissed the rank and file of Rome's artists by saying that hardly any of them deserved the title of *valent'huomo*, literally, a 'worthy man'. Caravaggio took pride in his own worth. The poems attacking Giovanni Baglione, in which he certainly had had a hand, made much of the gold chain awarded to his rival. The perceived injustice of the honour clearly rankled with Caravaggio as much, if not more, than anything Baglione had actually said or done. But by the summer of 1607, nearly a year after the murder of Tomassoni, Baglione had just been knighted and his stock had risen yet further. Caravaggio, by contrast, was still a fugitive from justice. Even if he were pardoned and allowed to return, he would be going back to Rome as a man in disgrace. But to return, himself, with a knighthood – and not just an honorific papal knighthood but a knighthood in the Order of St John, proudly wearing the eight-pointed cross on his chest – that would be very different. If he could manage that, he could face his rivals down.

Joachim von Sandrart tells an undoubtedly apocryphal tale about the cause of Caravaggio's decision to go to Malta, which, for all its evident fancifulness, may contain a kernel of truth. In Sandrart's story, Caravaggio's former employer Giuseppe Cesari, on horseback, passes him one day in the streets of Rome. Caravaggio challenges Cesari to a duel and tells him to dismount from his horse so that they can fight. But he is rebuffed:

> Giuseppe answered . . . that it was not fitting for a knight, named by the Pope, to duel with someone who was not a knight. With this politely cutting answer, he wounded Caravaggio more than he might have with his sword, for this talk so stunned and confused Caravaggio that he immediately (as he did not intend to defer the matter) sold all his belongings to the Jews for whatever he could get, and set out for Malta and the Grand Master with the purpose of soon himself becoming a knight . . .[46]

The tale is clearly a fiction, because Caravaggio was nowhere near Rome when he decided to go to Malta. But it has the ring of psychological truth. The unpalatable thought of lesser painters being dubbed knight may well have impelled him on his Maltese adventure.

Malta was not, however, a place where someone could simply turn up unannounced. The whole island was a fortress, and security was tight. No one was allowed in from the mainland without a passport and papers prepared by the order's network of receivers. The receiver in Naples was a high-ranking official named Giovanni Andrea Cape-ci.[47] Capeci would have had to gain approval from the Grand Master of the order on Malta itself before completing the necessary paper-work, and such permissions, especially for a fugitive from papal just-ice, were no simple matter. One of Caravaggio's friends in high places would have been needed to broker the arrangement with the Knights of Malta. Who helped him? There are a number of possibilities, because several people in the painter's network of patrons and protect-ors turn out to have had links with the Order of St John.

In the summer of 1607, at exactly the same time as Caravaggio chose to go to the island, two cousins of the noble Giustiniani family – avid collectors of Caravaggio's work in Rome – were on their way to Malta to offer the Grand Master a family property in Venosa, near Naples, as a naval base for the knights on the mainland. Perhaps they were prevailed on to put in a good word for the talented artist with a criminal record.

Ottavio Costa, the banker who had recently bought Caravaggio's second *Supper at Emmaus* while the artist was in hiding in the Alban Hills, also had connections with the Knights of the Order of St John. His wife's uncle was Ippolito Malaspina, an illustrious member of the heroic old guard of Malta, and something of a living legend. A veteran of the great Siege of 1565, Malaspina had gone on to captain one of the Maltese galleys at the Battle of Lepanto, in the year of Caravag-gio's birth. In 1603 he had been appointed commander of the papal fleet, as a result of which he temporarily delegated his responsibilities on Malta and moved to Rome for two years – years during which Caravaggio painted some of his most highly acclaimed Roman altar-pieces. Malaspina would certainly have known of the painter's work and may even have met him. By the summer of 1607 he had been re-appointed to a number of senior posts in the order, including Prior of Naples. He was very close to the Grand Master himself, a Frenchman named Alof de Wignacourt, having played an important part in Wig-nacourt's election in 1601. The possibility that Malaspina's advocacy might have been instrumental in Caravaggio's acceptance on Malta is strengthened by the fact that one of the first pictures the artist painted when he got there – another depiction of *St Jerome Writing* – was done for Malaspina himself: the Malaspina family crest is prom-inently painted into the right-hand edge of the canvas.

This was not the total of Caravaggio's contacts with the upper echelons of the order. The idea of going to Malta, to seek redemption for crimes committed, almost certainly emanated from his most constant guardians and protectors, the Colonna dynasty. A prominent member of the Colonna family had recently done exactly the same thing himself.

In 1602 Costanza Colonna's second son, Fabrizio Sforza Colonna, had been convicted of crimes considered so shameful that their precise nature was left unmentioned in the reports of the day. Following his arrest, he was taken to Rome and imprisoned while the pope considered his case. Costanza Colonna pleaded for mercy on her son's behalf. In deference to his rank, the pope decided to give the noble prisoner a second chance. He was sent to Malta in 'privileged exile', on condition that he remain on the island for at least three years, placing himself at the service of the Christian faith. By 1605 this black sheep of the Colonna family was deemed to have expiated his sins, and had been elected co-Prior of Venice, a post that he shared with his uncle, Ascanio Colonna. The following year he was made a member of the governing Venerable Council of the order and elevated to the rank of General of the Galleys. There could hardly have been a better way for the grandson of Marcantonio Colonna, hero of Lepanto, to complete his return from disgrace and exile.[48]

A less exalted version of the same process of redemption seems to have been planned for Caravaggio. Costanza Colonna, who had seen things go so well for her son on Malta, may well have been the driving force behind the whole scheme. She had long taken a virtually maternal interest in Michelangelo Merisi da Caravaggio, who was close to the same age as her own Fabrizio. What had worked for one difficult young man might work for the other.

A number of recently discovered documents place Fabrizio and Costanza Colonna in Naples in the summer of 1607. In fact they both arrived in the city just a matter of days before Caravaggio embarked for Malta. It has also emerged that he made the journey to the island in one of a flotilla of galleys commanded by none other than Fabrizio Sforza Colonna himself.

On his first voyage as General of the Galleys, Fabrizio Sforza Colonna had travelled to Barcelona to take delivery of a new flagship and a large number of slaves and convicts donated to the order by the Spanish crown. Discovering that the new Spanish flagship was poorly constructed, he had a replacement fitted out in the shipbuilding port of Marseilles. By the early summer of 1607 he was back in Italian waters, collecting his mother, Costanza, from the Torre del Greco near Naples, the spectacular seaside residence of the princes of Stigliano. The two of them carried on to Naples itself, where the final arrangements for Caravaggio's journey to Malta would soon be concluded.[49]

So it was that on 25 June 1607, bearing with him the good wishes of his protectress, Caravaggio embarked for the island fortress of Malta. It is not known whether his faithful assistant and rumoured lover, Cecco, accompanied him. Probably, he did not: Cecco appears in no more of Caravaggio's paintings after this date.

THE ISLE OF ST JOHN

The voyage to Malta was fraught with tension. The flotilla's first stop was Messina, in Sicily, where Fabrizio Sforza Colonna received an urgent warning from Grand Master de Wignacourt. Seven large galleys from the Barbary Coast had just been sighted in the waters off Gozo, Malta's sister island. Five of them had disembarked soldiers and mounted an unsuccessful attack on the order's garrison there. Wignacourt suspected that the enemy had received intelligence about the imminent arrival of the flotilla from Naples and intended to engage them in battle. He was concerned about 'the advantage that the enemy has because of the larger number of vessels and because our galleys are burdened and with provisions in tow'.[50]

By the beginning of July, the enemy vessels were still in Maltese waters, so Fabrizio Sforza Colonna continued to delay his departure for the last leg of the journey. Meanwhile, Grand Master Wignacourt sent a frigate from Malta to reinforce the flotilla. On 10 or 11 July the galleys of the order left Sicily. All on board would have been in a state of alert, fully armed for combat. In the event, the journey passed without incident. On 12 July, in the fierce heat of midsummer, Caravaggio arrived in the harbour of Malta's capital city, Valletta.

To a man in search of renewal and redemption, it must have been an inspiring sight. An entirely new city, built of honey-coloured limestone that glowed pink in the sun, Valletta had been constructed at breakneck speed in just forty years. After the turmoil of the Great Siege, the knights realized that they had to fortify the narrow headland known as the Xiberras Promontory, which connected the island's two principal harbours. The construction of the new capital by an army of slaves, on the steepest incline of the headland, had been an immense undertaking but once complete it meant that the knights' principal garrison was all but impregnable. It was named in honour of Jean de la Valette, Grand Master during the siege. The pope's best military engineer, Francesco Laparelli, was responsible for the plan. The sheer stone fortifications of the citadel rose directly from the craggy outcrop of the island itself, with the sea acting as a moat on both sides.

Within its walls, Valletta was laid out on the Renaissance model of the ideal city. The principal architect responsible for the buildings was Girolamo Cassar, who was from Malta but had studied in Rome. His palaces and churches were designed to reflect the knights' ideals of Christian sobriety and military discipline, with long, severe façades of rusticated stone. The streets were laid out in a grid, with nine thoroughfares running across the peninsula and twelve running from top to bottom. Their strict geometry was softened by gardens and fountains, providing shade and water. Getting from the harbour end of Valletta, up the steep hill to the centre of town, and to the grand Cathedral of St John, was hard work even for the fittest. (Centuries later, the club-footed English poet Byron would bid farewell to Malta with the words 'adieu, ye cursed streets of stairs'.)

Approaching Malta for the first time, Caravaggio was surrounded by symbols of the island's fierce rule of law. On the first promontory on the left of the harbour was the forbidding spectacle of a gallows. Within the harbour itself, prominent on the left-hand side, was the Castel Sant'Angelo, where many of the most famous events of the siege had taken place. By the time of Caravaggio's arrival, it had become a prison for disorderly knights. Another hallowed site from the recent Maltese past was the Castel Sant'Elmo, where so many members of the order had lost their lives in 1565. A late sixteenth-century German visitor to Malta, Hieronymus Megiser, noted that some of the rocks there were still visibly sprinkled with gore. The stains were pointed out with pride by his Maltese hosts, as the glorious blood of Christian martyrs.

Malta was a remote and harsh place, rocky and sun-parched, unlike anywhere Caravaggio had ever known. But it was also fertile, having been famous since antiquity for the quality of its cotton – Cicero had had his clothes made on Malta – as well as for the sweetness of its honey and its bounteous quantities of almonds, olives, figs and dates. As Megiser noted, the island encompassed two utterly distinct societies, 'Malta Africana' and 'Malta Europeana'. The world of the indigenous islanders had remained unchanged for centuries. Its people were dark-skinned, spoke a language incomprehensible to Europeans and lived in humble settlements much like the tribal villages of nearby coastal north Africa. Cosmopolitan Valletta was utterly different, a flammable blend of extreme Christian piety, simmering military aggression and barely contained sexual dissipation.

To the English poet and adventurer George Sandys, who unknowingly followed in Caravaggio's footsteps four years later, the two Maltas were indeed worlds apart:

> The *Malteses* are little lesse tawnie than the *Moores*, especially those of the country, who go halfe-clad, and are indeed a miserable people: but the Citizens are altogether Frenchified; the Great Maister, and major parts of the Knights being *French* men. The women wear long blacke stoles, wherewith they cover their faces (for it is a great reproch to be seen otherwise) who converse not with men, and are guarded according to the manner of Italy. But the jealous are better secured, by the number of allowed curtizans (for the most part *Grecians*) who sit playing in their doores on instruments; and with the art of their eyes inveagle these continent by vow, but contrary in practise, as if chastitie were only violated by marriage. They here stir early and late, in regard of the immoderate heat, and sleep at noone day.[51]

It is not known where Caravaggio lived during his time on the island. Prospective knights on their first tours of duty were given accommodation in the auberge belonging to their particular Langue, or country. Altogether there were eight Langues, of Italy, Provence,

Auvergne, England, France, Aragon, Castille and Germany. The Italian auberge, with its long façade decorated with trophies and escutcheons, was close to the main city gate of San Giorgio. But Caravaggio is unlikely to have lodged there with the other Italian novices, because when he first arrived no one other than his Colonna protectors seems to have known of his plan to be elevated to a knighthood. It appears from the archive that his desire for the Cross of St John was not communicated to the highest levels of the order until the winter of 1607. So he probably lived in the household of Fabrizio Sforza Colonna, at least during the first months of his stay.

Caravaggio was swiftly made aware of the sharp divide between public morality and the private behaviour of the knights and their companions. On 14 July, two days after his arrival on the island, a welcome party was thrown for him and a number of other new arrivals by a Sicilian knight named Giacomo Marchese. Marchese was overheard joking about a Greek painter who kept two wives. But for at least one of the other guests, it was no laughing matter. Judge Paolo Cassar, a doctor of civil and canon law, promptly denounced the unnamed painter to the Inquisition. On 26 July, Caravaggio was called by the Inquisitor, Leonetto Corbiaro, to answer questions about the identity of the alleged bigamist. He answered with his customary reticence, learned in the courts of Rome:

> About that which you ask me, most Reverend sir, I know nothing except that in the house of the Knight Fra Giacomo de Marchese there was staying a Greek painter who arrived with the galleys, but about the rest I have nothing to say concerning the said knight nor about anything which concerns the Holy Office [of the Inquisition] also I know nothing of the name of the said painter nor of which country he claims as his homeland.[52]

The case fizzled out, but it was a clear sign of how easy it could be to get into trouble with the law on Malta. Even more fearsome than the Inquisition was the Grand Master, Alof de Wignacourt, whose rule on the island was absolute. 'This man is a Pickard borne,' Sandys would write, 'about the age of sixtie, and hath governed eight years. His name and title, *The illustrious and most reverent Prince my Lord Frier Alosius of Wignian-court, Greate Maister of the Hospitall of*

Sainte Johns of Jerusalem: Prince of Malta and Goza [*sic*]. For albeit
a Frier (as the rest of the knights) yet is he an absolute Soveraigne, and
is bravely attended on by a number of gallant young gentlemen.'[53]
Like all Knights of Malta, Wignacourt was bound by vows of poverty
and celibacy. But he lived in grand style none the less, in the Grand
Master's Palace, an elegant building constructed around a courtyard
garden, with walls frescoed with scenes of the Great Siege by a minor
Italian artist named Matteo Perez d'Aleccio – who, like Caravaggio,
had fled to Malta after getting into trouble in Rome. Wignacourt surrounded himself with young page boys, the flower of the European
aristocracy. On his death, he bequeathed to the order more than 200
slaves and a fortune in ransom money.[54]

As supreme authority on Malta, Wignacourt was answerable only
to the pope. He presided over the Venerable Council of the order,
composed of the eight Conventual Bailiffs – one for each Langue –
and the Grand Priors. The Venerable Council framed the order's statutes. Wignacourt was also in charge of the Criminal Council, which
had the often demanding job of ensuring that those statutes were
obeyed. As the leader of an all-male elite fighting unit, especially
trained in privateering, pillage and kidnap, one of his main priorities
was simply to preserve order. This was by no means easy, and a blind
eye was diplomatically turned to certain habitual misdemeanours.
Wignacourt made no attempt to close down Valletta's many brothels:
in 1581, when one of his predecessors had attempted to eliminate
prostitution on Malta, the result had been a full-scale riot. But other
offences were dealt with swiftly and ruthlessly, on a sliding scale of
punishment.

The list of prohibitions and mandatory penalties is itself a testament to the difficulty of maintaining order among several hundred
proud Knights of Malta. Punishment for the offence of being incor-
rectly dressed, without the eight-pointed cross of the order, was the
'quarantaine', which insisted that the miscreant be confined to his
auberge for forty days, during which time he was to fast in penitence
and submit to regular public floggings by the vice-prior in the conventual church. Repetition of the same offence brought a three-month
prison sentence. The penalty for rowdy behaviour inside the auberges
was deprivation of seniority within the hierarchy of the knights.

Insults traded between brother knights in the Grand Master's presence meant the loss of three years' seniority. More serious crimes were punished by defrocking, the permanent deprivation of a knight's habit. This was the penalty ordained for a variety of offences, including assault on a fellow knight, heresy, apostasy, theft, duelling and the abandonment of comrades in battle.[55] If a knight killed in anger, he was sentenced to a traditional Maltese death. The procedure was described by George Sandys: 'If one of them be convicted of a capitall crime, he is first publicly disgraced in the Church of Saint John where he received his Knight-hood, then strangled and thrown into the sea at night-time.'[56]

It would be harder to enter the brotherhood of Malta than Caravaggio had perhaps imagined. Knights of Justice were the elite of the order, from whose ranks the Grand Crosses who sat on the Venerable Council were drawn, but to be considered for such a knighthood the candidate had to be able to prove unbroken noble lineage of two hundred years. Below Knights of Justice came Knights of Grace, but they too had to prove a high degree of nobility. Considering his humble origins, Caravaggio could only aspire to the still lower Knighthood of Magistral Obedience, which was reserved for men of merit – valent'huomini, to use his own favoured terminology – and awarded at the discretion of the Grand Master. But just before Caravaggio's arrival on the island, Wignacourt had introduced a statute putting an end to the conferment of such knighthoods. He had grown irritated by the number of applicants for them and felt they were cheapening the status of the brotherhood as a whole. Honorific knighthoods were viewed as being open to corruption, tradeable awards akin to a form of simony. On his travels in Palestine, Sandys was contemptuously amused by the sight of an apothecary from Aleppo being dubbed a knight in exchange for hard cash.

If Caravaggio were to become a Knight of Malta, special arrangements would have to be made by the Grand Master himself. Little is known about the artist's activities during his first several months on the island. But on the evidence of three pictures that he painted during the second half of 1607, he was working hard to impress those in the upper echelons of the order. With each new commission, he moved closer to the centre of power.

SIGNED IN BLOOD

Soon after establishing a workshop on Malta, Caravaggio painted a sombre devotional picture for Ippolito Malaspina. *St Jerome Writing* had the same subject as the picture painted for the papal nephew, Scipione Borghese, two years earlier. The image of the saint, this time, is less a generic old man and more the portrait of an actual individual. Spotlit in the gloom of his study, Jerome has wispy grey hair scraped across the sunburned crown of his head, deep wrinkles, a slightly cauliflowered right ear – emphasized by the raking light – and a dimpled, beak-like nose. In contrast with his coppery, weathered face, his bare torso is pale and white. His physique is lean, although the skin at his ribs and belly has begun to sag with age.

The saint looks down at the pages of the book in which he is writing. In his right hand he holds a quill, in his left an inkpot. On the desk before him lie three symbolic objects: a stone the colour of a bruise – the stone with which, according to his legend, he used to beat his breast; a tip-tilted skull, eyes gaping and teeth glinting; and a crucifix on which a stretched figurine of the agonized Christ is represented in shadowy foreshortening.

To the saint's right, his red cardinal's hat hangs from a rudimentary peg. All else is in shadow. Semi-nude, swathed up to the waist in a sheet of red drapery, Jerome the scholar-saint looks more like a military man sitting up in bed before first light, writing out the orders of the day. The sinews at the juncture of neck and shoulderblade are taut with nervous energy. Did Caravaggio model him on Malaspina himself? One of Wignacourt's closest advisers, Malaspina had been away from Malta for four years, and had returned on the same flotilla that had brought the artist to the island. Now in his late sixties, he had chosen to rededicate himself to the Order of St John, and to God. Caravaggio's picture was perhaps intended to commemorate that decision.

With its skilful foreshortenings, dramatic light and shade and compellingly lifelike depiction of dignified old age, the picture was a virtuoso performance and a demonstration of just what Caravaggio could do for the Knights of the Order of St John. Malaspina would eventually bequeath the *St Jerome Writing* to the chapel of the Italian Langue – it now hangs in the co-cathedral of St John in Valletta, having survived a heist in 1985, during which it was cut out of its frame with a Stanley knife – but originally he hung it in his house. Because Malaspina was in Wignacourt's immediate circle, the painting would soon have been seen by all the right people. More commissions followed.

In the autumn or winter of 1607 Caravaggio was approached to paint the likeness of one of the most senior and distinguished Knights of Malta, Fra Antonio Martelli. The picture, which now hangs in the Pitti Palace in Florence, is one of the most impressive of all seventeenth-century portraits. This depiction of an obdurate and forceful man, in lean old age, rheumy eyes gazing off into the distance, anticipates the mature portraiture of Rembrandt by some half a century. In the darkness of Caravaggio's Maltese studio, the air feels dense with thought. The old warrior, mouth set in an expression of habitual determination, looks out and away – but it is really as if he is looking *within*, sifting his own memories and remembering his old battles. His left hand rests on the pommel of his sword, a swiftly painted tangle of finely wrought metal, while in his right hand he holds a string of Rosary beads. These are the twin attributes of the Friar of War, dedicated at once to God and the profession of arms. Caravaggio has painted the hands so cursorily they seem unfinished. It was the sitter's face that fascinated him.

Martelli was seventy-four years old when Caravaggio painted him and had been a Knight of Malta for almost fifty, a doughty veteran of the Great Siege and numerous other battles and engagements. He had served, for many years, as Ferdinando I de' Medici's *consigliere di guerra*, his 'councillor of war'. He was a canny and gifted diplomat, the scion of an ancient Florentine family that had made the mistake of opposing the Medici earlier in the sixteenth century, and had paid the price. Martelli had undone the damage and re-established the influence of his family in the Grand Duchy of Florence. In the portrait he is dressed for winter, in a thick black monastic habit with a white long-sleeved shirt underneath. A large, eight-pointed cross of the Order of St John gleams on his chest in the half-dark. The habit marks him out as a Grand Cross of the order, the highest rank to which an elite Knight of Justice could rise. Martelli was indeed a member of the Venerable Council, an ally of Wignacourt and Malaspina. He had been appointed the order's Prior of Messina in 1606,[57] and was regarded in Medici circles as something of a phenomenon: as late as 1618, when Martelli was in his eighty-fifth year, the Grand Duke of Florence would appoint him General of Artillery in Tuscany. There is a strong sense of his formidable character in Caravaggio's portrait, even a hint of hero-worship about it. As a child, thanks to the plague, he had known few men on whom to model himself. A man like Martelli may have awoken in him not only admiration, but something resembling the emotion of filial respect.

By November or December, Caravaggio was painting the Grand Master himself. According to Bellori he depicted Wignacourt both seated and standing with a page, but only the second picture survives. It can be seen in the Louvre. The painting is somewhat damaged but remains none the less an impressive essay in a type of grand manner portrait originally pioneered by Titian in his work for the Spanish royal family more than half a century earlier. It is a more old-fashioned, stiff, conservative work of art than the portrait of Martelli, which may be a reflection of Alof de Wignacourt's unbending sense of his own importance. Instead of a monastic habit the Grand Master wears an ornate suit of mid sixteenth-century armour, a deliberate anachronism intended to evoke the glorious past, and in particular the heroism of the Great Siege. Bellori says the portrait was actually hung in the knights' armoury, where the similarly ornate armour of Jean de la Valette was also displayed, which must have reinforced the association. He holds the baton of high office in his gauntleted hands.

Wignacourt had a prominent wart on the left side of his nose, which Caravaggio has been careful to shroud in shadow. The Grand Master looks off to one side, but his look, unlike that of Martelli, is neither introspective nor retrospective. He looks to the future with necessary vigilance, the guardian of Christendom's frontline with Islam. While Wignacourt strikes a slightly creaking pose of authority, his adolescent pageboy enters the scene, stage right, with an expression of cool wariness in his wide and curious eyes. He holds the Grand Master's helmet against his downy cheek, allowing its plumes to caress the side of his face. The pageboy's identity is unknown, but a possible candidate is Alessandro Costa, son of Caravaggio's patron Ottavio Costa. He had travelled to Malta on the same flotilla as the artist, entering Wignacourt's entourage of pages on his arrival. Within the conventions of state portraiture, he represents innocent youth, in contrast with Wignacourt's wise old age. But his presence also adds an irregular, unexpected frisson of eroticism to the scene. Caravaggio's evident interest in the boy threatens to unbalance the composition.

By all accounts, Wignacourt was delighted by the portrait. The artist's biographers are unanimous in asserting that Caravaggio received the cross of the Order of St John as a direct reward for the Grand Master's portrait. Wignacourt may even have discussed the matter with him during sittings for the picture. If so, he would have made Caravaggio aware that there was a considerable stumbling block to the conferment of the honour. Having abolished the Knighthood of Magistral Obedience, the only kind for which Caravaggio might have been eligible, Wignacourt would have to appeal directly to Pope Paul V for permission to reinstate it: he was obliged to seek papal support whenever going beyond the letter of the order's statutes. That is exactly what he did.

On 29 December 1607 the Grand Master wrote to his ambassador in Rome, Francesco Lomellini. He briefed Lomellini on his desire to bestow knighthoods of Magistral Obedience on Caravaggio and one other person. He did not name the painter, simply referring to him as 'a person of great virtues, honourable, and respectful', and explaining that he wanted to give him a knighthood in order so as 'not to lose' him – '*per non perderlo*'. Wignacourt wrote separately to the historian of the Order of St John, Giacomo Bosio, who was then in Rome, urging him also to lobby for papal favour in the matter. In addition, Wignacourt's secretary, Francesco dell'Antella, wrote in support of the petition to grant the two knighthoods. The message was duly passed on to the pope himself:

Most Holy Father, the Grand Master of the [Order of the] Hospital of St John of Jerusalem wishes to honour some persons who have shown virtue and merit and have a desire and devotion to dedicate themselves to his service and that of the [Order of the] Hospital and does not have at the present moment any more suitable way of doing so; he therefore humbly begs Your Holiness to deign to grant to him, by a Brief, the authority and power for one time only to decorate with the habit of a

Magistral Knight two persons favoured by him and to be nominated by him; despite the fact that one of the two had once committed homicide in a brawl and despite that it is prohibited by the Chapter General of the Order that the habit of a Magistral Knight can be conceded any further. He begs to receive this request as a very special favour, because of the great desire he holds to honour such persons who have shown virtue and merit. And may the Lord preserve you for a long time.[58]

The request was granted at once. Papal permission was given in a missive of 7 February 1608, spelling out that 'It has pleased the Most Holy Father to approve for Aloph de Wignacourt Grand Master of the [Order of the] Hospital of St John of Jerusalem authority to present the habit of a Magistral Knight to two persons favoured by him despite the fact that one of the two committed homicide in a brawl.' On 15 February the letter reached Malta. Wignacourt had secured for Caravaggio his much coveted knighthood.

There were two conditions. Like any other novice, he could not be dubbed knight until he had spent a full year on the island, so he would have to stay until mid July to receive the honour. He would also have to pay a tribute known as the *passaggio* before he could be allowed to enter the brotherhood. Being a fugitive from justice, Caravaggio had little money, but Wignacourt had a solution to that as well. The Oratory of St John, attached to the co-cathedral of St John in Valletta, had only recently been completed. It was one of the most important buildings in Malta's new capital. But it had no altarpiece. If Caravaggio would supply one, the picture would be accepted in lieu of his *passaggio*.

The subject specified for the work was *The Beheading of St John*, which also meant a deadline before the end of summer. Wignacourt wanted to unveil the work on the Feast Day of the Decollation of St John – the day that marked his beheading – which was 29 August. Ideally the artist would have finished the work by July, so he could receive his knighthood exactly a year after his arrival on the island.

It is intriguing that Wignacourt should have omitted Caravaggio's name from his letter to the pope. Perhaps he had been tipped off that there were those in Rome who would lobby against the petition if they knew that it was to benefit Caravaggio; or perhaps he worried that Paul V might himself object, because conferment of a Maltese knighthood automatically commuted a capital sentence to one of exile. The reference to a man 'who had once committed homicide in a brawl' was a smokescreen: the phrase made it hard for anyone in Rome to connect the candidate for a Maltese knighthood with Caravaggio, who had killed a man not in a brawl but in a premeditated duel, which was a very different matter. It is possible that Caravaggio himself had lied about the murder to Wignacourt – duelling was banned on Malta and greatly frowned upon by the Grand Crosses of the order. Whether he did so or not, the Grand Master himself was being economical with the truth. It seems he was absolutely determined that the deal should go through.

Wignacourt was a dynamic and formidable Grand Master, with great aspirations for Malta. Caravaggio's portrait shows him as the proud absolute ruler of a brand-new city, founded on the monastic ideals of Christian chivalry. But he must have been conscious to a degree that Valletta was something of an artistic desert. Wignacourt had tried once before to address that deficiency, attempting but failing to lure an unnamed Florentine painter to Malta in 1606.[59] The Grand Master knew that it would be hard to tempt any truly sought-after artist to faraway, provincial, sun-baked Malta, in the shadow of the threat of Islam. But now fate had brought Caravaggio to the island. He had even come of his own accord.

The Grand Master's ambitions and the painter's needs might appear to have dovetailed perfectly: Wignacourt would get his great altarpiece, while Caravaggio would get his knighthood, and the death sentence that had hung over him for nearly two years would be lifted. But the painter may not have understood the true nature of the deal being dangled in front of him. That phrase in Wignacourt's first letter to his Roman ambassador Lomellini, in which he talks of knighting Caravaggio in order 'not to lose him', is telling. Not to lose him carries a further implication, which might seem obvious but has gone largely overlooked: to keep him. By giving Caravaggio a knighthood, Wignacourt would automatically acquire the power to do just that. Under the statutes of the order no Knight of Malta was allowed to leave the island, even for a day, without the Grand Master's permission.[60] For Caravaggio, his knighthood was a short-cut back to Rome.

But there is nothing to indicate that Wignacourt viewed it like that at all. It was just as likely his way of laying a trap. Having got a great painter to Malta, why should he ever let him go?

There was no reason why any of this would have dawned on Caravaggio until his actual arming as a Knight of Magistral Obedience. Only then need he be informed about the extent of the obedience required of him. Meanwhile, in the spring and summer of 1608, he concentrated on planning and painting the largest altarpiece of his entire career, *The Beheading of St John*. The daunting scale of the work, which was to be over ten feet high and more than fifteen feet across, meant that he probably had to change workshop.[61] In addition, models would have to be found and a few necessary props sourced: a butcher's knife, a gilded plate, a sheepskin and a length of rope.

The story of St John's martyrdom is told in the New Testament books of Matthew (14:3–12) and Mark (6:17–28). King Herod had thrown John into prison because he had dared to reprimand him for his illicit marriage to Herodias. Herod's consort plotted with her daughter, Salome, to bring about John's execution. At the king's birthday feast, Salome danced so seductively for Herod that he granted her anything she desired. She asked for the head of John the Baptist. An executioner beheaded the saint in his prison. The severed head was laid on a platter and given to Salome at the feast.

There were two main conventions for artists painting John's martyrdom. Either they depicted the moment when the dish was served up to a gloating Salome, or they depicted the instant before the beheading, with the executioner poised to strike. Caravaggio painted his own version of the latter subject, but imagined something even darker taking place. The scene is set in the gloomy courtyard of an oppressively harsh prison, beside a gateway built of massively heavy stone quoins and a barred window at which two prisoners huddle pathetically for a glimpse of the killing. The executioner is another in the line of Caravaggio's impassive, workmanlike killers. He leans over the body of his victim, whose hands are trussed cruelly behind his back. The executioner has laid down his sword, the cold steel of its blade glinting on the dull earth.

Shockingly he has made a botch of the job, cutting deep into the saint's neck, deep enough to sever the jugular, but leaving the head still attached to the trunk. Now he reaches behind him for the sharp-ened knife in the scabbard at his belt, which he needs to cut the last flap of flesh connecting John's head to his body. He grabs the saint by his hair so that he can get at the place he needs to with his knife. He might be a butcher working at his slab.

Does the saint still live? His pale face seems animated, as if he were in his last death agonies, recoiling from the gurgled, choking rush of his own blood. In the frozen world of Caravaggio's painting, he must wait forever for the *coup de grâce*. A swathe of red drapery has been thrown carelessly across his otherwise naked body. This sudden shock of colour in the prison gloom emphasizes the atrocious nature of what is taking place. It is like a pictogram or symbol of bloodletting in the dark. The martyr lies on a sheepskin, which symbolically makes of him a blessed Christian lamb, brought to sacrifice. The painter has contrived to pick out the martyr's naked left foot with a stray shaft of light. Surrounded by pools of darkness, placed next to some twisting coils of rope, it is almost like a still life detail – separate from the rest of the scene and yet emblematic of the poor and painfully solitary death which the saint endures.

The novices of the Order of St John listened to sermons and received instruction in the oratory for which Caravaggio's painting was des-tined. The place was both a school for the martyrs of the future and a burial ground for the martyrs of the past – the bones of the knights who had died at the Great Siege were interred beneath its stone-flagged floor. Within the oratory, novices were trained in the hard ways of the Knights of Malta and made to understand that they too might have to face death in a distant land at the hands of unbelievers. Caravaggio's altarpiece was designed to make sure that they could be under no illusions about what that might mean. A martyr's death brought the reward of eternal glory with the saints in heaven, but there would be nothing glorious about the death itself. It could be a death much like this one, a sordid act of butchery in a dark and lonely place. The picture is like a catechism, an asking of questions. Are you sure you have it in you to be a Knight of the Order of St John? Are you ready to die? To die like this?

Next to the executioner, underscoring Caravaggio's transposition of John's legend to a cruel present, stands the figure of a Turkish jailor with heavy black keys dangling at his belt. He directs operations with an air of weary impatience, pointing unnecessarily at the richly chased and gilded plate onto which the severed head must be placed. Beside him stands an old woman with her head in her hands, distraught at the spectacle of the martyrdom. She is another version of the goitrous peasant woman gazing piteously at the crucified body of the saint in *The Crucifixion of St Andrew*. She stands for Christian pity and prayer. The main group of five figures is completed by that of the serving girl who has been sent to collect the head.[62] Her pose has an eloquent woodenness about it. She is trying her best to carry out a task that appals her, affecting a mechanical workaday demeanour that the expression on her face belies. She stares fixedly down at the plate in her hands, pursing her lips like somebody desperately stifling the impulse to puke.

What she cannot bear to look at is the spurting of the saint's blood from the deep gash in his nearly severed neck. It is so thick that it resembles a skein of red wool laid on the ground. Beneath the main pool of coagulating gore, there lie some thinner threads of blood. Anyone looking closely at the picture sees that they have been made to spell out the letters of Caravaggio's own name: 'F. Michelangelo'. Inscribed in the blood of St John the Baptist himself, this is the only example of the artist's signature. He had never signed a painting before, and would never do so again.

This boldly idiosyncratic gesture has been subjected to a variety of anachronistic modern interpretations. It has been read, for example, as the veiled retrospective confession of Caravaggio, the murderer; and as a proto-Freudian token of his fetishistic obsession with violence and death. But the true meaning of the signature in blood is clear and unambiguous. The key to it lies in a tradition of Christian symbolism to which Caravaggio had already alluded earlier in his career. Years before, when painting *The Martyrdom of St Matthew* for the Contarelli Chapel in Rome, he had evoked the ancient link between martyrdom and baptism by having Matthew's blood flow into a baptismal pool. The blood signature alluded to the same association, although its meaning was subtly different. In *The Martyrdom of Matthew*, it was Matthew and Matthew alone who had been reborn into immortality through his own martyrdom. In *The Beheading of St John*, it is not only the martyr who gains eternal life. Caravaggio himself has been symbolically reborn, through his acceptance into the ranks of those dedicated to the martyred John the Baptist.

The Beheading of St John was Caravaggio's gift to the Knights of Malta, a due paid in lieu of his *passaggio* into the Order of St John. Its completion, therefore, marked his entry into the brotherhood of knights. Hence that prominent 'F' before his name. It stands for 'Fra', or 'Brother', the official prefix of any Knight of St John.[63] The artist's signature, written in John the Baptist's blood, was a public proclamation. It was Caravaggio's way of asserting that his own mortal sin, the murderous letting of a man's blood, had been washed away by the blood of his new patron saint. Now he could return to Rome, not as a criminal but as a proud Christian soldier.

COMPETING WITH MICHELANGELO

Caravaggio must have added his signature to the work some time shortly after 14 July 1608; because it was on that date, exactly a year and two days after his arrival on Malta, that he was invested with the habit of a Knight of Magistral Obedience and given the title 'Fra Michelangelo Merisi'. The address given by the Grand Master at the ceremony of the investiture can only have increased the artist's pleasure in his newfound status. In the Bull of his reception, Wignacourt went so far as to compare Caravaggio with Apelles of Kos, the celebrated painter of ancient Greece:

Whereas it behooves the leaders and rulers of commonweals to prove their benevolence by advancing men, not only on account of their noble birth but also on account of their art and science whatever it may be, so that human talent, hopeful of obtaining reward and honour, might apply itself to praiseworthy studies:

And whereas the Honorable Michael Angelo, born in the town Carraca, in the vernacular called Caravaggio, in Lombardy, having been called to this city, burning with zeal for the order, has communicated to us his fervent wish to be adorned with our habit and insignia.

Therefore, as we wish to gratify the desire of this excellent painter,

so that our island of Malta, and our order, may at last glory in this
adopted disciple and citizen with no less pride than the island of Kos
(also within our jurisdiction) extols her Apelles; and that, should we
compare him to more recent artists of our age, we may not afterwards
be envious of the artistic excellence of any other outstanding man of
equally important name and brush . . . and as we wish to comply with
the pious wish of the aforesaid Michael Angelo, we receive and admit
him, by the grace of God almighty and by a papal authorization especially granted to us for the purpose, to the rank of Brethren and Knights
known as Brethren and Knights of Obedience . . .[64]

This pretty sequence of tributes pays the greatest compliment of all
to Wignacourt himself, because if Caravaggio is a new Apelles, the
Grand Master is by implication a second Alexander the Great. The
author of the encomium, with its flowery phrases and polished rhetoric, was almost certainly Wignacourt's erudite secretary, Francesco
dell'Antella, who had also played a part in lobbying for Caravaggio's
knighthood some months earlier.[65] Dell'Antella was a learned Florentine, who for a Knight of Malta prided himself on his sophistication
and classical learning. He also took an unusually strong interest in
art. He was himself a gifted amateur draughtsman, who produced an
impressively detailed drawing of Valletta as one of the illustrations for
his friend Giacomo Bosio's history of the Order of St John. Dell'Antella
would eventually become an official member of the Accademia del
Disegno in Florence, the first Italian art academy, founded by Giorgio
Vasari in the mid sixteenth century.[66] Like Caravaggio, dell'Antella
was a proud and stormy man with a tendency to violence. He had even
killed Wignacourt's own nephew in a swordfight, but had been mag-
nanimously forgiven by the Grand Master on the grounds that he had
been unjustly provoked. This similarity of temperament and history
may have given the two men some affinity.

Perhaps as a gesture of gratitude to dell'Antella, perhaps to commission, Caravaggio painted a wry and learned cabinet picture for
him, *Sleeping Cupid*. The mischievous and malign child-god lies sleeping, one wing folded beneath him, the other reduced to the barely
perceptible rim of a feathery arc. In his left hand he limply holds a
bow, of Indo-Persian design, and a feathered dart of love. A dim light

illuminates the scene, suggestive of the first glimmers of dawn. The picture is a darker, drowsier, dreamlike version of the *Omnia vincit amor* painted in 1602 for Vincenzo Giustiniani. This time the Cupid is not an adolescent boy but a child, with the plump, fleshy body and heavy, lolling head of a toddler.

The painting is close in spirit to a poem about a statue of sleeping Cupid in Giambattista Marino's *La Galeria*, an anthology of verse inspired by works of art both real and imaginary. Marino was a close contemporary of Caravaggio, and had been a friend of his in Rome, so it is possible that the painter had the poet's verses in mind when he painted his picture.

Marino begins by warning the prospective visitor to his poetical museum against waking the image of the sleeping child:

> Guàrdati Peregrino
> non gli andar si vicino,
> nol desar, prega, ch'egli
> dorma in eterno pur, né mai si svegli.
> Se tu'l sonno tenace
> rompi al fanciul sagace,
> desto il vedrai più forte
> trattar quell'armi, ond'è
> e peggior che Morte.

> Look out, Pilgrim
> do not get so close,
> do not rouse him, pray that he
> sleeps forever and never wakes up.
> If you break the clever boy's sleep,
> right away you will see him yet more strongly
> take up those weapons that make him
> worse than death.[67]

Marino's sleeping child is lost in cruel dreams of deceptions, massacres and sufferings. Dawn is breaking and he will soon awake to visit more miseries of love on his countless victims. The poem ends with a question, and a joking reminder that the subject of all these fears and fantasies is after all merely a work of art:

Qual tu ti sia, che 'l miri,
temi non vivi e spiri?
Stendi securo il passo:
toccal pur, scherza teco, egli è di sasso.

Whoever you are, who gaze upon him,
do you fear lest he live and breathe?
Lengthen your stride with confidence, do not tiptoe,
Touch him even – I was teasing you – he is made of stone.

Caravaggio's painting also plays teasingly on the boundary between art and reality. The sleeping boy is an image, but of a disconcertingly lifelike kind. His teeth can be seen glinting behind his half-closed lips. The abandon with which his head is thrown back and the look of absorption on his face powerfully conjure the illusion of a real child caught up in a vivid dream. But there are other ways of looking at this picture too. Like Marino's poem, Caravaggio's painting looks back knowingly to the world of antiquity. Not only does it evoke the myth of Cupid; it also calls to mind the many ancient Greek legends about images of art so deceptively convincing that they seemed real – the painted grapes of Xeuxis which, as Pliny the Elder relates, fooled the birds into pecking at them, or the statue of a woman infused with such love by the sculptor Pygmalion that she actually came to life and stepped down off her pedestal. In painting the *Sleeping Cupid*, Caravaggio was making his own contribution to the imaginary art gallery of the classical past – and living up to the classical compliment that had so recently been paid to him at his investiture as a Knight of Malta. He had been dubbed the new Apelles, and now he was wittily acting the part.

There was yet another layer of allusion for the learned Francesco dell'Antella to enjoy as he contemplated his new possession, this time to a more recent work of art. The subject of Cupid asleep was famously associated with Caravaggio's namesake, Michelangelo Buonarroti. When Michelangelo was young, he had created a sculpture of a *Sleeping Cupid* so perfectly classical in spirit that he was able to pass it off as a genuine antique work of art. Giorgio Vasari tells the story:

[He] set himself to make from another piece of marble a Cupid that was sleeping, of the size of life. This, when finished, was shown ...

to Lorenzo di Pier Francesco [Medici] as a beautiful thing, and he, having pronounced the same judgement, said to Michelangelo: 'If you were to bury it under ground and then send it to Rome treated in such a manner as to make it look old, I am certain that it would pass for an antique, and you would thus obtain much more for it than by selling it here.' It is said that Michelangelo handled it in such a manner as to make it appear an antique; nor is there any reason to marvel at that, seeing as he had genius enough to do it, and even more.[68]

Michelangelo Buonarroti had created a sculpture of Cupid to rival the masterpieces of antiquity. Now Michelangelo Merisi was vying with him by emulating that very act of classical emulation. Implicit in the gesture was the Renaissance conceit of the *paragone*, a contest between different art forms. Michelangelo, the sculptor, had given tangible form to his *Sleeping Cupid*. Caravaggio, the painter, could not do that. But he could create a greater illusion of flesh and blood, and he could use his mastery of chiaroscuro to evoke the light of approaching dawn.

The *Sleeping Cupid* is essentially a *jeu d'esprit*. But it is also a vitally important painting for the understanding of Caravaggio's work as a whole, demonstrating his high degree of erudition and establishing beyond any doubt an explicit spirit of competition with Michelangelo, which had seemed at least implicit in so many of his Roman paintings, from *The Calling of St Matthew* onwards. Francesco dell'Antella made the comparison overtly when he went out of his way to show the picture to a great-nephew of Michelangelo named Francesco Buonarroti, who was also a Knight of Malta; and he then actually sent the work to Florence in the hope that the most celebrated member of the modern Buonarroti family, Fra Francesco's brother, the poet and dramatist Michelangelo the Younger, would give his opinion of it. Michelangelo the Younger clearly did see this rivalrous homage to his great-uncle's marble Cupid, because on 24 April 1610, dell'Antella wrote to him to say: 'I value now more than before my Cupid, after hearing the praise of your Lordship for which I kiss your hand.'[69]

APELLES IN PRISON

The perennially spiky Caravaggio was celebrated on Malta. In his own estimation he had always been a *valent'huomo*. Now he was truly being treated like one. Alof de Wignacourt was delighted with the painter's work for the order. According to Bellori, he was so impressed by the enormous new altarpiece for the Oratory of St John that 'as a reward, beside the honour of the Cross, the Grand Master put a gold chain around Caravaggio's neck, and made him a gift of two slaves, along with other signs of esteem and appreciation for his work'.[70] Finally, Caravaggio had got his own gold chain.

It may only have been at this moment of apparent happiness and prosperity that the full implications of being a Knight of Malta finally dawned on him. Not only was he bound to the island by the Grand Master's whim, but obliged to live in strict observance of the statutes of the order. Sexual indiscretions were liable to be tolerated as long as they were committed out of the public eye, but any other disorderly conduct would be ruthlessly dealt with under the knights' code of law. That meant no shouting or trading of insults, no fighting, no duelling with swords. For a man like Caravaggio, that was never going to be easy, especially in a town like Valletta. The city teemed with proud young noblemen from the different national Langues, intensely conscious of the most minute differences in rank and status. As Alof de Wignacourt himself remarked in a letter to the pope, 'It is impossible, in a place where so many are devoted to the profession of arms, and where so much importance is given to points of honour, that there should not be numerous fights and brawls.'[71]

Costanza Colonna and her son, Fabrizio Sforza Colonna, must have known that they were taking a calculated risk when they sent Caravaggio to Malta. Their hope must have been that the ruthless military discipline of the Order of St John would persuade him to keep his temper under control. Everything went to plan for a while, as Caravaggio painted for the central figures of the Maltese establishment. But the gamble did not pay off. The painter's pride in his knighthood came before his greatest fall from grace. Caravaggio's character had always been a volatile compound, an uneasy blend of Lenten piety and the raucous spirit of Carnival. This was never more true than on Malta.

It is impossible to know what triggered the outburst that undid him. Perhaps it was his shocked realization that Wignacourt indeed wanted 'not to lose him' – to chain him to the island, perhaps not forever, but for several more years. Whatever the cause, just weeks after admission to the Order of St John, Caravaggio lashed out against its authority. In the space of a few hours he went from hero to villain.

The early biographers are vague on the subject of what went wrong for Caravaggio on Malta. Mancini does not even mention the incident. According to Baglione, who was better informed, the cause of the trouble was an argument with a Knight of Justice: 'In Malta Michelangelo had a dispute with a Knight of Justice and somehow insulted him.'[72] Knights of Justice were higher ranking than mere Knights of Magistral Obedience. So Baglione may have meant to imply an argument over status, which was just the sort of 'point of honour' liable to cause the frequent fights between brothers of the order mentioned by Wignacourt in his letter to the pope.

Bellori's account is similar to Baglione's, except that in his version of the story Caravaggio's mercurial nature is the driving force behind the calamity. Like the hero of a Greek tragedy, he is a man ruinously undone by a fatal flaw of character: 'He lived in Malta in dignity and abundance. But suddenly, because of his tormented nature, he lost his prosperity and the support of the Grand Master. On account of an ill-considered quarrel with a noble knight, he was jailed and reduced to a state of misery and fear.'[73]

Caravaggio certainly committed an offence on Malta, one serious enough to merit imprisonment. But for centuries the exact nature of that offence remained a mystery. Generations of historians combed the archives in Malta, where the great books of statutes, crimes and punishments are still preserved in the library of the Order of St John, but to little effect. One of the volumes stored there revealed much about the aftermath of Caravaggio's crime, but nothing about the crime itself. Tantalizingly, a number of adjacent pages in that same book had been systematically and deliberately painted out with a thick layer of opaque pigment.

It was only in 2002, after the Maltese scholar Keith Sciberras had taken the initiative of X-raying some of those obscured pages, that the truth was revealed.[74] The painter had indeed become embroiled in an altercation with 'a noble knight', just as Bellori had indicated. Baglione turned out to have been right too. The aggrieved party was indeed a Knight of Justice, Fra Giovanni Rodomonte Roero, the Conte della Vezza. He was seriously injured in the incident.

One of several documents thus uncovered was a report of the preliminary results of an enquiry ordered by Grand Master Wignacourt and the Venerable Council on 19 August 1608. The purpose of that enquiry was to outline the events of a 'tumult' that had taken place the night before. The incident had involved several knights, some of whom had smashed open the door of the residence of the Organist of the Conventual Church of St John, Fra Prospero Coppini.

As a result of that preliminary enquiry, a criminal commission was set up to investigate the incident in more detail. The three investigators were Fra Philiberto de Matha, Fra Giovanni Gomes de Azevedo and Antonio Turrensi. They established that a brawl, involving seven knights altogether, had broken out in the house of Fra Coppini, but since he himself had not taken part, he was absolved. The commission found that Fra Giovanni Rodomonte Roero, the Conte della Vezza, had been the victim of an assault by six aggressors, including Caravaggio.

The artist's companions on the night in question included two senior figures in the Maltese hierarchy, both Knights of Justice like the victim, Roero. One was Fra Giulio Accarigi, who was originally from Siena but who had been a Knight of Malta since 1585. He had a reputation for violence and a criminal record to match, having spent two months in detention for assault in 1595 and a further two years in jail some ten years later. The other Knight of Justice involved was Fra Giovanni Battista Scaravello, from Turin, who had arrived on Malta in 1602 and had entered the Order of St John two years after that.

Two young novices were also implicated: Francesco Benzi, who had come to the island in 1606; and Giovanni Pecci, from Siena, who had arrived on Malta within a day of Caravaggio himself, on 13 July 1607. Both men would have known the painter as a fellow novice. One of the conditions of entry to the order was a rigorous programme of training in the selfsame Oratory of St John – also known as the

Oratory of the Novices – for which the artist had painted his altarpiece of *The Beheading of St John*. Benzi and Pecci would have prepared for their knighthoods alongside Caravaggio.

No eyewitness description of the fight has been found in the Maltese archives, so the parts played by those involved have to be deduced from the punishments each received. Accarigi and Scaravello seem to have taken minor roles. Each would eventually be given six months in jail, a relatively mild sentence in the harsh context of Maltese justice (although it is also possible that they were let off lightly on account of their rank). Benzi and Pecci were condemned to two and four years in prison respectively. The main culprits appear to have been Caravaggio himself and a certain Fra Giovanni Pietro de Ponte, who was a deacon of the church, and another frequent offender.[75] De Ponte was identified by the criminal commission as a prime mover of the assault. On the night of the fight he had been carrying a small pistol referred to as a *sclopo ad rotas*. It was a bullet or bullets from the *sclopo* that had inflicted serious wounds on Roero. De Ponte would be defrocked, deprived of his habit and denied forever his status as a Knight of Malta. Caravaggio was never sentenced for his part in the assault, for reasons that will become clear. But his crime was clearly deemed to be at least as serious as that of de Ponte, because the first report of the criminal commission into the case recommended that these two – but none of the others involved – be arrested immediately.

That report was submitted to the Venerable Council, whose members included Alof de Wignacourt, Fabrizio Sforza Colonna, Antonio Martelli and Ippolito Malaspina, on 27 August 1608. Present too would have been Wignacourt's secretary, Francesco dell'Antella, for whom Caravaggio had recently painted the *Sleeping Cupid*. But Malta's strict code of discipline, and the seriousness of the assault on the Conte della Vezza, would have given the artist's patrons and supporters no choice but to order his immediate arrest. On 28 August 1608 Caravaggio was seized and imprisoned within the forbidding precincts of the Castel Sant'Angelo.

The timing of his offence could not have been more perversely precise. Caravaggio had managed to get himself thrown into jail on the eve of one of the most important days in the calendar of the Knights of Malta: 29 August was the Feast of the Decollato, the day on which the order gathered in the Oratory of St John to remember the decapitation of its patron saint. In 1608, it was also the day Wignacourt had chosen to unveil Caravaggio's monumental altarpiece of *The Beheading of St John*. But instead of attending in his knight's robes, the painter now languished in an underground cell.

The 'tumult' cast a long shadow over the celebrations of the feast of the Decollato. To make matters worse a dispute had arisen between the confraternity responsible for arranging those celebrations, the Compagnia di San Giovanni Decollato, and the musicians of the Conventual Church – including, coincidentally, Fra Prospero Coppini, the organist whose door Caravaggio had helped to kick in. The musicians were unhappy about their pay and most of them went on strike, so that on the feast day itself neither Vespers nor the solemn Mass was sung in the oratory before Caravaggio's picture. The unveiling for which Wignacourt had planned so carefully could hardly have gone more badly wrong.

'A ROTTEN AND DISEASED LIMB'

Caravaggio spent the entire month of September detained in the *guva*, an underground cell cut directly into the rock of the Castel Sant'Angelo. It is a bell-shaped chamber, eleven feet deep, sealed by a heavy trap door, and reserved for knights who had been guilty of serious offences. The traces of their presence remain in the form of several melancholy graffiti, one of which records the last-known words of a sixteenth-century Scottish Knight of Malta, one John Sandilands: 'imprisoned forever, victim of evil triumphing over good – so much for friendship'.[76]

Caravaggio's own thoughts were less mournful and more pragmatic. Few had ever broken out of the Castel Sant'Angelo, while escape from the *guva* itself was unheard of, but he was determined to do so. Even if he could scale the walls of the rock-cut cell, he would then need to climb the ramparts of the castle itself. After that he would have to lower himself down a sheer 200-foot precipice to the sea. To do all this he would need help.

Getting off Malta itself would pose a whole tangle of other problems. Caravaggio would need a boat, skippered by a brave and corruptible captain. But the boat would be unable to collect him at the bottom of the castle cliff, because the only way to the open sea from there lay through the narrow opening of Valletta's Grand Harbour. Any vessel attempting to escape by that route would certainly have been spotted by the order's patrols. The journey would have to be made from one of the island's many small bays, and by night, to avoid detection. This meant that Caravaggio would have to swim round the promontory on which the Castel Sant'Angelo stood, then make his way to a quieter part of the island by foot, to wait for the vessel skippered by his accomplice. From there, the most logical destination would be Sicily, the nearest part of the mainland, some sixteen hours away with a favourable headwind.

Somehow, Caravaggio did indeed manage all of this. By the end of October 1608 he was in the Sicilian port town of Syracuse, some sixty miles from Malta. Bellori describes the artist's great escape in a single terse sentence: 'In order to free himself he was exposed to grave danger, but he managed to scale the prison walls at night and to flee unrecognized to Sicily, with such speed that no one could catch him.'[77] Baglione adds that a rope ladder was used in Caravaggio's escape, but neither writer makes any suggestions about who might have helped his getaway. He must have had help from someone on the inside in the Castel Sant'Angelo, but who that someone was remains a mystery.

Caravaggio was officially declared missing on 6 October, when

was heard the complaint of Lord Brother Hieronymus Varays, Procurator for the Treasury of the Order, made against brother Michael Angelo Marresi [sic] de Caravaggio who while detained in the prison of the Castle of St Angelo fled from it without permission of the most illustrious and most exalted Lord the Grand Master and departed secretly from the district, against the form of the Statute 13 concerning prohibitions and penalties: the most Illustrious and most exalted Lord the Grand Master and Venerable Council commissioned the Lord Brothers Joanni Honoret and Bladius Suarez that, through the agency of the Master Shield-Bearer, they should see that all due diligence is shown in finding out the said Brother Michael Angelo and in summoning him to appear, and should gather information about his flight . . .[78]

There is a strong implication here that an expeditionary force was sent to recapture Caravaggio and render him up to the Maltese court to face sentence both for the assault on the Conte della Vezza and for his defiance in fleeing the island. The Grand Master was known to be extremely severe on knights who transgressed Statute 13 of the order's legal code by leaving Malta without his permission. He insisted that all fugitives be returned to Valletta at once, preferably in secrecy. It was his normal practice in such cases to write to all the order's receivers in the major cities and ports of Europe to demand the immediate detainment of the renegade knight.[79] Yet seven weeks later Caravaggio was still at large in Sicily, having evaded whatever attempts had been made to rearrest him. On 27 November, his trial on Malta went ahead in his absence. The Venerable Council determined that he had escaped from prison using ropes. It decided to disgrace him and deprive him of his habit. At the same time, the council heard and passed judgement in the case of the August assault. Four of the six guilty knights were sentenced to jail terms, while the church deacon, Giovanni Pietro de Ponte, was to be defrocked like Caravaggio.

According to Maltese custom, criminal trials and ceremonial punishments were carried out in the Oratory of St John, where Caravaggio's *Beheading of St John* now hung directly over the main altar. So four days after the trial, on 1 December 1608, the ritual defrocking known as the *privatio habitus* took place in that very room. The archive records that 'a General Assembly was summoned of the Venerable Bailiffs, the Priors, Preceptors and Brothers in the Church and Oratory of St John our patron, at the sound of the bell, according to the ancient and praiseworthy custom of the Holy Order of St John of Jerusalem . . . the information inspected and carefully read out against Michelangelo Merisi de Caravaggio . . .'[80]

Wolfgang Kilian's mid seventeenth-century engraving of a criminal trial on Malta conjures up the scene of Caravaggio's *privatio habitus*. On either side of the Oratory of St John sit the massed ranks of the order's Grand Crosses. In December 1608 they would have included not only the artist's most prominent patrons such as Antonio Martelli, but also many other veterans of the great sea and land battles of recent European history – survivors of the Great Siege, of Lepanto, perhaps even the Spanish Armada. Before this assembly of heroes, Caravaggio's greatest humiliation was to take place.

In Kilian's engraving (see p. 328), the Grand Master sits, just as Alof de Wignacourt would have done, at the near end of the church. At the far end, the guilty knight kneels, directly beneath Caravaggio's depiction of St John's decapitation. Because Caravaggio was to be defrocked *in absentia*, a wooden stool draped with the habit of a Knight of Magistral Obedience would have been placed at the altar end of the church – more or less directly beneath Caravaggio's own signature, flowing in blood from the neck of John the Baptist.

Before the conclusion of the ceremony, there was one last formality to be gone through: 'The Lord Shield-Bearer ... repeated in a loud voice in the Public Assembly so that the said Brother Michael Angelo de Caravaggio being personally summoned once, twice, thrice and a fourth time, an abundant notice, did not appear nor as yet doth he appear ...' The oratory fell silent for the brief, necessary moment of Caravaggio's inevitable non-appearance. Then the robe of a Knight of Malta, so proudly but so briefly worn by him, was stripped from the stool by Grand Master Wignacourt himself, and the last damning words were written in the record: 'the said Brother Michael Angelo de Caravaggio was in the Public Assembly by the hands of the Reverend Lord President deprived of his habit, and expelled and thrust forth like a rotten and diseased limb from our Order and Society.'[81]

THE BURIAL OF ST LUCY AND A BLACK DOG CALLED CROW

Caravaggio was on the run for the second time in his life. His destination was the port town of Syracuse at the western edge of Sicily, where his old fellow apprentice, Mario Minniti, had established a thriving studio. Minniti had contacts in the town Senate. If they could be persuaded to look favourably on Caravaggio, they had the power to protect him from Maltese law. He had never been in more trouble than now. This time he had managed to alienate his entire network of

supporters, not only the Colonna and their allies, who had man-
oeuvred to get him to Malta, but also the formidable Alof de Wignacourt and his army of knights. Caravaggio desperately needed some
new friends in high places.

There is evidence that he took a deliberately circuitous route, landing at one of the island's smaller and more southerly ports, such as
Pozzallo or Scicli, before working his way north-east. En route, he
stayed in the little town of Caltagirone, some sixty miles inland from
Syracuse. A recently rediscovered eighteenth-century document
records that Caravaggio was seen visiting a church there, Santa Maria
di Gesù. He was impressed by the beauty of a sixteenth-century marble Madonna by Antonello Gagini on one of its altars. 'Whoever
wants her more beautiful, should go to heaven,' he reportedly said.[82]
Caravaggio was continuing to measure himself, as he had done
throughout his life, against the standard of Michelangelo and his
school: Gagini had been one of Michelangelo's most gifted pupils, and
was said to have assisted the sculptor on his final version of the tomb
of Pope Julius II, in the Roman church of San Pietro in Vincoli.

As the painter made his way from Caltagirone to Syracuse, he found
himself once more within a realm ruled distantly by Philip III of Spain.
The island had been praised for its warm climate and natural abundance since antiquity, but under the Spanish the majority of its people
suffered great privations and hardship. Part of the reason was Spain's
own economic crisis, caused by the sudden dwindling of its vast rev-
enues from the silver mines of Latin America, under the pressure of
competition from other European nations. A succession of Spanish
viceroys in Sicily were encouraged to bleed it of its natural resources.
The people became poorer as their rulers enriched themselves, concealing the true nature of this unequal transaction behind the grandest of
architectural façades. During the late sixteenth and early seventeenth
centuries, cities such as Syracuse, Messina and Palermo became stage-
sets for the performance of the rituals of absolute Spanish power.
Splendid new churches and palaces were built in an extravagant local
version of the Baroque style. Grand axial routes were ruthlessly cut
through the fabric of Sicily's medieval cityscapes, distracting attention
from the miserable lot of the poor, and allowing the rich to move
serenely through each city without ever seeing its warren of slums.

Travelling to Syracuse by land from the southern tip of Sicily was the best way of avoiding the pursuing knights, but Caravaggio exposed himself to other risks. Such was the discontent with Spanish rule that by the early years of the seventeenth century much of the island's interior had degenerated into lawlessness, with many regions at the mercy of competing clans of *banditti*. The Spanish authorities had retaliated against these roaming gangs with a degree of success, but travel in the rural hinterlands of Sicily was still considered dangerous by George Sandys in 1615: 'This Vice-Roy hath well purged the country of Bandities, by pardoning of one for the bringing in or death of another: who did exceedingly, and yet do too much infest it. Besides, the upland inhabitants are so inhospitable to strangers, that betweene them both there is no travelling by land without a strong guard; whom rob and murder whomsoever they can conveniently lay hold on.'[83] Despite the dangers, Caravaggio made it to Syracuse safely around the middle of October 1608.

The main source of information about Caravaggio's activities in Sicily is a manuscript of 1724 entitled *The Lives of the Messinese Painters*, written by a priest and amateur painter called Francesco Susinno. Susinno's sources were in the painters' studios of Sicily, where memories of Caravaggio's unprecedentedly emotive style of painting and perplexing personality were still strong more than a century after his death. In Susinno's words, Caravaggio 'was welcomed by his friend and colleague in the study of painting, Mario Minniti, a painter from Syracuse, from whom he received all the kindness that such a gentleman could extend to him. Minniti himself implored the Senate of that city to employ Caravaggio in some way so that he could have the chance to enjoy his friend for some time and be able to evaluate the greatness of Michelangelo, for he had heard that people considered him to be the best painter in Italy.'[84]

A commission from the Senate would mean protection from the Knights of Malta. The knights maintained an active presence in Syracuse, but so long as he was working for them, the city's fathers would look after him. Once again, Caravaggio's predicament would be his patrons' opportunity. Once again, he would be given the chance to paint his way out of trouble.

The timing of his arrival in Syracuse could hardly have been more opportune. Previously strained relations between the religious authorities and the Senate had improved in the early years of the seventeenth century, as a result of which the city had embarked on a vigorous programme of renovating its churches and monasteries, commissioning new altarpieces and boosting the cults of local saints.

One of the most actively venerated of those saints was the fourth-century martyr St Lucy, a native of Syracuse said to have met her end during the persecutions of the Emperor Diocletian. In the severe climate of the Counter-Reformation, with so many in the Roman Catholic faith calling for a return to the simple piety of the early Church, the cults of the ancient Christian martyrs were resurgent. A statue of St Lucy had already been placed on the ramparts of Syracuse, and the Senate had agreed to finance the creation of a costly silver reliquary to house some of her supposed remains. Not long before Caravaggio's arrival in the city, the authorities had also decided to restore the church most closely associated with her, the medieval basilica of Santa Lucia al Sepolcro. The church lay outside the city walls, having been built directly above the ancient Christian catacombs where, according to her legend, the virgin martyr had been interred. A local archaeologist and historian, Vincenzo Mirabella, had made a study of the site, re-emphasizing its significance in the sacred history of 'Syracuse the Faithful'. The newly restored church would need a painting telling the story of Lucy's martyrdom for its main altar. Who better to create it than 'the best painter in Italy'? The altarpiece that he produced can still be admired in the Franciscan church outside the old city walls.[85]

The subject given to Caravaggio was *The Burial of St Lucy*, the final episode in the story of her martyrdom and one seldom painted. There was a logic behind the choice. The civic and religious authorities of Syracuse were especially keen to reinforce the local cult of St Lucy, which had been severely damaged by the theft of the saint's remains during the Middle Ages. Rival cults of Lucy had been established elsewhere, most notably in Venice, where ownership of her relics was now being claimed. The authorities wanted Caravaggio's picture to remind the world that wherever her bones might have been taken, Syracuse was the original site of Lucy's miracles and the place where she had first been laid to rest.

The fullest account of her martyrdom is to be found in *The Golden Legend*. Lucy, a virgin of noble lineage, born in Syracuse, resolved to imitate the poverty and humility of Christ. She swore a vow of chastity and steadily gave away her possessions to the poor. Her former husband-to-be, a non-believer, failed at first to realize that she had converted to Christianity and suspected her of courting another man with her wealth. When she informed him that she was now a bride of Christ, he denounced her to a Roman judge named Paschasius. The judge punished the saint by giving her over to 'the ribalds of the town', instructing them 'to defoul her, and labour her so much till she be dead'. But when they came to take her away to a brothel, they could not move her. Paschasius sent for reinforcements, even for a team of oxen, but 'she abode always still as a mountain, without moving.' Then the judge ordered a great fire to be lit around her immobile form, commanding his torturers to pour boiling oil and resin on her. Throughout her ordeal, she prayed to God, so infuriating her tormentors that they thrust a sword straight through her throat. Even then she did not die, or even budge an inch, until Holy Communion was offered to her: 'Lucy never removed from the place where she was hurt with the sword, and died not till the priest came and brought the blessed body of our Lord Jesu Christ. And as soon as she had received the blessed sacrament she rendered up and gave her soul to God, thanking and praising him of all his goodness. In that same place is a church edified in the name of her . . .'

Caravaggio painted the moment just after St Lucy received communion and died. Having breathed out her soul, she lies on a bare expanse of ground. Her body is small, crumpled, pathetic. Her right arm is outstretched, the foreshortened hand reaching out like the hand of a beggar asking for charity. The other arm rests on her belly. Lucy's skin is pallid with death, her mouth slack. Her head lolls helplessly back. There is a deep gash in her neck, but no sign of burns. Her frail body is framed by the hulking figures of two gravediggers, stooping to plunge their spades into the earth. The contrast between the slight saint and the giants who have come to bury her is extreme and disconcerting. This was Caravaggio's way of continuing to suggest the brutality of Lucy's martyrdom – the death of a young woman at the hands of thuggish men – even in the moment of her burial.

The bull-necked, crop-haired gravedigger to the right, whose tightly draped buttocks have been given such rude prominence, is loutishly absorbed in his task. Were he to stand up, he would tower over all the other figures in the painting. He is a man-mountain, at least ten feet tall. His workmate is similarly gigantic but more aware of his surroundings. Veins bulge in the left forearm and right wrist, but, as he bends to dig, he loses concentration on the job in hand. He seems transfixed by the figure of the bishop, to the right of the scene, whose blessing hand is picked out by a ray of illumination. The toiling worker has suddenly become aware of the momentous, sacred nature of the ritual in which he is taking part. According to her legend, in her last moments Lucy had expressed the hope that her martyrdom might convert some of her tormentors to Christianity. In the figure of the second gravedigger, that hope is about to be realized. He has looked up, and seen the light.[86]

The picture has been much abraded by time, but its power and originality are undimmed. The strong illusion of reality is all the more impressive given the painter's bold distortions of scale and perspective. Clustered behind the body of the saint, a small group of mourners has gathered. Their faces and bodies are seen in fragments, occluded by shadow and the body of the first gravedigger, forming a collage of griefstruck response. To the right of the priest's blessing hand, a man's face has been abbreviated to little more than a furrowed brow and a pair of staring, anxious eyes; this may be a daringly cropped self-portrait. To the left, three more saddened faces appear. A bald man prepares to wipe tears from his eyes. Beside him, the much repainted figure of a woman stares impassively into space, while, between them, their bearded companion seems frozen by melancholy. At the feet of these three figures, Caravaggio has included a kneeling reprise of the old woman with her face in her hands from his recent altarpiece of *The Beheading of St John*.

The mourners are completed by a young man draped in a snaking length of red cloth, and a veiled elderly woman. His hands are clasped in front of him, at waist height, while hers are held up to her cheek. Both stare down with intense grief at the dead body on the ground in front of them. These last two mourners have been taken directly from the conventions of earlier Renaissance painting, in which

Mary and the Apostle John were depicted in exactly the same postures of grief. Caravaggio's use of this deliberate archaism evokes the Crucifixion and emphasizes the martyr's emulation of Christ. The wound in her neck and her outstretched left arm reinforce this chain of associations.

The picture has a hallucinogenic quality, the feeling again of a work painted from memory rather than from models. Just as the old woman with her head in her hands has been borrowed from Caravaggio's earlier *Beheading of St John*, the sinister figure in armour standing next to the blessing bishop is another version of Aegeas in *The Crucifixion of St Andrew*, painted in Naples in 1607. More than ever, Caravaggio's painting evokes the old, folk traditions of Italian polychrome sculpture. Lucy and those who mourn, bury and bless her could almost be mannequins of wax, dressed in real clothing and given real hair. The tall, bare room in which the burial takes place evokes the simple chapels of the old *sacro monte*, where stories of the life of Christ are told through assemblages of straining and struggling figures very much like these.

The artist may have drawn on older memories too. When plague had struck Milan in 1576 he would have seen many hasty burials and ragged funeral processions. The picture's iconography is ingeniously suggestive of hope and redemption, but its mood is overwhelmingly bleak. No angel descends to hymn the martyr's soul to heaven. Almost half the painting is dark bare stone, wall and arch both isolating and seeming to press down on the figures crowded around the dead body. The snapshot immediacy of the image, with its extremely innovative effects of cropping and occlusion, is suggestive of alienation and abandonment. Not until the middle of the nineteenth century, when Manet and Degas began to crop and cut their images in the name of capturing 'modern life', would there be anything to rival Caravaggio's weird dislocations in *The Burial of St Lucy*. The bishop and soldier, pushed to one side by the scything asymmetry of the composition, remain deeply ambiguous. Officially they stand for good and evil, light and dark, the compassionate Christian as opposed to the ruthless pagan response to a martyr's death. But they have been so brusquely sidelined by the artist that it is tempting to wonder whether he was opening the way to another view of what they might embody.

Church and state stand by, united in their ineffectiveness, as yet another innocent goes to the grave.

Perhaps with the priorities of the Senate of Syracuse in mind, Caravaggio also included a strong visual reference to the saint's original place of burial in his picture. The church of Santa Lucia was built directly on top of the city's ancient Christian catacombs, where according to legend her body had first been put into the ground. The high, arched interior in which he set *The Burial of St Lucy* was directly based on those actual catacombs, which he had visited for himself; in this way, he perpetuated the act of interment linking Lucy to the city, creating an illusion that made it look as though her body was forever about to be entombed beneath the church itself. However dark its mood, Caravaggio's painting was a brilliant stroke of propaganda for the city.

He started work on the altarpiece soon after arriving in Syracuse, probably at around the beginning of November. He must have worked extremely fast. The altarpiece was monumental in scale, the largest work of his Sicilian period and one of the largest pictures he had ever undertaken. Yet it was finished by the start of the following month, comfortably in time for St Lucy's feast day on 13 December. 'The big canvas came out so well that it became famous,' wrote Susinno; 'the idea behind it was so good that there are many copies in Messina and in other cities of the Regno.'[87]

The sources indicate that Caravaggio was in a state of nervous anxiety during much of this period. During his first weeks in Sicily, the galleys of the Order of St John were a constant and highly visible presence around the harbours of the island, including that of Syracuse.[88] Susinno records that 'Caravaggio was very distracted, restless, indifferent to his own existence: many a time he would go to bed fully dressed, with his dagger (from which he was never separated) at his side ... Even when dressed ordinarily he was always armed, so that he looked more like a swordsman than a painter.'[89] Baglione tells us that it was around this time that he acquired 'a black dog that was trained to play various tricks, which he enjoyed immensely'.[90] The animal was probably not just for amusement and company. Caravaggio gave it the ill-omened name of Corvo – 'Crow' – a raucous creature with an aggressive personality to match.

THE TYRANT'S EAR

Caravaggio may have painted *The Burial of St Lucy* in Mario Minniti's substantial workshop. It was quite unlike any of his own modest
studios. In pursuit of success and respectability, Minniti had rein-
vented himself as a gentleman-painter, employing an army of assistants to transfer his compositions from paper to canvas and adding
only the finishing touches himself. So busily productive was Minniti's
workshop that quality inevitably suffered. 'Many weak paintings by
him can be seen around,' wrote Susinno. 'If he had contented himself
with just a few public works he would have been as celebrated as
Caravaggio himself.'[91]

Caravaggio made at least one other acquaintance in Syracuse, with
whom he went on a foray to see some of the sights of the town:
Vincenzo Mirabella, antiquarian, mathematician and archaeologist.
Caravaggio may have sought his help in researching the Christian
catacombs of Syracuse, to give *The Burial of St Lucy* an authentically
antique setting: the catacombs were one of Mirabella's specialities,
and he would include a lengthy account of them in his book, the
Dichiarazioni della pianta delle antiche Siracuse, published in 1613.

Elsewhere in the same book, Mirabella would tell of how he took
Caravaggio to see another of the oldest sites of Syracuse, a huge grotto
said to have been used as a prison by the ancient tyrant Dionysus.
According to local folklore, Dionysus had ordered a deep and narrow
slit to be cut into the roof of this 'speaking cave', so named because of
its extraordinary acoustic qualities, which amplified noise in such a
way as to make the least sound perfectly audible. At the cave's single
entrance, the tyrant built a great gate, so that he could confine his
prisoners within. On the hilltop above the cave, perched directly over
the slit cut into its apex, he placed the house of his jailor. While his
captives languished hundreds of feet below, Dionysus could eaves-
drop on their every word. He could hear their admissions of guilt,
learn their plans, discover the names of their friends and allies.

After explaining all this to Caravaggio, Mirabella was struck by
the acuteness of the painter's response. 'I remember,' he wrote, 'when
I took Michelangelo da Caravaggio, that singular painter of our times,

to see that prison. And he, considering its strength, and showing his unique genius as an imitator of natural things, said: "Don't you see how the tyrant, in order to create a vessel that would make all things audible, looked no further for a model than that which nature had made herself to produce the self-same effect. So he made this prison in the likeness of an ear." Which observation, not having been noticed before, but then being known and studied afterwards, has doubly amazed the most curious minds.'[92] To this day, the great cave – now part of the Archaeological Park of Syracuse – continues to be known as 'The Ear of Dionysus'.

Judging by the portrait that serves as frontispiece to Mirabella's book, its author was a dapper and fashion-conscious gentleman with a self-consciously quizzical stare. He waxed his extravagantly long handlebar moustache and favoured the Spanish style of dress, wearing a high-necked lace ruff over a dark, finely embroidered shirt. But Mirabella was also highly respected by some of the best minds in early seventeenth-century Italy. A year after the publication of his book, he would be enrolled in Rome's foremost scientific society, the Accademia de' Lincei – named for that sharp-eyed animal, the lynx – after his friend Federico Cesi wrote a letter supporting his application to the great astronomer Galileo Galilei. In Cesi's words to Galileo, Mirabella was 'a knight from Syracuse, noble by birth and very rich, learned in Greek and Latin, man of letters and most erudite in Mathematics and primarily in the theory of Music, in which he is greatly esteemed and admired by his proposer. He has already published a worthy volume on the Antiquity of his birthplace with diligent description of the same . . .'[93] Mirabella subsequently became a friend and correspondent of Galileo himself. They exchanged letters about 'spots on the sun' and the astronomer lent 'the knight from Syracuse' telescope lenses on more than one occasion.

Mirabella was impressed by the empirical tenor of Caravaggio's thought, and by his evident interest both in acoustics and in the mechanism of the human ear. Their exchange gives a rare glimpse of Caravaggio not as a violent criminal, nor as a probable lover of young men and whores, but as an intellectual and sophisticate. This was the same man who, in Rome, had moved in a circle of speculative thinkers and connoisseurs such as Giulio Mancini and Cardinal del Monte – himself another correspondent of Galileo's – and who had befriended poets such as Giambattista Marino.

But Caravaggio's remarks about 'The Ear of Dionysius' seem also to have reflected his increasingly apprehensive state of mind. The tyrant's prison grotto was a potent image of his own contracting world – a 'speaking cave' where every movement was monitored by spies, every remark overheard by eavesdroppers. Behind the logic of his observation lurked a paranoid fear of surveillance and recapture.

LAZARUS RISING

Typically, the most strenuous efforts to recapture an errant Knight of Malta were made in the period leading up to his trial, and in theory the ceremony of the *privatio habitus* diminished the urgency of Wignacourt's campaign to get the painter back to Valletta.[94] But even if Caravaggio was aware of that, he did not feel safe in Syracuse. Despite the success of *The Burial of St Lucy*, Susinno records that 'the unquiet nature of Michelangelo, which loved to wander the earth, soon after led him to leave the home of his friend Minniti'. He departed more or less immediately after the work was finished, not even waiting to see it unveiled. By 6 December, a full week before the Feast of St Lucy, he was in the nearby city of Messina. There, he showed no sign of lowering his guard. He continued to wear his dagger and sword in public and to sleep fully clothed. Susinno wrote that 'his spirit was more disturbed than the sea of Messina with its raging currents that sometimes rise and sometimes fall.'

With a population of 100,000, Messina was as large and vibrant a city as Rome itself. North of Syracuse, it was separated by the narrowest of straits from Calabria on the mainland. Its port was one of the busiest in the Mediterranean. Messina was a town at the junction of east and west, Africa and Italy, and another centre of the thriving European slave trade. George Sandys described it as a stylish but dangerous place:

> the meanest artificers wife is clothed in silke: whereof an infinite quantity is made by the worme . . . The Gentlemen put their monies into the

common table (for which the Citie stands bound) and receive it againe upon their bils, according to their uses. For they dare not venture to keepe it in their houses, so ordinarily broken into by theeves (as are the shops and ware-houses) for all their crosse-bard windows, iron doores, locks, bolts, and barres on the inside: wherein, and in their private revenges, no night doth passe without murder. Every evening they solace themselves along the Marine (a place left throughout betweene the Citie walls and the haven) the men on horsebacke, and the women in large Carosses, being drawne with the slowest procession. There is to be seene the pride and beauties of the Citie. There have they their playhouses, where the parts of men are acted by women, and too naturally passioned, which they forbeare not to frequent upon Sundayes . . .[95]

Caravaggio's situation was awkward and fraught with danger. The galleys of Malta were in the waters of Messina throughout the last months of 1608. Not only that, but some time before 4 November Fra Antonio Martelli had taken up residence as the order's prior of the city. He is unlikely to have looked on Caravaggio's transgressions with a fond and forgiving paternal eye, but his ability to move openly against the painter was compromised because in the winter of that year the order was in litigation with the Senate of Messina, a state of affairs that continued for the duration of Caravaggio's stay in the city.

According to Susinno, Caravaggio's fame had preceded him. He must have won the favour of the Senate, because his services were immediately in demand: 'The new reputation of Caravaggio appealed to the sympathetic people of Messina, who always favoured strangers, and the impressive excellence of such a man was such that they wanted him to stay, and they gave him commissions.'[96] Emboldened by Fra Martelli's relative impotence, Caravaggio even had the cheek to present himself to his eager new clients as a fully fledged Knight of Malta. When the first of his Messinese altarpieces was consigned for delivery, the relevant document referred to the work as being 'by the hand of fr. Michelangeli Caravagio [sic] Knight of the Order of Jerusalem'.[97] Caravaggio was well aware that violation of the order's thirteenth statute meant inevitable expulsion, so he cannot simply have been acting in ignorance of his own disgrace.[98]

There are suggestions that the painter still hoped to win a pardon from Wignacourt. According to Bellori, 'hoping to placate the Grand Master, Caravaggio sent to him as a present the half-figure of Herodias with the head of St John the Baptist in a basin'[99] – a work that can tentatively be identified with a painting of a similar subject now in the National Gallery, London. But by continuing to pose as a Knight of Malta, he must have damaged his cause further. The stony-faced Fra Antonio Martelli is unlikely to have been impressed and reported back, no doubt, to the Grand Master. Alof de Wignacourt's desire to have Caravaggio forcibly extradited from Sicily can only have been strengthened by his insulting masquerade.

As Susinno suggested, the painter was soon hard at work for his new Messinese patrons. On 6 December a wealthy merchant named Giovan Battista de' Lazzari entered into an agreement to build and decorate the central chapel of the church of the Padri Crociferi, the 'cross-bearing fathers', a confraternity of hospitallers devoted to caring for the sick.[100] Determined to obtain the services of Caravaggio, the de' Lazzari family offered him a huge sum of money to paint the principal altarpiece for their new chapel, more than three times the fee he might have expected for an equivalent commission when he was at the peak of his fame in Rome. The proposed title was *The Madonna, St John the Baptist and Other Saints*, which suggests a rather static image of the type that would come to be known as a *Sacra Conversazione*, or 'sacred conversation'. Caravaggio must have disliked the subject, because in a play on his patrons' family name he made the counter-suggestion that they commission him to paint *The Resurrection of Lazarus* instead. The de' Lazzari accepted the proposal, and some time around the start of 1609 Caravaggio started work.

In Rome at the height of the Renaissance it had not been unknown for a famous artist to alter the terms of a commission. Michelangelo had famously plucked up the courage to tell Pope Julius II that his initial plan for the Sistine Chapel ceiling was 'a poor thing', replacing the pope's proposal of twelve apostles in a field of classical decoration with his own vastly more ambitious scheme of illustrations to the Book of Genesis. But in the provincial artistic milieu of Messina, Caravaggio's assertion of independence was still being talked about a hundred years later. Susinno was even more struck by it than he was by the huge fee that the painter was paid:

> When some wealthy members of the house of Lazzaro wished to build a new chapel for the church of the Padri Crociferi, they commissioned Caravaggio to paint a large canvas and agreed to pay the sum of 1,000 scudi. Caravaggio conceived the Resurrection of Lazarus, alluding to their family. Those noblemen were greatly satisfied, and the artist was given free rein to fulfil his creative fantasy. It is commendable to give liberty to great artists to operate at their own will, instead of tying both their hands when they are ordered to execute a certain work in this or that manner or form.[101]

Why, apart from this play on his patrons' name, did Caravaggio want to paint the story of Lazarus raised from the dead? It was a subject rarely depicted since the very early Renaissance. Following the conventions of Byzantine art, Giotto and Duccio had painted Lazarus, plague-spotted, rising from his tomb still wrapped in his grave clothes. In Caravaggio's later work, there is a powerful thrust towards both the subject matter and the style of much earlier Christian art. The only artist before him to have deliberately regressed in a comparable way had been – again – Michelangelo. With the creation of the *Rondanini Pietà,* late in life, Michelangelo had plunged his art back to the angular and ascetic forms of Gothic carving. Caravaggio's *The Resurrection of Lazarus* makes a similarly unorthodox statement of primitivist intent.

Light and dark, which Caravaggio had previously manipulated in the service of a beguilingly deceptive optical realism, now serve an altogether different purpose. Their function is simply to amplify meaning and feeling – to reduce, to pare away, to lose or annihilate everything irrelevant to the essentials of the story he wants to tell. Nine tenths of the painting is bitumen black, a great pit of darkness in which the action unfolds. It is the darkness of death. To the left, the deeply shadowed figure of Christ enters the sepulchre of Lazarus and with a gesture of his right hand bids the dead man to awake: 'Lazarus, come forth' (John 11:43). Around his shadowed form a gaggle of bystanders can be seen craning their necks for a view of the impending miracle.

Below Christ's beckoning hand, two swarthy and sunburned labourers lift the dead man's tombstone, while another raises the corpse from the grave. As the last of the three workmen stumbles forward, cradling the exhumed body, panic, disgust and wonder are mingled together on his face. Lazarus is an emaciated and green-tinged corpse, just plucked from the tomb and seemingly reluctant to wake from the sleep of death. Light streams into the sepulchre from behind Christ, flowing along the line of his outstretched right arm towards the right hand of Lazarus, which reaches as if involuntarily towards the source of illumination. His left hand reaches down, towards the bony litter of the sepulchre, a human skull and thighbone gleaming softly in the low light. He is caught between life and death, suspended at the very moment of his animation.

The parable of Lazarus was traditionally regarded as a miracle performed by Christ in prefiguration of his own crucifixion. In raising Lazarus from the tomb, Christ saved him from sin and death, just as by dying on the Cross, he would save mankind from Original Sin and open the way to salvation. Caravaggio was certainly aware of the theological parallel, since he has arranged Lazarus's body in the same configuration as that of Christ on the Cross. Lazarus's two sisters, Martha and Mary, gather around him like the mourners of Christ at the moment of his deposition. The detail of Martha's face, pressed so close to that of her reviving brother, was taken directly by Caravaggio from an ancient Christian prototype of the *Mater Dolorosa*, the Virgin Mary mourning the death of her son. Cheek pressed to cheek, eyes to mouth, mouth to eyes, the motif of two faces interlocked like pieces in a jigsaw puzzle had long been a standard trope of Byzantine painting. It was used, for example, by the twelfth-century master who painted the fresco of the *Lamentation* in the church of St Pantaleimon in modern-day Macedonia – and from Byzantium the device entered Italian painting in the thirteenth and fourteenth centuries. Caravaggio probably took the motif from an Italian source, and it is not impossible that he saw it in a Byzantine icon in Sicily.[102]

Just as he had done in *The Burial of St Lucy*, where the two central mourners derive from early Renaissance images of the Crucifixion, Caravaggio introduced a deliberate archaism from a much earlier tradition of art into *The Resurrection of Lazarus*. In both cases, he did so to evoke a parallel between the subject in hand and the Crucifixion of Christ. Perhaps he meant the gestures as acts of humility, a renunciation of his own illusionistic virtuosity, a penitential clipping of his own Icarus wings. He had always been an austere painter, a painter for, and of, holy poverty, but never more so than now. In emulation of Cardinal Borromeo, who had counselled a return to the austere values of the ancient Church, Caravaggio formulated his own modern version of a purged and primitive style. There is almost no colour in these works, almost no sense of space, just twisted groupings of figures arranged frieze-like in the convulsions of sorrow, melancholy or agonized bewilderment.

Lazarus was traditionally believed to have died of the plague. Hence the Italian word for a plague house, *lazzaretto* (the slang word for the Neapolitan poor, *lazzari*, shares the same etymology). Once again, as in *The Burial of St Lucy*, Caravaggio had painted a scene like many he must have witnessed during the darkest years of his childhood in Milan – a group of people gathered around a grave, lit by what seems like guttering torchlight. He had set himself the challenge of redeeming those memories of death and desperation, of transfiguring them into representations of the miraculous. In this, he cannot be said to have entirely succeeded.

For all his efforts, what is expressed in this last and darkest flowering of Caravaggio's art is anything but a simple and straightforward sense of piety. The shadowed figure of Christ in *The Resurrection of Lazarus* is another figment of the painter's memory, a second version of the statuesque Christ beckoning Matthew from shadow into light in the painter's very first large religious painting, *The Calling of St Matthew* in the Contarelli Chapel. But so shadowy is the Saviour's form that he might be missed altogether by the inattentive viewer. That kind of uncertainty, whether fully intended or not, has subversively worked its way to the very heart of the picture. Lazarus is suspended between death and life, extinction and salvation. As one hand reaches towards the light, the other extends down towards the tomb. His eyes are sightless, his body gripped still by *rigor mortis*. Will he truly be saved? All is still in the balance.

Whereas light flooded into Caravaggio's earlier religious paintings, here the illumination struggles to penetrate the gloom. The whole painting conveys a sense of just how hard it is truly to see – and perhaps believe in – salvation. Both men holding up Lazarus's tombstone look back with bewildered expressions at Christ, squinting and blinking in confusion. Above them, Caravaggio has included his own self-portrait. He gazes out of the picture, staring directly at the invisible source of light pulsing into the sepulchre, a look of yearning desperation on his face.

ADORATION, DESOLATION

Caravaggio's Sicilian biographer told colourful tales about how he painted *The Resurrection of Lazarus*. According to Susinno, Caravaggio asked for a room in the hospital run by the confraternity of the Padri Crociferi, hired some workmen, and arranged a grisly modelling class:

> in order to give the central figure of Lazarus a naturalistic flavour he asked to have a corpse dug up that was already in a state of decomposition, and had it placed in the arms of the workmen who, however, were unable to stand the foul odour and wanted to give up their work. Caravaggio, with his usual fury, raised his dagger and jumped on them, and as a result those unlucky men were forced to continue their job and nearly die, like those miserable creatures who were condemned by the impious Maxentius to die tied to corpses. Likewise Caravaggio's picturesque room could in some fashion be called the slaughterhouse of the same tyrant.[103]

This is surely a parable invented to illustrate the painter's reputedly excessive attachment to naturalism. Lazarus cannot have been modelled from a corpse in a state of decomposition, because his body is shown in the involuntary stasis of *rigor mortis*; that the painter could find the corpse of a real man who just happened to have died in a cruciform pose is less than plausible. The figure is an invention, although it seems likely enough that the three workmen were painted from local models, since their faces are unfamiliar from the rest of Caravaggio's work, and they do have the ungainly actuality of real individuals. Susinno tells an equally tall tale about a lost first version of the picture, which the painter supposedly slashed to ribbons with his dagger when a member of the de' Lazzari family had the temerity to criticize one or two elements. It is a story designed to perfect the caricature of the painter as a wild man of art, deranged by his own passions.

The biographer is more illuminating when he turns to the third and last of Caravaggio's surviving Sicilian altarpieces, *The Adoration of the Shepherds*. Long neglected, because so far off the beaten track, it is one of the most startlingly direct, wrenchingly emotional religious paintings of the seventeenth century. A sombre and profoundly personal work, it is the last great painting of Caravaggio's traumatic life. Susinno, who responded to it with heartfelt sincerity, believed it to be in fact the greatest of all his works:

> In this canvas he represented the Nativity with life-size figures, and this in my opinion is the best of all his paintings, because here this great naturalist abandoned his sketchy, allusive style and demonstrated his naturalism once more without the use of bold shadows ... This one great work of art would have been enough for Caravaggio's glory for centuries to come, because here he removed himself completely from dryness and from exceedingly dark tones. Instead, on the ground is a basket with carpentry tools alluding to St Joseph's trade. Above, on the right, the Virgin is seen stretched out on the ground, looking at the Christ child wrapped in cloth and caressing him. She is leaning on a haystack, behind which those animals are grazing; on the left side, at the foot of the Virgin, St Joseph is seated in attractive drapery, deep in thought. Nearby the three shepherds adore the newborn child; the first one has a staff in his hand and is dressed in a white garment, the second with his two hands joined in prayer shows a bare shoulder that looks like living flesh, and finally the third one looks on admiringly, his bold head painted marvellously. The rest of the canvas consists of a black background with rough wood that constitutes the shed. Indeed, the background was higher, and it was necessary to cut off a large section in order to fit the canvas into the chapel.[104]

Caravaggio's *Adoration of the Shepherds* is the most tragic of nativities. Mary has just given birth to her tiny, swaddled child. She slumps, exhausted from her labours, not against a haystack as Susinno mistakenly said, but against the side of a manger. Behind her, in the half dark, the biblical ox and ass stand patient and impassive. Mary is the *Madonna del Parto* – the 'Madonna of childbirth' – and also the Madonna of humility. She reclines on the bare earth of the cattleshed, strewn with strands of straw that catch the light like threads of gold. Those pieces of light are her only riches, but her eyes are closed to them. She is a refugee mother, utterly alone in the dark with her defenceless child.

Joseph is singled out by his halo, but he is not with her – he is with the shepherds, part of her audience. None of the men are truly with her, and there is no sense that any of them can help her. The bald shepherd closest to Mary and her child reaches out to touch them. But his hand is kept back from actually making contact, as if by an invisible force. The men are suspended in an eternal agony of empathy. Their faces radiate compassion and helplessness. What can be done? Does the world really have to be like this?

Once again, Caravaggio in Sicily reached back to the oldest popular traditions of Christian art. The motif of the tiny baby, crawling on his mother's body, pressing his face to hers and reaching to touch her with his little hand, is drawn from Byzantine art.[105] The whole scene has been conceived as another of the painter's assemblages of sculpturally realized figures, but this time what is evoked is not the sacred mountain with its chapels, but the tradition of the Christmas crib, begun by St Francis at the monastery of Greccio in the chill winter of 1223.

It is no coincidence that *The Adoration of the Shepherds* was painted for one of Messina's Franciscan churches. Such was the depth of the friars' attachment to Caravaggio's painting that they later fought tooth and nail to keep it. 'At various times princes have been attracted by this Nativity and sought to take it away,' wrote Susinno, 'but they were unable to do so because the Capuchin Fathers made an appeal to the Senate, which in those days was more important, and its authority made them realize that those Fathers were its only custodians. As a result the picture remained in Messina, and I can affirm in truth that this unique work is the most masterly painting by Caravaggio.'[106]

All of Caravaggio's great Sicilian pictures reach back – back to the oldest and most direct forms of Christian art, and back to his own oldest and most painful memories. Whether he was conscious of it or not, *The Adoration of the Shepherds* is an uncanny allegory of his own emergence into the dark world of Milan under plague back in the 1570s – born to a mother soon to be bereaved, born to be abandoned by all save her. That is why the men in the picture look on but cannot touch, like dreams or ghosts. They see the mother and child's abandonment, but can do nothing to assuage it. They are hardly in the same place, but in another shadowland. Iconographically, the gnarled and saddened men are Joseph and the shepherds. Emotionally, they are Caravaggio's father, his uncles, his grandfather – all the men in the family that he might have had, but lost. Caravaggio's own father's tools had been those of a simple stonemason. Here they are replaced by the equally humble tools of the carpenter, placed with such desolation to the other side of Mary.

The set square, the saw, the adze, the white rag, lie there unused, a *memento mori*, oblique memorial to an ordinary man who left an extraordinary child to fend for himself. This is Caravaggio's last still life. These are among his last truly meaningful, eloquent brushstrokes. The picture is almost unbearable.

'LIKE A CRIMINAL ESCAPING FROM HIS GUARDS'

It is hard to know what Caravaggio did during his time in Messina, other than paint. Susinno says that he paraded himself as a heretic: 'Apart from his profession, Caravaggio also went about questioning our holy religion, for which he was accused of being a disbeliever . . .'[107] But he also tells that dark story of the painter's visit to a Messinese church, where he refused holy water on the grounds that it was only good for washing away venial sins. 'Mine are all mortal' were Caravaggio's words, hardly those of a man untroubled by questions of salvation or damnation. Regrettably, there is no hard evidence about his beliefs. In religion, as in so much else, Caravaggio was perhaps a man divided – torn between doubt and faith, angry rebellion and sullen obedience.

He stayed longer in Messina than he had in Syracuse. He had won the favour of the Senate – which commissioned and paid for the *Adoration*, according to Susinno – and perhaps that added to his sense of security. But his behaviour remained erratic. 'He used to have his meal on a slab of wood, and instead of using a tablecloth, most of the time he would eat on an old portrait canvas; he was foolish and crazy, more cannot be said.'[108]

Susinno's weirdest story about Caravaggio concerns his alleged sexual interest in a group of adolescent schoolboys who used to play near the dry docks at the eastern end of Messina. It is an unusual anecdote in the context of the Sicilian author's *Lives*, which are not otherwise salacious:

> He used to disappear during holy days to follow a certain grammar teacher called Don Carlo Pepe, who escorted his pupils for recreation to the arsenal. There galleys used to be built . . . Michele went to observe the positions of those playful boys and to form his inventions. But the teacher became suspicious and wanted to know why he was always around. The question so disturbed the painter, and he became so irate and furious . . . that he wounded the poor man on the head. For this action he was forced to leave Messina. In short, wherever he went he would leave the mark of madness.'[109]

Having seemingly implied that the schoolteacher was accusing Caravaggio of an indecent interest in his pupils, Susinno himself asserts that the painter's real motive for following the boys was artistic. The priest-biographer ends up by writing off the whole incident as yet another instance of Caravaggio's mental instability. But because of its very oddity and untidiness, the story has the reek of truth. Caravaggio was hunted, haunted and lonely in Messina. It is by no means inconceivable that he should have sought companionship, even sexual solace, in the company of young men. Susinno's anecdote might even help to explain one of the most enigmatic and homoerotic paintings of Caravaggio's Sicilian period, his last depiction of *St John the Baptist*, now to be seen in the Borghese Gallery. Was this one of Don Pepe's pupils? Did Caravaggio persuade him to model for him, and perhaps more?

Placed in a cursory wilderness, landscape lost in shadow, accompanied by a cursory lamb of God, the boy reclines on a swag of red drapery and fixes the viewer with a sullen, sultry, knowing gaze. Is this really John the Baptist, prophet and seer, possessor of secret knowledge, or a swarthy Sicilian boy, older than his years and conscious of his sexual appeal? The artist still had the picture with him when he died: it was in the inventory of his last effects, which suggests that it was not painted to order but on impulse.

Caravaggio had evaded capture, first in Syracuse, then in Messina. He may have been forced to leave Messina because of the fracas with the schoolmaster, but he was probably planning to leave anyway because he suspected that his enemies were closing in on him. According to Bellori, 'misfortune did not abandon Michele, and fear hunted him from place to place. Consequently he hurried across Sicily and from Messina went to Palermo, where he painted another Nativity for the Oratorio of San Lorenzo . . . The Virgin is shown adoring her newborn child, with St Francis, St Lawrence, the seated St Joseph, and above an angel in the air. The lights are diffused among shadows in the darkness.'[110]

From this moment on in the painter's story, the light is diffused among a great many shadows. But certain facts are clear. As Bellori said, Caravaggio left Messina for Palermo, sometime around the height of summer 1609. Once again, he painted an altarpiece for the Franciscans, this time for an oratory in the possession of a confraternity known as the Compagnia di San Francesco. Perhaps in deference to the sensibilities of its members he painted a rather sweeter version of the heartbreakingly bare Adoration in Messina. The Virgin is still weary, still seated on the ground, but without the same sense of desolation and isolation. Comparison between the two works is no longer possible, since the Palermo version was allegedly stolen by order of a Sicilian Mafia boss in 1969, and has never been recovered.

Caravaggio did not stay long in Palermo. Within two months, at most, he was on the move again. By the middle of September 1609 he was back in Naples.[111] Baglione says he left because 'his enemy was chasing him'.[112] Bellori agrees: 'he no longer felt safe in Sicily, and so he departed the island and sailed back to Naples, where he thought he would stay until he got word of his pardon allowing him to return to Rome.'[113]

On his return to Naples, Caravaggio stayed in the Colonna Palace at Chiaia.[114] With its vast terraced gardens, close to the sea, it was an idyllic retreat from the cares of life, with the added bonus of thick walls. The fact that Caravaggio had evidently been accepted back into the Colonna fold suggests not only that Marchesa Costanza had forgiven him, yet again, but also that she had negotiated some kind of truce with Alof de Wignacourt and the Knights of Malta. Her own son, Fabrizio Sforza Colonna, remained in post as admiral of the Grand Master's galleys. He owed both his liberty and the rescue of his reputation to Wignacourt. In such circumstances, it would have been inconceivable for Costanza Colonna to have protected a known fugitive from the order. Whatever it involved, a deal must have been struck on Caravaggio's behalf. He would presumably have been required to send some paintings to the Grand Master, as well as putting an end to the absurd pretence that he was still a Knight of Magistral Obedience.

News that Caravaggio was back in Naples soon got around and offers of work followed. 'In Sant'Anna de' Lombardi he painted the Resurrection,' Bellori wrote.[115] The picture does not survive, because the chapel that once housed it in the Neapolitan church of the Lombards was destroyed by an earthquake at the turn of the nineteenth century. But documents and eyewitness accounts confirm that Caravaggio, himself a Lombard by origin, did indeed paint a large altarpiece of The Resurrection of Christ for Sant'Anna. To judge by the praise heaped on it, it was a strange and morbidly enthralling picture, the lost masterpiece of Caravaggio's later years.

Caravaggio's patron, Alfonso Fenaroli, had obtained the rights to the third chapel on the left side of the church on 24 December 1607, six months after the painter had left for Malta at the end of his first stay in Naples. Fenaroli must have commissioned the new altarpiece as soon as the artist arrived back from Palermo, probably sometime around the beginning of September 1609. Working in the abbreviated and fluent style of his Sicilian altarpieces, Caravaggio finished it before the end of the following month.[116] Nearly a hundred and fifty years later, the travelling French connoisseur Charles-Nicolas Cochin was bowled over by it. By then the picture had darkened with age, and the identity of its creator had been forgotten. Cochin had every reason to pass it over, but it seemed so bizarrely original, so memorable and so sinister, that it drew him in:

In the third chapel on the left, one sees a painting representing the resurrection of Jesus Christ. It is a singular invention, Christ is not even
shown rising into the air and he walks past the sentries [who guard the
holy sepulchre]. All of which gives a low idea of him, and makes him
look like a criminal escaping from his guards. Also, he has been given
the character of a scrawny suffering man. From a purely pictorial point
of view the composition is really beautiful and the style is strong and
felt with great taste. It is much blackened. No one knows the name of
the artist. This piece is beautiful.[117]

Only in these words is the vivid ghost of a great painting preserved.
Cochin was unaware of the painter's identity, his flight from Rome,
his escape from Malta, his restless peregrinations through Sicily – yet
still, purely from the power of his work, he sensed the depth of Caravaggio's unease. The painter had made Christ 'look like a criminal
escaping from his guards'. Just as he had done in his haunting Sicilian
pictures, Caravaggio was putting his own memories and emotions at
the heart of his work. Whatever he set out to paint – the death of a
martyr, the infancy of Christ or his resurrection – he always ended up
painting himself.

THE KNIGHT'S REVENGE

His work had never been bleaker or more emotionally naked. But in
the autumn of 1609 Caravaggio had some grounds for optimism. Alof
de Wignacourt seems to have been appeased, which lifted the threat
of sudden rendition to Malta, and negotiations were reopened for the
papal pardon that would allow him to return to Rome at last. Emboldened, perhaps, by the sense that his fortunes were about to change,
Caravaggio fatally let down his guard. He paid an ill-advised visit to
the Osteria del Cerriglio, a Neapolitan tavern frequented by artists
and poets and much celebrated in the popular literature of the time.

The Cerriglio was located in a narrow alleyway behind the Neapolitan church of Santa Maria La Nova. There are a number of theories about the original meaning of its name, which may have derived
from the *cierro*, local slang for the long forelock worn by the cut-throats

who were often to be seen there; from the merry appearance (*cera*) of those who had enjoyed its hospitality; from an oak forest (*cerrillo*) that had once stood nearby; from the *cerilleros*, the vagabonds and wastrels who caroused at the tavern; or simply from the name of its owner. It was famously a place where the wine flowed more freely than water, but a number of hitherto overlooked documents reveal that the Osteria del Cerriglio was also notorious as a brothel. Giulio Cesare Cortese, an exact contemporary of Caravaggio, wrote a mock-epic poem entitled *La conquista del Cerriglio*, in which the imaginary moment of the tavern's foundation is marked by 'huge orgies'.[118] Real orgies took place there too: another of the painter's contemporaries, Giambattista Basile, called it 'that place where the courtesans / wallowed / in front of disapproving passersby / stripping the gullible to the bone',[119] while yet another poet of the period, Giovan Battista del Tufo, added the detail that 'moreover, for gentlemen, / There is a door for entering secretly.'[120] The Cerriglio was especially popular among men seeking sex with other men, to judge by the insinuation in Basile's description of it as a place 'where Bacchus reigns and Venus is shunned'.[121]

The nineteenth-century Neapolitan poet, playwright and historian Salvatore di Giacomo, whose work on the underworld of seventeenth-century Naples has been largely forgotten, unearthed several incriminating references to the tavern in the archives of the city. 'The Cerriglio was not wholly frequented by well-mannered individuals, and the inn-keeper would often turn a blind eye if not turn his back altogether,' he wrote in his pioneering study of 1899, *Prostitution in Naples*.[122] Elsewhere, di Giacomo described just what 'gentlemen' such as Caravaggio might find when they walked though the brothel's discreetly concealed door and entered its upper rooms: 'These rooms nowadays would be called *higher chambers*. Since the end of the 16th century, by which time the Cerriglio was already famous, they had made up a separate quarter [of the tavern] ... in one of these little rooms, in circa 1671, a slave was caught practising what are nowadays referred to as certain psychopathic sexual acts, which were thought of in less scientific terms in the seventeenth century and punishable with beheading.'[123] The only sexual act punishable by beheading was sodomy. The Cerriglio clearly catered for a wide range of sexual appetites.

Caravaggio's problems arose when he tried to leave the tavern. He had been followed there by a group of armed men, who waited for him in the street outside as he took his pleasure within. As soon as he walked out of the door, they ambushed him. On 24 October 1609, a Roman newspaper included the following notice: 'Word has been received from Naples that Caravaggio, the famous painter, has been murdered. Others say disfigured.'[124] The rumour of his death turned out to have been exaggerated. He had not been killed, but he had been severely injured.

Within days of the publication of the newspaper report, Caravaggio's old friend and biographer, Giulio Mancini, put out his own antennae. Mancini did not yet know the full truth, but what he did know filled him with anxiety. He wrote to his brother Deifebo in Siena: 'It's said that Michelangelo da Caravaggio has been assaulted by 4 in Napoli and the witnesses say he has been given a facial scar. If so it would be a sin and is [the next word, which begins with a *d* but is illegible, could be 'disturbing' or 'a disgrace'] to everybody. Let God make it not so.'[125]

Mancini wrote that Caravaggio had been *sfregiato*, cut on the face, which in the honour code of the day was an injury inflicted to avenge an insult to reputation.[126] The same word had been used by the writer of the Roman news report. It lends both brief accounts of the assault a grim specificity, and explains the other detail gleaned by Mancini: that Caravaggio had been attacked by a group of four men. This was no drunken fracas but a premeditated act, a vendetta attack ruthlessly executed: three men to hold him down, one man to cut the marks of shame into his face.

Years later, the painter's biographers gave their own terse versions of what had happened. They were unanimous on two points. It was a coldblooded attack – a hit – and it was perpetrated by a man or a group of men from Malta.

Baglione's report of the assault at the Cerriglio follows seamlessly from his account of Caravaggio's incarceration on Malta and his subsequent escape. It is clear that Baglione believed the two episodes were linked as surely as cause and effect:

In Malta, Caravaggio had a dispute with a Knight of Justice and in some way affronted him. For this he was thrown into prison. But he escaped at night by means of a rope ladder and fled to the island of Sicily. In Palermo he executed several works, but because he was still being pursued by his enemy he had to return to Naples. There his enemy finally caught up with him and he was so severely slashed in the face that he was almost unrecognisable.[127]

Bellori, writing considerably later than Baglione, thought the cause of the assault lay elsewhere. In his account it was not the revenge attack of an insulted Knight of Justice, but a mission carried out by implication on the orders of Alof de Wignacourt:

> [Caravaggio] felt that it was no longer safe to remain in Sicily and so he left the island and sailed back to Naples, intending to remain there until he received news of his pardon so that he could return to Rome. At the same time seeking to regain the favour of the Grand Master of Malta, he sent him as a gift a half-length figure of Herodias with the head of St John the Baptist in a basin. These attentions availed him nothing, for stopping one day in the doorway of the Osteria del Cerriglio he found himself surrounded by several armed men who manhandled him and slashed his face.[128]

Francesco Susinno, writing still later, but from a position considerably closer to the events on Malta and Sicily, leaned towards Baglione's version of events: "The fugitive arrived in Palermo, and in that city also left excellent works of art. From there he moved again to Naples, chased there by his angered antagonist, and was badly wounded on the face."[129]

To these counterposed explanations of the attack may be added one other possibility: that its origins lay not in Malta but in Rome, and that it was carried out either by or on behalf of the aggrieved relations of the late Ranuccio Tomassoni. There is no suggestion that this was the case in any of the early biographies, nor in any contemporary source. In fact there is no hard evidence of any kind to support the hypothesis. But the theory has been advocated by at least one influential scholar of Caravaggio's life and work in recent years.[130]

A great deal of archival research has been done on Caravaggio over the past half-century. Many new discoveries have been made, and it is striking how in almost every case the historical facts have tended to

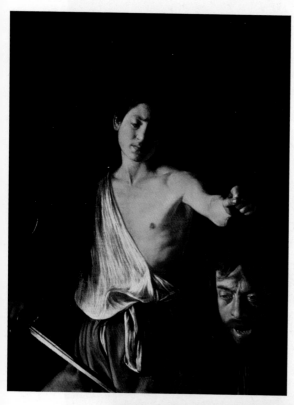

68. *David with the Head of Goliath*. Cecco as David, Caravaggio as the severed head of Goliath. Often misdated to the end of the painter's life, but actually painted in 1606 as a homicide's plea for clemency.

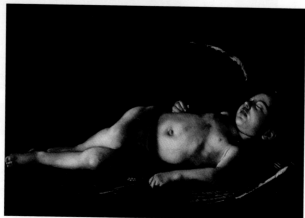

69. *Sleeping Cupid*. Painted in Malta for a Florentine humanist, this picture was inspired by a celebrated sculpture of the same subject by Michelangelo.

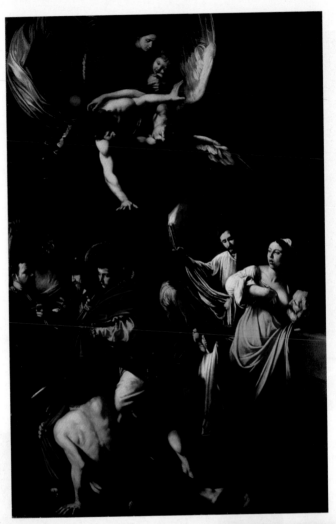

70. *The Seven Acts of Mercy*. 'This one dark street, scene of desperation and pain and death, is the painter's microcosm for the brutality of existence itself.'

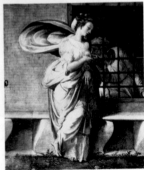

71. *Roman Charity* (detail) by Pierino del Vaga.

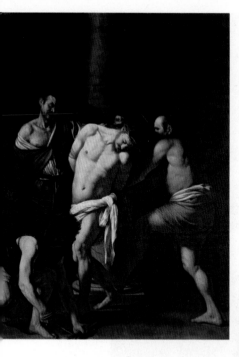

72. *The Flagellation*. Torture as a misbegotten act of intimacy.

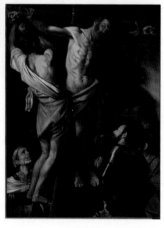

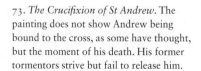

73. *The Crucifixion of St Andrew*. The painting does not show Andrew being bound to the cross, as some have thought, but the moment of his death. His former tormentors strive but fail to release him.

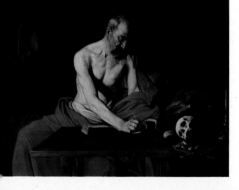

74. *St Jerome Writing*. Painted for one of the most senior Knights of Malta, a virtuoso demonstration of Caravaggio's gifts to the artist's new circle of patrons in the Order of St John.

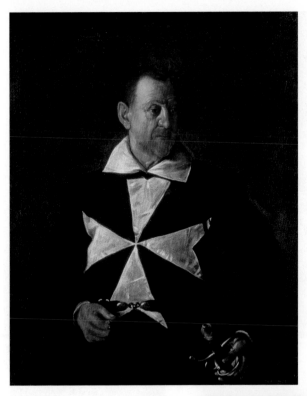

75. *Portrait of Fra Antonio Martelli.* 'This depiction of an obdurate and forceful man, in lean old age, rheumy eyes gazing off into the distance, anticipates the mature portraiture of Rembrandt by some half a century.'

76. *Portrait of Alof de Wignacourt, with His Pageboy.* Instead of a monastic habit, the Grand Master wears a suit of sixteenth-century armour, evoking the heroic defence of Malta at the great Siege of 1565.

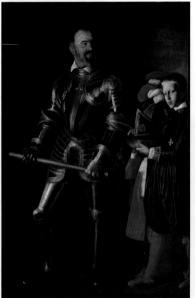

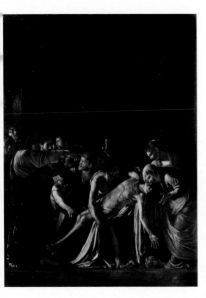

77. *The Resurrection of Lazarus.* 'Lazarus, come forth' (John 11). As Christ bids him to rise from the grave, Lazarus seems reluctant to wake from death.

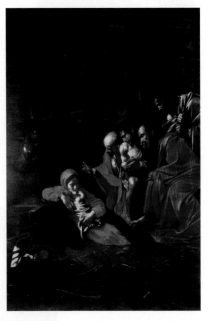

78. *The Adoration of the Shepherds.* The most tragic of nativities: Mary is a refugee mother utterly alone in the dark with her defenceless child.

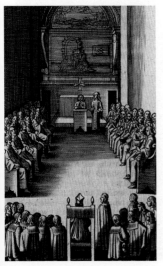

79. *A Knight of Malta being Defrocked* by Wolfgang Kilian (detail). The ceremony of *privatio habitus* took place directly beneath Caravaggio's altarpiece, which can just be made out here at the far end of the oratory.

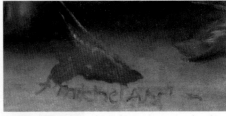

80. *The Beheading of St John* (endpapers – detail). In the blood gushing from the saint's neck, Caravaggio signed his name. It is his only signature on a painting.

81. *St John the Baptist*. Caravaggio's last known depiction of the saint, who was modelled on this occasion by a swarthy and sun-tanned Sicilian adolescent.

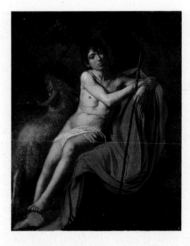

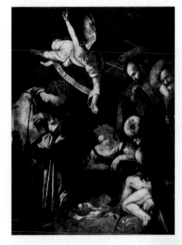

82. *The Adoration of the Shepherds*. Painted for a Franciscan confraternity in Palermo, the last of Caravaggio's Sicilian altarpieces was allegedly stolen by order of a Mafia boss in 1969. It has not been recovered.

83. *The Burial of St Lucy*. 'The picture's iconography is ingeniously suggestive of hope ... but its mood is overwhelmingly bleak. Almost half the painting is dark bare stone.'

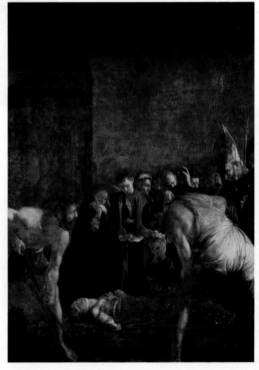

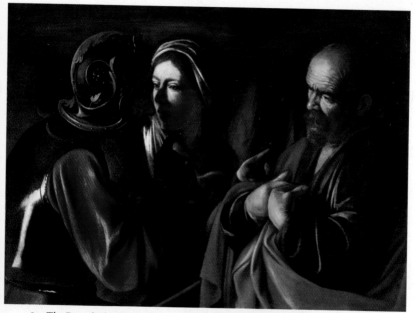

84. *The Denial of St Peter*. One of just two paintings that can be dated to after the painter's face was slashed in late 1609. The seriousness of his injuries is shockingly apparent in the work's ragged, fumbling style.

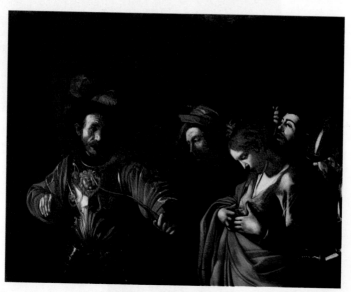

85. *The Martyrdom of St Ursula*. 1610, Intesa Sanpaolo Collection, the Gallery of Palazzo Zevallos, Naples, Oil on canvas, 56 x 70.9 in. (143 x 180cm).

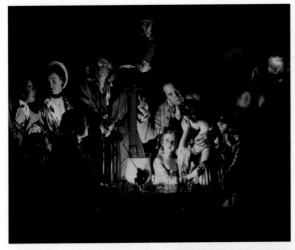

Caravaggio's influence reached forward to the Enlightenment, continued into the Romantic period and has infiltrated the DNA of modern cinema.

86. *Experiment on a Bird in the Air Pump* by Joseph Wright of Derby.

87. *The Raft of the Medusa* by Theodore Géricault.

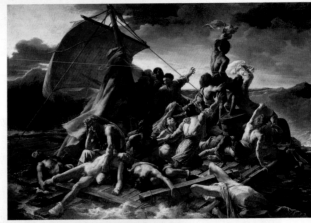

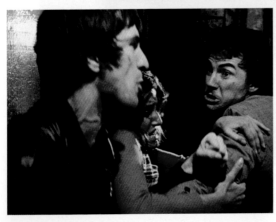

88. Still from *Mean Streets*, directed by Martin Scorsese.

confirm the accounts of one or other of Caravaggio's early biographers. Baglione has generally proved to be more accurate than Bellori, which is not surprising: he was part of Caravaggio's own circle, and although the two men were enemies they took more than a passing interest in each other's activities. Baglione knew who Caravaggio's friends and allies were in Rome, and understood the complicated and violent codes of honour by which he lived and died, whereas Bellori was simply baffled by them. A fairly straightforward process of elimination establishes Baglione's account of the assault in the Osteria del Cerriglio as the most credible explanation of the whole dark business.

The modern suggestion that Ranuccio Tomassoni's relations were the aggressors lacks merit on the grounds of chronology, geography and logic. The attack in the Cerriglio took place more than three years after Caravaggio had murdered Tomassoni. Even if it is assumed that the Tomassoni clan was still bent on revenge, which in this case would have been a dish served very cold indeed, it is unlikely that they would have attempted an attack on the painter in distant Naples: far better to wait until his heralded return to Rome, where they could watch his movements and plan their strike with a greater certainty of success. The most powerful argument against their involvement is the nature of the wounding Caravaggio suffered. He had been cut in the face. In the language of vendetta, the *sfregio* was punishment for an insult to honour and reputation. But the painter had murdered Tomassoni, not merely insulted him. An eye for an eye: if the Tomassoni had been behind the assault in Naples, Caravaggio would have been killed, not disfigured.

Bellori's suggestion that Alof de Wignacourt ordered the attack is equally illogical. Caravaggio had not personally insulted Wignacourt, nor had he attacked his reputation. True, he had defied the Grand Master's authority. But the appropriate punishment for that was extradition back to Malta. The facial wounding of an errant knight at a house of ill repute was not something Wignacourt would have sanctioned. His involvement seems even less likely, given that at the time of the attack Caravaggio was living in the household of the mother of Wignacourt's admiral of the fleet. The Grand Master was ruthless but he was also intensely pragmatic. If he had wanted satisfaction from Caravaggio, he would have taken it in the form of pictures.

Baglione's account, to which the Sicilian biographer Susinno subsequently gave his imprimatur, is the only one entirely consistent with the known facts of the case. It has the cold logic of vendetta, stressing the symmetry between insult given and punishment received, even in the author's choice of words. Baglione says Caravaggio had 'affronted' the Knight of Justice on Malta, a usage that etymologically conjoins insult with the notion of a metaphorical loss of face (*affronto*, the word used by Baglione, has the same root as *fronte*, Italian for 'forehead'). In revenge, Caravaggio's enemy literalized that same insult, slashing him in the face.

That enemy was, we now know, Giovanni Rodomonte Roero, the Conte della Vezza. We also know that he left Malta shortly after Caravaggio's escape from the island.[131] That too is consistent with Baglione's assertion that the painter was slowly but surely tracked by his enemy, who followed him to Sicily from Malta and finally caught up with him at the Osteria del Cerriglio. Since the facts to have emerged from the Maltese archive tally so exactly with the arc of Baglione's narrative, it is only logical to believe that the rest of his account is also correct. He asked the right questions of the right people, and he established the truth: it was indeed a vendetta, begun in Malta and finished in Naples.

Whatever the painter had said or done to him on the night of the fracas in Malta, Roero had been left with a burning sense of grievance. Maltese Knights of Justice were not known for their propensity to forgive and forget. The Conte della Vezza was evidently proud and mercilessly persistent. He had a team of accomplices. This was the man who hunted Caravaggio down, who stood over him as he struggled, who cut his face.

After exacting his bloody revenge, Roero vanished from historical view. That too seems to have been part of his plan. He may have been helped by friends within the Maltese judiciary. Shortly after the revenge attack, all details of Caravaggio's crime on Malta were carefully painted out of the archive there by an unknown hand.[132] In this way, the artist's name was obliterated from the great book of crimes and punishments. So too was the name of his victim and assailant. Having got his revenge, Roero meticulously covered his traces. Even Baglione, who plainly knew so much, never discovered the name of Caravaggio's assailant.

TWO LAST PAINTINGS

Caravaggio seems never to have fully recovered from the attack at the Osteria del Cerriglio. Crippled and perhaps partially blinded by his injuries, he went into the limbo of a long convalescence. On Christmas Day 1609, two months after the assault, Mancini's correspondence with his brother Deifebo communicated a solitary scrap of inconclusive rumour: 'It's said that Caravaggio is near here, well looked after, also that he wants to return to Rome soon, and that he has powerful help.'[133] Negotiations for a papal pardon may have been progressing, but in truth Caravaggio was nowhere near Rome. Mancini had been misinformed. The painter was in Naples, presumably at the Colonna Palace at Chiaia, fighting for his life. He would remain there for at least six months.

Mancini's letter apart, from October 1609 until May 1610 there is a striking absence of evidence about Caravaggio's activities. He apparently does nothing, says nothing. The archive falls silent, like a cardiograph flatlining. It then flickers briefly, but only twice. Each flicker takes the form of a painting.

The seriousness of Caravaggio's injuries is shockingly apparent in *The Denial of St Peter*, a melancholic and withdrawn devotional work painted some time in the summer of 1610.[134] It is a terminally raw and ragged thing – an image snatched from the pit of darkest adversity, painted by a man who could barely hold a brush. The stark and pared down style evolved in Sicily has been appallingly coarsened. Three figures, two men and a single woman, confront one another in the shallowest of spaces. The conception is subtle, the composition strikingly original and the mood bitterly sad. But such is the uncertainty of the handling that the whole image looks disconcertingly unfocused. It is still recognizably a Caravaggio, but the brushwork is so broad, the definition of forms so unsure, that the painter seems to have fallen prey to some form of essential tremor, an uncontrollable shaking of the hands, as well as perhaps to damage of the eyes.

The story that the painting illustrates is told in all four books of the New Testament. According to the gospels, Christ prophesied that his disciple Peter would deny him three times before the cock had crowed twice. On the day of Christ's arrest in the garden of Gethsemane, Peter followed his master into the courtyard of the high priest Caiaphas. He waited there as Christ was tormented by his accusers: 'And some began to spit on him, and to cover his face, and to buffet him, and to say unto him, Prophesy: and the servants did strike him with the palms of their hands. And as Peter was beneath in the palace, there cometh one of the maids of the high priest: And when she saw Peter warming himself, she looked upon him, and said, And thou also wast with Jesus of Nazareth. But he denied, saying, I know not, neither understand I what thou sayest.' Twice more, Peter was asked if he knew Jesus, and each time he gave the same answer: 'And the second time the cock crew. And Peter called to mind the word that Jesus said unto him, Before the cock crow twice, thou shalt deny me thrice. And when he thought thereon, he wept' (Mark 14:65–72).

Caravaggio has combined elements from all three denials in a single image. Behind the figures, a reddish-brown smudge and some scattered flecks of brighter pigment suggest the fire by which Peter warms himself, damp logs spitting sparks into the air. On the left, his face entirely in shadow, stands one of Caiaphas's guards. He looks like a dim memory of the malign soldier in the much earlier *Betrayal of Christ*, which had shown the moment directly before Peter's threefold denial. This soldier's red shirtsleeve is indicated in a few summary strokes of red paint with swiftly dashed-in highlights. A wedge-shaped piece of light fragments and disperses in the darkness of his armour. His face and hands are a blur. Beside him, a single girl stands in for both maids challenging Peter. She stares intently at the soldier while pointing at Peter with a half-sketched hand.

The most eloquent figure in the picture is Peter himself, his bald head creased with lines and his face carrying an expression of deep, glassy-eyed self-recrimination. He points both of his own hands towards himself, as if to complete the triple accusation. He denies Christ and hates himself in the same moment. A tear wells out of a corner of his half-hidden right eye. He is the embodiment of saddened guilt, a man who knows he has done wrong and can hardly bear to confront himself.

Against the odds, it is a moving and powerful image. Caravaggio has drawn on all his long-practised ingenuity. But his strategies are those of evasion. Crop the figures to extreme close-up, to avoid problems of anatomical articulation. Arrange the faces at odd or oblique angles, to obviate the need for accurate depictions of human physiognomy. Smother any awkward areas in blankets of shadow. Wherever gleams of illumination do pierce the darkness, they reveal the imprecision of the painter's touch. His draughtsmanship, the way he draws with the brush, has collapsed altogether. Peter's hands are like flesh-coloured mittens, his left thumb so botched it resembles the claw of an animal. Light flaring in darkness had once been Caravaggio's signature, the source of all his pictorial magic. Now it exposes his illness and incapacity, and shows us how that magic has evaporated.

Only one other painting survives by Caravaggio's hand. Darker still than *The Denial of Peter*, and yet more abbreviated in style, *The Martyrdom of St Ursula* is his last picture. Once more, a group of fragmentary figures has been arranged in a frieze-like composition within the shallowest of shadowy spaces. There is almost no light at all, and very little sense of scene or background, save for some shadowy drapery intended perhaps to signify the inside of a tent. It is a picture so entirely lacking in the connective tissue of illusion that it is like language without conjunctions or prepositions: killer's face, hands; shocked woman's eyes; victim stunned; two men watching.

The painting's subject is drawn from the life of St Ursula, as recounted in *The Golden Legend*. A chaste princess led 11,000 virgins on an ill-fated pilgrimage through Germany:

> And then all these virgins came ... to Cologne, and found that it was besieged with the Huns. And when the Huns saw them they began to run upon them with a great cry, and enraged like wolves on sheep, and slew all this great multitude. And when they were all beheaded, they came to the blessed Ursula, and the prince of them, seeing her beauty, so marvellous, was abashed, and began to comfort her on the death of the virgins, and promised to her to take her to his wife. And when she had refused him and despised him, he shot at her an arrow, and pierced her through the body, and so accomplished her martyrdom ...

The convention was to paint a vast crowd scene, an orgy of death. Caravaggio did the opposite. He envisaged the scene of Ursula's martyrdom as a horribly intimate ritual wounding. The murderous

Hun, who seems horrified by the result of his own actions, has just shot Ursula at point-blank range in the stomach. The victim of a sexual insult – 'she had refused him and despised him' – responds by subjecting the woman who had scorned him to a vile parody of pregnancy. Her swollen belly has been impregnated by the tip of an imperfectly painted arrow. She looks down with an expression of quiet surprise as blood spurts from the entry point, making a gesture with her hands that suggests she wants to part the flesh of her stomach still further. She is about to give birth to her own death.

Three others complete the group. Ursula's shocked maidservant hovers like a ghost between the killer and her mistress. In her left hand she holds the pole of a Christian banner, while with her right she reaches, too late, for the Hun's bow. A soldier in black armour, shown in half-profile, approaches to catch the martyr should she swoon or fall. Directly behind Ursula's stooped white mask of a face, another ghoulish face stares sightlessly into space. It is as if she has grown a second head. This is the last of all Caravaggio's self-portraits.

What did he mean by this strange, haunting device? To suggest his own sympathy for the martyr, his wish to die like her? Or was he painting his realization that he was actually dying – and dying, like her, from a revenge wound inflicted at close quarters? His mouth is half open, as though to suggest that he is gasping, that he feels the arrow piercing his flesh too. Had Caravaggio turned the whole scene into a proxy for his own traumatic ordeal at the Osteria del Cerriglio? The assassin has the weatherbeaten face of a warrior. Is he too a portrait, an image dredged up from painter's worst memories?

There are no answers to these questions. With the completion of the picture, darkness closes in on Caravaggio.

THE BOATMAN'S STORY

Caravaggio painted his last picture for Prince Marcantonio Doria of Genoa, who had probably sheltered him when he briefly fled Rome in the summer of 1605 after assaulting the notary Mariano Pasqualone. The prince, who had once tried to commission an entire fresco cycle from Caravaggio, had to content himself with a single canvas. He probably chose the subject of *The Martyrdom of St Ursula* in honour of his beloved stepdaughter Ursula, who like her namesake had committed herself to a lifetime of chastity by taking religious vows.

A small comedy of errors attended the delivery of the painting. It had been finished by 10 May 1610. But the very next day Doria's procurator in Naples, Lanfranco Massa, apologized to his master for having nearly ruined it: 'I thought to send you the painting of Saint Ursula this week, but to be sure that it was dry, I put it in the sun yesterday, and this instead caused the thick varnish which Caravaggio put on to liquefy; I want to obtain Caravaggio's opinion on how to do it so as not to harm it. Signor Damiano has seen it and was amazed, like all the others who saw it . . .'[135]

It took more than two weeks to put the picture right, but by the end of May it was ready for despatch from Naples to Genoa. On 27 May, Massa wrote to Prince Doria: 'I am sending with P. Alessandro Caramano on his boat a long box inside of which is the painting of *The Martyrdom of St Ursula*, carefully packed, for which [you] will be required to pay 50 soldi in conformance with the shipper's policy.'

The correspondence is completed by a shipper's manifest, dated the same day: 'Sr Lanfranco Massa has loaded in the name of God and of good fortune in the present port of Naples onto the *felucca* named *Santa Maria di Porto Salvo*, owned by Alessandro Caramano, a box containing the painting of *The Martyrdom of St Ursula*, made by the hand of Michel'Angelo [sic] Caravaggio, very well packed, in order to consign it in the same condition upon arrival in Genoa to Sr Marcantonio Doria who will pay two and one-half libri of that money should God carry it safely.' The manifest was signed by a certain Antonio Feraro, 'on command of the above stated Alessandro Caramano who does not know how to write'.

God and the illiterate boatman indeed carried the painting safely to distant Genoa. According to a note of receipt in the margin of Massa's second letter, it arrived on 18 June, precisely three weeks after it had left Naples. Three weeks after *that*, sometime around the second week of July, Caravaggio himself embarked on a *felucca* travelling from Naples to Rome.[136] He left from the Colonna Palace at Chiaia. He had three paintings with him, two of St John the Baptist and one of Mary Magdalen.

The timing of Caravaggio's departure suggests that he waited for Alessandro Caramano to return before leaving for Rome himself. He probably wanted to use Caramano for his own journey too. He was a trusted skipper, whose *felucca* had a sufficiently large hold to carry bulky pictures packed in wooden boxes. Caravaggio was very ill and no doubt more than a little apprehensive, so it made sense for him to choose a boatman whom he knew. But this time, the 'St Mary of the Safe Harbour' did not bring good luck.

According to Bellori, the painter felt confident to return to Rome because he had 'by then obtained his freedom from the pope through the intercession of Cardinal Gonzaga'.[137] The recently appointed Cardinal Ferdinando Gonzaga was the son of Vincenzo I Gonzaga, who had purchased Caravaggio's *Death of the Virgin*. The family may have hoped eventually to obtain more pictures from the artist in return for their support. But the young cardinal seems not to have dealt with the pope directly, approaching him instead through the papal nephew, Scipione Borghese. Borghese was already the proud owner of the artist's first version of *St Jerome Writing* as well as his *David with the Head of Goliath*. Insatiable collector that he was, Borghese agreed to help obtain Caravaggio's pardon, but only if the artist gave him his entire stock of unsold pictures as soon as he got to Rome.[138]

A Roman *avviso* of late July supports Bellori's report that Caravaggio had been granted his long-awaited pardon for the murder of Ranuccio Tomassoni some time before he left Naples, saying that the painter was travelling to Rome 'because His Holiness had lifted the *bando capitale* which he was under'.[139] But Baglione was not so sure: he makes it sound as though negotiations were still continuing, even as Caravaggio set out from Naples. The painter was travelling 'on the word of Cardinal Gonzaga, who was arranging his pardon from Pope Paul V'.[140] If the pardon had not yet been officially agreed, that may help to explain why things would go so badly wrong for him on his journey to Rome.

Each writer put a slightly different slant on what happened next.

In Baglione's telling, it became the parable of a fittingly miserable death, brought on by the painter's own impetuosity and the burning July sun:

When Caravaggio went ashore he was suddenly[141] arrested. He was held for two days in prison and when he was released, the *felucca* was no longer to be found. This made him furious and in his desperation he started out along the beach in the cruel July sun, trying to catch sight of the vessel which was carrying his belongings. Finally he reached a village on the shore and was put to bed with a malignant fever. He was completely abandoned and within a few days he died miserably – indeed, just as he had lived.[142]

Bellori gives a broadly similar account, although he emphasizes that Caravaggio was still in agony from the injuries he had received in the vendetta attack. He also embellishes the painter's detention on landing, turning it into a case of mistaken identity. The idea should not be taken too seriously, since Bellori probably just got it from misreading the phrase 'suddenly arrested' in Baglione's considerably earlier account:[143]

he boarded a *felucca*, and, suffering the bitterest pain, he started out for Rome ... When he went ashore the Spanish guard arrested him by mistake, taking him for another Cavaliere, and held him prisoner. Although he was soon released, the *felucca* which was carrying him and his possessions was no longer to be found. Thus in a state of anxiety and desperation he ran along the beach in the full heat of the summer sun, and when he reached Porto Ercole, he collapsed and was seized with a malignant fever. He died within a few days at about forty years of age ...[144]

Mancini gives much less detail. Wrongly and a bit strangely, since he knew better, he has Caravaggio leaving for Rome from Malta. He also omits the story of Caravaggio's imprisonment, release and desperate pursuit of the *felucca*, but agrees with Baglione and Bellori that the painter died at Porto Ercole:

He left with the hope of being pardoned and went to Civita Vecchia [Porto Ercole, to be precise, according to a marginal note in the text], where, stricken with a malignant fever, he died miserably and without care, at the height of his glory, being about thirty-five or forty years of age. He was buried nearby.[145]

Certain elements of the early biographers' accounts of Caravaggio's death are questionable. He certainly did not travel to Porto

Ercole on foot, for example. But in essence they got the facts right. What they said happened was, more or less, what actually happened.

The true sequence of events has been confirmed and fleshed out by two contemporary newspaper reports and a remarkable letter found in the state archive of Naples.

On 28 July a Roman *avviso* reported that 'There has been news of the death of Michelangelo Caravaggio, the famous painter, excellent in colouring and in drawing from nature, following his illness in Port' Ercole.'[146] Three days later, another Roman *avviso* confirmed the news, adding the detail that he had died at Porto Ercole 'while he was coming from Naples to Rome, having obtained the lifting of the death sentence he was under'.[147] The speed with which these reports appeared suggests that the writers may have received their information direct from Porto Ercole itself, which was a day's fast ride from Rome.

But the papal nephew, Scipione Borghese, had heard the news even quicker than the *avviso* writers. He knew that Caravaggio was dead as early as 23 July. But although he got his information with lightning speed, it was not entirely reliable, because Borghese's source wrongly told him that the painter had died not at Porto Ercole but on the little island of Procida, a day's sail west of Naples.[148] Presumably for that reason Borghese immediately wrote to the papal nuncio in Naples, Deodato Gentile, Bishop of Caserta, urgently demanding more intelligence. He wanted to know what had happened to poor Caravaggio. Even more pressingly, he wanted to know what had happened to the paintings in the dead man's luggage. As far as Borghese was concerned, they were now his property.[149]

The papal nuncio in Naples was indeed able to tell Scipione Borghese what had happened. His response to the papal nephew anticipates the accounts of Caravaggio's death given by both Baglione and Bellori by many years. Yet it turns out to match their descriptions of what happened so exactly, albeit with more detail, that it was in all probability their main source of information in the first place. What Gentile told Borghese became common knowledge in Rome.

Gentile's letter was dated 29 July. He began by acknowledging receipt of Borghese's request for information, which had reached him on 24 July.[150] He confessed that Caravaggio's death was 'completely new' to him. But he had made enquiries and found answers to the papal nephew's questions. He gave Borghese the full story of the painter's death, as he now understood it:

> Poor Caravaggio did not die at Procida, but at Port' Ercole, because having arrived with the *felucca*, in which he went to Palo, he was incarcerated by the captain there. In the uproar, the *felucca* went back out into the open sea and returned to Naples. Caravaggio stayed in prison, then freed himself by paying over a huge sum of money, and perhaps on foot reached Port' Ercole by land, where, falling ill, he departed this life.
>
> On its return, the *felucca* brought the things he'd left behind to the house of the lady Marchesa of Caravaggio, who lives at Chiaia, and from where Caravaggio himself had left. I immediately made sure the pictures were there, and found that there are no more than three, the two St Johns and the Magdalen, and they are in the above-mentioned house of the lady Marchesa, to whom I have sent [a message] straight away to ask that they be well looked after, so they are not ruined before they can be seen, or come into anyone's hands, since they were intended [for Your Lordship], and it is necessary to negotiate on Your Lordship's behalf with the heirs and creditors of the said Caravaggio and give them honest satisfaction.[151]

Deodato Gentile signed off with a promise to make sure that the paintings would end up in 'the hands of Your Most Illustrious Lordship'.

Despite this letter's dispassionate clarity, and despite the fact that it was written within days of the events that it describes, all kinds of arcane conspiracy theories about Caravaggio's death continue to proliferate.[152] He is said to have been the victim of a plot involving the Knights of Malta, or Costanza Colonna, or the pope himself – or all of them, acting fiendishly in concert. He is said to have been ambushed at sea, his body cut in pieces and dumped underwater in a sack. The proponents of such theories invariably claim that the information gathered by Deodato Gentile was nothing more than a smokescreen of falsehood and fabrication – a tall tale to cover up a murder. But there is no real reason to doubt the report that Gentile carefully filed to Scipione Borghese, who was not only one of the most powerful men in Italy but the head of the papal system of justice. Attempting to deceive such a man would have been foolhardy, and probably futile.

In truth, the supposed mystery of Caravaggio's death is nothing of the kind. Conspiracy theories are a distraction. Caravaggio's true fate was dark and dramatic enough to need no elaboration or reinvention. His last journey can now be clearly reconstructed, the cause of his death understood.

This is what happened.

Hoping that his pardon had been arranged, the painter set out from Naples to Rome on or around 9 July 1610. He left in a *felucca*, probably the *Santa Maria di Porto Salvo*, with his three paintings stowed in the hold. He is unlikely to have been the only passenger. A *felucca* was a two-masted boat with square-set sails and a spitsail, which could be rowed if winds were unfavourable. It was crewed by between six and eight men, and to hire one was expensive. The usual practice was for a skipper to wait until he had two or more customers going in the same direction before beginning a journey. It is probable that Caravaggio had a travelling companion who was going to Porto Ercole, or the boatman had a delivery to make there. Either way, Caravaggio knew that Porto Ercole was the boat's final destination.[153]

About a week after setting sail, the *felucca* carrying Caravaggio and his paintings docked at Palo, a high-security fort manned by a Spanish garrison, some twenty miles west of Rome. It was not the most common landing place for travellers to Rome, especially travellers wanting to arrive discreetly.[154] But Palo was a centre for the distribution and transportation of goods and materials, as well as a fortress.[155] It made sense for Caravaggio to land there because with his three heavy paintings in large boxes he needed a horse-drawn carriage or cart to complete his journey.

When he got to Palo, however, something went badly wrong. His papers may have been out of order, or perhaps he just made a remark the captain of the garrison did not like. Whatever it was, before his luggage could be unloaded, he was taken away to a holding cell. 'In all the uproar,' Deodato Gentile told Scipione Borghese, 'the *felucca* went back out into the open sea and returned to Naples.' Gentile's wording suggests a fracas, with Caravaggio resisting arrest, shouting and perhaps characteristically trying to draw his sword as he was forcibly restrained.

Avoiding further involvement in the scuffle, the skipper put out to sea again. He would indeed return to Naples, but not immediately. First, with his other customer, or to make his other delivery, he had to get to Porto Ercole, some fifty miles north and, depending on the wind, about a couple of days' journey by sea further from Rome, and from Naples.

Meanwhile, Caravaggio was forced to cool his heels in jail. The cause of his imprisonment may have been trivial, because he was allowed to buy his way out. At this point all the accounts become a little vague, or fanciful, suggesting there were no witnesses to what happened next. According to Deodato Gentile, Caravaggio, 'perhaps on foot, reached Porto Ercole by land'. Baglione elaborated that speculation into the maddened run of a desperate man along a parched coastline in the height of summer: 'in his desperation he started out along the beach in the cruel July sun, trying to catch sight of the vessel which was carrying his belongings.' The story clearly appealed to Bellori, who repeated it.

But it is obviously false. Assuming that Caravaggio got out of jail within a day of his arrest, he left Palo on 16 or 17 July. Scipione Borghese knew that he was dead by 23 July, which means that he actually died on 21 July at the very latest, and probably earlier. In other words, his journey from Palo to Porto Ercole can only have taken a few days, probably just a couple. But the distance between the two places is some fifty miles. In high summer, a man convalescing from serious injuries would have struggled to make that journey on foot in less than four or five days.[156]

Caravaggio may have been desperate, but he was not mad. Throughout his life he had shown a cool head in tight situations. It suited Baglione's purposes to invent the story of the enraged pursuit, because it paved the way for his smug ending – 'he died miserably – indeed, just as he had lived' – but the truth is that Caravaggio had to catch up with the boat because it was carrying the paintings that were the price of his compact with Scipione Borghese. If he did not, he could not return to Rome. He knew from conversations with the skipper, or with his travelling companion, that the boat had gone to Porto Ercole. Given the 'uproar' that had accompanied his arrest at Palo, he certainly could not count on the boat returning there with his possessions. So he had to go to find it.

Palo was a staging post, so even though the boat had a head start, he could easily get to Porto Ercole first. He would simply have to ride post along the coastal delivery route. With a change of horse, he might cover the whole distance in a single day. It would have been exhausting, but it was no insane race against fate. It was the logical thing to do. He left Palo probably on 16 or 17 July, and a day later arrived in Porto Ercole, another small coastal settlement, manned by a Spanish garrison. But the stress of his arrest at Palo, and the effort of getting to Porto Ercole to recover his paintings, finally broke him. In Porto Ercole, probably on 18 or 19 July, Caravaggio died.

The boat carrying his paintings arrived almost simultaneously, perhaps shortly afterwards. The skipper and crew soon learned the news of Caravaggio's illness and death. The painter was buried, hurriedly and without ceremony. In the heat of summer a body would decay quickly, so there could be no delay. Since he died alone, without relatives or friends to care for him, he was placed in an unmarked grave. His death was not recorded in the parish records. This has been regarded as a sinister omission by the conspiracy theorists. But there is an unsinister explanation for it. Porto Ercole's only priest was in dispute with the town fathers and on strike at the time. No deaths were recorded there in the summer of 1610.[157]

The boat carrying Caravaggio's possessions could do no more than return to Naples. Presumably the vessel left immediately. It was certainly back in Naples by 29 July, when Deodato Gentile reported to Scipione Borghese that Caravaggio's paintings had been returned to Costanza Colonna's palace.

The exact cause of Caravaggio's death is unknown. Deodato Gentile, writing just over a week after the event, simply said that he fell ill and departed life. On the evidence of the agonized self-portrait in *The Martyrdom of St Ursula*, and the shakiness of the hand that painted it, he was already unwell when he set out for Rome. The stress of his arrest, and the frantic ride to Porto Ercole in the extreme heat of July, was more than a man in his condition could take. Heat exhaustion, or perhaps a heart attack, may have been what finally killed him.

One question remains. Where did Deodato Gentile get his information? What was his source for all this close detail about the final journey and strange, sad death of a sick man trying to reach Rome from

Naples? Whatever it was, it was also the source on which the later biographers drew when they elaborated their own accounts of the painter's death. No one added anything meaningful to it, except red herrings like Bellori's mistaken arrest or Baglione's headlong footrace along the coast.

It might be thought that Gentile had put his feelers out in Porto Ercole, where the death had taken place, or had sent for information to Palo, where Caravaggio had been arrested. But he could have done neither of those things: the dates of his correspondence with Scipione Borghese preclude it. Borghese wrote to Gentile on 23 July and Gentile received the letter the following day. He replied to Borghese just five days later, on 29 July. It was two or three days by boat to Palo, the same again to Porto Ercole. By horse, even riding post, it would have taken at least four days in each direction, since it is two hundred miles from Naples to Porto Ercole. A week, more likely ten days, would have been needed to get there, make enquiries, and then report back. So Gentile must have found his information in Naples. Who could he have spoken to? Who would have known all this?

Only one person could have told the papal nuncio about what happened when Caravaggio landed at Palo. Only one person could have told him about the painter's death in Porto Ercole. That person was the boatman, who had just returned to Naples with the dead painter's belongings. His crew had accompanied him, but it was the owner of the boat whom Deodato Gentile would have brought in for questioning. The whole story must have been his testimony. Hence the use of nautical terminology – 'the *felucca* went back out into the open sea', he had said, *alto mare*[158] – as well as the ship's-eye perspective of the entire account. Hence too the vagueness after Caravaggio is arrested and the boat pulls off: that was the moment when the boatman lost sight of the painter.

The interview would have been short and to the point. The boatman was being accused of nothing and had nothing to hide. He had no reason to be evasive, so he simply told the truth as best he could.

Where did you take Michelangelo Merisi? Palo, the garrison. What happened there? Some kind of trouble. They arrested him. There was a real uproar, so it was best to take the boat on to Porto Ercole.

How did the painter get to Porto Ercole? The skipper does not know, so he shrugs and makes a guess, not thinking properly about the distances involved – 'perhaps on foot'.

What happened at Porto Ercole? He is not sure about that either, probably because the painter had died before he got there. But he does know that Caravaggio had fallen ill, and had died at that place. It had probably only just happened when the boatman arrived. He may even have been asked to identify the body, so they could bury it as soon as possible.

What about the paintings? Of course, he knows all about them. They are back at the Marchesa of Caravaggio's house, the palace at Chiaia, the one at the edge of the city, facing the bay. He had returned them just the day before. That is where he had taken them from in the first place, when the poor man had hired him.

Deodato Gentile could have had all this information second-hand from Costanza Colonna herself, because she must have quizzed the skipper of the *felucca* when he came back to her house in Naples, with the pictures but without Caravaggio. But he did not. Gentile makes it clear in his letter that he had *not* spoken to her, that he had only sent a message telling her to keep Caravaggio's pictures safe at all costs. Gentile's source can indeed only have been the captain of the *felucca* himself – the skipper, in all probability, of the *Santa Maria di Porto Salvo*.

Caravaggio appears for the first time as a flesh-and-blood human being in the documentary records through the fleeting testimony of a Roman barber-surgeon named Luca. The painter had been 'a stocky young man, about twenty or twenty-five years old, with a thin black beard, thick eyebrows and black eyes, who goes dressed all in black, in a rather disorderly fashion, wearing black hose that is a little bit threadbare, and who has a thick head of hair, long over his forehead'. That was in 1597. Less than thirteen years later, wounded and worn down, our last glimpses of Caravaggio are through the testimony of a humble boatman, Alessandro Caramano. Like Luca the barber's apprentice, Alessandro was just an ordinary man. He could not read and he could not write. But he could tell the truth about what he had seen with his own eyes.

Caravaggio had lived much of his life close to the margins of society, surrounded by poor and ordinary people. He painted them, staging the stories of the Bible with their bodies and their faces. He painted *for* them and from their perspective. In the end he died among them and was buried among them, in an unmarked grave. He was thirty-eight years old.

AFTERMATH

In Naples, Rome and Malta, people in high places briefly lamented the passing of 'poor Caravaggio'. Then they got into an unseemly scramble for his last few paintings.

Having been told by the boatman that the three pictures in the painter's luggage had been deposited with Costanza Colonna, Deodato Gentile had immediately written to her claiming them on Scipione Borghese's behalf. But he had been too late. The Knights of Malta had also found out about Caravaggio's death. On the very day that Gentile wrote to Costanza Colonna, the local prior of the Knights of Malta barged his way into her palace and forcibly confiscated the pictures. Caravaggio had been dead for only ten days, but an unholy row was already brewing over his last things.

On 31 July 1610, Gentile reported back to Borghese in Rome: 'Most Illustrious and Reverend Sir ... The Marchesa of Caravaggio has informed me that the paintings of Caravaggio are no longer in her house, but have been sequestrated by the Prior of Capua ... said prior is claiming that Caravaggio was a serving brother in his religious order, and that therefore all the spoils are his to take. The Marchesa says that this is all folly and vanity, and the prior is not right. I will do my best to find where they are kept, and use all diligence to secure them in the name of Your Illustrious Lordship ...'[159]

On the death of any Knight of Malta, his possessions indeed automatically reverted to the order. Suddenly it suited Wignacourt and his prior to pretend that Caravaggio's defrocking had never taken place, and that he had still been a Knight of Magistral Obedience when he died. But the marchesa, who knew very well that Caravaggio had been stripped of his knighthood, saw straight through this rather crude gambit. Hence her audible disgust for the prior and his men, turning up at her house and taking the paintings, as if she were a bankrupt and they were the bailiffs – it was indeed all *vanità*.

Deodato Gentile concluded his letter of 31 July by advising Borghese to write to Don Pedro Fernández de Castro, Conde de Lemos, who had recently taken over the post of Spanish viceroy in Naples. Don Pedro was the most powerful man in the city. Borghese followed Gentile's advice, informing the viceroy of the prior's false claims and appealing to him for help. But the wheels of Spanish diplomacy moved painfully slowly. It was mid August before Don Pedro swung, rather confusedly, into action. He told the impudent Prior of Capua that it was no good pretending that Caravaggio had died a Knight of Malta, and that he would have to surrender all claims to the pictures. But the Spanish viceroy had evidently failed to realize exactly what had happened. Somehow or other he had got it into his head that the paintings were still being argued over in Porto Ercole, some two hundred miles north. So he fired off a peremptory letter to the head of the Spanish garrisons in Tuscany, together with an inventory listing the works of art that he particularly wanted to secure:

Honoured Sir, I have been informed that the painter Michael Angelo di Caravaggio has died at Port' Ercole and that you have in your possession all his property, especially the items indicated in the inventory which accompanies this letter, the property having been taken over as a spolium under the pretext that the deceased was a member of the Order of St John, and that it belonged to the Prior of Capua who has declared that he has no right to this spolium inasmuch as the deceased was not a Knight of Malta; and thus I charge you that as soon as you receive this letter you send me the aforesaid property by the first *felucca* available, and especially the painting of *St John the Baptist*, and if by chance it has been disposed of or removed from the property for whatever reason, you shall endeavour by all means to see that it is found and recovered in order to send it well packed with the other property and deliver it here to the proper authority, and you shall carry this out unconditionally, informing me of the receipt of this letter. From my desk, Naples, August 19, 1610.[160]

It would be another five months before anything more was heard about the paintings. By then two of them had disappeared altogether, perhaps into the hands of Caravaggio's creditors, perhaps to Malta. The only work of art that anyone could locate for sure was a *St John*, which turned out to be the picture of the saint as an olive-skinned Sicilian boy painted at around the time Caravaggio had left Messina for Palermo. By the winter of 1610 it had found its way into the house of the Spanish viceroy, who seems to have become singularly reluctant to give it up.

On 12 December the beleaguered Bishop of Caserta, Deodato Gentile, was finally able to report further developments to Scipione Borghese. He apologized for still not having despatched the *St John*, which his lordship 'must have given up for lost', and explained the reasons. The viceroy had wanted to have a copy made of the painting for his own collection. In addition, there had been obscure problems with Caravaggio's inheritors and creditors – this part of the document is barely legible – and since he had left many debts there were people who had needed to be satisfied.[161] Gentile promised to press the matter and obtain the painting. Only in August of the following year did the papal nuncio finally manage to prise it from the grip of the Spanish viceroy and send it, at long last, to Rome. He apologized that it had been slightly damaged in all the toing and froing. The picture has remained in the Borghese collection ever since.

DOING JESUS LIKE CARAVAGGIO

The messy story of what happened to Caravaggio's last paintings is also a microcosm of his afterlife, and a parable illustrating his singularity as a painter. He had always been an outsider, a troublemaker, a difficult and dangerous man. Yet his art was so compelling, so original, so unforgettable, that people were simply transfixed by it. They fought to look at it, gathering in their hundreds every time a new altarpiece was unveiled, and they fought to acquire it, even though everything else about Caravaggio – his terseness, his weird dress sense, his violence, his sexual reputation, his unerring gift for getting into trouble – seemed so disconcerting and strange.

Caravaggio was not only the most disturbed but also the most unconventional of the truly great painters of the Italian tradition. His whole career ran counter to type, defiantly contradicting the patterns of training, patronage and even the actual practice of painting that were expected of a successful artist. It is clear that during his obscure early years, something went awry during his supposed apprenticeship to the Milanese painter Peterzano. Essentially, Caravaggio taught himself to paint. He may have picked up technical tips and clues in places like Giuseppe Cesari's studio, but his basic method was empirical. He looked at the way light falls, and at the way people behave. The fact that he was obliged to invent himself may partly explain his deep originality. The advantage of not having been taught was that he had nothing to unlearn.

Once he had begun to find his own way, Caravaggio painted with such force, such a stunning sense of drama, such a deep sense of humanity, that prestigious commissions flooded towards him. The simple truth is that he was a far greater painter than any of his contemporaries. But, despite winning the support of Cardinal del Monte, and despite his network of protectors within the Colonna family, he never found a secure place in the hierarchies of power and patronage. He painted as if the rich and the powerful were his enemies, as if he really did believe that the meek deserved to inherit the earth. Ultimately, he acted in the same way too. Only once in his life did he come close to achieving a truly settled position, a respected place among men of real power and influence, and that was on Malta. But almost as soon as he had been knighted, he managed to have himself thrown into jail. With hindsight it looks like a complete act of self-sabotage, as if he could not bear the thought of truly belonging and of walking the corridors of power.

Caravaggio was also unique among the great Italian painters in *how* he went about painting. He had no studio in anything like the conventional sense. He had the odd boy to help him, Cecco in particular, but essentially he painted all by himself. He did not draw. He never established a workshop with specialist assistants to help with the painting of drapery or landscape, as other artists did. He gathered around himself no real circle of pupils, and there were no acolytes to spread the word, no one to disseminate his methods and his beliefs. There were no portfolios of his drawings to pass around. There was nothing except his pictures themselves, and there were not very many of those because he had died so young. Under the circumstances, the vast impact of his work is all the more remarkable.

For more than a century and a half after his death, the classicizing critics of Europe's academic art tradition made a concerted and resolute attempt to blacken his name. According to their beliefs, much influenced by the strains of Neoplatonist philosophy, it was art's duty to present an idealized version of reality, and not – as Caravaggio was held to have done – merely to represent the real world in all its unregenerate ugliness. Bellori was the arch-exponent of the anti-Caravaggist movement in academic thought, but there were many others, notably the Spanish painter and author Vicente Carducho, who demonized Caravaggio as an anti-Christ of art, the antithesis to his saintly predecessor and namesake, the 'divine' Michelangelo. So influential was the rhetoric of Caravaggio's posthumous enemies that the great French seventeenth-century painter Poussin was persuaded that he had been 'sent into the world to destroy painting'.

Despite the sustained drive to denigrate and marginalize his work, Caravaggio's paintings were too profound and affecting to be suppressed. Gradually but inexorably, his dramatic sense of composition, his strikingly stark handling of light and dark and his sheer rawness of feeling worked themselves into the DNA of Western art. During the years immediately after his death, hardly a single important painter escaped his influence. Rubens, Velàzquez and Pietro da Cortona all echoed his compositions or copied his devices and traits. Within a generation, entire schools of so-called Caravaggisti established themselves in both Italy and the Netherlands. Partly perhaps because of the location of the French Academy in Rome, at the top of the Spanish Steps, and within easy walking distance of so many of his most important altarpieces, he would have an especially powerful impact on French art. His influence can be detected in the work of such widely differing French painters as Valentin de Boulogne and Georges de La Tour. There was a particularly strong resurgence of interest in his art during the Neoclassical and Romantic periods. In England, Joseph Wright of Derby's *Experiment on a Bird in the Air Pump* of 1768 transformed the scientific demonstration of the effects of a vacuum on a living creature into a hushed modern version of a miracle as painted by Caravaggio. In France, the self-appointed painter to the Revolution, Jacques-Louis David, painted the dead Marat slumped in his bath as if he were one of Caravaggio's spotlit martyrs, and in 1819 Theodore Géricault conceived arguably the first great masterpiece of French Romanticism, *The Raft of the Medusa*, as a modern, secularized version of an altarpiece by Caravaggio.

Towards the end of the nineteenth century Caravaggio's work did fall somewhat out of fashion. His paintings attracted relatively little attention from those pioneering the still embryonic discipline of art history, whose attentions were biased by the market. (The purpose of much early art historical research was to establish the provenance and therefore the value of pictures coming to auction, but, since nearly all of Caravaggio's major pictures were immovable altarpieces, very few of his works ever came up for sale.) Neither did his pictures seem especially interesting to painters of the early Modern period, such as Cézanne or, later, the Cubists and Futurists, because it was their stated ambition to flatten, distort and destroy the conventions of post-Renaissance illusionist painting. Caravaggio was too much of an 'optical' painter for their taste. They preferred the so-called Italian 'primitives', painters such as Giotto and Duccio, whose disregard for conventional perspective seemed closer to a Modernist aesthetic. They might have been interested in Caravaggio's late Sicilian pictures, which responded to powerful strains of primitivism in Counter-Reformation thought, but those paintings had fallen into neglect and were all but unknown by the early twentieth century. It is symbolic of this one period of genuine neglect that the young Picasso, for all his magpie eclecticism and positively Oedipal obsession with the art of the past, never showed the slightest interest in reworking or pastiching the art of Caravaggio. It was only when Picasso grew older that his attitude changed. In 1937, while working on *Guernica*, his agonized frieze of suffering inspired by the horrors of the Spanish Civil War, he told Salvador Dalí that he wanted the horse at the centre of the painting to have the same presence as the horse in Caravaggio's *Conversion of St Paul*: 'I want it to be so realistic – just like in Caravaggio – that you can smell the sweat.'[162]

Caravaggio's reputation was decisively rehabilitated for the twentieth century by the gifted and eloquent Italian art historian Roberto Longhi, who put on an extremely influential retrospective of the painter's work in 1951. Since then Caravaggio has become perhaps the most widely popular of all the Old Masters. In many respects he is the perfect painter for an age pruriently obsessed with the lurid private lives of famous people. His fame has never been greater, and his private life was nothing if not lurid. His many sins and misdemeanours, his irregularities and eccentricities, so long used to blacken his name, have now made him a posthumous celebrity. But the deeper pull is still that of his art.

Since Longhi staged his ground-breaking exhibition, Caravaggio's influence has continued to spread. But his work seems to have been less of an inspiration to those ploughing the increasingly conceptualist fields of fine art than to those working with photography and film. One of the few painters to have had a profound impact on disciplines other than painting itself, he may fairly be considered as a pioneer of modern cinematography. Pier Paolo Pasolini, who made some of the most powerful Italian films of the 1960s, was profoundly influenced by Caravaggio's sense of light, by his narrative directness, and by his casting of poor and ordinary working people in leading roles. Martin Scorsese, one of the most gifted American directors of the last forty years, has been disarmingly explicit about the depth of his own admiration for Caravaggio. He was introduced to the painter's work in the late 1960s by screenwriter Paul Schrader when they were working on *Taxi Driver*, his film about a vigilante killer taking on New York's underworld of drug dealers and whores. He sees Caravaggio very much with the eyes of someone looking for things he can use, borrow, adapt. In Scorsese's words, the long tradition of Caravaggio as a true artist's artist is both reincarnated and refreshed. It is worth quoting him at length:

I was instantly taken by the power of the pictures, the power of the compositions, the action in the frames, the way he designed the composition and the subject matter ... there was no doubt it could be taken into cinema because of the use of light and shadow, the chiaroscuro effect ...

Initially I related to the paintings because of the moment that he chose to illuminate in the story. *The Conversion of Paul*, *Judith Beheading Holofernes*: he was choosing a moment that was not the absolute moment of the beginning of the action, it's during the action, in a way. You sort of come upon the scene midway and you're immersed in it. It was very different from the composition of the paintings that preceded it, the Renaissance paintings. It was like modern staging in film. It was as if we had just come in the middle of scene and it was all happening.

It was so powerful and direct. It was startling, really. He would have been a great film-maker, there's no doubt about it. I thought, I can use this too . . .

So then he was there. He sort of pervaded the entirety of the bar sequences in another film I made around then, *Mean Streets*. There's no doubt about that. He was there in the way I wanted the camera movement, the choice of how to stage a scene. It's basically people sitting in bars, people at tables, people getting up, that sort of thing. *The Calling of Matthew*, but in New York! Making films with street people was what it was really about, like he made paintings with them. They weren't like the usual models from the Renaissance. They were people who were really living life. That's why it played into my mind in *Mean Streets* . . .

Then that extended into a much later film, *The Temptation of Christ*. Why couldn't we have people who lived on the street play apostles? They had been fishermen, Jesus was a carpenter. Caravaggio takes the Virgin Mary and has a prostitute play the Virgin Mary. She's a woman and the Virgin Mary's a woman. It's shocking and provocative. It doesn't judge the person. It doesn't make judgement on the prostitute when making her the Virgin and this is something very powerful and compassionate . . .

So in doing *The Last Temptation of Christ* the idea was that Jesus was going to be Jesus Christ on Eighth Avenue and 49th Street in New York, where we shot *Taxi Driver* those years ago. It hasn't changed much since then, it's a little better now, but really you might as well be in a den of iniquity most of the time. It was quite a place, especially at three and four in the morning. This is where Jesus would go. He wouldn't be hanging out on Park Avenue in New York. He'd be in the street with the crack addicts and the prostitutes. The idea was to do Jesus like Caravaggio.[163]

Epilogue

Caravaggio's contemporaries would doubtless have been amazed by the extent of his posthumous fame. Few of those who knew him could ever have imagined that he and his work would survive so far into the future, that he would be remembered so long after they had all been forgotten.

But it was true. Hardly any of the artists with whom Caravaggio had been close made any mark at all on posterity. His Sicilian friend Mario Minniti lived into his sixties, turning out quantities of mediocre altarpieces and making himself a small fortune, but no great reputation, in Messina. His old assistant Cecco Boneri established something of a career for himself as Cecco del Michelangelo, but soon slipped into near-total obscurity. The hot-headed architect Onorio Longhi, who had been his second in the duel, returned to Rome a year or so after Caravaggio's death, only to die himself five years later of syphilis.

Caravaggio's old enemy Giovanni Baglione lived long and prospered, winning numerous grand commissions from popes as well as princes and aristocrats. When he died he was nearly eighty, a Knight of Christ and a wealthy man. But he too would soon be forgotten – or at least remembered mostly for being Caravaggio's adversary and biographer. Orazio Gentileschi, who had once laughed along with Caravaggio at 'Johnny Baggage', was the only one of his close acquaintances to amount to much as an artist. A painter of considerable power and invention, he ended his career as a court painter to Charles I, dying in London in his mid seventies in 1639 just a few years before the start of the English Civil War. Orazio's daughter, Artemisia, who had been raped by Agostino Tassi, also became a gifted and successful painter in her own right.

And what of those with whom Caravaggio drank and dined, quarrelled and fought? What of those whom he loved and hated? What of the waiter with the cut face, the sharp-eyed barber-surgeon, the disgruntled notary? What of all the pimps and soldiers and the boys and girls who lived by selling their bodies? Some survived in his paintings, whether as villains or martyrs, torturers or apostles. Most disappeared without trace. But one fragment has survived: the last will and testament of Fillide Melandroni.

Fillide had been Caravaggio's first model. She was the disconcertingly sexy *St Catherine*, as well as the girl holding the flower up to her breast and gazing out with a smouldering, coquettish stare in the portrait he had painted of her in 1598. She was Fillide the courtesan, who perhaps won the heart and certainly lightened the purse of the Florentine aristocrat Giulio Strozzi.

In the summer of 1618, Fillide was thirty-seven or thirty-eight years old, close to the same age as Caravaggio when he died. She was still living in Rome, but by now she had her own house. She had clearly gone up in the world. But she was mortally ill, perhaps with the same form of venereal disease that had cut short the life of Caravaggio's friend Onorio Longhi. On 3 July she died.

Soon after, an inventory was made of her now considerable possessions. Her main reception room was decorated with gilded leather panels. At its centre stood a table covered with a Turkish carpet, and around the table there were eight leather-covered chairs. In the bedroom she had a large gilded four-poster bed with a green taffeta canopy and a chest containing some lengths of luxury fabric. She had books, vases, plants, an inkwell of silvered copper, a pearl necklace, twenty gold buttons and two gold pendants with pearls.

On 19 November her estate was settled and division was made of her goods. The will that she had made four years earlier was read out. It seems that she was happy for all her property to be sold and the proceeds parcelled out, in specified fractions, to her chosen legatees. But she wanted one particular object to go to one particular individual: 'Item: she states and declares that she has in her house a painting or portrait by the hand of Michelangelo da Caravaggio that belongs to Giulio Strozzi. She wishes it to be restored and consigned to Sr Giulio.'

Fillide's portrait by Caravaggio, the picture that would be consumed four centuries later by the flames of the Second World War, was the most precious thing that she had. She wanted it to go to Strozzi, her protector, who had allowed her to keep it for so long. Perhaps she liked the thought of being with him, in surrogate, after she died. Perhaps she still loved him.

From the inventory of her possessions and the terms of her will we may think that Fillide was not quite the same woman she had been when Caravaggio knew her. Once, she had shamelessly touted for business as a prostitute in the very shadow of the monastery of the Convertites, the religious foundation for the reform of prostitutes, and had assaulted her rival, Prudenza, in her house directly next door to it, screaming as she did so: 'You dirty whore! I want to cut you! I want to cut you!' Now, as well as the portrait by Caravaggio, her house contained three small devotional paintings: of the Nativity, of the Virgin Mary and of the Penitent Magdalen, the prostitute who mended her ways. Her will specified that she wanted to be buried in her parish church. At the end, as death approached, she left several legacies to religious institutions dedicated to the Virgin, so that Masses would be said for her soul after she had died, and a fifth of her entire legacy to the Convertites. The bequest was stipulated in the penultimate clause in her will, set down by the notary in black and white.

But who knows what Fillide really felt, or what she really believed. Like the dark-haired painter she had once known, she moved in that uncertain realm, 'between the sacred and the profane'.

Notes

PART ONE: MILAN, 1571-92

1. See Helen Langdon (ed.), *The Lives of Caravaggio* (London, 2005), pp. 89, 81.

2. The very structure of Bellori's *Lives of the Modern Painters, Sculptors and Architects* consigns Caravaggio to darkness. In arranging the engraved portraits that illustrated his book, Bellori made sure that the artists whom he truly valued be given dignifying attributes such as books or paintbrushes to hold. So for example Nicolas Poussin, one of Bellori's heroes, holds a book fixed with a fine clasp and gazes out with an expression of grave calm on his face. Caravaggio, by contrast, has his hand on the hilt of a sword and glares nervously sideways with the furtive and guilty eyes of a criminal. One of just twelve artists singled out for inclusion, he has been allowed his place at the table of art history. But he sits on the wrong side, a Judas among the true apostles. For an arresting interpretation of some of the fictional elements of the early biographies see 'Caravaggio's Deaths' by Philip Sohm, *Art Bulletin*, vol. 84, no. 3 (Sept. 2002), p. 452.

3. See Helen Langdon, *The Lives of Caravaggio*, p. 57.

4. Ibid., p. 41.

5. Ibid., p. 27.

6. See in particular M. Cinotti, *Novita sul Caravaggio* (Milan, 1983).

7. For the importance of Caravaggio's maternal relations and their contacts, Giacomo Berra, 'Il Giovane Michelangelo Merisi da Caravaggio: la sua famiglia e la scelta dell'ars pingendi', *Paragone*, vol. 53 (2002), pp. 40-128, is the invaluable source.

8. See Richard A. Goldthwaite, *Wealth and the Demand for Art in Italy 1300-1600* (Baltimore, 1993): 'Generally speaking ... the argument got shifted from the nature of nobility to the behaviour of the noble; and along the way, most of the essential elements of the traditional definition – arms, service, virtue, blood, economic activities – were qualified.' So many different ideas were 'bandied about the concept', the writer adds, 'that one could have it just about any way he wanted it'.

9. See Diarmaid MacCulloch, *Reformation: Europe's House Divided 1490–1700* (London, 2003), pp. 330–32.

10. See C. Hughes (ed.), *Shakespeare's Europe: Unpublished Chapters of Fynes Moryson's Itinery* (New York, 1967), p. 49; see also D. E. Zanetti, 'The Patriziato of Milan from the Domination of Spain to the Unification of Italy: An Outline of the Social and Demographic History', *Social History*, no. 6 (Oct. 1977), pp. 745–60.

11. See D. E. Zanetti, 'The Patriziato of Milan', pp. 750–52.

12. See Thomas Coryate, *Coryat's Crudities* (London, 1611), p. 102.

13. See 'Instrucciones de Carlos-Quinto a Don Felipe su hijo', in C. Weiss (ed.), *Papiers d'Etat du Cardinal de Grenvelle*, vol. 3 (Paris, 1842), pp. 267–318. My attention was brought to this document by John Hale, who cites it in his *The Civilisation of Europe in the Renaissance* (London, 1993), pp. 95–6.

14. See Agostino Borromeo, 'Archbishop Carlo Borromeo and the Ecclesiastical Policy of Philip II in the State of Milan', in John M. Headley and John B. Tomaro (eds.), *San Carlo Borromeo: Catholic Reform and Ecclesiastical Politics in the Second Half of the Sixteenth Century* (Washington, London and Toronto, 1988), pp. 85–111.

15. See Ludwig von Pastor, *The History of the Popes* (London, 1951), vol. 15, p. 108.

16. See Wietse de Boer, *The Conquest of the Soul: Confession, Discipline and Public Order in Counter-Reformation Milan* (Leiden, Boston and Cologne, 2001), p.73; Paolo Prodi, 'San Carlo Borromeo e il Cardinale Gabriele Paleotti: due vescovi della Riforma Cattolica', *Critica Storica*, 3 (1964), pp. 135–51.

17. See Agostino Borromeo, 'Archbishop Carlo Borromeo'.

18. See Diarmaid MacCulloch, *Reformation: Europe's House Divided*, pp. 411–12.

19. See E. Cecilia Voelker, 'Borromeo's Influence on Sacred Art and Architecture', in John M. Headley and John B. Tomaro (eds.), *San Carlo Borromeo*, pp. 173–87.

20. Ibid., p. 178.

21. See Wietse de Boer, *The Conquest of the Soul*, p. 43.

22. Ibid.

23. Ibid., p.122.

24. See Diarmaid MacCulloch, *Reformation: Europe's House Divided*, pp. 406–7.

25. See Wietse de Boer, *The Conquest of the Soul*, pp. 62–3: 'Confessors thus became quite literally law enforcement officers, who were to use their privileged access to the soul to assist in the application of church law. Having dispensed with such matters, they turned to the confession proper. But they continued to wear their uniforms as agents of discipline, constantly weighing

the need to deny absolution to those considered unwilling to mend their sinful ways ... if obstinacy was undeniable, the refusal of absolution was to be no empty threat. The Milanese confessor was to display the same combination of holy zeal and legal spirit that was characteristic of his bishop.'

26. See Ludwig von Pastor, *The History of the Popes* (London, 1930), vol. 19, p. 108.

27. See David Freedberg, *The Power of Images: Studies in the History and Theory of Response* (Chicago and London, 1989), p. 179. Freedberg's excellent account of traditions of visualization in Christian meditation gives passing mention to Borromeo (but not Caravaggio).

28. Ibid., p. 171.

29. Ibid., p. 168.

30. See Michael Baxandall, *Painting and Experience in Fifteenth Century Italy: A Primer in the Social History of Pictorial Style* (Oxford, 1972), p. 45: 'The painter was a professional visualizer of the holy stories. What we now easily forget is that each of his pious public was liable to be an amateur in the same line, practised in spiritual exercises that demanded a high level of visualization of, at least, the central episodes of the lives of Christ and Mary.'

31. Cited in Roger Fry, 'Flemish Art at Burlington House. I', Burlington magazine 50, 287 (Feb. 1927), p. 68.

32. See Michael Baxandall, *Painting and Experience in Fifteenth Century Italy*, p. 46.

33. See David Gilmore, *Aggression and Community: Paradoxes of Andalusian Culture* (New Haven, 1987), p. 161.

34. See Wietse de Boer, *The Conquest of the Soul*, p. 113.

35. Ibid., p. 114.

36. See M. Cinotti, *I pittori bergamaschi* (Bergamo, 1983), p. 235.

37. Ibid. Giovan Pietro, who is first mentioned in a document of 1578, died in childhood.

38. See Ann G. Carmichael, 'The Last Past Plague: The Uses of Memory in Renaissance Epidemics', *Journal of the History of Medicine and Allied Sciences*, vol. 53, no. 2, (Apr.1998), p. 143.

39. Ibid., p. 137.

40. See Paolo Bisciola, *Relatione verissima del progresso della peste di Milano, qual principio nel mese d'agosto 1576* (Ancona and Bologna, 1577). The translation here is that of Ann G. Carmichael in 'The Last Past Plague'.

41. See Ann G. Carmichael, 'The Last Past Plague', pp. 137, 141.

42. See Paolo Bisciola, *Relatione verissima del progresso della peste di Milano*.

43. See Fra Paolo Bellintano, *I due Bellintani da Salò et il dialogo della pesta di Fra Paolo*, F. Odorici (ed.), in Francesco Colombo (ed.), *Raccolta di cronisti e documenti storici lombardi inediti* (Milan, 1857), vol. 2, p. 296.

44. See ibid.; the story is singled out in Ann G. Carmichael, 'The Last Past Plague'.

45. See Paolo Bisciola, *Relatione verissima del progresso della peste di Milano*.

46. See M. Cinotti, , *I pittori bergamaschi*, p. 203.

47. For this document and the division of land, see ibid., pp. 235, 250, 206.

48. See Giacomo Berra, 'Il Giovane Michelangelo Merisi da Caravaggio'.

49. See *The Age of Caravaggio*, Royal Academy exhibition catalogue (London, 1985), p. 73.

50. The contract is quoted in M. Gregori, (ed.), *Gli affreschi della Certosa di Garegnano* (Turin, 1973), p. 10; I have used the translation offered in Helen Langdon, *Caravaggio: A Life* (London, 1998), p. 24.

51. Ibid., p. 57.

52. See Walter Friedlaender, *Caravaggio Studies* (Princeton, 1955), p. 233.

53. See Helen Langdon, *The Lives of Caravaggio*, pp. 89, 27.

54. The passage was first detected and deciphered by the art historian Maurizio Calvesi, author of a book aptly entitled *Le realtà del Caravaggio* (*The Realities of Caravaggio*) (Turin, 1990). I am grateful to him for sharing his insights with me.

PART TWO ROME, 1592–5

1. '*Bugiaronaccia poltrona puttana de tio te voglio tirare una pignatta de merda sul mostaccio ... fatti fottere dal boia e ho in culo te con quanti n'hai*': my attention was called to this passage by Alexandra Lapierre, who very kindly allowed me to examine her personal collection of transcripts from criminal archives concerning the activities of artists in late sixteenth- and early seventeenth-century Rome. She quotes the document, in a slightly different translation, in her historical novel *Artemisia* (London, 2000), p. 16, where it appears in the mouth of Agostino Tassi, a protagonist in her story – artistic licence, because it was actually uttered by another, now long-forgotten painter. The original document is dated 1602. She specifies its location in a note to her book; see pp. 369–70.

2. See James Fenton, 'Bernini at Harvard / Chicago Baroque', in *Leonardo's Nephew* (London, 1998), for a concise retelling of the story, which is rehearsed at fuller length in Charles Avery, *Bernini: Genius of the Baroque* (London, 1997).

3. See Helen Langdon, *The Lives of Caravaggio*, p. 57.

4. See *The Complete Works of Montaigne*, D. Frame (trs.) (London, 1958), p. 1,163.

5. Ibid., p. 1,164.

6. Ibid., p. 1,172.

7. Ibid., p. 1,143.

8. Ibid., pp. 1,142, 1,150.

9. Ibid., p. 1,142.

10. Ibid., p. 1,150.

11. See Helen Langdon, *Caravaggio: A Life*, p. 34; and Walter Friedlaender, *Caravaggio Studies*, p. 59.

12. See *The Complete Works of Montaigne*, p. 1,148.

13. I am grateful to Opher Mansour for allowing me to read his unpublished doctoral dissertation for the Courtauld Institute in London, 'Offensive Images: Censure and Censorship in Rome under Clement VIII 1592–1605', from which this information about Clement's Visitation is drawn.

14. This figure necessarily involves guesswork, but, given the sheer amount of artistic activity in Rome at the time, and given the size of many painters' and sculptors' workshops, it is likely to be on the low side.

15. Quoted in John Hale, *The Civilisation of Europe in the Renaissance*, p. 53.

16. See Giovanni Botero, '*The Reason of State*' and '*The Greatness of Cities*', trans. by Robert Peterson 1606, P. J. and D. P. Waley (trs.) (London, 1956), p. 38.

17. See *The Complete Works of Montaigne* p. 1,168.

18. My thanks again to Alexandra Lapierre for guiding me through the history of the artists' quarter and for sharing the fruits of her own research so generously in conversation.

19. See Helen Langdon, *The Lives of Caravaggio*, p. 41.

20. Ibid., p. 27.

21. The suggestion is made by Bellori in notes written while he was preparing his life of Caravaggio.

22. See Helen Langdon, *The Lives of Caravaggio*, p. 58.

23. See Giulio Mancini, *Considerazioni sulla pittura*, vol. 1 (Rome, 1956), pp. 226–7.

24. Ibid., p. 226.

25. See Helen Langdon, *The Lives of Caravaggio*, p. 41. I am grateful to John T. Spike for the suggestion – very plausible, I think – that the picture is a nocturne.

26. See for example the entries in *Caravaggio–Rembrandt*, Rijksmueum exhibition catalogue (Amsterdam, 2006), and *The Age of Caravaggio*, Royal Academy exhibition catalogue.

27. See Pliny, *Natural History*, Book 35, 64–6.

28. I am indebted to Maurizio Calvesi for this suggestion, made to me in conversation in September 2001. See Maurizio Calvesi, *Le realtà del Caravaggio*, and for an English language version of his interpretation see his *Caravaggio* (Florence, 1998), pp. 26–7.

29. The rabbi's name was Akiva. See Carl W. Ernst, *Interpreting the Song of Songs: The Paradox of Spiritual and Sensual Love* for a helpful guide through the theological intricacies of the centuries-long tradition of exegesis (www.unc.edu/-cernst/articles/sosintro.htm, 28 Oct. 2008).

30. St Teresa of Avila, 'Meditation on the Song of Songs', *The Collected Works of St Teresa of Avila*, vol. 2, Kieran Kavanaugh, OCD, and Otilio Rodriguez, OCD (trs.) (Washington, DC, 1980).

31. See Helen Langdon, *The Lives of Caravaggio*, p. 28.

32. Ibid., p. 49.

33. Ibid., p. 41.

34. It was painted on a light grey ground like a number of Caravaggio's earliest works, whereas the National Gallery picture was painted on a warmish ground, which accords with the painter's practice from around 1596.

35. All quotations from Sandrart taken from the translation given in Walter Friedlaender, *Caravaggio Studies*, pp. 263-6.

36. See Giorgio Vasari, *Lives of the Painters, Sculptors and Architects*, Gaston du C. de Vere (trs.), David Ekserdjian (ed.), vol. 1 (London, 1996), p. 860.

37. Cited in Peter Burke, *The Historical Anthropology of Early Modern Italy* (Cambridge, 1987), p. 98.

38. See Helen Langdon, *The Lives of Caravaggio*, p. 42.

39. See Helen Langdon, *Caravaggio: A Life*, p. 78. Langdon writes (and lectures) particularly well about Caravaggio's pictures of rogues. The idea that the cardsharps are rather like wasps in human clothing – see below – I owe to her.

40. See Helen Langdon, *The Lives of Caravaggio*, p. 42.

41. Mancini, cited in Howard Hibbard, *Caravaggio* (London, 1983), p. 350 (he was writing about the later version, a picture that he particularly loved, but his remarks are equally applicable to the painting owned by del Monte).

42. Cited in Todd P. Olson, 'The Street has Its Masters: Caravaggio and the Socially Marginal', in *Caravaggio: Realism, Rebellion, Deception*, Genevieve Warwick (ed.) (Delaware, 2006), p. 76.

43. The quotations reprinted here have been extracted from the essay 'Perceiving a Counter-Culture', in Peter Burke, *The Historical Anthropology of Early Modern Italy*, pp. 63-75. My summary of the different types of beggar is an abridged version of Burke's.

44. Ibid., pp. 65-71. My discussion of poverty, religion and politics throughout this section of the book owes a great deal to Burke's lucid analysis.

45. See Antonio Maria Cospi, *Il giudice criminalista*, pp. 374-7.

46. Ibid.

47. Cited in John F. Moffitt, 'Caravaggio and the Gypsies', *Paragone*, vol. 53 (2002), p. 141.

48. Cited in D. J. Gordon, 'Gypsies as Emblems of Comedy and Poverty', *Journal of the Gypsy Lore Society*, vol. 23 (1944), pp. 39–42.

49. Ibid.

50. See John F. Moffitt, 'Caravaggio and the Gypsies', p. 134.

51. Giuseppe Pavoni, Diário, 1589, pp. 29–30, cited in Kenneth Richards and Laura Richards, *The Commedia dell'Arte: A Documentary History* (Oxford, 1990), p. 74.

52. Ibid., p. 60.

53. Tommaso Garzoni, quoted in ibid., pp. 221–2.

PART THREE: ROME, 1595–9

1. See Helen Langdon, *The Lives of Caravaggio*, p. 42.

2. See Creighton Gilbert, *Caravaggio and His Two Cardinals* (Pennsylvania, 1995), p. 116.

3. See Helen Langdon, *Caravaggio: A Life*, p. 79.

4. See Zbgniew Wazbinski, *Il Cardinale Francesco Maria del Monte 1549–1626* (Florence, 1994), p. 77, cited in Helen Langdon, *Caravaggio: A Life*, p. 81.

5. Decorated with languorous, graceful figures and a flying putto, it is now one of the treasures of the British Museum.

6. He might have appreciated the French Romantic painter Delacroix's slashing cut through that particular Gordian knot: the observation that a painter's every brushstroke necessarily incorporated the act of drawing.

7. See Helen Langdon, *Caravaggio: A Life*, p. 96.

8. For del Monte, Mancini, health care and alchemy, see Silvia De Renzi, '"A Fountain for the Thirsty" and a Bank for the Pope: Charity, Conflicts and Medical Careers at the Hospital of Santo Spirito in Seventeenth-Century Rome', in *Health Care and Poor Relief in Counter-Reformation Europe*, Ole Peter Grell, Andrew Cunningham and Jon Arrizabalaga (eds.) (London, 1999), pp. 102–31.

9. De Renzi's scholarly study of the hospital (see above) concludes, ambiguously, that 'Reasons to apply for a job at the Santo Spirito could be various: a somewhat difficult-to-detect religious and moral commitment, and the more evident search for a prestigious position, were interwoven.'

10. See Creighton Gilbert, *Caravaggio and His Two Cardinals*, p. 205.

11. Ibid. Gilbert has done all scholars of Caravaggio and del Monte a service by so thoroughly exposing Amayden's untrustworthiness as a biographer.

12. The letter in question was discovered in the Florentine State Archives by the scholar Franca Trinchieri Camiz, who published it for the first time in

1991. See Franca Trinchieri Camiz, 'Music and Painting in Cardinal del Monte's Household', *Metropolitan Museum Journal*, no. 26 (Hartford, 1991).

13. See Franca Trinchieri Camiz, 'La "musica" nei quadri di Caravaggio', *Caravaggio. Nuove riflessioni, Quaderni di Palazzo Venezia*, vol. 6 (Rome, 1991).

14. See Keith Christiansen, *A Caravaggio Rediscovered: The Lute Player* (New York, 1990).

15. See Franca Trinchieri Camiz, 'La "musica" nei quadri di Caravaggio'.

16. See Claude V. Palisca, 'Musical Asides in the Diplomatic Correspondence of Emilio de' Cavalieri', *Musical Quarterly*, vol. 49, no. 3 (July 1963), p. 346.

17. See Keith Christiansen, *A Caravaggio Rediscovered: The Lute Player*, p. 26.

18. See the entry on Emilio de' Cavalieri in *The Grove Dictionary of Music* (Oxford, 2003).

19. See Zbgniew Wazbinski, *Il Cardinale Francesco Maria del Monte*, pp. 137–8.

20. See Creighton Gilbert, *Caravaggio and His Two Cardinals*, p. 116.

21. See Keith Christiansen, *A Caravaggio Rediscovered: The Lute Player*, p. 46.

22. See Helen Langdon, *The Lives of Caravaggio*, p. 63.

23. See Keith Christiansen, *A Caravaggio Rediscovered: The Lute Player*, p. 32.

24. See Franca Trinchieri Camiz, 'Music and Painting in Cardinal del Monte's Household', p. 220.

25. As Franca Trinchieri Camiz remarks, in 'Music and Painting in Cardinal del Monte's Household': 'the voice was well suited for solo performance because of its greater capacity for proper phrasing, which allowed the expression of the strong emotions in fashion during this period'(p. 221).

26. Ibid., p. 218; for a counter-example, see the very different, open-mouthed singers, accompanied by lutes and polyphonically hymning the infant Christ, in Piero della Francesca's *Nativity* in the National Gallery, London.

27. See Colin Slim, 'Musical Inscriptions in Paintings by Caravaggio and His Followers', in *Music and Context*, A. Shapiro (ed.) (Cambridge, Mass., 1995).

28. See Keith Christiansen, *A Caravaggio Rediscovered: The Lute Player*, p. 90. The translation given is that of Louis E. Lord.

29. The late seventeenth-century writer Pietro Paolo Bosca actually referred to it as a 'tantalus'. See P. P. Bosca, *De origine et statu Bibliothecae Ambrosianae* (Milan, 1672), p. 126. Cited by John T. Spike, *Caravaggio* (New York, 2001), in his CD-ROM catalogue entry on the *Basket of Fruit*.

30. Cited by John T. Spike, *Caravaggio*, in his CD-ROM catalogue entry on the *Basket of Fruit*.

31. My thanks to Maurizio Calvesi for this observation.

32. It is a fair assumption that the two pictures have the same history. So to trace one is, in effect, to trace both. *The Rest on the Flight to Egypt* is linked

to Olimpia Aldobrandini by an inventory of her collection compiled in 1611, which mentions 'A large painting of the Madonna's Flight into Egypt in a frame', albeit without naming the artist. The hypothesis that this is a reference to Caravaggio's painting is strengthened by circumstantial evidence. An inventory of 1622, listing pictures in the Villa Aldobrandini in Frascati, mentions 'A large painting on canvas of a Madonna embracing the child and a Saint Joseph . . . copy of Caravaggio'. The presence of this copy in one of the other residences of Olimpia Aldobrandini's family suggests that the original was indeed in her possession. The inventory reference is cited in John T. Spike's CD-ROM catalogue entry on *The Rest on the Flight to Egypt*.

33. See Helen Langdon, *The Lives of Caravaggio*, p. 28.

34. See Bernard Aikema, 'Titian's *Mary Magdalen* in the Palazzo Pitti: An Ambiguous Painting and Its Critics', *Journal of the Warburg and Courtauld Institutes*, vol. 57 (1994), p. 58.

35. See Colin Slim, 'Musical Inscriptions in Paintings by Caravaggio and His Followers'.

36. See John T. Spike in his CD-ROM catalogue entry on the *St Francis of Assisi in Ecstasy*.

37. See Helen Langdon, *The Lives of Caravaggio*, p. 63.

38. St Bonaventure's *Legenda maior* was one of the most readily available literary sources for painters working in the post-Tridentine period. It was the official biography of the saint, written in 1262. Bonaventure derived much of his information from the very first life of Francis, written by Thomas of Celano in c. 1230, just four years after the saint's death. See Pamela Askew, 'The Angelic Consolation of St Francis of Assisi in Post-Tridentine Italian Painting', *Journal of the Warburg and Courtauld Institutes*, vol. 32 (1969), pp. 280–386.

39. Cited in Pamela M. Jones, 'The Place of Poverty in Seicento Rome: Bare Feet, Humility and the Pilgrimage of Life in Caravaggio's *Madonna of Loreto* (c. 1605–6) in the Church of S. Agostino', in *Altarpieces and Their Viewers in the Churches of Rome from Caravaggio to Guido Reni* (Aldershot, 2008), p. 107.

40. *The Life of Teresa of Jesus: The Autobiography of St Teresa of Avila*, E. Allison Peers (trs.) (New York, 2004), Chapter 29.

41. Quoted in Radleigh Addington, *The Idea of the Oratory* (London, 1966), p. 3.

42. This is a confident assertion based on comparisons with known portraits of Caravaggio, but not a documented fact.

43. For the correspondence between Paravicino and Gualdo, see G. Cozzi, 'Intorno al Cardinale Ottavio Paravicino, a Monsignor Paolo Gualdo e a Michelangelo da Caravaggio', *Rivista storica italiana*, vol. 73 (1961),

pp. 36–68. I am indebted to Opher Mansour, who allowed me to see his translations of, and commentaries on, these letters, in his unpublished doctoral thesis submitted to the Courtauld Institute: 'Art, Offensive Images: Censure and Censorship in Rome under Clement VIII 1592–1605' (London, 2003).

44. It is often said that there is a hidden self-portrait reflected in the carafe – see, for example, Langdon, *Caravaggio: A Life*, p. 151. I have inspected the painting under high magnification and there is no such self-portrait in it.

45. See Helen Langdon, *The Lives of Caravaggio*, p. 43.

46. See n. 41 above.

47. See Giorgio Vasari, *Lives of the Painters, Sculptors and Architects*, vol. 1, p. 629.

48. See Helen Langdon, *The Lives of Caravaggio*, p. 93.

49. He did so, perhaps, because there was an established connection between that particular artistic style and alchemy. See my comments on Francesco de' Medici's *studiolo*, on p. 159 above.

50. Again, see n. 41 above. The resemblance to Ottavio Leoni's portrait of Caravaggio is, in my opinion, incontrovertible in the *Jupiter, Neptune and Pluto*. The identification with Francis is a little less certain but I am still confident that the saint is a self-portrait.

51. See Walter Friedlaender, *Caravaggio Studies*, p. 260.

52. Sandro Corradini discovered the case. With Maurizio Marini, he subsequently published the transcripts in full, together with a useful interpretative essay. See Sandro Corradini and Maurizio Marini, 'The Earliest Account of Caravaggio in Rome', *Burlington Magazine*, vol. 40, no. 1,138 (Jan. 1998), pp. 25–8.

53. The building still stands in Rome today. It is still a barber's shop!

54. See Helen Langdon, *The Lives of Caravaggio*, p. 92.

55. See Fiora Bellini, 'Tre documenti inediti per Michelangelo da Caravaggio', *Prospettiva*, no. 65 (Jan. 1992), pp. 70–71.

56. See Walter Friedlaender, *Caravaggio Studies*, pp. 263–5.

57. See Francesco Susinno, *Le vite de' pittori messinesi e di altri che fiorirono in Messina*, V. Martinelli (ed.) (Florence, 1960), p. 117.

58. See Rudolf and Margot Wittkower, *Born Under Saturn* (New York, 1963), p. 198. Orazio Gentileschi eventually prospered in France and Genoa in the 1620s. He was called to London in 1626 to become a painter at the court of King Charles I, who rewarded him with a generous stipend.

59. See G. P. Caffarelli, 'Famiglie romane', Biblioteca Angelica MS 1638, cc. 88r–v; cited (reliably) in Riccardo Bassani and Fiora Bellini, *Caravaggio assassino* (Rome, 1994), p. 13, n. 20.

60. ASR, Tribunale criminale del Senatore (TCS), reg. 1438, testimony of Onorio Longhi, 4 May 1595, cc. 20v–22v.

61. Ibid.

62. Ibid., reg. 444, testimony of Margherita Fannella, 4 May 1595.

63. Cited in Sandro Corradini, *Materiali per un processo* (Rome, 1993), document 15, 25–7 Oct., deposition by Stefano Longhi and others.

64. Ibid.

65. See Rudolf and Margot Wittkower, *Born Under Saturn*, p. 196.

66. See L. Pascoli, *Vite de' pittori, scultori ed architetti moderni* (Rome, 1730), vol. 2, pp. 512–13.

67. See ASR, TCS, reg. 1438, testimony of Onorio Longhi, 4 May 1595, cc. 20v–22v.

68. See Christopher Breward, 'Fashioning the Modern Self: Clothing, Cavaliers and Identity in Van Dyck's London', in *Van Dyck and Britain*, Karen Hearn (ed.) (London, 2009), pp. 34–5.

69. See Tommaso Garzoni, *La piazza universale di tutte le professioni del mondo* (Rome, 1996), pp. 1,263–83, for the following quotations.

70. ASR, Tribunale del governatore (TCG), reg. 483, witness statement of Anna Bianchini, 22 Apr. 1594, c. 144v; cited (reliably) in Riccardo Bassani and Fiora Bellini, *Caravaggio assassino*, p. 74, n. 5.

71. ASR, Archivio Sforza Cesarini, s. xii, b. 1b, filza 1, interrogationes et testes 1596–7, cc. n.n; cited (reliably) in Riccardo Bassani and Fiora Bellini, *Caravaggio assassino*, p. 53, n. 5.

72. Inventories show that she owned a painting of the Magdalen repenting by Caravaggio. The banker Ottavio Costa also owned a version of the same subject. Scholarly opinion is divided about who originally owned the Detroit painting but the balance of evidence currently available favours Olimpia Aldobrandini.

73. See Gregory Martin, *Roma sancta*, George Bruner Parks (ed.) (Rome, 1969), p. 143.

74. For Ranuccio Tomassoni, see Riccardo Bassani and Fiora Bellini, *Caravaggio assassino*, pp. 55–73.

75. For all the following testimonies see Sandro Corradini, *Materiali per un processo*, document 17.

76. Such figures appear with great frequency in northern European genre painting, especially Dutch art. Her tough, harsh face was probably modelled on a male Roman portrait bust.

77. See Carlo Cesare Malvasia, *Le vite de' pittori bolognese*, edition of 1678 (Bologna, 1841), vol. 1, p. 344.

78. His methods might be described as a kind of empirical Tintorettism, in the sense that they are the techniques a painter might evolve if he wanted to emulate Tintoretto but had never been trained in Tintoretto's actual methods – which were rather different, and certainly involved drawing.

79. See Walter Friedlaender, *Caravaggio Studies*, p. 264.

80. See Helen Langdon, *The Lives of Caravaggio*, p. 64. The idea that Caravaggio also used some kind of lens or camera obscura is a red herring. Caravaggio had plenty of enemies who would have no doubt taken pleasure in exposing him as a cheat, but no such device is mentioned by any of the early writers. Nor does anything like it appear in the only known inventory of his possessions.

81. Ibid., p. 33.

PART FOUR: ROME, 1599–1606

1. The document is reprinted and translated in Walter Friedlaender, *Caravaggio Studies*, p. 297.

2. See Herwarth Röttgen, *Il Caravaggio: ricerche e interpretazioni* (Rome, 1974), pp. 20–21; the translation is from John T. Spike, *Caravaggio*. The contract in question is the one signed by Giuseppe Cesari on 27 May 1591. As Cesari's successor, it seems highly probable that Caravaggio would have been made aware of Contarelli's wishes.

3. Quoted in Walter Friedlaender, *Caravaggio Studies*, p. 265.

4. See Helen Langdon, *The Lives of Caravaggio*, p. 69.

5. See for example Catherine Puglisi, *Caravaggio* (London, 1998), pp. 157–60.

6. See G. Urbani, 'Il restauro delle tele del Caravaggio in S. Luigi dei Francesi', *Bollettino dell'Istituto Centrale del Restauro*, vol. 17 (1966).

7. See Franca Trinchieri Camiz, 'Death and Rebirth in Caravaggio's *Martyrdom of St Matthew*', *Artibus et Historiae*, vol. 11, no. 22 (1990), pp. 89–105.

8. See E. Cecilia Voelker, Charles Borromeo's 'Instructiones fabricae et supellectilis ecclesiasticae', translation with commentary, dissertation, Syracuse University, 1977, pp. 250–51.

9. See Anti-Nicene Christian Library, *Translations of the Writings of the Fathers Down to AD 325. Volume 9: The Writings of Tertullian*, I, 25. Cited in 'Death and Rebirth in Caravaggio's *Martyrdom of St Matthew*'.

10. Titian's painting is lost, destroyed by fire, but its design can still be studied from prints.

11. See Walter Friedlaender, *Caravaggio Studies*, p. 300.

12. See, in particular, his thunderously inept contributions to the fresco cycle begun by Giorgio Vasari in the dome of Florence cathedral.

13. See Helen Langdon, *The Lives of Caravaggio*, p. 45. The translation here gives 'the style of Giorgione', which I have changed to 'idea' because the Italian word Baglione used was *pensiero*.

14. See Giorgio Vasari, *Lives of the Painters, Sculptors and Architects*, vol. 1, p. 641.

15. San Luigi dei Francesi was open to such innovations from outside. When Caravaggio accepted his commission, it was already one of the few churches in Rome to have a great Venetian canvas – by Jacopo Bassano – above its high altar.

16. See Helen Langdon, *Caravaggio: A Life*, p. 75.

17. See Sandro Corradini, *Materiali per un processo*, document 21, 7 Feb. 1601.

18. See Walter Friedlaender, *Caravaggio Studies*, pp. 269–70.

19. All the material from the investigation of Onorio Longhi in Oct. 1600, discussed below, is from Sandro Corradini, *Materiali per un processo*, document 15.

20. See above, p. 74.

21. Ibid., document 16, 20 Jan., deposition by Stefano Longhi and others.

22. Ibid., document 18.

23. Cited in John T. Spike, *Caravaggio*, in his CD-ROM catalogue entries for *The Conversion of St Paul* and *The Crucifixion of St Peter*; and Walter Friedlaender, *Caravaggio Studies*, pp. 302–3.

24. See Denis Mahon, 'Egregius in Urbe Pictor: Caravaggio Revisited', *Burlington Magazine*, vol. 93, no. 580 (July 1951), p. 226.

25. Caravaggio was familiar with the place too. He had convalesced in the Hospital of Santa Maria Consolazione in 1592–3, after being kicked by a horse.

26. Sixtus V; see Helen Langdon, *Caravaggio: A Life*, p. 181.

27. Quoted in John T. Spike, *Caravaggio*, p. 106.

28. See Helen Langdon, *The Lives of Caravaggio*, p. 88, where Bellori says that 'Caravaggio did not use cinnabar reds or azure blues in his figures; and if he occasionally did use them, he toned them down, saying they were poisonous colours.'

29. See Fiora Bellini, 'Tre documenti per Michelangelo da Caravaggio', pp. 70–71.

30. See Helen Langdon, *The Lives of Caravaggio*, p. 91.

31. See Charles Scribner III, 'In Alia Effigie: Caravaggio's London *Supper at Emmaus*', *Art Bulletin*, vol. 59, no. 3 (Sept. 1977), pp. 375–82, for an illuminating account of the youthful Christ and his theological significance.

32. The author's name was Gaspare Celio, whose book was published in Naples in 1638. He described the picture as 'a Pastor Friso, in oil, by Michelangelo da Caravaggio'. See the entry in John T. Spike, Caravaggio, CD-ROM catalogue entry no. 29.

33. See Conrad Rudolph and Steven F. Ostrow, 'Isaac Laughing: Caravaggio, Non-Traditional Imagery and Traditional Identification', *Art History*, vol. 24,

no. 5 (Nov. 2001), pp. 646–81. The article advances the theory that the painter meant to depict Isaac instead of St John. It also contains a very good summary of the hard documentary evidence that disproves its own argument.

34. 'Un quadro di San Giò: Battista col suo Agnello di mano del Caravaggio', cited in ibid., p. 649.

35. He described it as 'di San Giovanni Battista del Caravaggio'; cited in ibid.

36. See Helen Langdon, *The Lives of Caravaggio*, p. 72.

37. See Sergio Benedetti, 'Caravaggio's Taking of Christ: A Masterpiece Rediscovered', *Burlington Magazine*, vol. 135, no. 1,088 (Nov. 1993), p. 740.

38. See Niccolò Lorini del Monte, *Elogii delle piu principali S. Donne del sagro calendario, e martirologio romano* (Florence, 1617), p. 316. My attention was called to this passage by Pamela M. Jones's enlightening study of the pauperist context of Caravaggio's Rome in her book *Altarpieces and Their Viewers in the Churches of Rome from Caravaggio to Guido Reni*; see pp. 75ff. in particular.

39. Cointrel's nephew and heir, François, took possession of Cobaert's dull and stolid sculpture, eventually having it completed by another artist and placed in a chapel in SS Trinità dei Pellegrini, where he himself would eventually be buried.

40. See Irving Lavin, 'Divine Inspiration in Caravaggio's Two St Matthews', *Art Bulletin*, vol. 56, no. 1 (Mar. 1974), pp. 59–81.

41. See Helen Langdon, *The Lives of Caravaggio*, p. 45 for Baglione's remark, p. 66 for Bellori's.

42. Bellori's bald statement that the *Doubting Thomas* was painted for 'the Marchese Vincenzo Giustiniani' is supported by most of the available evidence. Giustiniani certainly owned the picture by 1606, because in the summer of that year he wrote a letter comparing his own, original *Doubting Thomas* by Caravaggio to a copy in Genoa. Baglione asserted that the *Doubting Thomas* was painted for Ciriaco Mattei, but this is probably a rare slip of the pen on his part. He may have confused the picture with *The Betrayal of Christ*, which certainly was painted for Ciriaco Mattei and which, oddly, Baglione does not mention at all. In summary, there is a remote possibility that the *Doubting Thomas* was painted for Ciriaco Mattei, then later acquired by Vincenzo Giustiniani. But the balance of probability favours a direct commission from Giustiniani himself. For a good analysis of the arguments and a precis of the relevant documents, see John T. Spike, *Caravaggio*, CD-ROM catalogue entry for *Doubting Thomas*.

43. See Walter Friedlaender, *Caravaggio Studies*, p. 264.

44. Inventory of 9 Feb. 1638; see John T. Spike, *Caravaggio*, CD-ROM catalogue entry for *Omnia vincit amor*.

45. The resemblance to Michelangelo's *Victory* was first noted by Walter Friedlaender, *Caravaggio Studies*, p. 93.

46. See Joachim von Sandrart, *L'Accademia Todesca della archittetura, scultura e pittura* . . . (Nuremberg, 1675). Quoted by Robert Enggass, 'L'Amore Giustiniani del Caravaggio', *Palatino*, vol. 11 (1967), pp. 13–19. This translation is from John T. Spike, *Caravaggio*.

47. The idea is advanced by Robert Enggass in the article cited in the previous note above. If this hypothesis is to be believed, Cupid does not trample the arts and sciences underfoot, but inspires them to flourish in the Giustiniani household. Such an interpretation is, however, flatly contradicted by the Giustiniani inventory of 1638, describing 'Cupid disparaging the world'. It is also at odds with the purely visual evidence of the painting. In particular, the discarded shell of an empty suit of armour cannot possibly have been intended by the painter as a compliment to the military prowess of his patron. Nor can Caravaggio's impishly provocative, full-frontally nude Cupid be plausibly transmuted into a Neoplatonic emblem of the Earthly Love that sparks man to Divine Creativity.

48. For an earlier conversation inspired by a painting of Cupid between the Venetian collector Gabriel Vendramin and the connoisseur Anton Francesco Doni, see Catherine Whistler, 'Titian's *Triumph of Love*', *Burlington Magazine*, vol. 151, no. 1,277 (Aug. 2009), n. 19, in which the author cites Doni's *I marmi* (Venice, 1552), vol. 3, fols. 40–41: '*e fra l'altro mi mostrò un leone con un Cupido sopra. E qui discorremo molto della bella invenzione, e lodassi ultimamente in questo, che l'amore doma ogni gran ferocità e terribilità à persone.*'

49. The Courtauld Galleries in London contain a particularly good example of two such chests in their original condition. As well as being embellished with complex narrative paintings about love, drawn from classical mythology, they are decorated with split pomegranates spilling their seeds, a kind of symbolic prayer for fertile married union.

50. See Charles Dempsey, '"Et nos cedamus amori": Observations on the Farnese Gallery', *Art Bulletin*, vol. 50, no. 4 (Dec. 1968), pp. 363–74.

51. See Helen Langdon, *The Lives of Caravaggio*, pp. 45–6.

52. See Karel van Mander, *Het Schilderboek* (Haarlem, 1604), cited in Beverly Louise Brown, 'The Black Wings of Envy: Competition, Rivalry and *Paragone*', in *The Genius of Rome*, Royal Academy exhibition catalogue, p. 251.

53. See Gianni Papi's essay 'Cecco del Caravaggio', in *Come dipingeva il Caravaggio: atti della giornata di studio*, Mina Gregori (ed.) (Milan, 1996).

54. This transcription was made from the original MSS of Symonds's travel journal by John Gash, who published it in the *Burlington Magazine*, vol. 140, no. 1,138 (Jan. 1998), pp. 41–2.

55. See Giorgio Vasari, *Lives of the Painters, Sculptors and Architects*, vol. 2, p. 418.

56. See Maryvelma Smith O'Neil's entertainingly revisionist study, *Giovanni Baglione: Artistic Reputation in Baroque Rome* (Cambridge, 2002), p. 17. I am indebted to her lucid account of the libels and their consequences, although not convinced by her suggestion that Baglione was an injured innocent in the affair.

57. These transcriptions of the poems are taken from Anthony Colantuono, 'Caravaggio's Literary Culture', in *Caravaggio, Realism Rebellion, Reception*, Genevieve Warwick (ed.) (Newark, 2006), p. 58.

58. Percy Bysshe Shelley's verse play *The Cenci* was inspired by these events.

59. See Maryvelma Smith O'Neil, *Giovanni Baglione: Artistic Reputation in Baroque Rome*, p. 13.

60. The libel trial documents were first published in full in G. A. Dell'Acqua and M. Cinotti, *Il Caravaggio e il sue grandi opere da S. Luigi dei Francesi* (Milan, 1971), pp. 153–7. The translation offered here is by Don Var Green and can be found in full in Maryvelma Smith O'Neil, *Giovanni Baglione: Artistic Reputation in Baroque Rome*, pp. 337–62. I have made a couple of slight alterations, to match my own translation of the two poems at the centre of the case, and in one or two instances have preserved the original Italian usages.

61. The document is printed in full in Maryvelma Smith O'Neil, *Giovanni Baglione: Artistic Reputation in Baroque Rome*, pp. 357–8.

62. See Sandro Corradini, *Materiali per un processo*, document 26.

63. See Maryvelma Smith O'Neil, *Giovanni Baglione: Artistic Reputation in Baroque Rome*, pp. 358–62.

64. Salini added the detail about the punch in the chest in a slightly later piece of testimony; I have inserted it here for the sake of clarity.

65. The document is reprinted in full in Maurizio Marini, *Michelangelo Merisi da Caravaggio 'pictor praestantissimus'* (second edition, Rome 1979), p. 472.

66. See Tullio Lazzari, *Ascoli in prospettiva* (Ascoli, 1722), p. 40.

67. The document is dated 6 June 1605. It is quoted, and photographically reproduced, in Maurizio Marini, *Michelangelo Merisi da Caravaggio 'pictor praestantissimus'*, p. 53.

68. See Sandro Corradini, *Materiali per un processo*, document 57. The translation is from Catherine Puglisi, *Caravaggio*, p. 420.

69. Nowadays many people have books they do not read, but books were so expensive in Caravaggio's time that ownership of a volume can be taken as an indication of familiarity with its contents.

70. See Helen Langdon, *Caravaggio: A Life*, p. 279.

71. See Walter Friedlaender, *Caravaggio Studies*, p. 280.

72. Ibid., p. 260.

73. Ibid., p. 249.

74. The translation is from ibid., p. 281; the fullest transcription of these documents is in G. A. Dell'Acqua and M. Cinotti, *Il Caravaggio e il sue grandi opere da S. Luigi dei Francesi*, p. 158.

75. G. A. Dell'Acqua and M. Cinotti, *Il Caravaggio e il sue grandi opere da S. Luigi dei Francesi*, p. 158.

76. See Walter Friedlaender, *Caravaggio Studies*, p. 281.

77. These officials were drawn from the lay population and elected to their posts by the noble families of the city. Hence they reflected the factionalism and competing dynastic ambitions that existed at the highest level of Roman society. During the so-called Vacant See, the interregnum between one pope's death and another's election – but only at that time – the *caporioni* were allowed to act as judges in the districts under their control. Trouble often ensued during these periods. See Laurie Nussdorfer, 'The Politics of Space in Early Modern Rome', *Memoirs of the American Academy in Rome*, vol. 42 (1997), pp. 161–86.

78. All this testimony is in Sandro Corradini, *Materiali per un processo*, document 41.

79. Ibid., document 47.

80. See Walter Friedlaender, *Caravaggio Studies*, p. 282.

81. The term 'house-scorning' was coined by Elizabeth S. Cohen. The discussion that follows is heavily indebted to her pioneering work in the field of seventeenth-century social history, especially the essay 'Honour and Gender in the Streets of Early Modern Rome', *Journal of Interdisciplinary History*, vol. 22, no. 4 (Spring 1992), pp. 597–625.

82. Louis Richeome, *The Pilgrime of Loreto*, facsimile of the 1629 edition, *English Recusant Literature 1558–1640*, vol. 285, D. M. Rogers (ed.) (London, 1976), p. 33.

83. Thousands of pilgrims visited Loreto every year and their experience was carefully orchestrated. The pilgrimage diaries of the Santissima Trinità dei Pellegrini, founded by Filippo Neri and supported by the patrons who paid for Caravaggio's *Madonna of Loreto*, the Cavalletti family, contain much information about the structure of a visit to Loreto. They strongly suggest that the painter wanted his picture to evoke an actual pilgrimage.

84. The placement of Caravaggio's works within the geography of Rome has received relatively scant consideration. Pamela Jones's essay, 'The Place of Poverty in Seicento Rome', included in *Altarpieces and Their Viewers*, contains a penetrating analysis of the significance of the geographical locations of some of Caravaggio's works.

85. See Helen Langdon, *The Lives of Caravaggio*, p. 90.

86. Ibid., p. 46.

87. See Walter Friedlaender, *Caravaggio Studies*, p. 284.

88. See G. A. Dell'Acqua and M. Cinotti, *Il Caravaggio e il sue grandi opere da S. Luigi dei Francesi*, p. 158.

89. It was left out of later editions.

90. See Jacob Hess, 'Nuovo Contributo alla vita del Caravaggio', *Bolletino d'Arte*, anno 26, ser. 3 (July 1932), pp. 42–4.

91. Rome's criminal archives include a report written by the constable who arrested her. See Sandro Corradini, *Materiali per un processo*, document 38.

92. If this is so (which is certainly possible), he would have been using the phrase in the same straightforward sense as the one-eyed Bolognese corporal, possibly called Paulo Aldato, who appears to say something similar in a later criminal action involving Caravaggio. Aldato (if that was his name) is reported as saying that he wanted to visit '*una sua puttana*' – one of his prostitutes – on a street nearby. There is no implication that Aldato was a pimp. See Sandro Corradini, *Materiali per un processo*, document 101.

93. He would later claim that he had tried to challenge Pasqualone to a fair and open fight, but probably only to put his own actions in a better light.

94. See Sandro Corradini, *Materiali per un processo*, documents 48–52, 54.

95. Giuliana Marcolini, 'Cesare d'Este, Caravaggio, e Annibale Carracci: una duca, due pittori e una *committenza* "a mal termine"', in *Sovrane passioni: studi sul collezionismo estense*, Jadranka Bentini (ed.) (Milan, 1998), pp. 23–4. Ruggieri's letter reporting Caravaggio's riposte was dated 2 Mar. 1605.

96. Had it not been for the discovery of Masetti's correspondence, the details of Caravaggio's trip to Genoa would have remained unknown. See Sandro Corradini, *Materiali per un processo*, document 53.

97. Ibid., document 55.

98. Ibid., document 56.

99. See Walter Friedlaender, *Caravaggio Studies*, p. 285.

100. Ibid.

101. See Sandro Corradini, *Materiali per un processo*, document 58.

102. Ibid., document 59. This is a slightly free translation; Masetti uses the phrase '*un' altra questione*', meaning 'another question'.

103. Ibid., document 67.

104. Ibid., document 68.

105. Ibid., document 71.

106. Carracci did eventually deliver his own picture for the duke, thought to be identical to the painter's *The Birth of the Virgin* now in the Louvre.

107. See Helen Langdon, *The Lives of Caravaggio*, pp. 73–4.

108. See Luigi Spezzaferro, 'La pala dei Palafrenieri', *Colloquio* (1974), which reprints the documents from the archive of the confraternity associated with the commission.

109. Ibid.; the translation is given in John T. Spike, *Caravaggio*, where the painting appears as entry no. 48. The same is true for the two documents that follow. For a reproduction of this document in Caravaggio's handwriting, see illustration no. 65.

110. See Helen Langdon, *The Lives of Caravaggio*, p. 90.

111. See Gabriele Paleotti, 'Discorso intorno alle imagini sacre e profane', in *Trattati d'arte del Cinquecento fra Manierismo a Controriforma*, vol. 2, P. Barocchi and P. Barocchi (eds.) (Bari, 1961), p. 370.

112. See Roberto Longhi, *Opere complete* (Florence, 1968), vol. 4, p. 58.

113. The date of *The Death of the Virgin* is disputed, but there are compelling reasons to place its completion close to the very end of Caravaggio's Roman period, i.e. around May 1606. Before the discovery of the contract for the painting, of 14 June 1601, the work was dated 1606 by most art historians on purely stylistic grounds. There seems little reason to reverse that view simply because of the discovery of the contract. It was common for paintings to be delivered late, sometimes years late (witness the travails of poor Fabio Masetti). The picture is certainly much closer in its *facture*, palette and mood to Caravaggio's later, post-Roman works than it is to such paintings of 1601-2 as *The Supper at Emmaus*. In my opinion, it was finished directly after the *Madonna of the Palafrenieri*, since it is painted in the looser, freer style of that picture's right half – the half containing St Anne – which directly prefigures the style of the artist's last years. As a compromise solution some experts have chosen to date the painting to 1604, but this seems perverse, bearing in mind both the picture's appearance and the existing documentary evidence. The first detailed reference to the picture occurs in a letter by Giulio Mancini, dated 14 Oct. 1606, in a context strongly suggestive of the picture having been finished just a matter of months earlier. Another reference to it from around the same time occurs in the correspondence of an agent working for the Duke of Mantua, who noted that the painters of Rome were complaining that they had not yet been able to see the painting. If it really had been finished as early as 1604, it would seem strange indeed that Caravaggio's friends and rivals had still not seen it all of two years later. In addition, in his biography of the painter Mancini explicitly connects its rejection with 'the trouble' that ruined Caravaggio's life, i.e., the killing of Ranuccio Tomassoni. It would therefore seem logical to assume that it was the very last picture the artist painted before his flight from Rome.

114. Saints should never be given the recognizable features of 'persons of ill repute', Paleotti had written. Gabriele Paleotti, 'Discorso intorno alle imagini

sacre e profane', p. 360. I am obliged to Opher Mansour for pointing out both these references to me.

115. See Giulio Mancini, *Considerazioni sulla pittura*, vol. 1, pp. 120, 132; see also Walter Friedlaender, *Caravaggio Studies*, p. 195.

116. See Michele Maccherini, 'Caravaggio nel carteggio familiare di Giulio Mancini' in *Prospettiva*, vol. 86 (1997), pp. 71-92.

117. See Sandro Corradini, *Materiali per un processo*, document 78. It is not clear what type of document this is; perhaps a journal.

118. See Helen Langdon, *The Lives of Caravaggio*, pp. 29-31.

119. Ibid., p. 52.

120. Ibid., p. 76.

121. See Peter Burke, 'Rome as Center of Information and Communication for the Catholic World 1550-1650', in *From Rome to Eternity: Catholicism and the Arts in Italy, c. 1550-1650*, Pamela M. Jones and Thomas Worcester (eds.) (Leiden, Boston and Cologne, 2002), p. 259.

122. See Sandro Corradini, *Materiali per un processo*, document 81.

123. The tennis courts were all destroyed in a fire during the eighteenth century. The site is now occupied by an underground car park. I am grateful to Maurizio Marini for showing me its exact whereabouts.

124. See Sandro Corradini, *Materiali per un processo*, document 85; the translation given here is from Walter Friedlaender, *Caravaggio Studies*, p. 286.

125. Ibid., document 82.

126. His report on the man's injuries can still be consulted in the 'Barbitonsores' section of the Roman State Archives. This document confirms that Caravaggio's ally in the fight had indeed been badly wounded. See ibid., document 80.

127. Ibid., document 83.

128. Ibid., document 84.

129. Ibid. document 95: '*initi duelli cum Michelangelo de Caravaggio ... ac pro presenti duello*'.

130. For the document discussed below, see ibid., document 101.

131. Ibid., documents 163, 164.

132. Ibid., document 145.

133. Ibid., document 111.

134. I am grateful to Sandro Corradini for talking me through this series of archival documents, which remain unpublished. For another precis of their contents, see Helen Langdon, *Caravaggio: A Life*, p. 313.

135. See Sandro Corradini, *Materiali per un processo*, document 109. Pontoni, who was a lawyer, also appears in document 17, testifying in the case of Fillide's knife attack on Prudenza Zacchia.

136. Ibid., document 151.

137. See Romolo Caggese (ed.), *Statuti della reppublica fiorentina. Volume 2: Statuto del podestà del anno 1325* (Florence, 1921); and *Volumen statutorem civitatis Maceratae*, facsimile reprint of the 1553 edition, Arnaldo Forni (ed.) ([n.p., n.d.]). I am indebted to Elizabeth S. Cohen and Thomas S. Cohen for allowing me to read their essay '*Sfregio*: Facial Mutilation as Expressive Act' when it was still in draft form. It was that essay that called my attention to the legal penalties cited in the statute books noted above.

PART FIVE: THE ALBAN HILLS, NAPLES, MALTA, SICILY, NAPLES, PORTO ERCOLE, 1606–10

1. See Helen Langdon, *The Lives of Caravaggio*, pp. 31, 76.

2. A picture in a private Roman collection has been put forward several times as a candidate, but it is so clumsy and sentimental that it cannot possibly have been painted by Caravaggio.

3. No documents relating to this work survive. It has been romantically placed at the end of Caravaggio's life – in the quatercentenary exhibition in Rome in 2010 it was once more dated to 1610 – but it was not among the pictures listed as being on the boat with him when he travelled to Rome for the last time in July of that year, and it is besides painted in a style quite different from that of Caravaggio's last-documented picture, *The Martyrdom of St Ursula*, now in the boardroom of the Banco di Napoli. Given that the style of the *David with the Head of Goliath* is so close to that of *The Seven Acts of Mercy* of 1606–7 in Naples – compare, for example, the handling of light in striated drapery in both pictures – and given that it indeed entered the Borghese collection (it can still be seen in the Villa Borghese in Rome), I believe that Caravaggio painted it expressly for Scipione Borghese to try to secure a pardon for his crimes. The identification of the severed head of Goliath as a self-portrait has been universally accepted, on the basis of visual comparison with Ottavio Leoni's portrait of Caravaggio in the Uffizi, and with other known self-portraits that occur within Caravaggio's *œuvre*.

4. Mancini is the source for this information: See Helen Langdon, *The Lives of Caravaggio*, p. 31.

5. It was only in 1613 that he ordered a frame to be made for it, according to a Borghese palace inventory: see the CD-ROM catalogue entry on the painting in John T. Spike, *Caravaggio*.

6. Sandro Corradini, *Materiali per un processo*, document 106, 23 Sept. 1606.

7. See George Sandys, *A Relation of a Journey* (London, 1615), pp. 253–4.

8. Cited by Jeanne Chenault Porter in 'Reflections of the Golden Age: The Visitor's Account of Naples', in *Parthenope's Splendor: Art of the Golden Age*

in Naples, published as Papers in Art History from the Pennsylvania State University, vol. 7, Jeanne Chenault Porter and Susan Scott Munshower (eds.) (Pennsylvania, 1993), p. 11.

9. See Giuseppe Galasso, 'Society in Naples in the Seicento', in *Painting in Naples 1606–1705: From Caravaggio to Giordano*, catalogue to the exhibition at the Royal Academy of Arts, London, Clovis Whitfield and Jane Martineau (eds.) (London 1982), p. 28.

10. It is probable that the open-weave Neapolitan canvases on which Caravaggio would paint some of his greatest pictures were of English origin: see Clovis Whitfield, 'Seicento Naples', in *Painting in Naples 1606–1705*, p. 19.

11. Benedetto Croce, *History of the Kingdom of Naples*, Frances Frenaye (trs.), H. Stuart Hughes (ed.) (Chicago, 1970), p. 116. Croce's text was first published as *Storia del regno di Napoli* (Bari, 1925).

12. Quoted in ibid., p. 120.

13. Quoted in Giuseppe Galasso, 'Society in Naples in the Seicento', in *Painting in Naples 1606–1705*, p. 25.

14. See ibid., *passim*.

15. See ibid., p. 25.

16. See Helen Langdon, *The Lives of Caravaggio*, pp. 76–7.

17. For the details and documents concerning this commission, see Vincenzo Pacelli, 'New Documents concerning Caravaggio in Naples', *Burlington Magazine*, vol. 119, no. 897 (Dec. 1977), pp. 819–29; and Vincenzo Pacelli, *Caravaggio: Le sette opere di misericordia* (Salerno, 1984), p. 102.

18. The quote is taken from the manuscript of C. De Lellis, *Aggiunta alla Napoli sacra del d'Engenio 1654–89*, cited in Vincenzo Pacelli, *Caravaggio: Le sette opere di misericordia*, p. 12.

19. See Ferdinando Bologna, 'Caravaggio: The Final Years', in *Caravaggio: The Final Years*, exhibition catalogue, the National Gallery (London, 2005), p. 22.

20. Tiberio del Pezzo was the member of the confraternity who signed the documents authorizing payment to Caravaggio, but since he was only a deputy his role is likely to have been marginal. For the documents concerning this commission, see Vincenzo Pacelli, *Caravaggio: Le sette opere di misericordia*, p. 102.

21. See pp. 250–53, above. Caravaggio painted Marino's portrait in 1600 or 1601. It does not survive.

22. See Estelle Haan, *From Academia to Amicitia: Milton's Latin Writings and the Italian Academies* (Philadelphia, 1998), p. 122.

23. Ibid., p. 119.

24. These documents are usefully summarized in John T. Spike, *Caravaggio*, in the CD-ROM catalogue entry on the picture.

25. See Helen Langdon, *The Lives of Caravaggio*, p. 77, where Bellori states that 'he was commissioned to do the *Flagellation of Christ at the Column* in the Di Franco Chapel of the church of San Domenico Maggiore.' There is another, half-length depiction of *The Flagellation* in Rouen that many scholars believe to be an autograph Caravaggio, but I am not convinced by it. Two other versions of the subject, one in Lucca and the other in a Swiss private collection, were published respectively by Roberto Longhi and Denis Mahon in the 1950s. I am not convinced by those paintings either.

26. See Vincenzo Pacelli, 'New Documents concerning Caravaggio in Naples', p. 820.

27. See Bernardo de Dominici, *Vite de' pittori, scultori ed architetti napoletani* (Naples, 1742–3), pp. 275–6. Cited in John T. Spike, *Caravaggio*, in his entry on *The Flagellation*.

28. This could be said to bring full circle that fruitful interplay between painting and sculpture already embodied by Caravaggio's own work. He himself had been powerfully influenced by the polychrome statuary of Lombardy and the *sacri monti*.

29. See Ann Tzeutschler Lurie and Denis Mahon, 'Caravaggio's *Crucifixion of St Andrew* from Valladolid', *Bulletin of the Cleveland Museum of Arts*, vol. 64 (Jan. 1977), pp. 3–24. The picture had reportedly found its way to a convent in Spain by 1972, and was on sale in the art market in Switzerland a year later; it was purchased by the Cleveland Museum of Art through the L. C. Hanna Jr Bequest in 1976. See the CD-ROM catalogue entry on the painting in John T. Spike, *Caravaggio*.

30. See *Caravaggio: The Final Years*, exhibition catalogue, p. 109. Keith Christiansen's entry on this particular painting also contains an outstandingly lucid account of the wider issues surrounding the much debated chronology of Caravaggio's later pictures.

31. The quotation is taken from *The Golden Legend* of Jacobus de Voragine, translated and adapted from the Latin by Granger Ryan and Helmut Ripperberger (New York, 1969), p. 13.

32. John Varriano, in his *Caravaggio: The Art of Realism* (Pennsylvania, 2003), notes that 'goiters are known to be geographically linked to mountainous places and were especially common in the region around Naples, the site where the earliest research on the disease was conducted.'

33. See Walter Friedlaender, *Caravaggio Studies*, p. 314.

34. It was taken there by Finson, who by that time had assumed sole ownership of the work. He subsequently bequeathed it to his friend and business partner, Vinck.

35. The picture was either sold or given to Emperor Josef II of Austria when he visited Antwerp in 1781.

36. See the CD-ROM catalogue entry on the painting in John T. Spike, *Caravaggio*, for the relevant documents.

37. For Mancini's correspondence in connection with the sale of *The Death of the Virgin*, see Michele Maccherini, 'Caravaggio nel carteggio familiare di Giulio Mancini', *Prospettiva*, vol. 86 (1997), pp. 71–92.

38. For Magno's correspondence with Chieppio, see Walter Friedlaender, *Caravaggio Studies*, pp. 308–10.

39. See Sandro Corradini, *Materiali per un processo*, document 110, 2–4 Nov. 1606.

40. See Maryvelma Smith O'Neil, *Giovanni Baglione: Artistic Reputation in Baroque Rome*, pp. 166–7.

41. Walter Friedlaender, *Caravaggio Studies*, p. 313.

42. Ibid., p. 313.

43. Giacomo Bosio, *Dell'istoria della sacra religione* (Rome, 1594–1602), vol. 3, p. 574. My attention was called to this and the following quotation by David M. Stone's article 'The Context of Caravaggio's *Beheading of St John* in Malta', *Burlington Magazine*, vol. 139, no. 1,128 (Mar. 1997), pp. 161–70.

44. Ibid., vol. 3, p. 574.

45. Helen Langdon, *The Lives of Caravaggio*, p. 79.

46. See Walter Friedlaender, *Caravaggio Studies*, p. 266.

47. Just a year before, at the start of 1606, Capeci had helped to organize another painter's journey to Malta. He had provided the artist in question, an unnamed Florentine, with canvases and pigments. He had also arranged his passage to the island via Messina in Sicily. For unknown reasons the painter from Florence never actually made it on to the island, but the episode strongly suggests that Capeci was involved in Caravaggio's transfer to Malta as well. See Keith Sciberras and David Stone, *Caravaggio: Art, Knighthood and Malta* (Malta, 2006), p. 22.

48. See Maurizio Calvesi, *Le realtà del Caravaggio*, pp. 132–3; Keith Sciberras and David Stone, *Caravaggio: Art, Knighthood and Malta*, p. 20; Helen Langdon, *Caravaggio: A Life*, p. 346.

49. Much of this sequence of events was established by the discovery of a long-overlooked letter of June 1607 in the Farnese deposit in the Naples State Archives, written by Alessandro Boccabarile, agent for Duke Ranuccio Farnese: 'Eight days ago five galleys of the Religion of Malta arrived here, from Provence, under the command of the Prior of Venice, brother of the Marquis of Caravaggio [i.e., Fabrizio Sforza Colonna]. He brought his mother, who was staying at the Torre del Greco with the Prince of Stigliano . . . The aforesaid galleys will leave for Malta once the Feast of St John is over, taking with them two unequipped galleys newly made in Provence, and above

all slaves . . .' This material was discovered by Antonio Ernesto Denunzio and published in the catalogue to the National Gallery's *Late Caravaggio* exhibition, p. 49.

50. Keith Sciberras's second chapter in *Caravaggio: Art, Knighthood and Malta*, entitled 'Virtuosity Honoured, Chivalry Disgraced', is an invaluable source of information about Caravaggio's time on Malta, much of it recently unearthed by Sciberras himself in the Maltese archives. For the documents concerning the journey to Malta, see p. 22.

51. See George Sandys, *A Relation of a Journey*, p. 234.

52. For these documents, see John Azzopardi's contribution to the catalogue *The Church of St John in Valletta 1578–98 and the Earliest Record of Caravaggio in Malta*, Fr John Azzopardi (ed.) (Malta, 1978).

53. See George Sandys, *A Relation of a Journey*, p. 230.

54. See Helen Langdon, *Caravaggio: A Life*, p. 345.

55. See Commander Denis Calman, *Knights of Durance* (Malta, 1963), p. 12.

56. See George Sandys, *A Relation of a Journey*, p. 230.

57. Martelli did not take up his position until 1608, when a Medici agent reported his arrival in the Sicilian port town: 'yesterday the galleys arrived here from Malta and with them Prior Martelli, who if much aged remains in excellent health.' For this quotation, see Keith Sciberras and David Stone, *Caravaggio: Art, Knighthood and Malta*, p. 89. Stone's account of Caravaggio's portrait of Martelli is clear and perceptive. The most informative essay on Martelli's life and career is by John Gash: 'The Identity of Caravaggio's Knight of Malta', *Burlington Magazine*, vol. 139, no. 1,128 (Mar. 1997) pp. 156–60. Some authors continue to question the picture's attribution to Caravaggio, others to doubt that it represents Martelli. But a mid seventeenth-century inscription in a Medici collection inventory records the name of the painting's sitter as Antonio Martelli and I see no reason to doubt that. He was a celebrated man and the painting probably hung in the Vasari corridor alongside other depictions of worthies and notables treasured by the Medici, which makes it all the more likely that the inventorist would have got his name right. It used to be thought that Martelli could not have been painted by Caravaggio on Malta in 1607–8 because of his appointment to the Priory of Messina in 1606, so the archival evidence showing that he did not actually leave for Messina until the autumn of 1608 is important. Last but not least, the nonpareil moral and intellectual force of the painting, its abbreviated style, its depth of chiaroscuro, even such details as the slightly blocky impasto highlights in the prominent sunburned ear of the sitter – all scream out late Caravaggio. I cannot see who else could possibly have painted the picture.

58. For these documents, see Fr John Azzopardi, 'Documentary Sources on Caravaggio's Stay in Malta', in *Caravaggio in Malta*, Philip Farrugia Randon

(ed.) (Malta, 1986), pp. 45–56; and Stefania Macioce, 'Caravaggio a Malta e i suoi referenti', in *Storia dell'Arte*, vol. 81 (1994), pp. 207–8. Helen Langdon, in conversation with me, has expressed second thoughts about whether this document actually refers to Caravaggio. She points out that Knights of Malta were so universally prone to violence that the reference to a homicide committed does not necessarily point the finger at Caravaggio alone as the intended recipient of one of the two knighthoods for which papal approval was being requested. However, given the scarcity of Knighthoods of Magistral Obedience awarded by Wignacourt – indeed, so great was his reluctance to award such knighthoods at all that he had all but abolished them – it seems highly unlikely that he gave two in the same year to men who had committed murder. In my opinion, the man mentioned in the document, and Caravaggio, are beyond all reasonable doubt the same person.

59. See n. 47 above.

60. I am indebted to Keith Sciberras for explaining this crucial sequence of points to me, in conversations on Malta in 2001.

61. It has been suggested that he may have painted the work *in situ*, in the Oratory of St John itself, but I think that is implausible on the grounds that the light in that space would have been so far from ideal, even in the summer months. There is no absolute proof either way, but I think it more likely that he found a space elsewhere and adapted it accordingly.

62. Some writers have identified her with Salome, others with Salome's mother, Herodias, Herod's consort. But she is dressed in the clothes of a serving wench. Everything about the way in which Caravaggio painted her indicates that she is meant to be seen as a member of the chorus, not as a leading player in the drama.

63. The inscription has occasionally been thought to imply the phrase '*fecit* Caravaggio', 'Caravaggio made this', rather than 'Fra Michelangelo'. But the fact that it was his reception painting into the Order of St John argues compellingly for the latter as the true reading.

64. Cited in John T. Spike, *Caravaggio*, pp. 209–10. Fr John Azzopardi published a photograph of the document, with transcription and translation, in 'Documentary Sources on Caravaggio's Stay in Malta', pp. 55–6.

65. I am grateful to John T. Spike for pointing out to me dell'Antella's probable authorship of the Bull, and for teasing out the implication that by praising Caravaggio as Apelles, it offers even higher praise to Wignacourt as his patron.

66. For dell'Antella's life and personality, see Helen Langdon, *Caravaggio: A Life*, p. 354; and Keith Sciberras and David Stone, *Caravaggio: Art, Knighthood and Malta*, p. 80.

67. I am indebted to Elizabeth Cropper's enlightening article about the links between Marino and Caravaggio: 'The Petrifying Art: Marino's Poetry and

Caravaggio', *Metropolitan Museum Journal*, vol. 26 (1991), pp. 193–212. For the connections between Marino's poem about sleeping Cupid and Caravaggio's painting, see pp. 199–200. The quotations are taken from Giambattista Marino, *La Galeria*, Marzio Pieri (ed.) (Padua, 1979), vol. 1, pp. 273–7. The translations given here are my own very slightly adapted versions of those given in Cropper's article.

68. See Giorgio Vasari, *Lives of the Painters, Sculptors and Architects*, vol. 2, p. 650.

69. Letter dated 24 Apr. 1610. See David Stone, 'In Praise of Caravaggio's *Sleeping Cupid*: New Documents for Francesco dell'Antella in Malta and Florence', *Melita historica*, vol. 12, pp. 165–77.

70. See Helen Langdon, *The Lives of Caravaggio*, p. 80.

71. See fn. 33 to Keith Sciberras's second chapter in *Caravaggio: Art, Knighthood and Malta*, for the full quotation in Italian. The translation given here is my own.

72. See Walter Friedlaender, *Caravaggio Studies*, p. 292. The translation given there is more faithful than that in Helen Langdon, *The Lives of Caravaggio*, pp. 52–3. Baglione's wording is important.

73. See Helen Langdon, *The Lives of Caravaggio*, p. 80.

74. I owe a debt of gratitude to Fr John Azzopardi for showing me around the Maltese archive, and allowing me to examine for myself the documents – both legible and obliterated – relating to Caravaggio's crime and punishment on Malta. Keith Sciberras, who also generously shared much information with me on my visits to the island, first published the results of his X-ray examinations under the title '"Frater Michael Angelus in tumultu": The Cause of Caravaggio's Imprisonment in Malta', *Burlington Magazine*, vol. 144, no. 1,189 (Apr. 2002), pp. 229–32. My account of the events surrounding Caravaggio's crime is, inevitably, hugely dependent on his pioneering research.

75. According to Malta's Liber Conciliorum for 1608–10, less than two years after the 'tumult' involving Caravaggio, De Ponte was sentenced for two months for fighting '*cum levi sanguinis effusione*' with a certain Fra Francesco Sarsale. See Keith Sciberras, '"Frater Michael Angelus in tumultu": The Cause of Caravaggio's Imprisonment in Malta', fn. 37.

76. I am grateful again to Fr John Azzopardi for helping to find the ladder and letting me into the *guva*. Keith Sciberras doubts that Caravaggio would have been kept in the *guva*, arguing that he would most probably have been detained in one of Castel Sant'Angelo's semi-open prisons. But, given Wignacourt's stated desire 'not to lose him', expressed in the petition to the pope for Caravaggio's knighthood, I share Fr Azzopardi's view that he would indeed have been confined in the *guva*, which was after all the most high-security of

the island's jails. It may also be worth noting that, according to a long oral tradition on Malta, the *guva* was Caravaggio's place of imprisonment.

77. Helen Langdon, *The Lives of Caravaggio*, p. 81.

78. See Faith Ashford, 'Caravaggio's Stay in Malta', *Burlington Magazine for Connoisseurs*, vol. 67, no. 391 (Oct. 1935), pp. 168-74.

79. See Keith Sciberras and David Stone, *Caravaggio: Art, Knightood and Malta*, p. 34.

80. See Faith Ashford, 'Caravaggio's Stay in Malta', p. 174.

81. Ibid.

82. The document was published by A. Spadaro, 'Il percorso smarrito e l'importante inedito: la presenza del pittore a Caltagirone', in *Foglio d'Arte*, vol. 8, no. 2 (1984-5), pp. 6-7; I was alerted to it by Gioacchino Barbera and Donatella Spagnolo's essay 'From *The Burial of St Lucy* to the Scenes of the Passion: Caravaggio in Syracuse and Messina' in the catalogue to the exhibition *Caravaggio: The Final Years*, pp. 80-87.

83. See George Sandys, *A Relation of a Journey*, p. 234.

84. Susinno's manuscript containing biographies of artists to have worked in Sicily, and particularly Messina, was first published by Valentino Martelli in Florence in 1960. Susinno's life of Caravaggio, which was included in that manuscript, was usefully reprinted and translated in Howard Hibbard, *Caravaggio* : see p. 381. Minniti had lived a chequered life since returning to his native Sicily in about 1604, at one point having been forced to seek sanctuary in the Carmelite monastery at Syracuse 'for a homicide casually committed' – for which see Francesco Susinno, *Le vite dei pittori messinesi* of 1724, Valentino Martelli (ed.) (Florence, 1960), p. 117. By the autumn of 1608 Minniti had long since redeemed himself, by painting numerous altarpieces for the religious institutions of Syracuse and Messina. He often worked for the Franciscans, which indicates that he had a close relationship with the order. His sister, Maria, was a Capuchin tertiary. See Gioacchino Barbera and Donatella Spagnolo, 'From *The Burial of St Lucy* to the Scenes of the Passion: Caravaggio in Syracuse and Messina' in the catalogue to the exhibition *Caravaggio: The Final Years*, p. 81.

85. See Susinno in Howard Hibbard, *Caravaggio*, p. 381; in fact, the church and its adjacent monastery were not assigned to the Minorite friars of the Franciscan order until 1618. But they had been lobbying to have the site restored and given to them for many years, so they are also likely to have had a strong say in the choosing of Caravaggio. The Franciscans were the poorest of the poor orders. They are likely to have been highly sympathetic to an artist whose work so aggressively insisted on the poverty of Christ and his early followers. Franciscan involvement also supports Susinno's account of the part played by Minniti in winning the commission for Caravaggio.

86. St Lucy's name was derived from the Latin word *lux*, meaning 'light', a fact that had not been lost on the early Church fathers. St Ambrose, in his commentaries on her martyrdom, noted that 'In Lucy is said the way of light.'

87. Susinno as reprinted in Howard Hibbard, *Caravaggio*, from which the translation used here derives. See p. 381.

88. See Keith Sciberras and David Stone, *Caravaggio: Art, Knighthood and Malta*, pp. 35–6.

89. Susinno as reprinted in Howard Hibbard, *Caravaggio*, from which the translation used here derives. See p. 386.

90. Ibid. The name of the dog is disclosed by Giovanni Baglione in a comic aside in a passage from his life of Caravaggio's follower Carlo Saraceni. See Giovanni Baglione, *Le vite de' pittori, scultori, architetti, dal pontificato di Gregorio XIII del 1572, fino a' tempi di Papa Urbano VIII nel 1642* (Rome, 1642), p. 147.

91. See Francesco Susinno, *Le vite dei pittori messinesi*, p. 119.

92. See Vincenzo Mirabella, *Dichiarazioni della pianta delle antiche Siracuse, e d'alcune scelte medaglie d'esse e de' principi che quelle possedettero* (Naples, 1613), p. 89. The whole passage is quoted in Italian in Maurizio Marini, *Michelangelo Merisi da Caravaggio 'pictor praestantissimus'*, p. 100. The translation given here is my own.

93. See Ferdinando Bologna, 'Caravaggio: The Final Years', in *Caravaggio: The Final Years*, p. 32.

94. See Keith Sciberras and David Stone, *Caravaggio: Art, Knighthood and Malta*, pp. 36–7.

95. See George Sandys, *A Relation of a Journey*, pp. 245–6.

96. Susinno as reprinted in Howard Hibbard, *Caravaggio*, from which the translation used here derives. See p. 382.

97. The documents recording this commission are now lost, presumed destroyed in the catastrophic earthquake that struck Messina in 1908. Before their destruction, they were transcribed and published. See V. Saccà, 'Michelangelo da Caravaggio pittore. Studi e ricerche', in *Archivio storico messinese*, vol. 7 (Messina, 1906), p. 58, and vol. 8 (Messina, 1907), p. 78.

98. There is proof positive that he was familiar with the knights' book of statutes in his Maltese altarpiece, *The Beheading of St John*. The image of the prison, with inmates, is clearly drawn from one of the illustrations in the order's book of statutes. See David M. Stone, 'The Context of Caravaggio's *Beheading of St John* in Malta', *Burlington Magazine*, vol. 139, no. 1,128 (Mar. 1997), pp. 161–70. It should also be noted that the document of consignment in which he is referred to as a Knight of Malta is dated June 1609, a full seven months after his expulsion from the order. It therefore seems highly unrealistic to argue that he did not know about his expulsion.

99. See Helen Langdon, *The Lives of Caravaggio*, p. 84. Caravaggio had made a similar plea for his head to Scipione Borghese just after the murder. The London picture is much weaker than the Borghese *David and Goliath*, however. It is not Herodias (or Salome) with the head, but a female servant.

100. See V. Saccà, 'Michelangelo da Caravaggio pittore. Studi e ricerche'. Caravaggio's name is not mentioned in the document of 6 Dec., but, given his strong association with the poor orders and charitable ministries, and given Susinno's remark that he left Messina soon after completing *The Burial of St Lucy*, which must have been ready by her feast day on 13 Dec., it is a reasonable assumption that Giovan Battista de' Lazzari had Caravaggio in mind from the start. Indeed, he may have been spurred to make his undertaking by the very opportunity that Caravaggio's arrival provided. I take the document of 6 Dec. as a *terminus ante quem* for Caravaggio's arrival in Messina from Syracuse.

101. Susinno as reprinted in Howard Hibbard, *Caravaggio*, from which the translation used here derives. See p. 382.

102. As George Sandys noted, the Eastern faith was tolerated in Sicily: 'Their religion is Romish yet there are not so few as ten thousand who are of the tollerated Greeke church.' See George Sandys, *A Relation of a Journey*, p. 238.

103. Susinno as reprinted in Howard Hibbard, *Caravaggio*, from which the translation used here derives. See p. 384.

104. Ibid. See p. 385.

105. It can be found in countless icons of the Virgin and Child, one of the most famous examples being Russia's most sacred icon, *Our Lady of Vladimir*, which was painted in Constantinople in the eleventh century and taken to Kiev a hundred years later to mark the conversion to Christianity of the peoples of Russia. Caravaggio will have been familiar with the motif from icons in Sicily, or from the rich traditions of Italo-Byzantine painting of the thirteenth and fourteenth centuries, examples of which were to be seen all over the Italian peninsula.

106. Susinno as reprinted in Howard Hibbard, *Caravaggio*, from which the translation used here derives. See p. 385.

107. Ibid. See p. 386.

108. Ibid.

109. Ibid.

110. Helen Langdon, *The Lives of Caravaggio*, p. 84.

111. I arrive at this date by common sense. We know that Caravaggio was seriously wounded by a gang of assailants in Naples in late Oct. 1609, as will be explained below, pp. 415–20. He was very badly injured indeed. The only two paintings that can be dated to after that time, *The Denial of Peter* and *The Martyrdom of St Ursula*, are so radically unlike his Sicilian paintings

that the difference can only logically be explained by incapacity and illness. We also know that Caravaggio painted a large altarpiece for the Fenaroli Chapel in Sant'Anna de' Lombardi during his second and last stay in Naples, i.e. after arriving there from Palermo in 1609. He cannot have painted it on his first visit to the city, because the patron had only acquired rights to the chapel on 24 Dec. 1607, when Caravaggio had already left Naples for Malta. In my opinion, it is clear from the visual evidence of *The Denial of Peter* and *The Martyrdom of St Ursula* that when he painted those works Caravaggio could barely wield a brush. On the empirical evidence of the pictures, his eyesight had been damaged as well as possibly his nervous system. It is therefore inconceivable that he could have painted any kind of large and ambitious altarpiece after the assault of late Oct. 1609. In other words, he must have painted the Fenaroli altarpiece in Naples before the wounding took place. Assuming he worked flat out, and assuming it was commissoned from him the moment he disembarked from Palermo, he still would have needed at least four to six weeks to paint it. Therefore, he must have been back in Naples from Sicily some four to six weeks before the wounding of late Oct. On that basis, I set a date some time around the first week of September for his return to Naples.

112. See Helen Langdon, *The Lives of Caravaggio*, p. 53.

113. Ibid., p. 84.

114. I make this assumption because we know for sure that Caravaggio *left* Naples from the Colonna Palace at the end of his second stay in the city, in July 1610: that fact is documented. Given that the early sources all say he went to Naples from Palermo because he was in fear of pursuit, it seems logical to suppose that he was at the Colonna Palace at Chiaia throughout his time there in 1609–10, under the protection of the Marchesa Costanza Colonna.

115. See Helen Langdon, *The Lives of Caravaggio* , p. 77.

116. For the reasoning behind these assertions concerning the date of the lost *Resurrection*, see n. 111 above.

117. See Charles-Nicolas Cochin, *Voyage d'Italie* ... (Paris, 1758), vol. 1, pp. 171–2; the passage is quoted in Maurizio Marini, *Michelangelo Merisi da Caravaggio 'pictor praestantissimus'*, p. 568.

118. '*orgie siffatte*': for a useful summary of the poem, see Giuseppe Ferrari, *Opuscoli politici e letterari* (Naples, 1852), p. 462. For the poem in full, see Giulio Cesare Cortese, *Opere* (Naples, 1666), 6 vols.

119. See Giambattista Basile, 'Talia, overo lo Cerriglio', *Egloca III, Le Muse Napolitane*, in *Collezione di tutti i poemi in lingue napoletane*, tome 21, vol. 2 (Naples, 1788), p. 267: '*Lloco le Cortesciane / Fanno lo sguazzatorio: / E all' uocchie de corrive, / A spesa de perdente / Ne sporpano tant' ossa ...*'

120. As cited in Salvatore di Giacomo, *La prostituzione in Napoli nei secoli XV, XVI e XVII: documenti inediti* (Naples, 1899), p. 82.

121. See Giambattista Basile, 'Talia, overo lo Cerriglio', p. 257. Basile's exact phrase is '*dove trionfa Bacco, dove se scarfa Venere*': *se scarfa* is Neapolitan dialect, which I translate as 'is shunned', having taken specialist advice from Nicholas Stone Villani, who kindly consulted a number of experts in historical Neapolitan usage on my behalf.

122. See Salvatore di Giacomo, *La prostituzione in Napoli*, p. 83.

123. Ibid., p. 119.

124. See Walter Friedlaender, *Caravaggio Studies*, p. 292.

125. See Michele Maccherini, 'Caravaggio nel carteggio familiare di Giulio Mancini', p. 83.

126. See p. 63 and p. 180, above.

127. This translation is broadly that given by Friedlaender in *Caravaggio Studies*, p. 236. I use the word 'affronted' instead of 'insulted', because it is closer to Baglione's usage in Italian, *affronto*, which I believe itself carries an implied meaning, as will be explained on p. 420, below.

128. This translation is again broadly that given by Friedlaender in *Caravaggio Studies*, p. 251. I have corrected Friedlaender's mistranscription of 'Herodias' as 'Salome'.

129. Susinno in Howard Hibbard, *Caravaggio*, p. 386.

130. Most notably Maurizio Marini. I am grateful to him for sharing his views with me during the course of a fascinating two days of excursions and peregrinations in Caravaggio's Rome in the autumn of 2001. I should add that when Marini expressed his view that the Tomassoni might have been responsible for the attack, Keith Sciberras had yet to publish the facts of Caravaggio's crime on Malta, which tilt the balance very much towards Malta as the source of the attack; in other words, Marini was not in possession of all the facts when we spoke.

131. See Keith Sciberras's second chapter in *Caravaggio: Art, Knightood and Malta*, fn. 49.

132. Keith Sciberras, who made the discovery of Caravaggio's crime on Malta, had to X-ray the book to get at the documents. In his account of his discovery, he notes that the records of the crime were covered over not long after they had been inscribed, i.e the coverings-over date from the early seventeenth-century, consistent with the idea that they might represent a cover-up arranged by Roero himself. See Keith Sciberras, '"Frater Michael Angelus in tumultu": The Cause of Caravaggio's Imprisonment in Malta', pp. 229–32.

133. See Michele Maccherini, 'Caravaggio nel carteggio familiare di Giulio Mancini', p. 83.

134. Only one other work in Caravaggio's entire known *œuvre* is painted in the sadly attenuated post-assault style of his last year, and that is *The Martyrdom of St Ursula*, discussed below, pp. 423–4. That picture is securely datable on the basis of original documents concerning its consignment. These two works are utterly distinct in style, and they clearly show a tragic falling off in the painter's manual dexterity that can only be accounted for by his injuries.

135. For all the documents concerning *The Martyrdom of St Ursula*, see Vincenzo Pacelli, 'Caravaggio 1610: la "Sant'Orsola confitta dal tiranno" per Marcantonio Doria', *Prospettiva*, vol. 23 (Oct. 1980), pp. 24–30. They are helpfully translated in John T. Spike, *Caravaggio*, in the CD-ROM catalogue entry on the picture.

136. The date of his departure can be inferred from the journey time by sea from Naples to Palo, where he tried to go on land with his things – roughly seven days – and the date of his death, which must have occurred sometime between 18 and 21 July 1610.

137. See Helen Langdon, *The Lives of Caravaggio* , p. 85.

138. The details of the deal emerge in Deodato Gentile's letter to Borghese about Caravaggio's death, of 29 July 1610; see below, p. 429.

139. See Walter Friedlaender, *Caravaggio Studies*, p. 292.

140. See Baglione's original Italian, as reprinted in Walter Friedlaender, *Caravaggio Studies*, p. 233. I have given my own translation.

141. Baglione uses the words *in cambio*, literally, 'in change', a phrase that has frequently been misleadingly translated as 'mistakenly', on the assumption that Baglione meant to imply that Caravaggio was arrested 'in exchange' (so to speak) of someone else. But in sixteenth- and early seventeenth-century Italian usage, *in cambio* is most frequently a phrase of emphasis with little actual meaning, carrying more or less the same thrust as 'in fact'. It can also sometimes imply the idea of a swift change, in which case the English word 'suddenly' is a good equivalent. Baglione probably meant it in this latter sense. The modern mistranslations take their cue from Bellori, who clearly based his own account of Caravaggio's death on that of his predecessor, Baglione. He himself seems to have misunderstood Baglione's use of *in cambio*, amplifying it into his own tale of a case of mistaken arrest – as will be discussed below, p. 427.

142. Apart from the word 'suddenly' – explained in the note above – I have used the translation given in Walter Friedlaender, *Caravaggio Studies*, p. 236.

143. See n. 141 above.

144. I have used the translation given in Walter Friedlaender, *Caravaggio Studies*, pp. 251–2.

145. Ibid., p. 258.

146. See Sandro Corradini, *Materiali per un processo*, document 138, 28 July 1610.

147. Ibid., document 140, 31 July 1610.

148. Much has been made of this reference to Procida, and many a paranoid theory has been erected on its shaky foundations. But whoever told Borghese that Caravaggio died there may just have been making a logical guess based on the knowledge that the painter had left from Naples. Boats from there hitting bad weather often took refuge in Procida. The English traveller George Sandys had exactly that experience when he left Naples to travel to Rome a few years after Caravaggio: he got caught in a storm and ended up making an unscheduled visit to the island before continuing on to Rome, via Nettuno.

149. Borghese's side of the correspondence has been lost. But the content of his letter of 23 July can be inferred from Gentile's letters back to him, which do still survive. All these documents were discovered by Vincenzo Pacelli, through brilliant sleuth work in the Neapolitan archives. They are conveniently brought together with much other archive material in Sandro Corradini, *Materiali per un processo*.

150. The courier must have travelled post haste, changing horses as he rode, since Naples is a little over 120 miles from Rome.

151. See Sandro Corradini, *Materiali per un Processo*, Document 139, 29 July 1610.

152. See, in particular, the fanciful closing sections of Peter Robb's quasi-biography of the painter, *M* (Sydney, 1998), in which the pope, Costanza Colonna and the Knights of Malta are held to have conspired to have Caravaggio assassinated. Vincenzo Pacelli, who located Gentile's correspondence with Borghese in the first place, also believes in a plot. In his view, the Knights of Malta, Costanza Colonna and Scipione Borghese conspired to have Caravaggio killed. He told me so in conversation in 2001. The plotters' motive, according to Pacelli, was their shared belief that Caravaggio had not only become an atheist but that he was using his most important commissions to profess, as it were, in subtle code, his heretical non-belief in God. The prime example given to me by Pacelli of a supposedly atheist painting infiltrated by Caravaggio into a Catholic church was *The Seven Acts of Mercy*. I am grateful to him for sharing his theories with me, but I have to say that I find them implausible.

153. I am indebted to the Maltese naval historian Joseph Scibberas for explaining how transport by *felucca* really worked in early seventeenth-century Italy.

154. When George Sandys went there from Naples a few years later, he went via the much sleepier port of Nettuno (see n. 148, above) to avoid detection as an Englishman and a Protestant.

155. I noticed this on a visit to Palo in 2001. The old fortress is still in existence, although nowadays it is a luxury hotel patronized by prominent Italian politicians, playboys and their supermodel girlfriends. The insignia of the old postal service can still be seen on the wall.

156. Besides, to make the journey on foot would have been to defeat its very purpose, which was to get to Porto Ercole preferably before or, at worst, at the same time as the boat. If Caravaggio had arrived four or five days after leaving Palo, the boat would already have got to Porto Ercole, unloaded and left. So if a horse or horses had not been available, there would have been no point in his even attempting the journey.

157. He refused to record any of the names of the dead for the entire year of 1610. I am grateful to Giuseppe La Fauci for showing me the book of the dead for the relevant period in the archives of the town, and for explaining the absence of records for the year in question. The death certificate that was 'found' in 2001 in Porto Ercole, a separate piece of paper with Caravaggio's name on it, is entirely inconsistent with the manner in which deaths were conventionally noted down in Porto Ercole – i.e., as entries in the book of deaths. I am sure that document is a forgery.

158. In Langdon, *Caravaggio: A Life*, p. 388, the author wrongly takes this phrase to mean 'high seas', as in tall waves, and suggests that a storm was brewing and the sea was swelling, which forced the boat to pull away from shore. However *alto mare* does not mean that; it simply means 'the open sea'.

159. See Sandro Corradini, *Materiali per un processo*, document 141, 31 July 1610.

160. See Walter Friedlaender, *Caravaggio Studies*, p. 293.

161. See Sandro Corradini, *Materiali per un processo*, document 144, 10 Dec. 1610.

162. Quoted in Carlton Lake, *In Quest of Dalí* (Michigan, 1969), p. 46.

163. Martin Scorsese's remarks have been directly transcribed from his conversations with the author in December 2005, which included an interview filmed for and subsequently transmitted by *The Culture Show* (BBC Television, directed by David Shulman).

Further Reading

Detailed references to nearly all of the many sources I have consulted in writing this book will be found in the Notes (see pp. 447–81 above). What follows here is a short list of texts that I would recommend to any non-specialist reader wishing to pursue an interest in Caravaggio and his world.

Wietse de Boer, *The Conquest of the Soul: Confession, Discipline and Public Order in Counter-Reformation Milan* (Leiden, Boston and Cologne, 2001). A fascinating, highly detailed account of the religious milieu created in Milan by Archbishop Carlo Borromeo during Caravaggio's youth.

Maurizio Calvesi, *Le realtà del Caravaggio* (Turin, 1990). For those who can read Italian, this is highly recommended. A broad-ranging, discursive study of many aspects of Caravaggio's life and work, full of biographical insights and intuitions that have been borne out, to a remarkable extent, by later documentary finds. Also worth reading for Calvesi's many ingenious iconographical interpretations of the pictures.

Sandro Corradini, *Caravaggio: materiali per un processo* (Rome, 1993). Hard work, requiring a mastery of demotic Italian as it was spoken in Caravaggio's day, as well the ability to read the judicial Latin used by the notaries of the time. Hard to get hold of too, since it was published in a tiny edition. But I cannot omit it from this list. Containing the fruits of more than two decades of privately conducted research in the archives of Rome, Corradini's book is the essential anthology of documents concerning the darker and more violent aspects of Caravaggio's life.

Walter Friedlaender, *Caravaggio Studies* (Princeton, 1955). Pioneering study of the painter's life and work, superseded in some respects by the research of later scholars, but still remarkably fresh, and full of wise and heartfelt responses to the individual paintings. Contains useful translations of numerous primary documents as well as dual-language versions of Mancini, Baglione and Bellori's biographies, and is supplemented by the short biographical remarks written by Karel van Mander and Joachim von Sandrart, also both in the original and in English translation.

Howard Hibbard, *Caravaggio* (London, 1983). Deeply unreliable on the facts of the painter's life, but still worth reading for some of the author's interpretations of the pictures themselves. Also contains a useful translation of Francesco Susinno's eighteenth-century life of Caravaggio.

Helen Langdon (ed.), *The Lives of Caravaggio* (London, 2005). A handy, pocket-sized edition of the three principal early biographies of the artist, by Giulio Mancini, Giovanni Baglione and Pietro Bellori.

Helen Langdon, *Caravaggio: A Life* (London, 1998). Much the best twentieth-century biography of Caravaggio, outstanding in particular on the painter's years in Rome. The last few chapters should be read with care, however, because some of Langdon's assumptions and conclusions concerning Caravaggio's later life have been overtaken by subsequent archival discoveries.

Roberto Longhi (ed. Giovanni Previtali), *Caravaggio* (Rome, 1982). For those who can read Italian, these are collected writings on the artist by arguably the greatest and certainly the most influential Caravaggio scholar of the twentieth century. Full of pithy, down-to-earth descriptions of the paintings.

Diarmaid MacCulloch, *Reformation: Europe's House Divided 1490–1700* (London, 2003). A brilliant, panoramic overview of the religious history of the period.

Maurizio Marini, *Caravaggio. Michelangelo Merisi da Caravaggio, 'pictor praestantissimus'* (Rome, 1989). Another for the reader of Italian. Marini's book draws together a great number of the primary documents relating to Caravaggio's paintings, and reprints many of them in facsimile.

John T. Spike, *Caravaggio* (New York, 2001). Somewhat marred by the author's attributional optimism (so much so that both the front and back covers of the book show pictures that Caravaggio never painted!). But the accompanying CD-ROM catalogue is tremendously useful, bringing together just about all the primary sources for all of the major paintings. In his catalogue Spike also furnishes remarkably long and comprehensive lists of bibliographical references for every single one of Caravaggio's paintings – a monumental endeavour, making his catalogue indispensable to anyone wanting to explore any particular work in great depth and detail.

Index

Merisi, Giovan Pietro (brother of C.) 45

Merisi (née Aratori), Lucia (mother of C.) 9; connections with Colonna clan 10, 12, 14; survives plague 44–5, 52–3; illness and death 57

Merisi, Ludovico (uncle of C.) 57, 76

Merisi, Michelangelo see Caravaggio

Merisi, Pietro (uncle of C.) 51

Messina 393, 402–13

Methodus Confessionis (confessors manual) 43

Michelangelo Buonarroti 33–4, 39, 57; *ignudi* paintings and C. 226–8, 241, Plate 47; St Peter's Basilica 67, 114; Sistine Chapel ceiling 160–61, 197, 226–8, 235–6, 240, 404; *Conversion of St Paul* and *Martyrdom of St Peter* 212, 214; *The Creation of Adam* 197, 240, Plate 39; *The Flagellation of Christ* (red chalk sketch) 345–6; *Judith and Holofernes* 181–2; *The Last Judgement* 225; *Pietà* 146, 279, 280, Plate 37; *The Rape of Ganymede* 124; *The Rondanini Pietà* 405; *The Sacrifice of Moses* 228; *Sleeping Cupid* 383–4; *Victory* 241

Milan 15–22, 24–8; Borromeo's *famiglia armata* 25, 35;

bubonic plague (1576-8) 44–52, 398; Lomazzo's cult of Bacchus 84; reputation as sin city 58; ruled by Spain 18–22, 58

Milton, John 341

Minniti, Mario 76–7, 82, 168, 256, 392, 394, 400, 443; models for C. 77, 86, 125, 154, 195, Plate 31

Mirabella, Vincenzo 395; the 'Ear of Dionysus' 400–402

miracle plays, influence on C.'s paintings 142

mirrors: alleged used as light reflector by C. 92, 272, 303; used for self-portraits 83–4, 272

mises-en-scène: in C.'s art 214, 280; sculptures 37–40, 201

models, courtesans and harlots 175–84, 288, 295–8, 305, 308, 311–12, see also prostitution

Modern art, little interest in C. 440

Montaigne, Michel de, description of Rome 65–7, 68, 70, 74

Montefeltro, Federigo da 76, 119

Montoya, Pedro 131, 132–3, Plate 24

Moryson, Fynes 17

Munster, Sebastian 235

murder, allegations about C. 58–9

Murtola, Gaspare, madrigal praising C.'s *Gypsy* 109–10

Museo di Capodimonte (Naples) 345